UBI SUMUS?

Naval War College
Historical Monograph Series
No. 11

The Historical Monograph series are book-length studies of the history of naval warfare, edited historical documents, conference proceedings, and bibliographies. They are the products of the Naval War College's historical studies and are based, wholly or in part, on source materials in the College's Naval Historical Collection. Financial support for research projects, conference support and printing is provided by the Naval War College Foundation.

Other volumes in the series are:

UBI SUMUS?

The State of Naval and Maritime History

Edited by

John B. Hattendorf
Ernest J. King Professor of Maritime History
Naval War College

NAVAL WAR COLLEGE PRESS
Newport, Rhode Island

1994

The cover illustrations are from the
collections of the Henry Eccles Library,
Naval War College, Newport, Rhode Island

Front: Paul Hoste, *L'art des Années Navales
ou Traité des Évolutions Navales* (Lyon, 1727).
Back: *L'art de Naviguer de M. Pierre de Medine
Espagnol* (Rouen, 1607).

Library of Congress Cataloging-in-Publication Data

Ubi sumus?: the state of naval and maritime history/edited by John
B. Hattendorf.
    p. cm.—(Naval War College hisotrical monograph series; no. 11)
    Includes bibliographical references
    ISBN 1-884733-04-2
    1. Naval art and science—History.   2. Naval history.
3. Navigation—History.   I. Hattendorf, John B.   II. Series: U.S.
Naval War College historical monograph series; no. 11.
V27.U23 1994
359'.009—dc20
94-34667
CIP

Contents

Acknowledgements

I would like to thank the International Security Studies program at Yale University and the Lynde and Harry Bradley Foundation for hosting the first Yale-Naval War College conference on naval and maritime history in June 1993. I am especially appreciative of the work and enthusiastic interest of Professor Paul M. Kennedy, Mark R. Shulman, and Anne Bitetti, who planted the seed for this volume.

At the Naval War College, Commander John W. Kennedy, Barbara Prisk and Jim Collins played key roles in making preparations for the conference. For their assistance during the final editing of the papers, I am particularly grateful to Lieutenant-Commander J.T. Dunigan, Barbara Prisk and Commander Roger Lerseth in the Advanced Research Department, Pat Goodrich at the Naval War College Press, Ian Oliver, Carole Boiani, Jerry Lamothe and typesetters Vicky Florendo and Allison Sylvia in the Visual Information and Publishing Branch.

The generous support of a donor to the Naval War College Foundation provided for publication of this book.

J.B.H.

Introduction

Ubi Sumus?
What Is the State of Naval and Maritime History Today?

John B. Hattendorf

Navigators need to ask "Where are we?" before they can ask "Where are we going?" Thus, the purpose of this volume is, to let naval and maritime historians ask "Ubi sumus?" rather than "Quo vadimus?"

A number of specialists in the United States have been deeply concerned that the serious historical study of man's relationships to and activities at sea has not had the firm institutional support that we believe it should have. In 1985, a group of American scholars involved in maritime studies saw that the field was close to extinction in this country and they suggested a national effort to revitalize and to coordinate work in the field. In response to this initiative, the Council of American Maritime Museums established a committee on higher education to examine the issue. In 1989, the committee reported that public education in the field was disadvantaged and that there was a general lack of awareness of the field within the academic community. For maritime museums, the lack of academic training in the subject was a serious, and even a critical, issue.[1] Many shared the committee's views and impressions of the situation in the United States and have tried to take steps toward a remedy. In the course of this, we have had little exact knowledge about the situation in other countries; our careful attention to them had been deflected by the hurdles of language and national boundaries. At best, we have known only what we have gained through fragmentary personal knowledge and our own experience in the course of individual research and reading. This volume is an attempt to take a step toward a broader and more basic analysis of the field, but in moving in this direction we are faced with a dilemma. It is the dilemma that nationality forces upon us. On the one hand, we are organized as scholars in terms of national structures, language, and institutions. On the other hand, our topic ranges across national borders as well as across standard academic boundaries.

---

[1] Council of American Maritime Museums, *Report of the Higher Education Committee: Survey Results*, Stuart M. Frank, Chairman (Sharon, Mass.: The Kendall Whaling Museum, April 1989).

More usually than not, it is national governments, national coordinating groups, state-funded museums, universities and libraries, foundations and navies, operating within the context of one country, that provide our wherewithal. Our first order of business, therefore, is to analyze the strengths and weaknesses of maritime and naval history in terms of scholarship, scope of teaching, supporting organizations, publishing houses, journals, and any other way in which our subject organizes itself. Thus, it is appropriate to ask our initial questions in national terms. We have asked the contributors to this volume to answer the following broad questions insofar as they apply to each individual country:

Who is teaching naval and maritime history, where is it being taught, and what facets of it are being taught?

Is this being done only in naval and merchant marine academies, government offices, and museums, or is it being done also in universities?

What organizations bring these studies together, or fail to: museums, universities, institutes, historical societies, journals?

What are the major intellectual trends in the literature on each country's maritime and naval history?

What period of history or aspects are covered best, and which are in need of more emphasis?

Is there a gulf between the study of military affairs on the seas and of non-military maritime history?

How do ideology and politics shape the debates about maritime and naval history?

The answers to these questions provide us with a basis for our enquiry to proceed. Yet, in some cases, these answers are themselves not always easy to find. As one naval officer in an Asian country wrote, "I seem to be like Don Quixote since such a task does not seem to have been even attempted ever before."

With a collection of responses on this series of questions, we can begin to compare and contrast the situation in various countries, and in that process, move above and beyond national boundaries, as appropriate to our subject. In doing this, we must see the subject of maritime and naval history more clearly. While we can not forget its national dimensions, we must be aware that sea history, maritime trade and naval rivalry touch on several nations simultaneously. At the same time, it is a theme that brings together a wide variety of different vantage points and disciplines. Within it, we find a dynamic interaction at a variety of levels. We can see relationships and trends between technological development and industry, the formation and growth of sciences, changing economic trends and financial instruments, politics, international relations, law, theories of economics and warfare, sociological and anthropological issues, along with reflections of cultural, intellectual, and religious impulses with additional perspectives to be found through art and literature. All of these are broad subjects in themselves, worthy of study in their own right, but defining them through their relationship to men and ships at sea provides us with a distinct series of related themes that we can follow over long periods of history. To my mind, this broad perspective justifies the academic pursuit of maritime and naval affairs as a subject. Lest I be misunderstood, I hasten to emphasize that the subject, as I see it, is not a closed category of human activity. Its academic legitimacy is to be found not in isolation from other types of history but in the breadth and range of historical interconnections which one can intelligibly make in following, over time, the varied developments surrounding ships, sailors, and their related enterprises.

At universities and in research institutions, it is appropriate to stress the academic value of our field and to discuss its state in terms of the highest historical scholarship. At the same time, however, there is a different level of attention to the subject that should not be ignored. Here, I want to draw attention to the importance which seamen themselves place on naval and maritime history. Their focus is designed to serve the maritime and naval profession. In this sense, it differs somewhat in emphasis and in objectives from that of the academic, while at the same time it shares much. In one respect, it is a means of maintaining an institutional memory for the organizations involved. On a larger scale, however, the history of a profession—for a professional within it—is clearly part of the specialized body of knowledge relating to its professional skills and practice as well as a tool for promoting the profession's special interests.

Since the nineteenth century, navies in particular have cultivated this approach. Naval historians such as Sir John Knox Laughton, Sir Julian Corbett, Captain Mahan, and Admiral Sir Herbert Richmond were certainly among the founding fathers of this method in the Anglo-American world. Illustrating the professional mode, Sir Herbert Richmond identified "three classes of individuals to whom an acquaintance of naval history is needful: the general public, the statesman, and the sea officer."[2]

The general public, he said, needs to understand the navy as an integral part of national and general history. For this audience, he stressed the need to promote an understanding of the Navy's role in maintaining a maritime country's security at sea.

The statesman, Richmond said, needs to understand how naval power has been employed, applied, and even misapplied. A statesman who understands

---

[2] H.W. Richmond, "The Importance of the Study of Naval History," *The Naval Review*, 27 (May 1939), pp. 201-18; quote from p. 201. The article was reprinted in *The Naval Review* 68 (April 1980), pp. 139-50.

these issues in history, Richmond argued, "would be more capable of undertaking the tremendous responsibilities attached to policy, preparation and direction of war than one to whom naval history is a closed book."[3]

The sea officer will gain several things from a study of naval history. First, he will find an understanding of the elements of the use of sea power. From this he can develop a foundation upon which to build up knowledge of naval war, starting from a record of practical experience rather than futuristic speculation. The officer will find naval history a groundwork of strategical study and a mental stimulant that will serve as a guide to conduct. Moreover, Richmond suggested, a study of tactics from the age of sail could have practical value for the modern officer in the twentieth century, when naval weapons and equipment changed beyond recognition. Even though the tactics of earlier times are themselves of little practical use to the present, a study of them reveals "the principles of the use of force and human nature, which expresses itself in its methods of command."[4] For the professional naval officer, the study of naval history brings out the need for clear thinking on a wide range of professional issues, while at the same time providing illustration, stimulation, and guidance to officers on the nature and character of naval command.

In other words, from a professional point of view, the general public should know enough about the history of naval and maritime affairs to appreciate and to support public expenditure on current programs; the statesman, to maintain, guide and use it appropriately; the sea officer, to understand the nature of the issues he faces and to absorb the ideals of the profession. Many of these points are ones which a professional academic would hesitate to endorse, seeking instead a broader and more dispassionate understanding of the maritime dimension in human affairs.

This book of essays had its origin in a two and a half-day joint Yale–Naval War College conference held in New Haven, Connecticut, at the invitation of Professor Paul M. Kennedy. This conference was limited by time and resources to focussing on the naval and maritime history of only eight countries: Canada, France, Germany, Italy, Netherlands, Spain, the United Kingdom, and the United States. Our thought in organizing this meeting was to have time for an exchange of ideas. Thus, it was convenient to limit both the size of our group and the number of papers presented. To encourage our discussion, we invited knowledgeable commentators to stir our thoughts on the issues, perhaps leading us in directions we had not previously examined. The countries that we chose for the conference are those where naval and maritime studies are highly active. Yet, maritime and naval history is still so specialized a field that we found difficulty in finding speakers and commentators for all the countries we wanted

---

[3] *Ibid.*, p. 203.

[4] *Ibid.*, p. 212.

to include. At the same time, we found that the division between maritime and naval studies in North America was so great that many specialists were unwilling to cross their self-imposed boundaries. In order to get a full understanding of the issues involved, we doubled the representation of papers from Canada and the United States.

Nevertheless, despite the practical restraints on what we could achieve, even in a very intense and busy conference, the papers were only the core of a larger project. Eight North American and European countries do not represent the world! To supplement our ideas, we solicited more essays, posing the same questions, from as many different countries as we could locate maritime and naval historians. Some did not respond; others, for one reason or another, were unable to provide essays. Reluctantly, we have had to accept the fact that we could not have complete representation and still publish a timely volume. Thus, despite the omission of so many African and Middle Eastern countries as well as Brazil, The People's Republic of China, Finland, Greece, Indonesia, Mexico, the Philippines, Russia, and Turkey, all of which have key maritime interests, this volume is large enough to suggest some of the main trends and issues in the current state of maritime and naval history.

As we look across the scope of the present state of maritime and naval history, we find a variety of situations, varying from country to country. In some, there are only a handful of professional seamen who are doing the heroic work of maintaining this field of historical work. Their work tends to center in the professional service academies, staff colleges, or in contributions from retired officers and merchant mariners. In other countries, the professional seamen have made links with academics and with research organizations that have helped to raise historical standards and broaden out understanding of events at sea. In other places, it is the museums that have taken the lead in research and writing, as well is in educating the public on the historical role of sea affairs. In a few places, maritime and naval history has become a subject for research and courses at the university level. Yet, perhaps, nowhere has it reached the highest level at which we would like to have it.

Overall, maritime and naval history is an area with tremendous potential for serious historical research, yet as a field, it often lacks methodological standards. Professional seamen have been the first to promote study in this area, finding it valuable for their own professional concerns. However, when interest in the field expands, too often it consists initially of only a fascination with ships or in some romantic notion of seafaring, rather than in broader, historical understanding. In order for the general study of maritime and naval history to reach a higher level, its focus must break out beyond a confined, self-contained and self-referenced view to make links with wider events and with trends of broad, general interest. Indeed, the best studies in naval and maritime history, up to this point, are those that specifically use naval and maritime affairs as examples, extensions or variations of already established general themes in topics like the history of science and technology or economic, social, political, international or intellectual history. Yet, maritime and naval history affairs are more than just stray examples. Man's activities at sea involve complex interrelationships of many strands in human affairs. When seen together, they constitute a broad theme within general history that should be neither isolated nor ignored. The development, over time, in the technologies of ships, the range of the nautical sciences, the skills and character of seamen, form the central strands of this theme as one traces its interaction with other areas of human activity.

Taken as a whole, the essays in this volume suggest both the strengths and weaknesses in the field of maritime and naval history. As a field, it is generally underdeveloped when compared to other historical topics. Nevertheless, some very important basic work has been done in laying the foundations for proper study: Significant progress has been made in establishing some key bibliographies and there are already available some important research guides to manuscript materials. Scholars have begun to publish critical editions of key documents and they are identifying, where available, the standard works which new research work can test and expand upon. Pressures from both within and without the maritime community are slowly opening its closed, self-referenced shell that was originally so valuable for early professional development. The wider contacts and perceptions benefit equally the modern professional seaman as well as the historian who wishes to observe them. In order to use them effectively, however, those who work in maritime and naval history must be more fully aware of progress that is being made toward improving methodology in the field.[5]

The teaching area is the least developed of all. Aside from professional academies which sometimes still deal with the subject only in outmoded hagiographic, romantic, or nationalistic styles, there are only a very a few serious academic courses that examine the broad historical implications of the subject. With a few exceptions, university courses have tended to ignore the natural international and comparative perspectives that maritime and naval affairs naturally involve. Few have attempted to deal in the alternative patterns to national history that such distinctive features of the subject as ocean currents and the pattern of maritime trade might suggest. Some of the rare academic chairs, designed to be filled by scholars who should be leading the teaching and work in the maritime and naval field at great research universities, are unfilled or diverted to specialists in distantly related themes. At universities, both undergraduate and graduate students approaching the broad spectrum of historical issues often entirely miss the maritime dimension. One hopes that, as methodology improves and more researchers and writers in maritime and naval history

---

[5]   This is the subject of another volume of essays: John B. Hattendorf, ed., *Doing Naval History: Essays Toward Improvement* (forthcoming).

demonstrate the wider dimensions of the field, they will provide the materials for teaching.

Where are we with the field of maritime and naval history? It is among the "youngsters" in the historical profession; it is a field that needs to become more sophisticated. By and large, we need to improve our methodologies and techniques as well as to consolidate the intellectual foundations for our field. To do that, we have the materials at hand. The following essays, however incomplete a collection, provide one basis for moving forward. These essays report where we are now, and with this knowledge, we can begin to look for new approaches and new linkages to improve the quality of future work in maritime and naval history.

1
The Ancient World

Lionel Casson

The history of the sea in ancient times is a fledgling discipline. It came into being, strictly speaking, only in the twentieth century.[1] To date, it has dealt almost exclusively with the technical aspects of ships. There are two reasons for this. The first is that, in this century, new disciplines were developed, such as archaeology, epigraphy, numismatics, art history, and, most importantly, marine archeology in the latter half of the century, and these have transformed our knowledge of the technical aspects, filling in what hitherto had been black holes. Inevitably, research has concentrated on these. The second reason is that, for the ancient world, we lack information on which to base meaningful exploration of larger historical aspects.

Until the dramatic revelations of Near Eastern archaeology, for the many centuries prior to ca. 1000 B.C., all ancient history, not merely the history of the sea, was a blank. And, for the centuries after that, naval history was hindered by a long-standing argument concerning the oarage of ancient war galleys, while maritime history was hindered by widely held misconceptions that the ancients used only relatively small sailing ships, that they clung to the coasts, that they were unable to sail against the wind.

Naval History

The first genuinely scholarly contribution to the history of the sea was Cecil Torr's *Ancient Ships*, published in 1895, in which Torr presented all the information that could be gleaned from Greek and Latin writers.[2] For maritime history it was a notable contribution, since it not only made clear that the ancients had ships of considerable size but provided details about their rig and equipment. Naval history, however, was another matter.[3] The standard warship of the

---

[1] Lionel Casson, *The Ancient Mariners*, 2nd ed. (Princeton: 1991). A presentation for the general reader of the maritime aspects of ancient history from the earliest beginnings to the end of the ancient world.

   L. Casson, *Ships and Seamanship in the Ancient World*, 2nd ed. (Princeton: 1986). A scholarly presentation with full documentation of all aspects of naval technology.

   Lucien Basch, *Le musée imaginaire de la marine antique* (Athens: 1987). Over 1,100 figures reproduce almost all the representations of ships that have survived from the ancient world.

[2] C. Torr, *Ancient Ships*. (Cambridge: 1895). A reprint edition (Chicago: 1964).

[3] William L. Rodgers, *Greek and Roman Naval Warfare*. (Annapolis: 1937; reprinted 1980). A

ancient world was a galley called a *trieres* in Greek and *triremis* in Latin—a trireme in our nomenclature. The first means "three-fitted," the second "having three oars," and centuries before Torr wrote, authorities had been arguing hotly over how this was to be understood. Most held that the *tri-* indicated there were three superimposed levels of oarsmen, and, since the evidence from written sources pointed in this direction, it was the view Torr followed. However, a British historian, W.W. Tarn, who wielded a skilled pen and was a master at polemics, in the early decades of this century convinced the scholarly world otherwise, that such an arrangement was impossible, that triremes must have had a single line of oars arranged in clusters of three. The problem was complicated by the fact that, in the fourth and third centuries B.C., ever bigger war galleys bearing similar nomenclature came into being, "four-fitteds," "five-fitteds," right up to a brobdingnagian "forty-fitted." The armchair experts of the nineteenth century, preferring logic to maritime reality, were convinced that, since a trireme was a ship with three levels of oars, the other names must embody this principle, and so from their drawing boards came reconstructions of ships with four levels of oars, ships with five levels, and so on up, monstrosities that would hardly stand up to a zephyr to say nothing of the rigors of a sea battle. Tarn, of course, insisted they were all one-level, even though this produced some meaningless arrangements.[4]

Tarn's views reigned until 1941, when a British scholar, John Morrison, published a watershed article in which, exploiting not only information from ancient writers but also some representations that he convincingly demonstrated were of triremes, ended the argument: the trireme did indeed have three levels of oars, the uppermost of which rowed over an outrigger. The *tri-* referred to the three oarsmen in a vertical line: the oarsman in the lowest level, the oarsman in the middle level seated above him, and the oarsman in the topmost level seated more or less over the one in the middle.[5] Four decades later, in the eighties, Morrison, with the aid of naval architect John Coates, directed the building of a replica of a trireme, the *Olympias*.[6] It was launched in 1987 and put through trials during subsequent years with spectacular success.[7]

---

comprehensive review of the major sea battles and the strategy and tactics involved. Much of the presentation requires revision on the basis of the evidence that has become available since the time of writing.

[4] Tarn's chief articles have been reprinted in the reprint edition of Torr, *Ancient Ships*.

[5] J. Morrison and R. Williams, *Greek Oared Ships 900–322 B.C.* (Cambridge: 1968). A fully illustrated study of the origin and development of the Greek war galley based on all surviving representations.

[6] J. Morrison and J. Coates, *The Athenian Trireme*. (Cambridge: 1986). A study of all aspects of the trireme—its development, construction, crews, equipment, use in battle. A chapter is devoted to the principles on which the building of the replica was based.

[7] J. Morrison and J. Coates, *An Athenian Trireme Reconstructed: The British sea trials of Olympias, 1987*. BAR [British Archaeological Reports] International Series, 486 (1989). A monograph that presents the results gained in the earliest trials. See also P. Lipke in *Archaeology* (March-April 1988), pp. 22–9.

What of the bigger ships, the "four-fitteds" and "five-fitteds" and so on? The ancients never went beyond three levels of oars. The best explanation of these galleys is that they had several men to each oar in one, two, or three levels, although exactly how many is a matter of guesswork. A "four-fitted," for example, may have had three levels with two men to the oar in the topmost and one each in the other two. A "nine-fitted" may have had three levels with three men to the oar in each, or two levels with five to the oar in the upper level and four to the oar in the lower. The huge "forty-fitted" was probably a catamaran, with three levels of multiple-rower oars in each hull (e.g., a top level of eight-man oars, middle level of seven-man oars, lowermost level of five-man oars).

These huge war galleys, no doubt about it, did exist and—save for the extraordinary "forty"—were by no means display pieces but saw action in many a battle; they were the ancient world's equivalent of dreadnoughts. This has been put beyond doubt by a recent dramatic archaeological find and the solving of a mystery posed by an earlier find. The dramatic find was the recovery in the waters off Athlit, a town on the coast of Israel near Haifa, of the ram of a warship (ancient war galleys had a projecting forefoot which was sheathed in bronze; this, the ram as it is called, was the vessel's key weapon).[8] It was a mighty casting with an overall length of just under seven and one-half feet and weighing somewhat more than a thousand pounds. The mysterious earlier find was a series of curious sockets carved in a retaining wall that formed part of a memorial monument set up by the Roman emperor Augustus to commemorate his naval victory over Mark Antony at the Battle of Actium in 31 B.C. The sockets were roughly graduated in size; the biggest was almost two meters wide and three-quarters of a meter high. We know that Augustus had included in the monument a display of rams removed from the enemy ships that had been taken. An American scholar, William Murray, noticing that the ram from Athlit would fit right into one of these sockets, realized that they must have held the rams that were displayed as trophies; they varied in size because they held rams from warships of different sizes. The socket nearest in size to fit the Athlit ram shows that this, for all its weight of one thousand pounds, must have come from a war galley of relatively modest size, a "four-fitted" or a "five-fitted"; the ram that fitted into the largest socket, three times as wide and proportionately bigger all around, must have been gargantuan.[9]

New studies have clarified how warships were manned (never by state-owned slaves but by free citizens or by hired rowers who were very well paid),[10] built,

---

[8]   L. Casson and J.R. Steffy, ed., *The Athlit Ram.* (College Station: Texas A & M University Press, 1991). A comprehensive report on the ram found off Athlit.

[9]   W. Murray and P. Petsas, *Octavian's Campsite Memorial for the Actian War.* Transactions of the American Philosophical Society, n.s. 79, pt. 4, (Philadelphia: 1989). Includes a detailed study of the sockets that held the trophy rams.

[10]   On the manning of warships, see Casson, *Ships and Seamanship* (1986), chapter 13; Morrison and Coates, *The Athenian Trireme* (1986), chapter 7; Chester Starr, *The Roman Imperial Navy 31 B.C.–A.D. 324*, 2nd ed. (Cambridge: 1960), chapters 3–5.

equipped, and maintained,[11] as well as the organization of the major fleets, that of Athens in the fifth and fourth century B.C.[12] and that of Imperial Rome in the first three centuries A.D.[13] In addition, the determining of the nature of the oarage of ancient war galleys, together with an appreciation of their size, has made possible a better understanding of the nature of naval battles.[14]

Maritime History

The development around the middle of this century of SCUBA diving has transformed our knowledge of ancient sailing ships, throwing light on critical areas about which we had hitherto been totally in the dark. It brought into being a new discipline, marine archaeology, in which archaeologist-divers locate ancient wrecks and dig those that repay excavation as carefully and scientifically as their colleagues on land dig sites.[15] By now they have identified and studied over a thousand ancient wrecks, most in more or less preliminary fashion, but a few they have excavated completely.[16] It soon became apparent that if a wreck had been carrying a cargo that could stand up to erosion, such as clay shipping jars or slabs of building stone or copper ingots and the like, the cargo would preserve from destruction the portion of the hull it lay over—and these remains have supplied vital information about an area which hitherto had been a blank, namely ancient shipbuilding. We now know that ancient shipwrights had their own special way of assembling a hull. They did not start with a skeleton of keel and frames and clothe this with planks, as has been Western practice since at least

---

[11] On equipment and maintenance, see Casson, *Ships and Seamanship* (1986), chapter 11, part 3, and chapter 16, part 2; Morrison and Coates, *The Athenian Trireme* (1986), chapters 8–9; Morrison and Williams, *Greek Oared Ships*, chapter 8.

[12] B. Jordan, *The Athenian Navy in the Classical Period*. Classical Studies, vol. 13 (Berkeley: University of California Publications, 1975). A presentation of what is known about the organization of Athens' fleet and its administration.

[13] Starr, *Roman Imperial Navy*. A masterly study of the administration and organization of the major fleets based in Italy and the provincial fleets based around the Mediterranean and elsewhere. In addition, Starr reviews the history of each.

[14] On the nature of sea battles, see Morrison and Coates, *The Athenian Trireme* (1986), chapters. 3–5; Casson and Steffy, *Athlit Ram*, chapter 7; Murray and Petsas, *Octavian's Campsite*, chapter 6 on the battle of Actium.

[15] P. Gianfrotta and P. Pomey, *Archeologia Subacquea* (Milan: 1981). A comprehensive review of the techniques of marine archaeology and the nature of their findings. See also *International Journal of Nautical Archaeology*. This journal, started in 1972, specializes in the publication of articles dealing with marine archaeology.

[16] G. Bass, ed., *A History of Seafaring Based on Underwater Archaeology*. (London: 1972). A review of underwater finds in both the Old and New World.

A. Parker, *Ancient Shipwrecks of the Mediterranean & the Roman Provinces*. BAR International Series, 580 (1992). An invaluable catalogue of over 1,250 wrecks found so far, giving for each all known details and a comprehensive bibliography. A series of terse introductory chapters summarizes marine archaeology's key findings to date.

G. Bass and F. van Doorninck, Jr., *Yassi Ada. I, A Seventh-Century Byzantine Shipwreck* (College Station: Texas A & M University Press, 1982). A comprehensive report of the results of a full-scale excavation of a small freighter that went down off the southwest coast of Asia Minor about A.D. 625.

the Middle Ages. They started with the creation of a shell of planks by fastening each plank to its neighbors by multiple mortise and tenon joints transfixed by dowels, and then strengthening the shell with the insertion of frames. The procedure goes back certainly to the fourteenth century B.C., and very likely earlier, and lasted throughout ancient times. During the best period, from at least the fourth century B.C. through the first A.D., the procedure was carried out with rigorous care: the mortise and tenons were set so closely that at times they were but a centimeter or so apart, the tenons fitted snugly in the mortises, each part above and below the seam was transfixed by a dowel to keep the joint from ever coming apart, and into this sturdy shell of planking was inserted a complete set of frames. One wreck, of a small coastal freighter that had gone down around 300 B.C. off Kyrenia on the north shore of Cyprus, was so well preserved that its excavators were able to construct a full-scale replica, *Kyrenia II*; in a series of voyages it demonstrated excellent sailing qualities, including the ability to make good progress against the wind. Not only merchant vessels but war galleys were built in this fashion, as was revealed by the bow timbers that were found encased in the Athlit ram.

After the second century A.D., the workmanship gradually got more careless: the joints were placed further apart, the tenons fitted loosely, and the frames were set further apart. A wreck of the seventh century A.D. clearly reveals changes in the direction of skeleton-first construction; a wreck of about A.D. 1025 shows the last step, full skeleton-first construction.[17]

Marine archaeologists have been busy as well in the investigation of ancient harbors and have provided welcome information about their shape, orientation, and construction.[18]

Europe and the British Isles

The discovery in western Europe and the British Isles of remains of boats in or along lakes and rivers has supplied firsthand evidence of the craft used there from early times through the period of Roman domination. Finds in Britain reveal that as early as the second millennium B.C., skilled boatbuilders were constructing planked craft at least 16 m long. Finds in Europe indicate that boatbuilders there may have been using a form of skeleton-first construction by at least the first century A.D.[19]

---

[17] On ancient shipbuilding, see Casson, *Ancient Mariners* (1991), chapters 3, 14; Casson, *Ships and Seamanship* (1986), chapter 10; Casson, "Greek and Roman shipbuilding: New Findings," *The American Neptune*, 45 (1985), pp. 10–9. On *Kyrenia II*, see Casson, *Ancient Mariners* (1991), p. 113 with bibliography, p. 227 and illustration, fig. 30. On the wreck of the 7th century A.D., see Bass and van Doorninck, *Yassi Ada*. On the wreck of A.D. 1025, see F. van Doorninck and J. R. Steffy in *International Journal of Nautical Archaeology*, 11 (1982), pp. 7–34; on pp. 26–8, Steffy provides a brief, but invaluable, survey of the gradual change in the ancients' method of shipbuilding.

[18] On harbors, see Casson, *Ships and Seamanship* (1986), chapter 16.

[19] E. Wright, *The Ferriby Boats: Seacraft of the Bronze Age* (London: 1990). A detailed report on the

Sea Power

As the above reveals, the emphasis in this century has been upon the technical aspects of maritime history: shipbuilding, harbor construction, naval tactics, fleet organization, etc. These subjects had hitherto been either totally or imperfectly known, and the emergence of fresh evidence provided by the newly developed technologies understandably gave them a leading role in scholarly research. But the larger historical issues have not been ignored. A recent study, following in Mahan's footsteps, surveys the influence of sea power on ancient history. A small book, it says just about all that one can currently and safely say on the subject.[20]

---

remains of several boats dating ca. 1300 B.C., including one that was 16 m long, that were found along the Humber River. They were made in skilled fashion of massive oak planks, bound edge to edge by lashings of yew withes.

P. Johnstone, *The Sea-craft of Prehistory* (Cambridge, Mass.: 1980). A worldwide survey, with chapters 11 and 12 dealing with the British Isles and Europe.

[20] Chester G. Starr, *The Influence of Sea Power on Ancient History* (New York: 1989).

2
Argentina

Captain Guillermo J. Montenegro
Argentine Navy, Retired

The state of naval and maritime history in Argentina is characterized by two general features:

First, research and publication on Argentine naval and maritime history has had, and still has, a strong emphasis on early nineteenth century naval history.

Second, naval and maritime history has remained mainly inside the realm of the sea-oriented community and with only a limited projection into the outside world.

There are several reasons for the preeminence of studies on early nineteenth century naval history:

- A long period of Argentine noninvolvement in international wars, between the Wars of Independence and the War against Brazil (1810–1828), and ending in 1982 with the Falklands/Malvinas War. In this long period, the only exceptions were the Anglo-French interventions in the 1830s and 1840s and the so-called War of the Triple Alliance, involving Brazil, Uruguay, and Argentina against Paraguay in 1864–70.

- A national sense of naval success in the early nineteenth century wars.

- A very limited naval participation in the civil wars that harried Argentina later in the nineteenth century.

- A very limited maritime development in the merchant marine, fishing and shipbuilding industries until the 1940s.

In spite of Argentina's geographical location and strong dependence on sea communications, Argentineans were not, and still are not, strongly sea-minded people. Using Mahan's concepts,[1] Argentina has a large, fertile territory, a comparatively small population, but the lack of natural harbors has worked

---

[1] Alfred T. Mahan, *The Influence of Sea Power upon History, 1660–1783* (Boston: Little Brown & Co., 1890), pp. 35–39.

against a smooth, self-sustained maritime development. This has led to the navy's initiatives, or navy-sponsored initiatives, to try to educate the public about the significance of sea power. The initiative in using naval and maritime history as a means of giving an overall view of early Argentine naval history came from a civilian, Anjel Justiniano Carranza, whose four volume work[2] was published in 1914–16. It covered the Wars of Independence and the War against Brazil. It was, and perhaps still is, the main reference work on that period. Later on, Teodoro Caillet-Bois, a retired naval officer working on an individual initiative basis wrote his well-balanced summary of Argentine naval history, with some hints on the maritime field, covering the period from colonial times up to the late 1920s.[3] A third pioneer was Héctor R. Ratto, also a retired naval officer, who published some works on early nineteenth century naval heroes.[4] Villegas Basavilbaso,[5] a former naval officer who went into the practice of law, made an important contribution in a small booklet of 35 pages, putting a Mahanian touch on the history of the wars of Argentine Independence. In parallel with these efforts, the Centro Naval (Naval Club), published some firsthand accounts by participants in early nineteenth century wars.[6] There was an American author, Lewis W. Bealer, who also made a contribution to early Argentine naval history by writing about the corsairs of Buenos Aires.[7]

The mid-1930s also witnessed the publication of the first significant work that focused on late nineteenth and early twentieth century Argentine naval history: *Los Viajes de la "Sarmiento,"*[8] depicting the twenty-nine round-the-world midshipmen training cruises performed by the well known square-rigger, ARA *Presidente Sarmiento*, between 1899 and 1931.

In addition to these publications, the Naval Museum, settled in 1892 in downtown Buenos Aires and later moved to El Tigre, on the outskirts of Buenos Aires in the early 1940s, gave an increasing momentum to spread the knowledge of naval and maritime history.

Besides researching, publishing, and spreading Argentine naval and maritime history, there was a deep interest within Argentine naval circles in foreign,

[2]   Anjel J. Carranza, *Campañas Navales de la República Argentina,* 4 vols. (Buenos Aires: Ministerio de Marina, 1914–16).

[3]   Teodoro Caillet-Bois, *Ensayo de Historia Naval Argentina* (Buenos Aires, 1929).

[4]   Héctor R. Ratto, *Hombres de Mar en la Historia Argentina* (Buenos Aires: Circulo Militar, 1934); Héctor R. Ratto, *Historia de Brown,* 2 vols. (Buenos Aires: Facultad, 1939).

[5]   Benjamín Villegas Basavilbaso, *La Influencia del Dominio del Mar en las Guerras de Emancipación Argentina* (Buenos Aires: Ministerio de Marina, 1935).

[6]   Antonio Somellera, *La Ultima Campaña de la Guerra con el Brasil* (Buenos Aires: Centro Naval, 1930); *Memorias del Almirante Guillermo Brown sobre las Operaciones Navales de la Escuadra Argentina de 1814 a 1828* (Buenos Aires: Centro Naval, 1936).

[7]   Lewis W. Bealer, *Los Corsarios de Buenos Aires* (Buenos Aires: Imprenta Coni, 1937). The original is a Ph.D. dissertation, University of California, 1935.

[8]   *Los Viajes de la Sarmiento* (Buenos Aires: Ediciones Argentinas, 1931).

contemporary naval history. The Russo-Japanese War and the First World War provided the subject for a massive amount of foreign literature which, in many cases, was translated and published either by the Centro Naval (Navy Club), the Naval War College (which was founded in 1934), or the Navy General Staff. In addition to purely historical works, contemporary authors dealing with naval and maritime strategy, such as Mahan, Corbett, Wegener, Groos, Di Giambernardino, and Castex, were also translated and published by the same naval-related presses.[9]

Two main naval-related periodicals were publishing, and still publish, a reasonable amount of historical work. One is the *Boletin del Centro Naval* (Naval Club Bulletin), founded in 1882, which publishes primarily original works and is a good source of Argentine naval and maritime history, as well as foreign naval affairs. The second periodical is the *Revista de Publicaciones Navales* (Naval Publications Review), founded in 1902. It is published by the Navy General Staff and is intended primarily for reproducing translations of significant articles appearing in foreign periodicals. As the reader may imagine, the 1920s and 1930s were full of essays about the First World War (including translations of some chapters of Corbett's *Naval Operations*).[10]

Historical literature about the Russo-Japanese War deserves special mention. On the eve of the war, Argentina sold to Japan two armored cruisers that were being built in Italy for the Argentine Navy. The ships became HIJMS *Nisshin* and HIJMS *Kasuga*. Commander Manuel Domecq García, senior Argentine officer supervising construction in Italy, traveled to Japan and was present in several actions, including the battle of Tsushima. Domecq García wrote a five-volume report which was printed by the Argentine Navy as classified matter and distributed amongst serving officers in the mid-1910s; and, it still remains one of the most interesting reports by a qualified, neutral witness.[11]

Another impulse came from the Navy League, founded in 1933, which worked hard to acquaint the general public with concepts such as sea power, sea interests, the navy itself, naval traditions and, of course, maritime history. The

---

[9]   Alfred T. Mahan, *Influencia del Poder Naval en la Historia. 1660–1783*, 2 vols. (Buenos Aires: Escuela de Guerra Naval, 1935); Alfred T. Mahan, *Estrategia Naval*, 2 vols. (Buenos Aires: Escuela de Guerra Naval, 1935); Julian S. Corbett, *Algunos Principios de Estrategia Marítima* (Buenos Aires: Escuela de Guerra Naval, 1936); Wolfgang Wegener, *La Estrategia Naval en la Guerra Mundial* (Buenos Aires: Estado Mayor General, 1935); Otto Gross, *La Doctrina de la Guerra Marítima según las Enseñanzas de la Guerra Mundial* (Buenos Aires: Estado Mayor General, 1935); Oscar Di Giambernardino, *El arte de la Guerra en el Mar* (Buenos Aires: Estado Mayor General, 1940); Raoul Castex, *Teorías Estratégicas*, 5 vols. (Buenos Aires: Escuela de Guerra Naval, 1938–1942).

[10]   Julian S. Corbett, "La Batalla de Las Malvinas" (Chaps. 28 and 29 in *Naval Operations*, vol. 1) *Revista de Publicaciones Navales* (Buenos Aires), 440 (July–September 1937), pp. 409–43; Julian S. Corbett, "La Batalla de Coronel" (Chap. 25 in *Naval Operations*, vol. 1), *Revista de Publicaciones Navales* (Buenos Aires), 441 (October–December 1937), pp. 677–91.

[11]   Manuel Domecq García, *Guerra Ruso-Japonesa 1904–05*, 5 vols. ([Buenos Aires: Ministerio de Marina], 1917).

Navy League started its own periodical, *Marina*, in 1934, which deals with both naval and maritime affairs, and, given its life span, it provides an interesting record for prospective researchers.

The Second World War produced a massive array of foreign naval historical works, but this time the Argentine Navy's participation was less significant in translating and publishing this literature than it was after the First World War. The "classic" periodicals, (*i.e., Boletin del Centro Naval* and *Revista de Publicaciones Navales*) kept on printing a large number of papers relating to the Second World War, some by Argentine authors.[12] On the naval side, Muratorio Posse's history of naval operations during the war was the main work, intended primarily as a textbook for the Naval War College.

The Navy-sponsored Instituto Browniano was founded in 1948. Its main task is to improve the knowledge about William Brown,[13] his deeds and his times. This Institute started publishing its own periodical, *Boletín del Instituto Browniano*, in 1950. Later on, in 1953, its name was changed to *Revista del Mar*. The commemoration of the centennial of Admiral Brown's death in 1957 led to the creation of a Naval Historical Center. This office started a long line of publications. Among the first we may cite a new edition of Carranza's *Campañas Navales*,[14] as well as Burzio's *Armada Nacional-Reseña Histórica de su Origen y Desarrollo Orgánico* and *Historia del Torpedo y sus Buques en la Armada Argentina*, Entraigas' *Piedra Buena-Caballero del Mar*, and Lenzi's *Carlos Maria Moyano-Marino, Explorador y Gobernante*.[15] The Naval Historical Center not only centralized historical research and publishing, but also took charge of the Navy Museum and two historic ships: The aforementioned ARA *Presidente Sarmiento* (former midshipmen training square-rigger) and the corvette ARA *Uruguay* (a sail and steam-propelled vessel which rescued the Swedish Nordenskjöld expedition from the Antarctica in 1904).

[12] See Guillermo J. Montenegro, "Research about the History of the Second World War in Argentina" in *Neue Forschungen zum Zweiten Weltkrieg*, ed. Jürgen Rohwer and Hildegard Muller (Koblenz: Bernard und Graefe Verlag, 1990), pp. 10–12.

[13] William Brown was an Irish Catholic who came to the Argentine service in the early 1810s and distinguished himself as a leader and fighter in the Wars of Independence and in the war against Brazil. He settled in Argentina, serving his adopted country loyally until his death. He is regarded as Argentina's chief naval hero.

[14] Anjel J. Carranza, *Campañas Navales de la República Argentina*, 4 vols., 2nd ed. (Buenos Aires: Departamento de Estudios Históricos Navales, 1962).

[15] Humberto F. Burzio, Armada Nacional-Reseña Histórica de su Origen y Desarrollo Orgánico (Buenos Aires: Departamento de Estudios Históricos Navales, 1960); Humberto F. Burzio, *Historia del Torpedo y sus Buques en la Armada Argentina 1874–1900* (Buenos Aires: Departamento de Estudios Históricos Navales, 1968); Raúl A. Entraigas, *Piedra Buena. Caballero del Mar* (Buenos Aires: Departamento de Estudios Históricos Navales, 1966); Juan H. Lenzi, *Carlos Maria Moyano: Marino, Explorador y Gobernante* (Buenos Aires: Departamento de Estudios Históricos Navales, 1962). Luis Piedra Buena and Carlos Maria Moyano were two pioneers involved in nation-building on the Patagonia area, the southern tip of Argentina, during the second half of the nineteenth century.

Works dealing with maritime history are not so numerous as the naval ones. Some focus on subjects such as the merchant marine and harbors, giving historical information as a by-product. In this first group, we may cite works by Russo and Ortiz.[16] A second group is of purely historical works, such as those by Pinasco, Madero, and González Climent.[17]

The Naval Historical Center undertook a significant effort to commemorate the Centennial of the Escuela Naval Militar (Naval Academy) in 1972. Two major works deserve mention: *Historia de la Escuela Naval Militar* and *Apuntes sobre los Buques de la Armada Argentina.*[18] As the reader may imagine, both dealt extensively with late nineteenth and twentieth century naval history. The late 1970s and early 1980s gave way to a series of works dealing with special aspects of twentieth century Argentine naval history. Among them were two articles published in German, "Latin American Dreadnoughts,"[19] by the American historian, Robert Scheina, as well as this author's "The Argentine Navy since 1945,"[20] and Arguindeguy's history of naval aviation.[21] The Naval Historical Center started a massive work in 1980: the ten-volume *Historia Marítima Argentina,*[22] covering both naval and maritime fields since early Spanish discoveries up to current times.

Among the periodicals, there are two more sources of interest to the historian. The first is the "Foreign Navies' Section" in the March issues of U.S. Naval Institute's *Proceedings.* This section has been published since 1980 and regularly carries references to the Argentine Navy. The second is *Boletín de la Escuela de Guerra Naval,* started by the Argentine Naval War College in 1969 (later on, in 1979, its name was changed to *Revista de la Escuela de Guerra Naval*). In the same style as the U.S. Navy's *Naval War College Review,* it has a varying portion of its pages dealing with historical issues, both Argentine and foreign. Another broad-scope work edited by the then Director of Naval History was published

---

[16] Luis A. Russo, *La Marina Mercante Argentina* (Buenos Aires: Facultad de Ciencias Económicas, 1938); Ricardo M. Ortiz, *Valor Económico de los Puertos Argentinos* (Buenos Aires: Losada, 1943).

[17] Eduardo H. Pinasco, *El Puerto de Buenos Aires: Contribución al Estudio de su Historia 1536–1898* (Buenos Aires: L. Lopez y Cia., 1942); Guillermo Madero, *Historia del Puerto de Buenos Aires* (Buenos Aires, 1955); Aurelio González Climent, *Historia de la Industria Naval Argentina* (Buenos Aires: Astilleros y Fábricas Navales del Estado, 1973); Aurelio González Climent and Anselmo González Climent, *Historia de la Marina Mercante Argentina,* 19 vols. (Buenos Aires, 1972–74).

[18] Humberto F. Burzio, *Historia de la Escuela Naval Militar,* 3 vols. (Buenos Aires: Departamento de Estudios Históricos Navales, 1972); Pablo E. Arguindeguy, *Apuntes sobre los Buques de la Armada Argentina,* 7 vols. (Buenos Aires: Departamento de Estudios Históricos Navales, 1972).

[19] Robert L. Scheina, "Lateinamerikanische Dreadnoughts" *Marine Rundschau,* 9 (1979), pp. 571–80.

[20] Guillermo J. Montenegro, "Die Argentinische Marine seit 1945," *Marine Rundschau,* 6 (1978), pp. 375–97.

[21] Pablo E. Arguindeguy, *Historia de la Aviación Naval Argentina,* 2 vols. (Buenos Aires: Departamento de Estudios Históricos Navales, 1980).

[22] Laurio H. Destefani, ed., *Historia Marítima Argentina,* 9 vols. to date, vol. 10 in press (Buenos Aires: Departamento de Estudios Históricos Navales, 1980–1993).

in 1984.[23] It is essentially an illustrated summary of Argentine history, depicting the contemporary naval participation.

The naval side of the Falklands/Malvinas War (1982) provided a large amount of British and American published works, but Argentine production has not been so significant. The main sources for the Argentine side of the naval war are several papers published by participating naval officers in *Boletín del Centro Naval*,[24] plus Busser's book on *"Operación Rosario."*[25] Other good sources showing an Argentine viewpoint are Scheina's article on "The Malvinas Campaign" and the chapters in his general history *Latin America*.[26] In addition, volume 10 of *Historia Marítima Argentina*[27] has a chapter on the Argentine naval participation in the war.

Scheina's *Latin América: A Naval History* gives very good coverage of twentieth century Argentine naval history, including the navy's intervention in Argentine internal politics in the mid-1950s. A recently begun project is going to fill an important gap in modern Argentine naval history: a history of the Naval War College. As mentioned before, the college was founded in 1934 and its development and its up and downs, have paralleled the Navy itself.

Naval and maritime history in Argentina is taught mainly at the navy's academies and schools. The institutions at which it is taught are: the Naval War College, the Naval Postgraduate School, the Naval Academy, and four navy-run high schools (called "Liceos Navales" in Argentina). A word should be said about the focus of this teaching. Due to the fact that, with the exception of the Falklands/Malvinas War, there was no actual Argentine war experience during this century, the analysis of World War II campaigns receive a good deal of attention, especially at the War College and Postgraduate School level. As the

---

[23] Enrique González Lonzieme, ed., *Evocación hacia el Futuro. La Armada en la Vida de los Argentinos* (Buenos Aires: Instituto de Publicaciones Navales, 1984).

[24] Luis Anselmi, "La Aviación Naval en las Malvinas" *Boletín del Centro Naval*, 735 (April-June 1983), pp. 117–38; Rodolfo Castro Fox, "La Tercera Escuadrilla de Caza y Ataque durante el Conflicto del Atlántico Sur (1982)," *Boletín del Centro Naval*, 734 (January-March 1983), pp. 1–9; Jorge Colombo, "Operaciones de aviones navales Super Etendard en la guerra de las Malvinas," *Boletín del Centro Naval*, 733 (October-December 1982), pp. 319–30; Carlos Molteni, "Malvinas . . . Así lo viví yo," *Boletín del Centro Naval*, 736 (July-September 1983), pp. 223–42; Norberto Pereiro, "La Segunda Escuadrilla Aeronaval de Sostén Logístico Móvil. Campaña Aérea en Malvinas" *Boletín del Centro Naval, 739* (April-June 1984), pp. 185–95; Miguel Pita, "Operaciones en la Guerra del Atlántico Sur en 1982. Intervención de la Brigada de Infantería de Marina No. 1," *Boletín del Centro Naval*, 739 (April-June 1984), pp. 117–54; Carlos Robacio, "El Batallón de Infantería de Marina No. 5 en las Malvinas," *Boletín del Centro Naval*, 735 (April-June 1983), pp. 139–62; César Trombetta, "Ocupación de las Islas Georgias durante el conflicto del Atlántico Sur en 1982," *Boletín del Centro Naval*, 735 (April-June 1983), pp. 107–15.

[25] Carlos Busser, ed., *Operación Rosario* (Buenos Aires: Atlántida, 1984).

[26] Robert L. Scheina, "The Malvinas Campaign" USNI *Proceedings*, 109 (May 1983), pp. 98–117; Robert L. Scheina, *Latin America: A Naval History, 1810–1987* (Annapolis: Naval Institute Press, 1987), Chapters 14 and 15.

[27] "El Conflicto Armado de 1982 con Gran Bretaña por las Islas Malvinas," Chapter 18 in *Historia Marítima Argentina*, ed. Laurio H. Destefani, vol. 10 in press.

reader may imagine, the Falklands/Malvinas War is also a principal field of study for those colleges. For both World War II and the Falklands/Malvinas War, the naval schools and colleges emphasize "the lessons," and not only "the facts." In recent times there has been a promising departure from this state of affairs: In 1990, the Catholic University of Buenos Aires and the Navy League started a jointly sponsored, two-year postgraduate course on "Sea Sciences." One of the subjects of the curriculum in this course is "Naval and Maritime History" (this is the word-by-word translation of the actual name in Spanish). The course is given at the Catholic University to students who are mainly civilians. Perhaps this is a short step, but it is a positive one towards moving naval and maritime history a little closer to the academic community.

As the reader may recognize, when approaching the end of this paper, naval and maritime history has remained mainly inside the realm of the sea-oriented community and has had a limited projection into the outside world. At the same time, research and publication on Argentine naval and maritime history is still dominated by a strong emphasis on the early nineteenth century. There is still a long way to go to fill the gaps in Argentine naval and maritime history, to integrate both of them, and to take naval and maritime history out of the professional, sea-oriented world and on to the general public. This is a significant challenge facing current and future Argentinians, as well as motivated foreign naval and maritime historians.[28]

---

[28] Two main references for future researchers are: Robert L. Scheina, "Unexplored Opportunities in Latin American Maritime History," *The Americas*, XLVIII (January 1992), pp. 397–406, and Héctor J. Tanzi, "Historiografía Naval" Chapter 15 in *Historia Marítima Argentina*, ed. Laurio H. Destefani, vol. 10 in press.

3

Australia

Commander James Goldrick and Sub-Lieutenant Alison Vincent
Royal Australian Navy

This paper aims to examine the status of naval and maritime history in Australia. Its scope extends not only to the research and teaching activities of tertiary institutions, but to work conducted under the auspices of the Royal Australian Navy and other government organizations, by maritime museums, and by societies and individuals, both professional and amateur. This survey highlights matters of importance rather than attempting a comprehensive coverage of the field and seeks to suggest the likely directions of further activity in the field.

The Navy and Naval History

The attitude of the Royal Australian Navy to historical studies tends to ambivalence. Although the RAN derives from the Royal Navy, and in tradition, organization, and culture is closely related to it, the RAN has long been uncomfortable with the apparent inconsistencies between much of the naval ethos and the developing Australian identity. This discomfort has been magnified by the fact that most of the active operations of the RAN were conducted on the basis of integration into the Royal Navy's or the United States Navy's operations, without a specific national identity above the level of individual ships

About the authors: James Goldrick is a warfare specialist commander in the RAN, presently in charge of the Navy's warfare officer training and tactical development at HMAS *Watson*. Having earned a BA (UNSW) and MLitt (University of New England), he has contributed articles to a variety of journals on contemporary and historical naval topics. His first book, *The King's Ships Were at Sea: The War in the North Sea August 1914–February 1915*, was published by the U.S. Naval Institute in 1984. Edited works include *With the Battle Cruisers* (1987), and co-editor of *Reflections on the Royal Australian Navy* (1991), and *Mahan Is Not Enough* (1993). Alison Vincent is a Sub-Lieutenant presently completing seaman officer training at HMAS *Watson*. She graduated BA (Honours) from University College of the University of NSW (the Australian Defence Force Academy) in 1991, her thesis being "Women are Here to Stay: The Reintroduction of the Australian Women's Services, 1942–1955."

or small squadrons. Thus, anniversaries which could be claimed by the RAN as significant to its history—such as the Battle of Cape Matapan (1941), Lingayen Gulf (1945), or the Korean War (1951–53)—are more often seen as belonging to the larger navies with which the RAN operated.

The history of the RAN has also been one of mixed success. Much of the Navy's effort in both wars went to trade protection work in subsidiary theaters which, while extremely important, was hardly glamorous or exciting. When the RAN was involved in first-line operations, particularly during the Second World War, this came at a time when naval forces were hard-pressed and heavy losses were experienced in holding the line against the Germans and the Japanese. Although there have been considerable efforts in recent years to focus the traditions of the Navy on events such as the sinking of the *Emden* and the successful passage by HMA Submarine *AE2* of the Dardanelles in 1915, there remains a certain reticence on the subject.

The other factor which has tended to overwhelm official support for naval history has been the deliberate concentration of the Australian War Memorial (AWM) on the activities of the First and Second Australian Imperial Force (AIF). Charged with both a memorial role and a duty as a museum and center for the production of the country's official war histories, the AWM was set on its path by the remarkable C.E.W. Bean, a journalist who was the official historian of the First AIF. The slant towards the Army was not unreasonable, considering the scale of Australia's contribution to the land conflict in both world wars, and it was certainly in proportion to the number of men and women involved.

Unfortunately, the fact that the official history task went in its entirety to the AWM prevented the RAN—and the other services—from developing a historical branch in the sense understood in the United States or Canada. Competent and comprehensive histories of the RAN in the First[1] and Second[2] World Wars were produced in good time, but these were commissioned works and the authors' formal involvement with naval historical studies ended with publication of their books. Since the RAN lacked the internal capacity to produce staff histories, there was never any development of a historical analyses section. Significantly, there was never any significant attempt to supplement the British naval staff monographs with the Australian perspective of operations in the Indian and Pacific Oceans.

Small and undermanned, the Directorate of Naval History within Navy Office came to function as a source of information, not a center for analyses. A succession of historical officers became highly expert in their ability to locate

---

[1]   A. W. Jose, *The Royal Australian Navy*, The Official History of Australia in the War of 1914–1918, series ed., Robert O'Neill, vol. 9 (St Lucia: University of Queensland Press in association with the Australian War Memorial, 1987). Reprint edition with minor corrections.

[2]   G. Hermon Gill, *Royal Australian Navy, 1939–1945*, The Official History of Australia in the War of 1939–1945 (Canberra: Australiian War Memorial, 1957, 1968), 2 volumes.

and distribute responses to specific questions of fact, but there were never the resources to do more. There were some attempts to centralize the historical effort within the Department of Defence, but the reality of the Directorate's role is now recognized by its incorporation as a section of the Directorate of Public Information.

More coherent interest in historical studies began to emerge with the formation of the Australian Naval institute in 1975 by a group of naval officers. While concerned primarily with contemporary issues, the institute resulted from an increasing belief within the Navy that the service required the development of a more active intellectual life. It accompanied moves within the RAN to extend the nascent degree program to more junior officers and to allow more arts degrees within a training scheme which had hitherto naturally emphasized technical studies. It was in the 1970s, too, that naval history became a formal part of the diploma-level Creswell Course which was undertaken by career seamen and supply officers not chosen for degree studies. This elective within the course did not, however, lead to further courses, and it remained a purely in-house activity until the end of the diploma program a decade later. More recent efforts in this area fall more properly within the frame of the following discussion of Australian tertiary institutions.

What did occur within the *Journal of the Australian Naval Institute*[3] was the publication of a small but steady stream of articles with historical focus. It was not the articles themselves that were so greatly important, but the interest in history that they generated within the Service. When a Maritime Studies Program was created within Navy Office under the direction of Commodore W.S.G. Bateman in the late 1980s, this included naval historical studies within its charter as part of an attempt to improve the RAN's "corporate memory." At the same time, the Australian Naval Institute embarked on a small oral history program, which is now beginning to bear fruit.[4]

Efforts by a number of naval officers and the support of the then Chief of Naval Staff in combination with the staff of the Australian War Memorial brought about a Naval History Seminar in 1989. This combined effort enjoyed international participation and the proceedings were published in 1991.[5] Shortly afterwards, a naval history workshop on the future of naval historical studies was staged in Sydney.

It is too early to assess the direct results of this workshop, which canvassed a range of issues. The key gap that has been identified, however, is the Navy's

---

3   Published quarterly. Membership in the Australian Naval Institute is available by writing to: The Secretary, Australian Naval Institute, PO Box 18, Campbell ACT 2601, Australia

4   The oral history has so far concentrated on former Chiefs of Naval Staff and interviews have been conducted with Admiral Sir Victor Smith and Vice Admiral Sir Richard Peek.

5   T.R. Frame, J.V.P. Goldrick, and P.D. Jones, *Reflections on the Royal Australian Navy* (Sydney: Kangaroo Press, 1991).

lack of a historical section that can focus not on public information services but on research and advice to policymakers. At the time of this writing, the subject remains under discussion within Navy Office. One project that is in hand is a history of Australian naval policy since Federation. Sponsored by the Chief of Naval Staff, this work is intended to provide a comprehensive treatment of the factors and considerations which have driven the development of policy in the last eighty years.

Non-Government Organizations—Naval

The Naval Historical Society of Australia was incorporated in Sydney in 1968 and included several state chapters. Formed by a band of retired officers, sailors, and naval enthusiasts, the Society did much to highlight interest in RAN history through its association with several memorials, a museum at Garden Island Dockyard, and the publication of a series of ships' histories, as well as a regular journal—the publication of which continues to this day. The early promise of the Society to become a focus for naval historical studies was not, however, fulfilled, largely because the organization remained preoccupied with the interests of veterans and enthusiasts. Australia's small population and the great distances between its chapters stifled initiative for joint action. Thus, the Society never acquired a substantial membership and therefore lacked the funds necessary to realize professional standing.

The same difficulties apply to the various naval museum ships such as the River-class frigate *Diamantina* in Brisbane and the Bathurst-class corvette *Castlemaine* in Melbourne. The small societies of enthusiasts who have done the remarkable work in preserving and displaying these ships are too small to conduct or sponsor other historical activity and their focus remains very much upon the ships and their crews.

A number of efforts have been made by professional associations to produce histories of their branch or specialization. They, too, have suffered from a lack of resources. Unable to employ professional researchers or writers, these semi-official histories have tended to be produced in a form that is of interest only to association members. For the naval historian, there is much good material but little more than that.[6]

Non-Government Organizations—Maritime

The leading organization in Australian maritime historical studies is undoubtedly the Australian Association for Maritime History, formed in May 1978. This body of over four hundred members has strong academic connections and is affiliated with the International Commission of Maritime History. Apart from sponsoring

---

[6] A history of the Radar branch has been written but not published, while the Anti-Submarine Officers' Association is in the course of producing a 1939–45 history of HMAS *Rushcutter* and the antisubmarine warfare branch.

many historical studies, the Association publishes the internationally circulated journal, *Great Circle*, which has achieved a sound reputation in historical circles and functions as the public forum for Australian maritime history, garnering high quality contributions from both Australia and overseas. The subject matter covers a wide spectrum of maritime affairs, although it has—to the chagrin of the editor, Dr. Graydon Henning of the University of New England—enjoyed relatively little support in the way of articles on Australian naval history. The Association publishes a quarterly newsletter and has sponsored several books, including *Shipping Arrivals and Departures, Sydney,* and the essay series, Minor Ports of Australia.

The Association's intent, which is to improve the status of maritime history studies, is demonstrated by its sponsorship of a conference on "New Directions in Maritime History" held in Fremantle, the port of Perth, in December 1993—the focal point of a week of activities staged under Western Australia's Maritime Year 1993 program. The organizers noted that the conference "is proposed to provide a full coverage of all major aspects of maritime history."

The Australian branches of the World Ship Society also deserve mention. This organization enjoys a healthy membership across the nation. While its focus is very much on the ships themselves, the Society has published a number of very useful monographs and represents a largely untapped source of data, both in the records and photographs held and in the membership itself.

Government Organizations

The Australian War Memorial holds responsibility for official histories and for the preservation and display of war relics. Official histories that address the naval component in the Vietnam War and the confrontation with Malaysia are now in the course of preparation. The bias towards the Army in the Memorial's displays has steadily declined, putting the roles of both the RAN and Royal Australian Air Force into perspective, and the Memorial sponsors naval research projects whenever it can. The truth is that few scholars have offered substantial proposals to the Memorial,[7] and there has been little more success with amateur efforts, several of which have been funded.[8] Apart from the 1989 Naval History Seminar, the annual history conferences of the War Memorial have enjoyed only very limited participation by naval historians.

The Australian National Maritime Museum at Darling Harbour in Sydney was long in gestation and was also the subject of some controversy because of cost over-runs in the construction of the museum buildings. Since its recent opening, however, the museum has definitely proved to be a public success. It

---

7   The major success has been *Where Fate Calls*, the book on the *Voyager* disaster of 1964 written by Tom Frame as the product of his PhD thesis at the Australian Defence Force Academy.

8   Projects on the World War II career of the cruiser *Australia* (1985), the earlier *Pioneer* (1986), and *Australia in the Boxer Rebellion* (1980) have not produced concrete results.

has succeeded in producing an exhibit program that reflects a fair balance in both traditional and more recent historical studies and covers both naval and maritime issues. The museum's interest in naval matters was displayed by its support for the 1989 Naval History Seminar and its sponsorship of a 1992 conference on the Battle of the Coral Sea. Several recent publications of works on maritime subjects reflect the broad approach taken by the museum, which will likely become a center for historical work in the future. A particularly encouraging sign is the museum's readiness to cooperate with other government organizations and with bodies such as the Australian Association for Maritime History.[9]

Tertiary Institutions

Maritime historical studies are in a generally healthy but limited state in Australia. Maritime history is quite often included as an aspect of study in economic, colonial, and Asian history, reflecting the nature of Australia's origins and environment. While few universities run complete courses, many teach maritime history as a component of other areas, although far fewer are active in naval history.

The topics that the various history departments teach tend, naturally, to reflect the specialties and interests of the academics concerned, and there is wide variety in the approaches adopted by the six institutions, which do place emphasis on maritime or naval history within their teaching programs; they are the Australian Defence Force Academy (University College of the University of New South Wales)(ADFA), the Australian National University (ANU), the University of Sydney, the University of Western Australia (UWA), the University of New England (UNE) and Bond University.

Although it has an obvious interest in defence-related subjects, ADFA attempts a balanced approach to naval and maritime history. In 1994, the academy's history department will introduce Australia's first undergraduate course on specifically naval history. This will be taught by Dr. Malcolm Murfett, a visiting lecturer from the University of Singapore and is to be a survey of the age of steam, covering the international naval history of the nineteenth and twentieth centuries. Naval history is also used as a component of politics units, notably in the undergraduate course on the "Politics of Australian Defence Policy." Postgraduate courses include several for the Master of Defence Studies program, such as "Seapower and Australian Society" (Dr. Anthony Bergin and Commodore W.S.G. Bateman), "Australian Defence Since Vietnam" (Dr. Graeme Cheeseman), "Armed Forces and Society" (Dr. Hugh Smith) and "Problems in the History of Australian Defence and Foreign Policy" (Professor John McCarthy). Some undergraduate courses include a component of foreign naval and maritime history, such as Dr. Stuart Lone's courses on Japanese and Chinese

---

[9]   In the case of the latter, the museum and the AAMH are cooperating to produce an index to vessel illustrations within *The Illustrated London News* in the nineteenth century.

history. A purely maritime course is offered on the maritime history of Southeast Asia from the eighteenth to the early twentieth centuries under the tutelage of Dr. Charles Glynn-Daniel.

The other universities place more emphasis on maritime history. The University of New England, however, teaches some naval history components in its courses and will increase its coverage with the introduction of a Master of Defence Studies course in 1994. The University of Sydney conducts undergraduate courses such as "Technology and Imperialism under the Southern Cross" (Dr. Macleod), "The Sea and History" (Associate Professor S.M. Jack) and "Australia and the World" (Associate Professor Meaney), while The Australian National University offers "Whaling History" (H.C. Forster). At Bond University, Dr. Ian Cowman conducts an undergraduate course on "Strategic Policy in Australia's Relations," which has a naval component.

Perhaps most prominent is the University of Western Australia, due largely to the energies of Professor Frank Broeze, who can fairly be described as a driving force in Australian maritime historical studies.[10] Until 1988, Professor Broeze taught a full-year course that incorporated three areas: the British Empire, Britain being overtaken by the USA, and the American Empire. The course covered naval development and merchant shipping, set within a framework of international political, technological, and economic change. Due to changes in university rules, Professor Broeze now teaches a semester-long course on "Maritime Australia." This study covers a wide variety of subjects, from ports and port cities to overseas trade and the Australian "surf culture."

Research and Publication

The extent of academic research and publication within Australia is rather wider than indicated by the availability of undergraduate and postgraduate courses. In a survey of maritime history in Australia, published in the *Australian Historical Association Bulletin* in late 1990,[11] Frank Broeze noted that the numbers of active researchers are increasing rapidly. Broeze suggested that Professor Geoffrey Blainey's book, *The Tyranny of Distance* (Melbourne, 1966), was seminal in focusing attention on the significance of the maritime element in Australia's development; his thorough survey of works in the field since that date indicates that exploration, shipping, and ports have been his primary topics.

Broeze also suggested that "gaping holes" in both maritime and naval history exist in regard to social and cultural history and that much work remains to be done in these areas. Australian historians need to continue the limited efforts made so far to connect Australian maritime history with that of the greater Pacific, Indian Ocean, and Southeast Asian regions.

---

10 The authors note their debt to Professor Broeze for his assistance with compilation of this paper.

11 Frank Broeze, "Maritime History in Australia," *Australian Historical Association Bulletin*, Numbers 64–65, October–December 1990. pp.43–53.

That research activity has increased is indicated by the fact that other journals in addition to *Great Circle* are publishing maritime material. In September 1992, the *Australian Economic History Review* published an issue entitled "Land and Sea," which featured five articles on shipping in Australia and New Zealand. Five more articles were published on maritime topics in *Studies in Western Australian History*.[12]

There is, however, a dearth of research in non-military academic circles into naval subjects. The Australian Historical Association annually prints a bulletin showing topics under research in universities. In 1992, there were virtually no naval projects listed. Perhaps the only university faculty member working in the field without direct professional connections to the Defence Force is Ian Cowman of Bond University, who is researching a history of the RAN.[13]

Books

The distinction between professional academic publications and those of amateurs becomes less discernible when the focus shifts from articles to books. Apart from the healthy number of authors within the universities themselves, several retired academics continue to produce good work, and this is supplemented by authors who, although not possessing formal training, are, nonetheless, highly capable historians. An attempt to recite a complete history of maritime publications in the last two decades would necessarily be incomplete, but a few are worth mentioning. Professor John Bach's two books[14] are important works, as is Frank Horner's study of French exploration,[15] and Marsden Horden's acclaimed study on Stokes.[16] Professor Oskar Spate completed his three-volume history of the Pacific[17] in 1988. Alan Frost produced his study on the early settlement[18] in 1980, a work complemented by Margaret Steven in 1983.[19] Tom Frame's study of the *Melbourne-Voyager* collision[20] was, by any standards, a best-seller and is shortly to appear in paperback. Other naval

[12] Volume 13 (1992).

[13] Ian Cowman presented a paper at the Institute of Historical Research in London in February 1991 entitled "Indecent Obsession: Australia's Search for a Blue Water Navy."

[14] John P.S. Bach, *A Maritime History of Australia* (Melbourne, Australia: Nelson, 1976); John P.S. Bach, *The Australia Station: A History of the Royal Navy in the South West Pacific, 1821–1913* (Kensington, N.S.W.: New South Wales Univ. Press, 1986).

[15] F.B. Horden, *The French Reconnaissance: Baudin in Australia 1801–1903* (Carlton, Vic.: Melbourne Univ. Press, 1987).

[16] Marsden Horden, *Mariners are Warned! John Lort Stokes and HMS **Beagle** in Australia 1837–1843* (Carlton, Vic.: Melbourne Univ. Press, 1989).

[17] O.H.H. Spate, *The Pacific Since Magellan* (Canberra: Australian National Univ. Press, 1979-1988).

[18] Alan Frost, *Convicts and Empire: A Naval Question 1776–1811* (Melbourne and New York: Oxford Univ. Press, 1980).

[19] Margaret Steven, *Trade, Tactics and Territory* (Carlton, Vic.: Melbourne Univ. Press, 1983).

[20] T.R. Frame, *Where Fate Calls: The HMAS Voyager Tragedy* (Sydney: Hodder and Stoughton, 1992).

works of interest include Robert Hyslop's two volumes on naval administration[21] as well as Ray Jones' work,[22] which covers the development of Australian naval aviation up until 1944 and which nearly constitutes a history of operational policy in the inter-war years.

These scholarly books are supplemented by a number of more or less popular works. While the majority of academic publications within Australia are essentially maritime in nature, it is ironic that the "popular" effort tends more towards naval subjects, either dealing with ships or war history. The retired journalist Frank Walker has produced books on the Australian involvement in midget submarine attacks on the *Tirpitz* and the sinking of HMAS *Armidale*. Other recent works have dealt with subjects such as the Japanese submarine campaign against Australia and the disastrous battle of Savo Island.[23]

Enthusiasts such as Ross Gillett and John Bastock have produced a number of beautifully illustrated and comprehensive guides to Australian warships, useful reference material for any historian. This emphasis on pictorial work is a feature of the Australian popular scene, and, although a maritime and naval photographic data base has yet to be assembled, the country is particularly rich in such material.

Facing the Future

The striking feature of any survey of the maritime and naval historical scenes in Australia is the fragmentation of activity and the division between military and civil spheres. The Australian Association for Maritime History has done much good work to bring together the maritime historians, and both its work and that of the National Maritime Museum will continue this process. It is not too much to assert that maritime history is now a thriving section of the discipline and is gaining increasing attention. Its broad appeal will continue to draw interest from special interest groups ranging from economists to conservationists to merchant mariners.

The difficulty will be to bring naval history into the mainstream of historical work. One of the obstacles to this process may be ideological; there are strong anti-military sentiments within much of Australian society and within intellectual circles in particular. The growth of conservation and peace organizations has led to increased interest in related topics, such as whaling and, for many, an aversion to military history as a whole. Such aversions can be overcome only if naval historians produce a far greater volume of substantial work than has

---

21 Robert Hyslop, *Australian Naval Administration 1900–1939* (Melbourne: Hawthorne Press, 1973) and Robert Hyslop, *Aye Aye, Minister: Australian Naval Administration 1949–1959* (Canberra: AGPS, c1990).

22 Ray Jones, *Seagulls, Cruisers and Catapults: Australian Naval Aviation, 1913–1944* (Hobart: Pelorus, c1989).

23 Denis and Peggy Warner with Sadao Seno, *Disaster in the Pacific* (Sydney: Allen & Unwin and Annapolis: U.S. Naval Institute Press, 1992).

occurred to date. The gaps in social and cultural studies which Professor Broeze has noted are particularly acute in the history of the Royal Australian Navy and efforts will have to be made to supplement the present activity, albeit limited, in the areas of naval policy and technical development. The process is beginning in a small way, largely under the auspices of the Australian Defence Force Academy, and there remains much to be done. Critical to this process will be the support that the Royal Australian Navy itself can give to historical studies.

4

Belgium

Christian Koninckx

To present and comment on a survey of maritime historiography, the very least one needs at one's disposal is an inventory summing up, preferably in a methodic way, monographs, articles, and reference works. Only then does a first evaluation of the printed output on maritime history become possible. Without a minimum of quantitative data, even the slightest analysis is unthinkable if it is to avoid being criticized as impressionable or unscientific. In short, an adequate and reasoned bibliography has to be available.

When a scientific committee[1] was set up in November 1979 within the Royal Belgian Academy of Sciences to promote research into Belgium's maritime history, one of the most important tasks facing it was to draw up a bibliography of published literature relating to all aspects of shipping, with special reference to Belgium, from the earliest times to the present day. In so doing, the committee was carrying on the tradition of the series, Bibliographie de l'histoire des grandes routes maritimes, which had already appeared.[2] Apart from the practical advantages of such a bibliography to research fellows and people interested in maritime history in general, once completed, it would make it possible to determine just how far research had progressed. Gaps could be traced and future research could be stimulated and pushed in new directions in order to fill those gaps. It is perhaps not superfluous to note that a bibliography really does offer a possibility for evaluation, although it is all too often neglected. In addition, all

---

1   *Wetenschappelijk Comité voor Maritieme Geschiedenis van de Koninklijke Academie voor Wetenschappen Letteren & Schone kunsten van België* (Brussels). This Committee represents Belgium in the International Commission for Maritime History. In fact, the Committee was not the only one and even not the first to promote maritime historical research in Belgium. The Royal Belgian Marine Academy, founded in 1935, includes a section for Maritime History & Archeology, which has been active since that time, if not the most active of the Marine Academy's five sections.

2   Bibliographie de l'Histoire des Grandes Routes Maritimes, edited by Charles Verlinden:
Tome I: *Allemagne, Danemark, France, Pologne* by H. Kellenbenz, K. Glamann, M. de la Roncière, R. Hervé and M. Malowist in *Boletin Internacional de Bibliografia Luso-Brasileira*, vol. IX, nos. 2 and 3 (1968).
Tome II: *Etats-Unis d'Amérique* by Philip Lundeberg in *ibid.*, vol. X, no. 4. (1969) and vol. XI, no. 1, (1970).
Tome III: *Espagne, Grèce* by F. Perez-Emid and F. Morales Padron in *ibid.*, vol. XIII, nos. 1 and 2 (1972).
Tome IV: *Grande Bretagne* by W.E. Minchinton in *ibid.*, vol. XIV, nos. 1, 2, and 3 (1973).
Tome V: *Océan Indien* by M. Roda (Saint-Denis-de-la-Réunion, 1976).

of us who are involved in maritime history must take advantage of the conclusions of workshops or seminars.

Methodology

As happens whenever a historical bibliography is compiled, a number of methodological problems arise. From the very beginning, one must set limits on the time span and geographical areas to be covered, as well as to consider the classification and the types of publications to be included. Where a maritime bibliography is concerned, one has to cope with similar methodological problems. Because of Belgium's general history, the case of Belgian maritime historiography is certainly not an easy one.

In fact, the problem of the delimiting periods of time is very closely connected with the geographical frame of reference. Throughout the ages, the provinces constituting present-day Belgium—call them regions, if you please—have frequently formed part of larger political entities. However, we consider historiography as Belgian, even when it deals with history before Belgium became a sovereign and independent state in 1830, as a result of the Congress of Vienna in 1815. But this does not make it any easier to evaluate the specific role played by Belgians among all the activities within and contributions to the domain of shipping, even though they may have been "Belgians" *avant la lettre*. To mention only a few, albeit very significant examples, the "Belgian" world of shipping and that of these foreign powers were closely interwoven as part of the Burgundian empire (1419–1477), subsequently under the rule of the Austrian (1477–1555) and Spanish Habsburgers (1555–1716), for a long time unified with the northern Netherlands, later still under Austrian regime, then called Austrian or Southern Netherlands (1716–1795), under French domination (1796–1814), and then, once again united, for the last but very short time, with the Northern Netherlands (1815–1830), and finally, under German occupation in the two world wars.

Consequently, it was not always possible to draw a clear distinction between genuinely local aspects and influences from abroad with a view to making an inventory of everything in print. In doubtful cases, therefore, it was wisely decided to include the publications.

Regardless of the foreign rulers—in some circumstances the interpretation given to the term "foreign" may be open for discussion—we may not overlook the fact that the Belgian provinces were not always the same entities as those recognized today. For many a year, our provinces, or part of them, were ceded, removed, or annexed. While this may be of less importance regarding the maritime history of the inland provinces—except in the case of inland navigation—the case is quite different with regard to the coastal areas. For example, one need look no further than to Zeeland Flanders and French Flanders or to Dunkirk in the South. The same kind of problem arises when considering the former colonies and overseas territories. Accordingly, the bibliography also includes literature relating to these areas, including the independent Congo, subsequently the Belgian Congo (1909) and, from 1960, the Republic of the Congo (called Zaire from 1971 onwards), the mandated territories of Rwanda and Burundi (1923–1962), the short-lived 18th century Banquibazar factory in Bengal, the polar stations in Antarctica (1897–), and so on.[3]

In short, literature on the whole world of ships and shipping was taken into consideration, so long as there was some clear relation with our part of the globe, either as a collective entity or through the presence of individuals from our regions. Because it is clear that maritime activities, in general, develop beyond national frontiers, there will be a great difficulty in the future in supporting the idea of a national historiography.

Classification

Another methodological aspect is related to the classification of the printed works on maritime history. The committee classified them under thirteen headings, convinced that this could be done in other ways too. No classification can give complete satisfaction, and ours is no exception to the rule. But the system finally adopted is modelled partly on that used for the catalogue in the library of the National Maritime Museum in Antwerp, and partly on that of the contents of the monumental *Maritieme Geschiedenis der Nederlanden* (Bussum, 1976–1979, 4 vols.). This major work stressed precisely how difficult it is to write Belgian maritime history without considering together the southern (Belgium) and northern Netherlands (Holland).

The main headings of the bibliography are as follows:

I. Generalities; II. Shipbuilding; III. Merchant shipping; IV. Naval shipping; V. Fisheries; VI. Inland navigation; VII. Ports and harbours; VIII. Seafarers; IX. Voyages of discovery and shipping routes; X. Navigation; XI. Maritime law; XII. Education—science—culture; XIII. Personalia.

Of course, there is a measure of overlap among certain of the main sections. For instance, merchant and naval shipping were for a long time closely linked; it is only in more recent times that the distinction has become clearer. The same can be said of inland and oceangoing shipping proper. In former times especially, though it is true even today, it was not always possible to make a clear distinction between the two. Coastal vessels can penetrate deep into inland waterways, just as inland vessels occasionally sail in coastal waters. This is closely bound up with the type of vessel used, but also with the depth of navigable waterways and with the increased dredging of ship canals to allow oceangoing ships deeper into the hinterland. Canal-building started under Grand-Duke Albert of Austria, at the beginning of the 16th century, to link the major cities with the North Sea, circumventing Dutch obstruction of the Scheldt.

---

[3] For example, Rio Nunez in Guinea (1848–1852) and Belgian occupation forces in the Rhineland (FRG) from 1945 on.

The problem of overlap is even more acute in connection with overseas territories. This is especially true of the Belgian Congo, since, in its dealings with the homeland, just about all the strongest and most important links were built up through maritime activity.

Evaluation of the Maritime Historiography

In processing the items for the bibliography, the committee discovered that Belgian maritime historiography has mainly focused on ports and harbours, accounting for close to 30 percent of the total production. This is not surprising perhaps, since Belgian ports have always played, as they still do, a continuing role in the maritime activity of the country. Even when foreign powers were ruling the country controlling or supervising the maritime traffic, ports and harbours were free to a greater or lesser extent to develop their activities. Not infrequently, the existence of Belgian ports, serving a wide hinterland, made them keenly pursued objectives if not targets.

The bibliographic heading "Ports and Harbours" includes port policy, port authority, infrastructure and equipment, port activities and pilotage as well. Because of their important networks, inland waterways and inland ports were included here, too. The particular attention paid to the history of ports is not surprising at all, since Belgium's economy was and still is highly dependent on its maritime traffic and on its easy connections with neighbouring countries. Thanks to a favourable topography, facilitating the development of inland navigation on the Scheldt and the Meuse, which are linked in turn by adequate canals, it is possible to reach from the sea, the Ruhr in Germany, the Swiss border via the Rhine, and, closer to home, the coal mines in Wallonia, where the industrial revolution started on the Continent. It is not necessary, perhaps, to underline the fact that the port of Antwerp was studied in depth; but Bruges in the Middle Ages, Zeebrugge in more recent times, and Ghent, too, were not overlooked. Attention was paid to Liège, which, like Antwerp, is located at one of the extremities of the well-known Albert Canal, linking the sea, the Scheldt, and the heavy industrial areas inland. Studies were also made of Matadi, the outer harbour of Léopoldville-Kinshasa, although its historiography cannot be compared with the research carried out on the metropolitan ports.

The arguments presented to explain the interest shown by historians in ports and harbours are reinforced by quantifying the historiography: Studies on merchant shipping comprise 11.2 percent of the total, with 9.85 percent devoted to inland navigation. This illustrates, once more, the evidence of Belgium's dependence on a maritime economy, based on a well-developed network of inland waterways that in turn have stimulated inland navigation for two centuries. One can, perhaps, observe the paradox more clearly if inland navigation is included in maritime historiography. Indeed, there are arguments for and against doing so. We have taken this into consideration in the present paper, because the heading appears in the already mentioned bibliography, although personally we believe that inland navigation is not part of maritime history, in a strict sense, and subsequently it is hard to insert it in the framework of maritime historiography. It is true, as we have already pointed out, that in earlier times the distinction between inland and oceangoing shipping was sometimes unclear. But when looking at what is listed under the heading "Inland Navigation," focusing as it does on inland shipping during the last century, on inland shipping to neighbouring European countries on the Rhine and in the colonies, representing all in all the majority of the items, we feel bound to assert that the terminology of maritime historiography is no longer appropriate. Once again, we are convinced that inland navigation would fit far more neatly into the framework of economic history.

One cannot make the same remark when speaking about merchant shipping. It is not surprising that a large quantitiy of publications deal with shipping during the 19th and 20th centuries. Navigation on the Scheldt became free from 1863 on—we recall that the Scheldt had been officially obstructed by the Dutch since 1648—and the gate to the seven seas opened only gradually for Antwerp. This development was amplified by the colonial era, starting from the end of the 19th century as far as Belgium is concerned.

It is appalling, however, to note the exaggerated interest historians have shown in the history of the 18th-century East India Company at Ostend, called the Ostend Company even though its Board of Trade was located in Antwerp. Appalling, because this company was very short-lived. It is little wonder, then, that its historiography should exaggerate its significance a little, compared to the great East India companies, abroad. However, the Ostend Company remains important for the country, and the huge interest shown in it can be explained by the availability of sources, since the archives are still preserved. However, interest in this topic contributes to the fact that maritime economic historiography is dominant.[4]

Looking at the other categories of Belgian maritime historiography: shipbuilding (4.57 percent), naval shipping (4.97 percent), seafarers (4.75 percent), discoveries (4.88 percent), navigation techniques (4.5 percent), maritime law (3.9 percent), we observe that historical research seems to have been directly proportional (see the diagram: Belgian Maritime History). Somewhat greater attention has been paid to the study of fisheries (6.29 percent) and to the topic of education, science and culture (5.89 percent).[5] The minor role played by naval history is self-explanatory due to the many foreign rulers; privateering was included here, also. In fact, a genuine Belgian Navy did not exist before the end

---

[4]   Percentages are related to the number of publications. If not the most ideal method, the approach is quite valuable as offering indications. Publications published from the 19th century until the eighties of the 20th century were considered.

[5]   Although we do not mention the subheadings here, all bibliographical items have been computed.

BELGIAN MARITIME HISTORY

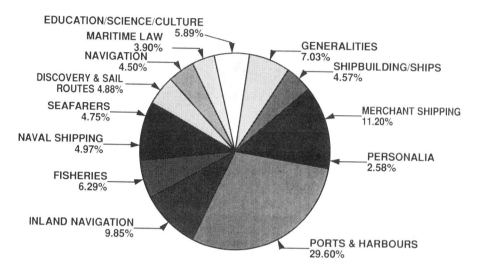

EDUCATION/SCIENCE/CULTURE 5.89%
MARITIME LAW 3.90%
NAVIGATION 4.50%
DISCOVERY & SAIL ROUTES 4.88%
SEAFARERS 4.75%
NAVAL SHIPPING 4.97%
FISHERIES 6.29%
INLAND NAVIGATION 9.85%
GENERALITIES 7.03%
SHIPBUILDING/SHIPS 4.57%
MERCHANT SHIPPING 11.20%
PERSONALIA 2.58%
PORTS & HARBOURS 29.60%

of the Second World War. Concerning Belgian participation in discoveries, the same remark can be made; maritime history in this category is principally limited to the contemporary period.

This very brief survey of Belgian maritime historiography cannot be concluded without a word about the heading "generalities," which includes such works as encyclopedias, reference works, dictionaries, bibliographies, inventories, catalogues, and so on; these works are the necessary tools for successful historical research. However, only Belgian production was taken into account here. We do not intend to analyse every subheading, but something has to be said about the inventories of records.

Looking at these, we observe that many important record collections had already been inventoried, even those of foreign repositories. This is the case of records kept in Paris concerning Belgian maritime history, as well as in Genoa, Venice, Florence, and Simancas, to cite just a few examples. But limiting ourselves to records kept in Belgium, we have to conclude that there is still a great many records available.

Nevertheless, we are inclined to state that maritime historical research has not made much progress in Belgium, in relation to what has been achieved in the Netherlands, a country of comparable size. But, it can be stressed that there is now a Belgium maritime bibliography, which is not yet the case in the Netherlands.

Perhaps, there is a lack of enthusiasm for maritime history, in general. Further, we have to point out the striking lack of maritime history in the programmes of Belgian universities and even in that of the Nautical College at Antwerp. When one considers scientific research in this area, it has to be said that it is very much limited to associations outside the universities, such as the Royal Belgian Marine Academy[6] at Antwerp and the Scientific Committee for Maritime History[7] in Brussels. However, the people involved are often members of both associations, simultaneously. In addition, there is, of course, the National Maritime Museum at Antwerp, housing in fact the Maritime Academy, and from which historical maritime research is also promoted.[8]

In view of these facts, it is hardly surprising that maritime history in Belgium is stagnating and still in its infancy. If this is a quite pessimistic view, our survey—and by the way, the bibliography, itself—offered the opportunity to make this statement.

---

6   Since 1935, the Academy has published a yearbook dealing mainly with maritime history.

7   The Committee established a series, entitled *Collectanea Maritima*, in which five volumes have already been published:

Vol. I: *Bibliography of Belgian Maritime History* (Brussels, 1984), on which the present paper is based.

Vol. II: *Source Material for the History of Antwerp Shipping Particularly the England Trade 1404–1485*, by G. Asaert (Brussels, 1985).

Vol III: *Nautisch en Hydrografische kennis in België en Zaïre. Historische Bijdragen* (Brussels, 1987), with English summaries.

Vol. IV: *Bijdragen tot de internationale maritieme geschiedenis* (Brussels, 1988), with English summaries.

Vol. V: *Proceedings of the international colloquim: "Industrial Revolutions and the Sea"* (Brussels, 1991).

8   *Nationa Scheepvaartmuseum, Antwerpen*, by A. de Vos, Coll. *Musea Nostra*, vol. 17, (Brussels, 1989).

5

Britain

N.A.M. Rodger

The most important single fact about naval and maritime history[1] in Britain today is conveyed by the awkward form of words which it is necessary to adopt as a title. "Naval and maritime" history is widely conceived as an amalgam or an uncomfortable hybrid of two distinct subjects, and not everybody would accept that the connections between the two are or ought to be very close. This seems to be a peculiarity of the English-speaking world, and it can be difficult to find words in English to express the unified subject of maritime history as it is understood in most European countries, or to translate into European languages the distinctions implied in English academic usage by "naval" and "maritime."[2]

This problem of definition is the key to the present state of the subject. All historians can agree that in principle history is a seamless web in which every country, every subject, and every period is bound closely to its neighbours; but for the practical purposes of study in school and university, it is necessary to divide it. Any subject that does not form one of the accepted divisions is at risk of becoming fragmented if not ignored. This has been the fate of naval and maritime history in Britain. Probably few historians, if pressed, would actually deny the significance of the sea in British history, but many of them would assume that it belonged naturally in someone else's department. The result has tended to be that particular aspects of maritime history have received attention in circumstances that tended to isolate them. Economic historians have studied the history of overseas travel and fisheries, but have ignored anything to do with warfare. Naval historians have studied battles and campaigns but supplied very little historical context in which to locate them and establish their significance. Military historians have in theory admitted the importance of the sea in warfare, but in practice very often ignored it. Students of strategic studies have plundered the recent past for case studies without penetrating far below the surface. The

---

[1] I am very grateful for the comments and suggestions of Dr. Michael Duffy, Dr. Stephen Fisher, Dr. R.J.B. Knight, Dr. A.D. Lambert, Dr. H.M.Scott, Professor Geoffrey Till, and Mr. David Williams.

[2] French *histore maritime*, German *Seegeschichte*, Dutch *Zeegeschiedenis*, Italian *storia marittima*, Spanish *historia maritima*, all refer to the history of man's use of the sea in general; in all these languages the word *marine* or *marina* is not limited to the fighting service alone.

result has been that naval and maritime history, especially in universities, has tended to be reduced to a number of disconnected minority interests in different departments, often departments which themselves are regarded as peripheral to the main business of the university.

In this context the breadth of the subject may be a practical disadvantage. It has been well said of naval history, and might be as well said of maritime history at large, that it is "a microcosm of national history; it is not a subject with its own particular technique, but an application of different subjects, each with its own technique, to a particular field. It has its own economic and constitutional history, its own legal problems and its own relations with diplomacy and politics. If national history may be compared to a cake, the different layers of which are different aspects of national life, then naval history is not a layer but a slice of the cake."[3] The breadth of the subject and the multitude of connections it has, or ought to have, with many areas of history, explain much of the importance and the excitement of the subject, but they also explain the difficulty of treating it in its entirety and the ease with which it can be parcelled out among many historians or history departments whose central interests lie elsewhere. However desirable it may be in theory to abolish academic demarcation lines, in practice there is no better way to get a neglected subject studied than to establish courses and departments dedicated to it.

It is only possible to explain how and why English-speaking historians have come to perceive the subjects of naval and maritime history as distinct by dipping briefly into the history of history as a serious scholarly pursuit in Britain. For our present purposes we may begin exactly a century ago in 1893, with the foundation of the Navy Records Society, which shows most of the characteristic features of its time. This was a period in which history was overwhelmingly the record of great men and of the state; it was the history of gentlemen, for gentlemen. Maritime history therefore naturally became naval history, and it was naval history with a purpose. The founders of the N.R.S. included some academics, notably its moving spirit, Professor J.K. Laughton,[4] but most of them were naval officers and civilians closely connected with the Navy who regarded naval history as directly relevant to their professional concerns. The study of history as a means of rediscovering the fundamental verities of naval strategy and tactics was a key element in the institutional and intellectual reforms which were then affecting the Navy. Young officers who thought seriously about their profession were likely to be interested in history, and they conceived of naval history as a source of guidance as well as inspiration, both in their own careers and in the reform of the Service at large. It is also probable that the foundation of the Society in 1893, just as Mr. Gladstone was fighting his last great political

---

[3] John Ehrman, *The Navy in the War of William III: Its State and Direction, 1689–1697* (Cambridge: 1953), p. xxii.

[4] Professor of Modern History at King's College London, formerly a Naval Instructor.

battle to cut the Navy Estimates, was not without political intent;[5] the former
Conservative First Lord of the Admiralty, Lord George Hamilton, was
prominent among its founders, and the then First Lord, Earl Spencer, whose
sponsorship of some of the admirals' demands did so much to drive the Prime
Minister from office, accepted the presidency.[6] Naval history was highly relevant
to the Navy of the day, and at times it had a radical, even subversive flavour, the
more so as many of the naval historians came to oppose the "matériel" school
of Sir John Fisher. They were prominent among the officers who in 1912
founded *The Naval Review* "to promote the Advancement and Spreading within
the Service of Knowledge relevant to the Higher Aspects of the Naval Profession," and the *Review* continued for many years to publish historical scholarship
of a high standard amongst papers on the current professional concerns of the
Navy.[7]

The subject which interested these early naval historians was essentially the
history of naval operations, often studied in close detail. Many of them—notably
Sir Julian Corbett and the then Captain H.W. Richmond[8]—were keenly
concerned to trace the relationship of the Navy to strategy and diplomacy: *The
Navy as an Instrument of Policy*, to use the title of one of Richmond's books. They
were not much interested in other aspects of naval history which did not echo
their current professional concerns, nor in the history of merchant shipping
except as an aspect of the defence of seaborne trade. Few of them were academic
historians,[9] indeed there were still few teachers of history in British universities,
but in spite of this the subject enjoyed the same high public esteem as the Navy
itself. The Council of the Navy Records Society in the first twenty years of its
life included King Edward VII and two royal princes, five Cabinet ministers,
eleven peers, twenty-seven admirals, four generals, and a variety of other
luminaries including two distinguished novelists (Kipling and Erskine Childers),

---

5   I owe this suggestion to Dr. Michael Duffy; it is also made by W.M. Hamilton, *The Nation and the
Navy: Methods and Organisation of British Navalist Propaganda 1889–1914* (New York: 1986).

6   *The Red Earl: The Papers of the Fifth Earl Spencer 1835–1910*, ed. Peter Gordon (Northamptonshire
Record Society Vols. 31 and 34, 1981–86) II, pp. 28–32, gives the background.

7   For example the studies of eighteenth-century campaigns by Commander J.H. Owen printed in the
1930s. It still prints historical articles, but would no longer claim to be a vehicle for original historical
scholarship.

8   Corbett's life has been written by Donald M. Schurman: *Julian S. Corbett 1854–1922: Historian of
British Maritime Policy from Drake to Jellicoe* (Royal Historical Society Studies in History No. 26: 1981).
Richmond has no less than three biographies: Arthur J. Marder, *Portrait of an Admiral* (London: 1952);
D.M. Schurman, "Historian in Uniform," in *The Education of a Navy: The Development of British Naval
Strategic Thought, 1867–1914* (London: 1965); and Barry D. Hunt, *Sailor-Scholar: Admiral Sir Herbert
Richmond, 1871–1946* (Waterloo, Ontario: 1982). See also, James Goldrick and John B. Hattendorf,
eds., *Mahan Is Not Enough: The Proceedings of a Conference on the Works of Sir Julian Corbett and Admiral
Sir Herbert Richmond* (Newport: 1993).

9   But the few were eminent; besides Laughton, the Society's early editors included S.R. Gardiner and
Sir Charles Firth.

two Directors of Naval Construction, two Princes of the Holy Roman Empire, the Secretary of the Admiralty, and the Lord Provost of Glasgow. No academic discipline, then or now, could boast of such social prestige.

After the First World War naval history tended to suffer from the public's disenchantment with all things military.[10] The Vere Harmsworth Chair in Naval history at Cambridge, endowed by Lord Rothermere in 1911, was converted to one of Imperial and Naval History in 1932; since then only one naval historian has held it, Sir Herbert Richmond, who was appointed in 1934 and was later elected Master of Downing College. Richmond's election was applauded by a previous holder of the chair as a signal that naval history would not be "pushed into the background," but that is exactly what happened.[11] In Cambridge, as also in Oxford and London, naval history continued to be regarded as a serious subject, but it was not a popular one. King's College London, which had agreed to found a department of naval history in 1913, was unable to find a scholar to continue Laughton's interests.[12] At the same time it ceased to be the mark of the intellectual naval officer to engage in serious research.[13] Richmond himself, who had written part of one of his most important books[14] while commanding HMS *Dreadnought*, had no successors in this respect. The Second World War had surprisingly little effect in changing this. Though the importance of sea power had again been convincingly demonstrated, weariness and distaste for war was hardly less marked in 1945 than it had been in 1918. In the 1940s several British university historians with interests in maritime history began their careers, notably C.N. Parkinson and A.N. Ryan at Liverpool, but the subject could not be said to have established itself as a subject in British universities. It was characteristic of the postwar years that while some maritime or naval historians rose to become professors (notably John Bromley at Southampton and Kenneth Andrews at Hull), scholars of ability were more likely to begin their careers as naval historians, but to advance by moving rapidly into other areas.[15] In

---

[10] John B. Hattendorf, "The Study of War History at Oxford, 1862–1990," in *The Limitations of Military Power: Essays presented to Professor Norman Gibbs on his eightieth birthday* (London: 1990), pp. 3–61, at pp. 26–7.

[11] Hunt, *Sailor-Scholar*, p. 217.

[12] *Ex inf.* Dr. A.D. Lambert.

[13] And not only naval officers: A.W. Tedder (the future Air Marshal) was a young official in the Colonial Service when he published *The Navy of the Restoration* (Cambridge: 1916).

[14] *The Navy in the War of 1739–48*, eventually published in 1920.

[15] John Ehrman (*The Navy in the War of William III*) is a notable example, though he also abandoned academic life for private scholarship. Others are Professor C.J. Bartlett of the University of Dundee (*Great Britain and Sea Power 1815–1853*, Oxford: 1963), Professor H.T. Dickinson of Edinburgh University ("British military and naval operations: Catalonia and Valencia, 1701–11," Durham M.A. thesis, 1963; his Ph.D. thesis was on "Henry St. John and the Struggle for the Leadership of the Tory Party 1702–14," Newcastle, 1968), Professor C.S.L. Davies ("Supply services of the English armed forces, 1509–50," Oxford D.Phil. thesis: 1964), Professor Bernard Dietz ("Privateering in North-West European waters, 1568 to 1572," London Ph.D. thesis: 1959), and Professor Norman Hampson of the University of Newcastle-upon Tyne (*La Marine de l'An II*, Paris: 1952).

Cambridge Captain S.W. Roskill, the official historian of the Royal Navy in the Second World War, and undoubtedly one of the most distinguished naval historians of this century, was offered a fellowship at Churchill College, but was never elected to the Harmsworth Chair for which he was so well qualified.[16]

The half century since the end of the Second World War has been marked by a rapid growth in the size and number of British universities, and an equally sharp decline in the size of the Royal Navy. For much of this period the study of warfare in any form attracted little interest in universities. The largest research institutions, with room for all sorts of minority interests, continued to produce some work, and in Oxford the Chichele Chair in the History of War sustained courses in military history and grand strategy which contained a naval element,[17] but until the late 1960s, naval history in universities had become almost invisible.[18] The period was, however, fruitful for the new subject of maritime history. Its practitioners were predominantly economic historians by training, appointed to positions in departments of economic history, and perhaps anxious to demonstrate the superior scientific rigour of a numerate discipline compared to the amiable vagueness of traditional historical scholarship. They did not feel they had much in common with naval history as it had generally been studied. Part of the problem here was that naval history was by this time being studied largely by people outside university departments, people who were by definition amateurs in the sense of not earning their living by scholarship, and also (it was often implied) in the sense of not matching professional standards. The derogative implications of the term "amateur" were not entirely unjustified, for naval history in the postwar years did indeed fall behind the professional standards of the academic world, as well as losing touch with its fashions. It was until recently a stronghold of the nationalist and triumphalist tradition, and it was late to be marked by such academic fashions as social history. It is still almost untouched by the spread of quantitative history, in spite of the existence of sources of unequalled richness. This made it easier for university historians to ignore the subject, and contributed to generations of history books which overlooked maritime, and especially naval, history or accorded it brief and embarrassed mention before turning to more agreeable matters. Another factor here may have been fear of the complex technology of the sailing ship: to tackle it was to risk making a fool of oneself before those who understood it, and perhaps also to risk lowering one's status before those historians for whom real history was the history of high politics and policy, and who shared the traditional English

---

[16] John Ehrman, "Stephen Wentworth Roskill, 1903–1982," *Proceedings of the British Academy*, LXIX (1983), p. 579–94, at pp. 589–91. His deafness would admittedly have hampered him in the chair, but it did not stop him teaching for the History Tripos.

[17] Hattendorf, *War History at Oxford*.

[18] Table 1.

view that technical expertise was what distinguished the player from the gentlemen.[19]

All this continued to be true throughout the 1950s and 1960s when British universities were expanding and creating new posts and departments. It only began to change in the 1970s, and was soon overtaken by a deepening crisis in university finance and morale. Faced with public hostility towards students and their teachers, dependent for funds on a government which identified universities as a cause of economic decline and talked seriously of closing some or even many of then as superfluous, academics entered a prolonged and uncomfortable period of change which shows no signs of ending. Among the many consequences have been departments and whole institutions closed, merged or struggling for survival; a collapse of morale in some quarters; the departure of some of the ablest and most ambitious for early retirement or the United States; and the loss of a generation of younger scholars unable to enter or make a career in the academic world. This has meant that there has been little money to spare for new ideas and new subjects. University departments have devoted all their attention to survival, meaning in practice the survival of their existing courses. Always conservative and bureaucratic institutions, difficult to steer onto new courses, British universities have until recently been in a particularly poor position to respond to new intellectual currents.

Among these has been the revival, change, and even to some extent the merging of naval and maritime history. By the 1980s the political climate in universities, following somewhat behind that of Britain as a whole, was turning more conservative, and both naval and military history were regaining some degree of respectability. The Department of War Studies established at King's College London in 1965 had a notable influence on military history, and in particular on the new theme of "war and society," which linked the hitherto old-fashioned world of military history with the post-war interest in social history. "Just as some thought war too serious a matter to be left to the generals," wrote Professor Geoffrey Best,

> so the history and scientific analysis of war seemed too serious a matter to be left to the military men and war enthusiasts who did most of the writing about it. Not that they had the whole of the field. The study of war has attracted, and still attracts, the attentions of scholars of the finest kind. But such men were to be found, no doubt reluctantly, in company with a huge crowd of narrower-minded writers, for whom "military historian" was the most complimentary title that could be found, military enthusiast or even war maniac often the more apposite. War and society studies began largely in reaction against that kind of stuff. Sometimes

---

[19] It is not irrelevant to note here that books on ship design are published in Britain not by academic presses but by specialist houses like Conway Maritime Press or Arms and Armour Press, whose products are associated by publishers and much of the learned public with the world of model-makers, train-spotters and collectors of all sorts of memorabilia, and are not reviewed in academic journals.

sinking to uniforms, badges and buttons, it rarely rose above campaigns and battles; it viewed them from the professional soldier's angle; it tended to extract the fighting side of war from its total historical context; and it usually meant a view of an army, navy or air force from within, little concerned about the nature of their connections with the society on whose behalf war was, nominally, being fought. Much might be learnt from such books about the way an army did the job set for it and, especially from between the lines, about the ways soldiers viewed themselves; little, however, about how soldiers got to be like that, and nothing at all about how armed forces fitted into, emerged from, and perhaps in their turn made impressions upon the societies to which they belonged.[20]

The election of Professor Michael Howard, former head of the Department of War Studies at the University of London, and subsequently Chichele Professor of the History of War at Oxford, to the Regius Chair at Oxford in 1980 did much to enhance the respectability of the new military history.[21] So did the skill with which Sir Michael handled the History Faculty at Oxford, still on his election inclined to be suspicious of a former soldier. At the same time some university scholars, notably Paul Kennedy, were making their names in naval history, or at least the naval aspects of economic history and high policy. These trends gathered pace in the late 1980s, with substantial contributions to naval history by established university scholars who had made their reputations in other fields.[22] During this decade the proportion of doctoral and other theses in naval history completed in British universities rose for the first time to a substantial fraction of those in "maritime" history.[23] What did not happen was any significant number of new appointments to university departments of scholars with such interests. When so few posts were being filled anyway, a department's major interests always took priority. The renewed vigour of the subject was indicated by the interest shown in it by established scholars rather than by new appointments. Only the King's College Department of War Studies could be said to have a continued, if not central concern for the subject, and in 1992 it appointed its first naval historian to a lectureship.[24] By contrast, the position of

---

[20] "Editor's Preface" to J.R. Hale, *War and Society in Renaissance Europe 1450–1620* (Leicester: 1985), p.7.

[21] It should be noted that the Regius Chair is in the gift of the Crown, not the University.

[22] David Loades, *The Tudor Navy: An Administrative, Political and Military History* (Aldershot: 1992); Bernard Capp, *Cromwell's Navy: The Fleet and the English Revolution 1648–1660* (Oxford: 1989); Loades is Professor of History at the University College of North Wales, Capp is Reader in History at the University of Warwick; they represent the schools of Sir Geoffrey Elton and Christopher Hill respectively. One might also cite the eminent military historian John Terraine's *Business in Great Waters: The U-Boat Wars 1916–1945* (London: 1989), though he has never held a university post.

[23] See Table 1: doctoral theses on naval subjects represented 18 percent of those in maritime history in general in the 1950s, 40 percent in the 1960s, and 42 percent in the 1970s and 1980s.

[24] Hitherto, the subject had been sustained by the volunteer and part-time efforts of two successive Professors from the Royal Naval College Greenwich, Bryan Ranft, and Geoffrey Till. It is also worth mentioning that on filling each of the last two vacancies in the Harmsworth Professorship, the electors were instructed not to ignore the claims of naval historians, though the chair was advertised in terms calculated to discourage them, and none was appointed.

maritime history, like that of all minority subjects in universities, tended to weaken. Several of its leading practitioners retired or died during the crisis years and were not replaced. Possibly it also suffered from a reaction against economics, by no means the most admired and respected academic discipline of the 1990s. The maritime historians had always been interested especially in the economics of trade and the business history of shipping firms, and had tended to see history from the perspective of the boardroom rather than the forecastle or the quarterdeck. They were not perfectly placed to profit from the post-war interest in social history.

University historians in general, preoccupied with survival in the 1980s, were taken somewhat by surprise by the rise in the popularity of history as a subject among the general public. At the very time when professors of history were publicly agonising over the future of their discipline, amateur historians of every age and condition were tackling a remarkable range of subjects with skills ranging from the negligible to the sophisticated, but with an enthusiasm which some academics had lost for ever. One engine driving this movement was the growth of local history among adults, and of school "projects," often in local history, among children. Another was the rapid rise in genealogy, which has been the route by which many beginners have advanced to historical knowledge of some sort, often no more than antiquarianism, but in some cases attaining the level of serious scholarship. Naval and maritime history has certainly participated in this popular revival. One interesting symptom of public enthusiasm has been the revival of the naval historical novel. Originally a product of the early nineteenth century, rediscovered in the 1940s by C.S. Forester, it has become a phenomenon of modern publishing and in Patrick O'Brian has produced one of the best modern English novelists. Another symptom has been the increase in the number of maritime museums and of people eager to visit them. The Merseyside Maritime Museum, the Scottish Maritime Museum, the Royal Naval Museum, the Submarine Museum and Chatham Historic Dockyard are among the best-known established within the last twenty years, and there are many smaller institutions. Coupled with them has been the rapid increase in the number of historic ships preserved and open to the public. Where a generation ago there was little more than the *Victory* and the *Cutty Sark*, there are now literally scores of preserved ships large and small. Among the most notable recent additions are the Tudor warship *Mary Rose*, the sailing frigates *Unicorn* and *Trincomalee* (ex-*Foudroyant*), Brunel's *Great Eastern*, Scott's *Discovery*, the cruiser *Belfast*, the Royal Navy's first submarine *Holland No. 1*, and its first ironclad battleship the *Warrior*. It is still an open question whether maritime history benefitted any more than, say, military history, country houses, or industrial museums from the boom years of the 1980s, and it is already clear that there is now a serious problem in generating sufficient income to support the number of ships[25] which has grown

---

25   And museums: some of the smaller maritime museums, notably the Exeter Maritime Museum, are known or rumoured to be in serious financial difficulties.

even faster than public enthusiasm, but on the most pessimistic assessment there is now a large public interest in maritime history which did not exist twenty years ago.

Until very recently, university history departments lacked the money and the freedom of manouvre to respond to it. Only now is this beginning to change, and one reason for the change is the growing tendency for university finances to be to some extent "market-driven." Universities are being obliged, some more reluctantly than others, to recruit growing numbers of students from a wider range of ages and qualifications than before and to compete for them on a basis on the range and quality of their teaching. Specialist post-graduate courses, until recently unusual in British university history, are proliferating, and it is becoming common for departments to be credited with part of the fees they bring to the university by recruiting people onto their courses. This gives them an incentive to identify and promote popular subjects and to tap the enthusiasm of amateur historians with the time (and, most importantly, the money) to engage in serious study. Among the fruits of this new situation is the Centre for Maritime Historical Studies at Exeter University, established in 1991, which combines existing lecturers from the separate departments of Economic and Social History, and History and Archaeology. It is still necessary to establish a special institution to associate naval and maritime historians,[26] but the early indications are that the Centre is drawing substantial numbers of students to its courses.

Maritime history is also attracting attention at other universities. At St. Andrew's, the Institute of Maritime Studies teaches an M.A. course in maritime archaeology and runs a seminar in maritime history. The University College of North Wales at Bangor now offers a B.A. degree in History and Marine Archaeology, which draws on Professor Loades's interest in naval history. The Economic and Social Research Council has funded two large studies of the Port of London by Professors Roseveare and Minchinton and Dr. Sarah Palmer of Queen Mary College London. But these new projects do not yet have an assured future, and it is not clear that departments and universities entering the field are doing more than balancing the loss of others. The pattern for many years has been of interest in maritime history generated by individual scholars, but that interest does not survive their departure. Southampton in Professor Bromley's time, Liverpool for much of the post-war period, were centres of maritime history and are so no longer.[27] The same may easily happen to other universities and colleges, and the same observation could be made of other minority subjects, such as diplomatic history, whose fortunes have depended on individual scholars rather than established departments. Indeed there is an obvious connection

---

[26] In Exeter, as in many universities, economic and "traditional" historians are in separate departments and buildings.

[27] Table 2 shows this quite clearly.

between foreign policy and naval history, and a number of historians[28] are prominent in the recent revival of both. Underwater archaeology has provided a notable intellectual stimulus to maritime history in recent years, but it has not done much to bridge the traditional division between historians and archaeologists, so that here again maritime history suffers from fragmentation.

It is a mistake, however, to concentrate on universities alone, for much of what institutional support the public enthusiasm for maritime history has received, has come from other institutions. This has been notably the case with the maritime museums. The National Maritime Museum has expanded its activities to run a range of lectures and courses, to support research fellowships in naval and maritime history, and to run a (heavily over-subscribed) conference for new researchers in maritime history. To some extent these are intended to replace the major scholarly projects for which curators nowadays seldom have time, as well as to provide a home for serious scholarship in subjects not supported by university departments. Other public institutions, notably the Public Record Office and the record offices of counties and cities, have provided facilities[29] for a large increase in interest in naval and maritime history. At the Public Record Office, where amateur historians make up more than three-quarters of the readers, naval and military records are the single most popular category of records used. Much of this use is not very sophisticated, but the amateur researchers, who include a significant minority of children, display an enthusiasm for research (and a respect for the archives) which are by no means universal among professionals. Moreover there is evidence that they are willing to explore a wider range of sources than professional historians, whose research tends to be confined to the record classes cited in other people's footnotes.[30]

Public institutions concerned to train officers for either the Navy or the merchant service have not made a notable contribution to naval and maritime history. The training of merchant navy officers ashore takes place in departments unconnected with history, by lecturers brought up as seafarers, engineers or naval architects, and there are only a few who maintain a serious interest in history.[31] The former Naval Historical Branch of the Ministry of Defence is too small and overworked to undertake scholarly projects of significance, and in recent years has been somewhat isolated from both academic and amateur historians. Young officers under training for the Royal Navy now spend only six months at the

---

[28] Such as Dr. Jeremy Black of Durham, Dr. Michael Duffy of Exeter, and Dr. Hamish Scott of St. Andrew's.

[29] But not necessarily with enthusiasm.

[30] P.R.O. statistics from the early 1980s suggest that amateur researchers consult about three times as many record classes as professionals, including many of value to the serious historian.

[31] Dr. Ian Buxton, Reader in Marine Transport at the University of Newcastle-upon-Tyne, is a notable exception.

Royal Naval College Dartmouth before going to sea,[32] and no serious attempt is made to cram history into a curriculum already grossly overloaded. Those officers who attend courses at the Royal Naval College Greenwich later in their career have some opportunity to make contact with naval history, but until recently it was unusual for them to take advantage of it. The Staff Course, however, has now been accredited as an M.A. degree, including options to study maritime history, and in this, the first year of the new course, about a score of officers have chosen to study some history. The Professor of History and International Affairs at Greenwich,[33] a historian of repute, is now teaching a significant amount of history (as distinct from strategic studies) for the first time since his appointment.

Outside public institutions, interest in naval and maritime history is sustained by several historical societies, notably the Navy Records Society, which still flourishes, and the Society for Nautical Research. The S.N.R. originally represented the amateur and antiquarian interest, especially in medieval shipping, which the Navy Records Society did not accept as respectable, or at least useful. Throughout its history it has acted both as a society of (in most cases) amateur enthusiasts, and as a vehicle for scholarship of a high standard. It is not always an easy balance to achieve, and for much of the past thirty years its journal, *The Mariner's Mirror*, has not been regarded in universities as a scholarly publication of the first rank, but under its present editor,[34] the quality of its articles has been excellent. At the same time it has not abandoned its original, not to say eccentric character, which has retained the loyalty of a society with a membership of over two thousand. Unusually, among either academic or amateur bodies, the S.N.R. has never accepted the division between "naval" and "maritime" history, and has always published material on an electric variety of "nautical" subjects and periods, but it is perceived by many "maritime" (meaning economic) historians as biased towards naval history, and this is certainly true of the interests of its membership. Undoubtedly the recent revival of *The Mariner's Mirror* owes something to healthy competition from the new *International Journal of Maritime History*.

The institutional division, and consequently the weakness, of naval and maritime history in Britain is in contrast to the situation in many other countries, and it is worth mentioning contacts with other countries to illustrate aspects of the subject in Britain. The biennial Anglo-French Naval Historians' Conferences, of which the fifth took place at Lorient in 1994, are now established and successful, but it is noteworthy that the initiative came from the French Service

---

[32]   But engineer officers spend four years at R.N.C. Manadon, where they take a degree which includes some non-technical courses.

[33]   Professor Geoffrey Till.

[34]   Dr. Michael Duffy of the Exeter Centre for Maritime Historical Studies, who has started the practice of "peer-review" of articles. The Review Editor, Dr. David Starkey, is also from the same Centre.

Historique de la Marine, which has published all the proceedings so far, and that no public or private body could at first be found to take responsibility for organising them in Britain, though the Society for Nautical Research has now assumed the burden.[35] Neither the Royal Navy nor any British university has shown interest. When the Dutch Navy organized a conference on the occasion of the third centenary of the 1688 revolution,[36] British historians were invited and the British government was represented diplomatically, but the only institutional response was made possible by the generosity of a commercial sponsor.[37] There appear to be no significant institutional links with maritime historians in Germany, Spain, or Italy, other than through the International Association of Maritime Museums. The Association of North Sea Societies, which organises a biennial conference,[38] provides an important connection between Britain, the Scandinavian countries, Germany, and the Netherlands, but it is largely confined to maritime historians in the narrow sense, particularly historians of the fisheries. The International Commission for Maritime History at its international level does not appear to regard naval history as forming part of its subject, though the British Committee (in conjunction with the S.N.R.) organises a lively and eclectic lecture series covering every aspect of the subject. In international relations, where institutional coherence matters, the picture is one of disorganisation and division.

If we turn from the question of who organises research, to what subjects are being studied and how, we find that naval and maritime history is in many respects flourishing. It is true that maritime history in the narrow sense is suffering from a smaller university base, but it remains strong, particularly in the nineteenth and twentieth centuries, the periods for which the materials survive for economic and quantitative analysis and for business history.[39] It has moreover been enriched by contact with imperial historians, who have long been interested in the economic causes and consequences of empire, and have lately noticed that it was ships which bound the British Empire together. The result has been some notable studies of merchant shipping in relation to wider issues.[40] A good

---

[35] The first British conference of the series, at Portsmouth in 1988, was organised by an *ad hoc* committee with much support from Hampshire County Council and Portsmouth City Council, but none at all from the Royal Navy.

[36] At the Koninklijke Instituut voor de Marine at Den Helder: its proceedings were published as *Navies and Armies: The Anglo-Dutch Relationship in War and Peace 1688–1988*, ed. G.J.A. Raven and N.A.M. Rodger (Edinburgh: 1990).

[37] *1688: The Seaborne Alliance and the Diplomatic Revolution*, the proceedings of a conference sponsored by Shell International Petroleum (National Maritime Museum: 1989).

[38] The last was at Aberdeen in 1993.

[39] Table 1 shows that the number of theses produced in maritime history has declined in recent years, but no more than the decline in university research in all subjects.

[40] For example Andrew Porter's *Victorian Shipping, Business and Imperial Policy: Donald Currie, the Castle Line and Southern Africa* (Royal Historical Society: 1986).

deal of valuable work is being undertaken, much of it by amateurs, in the history of the coasting trades and fisheries. For earlier periods it is more difficult to find evidence for commercial shipping, but there is a long and eminent tradition of extracting the history of medieval shipping and overseas trade from the Customs Ports Books.[41] It is particularly interesting to observe that historians of the sixteenth and early seventeenth centuries—a period in which it always made particularly little sense to distinguish naval and maritime history—are now treating overseas trade, exploration, piracy, privateering, and naval warfare as a common subject. There is still a tendency for scholars to stick to the records they are familiar with—the naval historians with the State Papers, the privateersmen with the High Court of Admiralty and so on—but the movement is in the right direction, and it is to be hoped that it will be imitated in other periods in which the academic demarcation lines have not been much crossed.

Naval history has undoubtedly suffered from its isolation from the academic world, but it has at least preserved an electric variety and profited from the explosion of popular interest in all aspects of history. The present century, especially the Second World War and more recent naval wars which are within living memory, continue to attract immense public enthusiasm and to justify large numbers of publications of varying levels of scholarship. The eighteenth and nineteenth centuries are attracting strong interest again, especially in such areas as the technical history of warships, where our understanding has been transformed by recent research. A number of outstanding younger scholars are working in seventeenth century naval history. Naval administration has received a good deal of attention, and such important auxiliary subjects as naval medicine have been attacked from various directions. "The Navy as an instrument of policy" is once again receiving serious attention and figures prominently in recent books on grand strategy and diplomacy,[42] as well as in the studies of economic historians[43] interested in the relationship between Britain's maritime, colonial, and economic expansion. The social history of the Navy, however, and of seafarers in general, remains largely unexplored, and the naval and maritime history of the Middle Ages is very much neglected. Moreover the study of actual warlike operations remains much less popular than hitherto, and study of tactics in battle is now completely abandoned.[44]

---

41 Dr. Wendy Childs of Leeds University is the best-known scholar now working in this field.

42 Such as H.M. Scott's *British Foreign Policy in the Age of the American Revolution* (Oxford: 1990).

43 Notably Professor P.K. O'Brien, now Director of the Institute of Historical Research of London University.

44 The recent publication of Brian Tunstall's *Naval Warfare in the Age of Sail: The Evolution of Fighting Tactics 1650–1815*, ed. Nicholas Tracy (London: 1990), is an apparent rather than a real exception, as the book was largely written in the 1930s.

A valuable collaborative work, *The New Maritime History of Devon*,[45] combines the work of a large number of maritime and naval historians. It is particularly encouraging not only that it attempts to span the full width of the subject, but that the editors have chosen contributors from a variety of institutions and walks of life other than universities.[46] Moreover, it was supported by the Leverhulme Trust and the British Academy as well as other national and local sponsors. This is one approach which evidently has the potential to heal many of the damaging divisions and weaknesses within the subject.[47] It is, however, a complex, expensive, and unwieldy one, and not likely to be suitable for general application; nor does the assembling of contributions, from many hands, on everything to do with the sea necessarily define the subject.

There remain many areas and periods of maritime history which have been neglected, but it may be suggested that the most urgent wants are less the coverage of neglected topics than the definition of the subject. At present, maritime history suffers from a lack of coherence. It is neither clearly identified as a discrete subject nor properly integrated into national and international history at large. It may seem paradoxical to suggest that a subject fragmented among many departments is yet not properly connected with any of them, but in practice it is easier to ignore a minority subject on the periphery of your own interests than a subject of major importance to others. If the importance of maritime history is to be recognized, it must be understood as forming an essential element in all sorts of history, but the best way of demonstrating that it does is to define it as a coherent subject in itself. Naval and maritime history would be stronger if it had more practitioners with the ability and the self-confidence to write big books, which would both define and project the subject. Here the lack of institutional base tells, for few historians outside universities (and fewer and fewer within them at present) have the time to write books on a grand scale. Many excellent books and articles on diverse aspects of the subject are being written, but we need historians able to take a large view and present the sweep of maritime history, both to a public hungry to read it and to the learned readers who need to be educated in its importance. At present journalists rush in where historians fear to tread, not always with happy results. In this connection it matters that no body in Britain giving grants for historical research, with the limited exception of the Leverhulme Trust, will accept applications from persons not holding full-time university posts. No other institution, not

---

[45] Vol. I, *From Early Times to the Late Eighteenth Century*, eds. Michael Duffy, Stephen Fisher, Basil Greenhill, David J. Starkey and Joyce Youings (London: 1992); Vol. II is not yet published. This work was begun before the formal institution of the Centre for Maritime Historical Studies but is closely associated with it.

[46] The contributors to the first volume are as follows: thirteen university historians, three university scholars of other subjects, two lecturers in other institutes of higher education, six museum staff, three officials of other public institutions, and five others.

[47] The possibility of a similar work on Cornwall is now being investigated.

even the British Museum, is regarded as a home of respectable scholarship. Without financial backing, few people will have the luck or ingenuity to support a big book.

It must also be said that not all historians are completely qualified to do so. Parochialism is a real weakness of both naval and maritime history in Britain, which is too often vigorous but narrow. This is a natural weakness in the self-taught amateur, and not as rare as it should be among people with an academic training. It is especially unfortunate that a subject which by its very nature is an international one, the history of the sea which brings men of different nations together in war and peace, is usually written from a national if not from a nationalist perspective. Though many British historians study the history of other countries, very few are interested in foreign navies.[48] Comparative studies of one nation with another are extremely rare, and much published work is still more or less monoglot.[49] This is not a problem confined to Britain, or to maritime history, but it is a serious flaw in any sort of scholarship.

So the state of naval and maritime history in Britain is in many respects vigorous and hopeful, but there remain notable weaknesses. The subject has never been more popular among the general public, and its inclusion in the new National Curriculum for English schools ought to ensure that it remains so. University departments that recognize and exploit this popularity ought to profit by doing so as well as strengthen the subject in process. At the same time it would be rash to ignore the existence of prejudice against it among academics of an older generation, meaning the generation now at the head of their profession. At a time when university departments are being graded on the quality of their research by committees of their peers, departments fear that exploiting vulgar popularity will earn them a low mark and lose them research funds. This matters, because no institutions outside universities are likely to be able to provide the support the subject needs if its importance is to be recognised. The national museums, especially the National Maritime Museum, are hard-pressed to cover their core responsibilities and unlikely to be able to increase their backing. The Navy sees almost no value in the study of history for its officers and is indifferent to the rise of popular interest in naval history, which, with imaginative handling, might do much for the Navy's popular constituency. Maybe the Navy's decision to participate in the celebration of the fiftieth anniversary of the Battle of the Atlantic in May

---

[48] An exception is R.A. Stradling of the University of Wales, Cardiff, author of *The Armada of Flanders: Spanish Maritime Policy and European War 1568–1668* (Cambridge: 1992).

[49] Capp's *Cromwell's Navy* recently offered an unfortunate example; the author was unaware of Hans-Christoph Junge's *Flottenpolitik und Revolution: Die Enstehung der englischhen Seemacht während der Herrschaft Cromwells* (Stuttgart: 1980), which had already covered much of the same ground.

1993 marks a change of heart, but we are still very remote from any official support for naval or maritime history.

Of all the desiderata, it may be suggested, the most to be wished for is some large books, conceived of with breadth and imagination, written with a skill to attract the general public, founded on scholarship which will compel academic acceptance, and sold too widely to be ignored. This may seem a tall order, but it has been done in our own day by historians, including one who made his name in naval history,[50] and it could be done again. What maritime history needs is essentially the same as history in general needs—a strong scholarly base linked to wide popular interest. A good deal of that is in place already, but the situation will remain unsatisfactory until the subject is better recognized in universities.

Table 1: University Theses by Subject, 1900–1990

	Naval	Maritime	Both	Total
1900-09	0	4+5	1+1	5+6
1910-19	0+5	1+12	2+1	3+18
1920-29	1+5	5+39	4+4	10+48
1930-39	6+12	36+50	4+8	46+70
1940-49	5+3	11+20	5+0	21+23
1950-59	6+11	55+40	6+5	67+56
1960-69	29+17	58+37	9+3	96+57
1970-79	56+14	96+61	14+9	166+84
1980-90	50+12	86+41	11+2	147+55
Totals	**153+79**	**352+305**	**56+33**	**561+417**

Source: *A Select Bibliography of British and Irish University Theses about Maritime History, 1792–1990*, eds. David M. Williams and Andrew P. White, International Maritime Economic History Association, Research in Maritime History No. 1 (St. John's: Newfoundland, 1991).

The figures in table 1 are for doctoral theses plus masters' theses (including B.Litt. and B.Phil.). In this table "Naval" includes combined operations, grand strategy and war planning; "Maritime" includes commercial shipping, overseas trade, fisheries and ports (other than dockyard ports); "Both" includes piracy, privateering, seaborne trade in wartime, and the connections between commerce, strategy, and policy. Economic geography, maritime law, and tourism are not included. Theses dealing with periods less than twenty years earlier than the date of submission have been excluded as dealing with current affairs rather than history. The classifications are based on the thesis titles and are inevitably subjective, so the figures should be taken as indicative only.

---

[50] Paul M. Kennedy, author of *The Rise and Fall of British Naval Mastery* and *The Rise and Fall of the Great Powers*.

Table 2: Theses of Selected Universities, 1900–1990

	Liverpool	Exeter	London	Oxford	Cambridge	St. Andrew's	Wales
1900-09	0	0	5	3	0	0	1
1910-19	1	0	11	1	0	0	3
1920-29	1	0	22	6	4	0	7
1930-39	6	0	45	27	4	0	8
1940-49	1	0	12	5	4	0	2
1950-59	6	0	51	17	13	0	5
1960-69	11	4	65	15	19	1	6
1970-79	16	19	59	32	24	5	9
1980-90	6	6	48	22	12	7	4
	48	29	318	128	80	13	45

In this table the theses are those listed in table 1 from the three most prominent "research universities" and some others with interests in maritime history.

6

Maritime History in Canada
The Social and Economic Dimensions

Lewis R. Fischer and Gerald E. Panting

Canada is a nation with a significant maritime heritage. The aboriginal peoples who first occupied the land were overwhelmingly maritime in orientation. The earliest Europeans to visit the shores of the "New Found Land" were attracted principally by the lure of maritime resources, and they built the richest fishery in the world. The non-aboriginal portion of the population was comprised overwhelmingly of intra-continental migrants, most of whom arrived by sea. Until the coming of the railways in the middle of the nineteenth century, settlements almost always abutted water, and the penetration of the great North American landmass utilized the system of rivers and lakes that cut deeply into the continent. In the nineteenth century Canada built upon its comparative advantages to amass the third largest merchant fleet in the world. In the current century, offshore resources, especially oil, offer the promise of the latest in a series of resource booms that have shaped much of the Canadian experience.

Given the importance of marine features to its history—and as one of the few countries in the world to border on three oceans—it might be imagined that maritime topics would occupy a central place in the national consciousness. Such an assumption, however, would be erroneous. That maritime interests have always been peripheral to Canadians reflects a reality similar to that in the United States: the main currents of our historical thought have always been concerned with the dramatic saga of filling what Europeans perceived to be an "empty" continent. As in the U.S., the North American landmass has been associated with progress and opportunity; the sea, on the other hand, has been a moat which protects us from the depravity from which our ancestors fled in the old world. Moreover, as a non-imperialist nation, Canadians have never seen the sea as a route to expansion, as have the people of many other nations.[1]

---

[1] Canadian expansionism has assumed an economic rather than a political character. In particular, this has been reflected in the penetration by Canadian banks into certain parts of the Caribbean and Canadian resource companies into various parts of Latin America. But as a nation which has traditionally been more concerned with protecting its sovereignty from the American leviathan, the activities of Canadian businesses overseas remain virtually unknown to the majority of the population.

As a result, maritime history in Canada has not been blessed with a surfeit of public support. To make matters worse, the subject has been largely ignored in Canadian universities. While in part this reflects the state of public interest, much of the responsibility for this state of affairs rests with those who have chosen to study maritime subjects. Many of the questions posed by maritime historians have not been illuminated by mainstream scholarly ideas or debates, and a good deal of maritime history in Canada—as in most of the rest of the world—has been compromised by an unhealthy dose of antiquarianism. These characteristics have often made it difficult for the bulk of the historical profession to take maritime history seriously.

Fortunately, there is evidence that the constraints which have prevented maritime history from being central to the way we think about the past are being overcome. A new awareness of the importance of the maritime past has been reflected in the past two decades by the construction of major new maritime museums in Halifax and Kingston, Ontario, as well as the opening of a spate of smaller museums elsewhere. As well, many of our more established museums, such as the Maritime Museum of British Columbia, are undergoing significant facelifts and expansions, even in a time of general fiscal restraint. Maritime heritage organizations and societies for marine enthusiasts grew substantially in the 1980s and show no signs of stagnation in the 1990s.

The scholarly community has also been part of this ferment. A new generation of scholars is finally asking questions of interest to other historians, who are conversely beginning to comprehend the way that the fruits of maritime historical research can illuminate their own scholarship. These relatively new phenomena have led to an expansion in the number of scholars willing to identify themselves as maritime historians as well as to growth in the number of courses and programs offered.

All of this makes us reasonably optimistic about the state of maritime history in the Dominion. This paper presents evidence to support this assessment. Our concern is with the state of non-naval maritime scholarship in Canada. Despite the intellectual artificiality of separating naval and non-naval maritime scholarship, as a heuristic tool this division has some justification.[2] This is because in important ways the Canadian contribution to the study of the social and economic aspects of maritime history has been relatively greater than in many

---

[2] To refer to the non-naval side of the topic, we will generally use the term "maritime history." This conforms to the distinction between naval topics and the remainder of the historical study of man's relationship to the sea first suggested by the Robert G. Albion in his series of bibliographies; see *Maritime and Naval History: An Annotated Bibliography* (Cambridge, Mass.: 1951). This semantic convention was enunciated even more clearly by Robin Craig in his editorial in the first issue of the journal *Maritime History*, I (1971), pp. 1–3, and by the late Ralph Davis in his review essay, "Maritime History: Progress and Problems," in Sheila Marriner ed., *Business and Businessmen: Studies in Business, Economic and Accounting History* (Liverpool: 1978), p. 169. We are grateful to David M. Williams for drawing these references to our attention.

other nations. While this is certainly not true if measured by the quantity of scholarly output, the judgement is defensible when Canadian scholarship is placed in international perspective. Although space does not permit us to set out the complete international context, a careful comparison of the Canadian contribution with what is described elsewhere in this volume will, we believe, sustain this point.

We make no pretence in this essay to being complete, and we apologize that so much of importance has necessarily been omitted. Our focus is on Canadian scholars and scholarship, and we have little to say about maritime history in its more "popular" manifestations. This same caveat extends to our discussion of historians, university programmes, and historiography. For the most part we intend to focus on those areas in which we believe Canadians have made particularly significant contributions and to a lesser extent on areas in which Canada has been especially weak; we generally exclude the great middle ground from consideration. Likewise, we will have little to say about non-historians who probe the maritime past except where they have had a demonstrable influence on the work of historians. Although we recognize the legitimate role of those from other disciplines, to make the subject manageable requires us to sharpen our focus.

We begin by examining the Canadian scholarly community with an interest in maritime history. The place of maritime history in Canadian universities is dealt with in the second part.[3] The third section discusses scholarly organizations and journals dealing with maritime history. The final part of the paper focuses on some important Canadian contributions in the realm of scholarly publishing. Although our focus will be on scholarship about Canada written by Canadians, it would be parochial to ignore the contributions of non-Canadians who have written about this country or the achievements of those who have focused on the historical experience elsewhere. Because our purpose is to present a picture of the state of maritime scholarship in Canada today, we will limit our discussion in the last section to works written since the mid–1970s, with a particular emphasis on what has been produced in the last decade.

Canadian Maritime Scholars

One of the authors present has conducted several surveys in the past few years of Canadian maritime scholars. They are worth citing here, both as an introduction to the Canadian maritime scholarly community and as a context in which to place it. In 1987 the Canadian Nautical Research Society (CNRS), the Canadian sub-commission of the International Commission for Maritime History (ICMH), published a research directory in its newsletter, *ARGONAUTA*. A

---

[3] While the term "scholarly community" in this paper includes historians employed not only in universities and community colleges but also in archives and museums, we do not intend in this essay to discuss the state of Canadian museums and archives.

breakdown of the directory shows that approximately two-thirds of the scholarly membership had a primary focus on maritime rather than naval topics.[4] An analysis of an updated directory published in 1990 yielded similar results.[5] While the membership of CNRS is not perfectly representative of Canadian maritime scholars, we estimate that about 90 percent of the historians who have made maritime topics a significant part of their research are included in one or the other of the directories.[6] The naval to non-naval ratio underscores the relative importance of non-naval topics in Canada. This is in stark contrast to findings elsewhere. A breakdown of the U.S. membership in the North American Society for Oceanic History (NASOH) shows that the relationship between naval and non-naval scholars is almost exactly the obverse of Canada. And a published study of German maritime historians shows that the vast majority have naval rather than maritime interests.[7] Canada is thus somewhat unique in having such a high proportion of maritime specialists.

A spatial analysis of the interests of Canadian maritime scholars suggests its strengths and weaknesses. The largest concentrations were concerned with the East Coast and the Great Lakes–St. Lawrence system; together, they comprised the geographic foci of about two-thirds of Canadian maritime scholars. The Arctic and the West Coast account for almost a quarter, although the proportions would be higher if we included scholars interested in contemporary events in the Arctic and non-historians for the West Coast. About 10 percent of Canadian maritime scholars are interested in international maritime history. The international component is certainly higher than in most European countries, although it is not clear if it is higher than in the U.S. Nonetheless, it reflects a condition to which we will return later in the paper: the fact that some Canadian scholars have attempted to study maritime history in a larger, less place-specific context than is the case in many other nations. Not surprisingly, the largest components of this international group have been interested in topics such as merchant shipping and exploration.

In a nation which by world standards has a relatively short history, it is not surprising that the vast majority of Canadian maritime historians have focused on the nineteenth and twentieth centuries. Those scholars who study earlier

---

[4] For a full discussion of the interests of members, see Lewis R. Fischer, "Maritime History around the World: Canada, *ARGONAUTA*, V, no. 2 (March 1988), pp. 2–4. The directory appeared in *ARGONAUTA*, IV, no. 4 (October1987). For an opposing view, see Eric W. Sager, "Counterpoint," *ARGONAUTA*, V, nos. 2–3 (June-September 1988), pp. 6–7.

[5] *ARGONAUTA*, VII, Special Supplement (October 1990).

[6] This estimate is, of course, somewhat arbitrary, since maritime history cuts across a variety of other sub-disciplines. We make this estimate based upon our knowledge of the field rather than on any precise empirical criteria.

[7] See Rolf Walter, "Maritime History in Germany," *Maritime Economic History Group Newsletter*, I, no. 2 (September 1987).

periods tend to be concentrated in exploration, ethno-history, and the fisheries of the East Coast and the St. Lawrence River.

The vast majority of Canadian maritime historians writing scholarly works are employed in universities. Unlike in many European nations, Canadian maritime museums have not traditionally funded research posts only tangentially related to the mounting of exhibits.[8] A similar survey taken twenty or thirty years ago would likely have found a larger contribution from archives, but the professionalization of archival work has reduced the number of historians employed in such repositories who are able to devote a significant amount of time to scholarship. Since maritime scholarship in Canada has clearly been concentrated in universities—and since it is in the universities that new maritime historians are being trained—an examination of the place of maritime history in academe is essential for comprehending the state of the field.

Maritime History in Canadian Universities

At an international congress in the mid–1980s, an informal poll was taken among the maritime historians in attendance concerning their training. Not surprisingly, the overwhelming majority indicated that their graduate preparation was in something other than "maritime history." On one level, this is not surprising. After all, the techniques of business history can be applied equally well to studying a steel company or a shipping firm; the insights of social history are applicable to both landward and maritime-oriented groups; and so on. Indeed, maritime historians need to admit that their field has no discrete boundaries to separate it from other historical experiences and no particular set of insights or approaches which mark it as a distinct historical sub-discipline. Yet it is also true that a focus on the relationship between man and the sea provides a clear distinction from which to build a sub-discipline. Moreover, maritime history has spawned a literature which, if not wholly separate from other realms of history, at least contains some common characteristics. This suggests that it ought to be possible to develop undergraduate and graduate programs in maritime history and hence to produce a body of graduates with unique perspectives and knowledge.[9] Such programs will of course not be isolated from other parts of the discipline; rather, they will borrow insights and approaches where necessary.

If we accept that it is legitimate to offer programs in maritime history, we must also concede that Canada has been slow to develop identifiable courses and programs in the field. This does not make the country unique; indeed, a survey

---

[8]   Although some European museum people might take exception to this characterization, it must be assessed comparatively. It is unquestionable that relative to conditions in North America museum employees in Europe (at least outside Britain) in general have more time for research.

[9]   Another argument for providing training in maritime history is that traditional preparation, organized as it is for the most part around national histories, may not be the most appropriate approach for understanding what is, after all, one of the most international of phenomena.

of the state of the teaching of maritime history in most other countries would produce strikingly similar results. It is therefore safe to say that the majority of the next generation of maritime historians will be trained in more or less the same way as were their predecessors.

But this will not be true for the entire new generation of Canadian maritime historians. The number of universities which offer regular courses in maritime history is increasing gradually and currently includes Dalhousie and Queen's University, as well as the Universities of Calgary, British Columbia, and Victoria. A number of others offer maritime courses on an irregular basis. But the school with the greatest commitment to maritime history is Memorial University of Newfoundland, which is the only institution in North America to offer a regular program of both undergraduate and graduate courses in the field. Indeed, to our knowledge, only the University of Leiden in the Netherlands offers comparable training.[10]

Memorial's core undergraduate program is not all-inclusive. Instead, it focuses on the maritime history of the North Atlantic since 1450. In addition, there are a series of advanced seminars in specific aspects of maritime history and a variety of supplemental cognate courses. On the graduate level, Memorial offers a series of seminars leading to both the MA and PhD degrees. Since the program is relatively new, it is too early to judge its success with any degree of confidence. But it does represent an acceptance of the significant role that maritime history has to play in the training of undergraduate and graduate students.

In early 1991 we did a survey of graduate theses currently in progress in maritime history at Canadian universities. To compile this overview, we contacted every director of graduate history programs at all Canadian universities. Although some failed to respond, most did. At the time there were seventeen theses underway, nine of which were on non-naval topics. Of the latter group, six were being pursued at Memorial (four PhDs and two MAs); the others were being written at the Universities of Guelph, New Brunswick, and York.[11]

It is clear that regardless of how the Memorial program evolves, many (and perhaps most) future Canadian maritime historians will be trained in traditional ways. Basically, this means that they will write maritime theses at a variety of universities. Although many will be supervised by maritime historians, they will not be trained specifically in maritime history.

Canadian Maritime History Organizations and Journals

In most nations in which maritime history has a reasonably high profile, there are a variety of organizations to encourage and promote its study. Many such

---

[10] In the U.S., the Williams College program may develop similarly, as may East Carolina's program, if that school is ever granted approval to offer the PhD. Texas A&M offers a similarly comprehensive program in nautical archaeology.

[11] The graduate student research directories appeared in *ARGONAUTA*, VIII, No. 1 (January 1991) and no. 2 (April 1991).

groups, such as the World Ship Society and the Steamboat Historical Society, are unabashedly popular in orientation, providing a home for enthusiasts and only occasionally promoting what we recognize as scholarship. Others, such as the Society for Nautical Research (SNR) in Britain, are umbrella organizations which cater to both enthusiasts and scholars. There are relatively few maritime organizations which are devoted solely to scholarly work.

Canada has some of each type of organization. Those that have enjoyed the most rapid growth in the past two decades are almost certainly the support groups which have evolved around maritime museums and heritage societies. While they deserve recognition for the important work they have done in helping to alter the public consciousness, their accomplishments fall outside the purview of this paper. In keeping with the focus enunciated in the introduction, we would like to concentrate here on the second two categories.

Canada's equivalent to the SNR, or to NASOH in the U.S., is the Canadian Nautical Research Society (CNRS), which is also the Canadian national commission of the International Commission for Maritime History.[12] Current membership is approximately three hundred, about one-third of whom are actively engaged in scholarly research and writing. While CNRS is far from the largest of the twenty-three national commissions that comprise ICMH, a reflection of its success is that it has roughly twice the membership of NASOH, although Canada's population is only one-tenth that of the United States.[13] CNRS seeks to promote interest in maritime history through an annual conference, a series of awards for books and articles to honour excellence in Canadian maritime history, and by publishing both a quarterly newsletter, *ARGONAUTA*, and a quarterly scholarly journal, *The Northern Mariner/Le Marin du nord*.[14] CNRS members also frequently are members of other marine organizations, although the goals of many of these societies tend to be popular rather than scholarly. Many Canadian maritime historians are also members of NASOH. Indeed, NASOH's immediate past president, Barry Gough, is a distinguished Canadian maritime historian.

To achieve its goal of promoting Canadian maritime scholarship, the publication of *The Northern Mariner/Le Marin du nord* is probably the most significant activity of CNRS. *TNM/LMN*, which began in 1991, accepts both naval and maritime articles. Its first ten issues have contained a variety of essays on maritime historical subjects, including Canadian whaling, fishing, harbour development, shipbuilding, merchant shipping, and the Arctic. Especially significant has been

---

[12] Like CNRS, NASOH is a national commission affiliated with ICMH. SNR, on the other hand, is not the British national commission.

[13] Lest the comparison prove offensive, we should admit that about 10 percent of the CNRS membership is drawn from abroad, with the U.S. providing the largest component. But it is also the case, as we suggest below, that many Canadians are members of NASOH.

[14] Both of these publications are published at Memorial University of Newfoundland and edited by Lewis R. Fischer, Gerald E. Panting, and Olaf U. Janzen.

the development of what is arguably the most comprehensive maritime book review section in the world. *TNM/LMN* has been averaging about sixty reviews per issue; its policy is to attempt to review all books on Canadian maritime history and the most important volumes published elsewhere, including a number written in languages other than English.

Also important for promoting the scholarly study of Canada's maritime past are the Keith Matthews Awards, presented annually to the best book and best article either on a Canadian marine subject or by a Canadian on a foreign topic. There are also honourable mentions awarded at the discretion of the committee. The book award, which was inaugurated in 1984, has gone to non-naval books about half the time. The article award, which began in 1985, has been dominated by non-naval essays.[15]

Canada also occupies a key role in the umbrella organization of which CNRS is a part, the International Commission for Maritime History. The Secretary-General of ICMH is currently Canadian, which means that the secretariat of the largest international maritime and naval organization is in Canada. ICMH's newsletter, *ICMHNews*, is edited at Memorial University of Newfoundland. Moreover, the next quinquennial congress of the ICMH, traditionally the largest maritime history conference in the world, will be held in Montréal in 1995 and is being organized by a Canadian. This prominent role in ICMH helps to ensure greater visibility for Canadian scholarship in international circles.

Canadians also play significant roles in the only international maritime history organization solely for scholars. This is the International Maritime Economic History Association (IMEHA), which is concerned principally with the economic and social aspects of maritime history. Founded in 1986, one of the two Vice-Presidents is a Canadian, as are both the Secretary and the Treasurer. As with the ICMH, the secretariat of the IMEHA is located at Memorial.

The IMEHA also sponsors an international scholarly congress every four years. The First International Congress of Maritime History, held in Liverpool, England, in August 1992 attracted more than one-hundred scholars from over thirty nations. Fifteen percent of the papers were presented by Canadians.[16]

In addition, the IMEHA publishes the leading scholarly journal in maritime history, the *International Journal of Maritime History*. Although the *IJMH*, which began publishing in 1989, has an international focus, it has included a respectable sample of Canadian maritime writing. The IMEHA also publishes monographs,

---

[15] It is worth noting, however, that Marc Milner, who contributes an essay on Canadian naval history to this volume, was a winner of the article award in 1989 for his essay "The Implications of Technological Backwardness: The Royal Canadian Navy: 1939–1945," *Canadian Defense Quarterly*, IX, no. 3 (Winter 1989).

[16] The Second International Congress of Maritime History will be held in Amsterdam in 1996; the third will be in Esbjerg, Denmark, in the year 2000.

bibliographies and reprints in a regular series entitled Research in Maritime History. Both are edited and published at Memorial.[17]

There is one other Canadian maritime journal that publishes a reasonable proportion of scholarly essays. *FreshWater*, a journal of Great Lakes maritime history published at the Marine Museum of the Great Lakes in Kingston, has in a short time attained a reputation for scholarly publishing at least equal to its American counterpart, *Inland Seas*. But because its subscription list is heavily weighted toward museum supporters, it is unlikely that *FreshWater* will ever become primarily a scholarly journal.[18]

On balance, we feel safe in asserting that Canadian maritime historians are well-served by the existing maritime organizations and journals in the country. Although precise comparisons are difficult, given the size of the community we would judge that Canadian maritime scholars are served at least as well as any comparable group in the world.

Recent Canadian Contributions to Maritime Historical Scholarship

Any judgement about the state of Canadian maritime history scholarship depends on the approach adopted. For example, within the country some geographic regions, such as the East Coast, have been reasonably well-served while others, such as the West Coast, have been studied less adequately by scholars. Canadians have made major contributions in the histories of merchant shipping, methodology, fishing (including whaling and sealing), and maritime social and economic history, but have been relatively neglectful of topics such as the history of shipping firms and the impact of technological change. Among Canadian scholars whose focus has been outside the country, it is more difficult to discern any particular specialties.

Ultimately, though, a balanced evaluation depends on the choice of criteria. If we assess their contribution to national scholarship, Canadian scholars fare better than if we use international recognition as a standard. This should not be taken as a criticism, however, since there is little doubt that a similar verdict could be made about maritime historians virtually anywhere. Our view is that on balance the Canadian contribution has been above average. To support this contention we examine below some of the main trends in recent Canadian maritime scholarship.[19]

---

[17] The Editor-in-Chief of the *International Journal of Maritime History* is Lewis R. Fischer, who also is series editor of Research in Maritime History.

[18] *FreshWater* is edited by a board including Maurice D. Smith, M. Stephen Salmon, Walter Lewis, Ken Macpherson, and Gordon D. Shaw.

[19] The organization below is based loosely on a number of topics. The discerning reader will recognize that many of the works discussed could have been included in two or more categories. To avoid repetition, however, we have discussed particular books and articles only once.

One of the topics in which Canadians have made internationally recognized contributions is the history of merchant shipping, especially on the East Coast. Twenty years ago the recognized authority on the subject was still Frederick William Wallace, whose romantic and often antiquarian books dated from the 1920s.[20] That this has changed is largely, but not entirely, due to the work of individuals associated with the Atlantic Canada Shipping Project (ACSP) at Memorial University of Newfoundland. Since both of the present authors were associated with this project, we feel compelled to admit that its reputation and output were at least as much a function of the resources available as the people involved. This is not to deny that the ACSP benefitted from the talents of some exceptional scholars, especially the late Keith Matthews, who conceived of the study in the first place; the late David Alexander, who provided much of the intellectual direction; and Eric W. Sager, who has gone on to become one of the most prolific and insightful maritime historians not only in Canada but also in the world. Yet without the benefit of six years and more than $1 million, this project to examine the rise and decline of the eastern Canadian shipping industry in the nineteenth century would never have produced the results it did.

The best place for a neophyte to begin to understand the contributions of the ACSP is with Eric Sager and Gerry Panting's *Maritime Capital*, which not only summarizes many of the project's conclusions but also extends the analysis in new directions.[21] Yet a full appreciation of the topics investigated by those associated with the project requires more comprehensive reading. The micro-level work of the ACSP can be found in six volumes of essays, which include not only contributions from project members but also papers by a wide range of national and international scholars for context.[22] In addition, there are a series of other publications which contain material and insights not found in *Maritime Capital*.[23]

---

[20] See Frederick William Wallace, *Wooden Ships and Iron Men* (London: 1924); Wallace, *In the Wake of the Wind Ships* (Toronto: 1927); Wallace, *Record of Canadian Shipping* (London: 1929).

[21] Eric W. Sager with Gerald E. Panting, *Maritime Capital: The Shipping Industry in Atlantic Canada, 1820–1914* (Montréal: 1990).

[22] Keith Matthews and Gerry Panting, eds., *Ships and Shipbuilding in the North Atlantic Region* (St. John's: 1978); Lewis R. Fischer and Eric W. Sager, eds., *The Enterprising Canadians: Entrepreneurs and Economic Development in Eastern Canada, 1820–1914* (St. John's: 1979); David Alexander and Rosemary Ommer, eds., *Volumes not Values: Canadian Sailing Ships and World Trades* (St. John's: 1979); Rosemary Ommer and Gerald Panting, eds., *Working Men Who Got Wet* (St. John's: 1980); Lewis R. Fischer and Eric W. Sager, eds., *Merchant Shipping and Economic Development in Atlantic Canada* (St. John's: 1982); and Lewis R. Fischer and Gerald E. Panting, eds., *Change and Adaptation in Maritime History: The North Atlantic Fleets in the Nineteenth Century* (St. John's: 1985).

[23] Chief among these are a series of works by Eric W. Sager and Lewis R. Fischer, including "Patterns of Investment in the Shipping Industries of Atlantic Canada, 1820–1900," *Acadiensis*, IX, no. 1 (Autumn 1979), pp. 19–43; "Atlantic Canada and the Age of Sail Revisited," *Canadian Historical Review*, LXIII, no. 2 (June 1982), pp. 125–50; and *Shipping and Shipbuilding in Atlantic Canada, 1820–1914* (Ottawa: 1986). See also David Alexander and Gerald Panting, "The Mercantile Fleet and Its Owners: Yarmouth, Nova Scotia, 1840–1889," *Acadiensis*, VII, no. 2 (Spring 1978), pp. 3–28; Rosemary Ommer, "Anticipating the Trend: The Pictou Ship Register, 1840–1889," *Acadiensis*, X, no. 1 (Autumn 1980), pp. 67–89; Ommer,

Given the complexity and cost of the ACSP, it is not surprising that it has failed to stimulate comparable studies of other Canadian fleets. This point notwithstanding, it is nonetheless disappointing that scholarly research on merchant shipping in other parts of the country has been disappointing. The best recent work on the St. Lawrence has been done by Jean Leclerc.[24] On Canadian merchant shipping on the Great Lakes the contributions by Steven Salmon, Walter Lewis, and Kenneth Mackenzie have been first-rate, but merchant shipping on the Lakes has by and large been left to the popularizers.[25] For the west coast, there is no comprehensive work, although the recent volume by Ken Coates and Bill Morrison and a preliminary essay by Eric Sager give a good feel for what might be done.[26] If the approach of the ACSP to merchant shipping has not been emulated for other parts of the country, it has been applied to Norway and the international economy by Lewis Fischer in collaboration with Helge Nordvik.[27]

But aside from the ACSP, the most important work on merchant shipping done by Canadians has been on foreign fleets. Richard W. Unger is an acknowledged authority on medieval shipping, concentrating mostly on the Low Countries.[28] Jake Knoppers, a pioneer in applying computer-assisted analysis to maritime history, has written a seminal work on the shipping involved in eighteenth-century Dutch trade with Russia.[29] And David Eltis has made important contributions to the ongoing debate about shipping in the slave trade.[30]

"The Decline of the Eastern Canadian Shipping Industry, 1880–95," *Journal of Transport History*, V, no. 1 (March 1984), pp. 25–44.

[24] Jean Leclerc, *Le Saint-Laurent et ses pilotes 1805–1860* (Montréal: 1990).

[25] See, for example, M. Stephen Salmon, "'Rank Imitation and the Sincerest Flattery': The Dominion Marine Association and the Revision of the Canadian Coasting Regulations, 1922–1936," *The Northern Mariner/Le Marin du nord*, I, no. 3 (July 1991), pp. 1–24; Kenneth S. Mackenzie, "C.C. Ballantyne and the Canadian Government Merchant Marine, 1917–1921," *The Northern Mariner/Le Marin du nord*, II, no. 1 (January 1992), pp. 1–13.

[26] Ken Coates and Bill Morrison, *The Sinking of the Princess Sophia: Taking the North Down with Her* (Toronto: 1990); Eric W. Sager, "The Shipping Industry in British Columbia from 1867 to 1914," *The Northern Mariner/Le Marin du nord*, III, no. 3 (July 1993), pp. 45–50.

[27] See, for example, Lewis R. Fischer and Helge W. Nordvik, "A Crucial Six Percent: Norwegian Sailors in the Canadian Merchant Marine, 1863–1913," *Sjøfartshistorisk Årbok, 1984* (Bergen: 1985), pp. 139–59; "Myth and Reality in Baltic Shipping: The Timber Trade to Britain, 1863–1908," *Scandinavian Journal of History*, XII, no. 2 (Summer: 1987), pp. 99–116; and "Finländere i den Kanadensiska Handelsflottan, 1863–1913," *Historisk Tidskrift för Finland*, LXXIII, no. 3 (1988), pp. 373–94. As with the ACSP, much of their work is based on large-scale data sets.

[28] See, for example, Richard W. Unger, *The Art of Medieval Technology: Images of Noah the Shipbuilder* (New Brunswick, N.J.: 1991); Unger, "The Tonnage of Europe's Merchant Fleets, 1300–1800," *American Neptune*, LII, no. 4 (Fall 1992), pp. 247–61; Unger, "Marine Paintings and the History of Shipbuilding," in David Freedberg and Jan DeVries, eds., *Art in History, History in Art: Studies in Seventeenth Century Dutch Culture* (Los Angeles: 1991), pp. 75–93; Unger, "Integration of Baltic and Lower Countries Grain Markets," *Interactions of Amsterdam and Antwerp with the Baltic Region, 1400–1800* (Leiden: 1983), pp. 1–10.

[29] Jake V.T. Knoppers, *Dutch Trade with Russia from the Time of Peter I to Alexander I: A Quantitative Study of Eighteenth Century Shipping* (2 vols., Montréal: 1976).

[30] See, especially, David Eltis, *Economic Growth and the Ending of the Transatlantic Slave Trade* (Oxford: 1987).

The other contribution of the ACSP was in pioneering techniques in the computer-assisted quantitative analysis of large masses of historical material. Indeed, some of its data sets remain among the largest yet created by historians. Here the spin-offs have been slightly more encouraging; the software and techniques developed by the project have been used in Canada by the Marine Museum of the Great Lakes and abroad by the National Maritime Museum in the United Kingdom and the Bergen Maritime Museum in Norway.[31] Lewis Fischer has also used ACSP material as part of the data base for an international study of maritime wages in the nineteenth century.[32]

Fishing has also attracted a good deal of recent Canadian interest. Although no one has yet expanded on the seminal work of the late Keith Matthews on the seventeenth and eighteenth-century migratory fishery from the west of England,[33] there has been a flurry of work on the French period on the East Coast, in particular by Jean-François Brière, Olaf Janzen, and Laurier Turgeon.[34]

[31] The best introduction to the project's methodology is Lewis R. Fischer and Eric W. Sager, "An Approach to the Quantitative Analysis of British Shipping Records," *Business History*, XXII, No. 2 (July 1980), pp. 135–51.

[32] For some examples of the study of international wages, see Lewis R. Fischer, "International Maritime Labour, 1863–1900: World Wages and Trends," *The Great Circle*, X, no. 1 (Spring 1988), pp. 1–21; "Seamen in a Space Economy: International Regional Patterns of Maritime Wages on Sailing Vessels, 1863–1900," in Stephen Fisher, ed., *Lisbon as a Port Town, the British Seaman and Other Maritime Themes* (Exeter: 1988), pp. 57–92; "Seamen in the Industrial Revolution: Maritime Wages in Antwerp during the Shipping Transition, 1863–1900," *Collectanea Maritima*, V (1991), pp. 331–42; "Around the Rim: Seamen's Wages in North Sea Ports, 1863–1900," in Lewis R. Fischer *et al.*, eds., *The North Sea: Twelve Essays on the Social History of Maritime Labour* (Stavanger: 1992), pp. 59–78. In collaboration with Helge W. Nordvik, Fischer has also completed a number of wage studies of the Norwegian maritime sector; see, for example, Fischer and Nordvik, "From Namsos to Halden: Myths and Realities in the History of Norwegian Seamen's Wages, 1850–1914," *Scandinavian Economic History Review*, XXXV, no. 1 (1987), pp. 41–65; "Wages in the Norwegian Maritime Sector, 1850–1914: A Re-Interpretation," in Lewis R. Fischer, Helge W. Nordvik and Walter E. Minchinton, eds., *Shipping and Trade in the Northern Seas, 1600–1939* (Bergen: 1988), pp. 14–35; "Regional Wages in the Age of Sail: The Price of Sailing Ship Labour in Towns along the Oslofjord, 1899–1914," *Norsk Sjøfartsmuseum Årsberetning 1987* (Oslo: 1988), pp. 159–86; "Salaries of the Sea: Maritime Wages in Stavanger, 1892–1914," *Stavanger Historisk Årbok 1987* (Stavanger: 1988), pp. 103–32; "Norwegian *Matroser*. Seafarers and National Labour Markets in Norway, 1850–1914," *Scandinavian-Canadian Studies*, IV (1989), pp. 58–81; "The Regional Economy of Late Nineteenth Century Norway: Maritime Wages as a Measure of Spatial Inequality, 1850–1914," in Illka Nummela, ed., *Sitä Kuusta Kuuleninen* (Jyväskylä: 1990), pp. 89–112.

[33] Keith Matthews, "A History of the West of England-Newfoundland Fisher" (unpublished D.Phil. thesis, Oxford University, 1968).

[34] Among Brière's most important contributions are *La Pêche française en Amérique du Nord au XVIII siècle* (Montréal: 1990); "The Safety of Navigation in the 18th Century French Cod Fisheries," *Acadiensis*, XVI, no. 2 (Spring 1987), pp. 85–94; "Le commerce triangulaire entre les ports terre-neuviers français, les pêcheries d'Amerique du nord et Marseilles au XVIIIe siècle," *Revue d'Histoire de l'Amérique Francaise*, XL, no. 2 (September 1986), pp. 193–214; and "Pêche et politique à Terre-Neuve au XVIIIe siècle: la France véritable gagnante du traité d'Utrecht?" *Canadian Historical Review*, LXIV, no. 2 (June 1983), pp. 168–87. Olaf Janzen's meticulous work can be sampled in "'Une Grande Liaison': French Fishermen from Île Royale on the Coast of Southwestern Newfoundland, 1714–1766—A Preliminary Survey," *Newfoundland Studies*, III, no. 2 (Fall 1987), pp. 183–200; "The American Threat to the Newfoundland Fisheries, 1776–1777," *American Neptune*, XLVIII, no. 3 (Summer 1988), pp. 154–64; "'Une Petite Republique' in Southwestern

For the nineteenth century there are recent books by Shannon Ryan and Rosemary Ommer, the former focusing on the marketing of Newfoundland cod overseas and the latter on the rise and decline of Jersey-dominated fishing in the Baie des Chaleurs.[35] Sandy Balcom's study of the Lunenburg fishery, which originated as graduate thesis at Memorial, also has much to recommend it.[36] The sociologist Peter Sinclair has produced a string of books and articles on the nineteenth and twentieth-century Newfoundland fishery and its communities.[37] A recent superb collection of essays puts the credit system which bound labour to the fisheries in international perspective.[38] For the more recent Newfoundland fishery, the *magnum opus* is David G. Alexander's *The Decay of Trade*.[39]

While the Great Lakes fisheries have received much less attention from historians,[40] the West Coast has been better served. Of particular importance is the collaborative volume written by Patricia Marchak, Neil Guppy, and John McMullan, which not only examines the history of the industry but also advances important theoretical considerations.[41] Several works by Dianne Newell have added to our understanding of the Pacific salmon fishery.[42] The most important Canadian contributions to foreign fishing history have unquestionably been Laurier Turgeon's work on France and Daniel Vickers' series of studies on colonial Massachusetts.[43]

Newfoundland: The Limits of Imperial Authority in a Remote Maritime Environment," in Lewis R. Fischer and Walter Minchinton, eds., *People of the Northern Seas* (St. John's: 1992), pp. 1–33; and "'Bretons . . . sans scruple': The Family Chenu of Saint-Malo and the Illicit Trade in English Cod during the Middle of the 18th Century," in *Proceedings of the Fifteenth Meeting of the French Colonial Historical Society* (Lanham, Md: 1992), pp. 189–200. Turgeon's best essay on the Canadian east coast fishery is "Colbert et la pêche française à Terre-Neuve," in Roland Mousnier, ed., *Un Nouveau Colbert* (Paris: 1985), pp. 255–68.

[35] Shannon Ryan, *Fish Out of Water: The Newfoundland Saltfish Trade, 1814–1914* (St. John's: 1986); Rosemary E. Ommer, *From Outpost to Outport: A Structural Analysis of the Jersey-Gaspé Cod Fishery, 1767–1886* (Montréal: 1992). Nicolas Landry, "Les pêches canadiennes au XIXe siècle," *The Northern Mariner/Le Marin du nord*, II, No. 4 (October 1992), pp. 23–30, is a recent review essay which puts the writings on the nineteenth-century eastern Canadian fishery in perspective.

[36] B.A. Balcom, *History of the Lunenburg Fishing Industry* (Lunenburg: 1987).

[37] The most historically-minded of these is Peter R. Sinclair, *From Traps to Draggers: Domestic Commodity Production in Northwest Newfoundland, 1850–1982* (St. John's: 1985).

[38] Rosemary Ommer, ed., *Merchant Credit and Labour Strategies in Historical Perspective* (Fredericton: 1990).

[39] David Alexander, *The Decay of Trade: An Economic History of the Newfoundland Saltfish Trade, 1935–1965* (St. John's: 1977. Many of Alexander's seminal essays on the fishery and other matters were collected posthumously in Eric W. Sager, Lewis R. Fischer and Stuart O. Pierson, comps., *Atlantic Canada and Confederation: Essays in Canadian Political Economy* (Toronto: 1983).

[40] An exception is A.B. McCullough, *The Commercial Fishery of the Great Lakes* (Ottawa: 1989).

[41] Patricia Marchak, Neil Guppy, and John McMullan, *Uncommon Property: The Fishing and Fish-Processing Industries in British Columbia* (Toronto: 1987).

[42] See, for example, Dianne Newell, ed., *The Development of the Pacific Salmon-Canning Industry: A Grown Man's Game* (Montréal: 1989).

[43] Turgeon's most important work is "Le temps des pêches lointaines, Permanences et transformations

In recent years there has also been a flurry of publications dealing with whaling and sealing. On the east coast, Chesley Sanger and Anthony Dickinson have virtually re-written the history of shore-based whaling in Newfoundland.[44] In addition, they have made important contributions to our understanding of this activity on the Pacific coast and Sanger has also written on international whaling.[45] The West Coast has also been blessed with a superb history of whaling by the American scholar, Robert Lloyd Webb.[46] While less scholarly—but ironically more popular—a work that has appeared in recent years on the Arctic, a book by Dorothy Harley Eber, has deepened our understanding of the human dimension of this important industry.[47] The most impressive body of work on a non-Canadian topic has been Danny Vickers' magnificent work on Nantucket whalemen.[48]

On sealing, the place to begin is with Tony Busch's *The War against the Seals*, a comprehensive account of the development of this important, if currently unpopular, occupation.[49] Jim Candow's study of the development of the Newfoundland seal fishery is the standard source on the topic, but should

(vers 1500–1850)," in Michel Mollat, ed., *Histoire des Pêches Maritimes en France* (Toulouse: 1987). For a flavour of Daniel Vickers' achievements, see "Merchant Credit and Labour Strategies in the Cod Fishery of Colonial Massachusetts," in Ommer, ed., *Merchant Credit and Labour Strategies in Historical Perspective*, pp. 36–48; and "'A Knowen and Staple Commoditie': Codfish Prices in Essex County, Massachusetts, 1640–1775," Essex Institute *Historical Collections*, CXXIV (1988), pp. 186–203.

[44] Their key essays include "The Origins of Modern Shore Based Whaling in Newfoundland and Labrador: The Cabot Steam Whaling Co. Ltd., 1896–98," *International Journal of Maritime History*, I, no. 1 (June 1989), pp. 129–57; "Modern Shore-Based Whaling in Newfoundland and Labrador: Expansion and Consolidation, 1898–1902," *International Journal of Maritime History*, II, no. 1 (June 1990), pp. 83–116; and "Expansion of Regulated Modern Shore-Station Whaling in Newfoundland and Labrador, 1902–03," *The Northern Mariner/Le Marin du nord*, I, no. 2 (April 1991), pp. 1–22; "Modern Shore-Station Whaling in Newfoundland and Labrador: The Peak Season, 1904," *International Journal of Maritime History*, V, no. 1 (June 1993), pp. 127–54.

[45] C.W. Sanger and A.B. Dickinson, *"They Were Clannish as Hell": Origins of Modern Shore-Station Whaling in British Columbia—The Newfoundland Factor* (Halifax: 1991); and "Newfoundland Involvement in Twentieth-Century Shore-Station Whaling in British Columbia," *Newfoundland Studies*, VII, No. 2 (Fall 1991), pp. 97–123; Sanger, "'On Good Fishing Ground but Too Early for Whales I Think': The Impact of Greenland Right Whale Migration Patterns on Hunting Strategies in the Northern Whale Fishery, 1600–1900," *American Neptune*, LI, No. 4 (Fall 1991), pp. 221–40; Sanger, "'Saw Several Finners But No Whales:' The Greenland Right Whale (Bowhead)—An Assessment of the Biological Basis of the Northern Whale Fishery during the Seventeenth, Eighteenth and Nineteenth Centuries," *International Journal of Maritime History*, III, No. 1 (June 1991), pp. 127–54.

[46] Robert Lloyd Webb, *On the Northwest: Commercial Whaling in the Pacific Northwest, 1790–1967* (Vancouver: 1988).

[47] Dorothy Harley Eber, *When the Whalers Were up North: Innuit Memories from the Eastern Arctic* (Montréal: 1989).

[48] See Vickers, "Nantucket Whalemen in the Deep-Sea Fishery: The Changing Anatomy of an Early American Labor Force," *Journal of American History*, LXXII (1985), pp. 277–96; and "The First Whalemen of Nantucket," *William and Mary Quarterly*, Third series, XL (1983), pp. 560–83.

[49] Briton C. Busch, *The War against the Seals: A History of the North American Seal Fishery* (Montréal: 1985).

be supplemented by several works by Shannon Ryan and Chesley Sanger.[50] Anthony Dickinson has published several works on sealing outside of Canada.[51]

Another area which has received attention is maritime social history. Borrowing insights from the social sciences, some talented scholars are beginning to use them to illuminate previously dark corners of the maritime experience. Any discussion of the writing of maritime social history by Canadians must begin with books by Eric Sager and Judith Fingard. Sager's *Seafaring Labour*, which appeared in 1989, is a pathbreaking analysis of life at sea which does for the nineteenth century what the American historian Marcus Rediker did for the eighteenth and the British historian Nicholas Rodger did for the Royal Navy.[52] Judith Fingard's *Jack in Port* is a penetrating study of the "sailortowns" in Halifax, Saint John and Québec.[53] Both have been widely cited and emulated overseas. We suspect that the same will be true for Sager's new book, *Ships and Memories*.[54]

Sager and Fingard have not, however, made the only significant contributions. Gilles Proulx, for example, has written an under-rated volume on conditions at sea in the trade between France and New France.[55] And of special note is a recent collection of essays which brings many of the best Canadian and American scholars into the field.[56] Canadian social historians also have had a special interest

[50] J.E. Candow, *"Of Men and Seals": A History of the Newfoundland Seal Hunt* (Ottawa: 1989); Shannon Ryan, *Seals and Sealers: A Pictorial History of the Newfoundland Seal Fishery* (St. John's: 1987); Ryan, "The Industrial Revolution and the Newfoundland Seal Fishery," *International Journal of Maritime History*, IV, no. 2 (December 1992), pp. 1–44; Ryan, "Newfoundland Sealing Disasters to 1914," *The Northern Mariner/Le Marin du nord*, III, no. 3 (July 1993), pp. 15–43. Ryan is currently writing a history of the seal fishery which should supersede previous works. See also Chesley W. Sanger, "The 19th Century Newfoundland Seal Fishery and the Influence of Scottish Whalemen," *Polar Record*, XX (1980), pp. 231–52; Sanger, "Dundee Steam-Powered Whalers and the Newfoundland Harp Seal Fishery," *Newfoundland Studies*, IV, no. 1 (Spring 1988), pp. 1–26; Sanger, "Changing Resources and Hunting Grounds of Scottish Whaling-Sealing Vessels in the Second Half of the Nineteenth Century," *Scottish Geographical Magazine*, CVII, no. 3 (1991), pp. 187–97.

[51] See especially Anthony Dickinson, "Some Aspects of the Origin and Implementation of the Eighteenth-Century Falkland Islands Sealing Industry," *International Journal of Maritime History*, II, no. 2 (December 1990), pp. 33–68.

[52] Eric W. Sager, *Seafaring Labour: The Merchant Marine of Atlantic Canada, 1820–1914* (Montréal: 1989); Marcus Rediker, *Between the Devil and the Deep Blue Sea: Merchant Seamen, Pirates, and the Anglo-American Maritime World, 1700–1750* (Cambridge: 1987); N.A.M. Rodger, *The Wooden World: An Anatomy of the Georgian Navy* (London: 1986). The importance of the Sager and Rediker books can be seen most clearly by consulting the "Roundtable" feature in the *International Journal of Maritime History*. This format features six to eight analyses of the book under consideration, with a response by the author. The roundtable on Sager's book appeared in *International Journal of Maritime History*, II, no. 1 (June 1990), pp. 227–74, while the roundtable on Rediker was in I, no. 2 (December 1989), pp. 311–57.

[53] Judith Fingard, *Jack in Port: Sailortowns of Eastern Canada* (Toronto: 1982). For a perspective that dissents from some of her main conclusions, see Richard Rice, "Sailortown: Theory and Method in Ordinary People's History," *Acadiensis*, XIII, No. 1 (Autumn 1983), pp. 154–68.

[54] Eric W. Sager, *Ships and Memories: Merchant Seafarers in Canada's Age of Steam* (Vancouver: 1993).

[55] Gilles Proulx, *Between France and New France: Life aboard the Tall Sailing Ships* (Toronto: 1984).

[56] Colin Howell and Richard Twomey, eds., *Jack Tar in History* (Fredericton: 1991).

in labour relations, and a spate of books have appeared in the past few years on the histories of Canadian maritime unions.[57] Internationally, the work by T.J.A. LeGoff on eighteenth-century French mariners and Lewis Fischer on Norwegian seamen is part of this same trend.[58]

The history of maritime exploration has also enjoyed a rebirth in recent years, particularly on the West Coast. Although the Columbia quincentenary did little to inspire a renewed interest in exploration history on the East Coast,[59] the two hundredth anniversary of George Vancouver's voyage and a series of anniversaries of Spanish exploration had a more important impact in the West.[60]

Finally, we would like to draw attention to an approach in which Canadians have taken a particularly important international role. This is the attempt to treat maritime history in its broad international context. Although maritime history has almost always been studied in particular local, regional, or national contexts, it has an equally important international dimension. One Canadian scholar who has chosen this approach is the economic historian C. Knick Harley, who has contributed important analyses on such subjects as trends in maritime productivity and international freight rates.[61] The imperial historian, Ian K. Steele, who has written a superb book on seventeenth and

---

[57] Among the most influential have been John Stanton, *Life and Death of a Union: The Canadian Seamen's Union* (Toronto: 1978); Jim Green, *Against the Tide: The Story of the Canadian Seamen's Union* (Toronto: 1986); William Kaplan, *Everything that Floats: Pat Sullivan, Hal Banks and the Seamen's Unions of Canada* (Toronto: 1987); Sue Calhoun, *A Word to Say: The Story of the Maritime Fishermen's Union* (Halifax: 1991).

[58] See, for example, T.J.A. LeGoff, "Le rerecrutement géographique et social des gens de mer bretons à la fin de l'Ancien Régime," in *La Bretagne, une province à l'aube de la Révolution* (Brest: 1989); LeGoff, "Les gens de mer devant le système des classes, 1755–1763: resistance ou passivité?" *Revue du Nord*, I (1986), pp. 463–78; LeGoff, "L'impact des prices effectuées par les Anglais sur la capacité en hommes de la marine française pendant le guerres de 1744–1748, 1755–1763, 1778–1783," in Martine Acerra et al., eds., *Les marines de guerre européennes XVII-XVIIIe siècles* (Paris: 1985), pp. 103–22; Fischer, "Fish and Ships: The Social Structure of the Maritime Labour Force in Haugesund in the 1870s," *Sjøfartshistorisk Årbok, 1986* (Bergen: 1987), pp. 139–70; Fischer, "The Sea as Highway: Maritime Service as a Means of International Migration, 1863–1913," in Klaus Friedland, ed., *Maritime Aspects of Migration* (Köln: 1990), pp. 293–307.

[59] An exception is J.C.M. Oglesby, "In Search of Christopher Columbus," *The Northern Mariner/Le Marin du nord*, II, no. 4 (October 1992), pp. 37–41.

[60] See, for example, Christon I. Archer, "The Voyage of Captain George Vancouver: A Review Article," *BC Studies*, No. 73 (Spring 1987), pp. 43–61; Archer, "The Voyages of the *Columbia* to the Northwest Coast, 1787–1790 and 1790–1793," *BC Studies*, no. 93 (Spring 1992), pp. 70–81; John Kendrick, *The Voyage of Sutil and Mexicana, 1792: The Last Spanish Exploration of the Northwest Coast of America* (Spokane: 1991); Kendrick, *The Men with Wooden Feet: The Spanish Exploration of the Northwest Coast* (Toronto: 1985); Barry Gough, *The Northwest Coast: British Navigation, Trade and Discoveries to 1812* (Vancouver: 1992).

[61] C.K. Harley, "Ocean Freight Rates and Productivity, 1740–1913: The Primacy of Mechanical Invention Reaffirmed," *Journal of Economic History*, XLVIII, no. 4 (December 1988), pp. 851–75; Harley, "Coal Exports and British Shipping, 1850–1913," *Explorations in Economic History*, XXVI, no. 3 (July 1989), pp. 311–38.

eighteenth-century trans-Atlantic communication would also fall into this category.[62] So, too, would much of Lewis Fischer's work on nineteenth-century international shipping.[63]

Despite all the scholarly activity in recent years, there are some rather large gaps in our knowledge of Canadian maritime history. One which can be inferred from this brief survey is the maritime history of the West Coast, which has by and large been the preserve of popular historians rather than scholars. Another is the business history of shipping. Aside from some of the work cited previously by Gerry Panting, there are virtually no scholarly studies of Canadian maritime businesses. But some Canadians have adopted a business history perspective to delve into non-Canadian topics. The best and most prolific of these scholars is William D. Wray, whose work has become the standard interpretation on late nineteenth and twentieth-century Japanese shipping, especially the NYK.[64] Also important is the contribution of Jack Bosher, who has written an important book on the structure of the La Rochelle business community that traded with Canada in the first half of the eighteenth century.[65] Lewis Fischer has recently begun a project to examine the business history of modern shipbroking.[66] And J.D. Alsop has

---

[62] Ian K. Steele, *The English Atlantic 1675–1740: An Exploration of Communications and Community* (New York: 1986).

[63] See especially Lewis R. Fischer and Helge W. Nordvik, "Maritime Transport and the Integration of the North Atlantic Economy, 1850–1914," in Wolfram Fischer, R. Marvin McInnis, and Jürgen Schneider, eds., *The Emergence of a World Economy, 1500–1914* (Wiesbaden: 1986), pp. 519–44; Fischer, "A Flotilla of Wood and Coal: Shipping in the Trades between Britain and the Baltic, 1863–1913." In Yrjö Kaukiainen, ed., *The Baltic as a Trade Route: Competition between Steam and Sail* (Kotka, Finland: 1992), pp. 36–63. Many of his works cited previously also fit this description.

[64] Wray's most important work is *Mitsubishi and the N.Y.K., 1870–1914: Business Strategy in the Japanese Shipping Industry* (Cambridge, Mass.: 1984), which is the first of a projected three-volume set. See also his "The NYK and World War I: Patterns of Discrimination in Freight Rates and Cargo Space Allocation," *International Journal of Maritime History*, V, no. 1 (June 1993), pp. 41–63; "Kagami Kenkichi and the N.Y.K., 1929–1935: Vertical Control, Horizontal Strategy, and Company Autonomy," in Wray, ed., *Managing Industrial Enterprise: Cases from Japan's Prewar Experience* (Cambridge, Mass.: 1989), pp. 183–227; "NYK and the Commercial Diplomacy of the Far Eastern Freight Conference, 1896–1956," in Tsunehiko Yui and Keiichiro Nakagawa, eds., *Business History of Shipping: Strategy and Structure* (Tokyo: 1985), pp. 279–311; and "'The Mitsui Fight,' 1953–1956: Japan and the Far Eastern Freight Conference," in Lewis R. Fischer and Helge W. Nordvik, eds., *Shipping and Trade, 1750–1950: Essays in International Maritime Economic History* (Pontefract: 1990), pp. 213–34.

[65] J.F. Bosher, *The Canada Merchants 1713–1763* (Oxford: 1987). See also Bosher, "The Imperial Environment of French Trade with Canada, 1660–1685," *English Historical Review*, CVIII, No. 1 (January 1993), pp. 50–81.

[66] Lewis R. Fischer and Anders M. Fon, "The Making of a Maritime Firm: The Rise of Fearnley and Eger, 1869–1917," in Lewis R. Fischer, ed., *From Wheel House to Counting House: Essays in Maritime Business History in Honour of Professor Peter Neville Davies* (St. John's: 1992), pp. 303–22; Fischer and Helge W. Nordvik, "The Growth of Norwegian Shipbroking: The Practices of Fearnley and Eger as a Case Study, 1869–1914," in Fischer, ed., *People of the Northern Seas*, pp. 135–55. Fischer and Nordvik, "From Broager to Bergen: The Risks and Rewards of Peter Jebsen, Shipowner, 1864–1892," *Sjøfartshistorisk Årbok, 1985* (Bergen: 1986), pp. 37–68, also adopts a business history approach.

shed a good deal of light on the business practices of traders during the slave trade period.[67] A third topic which remains relatively untouched is technological history. Most of what has appeared have been narrow studies of single vessels or types of ships. Nonetheless, there has been some important recent work on the history of canal technology on the Great Lakes.[68] Also worth consulting is Bill Wray's essay on the transition from sail to steam in Japan and Knick Harley's paper on the same topic in Britain.[69]

Despite these lacunae, in general the state of Canadian maritime scholarship is healthy. Indeed, the exponential increase in published works in the past two decades has gone far to alleviate gaps in our knowledge. If the trend continues—and there is no reason to believe that it will be reversed—it may be that even some of the neglected topics identified here will find their scholars in the near future.

Conclusion

This essay has rendered some positive judgements on the state of Canadian maritime history. A mere two decades ago it would have been difficult to make such optimistic assessments. But the state of Canadian maritime history is much healthier today than any realistic observer would have predicted. The principal reason for this improvement is not funding, because Canadian universities have hardly been immune from the cutbacks and retrenchment that have haunted post-secondary institutions around the world in the past few years. Instead, the impetus behind the advance of the discipline has come from people. The increased awareness of the importance of maritime heritage by the general public has been part of this. But most of the credit must go to the maritime historians who, through hard work, have built respectable programs and organizations as well as a world-class body of scholarly literature. They are to be found in colleges and universities from coast to coast.

In the late 1970s, an eminent British maritime historian could identify the essence of what we believe has underpinned this resurgence of scholarly interest in maritime history in Canada. Robin Craig, then of University College, London, reminded participants at the Third Conference of the Atlantic Canada Shipping Project that the most recent ACSP volume was entitled *The Enterprising Canadians*. Noting the impressive work that was being done not only in St. John's but also elsewhere in Canada, he exclaimed "I will say Amen to that." It

---

[67] See, for example, J.D. Alsop, "The Career of William Towerson, Guinea Trader," *International Journal of Maritime History*, IV, no. 2 (December 1992), pp. 45–82.

[68] Brian S. Osborne and Donald Swainson, *The Sault Ste. Marie Canal: A Chapter in the History of Great Lakes Transport* (Ottawa: 1986); Robert W. Passfield, *Technology in Transition: The "Soo" Ship Canal, 1889–1985* (Ottawa: 1989).

[69] William D. Wray, "Shipping: From Sail to Steam," in Marius Jansen and Gilbert Rozman, eds., *Japan in Transition: From Tokugawa to Meiji* (Princeton: 1986), pp. 248–70; C.K. Harley, "The Shift from Sailing Ships to Steamships, 1850–1890: A Study in Technological Change and Its Diffusion," in C.N. McCloskey, ed., *Studies on a Mature Economy: Britain after 1840* (London: 1971), pp. 215–34.

is indeed by their enterprise that Canadian maritime historians have earned the positive evaluation in this paper.

7

The Historiography of the Canadian Navy
The State of the Art

Marc Milner

O f all the nations under discussion in this volume, Canada scarcely ranks as a naval power in the historical sense. The Canadian Navy dates only from 1910, and although it had flexed its nascent "sea power" muscle during convoy duty in the First World War, only in the Second World War and the Cold War did it show strength of any international importance. As a nation Canada has fought no wars on its own, nor have its armed forces been the object of particular enemy attention. Indeed, one might say that Canada has no independent national naval history at all. Moreover, as a distinct field of scholarship, Canadian naval history is a very recent phenomenon. It is also, at present, a sub-field of Canadian military history, and as such is poorly integrated into the wider maritime history of the country. Not surprisingly, the brevity and peculiar nature of Canada's naval history have profoundly shaped its historiography and the extent to which Canadian naval history is taught.[1]

For these reasons, any discussion of the state of Canadian naval history must be prefaced by a short discourse on the nature of that history. Perhaps more than other nations, Canada's naval history is but a thin thread in a much larger tapestry. This situation is somewhat paradoxical, since by the end of the nineteenth century Canada had become a very considerable maritime state, as Professors Panting and Fisher demonstrate. But Canada—like its antecedents, the British North American colonies—rested secure in the bosom of British sea power. With the mother country as the predominant naval power in the world, it would have been absurd for the new self-governing Dominion of Canada to even try to develop its own navy in the nineteenth century. Quite apart from the fact that Britain retained responsibility for Canadian foreign affairs, the metropolitan power, whether French or British, had always been responsible for the maritime security of its North American colonies. It was the colonists' task to defend the land frontier, and so it remained after 1867 when the new Dominion's military efforts were devoted to the raising of militias. Paradoxically then, Canada was a

---

[1] I am especially grateful to J.A. Boutilier, W.A.B. Douglas, M. Hadley, R. Sarty, and D. Zimmerman for their comments on the draft of this paper. The final conclusions, errors or omissions remain entirely my own.

"British" nation, dependant upon the sea for her well-being. Though many of her people followed the sea, her military heritage was decidedly continental in flavour.[2]

The founding of the Royal Canadian Navy in 1910 did little to alter that situation. The debate over the establishment of a naval service reflected the increasing ambiguity over Canada's constitutional position: should Canada simply give money to Britain to support her naval armaments race with Germany, or establish a Canadian branch of the Imperial Navy. A Canadian Navy might keep problems at arm's length, it was argued, but conversely, it also might draw Canada into confrontations which might otherwise be avoided. Something also had to be done about policing Canada's fishing grounds. It is a moot point whether it was German hostility in war or the American threat to the fisheries that was more responsible for the establishment of the RCN.[3] Sir Wilfrid Laurier's Liberal government prevailed and the RCN was born on 10 March 1910. The issue of a tiny local navy—too small to fight and big enough to get into trouble—was so contentious that the 1911 federal election was fought partly around it. The Conservatives, who favoured direct financial aid to Britain, won the election. But Robert Borden's government could not bring itself either to nurture the new navy or abolish it entirely.

The RCN's tenuous existence in the defence firmament lasted for the next thirty years. The First World War did nothing to salvage it from obscurity. The fleet in 1914 consisted of two aged cruisers acquired for training purposes. One of these, *Rainbow*, was at sea off Vancouver Island when war was declared. Slow, tired, under-gunned and equipped only with sand-filled training rounds, *Rainbow* was ordered to search for von Spee's powerful East Asiatic squadron of modern cruisers off the U.S. coast. Admonished by Ottawa to "Remember Nelson and the British Navy," she got by all accounts to within fifty miles of at least one German ship (*Leipzig*), but the enemy "escaped."[4] What Edwardian writers would have made of *Rainbow*'s valiant and utterly futile end at the hands of such powerful ships we can only guess. But no gallant tradition of death and

---

[2] For a discussion of this issue see, Roger Sarty, "Canadian Maritime Defence, 1892–1914," *Canadian Historical Review*, vol. LXXI, December 1990, pp. 48–73.

[3] The debate over German naval armaments and the need to assist the Mother Country is the traditional context for the Canadian naval debate of 1909–1910, for example in Gilbert Tucker's *The Naval Service of Canada*, volume I (Ottawa: King's Printer 1952). The problem of fisheries protection—although not to the exclusion of the German problem—has been the focus of much recent debate, as in Richard Gimblett's "'Tin Pots' or Dreadnoughts?: The Evolution of the Naval Policy of the Laurier Administration, 1896–1910," unpublished MA thesis, Trent University, 1981. And then there is the "Sarty Thesis": the little known, but sophisticated and sound, view that the development of a small Canadian navy in the early 20th century was crucial to the perfection of Canada's existing system of coast defence based on long range gunnery—what might be called, "the Navy as an outgrowth of coast artillery theory" of the origins of the RCN. See Roger Sarty, "'There will be trouble in the North Pacific': The Defence of British Columbia in the early Twentieth Century." *B.C. Studies*, 61, Spring, 1984, pp. 3–29.

[4] Tucker, I, pp. 261–79.

glory befell the fledgling service. Instead, Canada poured troops onto the western front, where the Canadian Corps earned an enviable reputation for its fighting effectiveness. The First World War also produced a number of internationally famous Canadian airmen, with the likes of Bishop, Collishaw, and Barker household names within Canada and throughout the Empire by 1918. Nothing in the RCN's wartime experience compared; most of it was a dreary war of patrols. Even the U-boat operations of 1918 off the east coast failed to feed the public imagination with images of Canadian naval heroes. Quite the contrary, newspapers unfairly maligned the RCN for its supposed bungling and post-war critics accused the Navy of incompetence, "culpable negligence" and worse.[5]

The Navy nearly disappeared in the inter-war years despite some attempts to put the RCN on a firmer footing after the war. At the height of the Depression, the General Staff, dominated by the Army and the Air Force, voted to reduce the RCN to care and maintenance status; ships laid-up, recruiting and training halted, and bases all but closed. Though it was ultimately saved, the RCN never forgot its brush with extinction and came to see that its principal enemies were perhaps those closest to home.

As another major war loomed on the horizon in the late 1930s, another Liberal government, this time under W.L.M. King, saw the RCN as a marvelous vehicle for contributing to imperial security without sending thousands of troops overseas again. Although King could not forestall public clamouring for another big Canadian army on the western front once the war got underway, he did develop a very large navy (and a large air force as well). The Navy, in particular, suited King's desire to involve Canadian industry in war production, because many of the basic ships needed for the escort fleet could be built in Canada. By 1943 fully half of the Allied escorts in the main theatre of the Atlantic war were RCN, and by the end of the Second World War Canada—for a brief moment— had the third largest navy in the world.

The wartime fleet was overwhelmingly small-ship and reservist in flavour. The ships themselves were almost all war-built for basic escort roles and had little long-term value to the post-war Navy. Their crews too were "hostilities only." Only 5,000 of the Navy's wartime personnel strength of nearly 100,000 belonged to the professional naval service. Not surprisingly, the tiny fraternity of professional RCN officers used the war to secure the basic elements of a balanced post-war Navy and kept most of its own personnel in "proper" warships: fleet class destroyers, cruisers, and the like. This dichotomy of wartime experience between the reservists in small ships battling U-boats and the RCN waging a struggle for long-term viability coloured not only the conduct of the war itself, but also much of the writing that followed.[6]

---

[5]   See M. Hardley and R. Sarty, *Tin-Pots and Pirate Ships* (Kingston/Montreal: McGill-Queen's Press, 1991), p. 301.

[6]   See for example W.A.B. Douglas' seminal piece, "Conflict and Innovation in the Royal Canadian

The expansion of the RCN during the Second World War was a remarkable accomplishment—truly staggering by Canadian standards and a significant event in naval history in general. For the RCN, however, it was a precarious victory, and the Navy's fortunes were salvaged only by the advent of the Cold War. Under King's successor, Louis St. Laurent, post-war Liberal governments built a large and capable navy in the 1950s. To a considerable extent this early Cold War fleet was simply an outgrowth of the wartime experience. Moreover, the wave of new construction and modernization of reserve vessels that followed the Korean War was part of a general military expansion. While the Navy was large and modern by the early 1960s, in terms of budgets and personnel the RCN remained clearly in third place within the Canadian defence establishment. Little new was added after the early Cold War building boom, and by the 1980s the Navy faced block obsolescence. The last deep freeze in the Cold War produced orders for a new fleet in the mid-1980s, which is just now being completed. None of the new ships saw service in the Gulf War, where the Navy fought largely without incident and without loss. It is too early to tell just how the Navy will fare in the new world order.

Several key points affecting the development of Canadian naval historical writing emerge from this very brief survey. The first—and most obvious—is that the history itself is only some eighty years old. It is difficult, although by no means entirely impossible, to push the antecedents of the RCN much further back than 1900. Secondly, much of that history is uneventful. Apart from the Second World War and the early years of the Cold War, the RCN has lived a low-key, often marginal existence. The third point is that since the Navy's founding in 1910, Canada has acted within the confines of much larger international organizations, initially the British Empire and latterly NATO and the UN. This has left little scope for distinctly Canadian naval operations and none whatever for distinctly Canadian wars. Where other nations might well have resorted to gunboat diplomacy abroad to secure their national interests, Canada has been able to rely on collective action. After all, who was Canada likely to fight—on her own—in the twentieth century? Canadian naval history—as presently structured—is, therefore, drawn from a very narrow base in space and time. Ironically, the only uniquely Canadian naval missions in defence of Canadian sovereignty have been typically directed at our friends in peacetime. The final point is that for the first sixty years of its existence the RCN defined itself within a largely British context. Until 1939 the RCN was simply a flotilla of the Imperial Navy; training, uniforms, equipment, ships, tactics, doctrine were all British, and Canadian officers appeared on a combined Empire and Commonwealth seniority list. This was much less so after 1945. But the notion of

---

Navy 1919–1945," in G. Jordan, ed., *Naval Warfare in the Twentieth Century: Essays in Honour of Arthur Marder* (New York: Crane Russack, 1977), pp. 210–32, for a discussion of the tension between fighting the war against the Germans and the battle for long-term viability at home.

the RCN as a direct descendant of Nelson's Band of Brothers survived in the RCN until the full effects of armed forces unification were felt in the early 1970s, and even now Nelson's ghost surfaces on occasion.

It is important to understand, therefore, the very restricted nature of the Canadian naval experience, its very "British" character, and the importance of Canada's powerful militia tradition when assessing the development of Canadian Navy historiography.

While many recent works on the origins and early days of the RCN take their accounts back into the latter stages of the nineteenth century, the colonial period and great age of sail have not been embraced as part of Canadian naval heritage. In part this is because the Canadian military establishment has been loath to adopt any of the military or naval traditions of the French era. The work of Guy Freqault on the first distinctly Canadian naval hero, Pierre le Moyne d'Iberville, and Jacques Mathieu's work on French naval building in Quebec in the eighteenth century remain solidly part of Canadian colonial history.[7] D'Iberville, a native son of New France, sailed his lone ship *Pelican* into Hudson's Bay in 1697 and in a brilliant action with three English ships sank two and secured command of the area, a feat unremembered in the myths and culture of the Canadian navy.[8] In fairness, though, the British colonial period also stands outside of mainstream Canadian naval history, despite the efforts of W.A.B. Douglas, Faye Kert, Richard Wright, and others.[9] Even the substantial body of work done by Barry M. Gough on naval activity in British North American waters during the nineteenth century, such as his *The Royal Navy and the Northwest Coast of North America, 1810–1914* (1971), fall into imperial, colonial or maritime history, not naval.[10]

The failure of the often desperate and typically disparate naval efforts of the colonists of New France and British North America to find resonance within Canadian naval history remains enigmatic. Among academics this disconnection is almost certainly due to the fact that the study of history itself is subdivided into fields which often do not talk to one another—like military and colonial history. But the Navy, too, cleaving first to its Royal Navy lineage and involved in a constant battle to maintain its blue-water capability, finds little of value in these puny antecedents. The result is that Canadian naval history as presently

---

[7]   Guy Fregault, *Pierre le Moyne d'Iberville* (Montreal/Paris: 1968), and Jacques Mathieu, *La Construction Navale Royale a Quebec, 1739–1759* (Quebec: 1971).

[8]   A replica of *Pelican* was launched in Montreal in 1993.

[9]   W.A.B. Douglas, "The Anatomy of Naval Incompetence: The Provincial Marine of Upper Canada before 1813," *Ontario History*, LXXXI, 1979, pp. 3–26, and "Nova Scotia and the Royal Navy, 1715–1766," unpublished Ph.D. dissertation, Queen's, 1973; Faye Kert, "The Fortunes of War: Privateering in Atlantic Canada in the War of 1812," Unpublished MA Thesis, Carleton University, 1986, Richard J. Wright, "Green Flags and Red-Coated Gunboats: Naval Activities on the Great Lakes during the Fenian Scares, 1866–1870," *Inland Seas*, XXII, no. 2, Summer 1966, pp. 91–110.

[10]   Barry M. Gough, *The Royal Navy and the Northwest Coast of North America, 1810–1914* (Vancouver: UBC, 1971) and *Gunboat Frontier: British Maritime Authority and Northwest Coast Indians, 1846–90* (Vancouver: UBC, 1984).

constituted derives none of its traditions from the age of sail—the key formative period for many of the navies of the world.

Moreover, nothing occurred in RCN history prior to 1939 to save it from obscurity, particularly when set against the deeply entrenched national militia tradition and the tremendous accomplishments of the Canadian Corps in the First World War. Prior to 1939 legitimacy for the RCN derived from its connection with the RN. But set against the RN standard—the only measure suitable among Canadians until a generation ago—there was not much to say of Canada's experiment in naval power before the Second World War.

The first thirty years of RCN history were thus seen as something of a wasteland; little but policy and unfulfilled dreams. By contrast, the scope and scale of the RCN's Second World War accomplishment captured the imagination of the first generation of post-1945 historians—and with good reason. The RCN rose from utter obscurity to a global standing in a few short years. And while the wartime fleet had not been a balanced one in the traditional sense, the acquisition of heavy cruisers and light fleet carriers at the very end of the war gave promise that one day it would be. Further, Canada had demonstrated her naval potential in time of crisis, and the myriad of small ships required of modern naval warfare gave Canada tremendous leverage. Not surprisingly, the RCN's post-war official histories, Gilbert Tucker's *The Naval Service of Canada* (two volumes, 1952) and, more especially, Joseph Schull's *The Far Distant Ships* (1950, reprinted in 1990), were celebrations of Canadian accomplishment.[11] Tucker's first volume covered naval developments up to 1939 and seemed to say all that was needed about that colourless period. His second volume, on naval administration ashore between 1939 and 1945, chronicled the growth of the RCN's institutions as they coped with the rapid expansion of the fleet. Tucker planned a series of three operational volumes on the war, but these were axed by the Naval Staff and a Minister of Defence, who were not interested in a detailed accounting of the exploits of reservists in small, hastily built escorts.[12] What the Navy wanted, and what it commissioned Schull to write, was a popular history which would foster support for post-war naval expansion plans. Schull's delightfully written *The Far Distant Ships* was therefore long on colour and short on analysis or context. To what extent it helped in the building boom of the RCN during the 1950s is an interesting—and unexplored—historical question.

What is clearer is that the combination of Tucker and Schull—both official histories—satisfied the need for information on the wartime RCN for a genera-

---

[11] G.N. Tucker, *The Naval Service of Canada: Its Official History*, volume I, *Origins and Early Years* and volume II, *Activities on Shore during the Second World War* (Ottawa: King's Printer, 1952), and Joseph Schull, *The Far Distant Ships: An Official Account of Canadian Naval Operations in the Second World War* (Ottawa: King's Printer, 1950), reprinted by Stoddart of Toronto in 1990.

[12] See C.P. Stacey, "The Life and Hard Times of an Official Historian," *Canadian Historical Review*, LI, no. 1, March 1970, pp. 21–47.

tion. Two other monographs on RCN history appeared over that period, Thor Thorgrimsson and E.C. Russell's *Canadian Naval Operations in Korean Waters, 1950–1955* (1965), and J.D.F. Kealy and E.C. Russell's *A History of Canadian Naval Aviation* (1967).[13] These too were official histories, and it is possible to see them both as celebrations of Canadian naval maturity and broadsides in the on-going budgetary battles of the 1960s. Until the 1980s these official histories constituted the total of scholarly monographs on RCN history.

The lack of scholarly monographs on the Navy—or even wider academic interest in the RCN by non-government historians in the twenty-five years following the war—is hard to explain. It may be that the RCN's wartime experience failed to capture anyone's imagination. Certainly the notion of Canada as a sea power was a new—and perhaps transitory—experience, and few Canadian academics were interested in the subject. Gerald Graham, a Canadian who became a distinguished historian of imperial Britain, had served briefly as an official historian during the war, but he preferred to concentrate on the intellectually more rewarding delights of the British Empire. So, too, did Donald Schurman. A veteran of the RCAF, Schurman was drawn to naval history through an interest in the intellectual roots of twentieth-century British maritime strategy. Both of these men, Graham and, perhaps more so Schurman (whose career has been spent at the Royal Military College of Canada and Queen's University, both in Kingston), profoundly influenced the way in which aspiring Canadian academic naval historians viewed their field.[14] Both foreswore the particular in favour of breadth and depth, emphasising the larger context of naval history. It seems fair to say that the very recent nature of Canada's expression of sea power and Tucker and Schull's emphasis on the uniqueness of the Canadian experience failed to stir them. Moreover, while the Army's historical section under C.P. Stacey nurtured a coterie of young historians who went on to academic posts—Reg Roy, George Stanley, Jack Hyatt, Don Goodspeed to name a few—the collapse of Tucker's project in the late 1940s left Canadian naval history in the hands of a few devoted amateurs in the naval historical section.[15] In the end, however, perhaps the most compelling reason for the

---

[13] Thor Thorgrimsson and E.C. Russell, *Canadian Naval Operations in Korean Waters, 1950–1955* (Ottawa: Queen's Printer, 1965) and J.D.F. Kealy and E.C. Russell, *A History of Canadian Naval Aviation, 1918–1962*, (Ottawa: Queen's Printer, 1965)

[14] Schurman's influence has been unquestionable; among his former pupils was the late Barry Hunt, who taught naval history at RMC for twenty years and Schurman's friend and former colleague at RMC W.A.B. Douglas, has for the last twenty years been writing *the* official history of the Canadian Armed Forces. Gerald Graham's influence has been perhaps less direct, but no less profound. Much of recent academic activity on the RCN has been at the University of New Brunswick, where one of Gerald Graham's former students, Dominck S. Graham, ran the military history program until 1986. Milner and Zimmerman were products of that program, which Milner now runs. The latest UNB naval historian, Michael Hennessey, has taken the late Barry Hunt's position in the History Department at RMC.

[15] J.M.S. Careless left the naval historical section to pursue a career in Canadian history at Toronto.

dearth of published material on the RCN in the generation after 1945 is that the files were still closed to everyone except the official historians.

It was possible, therefore, until 1970, to count the number of monographs on RCN history on the fingers of one hand—and all of them were government publications. There were a few memoirs of note,[16] a few articles, some passages on the RCN in Don Goodspeed's *The Armed Forces of Canada, 1867–1967* (1967), and some wartime public relations publications. But apart from the official histories, the only thing that passed for serious scholarship on the RCN were the sections in James Eayrs' first two volumes of *In Defence of Canada* (1964 and 1965).[17]

Several things conspired to alter this complacency during the 1970s. Perhaps the most important was that sometime between 1960 and 1980 Canada cast off its colonial mentality and Canadians started measuring the RCN in its own right, as the service of an independent, sovereign state. This was facilitated by armed forces unification, announced in 1964 and put into effect on 1 January 1968. With that the Royal Canadian Navy ceased to exist, becoming "Maritime Command" of the new Canadian Armed Forces and adopting the new standard green uniform of the combined forces. Unification shook the navy to its very core, forced a process of redefinition, and forced the retirement of many of the last wartime veterans who either did not or could not accept Canadianization of the Navy. The Navy, which had seen itself in 1960 as more Royal than Canadian, was by 1980 distinctly Canadian in outlook—right down to its green uniforms and the replacement of Trafalgar Day in favour of Battle of the Atlantic Sunday as the feast day of the Canadian fleet. The Navy has since gone back into distinctive naval uniforms, derived—appropriately enough given its new "imperial" orientation—largely from those of the United States Navy.[18] Concurrent with this altered state within the Navy and the nation was the opening of wartime archive material which allowed non-official historians a more critical look at the Navy's most significant experience—the Second World War.

The need to look more closely at the RCN's Second World War experience—and the inadequacies of Tucker and Schull on the subject—had been evident for some time. The only critical assessment of the RCN's contribution to the actual fighting to appear in the generation after 1945 came from the pen

---

[16] See Alan Easton's superb wartime memoir *50 North* (Toronto: Ryerson, 1963), William Sclater's excellent *Haida* (Toronto: Oxford UP, 1946), and W.H. Pugsley's two volumes on the lower deck, *Saints Devils and Ordinary Seaman* (Toronto: Collins, 1945) and *Sailor Remember* (Toronto: Collins, 1948).

[17] James Eayrs, *In Defence of Canada: From the Great War to the Great Depression* (Toronto: Univ. of Toronto, 1964) and *In Defence of Canada: Appeasement and Rearmament* (Toronto: Univ. of Toronto, 1965).

[18] Much of the old RN tradition still survives, however, as evidenced by the practices outlined in Lt.(N) Graeme Arbuckle's *Customs and Traditions of the Canadian Navy* (Halifax: Nimbus Publishing Ltd., 1984). Indeed, one is hard-pressed to find anything distinctly Canadian in the customs and traditions which Arbuckle describes.

of Captain Donald Macintyre, RN. One of the war's best escort commanders and a naval historian of note, Macintyre savagely attacked the RCN's wartime operational efficiency in his memoir *U-Boat Killer* (1956).[19] Macintyre charged the RCN with bungling incompetence, described its fleet as "travesties of warships" and accused the Canadian naval staff as bent on nothing more than placing the maximum number of RCN ships on operational plots.

The issue of the fleet's efficiency was addressed briefly in C.P. Stacey's official volume on Canadian defence policy during the war, *Arms, Men and Governments* (1970).[20] However, by the 1970s the conventional wisdom on the wartime RCN was a blend of both the Canadian and Macintyre themes; the Navy had been big, but probably misguided. The difficulties of such a limited Canadian literature and its concentration on the peculiarly Canadian exploits of the war years were demonstrated in 1979 with the publication of John Swettenham's *Canada's Atlantic War*. Swettenham, one of Canada's best known military historians, produced a very conventional account of the war at sea into which he attempted—without much luck—to integrate the Canadian story. What he achieved in the end was the standard British interpretation of events, punctuated by Canadian incidents. In that sense, *Canada's Atlantic War* accurately reflects the state of the art—at least with respect to Second World War history—at the end of the 1970s. It was hardly Swettenham's fault.

By the 1970s, however, Canadians were beginning to awaken to their naval history largely, although by no means exclusively, through the experience of the Second World War. Several major research projects were underway and the voice of veterans began to be heard in the first of what has become a fairly steady stream of memoirs and nostalgia. In 1972 the first postwar graduate master's thesis in RCN history was completed, and another followed by the end of the decade.[21] By the end of the 1970s two doctoral dissertations were underway,[22] and the appearance of two new wartime naval memoirs, James Lamb's *The Corvette Navy* (1977) and Hal Lawrence's *A Bloody War* (1979) marked the beginning of a series of books by these two writers and the commencement of a significant memoir phase in the field.[23] The decade also brought the first

---

19 Captain Donald Macintyre, *U-Boat Killer* (London: Weidenfeld and Nicholson, 1956).

20 C.P. Stacey, *Arms, Men and Governments: The War Policies of Canada, 1939–1945* (Ottawa: Department of National Defence, 1970).

21 W.G. Lund, "Command Relationships in the North West Atlantic, 1939–1943," unpublished MA thesis, Queen's University 1972 and M. Milner "Canadian Escorts and the Mid Atlantic, 1942–1943," unpublished M.A. thesis, University of New Brunswick, 1979. See W.A.B. Douglas, "Canadian Naval Historiography," *Mariner's Mirror*, 70, no. 4, November 1984, pp. 349–62, for a list of other theses and dissertations in related fields, such as imperial maritime history.

22 Marc Milner, "No Higher Purpose: The Royal Canadian Navy's Mid-Atlantic War, 1939–1943," University of New Brunswick, 1983 (and published by University of Toronto Press in 1985 as *North Atlantic Run*) and Thomas Richard Melville, "Canada and Sea Power: Canadian Naval Thought and Policy, 1860–1910," unpublished Ph.D., Duke University, 1981.

23 James B. Lamb, *The Corvette Navy: True Stories from Canada's Atlantic War* (Toronto: Macmillan, 1977) and

serious, scholarly questioning of the Navy's wartime policy in the form of W.A.B. Douglas' seminal article in Arthur Marder's festschrift.[24]

If the 1970s was the decade of gestation, the birth of modern Canadian naval historical writing (it cannot truly be called a renaissance) dates from a historical conference convened in 1980 at Royal Roads Military College, Victoria BC. The conference was the work of Dr. Jim Boutilier, a member of the RRMC Department of History and Political Economy. Boutilier was spurred by what he saw as the astonishing failure of both historians and naval personnel to analyze RCN history. His solution was to get the Navy and a few scholars together to think and write about the subject for a conference convened in March 1980, the first on RCN history. It brought together many—if not most—of the surviving senior officers of the RCN, who dominated the program. Of the nineteen speakers during the three day conference, eleven were "Old Salts" speaking largely within their own sphere of expertise. Among the more innovative elements of Boutilier's conference were papers on RCN history prior to 1939, especially its origins. Significantly, no paper dealt with operations in the First World War.[25]

"The RCN in Retrospect" Conference was not an academic tour de force, but it met Boutilier's expectations; the Navy awoke to its history.[26] The publication of the conference proceedings in 1982 marked a watershed in RCN historiography. When Alec Douglas produced his review of Canadian naval history for the *Mariner's Mirror* in 1984, he could count the five volumes of official history, the proceedings of Boutilier's conference, a few more memoirs (including the first of a series of collective reminiscences published as *Salty Dips* by the Naval Officers Association of Canada (Ottawa Branch)), "a half dozen theses," a number of scholarly articles, and the first volume of Jeff Brock's two-volume memoir, *The Dark Broad Seas* (1981) and *The Thunder and the Sunshine* (1983), the only memoir of any substance—however fanciful—by a senior RCN officer.[27] Douglas tactfully omitted reference to another memoir and the only biography ever written on a Canadian naval officer. H.N. Lay's *Memoirs of a Mariner* (1982) had potential to make a major contribution to the field, but spoke more to his family than to those interested in the Navy. J.M. Cameron's *Murray: The Martyred Admiral* (1980), was a seriously flawed attempt to vindicate the career of the RCN's most famous operational commander, R.Adm. L.W.

Hal Lawrence, *A Bloody War: One Man's Memories of the Canadian Navy 1939–45* (Toronto: Macmillan, 1979).

[24] For a full reference see footnote 6.

[25] The conference proceedings were published as *The RCN in Retrospect* (Vancouver: Univ. of British Columbia Press, 1982). The table of contents is unaltered from the list of speakers.

[26] The model was used later by Commander James Goldrick, RAN, to spur interest in Australian naval history. The proceedings were published as *Reflections on the Royal Australian Navy*, T.R. Frame, J.V.P. Goldrick and P.D. Jones, eds. (Kenthurst, NSW: Kangaroo Press, 1990).

[27] As discussed in W.A.B. Douglas, "The prospects for Naval History," *The Northern Mariner*, vol. 1, no. 4, October, 1991, p. 19.

Murray, who moved to England in 1945 after rioting servicemen destroyed much of downtown Halifax. Cameron's hagiographic account of Murray's life is notable only because it remains the only biography ever published on a Canadian naval figure.[28] Douglas' 1984 listing also neglected two substantial recent books on RCN history, Fraser Mckee's *The Armed Yachts of Canada* and Macpherson and Burgess' *Ships of Canada's Naval Forces, 1910–1980*.[29]

Alec Douglas gave this burgeoning field a push in 1985 with his own conference commemorating the 75th anniversary of the founding of the RCN. He filled the program with a largely academic crowd. Among their contributions were the first serious scholarship on the First World War since Tucker's Volume One and the first serious academic work on the post-1945 period to emerge since Eayrs' earlier material in the 1960s.

The proceedings of "The RCN in Transition" Conference were published in 1988,[30] when the stream of publications in Canadian naval history had—to use Douglas' words—"turned into a torrent." By 1991 Douglas was able to list[31] as many substantial publications in the seven short years since his *Mariner's Mirror* article appeared as had been published in the previous 74 years of RCN history combined. The first scholarly monographs on Canadian naval history by academic historians were published in 1985, both dealing with the Second World War: Michael Hadley's *U-Boats Against Canada* and Marc Milner's *North Atlantic Run* (the latter was one of the two Ph.D. dissertations completed on RCN history up to that point). David Zimmerman's *The Great Naval Battle of Ottawa* (1989) had also begun as a Ph.D. dissertation (the third in RCN history) at the University of New Brunswick.[32] Amid this torrent of new publications were more memoirs[33] and David Perkins' monograph on Canadian submariners in the First World War, Alan Snowie's history of the carrier *Bonaventure*, and some popular and privately published histories of individual ships and ship types.[34] Indeed, there was enough scholarship available by the late 1980s to

---

[28] Rear-Admiral H. Nelson Lay, OBE, CD, RCN (Retd), *Memoirs of a Mariner* (Stittsville, Ontario: Canada's Wings, 1982) and James M. Cameron, *Murray: The Martyred Admiral* (Hantsport, NS: Lancelot press, 1980).

[29] Fraser McKee *The Armed Yachts of Canada* (Erin, Ontario: Boston Mills, 1983), and Ken Macpherson and John Burgess *The Ships of Canada's Naval Forces, 1910–1981* (Toronto: Collins, 1981).

[30] W.A.B. Douglas, ed., *The RCN in Transition* (Vancouver: University of British Columbia, 1988).

[31] See Douglas, "The Prospects for Naval History," *The Northern Mariner*, vol. 1, no. 4, October 1991.

[32] Michael L. Hadley, *U-Boats Against Canada: German Submarines in Canadian Waters* (Montreal/Kingston: McGill-Queen's, 1985), Marc Milner, *North Atlantic Run: The Royal Canadian Navy and the Battle for the Convoys* (Toronto: Univ. of Toronto Press, 1985), and David Zimmerman, *The Great Naval Battle of Ottawa* (Toronto: Univ. of Toronto Press, 1989).

[33] Gordon W. Stead, *A leaf Upon the Sea: A Small Ship in the Mediterranean* (Vancouver: UBC, 1988), James B. Lamb, *On The Triangle Run* (Toronto: Macmillan, 1989), Hal Lawrence's *Tales of the North Atlantic* (Toronto: McClelland and Stewart, 1989) and *Victory at Sea* (Toronto: McClelland and Stewart, 1990), *Salty Dips* volumes I and II, Anthony Law, *White Plumes Astern* (Halifax, NS: Nimbus Publishing, 1989) and Frank Curry, *The War at Sea* (Toronto: Lugus, 1991).

[34] David Perkins, *Canada's Submariners, 1914–1923* (Erin, Ontario: The Boston Mills Press, 1989),

permit the writing and publication of Tony German's *The Sea Is at Our Gates*, the first popularly written comprehensive one-volume history of the RCN.[35]

The 'eighties, then, mark a major watershed in the historiography of the RCN. Since then the pace has not slackened. There is no space here to list all of the new work, but some key works warrant mention. In 1991 the first scholarly monograph on pre-1939 RCN history appeared: *Tin-Pots & Pirate Ships: Canadian Naval Forces & German Sea Raiders 1880–1918*, by Michael Hadley and Roger Sarty.[36] The heavy emphasis on the Second World War has continued apace, and many new, young scholars are entering the field. In recent years substantial scholarly articles on the RCN have appeared in *The Mariner's Mirror, The Northern Mariner, The Canadian Historical Review, The Canadian Defence Quarterly, Military Affairs, Canadian Military History, The Naval War College Review*, and *The RUSI Journal*. Many of these new historians are working on the Cold War era, for which the documents are becoming available.[37] Others are pushing their research back into the pre-1939 period, and volume I of the forthcoming new official history of the RCN will go a long way to filling that crucial gap.[38] Work is underway at the University of Victoria on the social history of the pre-1939 Navy and an official account of the Gulf War is forthcoming from the Department of National Defence.

Alan Snowie, *The "Bonnie"* (Erin, Ontario: the Boston Mills Press, 1987) and, for example, Tom Blakely's privately published *Corvette Cobourg: The Role of a Canadian Warship in the Longest Sea Battle in History* (Cobourg, Ontario: Royal Canadian Legion Branch No. 133, nd), and Ken Macpherson's *River Class Destroyers of the Royal Canadian Navy* (Toronto: Charles Musson, 1985), and *Frigates of the Royal Canadian Navy* (St. Catharines, Ontario: Vanwell, 1989).

[35] Commander Tony German, *The Sea is at Our Gates: The History of the Canadian Navy* (Toronto: McClelland and Stewart, 1990). German's book was accompanied by a video tape as part of the attempt to popularize the Navy's history among a younger generation. See also Jack Macbeth's *Ready, Aye, Ready: An Illustrated History of the Royal Canadian Navy* (Toronto: Key Porter Books, nd).

[36] Published by McGill-Queen's Univ. Press of Montreal and Kingston.

[37] See for example Peter T. Haydon's, *The 1962 Cuban Missile Crisis: Canadian Involvement Reconsidered* (The Canadian Institute of Strategic Studies, 1993), which contains new information on the RCN's role, as does his chapter, "The RCN and the Cuban Missile Crisis," in M. Milner, ed., *Canadian Military History* (Copp Clark Pitman, 1993), pp. 349–67.

[38] See B.J.C. McKercher, "Between Two Giants: Canada, the Coolidge Conference and Anglo-American Relations, 1927," in *Anglo-American Relations in the 1920s*, B.J.C. McKercher, ed., (Edmonton: Univ. of Alberta Press, 1990), pp. 81–124, Michael J. Whitby, "In Defence of Home Waters: Doctrine and Training in the Canadian Navy during the 1930s," *Mariner's Mirror*, May 1991, pp. 167–77, and a series of works by Roger Sarty; "The Naval Side of Canadian Sovereignty, 1909–1923," *The Niobe Papers*, volume IV, F.W. Crickhard and K. Orr, eds. (Halifax, NS: Nautical Publishing, 1993): "The Origins of Canada's Second World War Maritime Forces, 1918–1940, papers of the 1990 Society for Military History AGM (forthcoming), "'Entirely in the hands of the friendly neighbour': The Canadian Armed Forces and the Defence of the Pacific Coast 1909-1937," in D. Zimmerman, ed., *Redirection: Defending Canada, the Pacific Perspective* (forthcoming), and "Mr. King and the Armed Forces, 1939," paper to the Canadian Committee for the History of the Second World War, Elora, Ontario 1989. Sarty is also the principal author of the pre-1939 volume of the new official history of the RCN.

Ships, too, remain a source of interest, especially Second World War escort vessels and two major books on Canadian corvettes appeared in 1993.[39] If there is a major gap in the current state of Canadian naval historiography, it would be on the role of individuals. At present only one biography, that of Engineer Rear Admiral G.L. Stephens, is in the wind, as are a couple of memoirs by retired senior officers.

A complex and comprehensive Canadian naval historiography is, therefore, a very recent phenomena. Probably for that reason there is little evidence that Canadian naval history is yet widely seen as a viable field of instruction for academic credit in Canada. Military history, of which naval history in Canada is a part, is offered as a bona fide academic subject at only a few Canadian universities and within the three military colleges. The emphasis in such courses is usually on Canada's military past or on the broader international military experience, approaches which are strongly biased towards land warfare. Few of those who teach military history in Canada have either the expertise or the interest to separate Canadian naval history from the general pattern of the nation's military history. In that sense, the Canadian Navy's experience remains an aberration even in Canadian military history courses; an obligatory reference in an otherwise traditional survey of Canada's long and colourful army heritage.

Those, like this writer, who teach both Canadian military history and courses in the history of sea power, also invariably set the Canadian naval story in a much wider context. It forms a piece, sometimes bigger, usually quite small, of a much larger tapestry. Perhaps surprisingly, Canadian naval historians accept such an approach as a given. They do not see an independent existence for the RCN outside of the large context of either the empire or the collective security organizations joined since 1945. In that sense, Canadian naval history is always subordinated to another mainstream military or naval (sea power) field. In only one instance—from what could be determined—has the focus been reversed and a Canadian naval history course been given for academic credit. In 1991, Michael Hadley, of the Germanic Studies Department at the University of Victoria, gave a one-time term-length honours seminar on naval history funded by the university's Military and Strategic Studies Program. Hadley was given the liberty by the Department of History to do whatever he wished in a seminar on sea power, so he turned it into a case study using the RCN as the model. The course, "The Canadian Navy and the Major Powers," has since became a regular undergraduate offering.[40] Apropos of the comments made earlier here, there is

---

[39] John Harland and John Mackay's *The Flower Class Corvette Agassiz* (Anatomy of the Ships Series) (London: Conway, 1993) and Ken Macpherson and Marc Milner's *Corvettes of the Royal Canadian Navy* (St. Catharines, Ontario: Vanwell, 1993).

[40] Information courtesy of Michael Hadley, who, in addition to being an accomplished historian in his own right, is also a retired naval reserve captain.

no indication that Canadian naval history is ever taught within the context of Canadian maritime history.

It remains to be seen whether Hadley's course itself is an aberration or a reflection of the maturity of Canadian naval historical writing. In 1980 it was possible to conduct a couple of individual seminars on aspects of Canadian naval history, especially its origins and the controversy over fleet efficiency, as part of a course on naval or Canadian military history. But it would have been difficult to do more. Hadley demonstrated that by 1990 it was possible to mount at least a term length course for academic credit on Canadian naval history. It is ironic, and indicative of the strong contextual bias evident among naval historians (writ large) within Canada, that many of them consulted for this paper could still not see the merit in offering a course in Canadian naval history. Maybe they are right, since much remains to be done. Important new scholarship on the early Cold War will emerge within the next few years with Ph.D. theses from Mike Hennessey and Shawn Cafferky. Hennessey's work, in particular, draws together many of the elements of national naval and maritime policy and will help bridge that gap between naval history proper and the wider fields of which it is a part.[41] There are now a number of substantive articles available on the inter-war years and a new and thorough volume of official history in the wings. Hadley and Sarty's *Tin-Pots and Pirate Ships* seems to have satisfied interest in the First World War for the time being. However, despite their efforts a comprehensive monograph on the Navy prior to 1914 is still needed. So too is some way of bridging the gap between the events of the twentieth century and all that went before. Perhaps when the Navy finds its roots in the age of sail and in the larger context of Canadian history, Canadian naval history will truly have come of age.

---

[41] See for example his, "Canada, The Navy and the Shipbuilding Industry: Plus ça Change?" in Michael A. Hennessey and Kenrick G. Hancox, eds., *Canada, the Navy and Industry* (Toronto: Canadian Institute for Strategic Studies, March 1992); "The State as Innovator: Controlling Command Technology for Warship Production in Canada, 1949–1965," in Peter A. Baskerville, ed., *Canadian Papers in Business History*, vol. II (Victoria, BC: Public History Group, University of Victoria, 1993); and "Post-War Ocean Shipping and Shipbuilding Policy in Canada: An Agenda for Research," *The Northern Mariner*, vol 1, no. 3, July 1991.

8

Chile

Captain Carlos Tromben, Chilean Navy

Chile's naval and maritime history can be traced in a vast bibliography whose main titles are included in this paper. This history is the result of the work of Chilean and foreign researchers and authors, who through the years have shown their interest in describing, documenting, and analyzing the facts and ideas related to these topics.[1]

The period before Ferdinand Magellan discovered Chile's southern tip in 1520 and Diego de Almagro explored the central zone in 1536, has not been the subject of in-depth studies, probably because the major source materials are in Spanish archives. The aboriginal civilizations were less developed, if compared with the degree reached by the people of what is today Peru, Mexico, and Central America. In spite of this, Chile's native inhabitants were skilled coastal navigators, due to the fact that they obtained an important part of their food from the sea.

Likewise, Hispanic presence in Chile is a subject that has not been thoroughly investigated. Only recently, with Spanish support in connection with the celebration of the quincentenary of Columbus's arrival in America, one of the interesting aspects of this period, the Hispanic forts at Valdivia and Corral, are being studied and restored. For Chilean scholars, the major problem is that most of the related documentation is in Europe.

The war for independence, which took place intermittently between 1811 and 1826, was full of naval events. These naval events were at the forefront of

---

[1] Histories that include general aspects of Chilean maritime affairs are:

Francisco Antonio Encina, *Historia de Chile desde la prehistoria hasta 1891* (Santiago: Nascimento, 1940-1952); Jaime Eyzaguirre, *Historia de Chile* (Santiago, 1965); Jay Kingsbruner, Chile, a historical interpretation (New York: Harper Torch Book, 1973); José M. Martínez-Hidalgo y Teran, *Enciclopedia general del mar* (Barcelona: Garriga, 1968), 8 volumes; Benjamín Subercaseaux, *Tierra de océano* (Santiago, nd); Gonzalo Vial, *Historia de Chile 1891–1973* (Santiago: Santillana, 1984).

Early naval histories and chronicles of Chile include:

Luis Novoa de la Fuente, *Historia naval de Chile* (Valparaiso: Imp. de la Armada, 1944); Francisco Rojas M., *Administración naval de Chile comparada: su desarrollo, evolución y organización 1817–1932* (Santiago: Imp. Chile, 1934); Carlos Sayago, *Crónicas de la Marina militar de Chile* (Copiapó: Imp. de la Unión, 1864); Alberto Silva Palma, *Crónicas de la Marina chilena* (Santiago: Talleres del estado Mayor Jeneral, 1913); Horacio Vio Valdivieso, *Manual de historia naval de Chile* (Valparaiso: Imp. de la Armada, 1972).

opening the Chilean economy to international trade, spawning the birth of a strong maritime activity.[2] The new state that emerged out of the far off and, probably, the poorest of the Spanish colonies, with its particular geography of extended and fragmented coasts, attracted the attention of many Europeans and Americans, who registered their experiences in memoirs or narratives that have become the main historical source for this period.[3] Among the many authors was Mary Graham, a dynamic and learned British woman, who arrived in Valparaiso on board a ship commanded by her husband, who passed away a few days before their arrival. She stayed in this country for a prolonged period and depicted the facts, people, and customs of the period between 1822–23 in a very interesting book.[4]

Another important author of this era is John Miller, who penned the memoirs of his brother, General William Miller, who held a high command post in what has become the Chilean Marine Corps.[5]

Famous for his memoirs on the Chilean independence period is Admiral Thomas Alexander Cochrane, who came to Chile from England at the invitation of General Bernardo O'Higgins. In the four years that Admiral Cochrane remained in command of the fleet—created with great effort by Chile—he was able to eliminate completely the Spanish naval presence in the American Pacific.[6] While in command, he proposed several initiatives that failed to come to fruition due to the internal conflicts that were present during General Bernardo O'Higgins' term of rule. His memoirs, published in London several decades later, are interesting, detailed, and valuable, allowing historians to understand this distinguished mariner and his times.[7]

Another important source on this period is the papers of General Bernardo O'Higgins, a thirty-three volume work, edited by the Chilean Government and published in 1950,[8] containing many letters and documents related to the founder of the Chilean Navy, who was an important ruler of those initial days.

---

[2]   Fernando Campos Harriet, *Los defensores del rey* (Santiago: Andrés Bello, 1958); Brian Loveman, *Chile the legacy of spanish capitalism* (New York: Oxford University Press, 1979).

[3]   J.F. Coffin, *Diario de un joven norteamericano detenido en Chile durante el periodo revolucionario 1817–1819* (Santiago: Imp. Elzeveriana, 1898); *Coleccion de Historiadores i de Documentos relativos a la Independencia de Chile* (Santiago: varios impresores, 1900-1937), 30 volumes.

[4]   María Graham, *Diario de mi residencia en Chile en 1822* (Santiago: Del Pacífico, 1956).

[5]   John Miller, *Memorias del general Miller al servicio de la República del Perú* (Santiago: Imp. Universitaria, 1912), 3 volumes.

[6]   Books on the subject viceadmiral Thomas Alexander Cochrane:
James Blakwood, *The life and daring exploits of Lord Cochrane* (London: Paternoster Row, 1861); Enrique Bunster Tagle, *Lord Cochrane* (Santiago: Zig-Zag, 1942); Francisco García Reyes, *La primera escuadra nacional* (Santiago, 1860).

[7]   Thomas Cochrane, Earl of Dundonald, *Autobiography of a Seaman* (London, 1860); *Narrative of Service in the Liberation of Chile, Perú and Brazil from Spanish and Portuguese domination* (London: James Ridway, 1859), 2 volumes.

[8]   Archivo Nacional, *Archivo de Don Bernardo O'Higgins* (Santiago: Nascimento, 1946–50), 33 volumes.

These volumes abound in material related to the difficulties of creating a fleet and merchant navy in a country that lacked resources and was worn out by war.

Admiral Cochrane returned to England at the end of Spanish dominion of what was then Chile and Peru. The Chilean Navy experienced a period of neglect. Nevertheless, foreign travellers and scientists still kept coming, and they left impressions on a variety of different matters, particularly about Chilean maritime geography.[9]

The next conflict involving the Chilean Republic was the war against the Peru-Bolivian Confederation, but the actors involved in this war left no books describing the maritime campaign in particular, in spite of its importance in dismantling the Confederation.

Something similar happened in Chile and Peru's joint war against Spain between 1865 and 1866. However, many years later, the commander of the Chilean-Peruvian naval force, Rear-Admiral Juan Williams Rebolledo, wrote about the events in which he participated.[10]

In contrast, the War of the Pacific, 1879–1883, inspired many books of narrative, documents, and analysis on the most serious foreign conflict that Chile had faced since its independence. The writers were either civilian historians or members of the Navy.[11] Among the first were Diego Barros

---

[9]   Eugenio Pereira Salas, *Las actuaciones de los oficiales navales norteamericanos en nuestras costas, 1813–1840* (Santiago: 1935); Eduard Poepping, *Testigo en la alborada de Chile: 1826-1829* (Santiago: Zig-Zag, 1960); William Bennet Stevenson, *A Historical and Descriptive of Twenty Years of Residence in South America* (London: Hurst, Robenson & Co., 1825), 3 volumes.

[10]   Benjamín Vicuña Mackenna, *Historia de la guerra de Chile con España* (Santiago: 1883); Juan Williams Rebolledo, *Guerra del Pacífico: Breve narración histórica de la contienda de Chile y Perú contra España (1865–1866)* (Santiago: Imp. Elzeveriana, 1901); Herbert W. Wilson, *Ironclads in action* (London: Marston Low, 1896); Pedro Novo y Colson, *Historia de la Guerra contra España en el Pacífico* (Madrid: 1882).

[11]   Books about the war between Chile, Peru and Bolivia started in 1879:
Correspondencia de Don Antonio Varas sobre la Guerra del Pacífico (Santiago: Imp. Universitaria, 1918); Arturo Cuevas, *Estudio estrategico sobre la campaña marítima de la guerra del Pacífico* (Valparaíso: Imp. de la Armada, 1901); Miguel Grau, *Correspondencia general de la Comandancia de la 1ª División Naval* (Santiago: Imp. de la Librería de "El Mercurio," 1880; Joaquin Larraín Zañartu, *El 21 de Mayo. Homenaje de "La Patria" a los héroes de "La Esmeralda" y "La Covadonga", en el primer aniversario del glorioso combate de Inquique* (Valparaiso: Imp. de "La Patria," 1880; Jacinto Lopez, *Historia de la guerra del guano y del salitre; o Guerra del Pacífico entre Chile, Bolivia y Perú* (New York: De Laisne and Rossboro, 1931); Francisco A. Machuca, *Las cuatro campañas de la Guerra del Pacífico* (Valparaiso: Imp. Victoria, 1927); Clements Markham, *History of the War between Perú and Chile* (London: Sampson Low, Marston, Searle Rivington, 1883); Lieutenant W.T.B.M. Mason, USN, *War on the Pacific Coast* (Washington: 1883); Nicanor Molinari, *Asalto y toma de Pisagua, 2 de noviembre de 1879* (Santiago: Imp. Cervantes, 1912); Nicanor Molinari, *Asalto y toma de Pisagua, 2 de noviembre de 1879* (Santiago: Imp. Cervantes, 1912); Pedro Nolasco Prendez, *La Esmeralda* (Santiago: Imp. de la República de Jacinto Núñez, 1879); Juan Williams Rebolledo, *Guerra del Pacífico: Operaciones de la escuadra mientras estuvo a las órdenes del contra-almirante Williams Rebolledo, 1879* (Valparaiso: Imp. del Progreso, 1882); Herbert W. Wilson, *Battleships in Action* (London: Marston Low, 1927).
Much writing on this period focuses on Arturo Prat:
Arturo Prat I El Combate Naval De Iquique (Santiago: Imp. Gutenberg, 1880); José Toribio Medina, *Arturo Prat* (Valparaiso: Imp. de la Armada, 1952); Marfisa Muñoz Yurazeck, *Arturo Prat* (Santiago: Imp. Universitaria, 1914); Juan Peralta Peralta, *Arturo Prat Chacón: Héroe del Mar* (Valparaiso: Imp. de la Escuela

Arana[12] and Benjamin Vicuña Mackenna.[13] Others include the already mentioned Admiral Juan Williams Rebolledo, who wrote another book about his participation as commander of the fleet in the early part of the war,[14] and Vice-Admiral Luis Uribe Orrego, who was a lieutenant at the beginning of the conflict.[15] The latter's works refer not only to this war, but to the complete history of the Chilean Navy and Merchant Navy. Pascual Ahumada Moreno[16] and Justo Abel Rosales[17] compiled documents that are an interesting source for consultation about this period.

In spite of the Chilean victory in the War of the Pacific, some logistic and organizational weaknesses were acknowledged. These facts, together with the rapid evolution of navies, gave way to a stage of great intellectual and professional development within the Chilean Navy. At the same time, the armed forces participated in the positive educational development that was taking place in the country. As a result of this, in 1885, the Naval Circle [Circulo Naval] was established. Initially chaired by Vice-Admiral Uribe, it is an organization dedicated, among other things, to debate and to publication of developments in the naval and maritime sciences. The *Navy Review* [*Revista de Marina*] originated in this organization, and for over a century, historians and analysts have written and published uninterruptedly in its pages. This bimonthly publication is an important source for those who want to get acquainted with Chilean naval history and the professional activities of the following generations.

At the end of the nineteenth century, there was a bloody civil war that took place in 1891, and there were acute tensions in Chilean relations with Argentina and the United States of America. The Chilean Navy reached an important new stage, as the fleet gained power and obtained the consensus of support for its activities in controlling the sea, so important for a country with a geographic configuration like Chile.[18]

Naval, 1953); Arturo Prat Chacón, *Observaciones a la lei electoral vijente* (Valparaiso: Imp. de "El Mercurio", 1876); Juan Simpson, *Algunos rasgos inéditos de la personalidad de Arturo Prat* (Valparaiso: Imp. Victoria, 1925); Carlos Toledo de la Maza, *Arturo Prat: Vida y obra de un hombre ejemplar* (Valparaíso: Ediciones Prat, 1975).

[12] Diego Barros Arana, *Historia General de Chile* (Santiago: Rafael Jover, 1884-1902), 16 volumes.

[13] Benjamin Vicuña Mackenna, *Las dos Esmeraldas* (Santiago: 1879).

[14] Juan Williams Rebolledo, *Guerra del Pacifico: Operaciones de la escuadra mientras estuvo a las órdenes del contra-almirante Williams Rebolledo* (Valparaíso: Imp. del Progreso, 1882).

[15] Luis Uribe Orrego, *Los combates navales en la Guerra del Pacífico: 1879–1881* (Valparaiso: Imp. de la Patria, 1886); *Neustra Marina militar* (Valparaiso: Tipografia de la Armada, 1910).

[16] Pascual Ahumada Moreno, *Guerra del Pacífico* (Valparaiso: Imp. del Progresso, 1884–1891), 8 volumes.

[17] Justo Abel Rosales, *La apoteosis de Arturo Prat i de sus compañeros de heroísmo muertos por la patria el 21 de mayo de 1879* (Santiago: Imp. de los Debates, 1888).

[18] Julio Bañados Espinosa, *Balmaceda: su gobierno y la revolución de 1891* (París: Librería de Gernier Hermanos, 1894); José Miguel Barros Franco, *Apuntes para la historia diplomática de Chile: el caso del Baltimore* (Santiago: Casa Nacional del Niño, 1950); Maurice H. Harvey, *Dark Days in Chile* (London: 1892); Antonio Iñiquez Vicuña, *El golpe de estado y la revolución, primero y siete de enero 1891* (Santiago: Imp. Victoria, 1891); Emilio Rodriguez Mendoza, *Ante la descendencia* (Santiago: Imp. Moderna, 1899);

To the publications of Admirals Williams and Uribe, we may add those of Captain Francisco Vidal Gormaz that refer to scientific matters and the story of the explorations performed by Spanish navigators in the southern tip of Chile, based in documental reseach done by this notable naval hydrographer in Spain. At the turn of the century, the trend increased toward more critical, historical, and scientific research, supported by many officers who were sent to study in European countries with greater naval development. The arrival of British officers in Chile, who came to act as instructors, promoted this trend toward professional improvement by creating the Naval War College and other initiatives. This increased the spreading of the doctrines on sea power developed in Europe and in the United States, particularly those of Captain Alfred T. Mahan. Since that time, there has been a tendency to analyze past events, stressing these doctrines.

In Chile, during the first half of this century, a new generation of naval historians and analysts developed. Among them were Rear Admirals Luis Langlois Vidal,[19] Alejandro Garcia Castelblanco,[20] and later, Captain Horacio Vio Valdivieso.[21] Simultaneously, the First World War and the serious political events of the 1920s and 30s, with their repercussions in the Chilean military, gave origin to different articles published in the *Revista de Marina* and to the memoirs of Admirals Jose T. Merino Saavedra,[22] and Edgardo von Schroeders Sarratea.[23] By mid-century, Vice Admiral Juan Agustin Rodriguez Sepúlveda[24] finished his work of historical research, reaching a wide audience.

The Chilean Academy of History, a center for the study and publication of history, was founded in 1933. Among its membership are notable researchers and specialists in naval history. One of its founding members was the already mentioned Admiral Garcia Castelblanco. Other members that joined the academy later were Captain Rodrigo Fuenzalida Bade, author of a large work on the history of the Chilean Navy,[25] and Dr. Carlos López Urrutia, who lives

Fanor Velasco, *La revolución de 1891: Memorias de don Fanor Velasco*, 2nd ed. (Santiago: Dirección General de Talleres, 1925); P. Wycroff, "The Chilean Civil War, 1891" U.S. Naval Institute *Proceedings* 88 (October, 1962), pp. 58–63.

[19] Luis Langlois Vidal, *Influencia del poder naval en la historia de Chile desde 1810 a 1910* (Valparaiso: Imp. de la Armada, 1911).

[20] Alejandro García Castelblanco, *Estudio crítico de las operaciones navales de Chile* (Valparaíso: Imp. de la Armada, 1929).

[21] Horacio Vio Valdivieso, *Reseña histórica de los nombres de las unidades de la Armada* (Santiago: 1938); Manual de Historia Naval de Chile (Valparaiso: Imp. de la Armada, 1972).

[22] Jose T. Merino Saavedra, *La Armada Nacional y la dictadura militar. Memorias del último Director General de la Armada* (Santiago: Imp. de la Dirección General de Prisiones, 1932.)

[23] Edgardo von Schroeders, *El delegado del gobierno y el motin de la escuadra* (Santiago: Imp. y Litografia Universo, 1933).

[24] Juan Agustin Rodríguez Sepúlveda, *Crónicas nacionales y navales* (Valparaiso: Imp de la Armada, 1953.)

[25] Rodrigo Fuenzalida Bade, *La Armada de Chile desde la alborada al sesquicentenario* (Santiago: Talleres Empresa Periodística "Aquí Está," 1978), 4 volumes; *Marinos ilustres y destacados del pasado* (Santiago: Sipimex Ltda., 1985).

and teaches in the United States and is the author of several books and articles on the same topic.[26] The current commander in chief of the Chilean Navy, Admiral Jorge Martinez Busch, author of an extensive bibliography on historical and geopolitical matters, recently joined the Chilean Academy of History.

Throughout its existence, the Chilean Academy of History has contributed to the research of many aspects related to naval and maritime history, the publication of the O'Higgins archives among them. One of the academicians that participated, Luis Valencia Avaria, has published books and articles specializing on the independence period and on the efforts of the O'Higgins government to create the Chilean Navy. Another academician, Alamiro de Avila Martel, completed several month's of research in English and Scottish archives on Admiral Cochrane, sponsored by the academy, and later published a biography.[27] A collection of edited documents is awaiting publication.

It is worthwhile noting that the academician Gabriel Guarda Geywitz has developed part of his work on the history of architecture and urbanization in Chile considering the Spanish fortifications at the south of the country, where many important events related to the Chilean Navy took place. One of his books treats the topic of the seizure of Valdivia during the War of Independence.

The civilian researchers who are more oriented toward naval history are at the Catholic University of Chile (Universidad Católica de Chile) in Santiago. Some of these individuals include Professors Roberto Hernández Ponce, Ximena Rojas Valdés, and Emilio Meneses Cuiffardi. The latter is a political scientist oriented toward topics in geopolitical and international relations. He has published a book on difficulties in the naval relations between Chile and the United States.[28]

David Mahan Marchese, M.D., has done a great and valuable research effort on naval historiography and iconography.[29] He is in possession of a private collection that is the widest and best organized in the country, collaborating with many researchers on the subject.

In the field of Chilean maritime history, Admiral Uribe and Claudio Véliz have publications on the merchant navy.[30] Also worth mentioning in this context are Pedro Sapunar, Jorge Lira, Mateo Martinic, and Manuel Fernández, who have referred to the history of Chilean ports in different periods of this century.

El Mercurio publishes, in several of its newspapers, a supplement entitled Our Sea (Nuestro Mar), under the direction of Rear Admiral Francisco Ghisolfo Araya, Chilean Navy (retired), who is a prolific author of essays on historical,

---

[26] Carlos López Urrutia, Historia de la Marina de Chile (Santiago: Andrés Bello, 1969).

[27] Alamiro de Avila Martel, Cochrane y la independencia del Pacífico (Santiago: Universitaria, 1976).

[28] Emilio Meneses Ciuffardi, El factor naval en las relaciones de Chile y EE. UU., 1881–1951 (Santiago).

[29] David Mahan, La Marina de Chile: Proyecto de ensayo Bibliográfico (Valparaiso: 1974).

[30] Claudio Véliz, Historia de la Marina Mercante de Chile (Santiago: Universidad de Chile, 1961).

strategic, and tactical topics. This publication characteristically publishes interesting articles on naval and maritime activities. Otherwise unavailable background information can also be found in its pages.

In Chile, in general terms, there is a trend to treat naval and maritime subjects without any distinction between them. The Chilean Navy has a special concern for the latter. Furthermore, there is a branch of the Navy that performs the coast guard function, and merchant marine officers are educated at the Naval Academy.

The *Naval Review* [*Revista de Marina*], normally publishes articles on subjects relating to naval history. In addition to this *Review*, the Chilean Navy publishes *Lookout* [*Vigia*], which includes similar topics, although graphically treated and in a lighter manner, providing both knowledge and entertainment. It also includes notes on current naval and maritime situations that will become future sources of information for historians.

Several books relating to the special branches of the Chilean Navy have been published during the last decade, some of them with many illustrations and references. Such is the case of books about naval aviation,[31] naval engineering,[32] supply,[33] the submarine force,[34] and naval artillery,[35] and Marine Corp.[36]

English speaking countries have developed recently an interest in Chilean naval history. Different factors might account for this interest. In the case of British authors, the reason might lie in the important naval influence their country exerted in the days of the independence, when many British officers and personnel came here, either with Cochrane or by themselves, and in the great amount of naval shipbuilding that was performed by British shipyards for the Chilean Navy by the middle of the past century. Later, at the beginning of this century, through the First World War, and even after this conflict, British instructors came to Chile, while a great number of Chilean officers were educated in Britain and in Europe.

The work of Philip Somervell on the subject is quite important.[37] We can also name Adrian English, who is a journalist who publishes articles on

---

[31] Carlos Tromben Corbalán, *La Aviación Naval de Chile* (El Belloto: Comandancia de Aviación Naval, 1987).

[32] Carlos Tromben Corbalán, *Ingeniería naval, una especialidad centenaria* (Valparaiso: Imp. de la Armada, 1989).

[33] Francisco Astudillo Tapia, y Fernández A., Marco *Historia de la especialidad de Abastecimiento, 1818–1940* (Valparaiso: Imp. de la Armada, 1991).

[34] Armada De Chile, *Fuerza de Submarinos* (Concepción: Comandancia en Jefe de la Fuerza de Submarinos, 1992).

[35] Juan Anderson Diaz, *Centenario de la Escuela de Armamentos, 1892–1992* (Valparaiso: Imp. de la Armada, 1992).

[36] Curpo de Infantería de Marina (Santiago: Sipimex Ltda., 1994).

[37] Philip Somervell, "Amistad naval anglo-chilena", *Revista de Marina,* 102: 767 (July-August, 1985), pp. 481–93.

the Chilean Navy in specialized reviews; in time they will be a source of historical data.[38]

The Chilean Navy has also been a subject of study in the U.S. Besides the articles of the aforementioned Dr. Carlos López, we should mention the books by William Sater[39] and Robert L. Scheina[40] and others who have written their degree theses for different American and British universities.[41] All of these scholars share a curiosity for this small country with its huge coastline that throughout its history has had a rather important naval force compared to its territorial size and which, by the end of the last century, was even able to threaten the emerging naval superiority of the United States in the Pacific Ocean. A subject of interest for American authors is the participation of the Chilean Navy in internal conflicts and the influence exerted by the U.S. Navy, particularly since the Second World War, when Great Britain notably decreased its presence in this part of the world, but Americans have also done some substantial work on earlier periods.[42]

An interesting book on Chilean sea power [El Poder Naval Chileno], was published to celebrate the centennial of the Revista de Marina.[43] Several distinguished historians and analysts, some of them already mentioned, directed by Captain Claudio Collados Núñez, reviewed the historical evolution of the concept of sea power in Chile from different perspectives.

Currently, there is no official professorial chair in maritime and naval history, except at the Naval Academy. The Chilean Navy focusses research in the field in the Historical Division of the Naval Museum and Historical Archives, and Naval History Bureau in the General Secretariat of the Navy. These two centers of work, research, and analysis are supporting several current research projects to be published.

The transfer of the Naval Museum (which until 1967 had been occupied by the Naval Academy) to its current building in Valparaiso meant not only

---

[38] Adrian J. English, Armed forces in Latin America (London: Jane's Publishing Co., 1984).

[39] William F. Sater, The Heroic Image in Chile: Arturo Prat, Secular Saint (Berkeley: Univ. of California Press, 1973).

[40] Robert L. Sheina, Latin America: a Naval History 1810–1987 (Annapolis: Naval Institute Press, 1987); The Influence of Sea Power Upon Latin America: A bibliography (2nd ed. Offset, 1972); "Indigenous Latin America Sea Power" Ph.D thesis, Catholic University of America, 1976).

[41] Robert N. Burr, By Reason of force: Chile and Balance of Power in South America, 1830–1905 (Berkley: Univ. of California Press, 1967); David J. Cubitt, "Study of the Naval Aspects of the War of Independence of Chile" (Portsmouth, UK: Portsmouth Polytechnic, 1978-79); D.J. Cubitt, Lord Cochrane and the Chilean Navy (1818–1823), with an Inventory of the Dundonald Papers relating to his service with the Chilean Navy (University of Edinburgh); Leland Henschel Jackson, "Naval Aspects of the War of the Pacific" (M.A. thesis, University of Florida, 1963); Donald E. Worcester, "Sea power and Chilean Independence" (thesis, University of Florida.)

[42] Edward Baxter Billingsley, In Defense of Neutral Right: the United States Navy and the Wars of Independence in Chile and Perú (Chapel Hill: Univ. of North Carolina Press, 1964); Hanson U. Hancock, A history of Chile (Chicago: Sergel and Co., 1983); Robert Hart, The Great White Fleet (Boston: Little Brown & Co., 1965); Robert Erwin Johnson, Thence round Cape Horn (Annapolis U.S. Naval Institute, 1963). For the recent period, see Robert L. Sheina, Latin America: A Naval History.

[43] Armada de Chile, El poder naval chileno (Santiago: Alfabeta, 1985).

the renewal of the museum's exhibits in accordance with latest standards for museums, but the creation of the specialized Historiography Division, headed by Professor Jorge Garin Jiménez (who has been involved in a research at the National Archives) to select and to classify naval and maritime-related material. The first volume of the papers of Vice-Admiral Thomas A. Cochrane is the fruit of this work, jointly developed with the Naval History Bureau of the General Secretariat of the Navy. It will be published soon with the sponsorship of the office of the commander in chief of the Navy.[44]

The Chilean Navy has two other important on-going projects. The first consists of continuing research at the National Archives, and in other places, in order to make available the most important documents, enabling specialized researchers to use them. The second is a project to remodel an additional part of the old building of the Naval Academy, supplementing the current Naval Museum with a library and archive for naval and maritime history.

As a final consideration we can add that the independence period and, in general, all of the last century have been treated in depth by Chilean naval and maritime historiography, probably because it was mainly a time of external conflicts and it is easier to agree on their interpretation. By the same token, recent events are less addressed, probably because naval and even maritime affairs are related to internal political problems or other aspects that are subject to the most different interpretations.

There are many newspaper and specialized review articles, together with professional theses written by naval and military officers about the events of the 1920s and 30s.[45] The published institutional histories for this period cover controversial matters lightly, but there is very little published about the following decades. Due to a lack of perspective, it is certainly not easy to provide a fair historical judgment on recent events. Nevertheless, this should not be an excuse to dispense with the personal viewpoints of recent events, as authors such as Admirals Uribe and Williams did in the past century or as von Schroeders and Merino Saavedra did at the beginning of this one. The works of Admirals Ismael Huerta Diaz[46] and Sergio Huidobro Justiniano,[47] especially Admiral Huerta's work, which is undeniably valuable in literary and documentary terms, seem to be isolated

---

[44] Jorge Garín Jiménez, Archivo Histórico Naval, Volume I Book I: Vicealmirante Thomas Alexander Cochrane (Valparaíso: Imp. de la Armada, 1993).

[45] Ricardo Donoso, *Alessandri, agitador y demoledor* (Mexico: 1954); Ernesto González, *El parto de los montes o la sublevacion de la marineria* (Santiago: Talleres Gráficos "Cóndor," 1932); Leonardo Guzmán Cortés, *Un episodio olvidado de la historia nacional, julio-noviembre de 1931*, (Santiago: Anrdés Bello, 1966); Antonio Quintanilla, *Memorias del general Quintanilla* (Santiago: 1960); Ramón Vergara Montero, *Por rutas extraviadas* (Santiago: Imp. Universitaria, 1933); Lorenzo Villalon Madrid, *Combate naval de Inquique, Valparaíso 21 de mayo e 1925* (Valparaíso: Fisher e Ihnen, 1925).

[46] Ismael Huerta Díaz, *Volvería a ser marino* (Santiago: Andrés Bello, 1988).

[47] Sergio Huidobro Justiniano, *Decisión Naval* (Valparaíso: Imp. de la Armada, 1989).

efforts that find their way amid many newspaper publications and books that treat these subjects partially or antagonistically. The lack of good analytical and interpretative works on the naval aspects of recent events is a void that we cannot but regret.

9

Denmark

Hans Christian Bjerg

Denmark commands a significant maritime geostrategic position. It is beyond dispute that this position has played a decisive role in the development of our country and has given it the essence of its historical identity.

It's curious, therefore, to observe that the maritime aspect of Danish history has been assigned a relatively humble position in historical literature, research, interpretation, and consciousness. Apparently, in the general consciousness of the Danish people, their country is more an agricultural nation than a maritime one.

Fortunately, that state of affairs seems to be changing. In the last three decades the interest for naval and maritime history has increased significantly in Denmark.

One of the reasons for the previous lack of comprehensive research in naval and maritime history in Denmark is that we used to speak about maritime issues in terms of traditional grievances. We did not consider the maritime cultural concept as a whole, wherein all the diffuse but important maritime aspects come together.

It would be fair at this point to note that the situation described above is obviously not unique to Denmark.

The Museums

The Royal Danish Navy has maintained museum collections since the eighteenth century. Still, the public was not normally given access to these collections and therefore a general interest in naval history was not stimulated.[1]

---

[1] R. Steen Steensen, *Orlogsmuseet* Marinehistorisk Selskabs Skrifternr, 6 (København: 1961), and Hans Chr. Bjerg, "Den marinehistoriske forskning og Søværnets museumsproblemer," in *Marinehistorisk Tidsskrift* no. 1, 1973, pp. 7–18.

Hans Christian Bjerg graduated from the University of Copenhagen in 1971. He was Assistant Keeper at the Danish National Archives 1971–81, Consultant on Naval History of the Royal Danish Navy in 1974, Lecturer in Naval History at the Royal Naval Academy in Copenhagen in 1975, and Chief Archivist and head of the Military Archives in 1981. He is author of several books and articles about naval history and was editor of the *Danish Naval Historical Review* from 1967 to 1978. He has been a member of the board of the Society for Danish Naval History since 1964.

The first maritime museum was founded in Denmark in 1914. It was named The Museum for Trade and Shipping, (Handels og Sefartsmuseet) and was located in the old castle of Kronborg, near Elsinore. For a long time this museum was the center for the only research in maritime history officially undertaken in Denmark.

Starting in 1958, parts of the naval collections were put on permanent exhibition. That exhibition eventually evolved into a genuine museum. The Royal Naval Museum [Orlogsmuseet] finally moved into its own building in Copenhagen in 1989. Unfortunately, due to lack of financial support, the opportunities for the Royal Naval Museum to initiate and attract research projects in naval history has been restricted.

In 1964, The National Museum established a special laboratory for ship history, primarily to develop research on the ships during the Viking age and in the Early Middle Ages. A Viking museum was connected to this laboratory in 1968 and is located in Roskilde on Zealand. Since 1993 this museum's activities have expanded and should develop into a more ambitious Research Center for Maritime Archaeology, which will be supervised by a special council of experts.[2]

In 1908 the a screw frigate *Jylland*, which had been launched in 1860, was stricken by the Royal Danish Navy in order to be scrapped. Instead, the frigate was bought by a group of private individuals who, for a period, used it as a floating exhibition platform. In 1960 it was placed at Ebeloft on Jutland and opened as a museum ship. At the end of the 1980s, support from a private foundation made it possible to completely restore the ship. That process was finished in early 1994. The ship is a success as a museum and it has stimulated an interest for the special development of warships and the history of the Navy and its men.[3]

In 1993 an integrated maritime museum was open for the public in Aaiborg on Jutland. There it is possible to visit a submarine and a fast patrol boat and to view collections showing the nation's general maritime and naval development.

It warrants mention that the Arsenal and Arms Museum [Tejhusmuseet] in Copenhagen also contains rich collections related to naval development and that the historians of that museum have also contributed to research and publishing of naval history.

Within maritime ethnology and the development of fishing, which also had an important role for the country's economy, The Museum for Fishing and Shipping [*Fisker i og Sefartsmuseet*] at Esbjerg on Jutland has made exceptional studies in the research of this aspect of our history.

[2]   Olde Crumlin-Pedersen "Marinarkæologisk Forskningscenter i Roskilde—en aktuel orientering," in *Fortid og Nutid* (1994), pp. 24–52.

[3]   The history of the museum ship can be found in R. Steen Steensen, *Fregatten Jylland*, Marinehistorisk Selskabs Skrifter (København: 1965); and F.H. Kjøolsen, "The Old Danish Frigate," in *Mariner's Mirror* (1965) pp. 27–33.

All in all, the museum situation in Denmark regarding the nation's naval and maritime history is more favorable today than ever.

Instruction and Education

One of the reasons for the lack of the interest on naval and maritime history in general in Denmark is due to the fact that there has never been a Chair on this subject at the Danish Universities. Of course, courses in maritime aspects of certain disciplines have been held. But the concept as such has never been object for profound and comprehensive research. As of this writing, only three doctoral dissertations have been prepared in this field.[4]

The situation at the universities for the last two decades seems to be following the general trend noted above. In advanced classes in history, several now choose to prepare papers about relevant naval and maritime subjects and related problems.

There is, however, no formal education or instruction on the maritime history at the schools for the merchant marine and shipping. Only at the Royal Naval Academy do they provide regular instructions and lectures on Danish Naval History and development of the naval tactics during the ages. But, once again, there is no formal chair. The lectures are given by the historical adviser of the Royal Danish Navy, who is a naval historian and also head of the military archives in Denmark.

Organizations

For many years the only forum for discussions about naval and maritime history was the so-called Society of Naval Lieutenants (See-lieutenant-Selskabet), founded in 1784. In the beginning, only lieutenants of the Navy could be members. Later, all naval officers of the line could be members. The Society is a closed circle and is only visible for the public through the Society's the *Naval Review* [*Tidsskrift for Sevssen*], which the Society has published since 1856 when it took over from private sources who had published it since 1826. Now it is one of the oldest reviews on naval affairs in the world.

In 1951 a small group of interested naval officers and historians founded the Naval Historical Society (Marinehistorisk Selskab). Their intention was to stimulate research in, and interest for, the history of the Royal Danish Navy. Furthermore, another goal was to develop a naval museum where the rich collections of the Navy could be shown to the public.

Ever since 1951 this society has been the primary forum for discussions on primarily naval history and, to a lesser extent, on maritime history in general.

---

[4]   Henning Henningsen, *Crossing the Equator: Sailor's Baptism and Other Initiation Rites* (Copenhagen: 1961); Ole Feldbæk, *India Trade under the Danish Flag 1772–1808* (Scandinavian Institute of Asian Studies Monograph Series no. 2) (Copenhagen: 1969); Anders Monrad Møeller, *Fra Galeoth til Galease. Studier i de kongerigske provinsers søfart i det 18. årh.* (København: 1981).

From its inception, the society published books on Danish naval history. In 1967 it began to publish the *Naval Historical Review* [*Marinehistorisk Tidsskrift*], for which the first editor was the present author. This *Review* has fulfilled its purpose and has really stimulated research on naval historical matters. Today the *Review* constitutes an important forum for naval and maritime matters.

From 1959–73, a naval officer was attached to the naval staff as a consultant on historical questions. In 1974 a civilian historian became the consultant of the Navy on naval historical matters and has, in reality, worked as the official naval historian.

The Board of Marinehistorisk Selskab discussed in 1971 the general condition of naval historical research in Denmark and how it could stimulate general interest in seeing naval and maritime history as a whole and as aspects of the same overall concept. The discussions were also inspired by the development in Sweden of an official council for maritime research in 1971–72. As a consequence, the Board decided to initiate the First Danish Conference on Maritime History in March 1974. The purpose of the conference was to develop a baseline for research on Danish maritime history and to investigate the possibilities for coordinating the efforts of the different disciplines.

The result of the conference was the creation of the Contact Committee for Danish Maritime Historical and Social Research, which, since 1974, has arranged a biennial conference for maritime research. Furthermore, the committee had taken the initiative to publish surveys periodically of on-going research as well as a guide to where sources for maritime history can be found. Each year the Committee publishes a bibliography of books and articles related to naval and maritime matters.[5]

Naval History Research and Literature

The research and publishing of Danish naval history, until the second part of the present century, has been dominated by naval officers. The literature on these matters was characterized by general works and very few special investigations. As a matter of fact, very few educated historians had previously dared to step into the field.

One who did was H.D.Lind, a vicar, who in the last decades of the nineteenth century has published works about the sixteenth and seventeenth century Danish Navy. His works are still used as textbooks today.

The first survey of relative modern Danish naval history was printed in small booklet form in 1818 by W.A. Graah, a naval officer.[6] After comprehensive studies of the archives, another naval officer, H.G. Garde, published a four-volume history of the Dano-Norwegian Navy dating from 1500.[7] The edition

---

[5]   Hans Christian Bjerg, "Den maritimhistoriske forskning i Denmark," in *Fortid og Nutid* XXVI (1976), pp. 392–7.

[6]   W.A. Graah, *Udkast til Danmarks Søekrigshistorie* (København: 1818).

[7]   H.G. Garde, *Efterretninger on den danske og norske Sømagt*, bd. I-IV (København: 1832–35).

was not a continuous history, but rather a chronological synthesis of periodic information. It does, however, remain a useful work.

Garde expressed the hope that its publication would inspire historians to write about Danish naval history, but he was to be disappointed. It was Garde himself who would, in 1852 and 1861, publish two general works on the history of the Danish Navy, covering the period 1500–1814.[8] He later brought that history up to 1848.[9] General works on Danish naval history were not produced until 1875 and 1906 respectively. The authors, once again, were naval officers.

The same was the case when a new general naval history was published in 1934. A two-volume publication emerged in 1941–42, following the same model. The two last mentioned books must be considered in view of the existing political context. With regard to the first publication, it must be noted that, in the 1930s, the wave of disarmament nearly strangled the Navy in Denmark, and the naval officers had to profile their occupation. When the two-volume work was published, Denmark was occupied by German troops, and one purpose of the publication was apparently to emphasize the long history of Denmark and the strength of the national will which, over the ages, had been secured by the Navy.

The last publication in the list of general books about history came in 1961-62.[10] It followed the same model as its predecessors, but for the first time, some of the contributors were civilian historians. This was apparently a result of the efforts of Marinehistorisk Selskab since 1951. The general works did not communicate new knowledge to the naval history other than the contemporary activities of the Royal Danish Navy.

The increase of interest in naval history from the beginning of the 1970s produced a demand for new knowledge about naval history. Therefore, the time for general works had passed and several books and articles about special and narrower subject areas based on a scientific approach emerged. However, one general work from this period was produced. It is a two-volume book about the shipbuilding activity in the Danish-Norwegian Navy in the period of the sailing warship, 1690–1860, which was published in 1980.[11] That book revealed the richness of the huge collections of technical drawings and plans which existed in the naval files of the Danish National Archives. It has contributed to our knowledge of an important aspect of our maritime heritage which had not been

---

[8]   H.G. Garde, *Bidrag til Sømagts Historie 1700–1814* (København: 1852), and *Den dansk-norske Sømagts Historie 1535–1700* (København: 1861).

[9]   H.G. Garde, "Bidrag til Sømgtens Historie 1814–48," *Historisk Tidskrift*, 3.Rk. V. Bd. (1866–67), pp. 165–216.

[10] *Flåden gennem 450 Ar*, Red. af R. Steen Steensen, G. Honnes de Lichtenberg og M. Frils Møller, (København, 1961) (vol. 1), and *Flåden - administration, teknik og civile opgaver*, Red. af K.G. Konradsen, G. Honnens de Lichtenberg og M. Frils Møller, (København, 1962) (vol. 2).

[11] Hans Christian Bjerg and John Erichsen, *Danske Orlogsskibe 1690–1860, Konstruktion og Dekoration*, Bd. I-II (København: 1980).

researched previously. It also inspired basic studies about technical development in Denmark where, for a long time, the Naval Shipyard in Copenhagen was the largest workplace in the country. In the 1980s, profound and comprehensive studies were published on the ships and shipbuilding of the Danish Navy in the seventeenth and the eighteenth centuries.[12]

Now we also have a comprehensive knowledge on the Navy in the last part of the seventeenth century, thanks to discussions among the Danish naval historians about the course of the Naval Battle of Køge Bugt on the 1st of July 1677. This discourse has brought many new facts to light on that period.[13] Contemporary research also exists on the last part of the eighteenth century and on the first decade of the nineteenth century.[14]

Much remains to be done. For example, we still need modern research on the administration of the Navy, its political role, the social conditions for the officers and the crews, and among other things, new investigations on the naval battles fought by the Navy.

In 1975 the present author published *A Bibliography of Danish Naval History from 1500–1975* [*Dansk Marinehistorisk Bibliografi 1500–1975*]. It lists 2,086 items, most of them small articles and booklets. Unintentionally, the bibliography became a chronicle of the status of Danish naval history prior to the increasing interest which appeared in the 1970s. Since then, there have been around 500 items published, which, on average, are far more detailed and extensive than most of the items listed in the mentioned bibliography. It is not surprising, therefore, that a revision to that bibliography is planned for publication in the next two to three years.

Danish naval historians realize today that a lot of trends common to other European naval development can be recognized in the Danish materials. But they are also of that opinion that knowledge of the development of the small Danish Navy can provide important pieces to an understanding of the general puzzle. Heretofore, very few books or articles on Danish naval history have been published in English or another major language. It is, therefore, the claimed intention of Danish naval historians today to publish more in English in the future.

Maritime History Research and Literature

As compared to naval history, maritime history has thus far been characterized by general surveys and sporadic scientific research. It is worthwhile to observe

---

[12] See for instance, Niels M. Probst and Frank Allan Rasmussen in several articles in *Marinehistorisk Tidsskrift* in the 1980s and 1990s.

[13] Jørgen H. Barfod, *Niels Juel, liv og gerning i den danske søetat* (Arhus: 1977). The discussions about the Battle of Køge Bugt can be followed in articles in *Tidsskrift for Søvæsen og Marinehistorisk Tidsskrift* in the beginning of the 1950s and from 1977 and on.

[14] Ole L. Frantzani Trualan tra vat. *Dansk-norsk flådepolitik 1769–1807*, Marinehistorisk Selskabe Skrifter, no. 16 (København: 1980) and Ole Feldbæk, *Slaget på Reden* (København: 1985).

that the two disciplines have followed separate tracks. But, in general, the interest in maritime history has been greater than that shown for naval history.

In 1919 a huge book in two volumes was published. The title was *The Shipping and Trade of Denmark during the Ages* [*Danmarks Søfart og Søhandel fra de ældste Tider til vore Dage*]. The contributors were esteemed historians, naval officers, and men working with the shipping trade. For a long time this book represented the general knowledge of the maritime history of Denmark, but did not inspire further research.

Research and writings about maritime history have concentrated around the *Handes og Søfartsmuseet* and its yearbook, the articles which represent the main part of the published maritime history up to current times. A lot of information may also be found in the jubilee publications of the different Danish shipping companies.

Denmark and the Sea [*Danmark og Havet*] was the title of a general two-volume book about the maritime history of Denmark and the maritime contemporary institutions in the country. It was published in 1948.

The 1970s were also a breakthrough for the maritime historical interest and research centered around the Conference for Maritime History and the Contact Committee mentioned above. In 1980 the Contact Committee began to publish the *Maritime Contact* [*Maritim Kontakt*], which now, in addition to the yearbook of the Museum for Trade and Shipping, is the main forum for published maritime research in Denmark. One of the few doctoral dissertations on maritime history was published in 1981.[15]

The situation for maritime historical research in Denmark is, therefore, generally in very good shape at the moment. An example of this is the working plan for a general and comprehensive work on the maritime history of Denmark, which is going to be published within the next 3–4 years in 4–5 volumes, written by historians who belong to the new school that emerged after the 1970s. It is expected that this new history will compile all the new knowledge provided by the modern and scientific research approach.

---

[15] By Anders Monrad Møller, cfr. note 4.

10

Dominican Republic

Cesar A. De Windt Lavandier
Rear Admiral, Dominican Republic Navy, Retired

Following twenty-two years of Haitian military occupation, Dominican Republic independence was proclaimed on 27 February 1844. On that very same day, Commander Juan Alejandro Acosta took possession of the port facilities at the Harbor on the Ozama River, and the Dominican Navy, known as the National Fleet, was born.

The Navy was initially composed of five converted merchant ships provided by three Dominican businessmen, and was organized by its founders, Commanders Juan Bautista Cambiaso and Juan Bautista Maggiolo. The first ship to carry the Dominican banner was the schooner *Leonor*, which departed Santo Domingo on 2 March 1844 bound for Curacao. Her mission was to return previously exiled patrician Juan Pablo Duarte, the founder of the Dominican Republic, to his newly independent homeland.[1]

The Navy's first five converted merchant vessels were soon joined by seven other ships that had been purchased for use in the new nation's defense. The Dominican Navy then comprised twelve ships, with attendant Naval Artillery and Naval Infantry units from 1844 to 1861. It was to play a leading role in securing the independence of our fledgling country. This was particularly true during the war between the Dominican Republic and Haiti from 1849 to 1850, when the Navy successfully met the Haitian Navy in combat while transporting substantial quantities of troops and supplies in that conflict.

Despite this proud and significant introduction, however, much of the Dominican Republic's naval and maritime history has fallen into a state of neglect in recent times. It is this issue which merits our attention.

Authentic historiography in the Dominican Republic began with Jose Gabriel Garcia who, during the last decade of the nineteenth century, wrote wrote four volumes in a compendium of the history of Santo Domingo dating back to the arrival of the Spaniards to the islands.[2] Garcia, it should be noted, also served as

---

[1]   Duarte was destined to be exiled again that same year by his Dominican rival, Pedro Santana, and would lead a wandering lifestyle, largely in Venezuela, until his death in 1876. Still, he is widely regarded as the founder of the Dominican independence movement.

[2]   Jose Gabriel Garcia, *Historia Moderna De La Repubica Dominicana* (Santo Domingo: Garcia hermanos,

an artillery lieutenant in one of the warships that fought against the Haitian forces during the 1849–50 war. He took part in the naval battle of Aux Cayes off the southern coast of Haiti in December 1849, from which the Dominican Republic emerged victorious.

Antonio del Monte y Tejada, another author who actually preceded Garcia, made reference to the Dominican Corsairs activities from 1738 to 1760.[3] Both writers based their ideas on their studies of the West Indian Chronicals. Since Garcia did not have access to many primary sources of information, it is possible that he used del Monte y Tejada's notes, as Antonio had traveled to Havana, Cuba to conduct extensive research in the official files and deposits held there.

Also ranking among the noteworthy researchers of our history is Emilio Rodriquez Demorizi, who, most notably, made reference to the evolution of our merchant marine as well as the Dominican Navy in many of his books.[4]

In fact, in our country the military affairs dealing with seafaring events are very closely related to non-military maritime issues. All matters associated with port authorities are in the hands of the military officials. Since the Dominican Republic is a small nation, the Navy supervises all activities concerning all of our ports of call, including trade, defense and security. Thus, our naval heritage is very much a part of our national history.

Unfortunately, there is no institution in the Dominican Republic, governmental or private, intended solely to teach our naval history. The only entity currently teaching maritime history is the Dominican Naval Academy, and even those courses are taught under precarious conditions. Appropriate research facilities are nonexistent, and the lack of resources, materials, and primary documents prevent students from obtaining a validated understanding of that history.

The Academy of History (Academia de la Historia de la Republica Dominicana) is an official institution founded by a group of prominent and distinguished historians dedicated to the study of the history of the two countries sharing the island of Hispaniola: the Dominican Republic and the Republic of Haiti. As such, it concerns itself with many aspects of the island's history, but it has not undertaken the study of either the Dominican Navy or its merchant marine.

Several individuals in the private sector have accumulated documents relating to events that took place during our War for Independence and those chronicling the Dominican Republic's naval participation in World War II, but those efforts have not enjoyed the support of our public institutions.

1893–1906; reprint 1968), 4 vols.

[3] Antonio del Monte y Tejada, *Historia de Santo Domingo* (1890; reprint: Ciudad Trujillo, 1952–1953), 3 vols.

[4] See, for example, Emilio Rodriguez Demorizi, *Hostos en Santo Domingo* (Ciudad Trujillo, 1939–1942), 2 vols.

In my personal opinion, our country is in great need of institutions that promote the studies of naval historiography. For example, the creation of a special department at Universidad Autonoma de Santo Domingo, the oldest university in the New World and a very prestigious institution, to study maritime and naval history would be extremely important.

It would also be possible to integrate a special branch for the study of maritime history with the collaboration of other international organizations with our government. Proposals for such a development could be made through the Museum of History and Geography or through the Academy of History of the Dominican Republic.

The absence of a sound and vigorous branch of maritime history in the Dominican Republic is due largely to the imperatives of national priorities; we are a small and poor country and must husband resources accordingly. The potential for cooperative or collaborative efforts with international organizations dedicated to maritime research may provide the opportunity to overcome the resource limitations and permit us to more thoroughly develop and better understand this important aspect of our nation's history.

11

France

Hervé Coutau-Bégarie

For much of the twentieth century, France has maintained a leading role in the study of history. At the turn of the century, the positivist school helped decisively to settle the emerging rules of scholarly history. In the 1930s, the Annales school played a leading role in the revival of historical studies with its interests in economy and social history. Today, Fernand Braudel, Emmanuel Le Roy-Ladurie, and Pierre Chaunu are well known to the international community of historians.[1] Yet, despite this rich relationship with historical studies in general, it is not at all certain that the same positive observations can be made about the influence of the French school on maritime history.

Such an assertion may be surprising. France, after all, has played an important role in the International Commission of maritime history. It was through French influence that the revision of the *Glossaire nautique* by Jal, and the creation of a maritime history working group five years later at the Stockholm Congress, was approved at the 10th International Congress of Historical Sciences in Rome in 1955. The first international symposia were organised in Paris from 1956 to 1959 by the Académie de Marine, the Comité de documentation historique de la Marine, the Centre national de la recherche scientifique and the IVe Section de l'Ecole pratique des Hautes Etudes. Subsequent symposia have taken place all over the world, but the mainspring has always been a French source. Symposia products were also for some time published by the S.E.V.P.E.N. in France, in a collection known to all maritime historians.

Given all this, how could one have doubts as to the influence of French maritime historiography? The balance sheet is impressive, but it is essentially the work of one man: Michel Mollat, President of the International Commission of Maritime History for twenty-five years. Mollat authored many books, served as the head of the working groups for the revision of the *Glossaire nautique*, of a survey concerning the marine ex-votos, and of a bibliography of oceanic routes. He was a leading figure in dozens of national or international symposia and, finally, was founder of the Laboratorie d'Histoire maritime. An entire article devoted just to his work would not suffice to relate his contribution to maritime

---

[1] Hervé Coutau-Bégarie, *Le phénomène Nouvelle Historie, Grandeur et décadence de l'école des Annales* (Paris: Economica, 2e éd., 1989).

history. Following him are those who are today known to the international community: Jean Meyer, Etienne Taillemite, Jean Boudriot, and Philippe Masson.

But French maritime historians have been unable to establish a common methodological approach with which to challenge the Anglo-Saxon hegemony in this field. The reasons for this situation are, of course, complex. First, we have to consider the absence of a structure around which French maritime historians could gather. For instance, there is no counterpart to the British Navy Records Society in France. The Commission francaise d'Histoire maritime (CFHM), is relatively new, dating back only to 1976, and its means have always been very modest. For various reasons, the integration of the Commission into the Comité de documentation historique de la Marine, which was logically appropriate, has not been possible.

Furthermore, there is no real center for research within academia except the Laboratoire d'histoire maritime. That laboratory was created in 1973 by Michel Mollat at the Sorbonne when the IVème section de l'Ecole pratique des Hautes Etudes was finally integrated into the Centre National de la Recherche Scientifique.[2] Additionally, no journal of maritime history enjoying the same importance as the *American Neptune* or the *Mariner's Mirror* exists in France. As a result, the professional articles which are produced are dispersed in various reviews, the most important of which do not give them the space or attention they deserve.

In 1979, the CFHM began publication of a *Chronique d'histoire maritime*, which, in fact, is more a simple bulletin than a true review. Of course, we have the excellent review, *Neptunia,* published by the Musée de la Marine, but it is more interested in archeology than in history, and its size prohibits the publication of extensive articles. The review *Marins et Océans*, published for the first time by the CFHM in 1990, was stopped after the third issue with a change in the Commission's editorial policy. The same situation exists in the publishing of other scholarly maritime and naval history; for instance, the well-known S.E.V.P.E.N. no longer exists after having once been the publishing resource for substantive studies.

The Service historique de la Marine publishes certain works, but only when they are the result of researchers using the documents kept by that Service. Some works remain unpublished, particularly if they are extensive, unless it is possible to adopt the imperfect solution of the anastatic process. For example, the work on the Chinese Navy by Jacques Dars was published more than twenty years after its examination by the university, and the book by Claude Huan on the Soviet Navy in the Arctic during the 1940-1945 war waited more than ten years for a publisher. These are but two examples among others.

This lack of structure has created an unfortunate separation between naval history and maritime history. The former has suffered from a long-lasting

---

[2]   Naturally there are other centres of research having fewer resources such as Centre d'historie des Espaces atlantiques in Bordeaux under the supervision of Paul Butel.

prejudice against military history, anathematised by the Annales school.[3] The study of naval history has been relegated for decades to retired naval officers or ship lovers, interested in the ships themselves. Thus, naval history has long focused on technique and tactics and emphasized activities of ships-of-the-line or the actions of privateers in the *guerre de course*. Maritime history, on the other hand, survived by adapting itself to external subjects such as economic history, through which its revival began.

In a *Revue historique* article in 1971, Professor André Martel foresaw a revival of military history in France. It is not going too far to say that a similar occurrence has been observed for the last two decades in the studies of naval and maritime histories. Both have finally reached, if not unity, at least a complementarity which allows them to coexist in academia. The number of studies has increased in various spheres. Today, French maritime history covers almost all historical research fields, although, unfortunately, some important areas exhibit weakness or obsolescence. As an initial conclusion, therefore, we may say that the results of this progress remain mixed.[4]

The distinction between naval history and maritime history has given rise to some disputes. The most common point of view, in accordance with the etymology currently being accepted, is that naval history should include everything which concerns the ships themselves, while maritime history would be more one of the environment. It does not seem necessary to debate that question here, but to remain with the commonly accepted interpretation, naval history means the history of the military forces used at sea, while maritime history concerns all the rest. This division has the advantage of being easily understandable and also corresponds in a certain way to an institutional reality which is almost sociological: naval historians form a particular group in which academics remain a minority; maritime historians are much more numerous and more diversified, while at the same time more closely connected to academia.

Naval History

Before 1940, France seemed to have a promising and solid base in naval history. Famous historians had dedicated their studies to it: Lacour-Gayet wrote a whole set of volumes on French maritime and colonial policy before the Revolution. Charles de la Roncière wrote a monumental, six volume *Histoire de la marine française*. Although his history was never completed, the final volume he produced, concerning Louis XIV's navy, is still considered a reference for today's research.

---

[3]   Hervé Coutau-Bégarie, "L'histoire militaire face à la nouvelle histoire," *Stratégique*, 18, 1986.

[4]   This statement is in no way exhaustive. Its aim consists in bringing tendencies to the fore and in not seeking an exhaustive evaluation. The only works mentioned are the most important or the most significant as such.

The historical method also remained highly regarded in French naval circles despite the consequences of the First World War. Officers studying at the Ecole de guerre navale were typically required to write a thesis, and most often they were of a historical nature, with a predilection for works on the seventeenth and eighteenth century periods. For this reason, we have a number of important studies based on archival research and presenting original interpretations which have been brought to the attention of the public by historians since the Second World War.[5]

This tradition continued through the 1950s, with an inclination towards contemporary history. Then, in the following decade, it was interrupted when military teaching turned from history and gave priority to technical subjects. This lack of interest, demonstrated by both the Navy and academia, was very harmful to the progress of research. It was only in the 1980s that naval history was revived and claimed its rightful place among historical studies.

Contemporary Naval History. Contemporary naval history reached an exceptional level of development in France between the two world wars, when the memory of the First War was still vivid, furthering the publication of works on naval warfare. The undisputed leader of that form of literature was Paul Chack, who published a number of small works with much success, and which have recently been collected in one volume by Jacques Antier.[6] Simultaneously the Service historique de la Marine, created in 1920 by Captain Raoul Castex, began publishing some strategical studies through its historical section. Other purely historical studies, written primarily by Captains Adolphe Laurens and Louis Guichard, are remarkable for the way the authors scrupulously used official records. These works remain useful today.[7]

This worthy historical effort was brought to a sudden halt by the Second World War. Of course, at the end of that war, just as in 1918, a number of popular works on naval war emerged. Some of them have achieved great success, particularly those by Jacques Mordal (pen name of naval doctor Hervé Cras, who also wrote several other works on the Second World War). At the same time, just as in 1918, the historical section of the Service historique de la Marine, renewed publication of historical studies through official histories. Cras and Captain Caroff wrote most of those studies, which deal with almost all the theaters of operation: Mediterranean, Atlantic, the Channel, North Sea, and

[5]   See for instance the works listed in the bibliography of Philippe Masson, *Histoire de la Marine* (Paris: Lavauzelle, 1982, volume I).

[6]   Paul Chack et Jean-Jacques Antier, *Histoire maritime de la première guerre mondiale* (Paris: France-Empire, 1970 in 3 volumes and 1992 in one volume).

[7]   Adolphe Laurens, *Histoire de la guerre sous-marine allemande* (Paris: Editions maritimes et coloniales, 1930); *Le commandement naval en Méditerranée* (Paris: Payot, 1931); *Précis d'histoire de la guerre navale* (Paris: Payot, 1929); Louis Guichard, *Histoire du blocus naval 1914–1918*, (Paris: Payot, 1929).

Indochina. Other similar works have been devoted to certain postwar events, particularly the colonial war in Indochina and the Suez crisis.[8]

Unfortunately, this effort was stopped in the 1960s for several reasons. The primary one was the lack of resources available to the Service historique de la Marine, but the slow progress of granting access to official records or documents to unofficial researchers also contributed to the problem. Thanks to the 1979 change in French national security law, which reduced the required time delay for opening records to the public from fifty to thirty years, part of the access problem has been alleviated. Still, we must contend with the fact that many of our historical records suffered significant disorder, or even destruction, both during the 1940 French collapse and during military actions before and after Liberation. Therefore, reconstitution of naval archives has been difficult and only partially successful. Additionally, some of the series in the French naval archives are incompletely listed or without detailed inventories. This, of course, further complicates the researcher's task.

Despite the various limitations, the contemporary period is the best studied. Among the best works are those by Philippe Masson, head of the historical section of the Service historique de la Marine, and those by Claude Huan, dispersed through many articles and conference papers.

A number of French researchers have extended their consideration of maritime issues beyond France. Here too, Captain Claude Huan has studied Soviet and German naval history in a number of important articles and begun a history of the German-Soviet war, the first volume of which has just been published.[9] Captain François-Emmanuel Brézet chose to study the Imperial German Navy; his original analysis of the Jutland battle[10] replaces the famous book by Captain Georg von Hase, *La bataille du Jutland vue du Derflinger*, which had impressed many French naval officers in the 1930s.[11]

We are, however, unable to mention any noteworthy study on the Royal Navy (contrary to what happens on the other side of the Channel), or on the

---

8   Hervé Cras, *Les forces maritimes du Nord*, 1955; C.F. Caroff, *Le théâtre atlantique*, 1958–1959; *Le théâtre méditerranéen*, 1960; *Les formations de la marine aux armées*, 1953, rééd. 1984; *La campagne de Norvège*, 1955, rééd. 1986; Hervé Cras, *L'armistice de juin 1940 et la crise franco-britannique*, 1959; C.F. Caroff, *Les débarquements alliés en Afrique du Nord (Novembre 1942)*, 1960, rééd. 1987; André Reussner, *Les conversations franco-britanniques d'Etat-Major (1935–1939)*, 1969; V.A.E. Chaline et C.V. Santarelli, *Historique des Forces navales français libres*, t. 1, 1989; Jacques Michel, *La marine française en Indochine de 1939 à 1956*, 1972–1977, rééd. 1991–1992; Philippe Masson, *La crise de Suez*, 1966.

9   Claude Huan, *La marine soviétique en guerre. I Arctique* (Paris-Caen: Economica-Mémorial, 1990). Two other volumes will follow: one for the Black sea, another for the Baltic. Huan has already published a great number of studies, mainly in the 1960s in *Revue Maritime*.

10   This author has previously published important articles: "Une flotte contre l'Angleterre. La rivalité navale anglo-allemande 1897-1914" in *Marins et Océans I* (Paris: 1991); "Le croiseur de bataille: mythe ou réalité," in *Marins et Océans II* (Paris: 1992).

11   F.E. Brézet, *Le Jutland 1916* (Paris: Economica, 1992).

navies of Italy and Japan. Contemporary naval history in France remains markedly introverted.

Despite the individual efforts noted above, there are a considerable number of lacunae in contemporary French naval history. It is, for instance, obvious that biographical research lags in France. Most of the British admirals of the First World War had their biographies written; this is not the case for the French admirals. Admiral Guépratte, well known for his gallantry during the First World War, was the only one to be the subject of biographies, but they are all too often anecdotal or hagiographic. None of the chiefs of the naval staff nor the commanders-in-chief of the French fleet have been accorded this honor.

With regard to the Second World War, only two admirals, Castex[12] and Darlan,[13] have had biographies published; the former as a naval thinker and the latter for his political importance. This course of events seems surprising, particularly when we recall the important role played by several other admirals, such as de Laborde, Commander in Chief of the French High Sea Forces at the time of the scuttling of the French Navy in Toulon in November 1942; or Muselier, Commander of the Free French Naval Forces until his break with de Gaulle; or Abrial, who defended Dunkirk, was governor of Algeria after 1940, and Secretary of State for the Navy during the dramatic events leading to the scuttling of the fleet.

There are many more examples of the lack of biographical research of French naval history in France. Through the work of Philippe Masson, we do have a general history of the French Navy during the Second World War.[14] This work replaces the obsolete and inadequate one by Admiral Auphan and Jacques Mordal,[15] whose work suffered from the research restrictions noted earlier. The history by Philippe Masson is a synthesis of complementary investigations into the mass of documents kept in Vincennes. There is no comparable work for the First World War, which has been widely neglected since the death of Henri Le Masson. The fundamental reference about the Navy of the *Belle Epoque* remains American Theodore Ropp's work, written between the two wars at the time when the public record offices were closed (although there is a study in progress by Admiral Ausseur).[16] Another key work is the study by Genevieve Salkin on naval attachés, bringing to naval history the methods of prosopography.[17]

---

[12] Hervé Coutau-Bégarie, *Castex le stratège inconnu* (Paris: Economica, 1985).

[13] Hervé Coutau-Bégarie et Claude Huan, *Darlan* (Paris: Fayard, 1989), followed by *Lettres et notes de l'amiral Darlan*, (Paris-Caen: Economica-Mémorial, 1992).

[14] Philippe Masson, *La marine française et la guerre 1939–1945* (Paris: Tallandier, 1991).

[15] Amiral Auphan et Jacques Mordal, *La marine française pendant la seconde guerre mondiale* (Paris: Hachette, 1958).

[16] Unpublished for a long time, this book has been magnificently edited by Stephen Roberts: Theodore Ropp, *The Formation of a Navy* (Annapolis: Naval Institute Press 1987).

[17] Geneviève Salkin-Laparra, *Marins et diplomates. Les attachés navals 1860–1914* (Vincennes: Service historique de la Marine, 1990).

Another work by Philippe Masson concerns the postwar mutinies,[18] but no fundamental study exists on naval law.[19] A thesis on interwar naval policy was abandoned, but we shall soon have a book published, unfortunately posthumously, by Admiral de Lachadenède, which considers the French Navy during the Spanish Civil War.[20] As for the study of the officer corps by Ronald Chalmers Hood, it is slightly exaggerated and warrants some revision.[21]

Today, ships' histories are pursued by passionate specialists. One of the best is Robert Dumas, the matchless connoisseur of the battleships.[22] While the French Fleet Air Arm looks forward eagerly for a historian,[23] Henri Le Masson, publisher of the *Flottes de Combat* and a renowned historian, produced several remarkable studies on the history of the light craft and of submarines from a broader perspecive than that usually employed.[24] Captain Huan is also working on a revised history of French submarines.[25]

The history of French naval thought actually lay essentially fallow until the launching of the international programme under the supervision of the Fondation pour les Etudes de Défense Nationale (FEDN), to which historians from eleven countries contributed.[26] The studies on naval disarmament, which proliferate in the Anglo-Saxon world, are very rare in France. The Washington Conference aroused the attention of a German historian who has written a thesis on the subject.[27] The London Conferences also await a French historian's approach.[28]

---

[18] Philippe Masson, *La marine française et la mer Noire* (Paris: Publicatioons de la Sorbonne, 1982).

[19] Captain Huan is working on this subject.Philippe Masson, *La marine française et la mer Noire* (Paris: Publications de la Sorbonne, 1982).

[20] René Sabatier de Lachadenède, *La marine française et la guerre civile d'Espagne* (Vincennes: SHM, 1994).

[21] Ronald Chalmers Hood, *Royal Republicans, French Naval Officers Corps between the Wars* (Batan Rouge: Louisiana Univ. Press, 1985).

[22] Robert Dumas, *Les cuirassés de 23 000 tonnes* (Brest: Editions de la Cité, 1980); *Le cuirassé Jean Bart* (Bourg-en-Bresse: Marine Editions, 1992).

[23] Let us mention the recent creation of an Association pour la recherche de la documentation sur l'histoire de l'aéronautique navale (ARDHAN), 3 Avenue Octave Gréard. 00300 Armées.

[24] Henri Le Masson, *Du Nautilus au Redoutable* (Paris: 1960); *Histoire du torpilleur en France* (Paris: Académie de Marine, 1966).

[25] L'AGASM (Association générale des anciens sous-mariners) has a remarkable review of little diffusion, *Plongée*, which has published several issues treating of highly technical questions on submarines of the main sea powers.

[26] France, Great Britain, Germany, Italy, Belgique, Portugal, Rumania, Sweden, Finland, United States, Argentina. Three volumes have been published under the title *L'évolution de la pensée navale*, (Paris: FEDN, I, 1991; II, 1992; III, 1993). At least two other volumes are programmed.

[27] Hannsjorg Kowar, *Die Französische Marinepolitik 1919–1914 und die Washingtoner Konferenz* (Stuttgart: Hochschulverlag, 1978); a digest of this work is about to be published in French.

[28] The study by Maurice Vaïsse, *Sécurité d'aboard* (Paris: Pédone, 1980) is most particularly dedicated to general disarmament according to the rules of the SDN.

Today, some famous events need reinterpretation. For instance, the 1916 Athens affair still provokes a misplaced reserve in historical circles. Nobody wants to shed light on the causes which resulted in that show of force which culminated in tragic failure. That is not so for the Mers el-Kébir episode, but, even fifty years later, that tragedy warrants historical clarification. For instance, all existing sources continue to give the erroneous number of losses as 1,294 killed, while many aspects of the decision-making process are left undisclosed.[29] The same can be said of the scuttling of the French fleet in Toulon. A number of important messages between Toulon and Algiers remain unknown, while everyone tells the legend of a major SS operation, which participated with only a small detachment.

The deficiencies of French contemporary naval history are, in fact, logical, if we take into account the lack of interest which surrounds naval strategy in France. The tradition personified by Admiral Castex in the interwar years and following the renowned authors at the turn of the century, Admirals Daveluy and Darrieus, has fallen by the wayside. There is not a single work concerning French naval strategy, outside some historical works, since Espagnac du Ravay's 1941 essay, *Vingt ans de politique navale*, written by order of Admiral Darlan. By contrast, consider, for instance, that in the 1970s and 1980s, approximately ten books concerning naval strategy were published in England by authors such as Sir James Cable, Eric Grove, and Rear-Admiral Richard Hill.

This is the result of a political censorship enduring from the memory of the Second World War (as exemplified by the absence of a commemoration of the fiftieth anniversary of Mers el-Kébir, the official celebration of which was strictly the work of the British). It is due also to an instinctive suspicion towards any reflection that could threaten the delicate consensus about defence policy. Furthermore, it is the consequence of a sensitive juxtaposition of hierarchical interests, divided between a lack of interest for genuine research and a particular interest in preventing even a muffled criticism of its actions. The freedom of expression that favored research on strategy and history through the 1930s simply does not exist anymore. There is, of course, the beginning of a scholarly interest in French naval strategy following 1945, but the results of these efforts are still undetermined.[30]

Contemporary naval history, despite all, is tied to an understanding of previous periods.

Ancient Naval History. The deficiencies in French maritime and naval historiography are particularly manifest with regard to antiquity. We can note only a few works, which are generally governed by an archeological approach.

---

[29] Hervé Coutau-Bégarie et Claude Huan, *Mers el-Kébir. La rupture franco-britannique*, (Paris: Economica, 1994).

[30] For example, studies still unpublished by Philippe Ouérel on the naval policy of the 4th Republic and Jean-Marc Balenci on naval diplomacy in the Indian ocean since 1967.

The most impressive study concerning Roman history was presented by Michel Reddé, and focused on the Roman Imperial Navy.[31] This monumental work stands out because of a very erudite analysis of the infrastructure of naval bases at the disposal of the Roman Navy. On the other hand, it must be noted that his consideration of naval tactics and strategic employment of fleets was somewhat thin; Reddé did not take a keen interest in these important aspects of naval warfare. It is to Jean Pagès' works that one must turn for treatment of those features of ancient naval warfare.

There has been little work on Greek naval history (with the singular exception of a small book by Jean Rougé, who presented a very short synthesis of the subject) until the studies by Jean Pagès on naval thought, armament, tactics, and thalassocracies. Still, these articles, dispersed in different publications, provide materials for synthesis in future publications.[32]

The current disinterest in ancient naval history contrasts notably with the nineteenth when Admiral Jurien de la Gravière, Admiral Serre, and Professor Cartault acted as pioneers in the field. Historians of ancient naval wars still appreciate their studies, despite their age. One must also note that there is a recent work in French on ancient ships, *Le Musée imaginaire de la marine antique*. It was, however, written by Lucien Basch, a Belgian specialist, and to credit his excellent work to the French school would be inappropriate.

Medieval Naval History. Medieval history is just slightly better off. Here again, there are only a few names worthy of mention. One, of course, must be Professor Mollat, whose interests lay more in maritime history than in naval history. Nevertheless, he contributed to naval history in a number of his works.[33] Another historian, Anne Martin-Chazelas, has shed light on the question of the Clos des Galées, which was the first real attempt to establish a naval dockyard in France. Her study, however, is based on a set of unique documents. Furthermore, the life of Jean de Vienne still awaits a sound biography.

Some incidents mentioned in the works by Charles-Emmanuel Dufourq on Catalonia, Michel Balard on Genoa, Freddy Thiriet on Venice, and Clause Cahen on the Crusades make one regret the absence of naval historical studies on those subjects.[34] Maurice Lombard has opened new avenues for consideration

---

31 Michel Reddé, *Mare Nostrum Les infrastructures de la marine romaine à l'époque impériale* (Rome: Ecole française de Rome, 1987).

32 Jean Pagès, "La pensée navale athéienne au Ve siècle" in Hervé Coutau-Bégarie, *L'évolution de la pensée navale I*, 1991; "La pensée navale hellénistique" in *L'évolution de la pensée navale II* (Paris: FEDN, 1992); "Les armes navales dans l'Antiquité," *Marins et Océans II* (Paris: FEDN,1991); "Etudes sur le combat naval antique," *Marins et Océans III*, 1992; "Y a-t-il eu une pensée navale romaine?" *L'évolution de la pensée navale III*; "Les Thalassocraties antiques" et "Géostratégie maritime d'Athènes" in Hervé Coutau-Bégarie, *La lutte pour l'empire de la mer* (Paris: 1993).

33 For instance, *La vie quotidienne des gens de mer en Atlantique, Moyen-Age-XVe siècle* (Paris: Hachette, 1983).

34 See Economic History in the present paper.

in his work, but they, too, have not been pursued.[35] In France, there are no works comparable to those of Lewis or Pryor.[36]

It is important when discussing this era to mention the activities of scholars devoted to research of Byzantine history and among these, particularly Hélène Archweiler, with her primary work on this subject, *Byzantium and the Sea*.[37] This enormous work, almost exhaustive for all that concerns the structure and the organization of the Byzantine navy, has, unfortunately, serious shortcomings in the areas of tactics and strategy. We find the same institutional tendencies in the works of Hélène Antoniadis-Bibicou.[38] For example, the nearly total absence of reference to the very rich Byzantine naval thought, which is known only by the work of Alphonse Dain, who is preoccupied with establishing a critical edition of historical texts and providing a philological study of them without trying to single out main trends in tactical or strategic terms.

Very few works can be mentioned on Arab or Ottoman naval histories in the Mediterranean. One exception, Michel Lesure, has devoted several works to the Ottoman fleets and to Turkish naval thought.[39] It is symptomatic to note that the remarkable work by John Guilmartin on galley warfare has made little impact in France.[40]

Modern Naval History. Modern naval history is, save for the contemporary era mentioned above, the period best represented in French historiography. It is the period in the French Navy's heritage which has the richest and most interesting information. Richelieu is the true founder of the modern French Navy, and nineteenth century historians have already emphasized the Cardinal's impact on naval issues. Following Richelieu, the credit for the resurrection of the French Navy during the reign of Louis XIV belongs to Jean Baptiste Colbert. The question has been entirely reexamined during the last two decades. Cardinal Richelieu has been subject of several studies, but the most interesting results, covering the end of the seventeenth and eighteenth centuries, have been achieved by Jean Meyer and his colleagues, who have worked since the 1970s with the group at the Laboratoire d'histoire maritime (CNRS Paris-Sorbonne). Jean Meyer started his career as historian of nobility, but his research turned

---

[35] Maurice Lombard, *Espaces et réseaux du haut Moyen-Age* (Paris-La Hayre: Mouton, 1972).

[36] Archibald Lewis, *Naval Power and Trade in the Mediterranean, AD 500–1100* (New Jersey: Princeton Univ. Press, 1951) and John H. Pryor, *Geography, Technology, and War: Studies in the Maritime History of the Mediterranean 649–1571* (Mass.: Cambridge Univ. Press, 1988).

[37] Hélène Archweiler, *Byzance et la mer* (Paris: Presses Universitaries de France, 1966).

[38] Michel Lesure, *Lépante* (Paris: Gallimard-Julliard, Archives, 1974).

[39] *Ibid.*

[40] John Guilmartin, *Gunpowder and Galleys, Changing Technology and Mediterranean Warfare at Sea* (Mass.: Cambridge Univ. Press, 1974). Jean Pagès prepares a translation accompanied by commentaries of *Della Milizia Marittima* (1542) composed by the Venitian admiral Da Canal who, in the third book, exposes the tactics of the Venetian fleet at Lepanto (1572).

progressively towards naval history, where he has achieved very important results, and has compiled his studies in works of synthesis written in collaboration with Martine Acerra.[41] Daniel Dessert produced a revisionist work on the navy of Louis XIV. It is a very remarkable work, though unfortunately it is marred by hostility to Colbert. The systematic study of the documents dealing with the shipyards, and maritime administration, particularly the records of the Inscription maritime (administration of the French professional seamen created by Colbert), has opened new avenues to maritime scholarship, which are quite different in many aspects from those obtained through the classical approach founded on the studies of naval campaigns and ministers' papers. For example, this new approach has ended the myth about the effects of the battle of la Hougue and partly rehabilitates Pontchartrain's reputation.

André Corvisier observed at the beginning of the 1970s that the revival of military history was achieved by means of the history of military men; in other words, through social history applied to the army. A similar approach may be observed in naval history, particularly in modern times. Indeed, naval history benefits directly from the results of research in economic and social history. In terms of social history, one can see this in the monographs on ports, such as those produced by Alain Boulaire on Brest, by Martine Acerra on Rochefort, and by Jean Peter on Toulon. In his thesis on *la guerre de course,* Philippe Villiers succeeded in reviving the subject from a military point of view, largely by using methodologies belonging to economic history.[42]

The studies on social history are widely dispersed at the extremeties of the naval hierarchy. They range, on the one hand, from lower work by André Zysberg on galley rowers,[43] and Alain Cabantous' study on mutineers and deserters,[44] to several studies on officers, most particularly on admirals. The thesis by Jacques Aman on "blue" officers was widely noted when it was published in 1976.[45] More recently, we have the enormous work by Michel Vergé-Franceschi on flag officers, which is full of details on admirals' genealogies.[46] Unlike earlier studies, these works do not focus on tactics or strategy.

[41]   Martine Acerra et Jean Meyer, *La grande époque de la marine à voile* (Rennes: Ouest-France, 1988); *Marine et Révolutions* (Rennes: Ouest-France, 1991). Let us mention also his contribution "L'Europe et le mer," in André Corvisier et al., *L'Europe à Louis XVI*, 1990. On "la guerre de course," see the posthumous work by Auguste Toussaint: *Avant Sucouf; Corsaires en océan Indien* (Aix: Publications de l'Université d'Aix-Provence, 1989).

[42]   Patrick Villiers, *Le commerce colonial atlantique et la guerre d'Indépendance américaine*, 1976 and *Marine royale, corsaires et traffic dans l'Atlantique de Louis XIV à Louis XVI*, 1990. On "La guerre de course"; the posthumous work by Auguste Toussaint, *Avant Surcouf: Corsaires en l'océan Indien* (Aix: Publications de l'Université d'Aix-Provence, 1989).

[43]   André Zysbert, *Les galériens* (Paris: Le Seuil, 1987).

[44]   Alain Cabantous, *La vergue et les fers. Mutins et déserteurs dans la marine de l'ancienne France* (Paris: Tallandier, 1984).

[45]   Jacques Aman, *Les officiers bleus dans la marine française au XVIIIe siècle* (Paris-Genève: Droz, 1976).

[46]   Michel Vergé-Franceschi, *les officers générations de la marine au XVIIIe riécle* (Paris: Librarie de l'Inde, 1990).

It must be pointed out that the studies which formerly would have been labelled "naval," that is to say, focused on tactics and strategy, are not insignificant. The research led by Jean Meyer and his colleagues, specially those on ports and naval bases, gave historians a better understanding of the logistical imperatives which weighed heavily on navies in the days of sailing ships. Research on galley rowers have also allowed scholars to create a model which explains the way galleys were manned and operated in battle (Zysberg, for that purpose, obtained assistance from a physicist). The research concerning officers and, particularly, admirals has brought to light masses of documents that provide a better view on naval operations. Finally, it is important to mention the fundamental contribution that Jean Boudriot has made, which offers new insight on the technical aspects of battleships.[47] Boudriot's contribution is fully as important as J.S. Morrison's on the problem of the trireme.

Besides the works which disassociate themselves from the old approach, one can not ignore the persistence or, rather, the revival of studies having a more traditional perception; that is to say, a viewpoint centered on tactics and strategy. First among them are those by Captain F. Caron on the capitulation of Louisbourg in 1758 and on the War of Independence, to which he will soon add a work on Suffren's campaigns.[48] François Caron has reached conclusions which have been disputed by some Anglo-Saxon authors, but his detailed knowledge of seafaring has helped him to take the lead in certain, little understood aspects of naval warfare, such as the problem of the continuity in the line-ahead battle formation.[49]

Other studies are in process. Michel Depeyre is writing an anxiously awaited thesis, the first of its kind, on naval thought during the seventeenth and eighteenth centuries.[50] There is also a revival of biographical studies after several decades of indifference. The well-written and popular biographies based on rather limited documentation by Jean de la Varende have been followed by new studies on Duquesne by Michel Vergé-Franceschi,[51] and on Tourville by Marc Vigié.[52] Suffren has been the subject of less convincing biographies.

The period of the French revolution and the Imperial period have traditionally remained the field of a very learned but isolated group of historians.

[47] Jean-Boudriot, *Le vaisseaux de 74 canons* (Paris: 4 vol., 1976–1978); *Les vaisseaux de la Compagnie des Indes* (Paris: 1990).

[48] François Caron, *La guerre incomprise ou les raison d'un échec. Capitulation de Louisbourg* (Vincennes: SHM, 1983). *La victoire volée. Bataille de la Chesapeake* (Vincennes: SHM, 1989). Jacques Aman, *Une campagne navale méconnue à la veille de la guerre de Sept Ans. L'escadre de Brest en 1755* (Vincennes: SHM, 1986).

[49] See his study on "Le vicomte de Grenier: Héritier de Bigot de Morogues ou disciple de Suffren?" in *L'évolution de la pensée navale III* (Paris, 1993).

[50] See his articles on Hoste and Clerk in *L'évolution de la pensée navale I et II*.

[51] Michel Vergé-Franceschi, Abraham Duquesne, *huguenot et marin du Roi Soleil* (Paris: France-Empire, 1992).

[52] Marc Vigié, *Tourville* (Paris: Fayard, 1993).

Marc Vigié, *Tourville* (Paris: Fayard, 1993).

Following A. Thomazi and Captain Muracciole, Rear-Admiral Maurice Dupont has just crowned his extensive research[53] with a biography of Decrès, Minister of the Imperial Navy Department.[54] The nineteenth century is not so well represented, despite an extensive field of research which has scarcely been explored. Bernard Lutun is currently working in this area.[55]

The Contribution of French Orientalists. France has always had a great interest in the Far East, but naval studies in that area, while important, are few in number. Arab sources have been studied by Rear Admiral Henri Labrousse in articles recently gathered in a single volume concerning, principally, the Red Sea.[56] Chinese naval history has benefited from the thesis by Jacques Dars, although it was long delayed in publication, as mentioned earlier. Dars deepened the intuitive ideas of Lo Jun Pang, whose pioneer work dealt with the expansion of the Chinese Navy from the Song period to the Ming period.[57] It is a very highly focussed work, but one of very high quality.

Compared to what is typical practice in Great Britain and the United States, the results achieved by French naval historians are, all in all, rather poor. The chasm which has for so long divided the Navy and acadamia, the lack of tradition in maintenance of archives, and the destructive effects of domestic and international disruptions have taken their toll on French sources. The harmful effect of this combination of factors continues to hamper research.

For instance, we must observe that the continued publication of important documents has never been the rule in France. The Fench naval classics, from Hoste to Castex, have not been republished. The memories of most of the great sailors cannot be found today, and there are no collections of documents similar to those so frequently found in political, administrative and economic history. This is a real and eminently prejudicial deficiency, for which there appears to be no solution whatsoever.

All the same, French naval history remains largely inward-looking. However, it is true that international contacts are increased, as demonstrated by the Franco-British symposium on maritime history, held since 1986 on the initiative of the Service historique de la Marine,[58] as well as many other symposia.[59] But, it is impossible to mention any wide-ranging study on Great Britain, Italy, or Japan. Claude Huan's research on the *Kriegsmarine* and the Soviet Navy are an exception.

---

[53] Particularly his very important contribution to the *Dictionnaire Napoléon*, by Jean Tulard, (Paris: Fayard, 1987).

[54] Amiral Maurice Dupont, *L'amiral Decrès et Napoléon* (Paris: CFHM-Economica, 1991).

[55] An enormous work of almost 1,000 pages on the Guérigny forges; "L'épuration dans la marine 1814–1817." *Revue historique* 285 (1992).

[56] Amiral Labrousse, *Récits de la mer Rouge et de l'océan Indien* (Paris: CFHM-Economica, 1992).

[57] Jacques Dars, *La marine chinoise du Xe siècle au XIV e siècle* (Paris: CFHM-Economica, 1992).

[58] The acts have been published by the Service historique de la Marine: *Guerres et paix, 1660–1815* (1986); *Les empires en guerre et en paix 1793–1860* (1988); *Français et Anglais en Méditerranée 1789–1830* (1990).

[59] *Les marines de guerre européennes au XVIIIe siècle* (Paris: Presses de l'Université de Paris-Sorbonne,

Such an attitude contrasts sorely with the numerous contributions coming from abroad which have been beneficial to the French naval history. Consider, for instance, the works of Jenkins, Bamford, Symcox, T. Le Goff, Dull, Halpern, Ropp, Kowark.[60]

Nevertheless, a perceptible improvement has been observed during the last two decades as the summary sketched out here shows. For several years we have had at our disposal some instruments of research which were previously lacking and which now signal new developments. Rear Admiral Frémy has published a splendid dictionary of ships.[61] Etienne Taillemite, for his part, is the author of an exhaustive but eminently readable dictionary on French sailors.[62] In the same period, we have witnessed the publication of a vast synthesis concerning the history of the French Navy by Philippe Masson. It is rather paradoxical that, previously, the primary reference was the work of a British historian, H.E. Jenkins, which was published in 1973 and translated into French five years later.[63] In that book, Jenkins expressed the perfect synthesis of the traditional points of view, certain of which were being challenged by the conclusions of more recent research.[64] Philippe Masson's book was followed by one of Etienne Taillemite in such a way that we have at hand two works with diverging views on the same subject.[65] They provide a genuine basis for setting aside the caricature suggesting that "if France is not ashamed of her Navy, the Navy has some grounds to be ashamed of France" (Jenkins). It is wrong to say, notwithstanding a few exceptions, that the French governments have never understood their Navy. Masson would better accuse the naval men themselves, with their lack of great leaders and with a chronic lack of discipline in the officer corps. For his part, Etienne Taillemite considers first the structural handicaps, the insufficient coastal populations, the lack of good Channel harbours. All this remains a problem of determinism which must be considered anew.

1985); *Fleurieu et la marine en son temps* (Paris: CFHM-Economica, 1992); *Marine et technique au XIXe siècle* (Paris: IHCC-SHM, 1989); *Les marines de guerre du dreadnought au nucléaire* (1988), (Paris: IHCC-SHM, 1991).

[60] Paul W. Bamford, *Forest and French Sea Power 1660–1783* (Toronto: Univ. of Toronto Press, 1956); Jonathan Dull, *The French Navy and American Independence: A Study in Arms and Diplomacy 1774–1781* (New Jersey: Princeton Univ. Press, 1975); Paul R. Halpern, *The Mediterranean Naval Situation 1908–1914* (Cambridge: Harvard Univ. Press, 1971); Hannsjörg Kowark, *Die Französische Marinepolitik 1919–1924 und die Washingtoner Konferenz* (Stuttgart: Hochschulverlag, 1978); T.J.A. Le Goff, "Problèmes de recrutement de la marine française pendant la Guerre de Sept Ans," *Revu Historique*, 283 (1990), pp. 205–33; Theodore Ropp, *The Development of a Modern Navy: French Naval Policy 1871–1904.* Edited by Stephen S. Roberts (Annapolis: Naval Institute Press, 1987); and Geoffrey Symcox, *The Crisis of French Sea Power 1688–1697: From the guerre d'escadre to the guerre de course* (The Hague: Martinus Nijhoff, 1974).

[61] Raymond Frémy, *Des noms sur la mer* (Paris: ACORAM, 1991).

[62] Etienne Taillemite, *Dictionnaire des marins français* (Paris: Editions maritimes et d'outremer, 1982).

[63] H.E. Jenkins, *Histoire ignorée de la marine française* (Paris: Albin Michel, 1978).

[64] Philippe Masson, *Histoire ignorée de la marine* (Paris: Lavauzelle, volume 1, 1982 and volume 2, 1983).

[65] Etienne Taillemite, *Histoire ignorée de la française* (Paris: Perrin, 1988).

But, again, we must not forget that those very few works are insignificant compared with the flowering of those in other branches of the French historical research. It simply indicates that a vast area of historical research remains to be carried out.

Maritime History

If naval history has a clearly delimited field of research, the same does not hold true for maritime history. At different levels, all human activities have something to do with the sea in such a way that maritime history deals with all fields of historical research. Despite its slow development in France, maritime works are numerous, and it is difficult, within the scope of this paper, to provide an indicative example. Therefore, it seems better to look to the main tendencies of research by theme rather than by period.

Bibliographies and Aids to Reseach. Maritime bibliography was overlooked for a long time. Finally, in the 1970s, it required a remarkable collection through the work of Jean Polak, which is well-known and used among the French maritime historians. One can follow it through all the different categories in the *Bibliographie ennuelle de l'histoire de France*.

Some remarkable work has been done to inventory archival sources. Etienne Taillemite and Philippe Henrat have done this for the Archives Nationales. The Service Historique de la Marine has made a similar great effort but, for lack of money, the inventories made during the last few years, particularly those concerning contemporary events, have not all been published.

Among these means of research, while we must regret the absence of ships lists or the lack of biographical dictionaries (the one by Taillemite being mostly centered on naval officers), we still must mention one of the most interesting efforts in contemporary maritime history: the revision of the *Glossaire nautique* by Jal, initiated by Professor Michel Mollat du Jourdin and pursued under Christiane Villain-Gandossi's leadership within the scope of a seminar comprising several dozens of specialists. As of this writing, six sections have been published, as far as the letter "I," and a seventh has gone to press. It is needless to insist here upon the exceptional importance of such a revision. Nevertheless, one must keep in mind that the original work contains much information that is not included in the revised edition.

In the same vein, but on a different subject, we must point out another undertaking initiated by Michel Mollat: the survey of the votive ships. This investigation, started in the 1970s within the Laboratoire d'histoire maritime, is now completed. Such a work is extremely useful, not only for art history, but also for the history of ship-building and for the history of seafaring peoples. Unfortunately, because of budget difficulties, we regret that nothing of it has yet been published.

General Works. We have a clear idea of the ground lost by French maritime history when we perceive the scarcity of that kind of work. *Marine et Océans* by Philippe Masson, which concerns only the contemporary period, is an exception.[66] There is no recent scholarly synthesis on maritime history except the very recent work by Michel Mollat: *L'Europe et la mer*.[67] It is clear that there are no general studies in French about the history of the oceans. *L'Histoire de l'Atlantique* by Jacques Godechot dates back to 1947 and, so far, has not been replaced. On the Indian ocean, we have *Histoire de l'océan Indien* (1961) by Auguste Toussaint. The author died before completing the second edition. Such an important work, still partly obsolete, can only be completed by fragmentary eighteenth century studies and by others on the history of the Mascarenhas Islands.[68] We may well ask if Auguste Toussaint, although born in Mauritius and a French-speaking historian, may be considered as belonging to the French maritime history, rather than to that of Mauritius.

We have no general French study on the Pacific ocean. On the other hand, it is much more surprising when we see the lack of a similar work on the Mediterranean; the sea so close and so dear to the heart of many Frenchmen. The principal work of Fernand Braudel, *la Méditerranée et le monde méditerranéen à l'époque de Philippe II*, belies the lack of general study on the Mediterranean in French. However, we must mention Jean René Vanney, author of an erudite study on the Southern Seas, which helped to fill the gap.[69] In spite of all, there is much to do in order to ensure that non-specialists might easily have sufficient documentation at hand. The bibliographical references at the end of Vanney's book contain a warning which could be valid for many oceans of the world: "The place occupied by the often translated French works is so modest that a grave question is posed as soon as we want to facilitate an easy access for the non-specialist."[70]

What is true for the regional synthesis is also true, to a large extent, for very particular studies.[71] French maritime studies are very much in need of works designed to put within easy reach of the readers research results which, in spite of all, are still going on very actively.

Underwater Archeology. Naval archeology has been somewhat neglected by academia, but it has succeeded in becoming implanted in the CNRS and also in the Ministère de la Culture. The benefit of this was the creation in 1970 of the Department of submarine archeological research (DRASM), which from that

---

[66] Philippe Masson, *Marine et océans* (Paris: Imprimerie nationale, 1982).

[67] Michel Mollat du Jourdin, *L'Europe et la mer* (Paris: Le Seuil, 1993).

[68] Auguste Toussaint, *Histoire de l'océan Indien* (Paris: Presses Universitaires de France, 1961); *L'océan Indien au XVIIIe siècle* (Paris: Flammarion, 1973); *Histoire des iles Mascareignes* (Paris: Berger-Levrault, 1972).

[69] Jean-René Vanney, *Histoire des mers australes* (Paris: Fayard, 1986).

[70] *Ibid.*, p. 699.

[71] Philippe Masson's book, *Grandeur et misère des gens de mer* (Paris-Limoges: Lavauzelle, 1986), is an exception.

time has managed all underwater finds. The results of that research have appeared in *Gallia* and in *Gallia Informations*. A review of underwater research, *Cahiers d'archéologie subaquatique,* began publication in 1972 and, in 1977, CNRS commenced publishing another, *Archéonautica*. The research covers, at the same time, harbours and ships; the wreck called épave de la madrague de Giens (1st c. B.C.) for instance, has been the subject of a very careful research. Among the prominent scholars are Patrice Pomey for ancient archeology and Eric Rieth on medieval archeology. These authors recently presented an overall survey of researches in process during a recent symposium on maritime heritage.[72]

Additionally, as a matter of interest, we must not forget to mention the archeological excavations near Bercy. These two 4,500-year-old dugouts were recently brought to light thanks to a research group of the Vieux Paris.[73] In yet another area, Gabriel Camps has published the results of his research on early navigation in the Mediterranean in several articles.

Modern naval archeology in France today is brilliantly represented by Jean Boudriot. All maritime historians know his works (I have already mentioned those on the 74-gun ships-of-the-line, and on the French vessels of the Compagnie des Indes), among others on merchant ships. Jean Pierre Moreau has worked on finds in the Caribbean and specialized in archeological treasures.[74]

With regard to contemporary naval techniques, we could bring together with industrial archeology certain research on the first steamships, or those on the passengers ships, which have always been popular with the public.

Without commenting on the relationship between maritime history and interior navigation history, it is important to remember, just as a matter of interest, the very active groups working on river history today.[75]

Finally, we must speak of the efforts in favour of the maritime preservation. Without coming under maritime history, in the strict sense, preservation is closely linked to it. The international symposium held in Nantes in 1991, organised by both the Ministère de la Culture and the CFHM, provided a summation of work and the recent initiatives taken in a long neglected area of historical research. The symposium papers, just published, define a part for maritime historians in the process of restoring maritime heritage.

Economic History. Economic history was one of the strong points of the Annales school, and it is only natural that the maritime trade benefited from its study. This is clearly demonstrated by the important theses published between the 1950s and 1970s which cover all the periods. Regarding antiquity, the work

---

[72]   *Le patrimoine maritime et fluvial* (Paris: Colloques du patrimoine, 1993).

[73]   There is also the discovery of the Henri Cosquer cave, but that only indirectly concerns maritime history.

[74]   Jean-Pierre Moreau, *Giude des trésors archéologiques sous-marins des petites Antilles* (Paris: J.-P.M., 1988).

[75]   Most particularly, the numerous works by François Beaudouin.

by Jean Rougé on Roman sea-trade,[76] followed by the less imposing, but very rich work by Julie Vélissaropoulos on ancient greek maritime institutions set the stage.[77] Considering the medieval period, the fundamental thesis by Michel Mollat on Norman trade,[78] and the publication, fifteen years later, of a study by Henri Touchard on the commerce of Brittany[79] as well as one on the Bordeaux trade by Jacques Bernard, continue the tradition.[80]

The Mediterranean has been the subject of several important studies; Henri Bresc on Sicily,[81] Jean-Claude Hocquet on Venetian salt trade,[82] Jacques Heers on Genoa,[83] Jean Delumeau on Rome,[84] Michel Balard on Genoese Romania[85] and, finally, Freddy Thiriet on Venetian Romania.[86] Spain has been less studied than Italy, but we cannot ignore the work of Charles-Emmanuel Dufourcq on Catalonian Spain and the Maghreb,[87] and another on Valencia by Catherine Guiral.[88] The north of Europe, in comparison, has received much less investigation than the Mediterranean. Still, there are at least two important studies: one by Stéphane Lebecq on the medieval Frisians, which is an exemplary collaboration between the use of written sources and archeology,[89] and another by Philippe Dollinger on the Hanse, which extends substantially into modern times.[90] For this last period we have in the first place, the monumental and justly famous thesis by Pierre Chaunu on Sevilla,[91] those by Frédéric Mauro on Portugal and the Atlantic,[92] Victor Magalhaes-Godinho in the Indian ocean,[93]

---

[76] Jean Rougé, *Recherches sur l'organisation du commerce maritime en Méditerranée sous l'Empire romain* (Rome: Ecole fraçaise de Rome, 1966).

[77] Julie Vélissaropoulos, *Les nauchléres grecs. Recherches sur les institutions maritimes en Gréce et dans l'Orient hellénisé* (Paris-Genéve: Minard-Droz, 1980).

[78] Michel Mollat, *Le commerce maritime normand à la fin du Moyen-Age* (Paris: Plon, 1952).

[79] Henri Touchard, *Le commerce maritime breton à la fin du Moyen-Age* (Paris: Les Belles-Lettres, Annales littéraires de l'Université de Nantes, 1967).

[80] Jacques Bernard, *Navires et gens de mer à Bordeaux vers 1450 - vers 1550*, (Paris: S.E.V.P.E.N., 1968).

[81] Henri Bresc, *Un monde méditerranéen. Economie et société en Sicile 1300–1450* (Rome: Ecole française de Rome, 1986).

[82] Jean-Claude Hocquet, *Le sel et la fortune de Venise, 1200–1650* (Lille: Presses de l'Université de Lille, 1978–79).

[83] Jacques Heers, *Gênes au XVe siècle* (Paris: S.E.V.P.E.N., 1961).

[84] Jean Delumeau, *Vie économique et sociale de Rome dans la seconde moitié du XVIe siècle* (Paris: S.E.V.P.E.N., 1957–1959); *L'alun de Rome* (Paris: S.E.V.P.E.N., 1962).

[85] Michel Balard, *La Romaine génoise, XIIe début de XVe siècle* (Rome, Ecole française de Rome, 1978).

[86] Freddy Thiriet, *La Romanie vénitienne au Moyen-Age. Le développement et l'exploitation du domaine coloniale vénitien, XIIe-XVe siècle* (Paris: de Boccard, 1975).

[87] Charles-Emmanuel Dufourcq, *L'Espagne catalane et le Maghreb*, (Paris: Presses Universitaires de France, 1965).

[88] Catherine Guiral, *Valence, port méditerranéen* (Paris: Presses de la Sorbonne, 1975).

[89] Stéphane Lebecq, *Marchands et navigateurs frisons du Haut-Moyen-Age* (Lille: Presse Universitaire de Lille, 1983).

[90] Philippe Dollinger, *La Hanse* (Paris: Aubier, 1968).

[91] Pierre Chaunu, *Séville et l'Atlantique* 12 vol. (Paris: S.E.V.P.E.N., 1955-1960).

[92] Frédéric Mauro, *Le Portugal et l'Atlantique* (Paris: S.E.V.P.E.N., 1960).

[93] Victor Magalhaes-Godinho, *L'économie de l'empire portugais au XVe et au XVIe siècle* (Paris: Fondation Gulbenkian, 1969).

and those on the French trade during the eighteenth century by Paul Butel,[94] Charles Carrière,[95] Christian Huetz de Lemps,[96] Louis Dermigny,[97] Jean Tarrade[98] and, finally, the very recent one by Jean Ducoin.[99]

The contemporary period has received much more attention by the economists and historians. For example, I note the work of Jean Heffer on New York harbour during the second half of the nineteenth century, who employed the methods of New Economic History. All the works just mentioned above are the best known and are directly focused on maritime history. There are, however, many others which also consider sea-trade. The slave-trade, which no one dares put under the single heading "Economic History," has given impetus to rather numerous studies of mixed interest.[100]

There is also a branch of maritime history which is all too often forgotten: the history of fishing. It is usually left to local historians who have produced works not easily accessible: we cannot, however, ignore important contributions in this field, such as the one by Thierry du Pasquier on the French whaling industry.[101]

Among all these works published during the last years, we must preserve a special place for those concerning the history of Marseilles. This is largely because of their quality, but it is also thanks to the support constantly provided historians by the Chamber of Commerce of this premier French port. This fortunate collaboration has allowed publication of numerous works in a unique situation in France. Just the same, there are also numerous histories of coastal towns.[102]

History of the French Seafaring People. Social history has been another strong point of the Annales school, but it may be that maritime history has not benefited from this as much as it has from economic history. Among the regional studies, which have so much for French historians, some theses deal with maritime populations. The northern part of France has an advantage by virtue of the 1963 work by Jacques Toussaert on the population of the Flemish coast at the end of Middle Ages,[103] and more recently another by Alain Cabantous,

94   Paul Butel, *Les négociants bordelais au XVIIIe siècle. L'Europe et les îles* (Paris: Aubier, 1974).

95   Charles Carrière, *Négociants marseillais au XVIIIe siècle. Contribution à l'étude des économies maritimes* (Paris: 1973).

96   Christian Huetz de Lemps, *Géographie du commerce bordelais à la fin du règne de Louis XIV* (Paris: La Haye, Mouton, 1975).

97   Louis Dermngy, *La Chine et l'Occident. Le commerce à Canton au XVIIIe siècle* (Paris: S.E.V.P.E.N., 1964).

98   Jean Tarrade, *Histoire du commerce atlantique au XVIIIe siècle*, thèse inédite (1976).

99   Jean Ducoin, *Naufrages, conditions de navigation et assurances dans la marine de commerce. Le cas de Nantes et de son commerce colonial avec les ils britanniques* (Paris: Librairie de l'Inde, 1993).

100   Parmi les plus récents, Jean-Michel Deveau, *La traite rochelaise* (Paris: Karthala, 1990); Serge Daget, *La traite des Noirs* (Rennes: Ouest-France, 1990).

101   Thierry du Pasquier, *Les baleiniers français de Louis XVI à Napoléon* (Paris: H. Veyrier, 1990).

102   See the series edited by Lindt and published in Toulouse.

103   Jacques Toussaert, *Le sentiment religieux en Flandre maritime à la fin du Moyen-Age* (Paris: Plon, 1963).

which covers an adjacent region in more modern times.[104] Still, one would expect to find a greater number of studies concerning the coastal regions. In fact, many often give only a secondary place to maritime subjects.

The revival in understanding seafaring populations was accomplished through the history of mentalités. Alain Cabantous has made an important contribution to this subject.[105] It is a field in which many promising points of view have recently been observed, for example, in Alain Corbin's original consideration of the coastal region during the nineteenth century.[106] The path followed by Corbin is particularly interesting, since he started with a study on a mountainous region far from the sea.

This very short account should be considerably extended by listing all the studies that dealt incidentally or substantially with social history, and this is also the case with almost all of the studies under the rubric of economic history. The work by Michel Mollat, which bears a significant subtitle, "Studies of Economic and Social History," is typical of the Annales school. Among recent works which illustrate this connection, there is the thesis on the merchants of St. Malo by André Lespagnol.[107] To all this, one could add other numerous works, symposia proceedings or books belonging to the much known series, *La vie quotidienne des gens de mer dans l'Atlantique, IXe–XVIe siècle* by Michel Mollat; *La vie quotidienne dans les ports méditerranéens*, by Charles-Emmanuel Dufourcq, or *La vie quotidienne à Bordeaux au XVIIIe siècle* by Paul Butel and Jean-Pierre Poussou.[108]

Colonial history. There is a close relation between maritime history and colonial history, the latter being called in France today, "overseas" history. During the nineteenth century, the dependence of maritime and colonial affairs on a single ministry was institutional in France but has since been abandoned. Nevertheless, the bond between them has remained present in academia. During recent years, colonial history has enjoyed a brilliant revival, reaching a peak at the end of the 1980s with several remarkable works. In particular, one by Philippe Haudrère, *La Compagnie française des Indes 1719–1795*, and another by Jacques Weber *Les établissements français en Inde au XIXe siècle 1816–1914*, were both submitted for consideration within a period of several weeks in 1987.

These two theses confirm the vitality of the French research on the Indian Ocean. Additionally, a group led by Jean Aubin started a publication, *Mare*

[104] Alain Corbin, *Le territoire du vide. L'Occident et le désir du rivage 1750–1850* (Paris: Aubier, 1988).

[105] Alain Cabantous, *Dix mille marins face à l'océan. Les populations maritimes de Dunkerque au Havre vers 1660–1794* (Paris: Publisud, 1991).

[106] Alain Corbin, *Le ciel dans la mer. Christianisme et civilisation maritime XVe-XIXe siècle* (Paris: Fayard, 1990).

[107] André Lespagnol, *Ces Messieurs de Saint-Malo. Une élite négociante au temps de Louis XIV* (Saint-Malo: L'Ancre de Marine, 1991).

[108] See for instance, the Symposium of Boulogne on the seafaring populations; the proceedings were published in a special issue of *Revue du Nord*, 1986.

Luso-Indicum, in the 1970s. There also are a number of works by Geneviéve Bouchon on India during the Portuguese investiture. The French have also taken an active part in researching South-East Asian history, the maritime aspect of which is clearly evident. This sector has also a specialized review, *Archipel*, and has recently benefited by the monumental thesis on Java by Denys Lombard.[109]

Nineteenth-century colonial history has generated many works, some of which contribute to the maritime dimension; consider, for instance, those by Jean-Louis Miège, former president of the CFHM. The idiological aspect in some of them was denounced several years ago by François Caron,[110] and provoked a controversy with Charles-Robert Ageron,[111] but this must not overshadow their important role in the development of maritime history.

The history of explorers cannot be ignored either. Jehan Desanges has produced a very important study of the Roman activity along the african coast.[112] But nothing exists yet in French which equates to the remarkable analytical editions of the ancient *Peripli* that have just been published in English. Michel Mollat studied medieval sea voyages and edited a volume on the Verrazano voyage; Etienne Taillemitte, for his part, edited the diary of La Pérouse; Admiral de Brossard did the same with the journal of Bougainville; and Numa Broc did so with the journal of Pager. Special mention must also be made of Jean-Pierre Faivre, for his important study of the South Pacific during the first half of the nineteenth century.[113]

A very productive and specialized branch also contributes to the work on the explorers. For instance, the history of map-making, as exemplified by Mireille Pastoureau's *Voies Océanes*,[114] or the oft-ignored thesis by Yoro K. Fall on Majorcan portolan charts (showing that certain coasts were known before the dates of their official discovery), add substantially to our body of knowledge.[115] For the contemporary period, Jacqueline Carpine-Lancre has published a number of works on oceanography.[116]

A good example of the link existing between both disciplines is the history of naval and colonial medicine. This is a specialized subject, but demonstrates the evolution of maritime history in France. As General medical doctor Niaussat,

---

[109]   Denys Lombard, *Le carrefour javanais* (Paris: Editions de l'EHESS, 1990).

[110]   François Caron, *La France des patriotes*, volume V of *Histoire de France* by Jean Favier (Paris: Fayard, 1987).

[111]   This is clarified in a long letter which has remained unpublished but is widely known.

[112]   Jehan Desanges, *Recherches sur les activitiès des Méditerranéens le long des côtes africaines* (Rome: Ecole française de Rome, 1980).

[113]   Jean-Paul Faivre, *L'expansion française dans le Pacifique, 1800–1842* (Paris: Nouvelles éditions latines, 1953).

[114]   Mireille Pastoureau, *Voies océanes. Cartes marines et grandes découvertes* (Paris: Bibliothéque nationale, 1992).

[115]   Yoro K. Fall, *L'Afrique à la connaissance de la cartographie moderne*, (Paris: Karthala-CRA, 1982).

[116]   Jacqueline Carpine-Lancre, *Souverains océanographes: Dom Carlos Ier roi de Portugal et Albert Ier prince de Monaco* (Paris-Lisbonne: Fondation Gulbenkian, 1992).

one of the leaders of the naval and colonial medicine, put it, "It has been, if not ignored, at least neglected . . ." until a recent date.[117] Here, France was unquestionably behind Great Britain, Germany, or Italy. There are only several isolated individuals, (General medical doctor Carré on history of the naval medical schools, Dean Jean-Pierre Kernéis on medical officers serving at sea, and Professor Pierre Huard on the Far East) who can be cited in this field. Even so, starting around the 1980s, we have observed several efforts in that field, along with the organization of conferences on the history of naval and colonial medicine and with the increase in the number of studies under the auspices of Niaussat or Carré. Historians have stood somewhat apart from this process, largely because of their lack of technical knowledge. Unfortunately, Jacques Leonard, who was the exception, was not able to create a viable school because of his untimely death.

★   ★   ★

This brief survey cannot pay homage to all the numerous authors who contributed to, enhanced, and revived the knowledge of maritime history in its diverse aspects. To the individual studies cited here, one must add a great number of essay collections, particularly when considering the numerous symposia and countless articles of high quality that have been produced. We hope, however, that a vision of a French maritime and naval history, after a too long period of marginalization, will emerge, fully integrated into the historical studies pursued in academies and in the CNRS, including the irreplaceable contribution of the amateurs, particularly those belonging to learned societies or coming from the maritime professions. There are considerable deficiencies in the field, but there is no doubt that maritime history is one of the most promising fields for future work and development in the years to come.

---

[117] Cf. P.M. Niaussat, "A propos d'une disciple historique trop méconnue: l'histoire de la médecine navale et d'outremer," *Chronique d'histoire maritime*, 1er semestre 1984, no. 9.

12

Germany

Kapitän zur See Dr. Werner Rahn, German Navy

Before we deal with naval history and the history of shipping in Germany, a few preliminary remarks of a linguistic nature and definitions with regard to contents are called for in order to prevent any misunderstandings.

Military History and Naval History: Some Remarks on Basic Terms

The German term *Schiffahrtsgeschichte*, literally translated as the "history of shipping," can, without hesitation, be equated with the Anglo-Saxon term "maritime history." This field of research centers on the ship as a system of transportation with its economic, social, and technological context. The development, construction, operation and handling, manning, and ultimately the fate of the ship as well as many other spheres are fields of research in "maritime history."

If we take the terms "military history" and "naval history," it is clear and simple to most Anglo-Saxon historians what these terms involve. In the case of "military history," research interest focuses on land forces, i.e. the army, while in the case of "naval history" this interest focuses on naval forces or—to put it in more general terms—the navy as an armed service. Both these spheres are subordinate elements of general history, in particular that of strategy and politics.

In contrast, since 1945 in Germany, the term "military history" has come to be accepted as a generic term for that part of the study of history whose central subjects of research are the armed forces and war.[1] Military history deals with the evolution and structure of the armed forces and their position in state and society. Military history studies the importance of armed forces as a means of policy and as an instrument of state authority. It analyzes the problems associated with the exercise of command and control over armed forces in peacetime and in war at the various levels.

---

[1] A recent summary of the development of military historiography in Germany may be found in Roland G. Foerster, "Military History in the Federal Republic of Germany and the Bundeswehr," in David A. Charters, Marc Milner, and J. Brent Wilson, eds., *Military History and the Military Profession* (Westport, Conn. and London: Praeger, 1992), pp. 191–210.

In this sense, "naval history" in Germany is taken to mean that part of military history which focuses its study of the above-mentioned fields of research on the "navy" as an armed service. When the term "military history" is used in the following basic remarks, it always includes "naval history."

However, when dealing with the above-mentioned fields of research, there is one sphere that must not be neglected, as it is the greatest challenge for military history—I am referring to war! Ultimately, armed forces are raised, equipped and trained so that they can one day be sent into battle.[2] Thus, it is not only legitimate but imperative that military history also deal with war and warfare in the widest sense. This approach to research would appear, on the face of it, to be self-evident; however, many years ago, John Keegan, in his seminal book *The Face of Battle*, pointed out critically that many professional historians are shy of exploring and portraying the profundities and realities of the phenomenon of "war."[3] This inhibition is also widespread in Germany.

Generally speaking, it can be expected of the military historian that he also has a certain affinity with the subject of his research, namely the military, and that he possesses a modicum of basic theoretical—and if possible also practical—knowledge about the military in the same way that we naturally expect an economic historian to have a sound basic knowledge of economic theory. John Keegan is thus justified in demanding that the military historian should spend as much time as possible among military personnel, "because the quite chance observation of trivial incidents may illuminate his private understanding of all sorts of problems from the past which will otherwise almost certainly remain obscured."[4]

The same is true for naval history. A historian who studies the origins and use of naval forces will find that his research profits greatly if he has ever had the opportunity to spend some length of time aboard a warship. He will find it easier to evaluate and integrate most of his sources, such as reports, memoranda, and planning documents from all levels of naval command. This is true especially since some structural factors for the building and deploying of naval forces change only very little over time.

Like any historian, the naval historian bears a great responsibility in his striving after historical truth, if he wants to be taken seriously. This striving will never be free of subjective values. The uncritical patriotic history which used to glorify military and naval actions and successes is a thing of the past. Today, some military historians tend to judge personalities, events, and structures according to today's moral categories, and they end up "putting the past on trial, and since the critical historian, armed with his generation's self-confidence or with his

---

[2]   See Carl von Clausewitz, *Vom Kriege*, Erstes Buch, II: "*Der Soldat wird ausgehoben, gekleidet, bewaffnet, geübt, er schläft, ißt, trinkt und marschiert, alles nur, um an rechter Stelle und zu rechten Zeit zu fechten.*"

[3]   John Keegan, *The Face of Battle* (London: Jonathan Cape, 1976), p. 29.

[4]   *Ibid.*, p. 34.

progressive concept of the future, knows everything better, in this trial he will be prosecutor, judge and legislator all in one."[5]

Research into German Naval History after 1945

After 1945, the documents of the German Navy, preserved almost in their entirety, were available initially only to the Allied forces' historical research sections. The files were transferred onto microfilm on a large scale; where more than one original copy existed—e.g., several original copies of war diaries—the British kept copy no. 1, while the second copy went to Washington D.C. This was the case with numerous U-boat war diaries and the War Diary of the Naval Staff. The Allied historians evaluated the material for their respective official accounts of World War II, as is apparent from numerous references in the various volumes.[6] In most cases, however, the evaluation was confined to strategic and operational sectors in order to make the Allies' corresponding actions and reactions more easily understandable.

On the German side, initially, only former naval officers were allowed access to selected files. On behalf of the British Admiralty or the U.S. Navy, they compiled special operational and tactical studies that seemed necessary given the fact that a conflict with the Soviet Union could no longer be ruled out.[7] The long-serving Head of the Historical Research Department of the Navy, Vice Admiral Kurt Assmann, for example, worked in London writing an account of the naval war in the Arctic Sea from the German point of view.[8] Grand Admiral Karl Dönitz's son-in-law, Commander Günter Hessler, was given unlimited access to all files of the Naval Staff and the U-boat Command, in order to write a comprehensive operational history of the Battle of the Atlantic. Hessler performed this task in an outstanding manner and produced an operational history which comprises an abundance of material and provides precise references throughout, and which will surely remain unequaled for a long time to come. The British Admiralty had the three-volume study translated, and from 1950 onwards had it distributed among the Royal Navy as Confidential Book C.B. 4523, later renamed B.R. 305. The third volume, covering the period June 1943 to May 1945, was, however, not published until 1977. For the translation,

---

5   Thomas Nipperdey, "Wozu Geschichte gut ist," *Militärgeschichtliche Mitteilungen*, 41 (1987), pp. 7–13, quotation p. 9.

6   See, for example, Stephen W. Roskill, *The War at Sea 1939–1945*, vol. I, *The Defensive*, (London: HMSO, 1954), pp. xix, 51–60.

7   See Christian Greiner, "'Operational History (German Section)' und 'Naval Historical Team,' Deutsches militärstrategisches Denken im Dienst der amerikanischen Streitkräfte von 1946 bis 1950," in Manfred Messerschmidt, Klaus A. Maier *et al.*, eds., *Militärgeschichte. Probleme—Thesen—Wege*, (Stuttgart: DVA, 1982), pp. 409–35.

8   Vizeadmiral a.D. Kurt Assmann, "Die deutsche Kriegführung gegen den englisch-russischen Geleitverkehr im Nordmeer 1941–1945," (unpublished manuscript, Bundesarchiv-Militärarchiv, Freiburg: RM 8/1126).

the German original version was somewhat abridged. It was not until 1989 that the British Ministry of Defence decided to publish the study in the form of a facsimile edition.[9] The German Military History Research Office[10] is currently preparing the publication of the original German version.

The favorable source situation—due to the fact that the majority of the naval documents were soon accessible and were extensively transferred onto microfilm—at an early stage prompted a number of historians in America to deal with the individual phases and problems of German naval history. In addition, this group of documents provided an excellent starting point for studying the German conduct of war and politics during World War II.

From among the numerous research studies, this article will mention only the works of Keith W. Bird, Holger H. Herwig, Daniel Horn, Ivo Nikolai Lambi, L.W. Lewis, Janet M. Manson, Eric C. Rust, Allison W. Saville, Charles Thomas, Gerhard L. Weinberg, and Gary Weir.[11]

Any new research into German naval history will first of all fall back on a book which has been available since 1985 and which is likely to be used not only as an indispensable aid but in many cases also as a sound guide: I am referring to Keith W. Bird's bibliography, which he compiled in an exemplary manner, entitled *German Naval History. A Guide to the Literature.*[12] This work completely covers and comments on the entire German naval literature of the nineteenth and twentieth centuries. In addition, it is a comprehensive research report which contains only few gaps. Bird not only lists sources and literature, but also provides a comprehensive academic historical survey to which the individual titles are allocated accordingly. Bird divides German naval historiography from the nineteenth century to the present into six periods, and the demarcation lines between the periods are generally undisputed. In this context, only the last two periods are of interest: the period from 1945 to 1965 and the period from 1965 to the present. For research in Germany, the year 1965 constituted a turning

---

[9] Ministry of Defence (Navy), *German Naval History: The U-Boat War in the Atlantic, 1939–1945.* Facsimile edition with Introduction by Andrew J. Withers, 3 parts in 1 volume (London: HMSO, 1989).

[10] Militärgeschichtliches Forschungsamt or MGFA.

[11] For complete bibliographical datas of their publications up to 1984, see Bird, Keith W., *German Naval History. A Guide to the Literature* (New York, London: 1985). Cf. further Janet M. Manson, *Diplomatic Ramifications of Unrestricted Submarine Warfare, 1939–1941* (New York: Greenwood Press, 1990), Gary E. Weir, *Building the Kaiser's Navy: The Imperial Naval Office and German Industry in the von Tirpitz Era, 1890–1919* (Annapolis: Naval Institute Press, 1992), Eric C. Rust, *Naval Officers under Hitler: The Story of Crew 34,* (New York: Praeger, 1991) and for the recent publications of Holger H. Herwig: "The Failure of German Sea Power, 1914–1945: Mahan, Tirpitz, and Raeder Reconsidered," *The International History Review,* February 1988, pp. 68–105; "Wolfgang Wegener and German Naval Strategy from Tirpitz to Raeder" Introduction to Wolfgang Wegner, *The Naval Strategy of the World War,* Classics of Sea Power series (Annapolis: Naval Institute, 1989), pp. xv–lv; "The Influence of A.T. Mahan upon German Sea Power," in John B. Hattendorf, ed., *The Influence of History on Mahan,* (Newport, R.I.: Naval War College Press, 1991), pp. 67–80.

[12] Keith W. Bird, *German Naval History. A Guide to the Literature* (New York: Garland, 1985).

point in that the process of returning most of the naval documents to Germany was concluded in that year. Only the U-boat files of World War II remained until 1978 in the custody of the British Ministry of Defence, which was very restrictive in allowing use of these documents.

Besides the already mentioned naval officers who worked for the British Admiralty or for the U.S. Navy, Walther Hubatsch, in 1956–57, was the first German civilian historian to be allowed access to the German naval files in London; he could, however, only evaluate them in parts. His findings resulted in the book *Der Admiralstab und die obersten Marinebehörden in Deutschland 1848–1945* (Naval Staff and Supreme Naval Commands in Germany 1848–1945).[13] This book and other works by Hubatsch determined for a long time how the historical development of the Navy was viewed, not least by the Navy itself! Thus, initially, one book remained largely unnoticed, a book that was published in 1965 and which Bird justly calls a "turning point": It is Jonathan Steinberg's work, *Yesterday's Deterrent. Tirpitz and the German Battle Fleet*. For the first time since 1945, Steinberg—who consulted an extensive wealth of original sources—examined the background against which, in the late nineteenth century, Tirpitz was appointed Secretary of the Navy and Germany began building a battle fleet.

After the return of the naval documents to Germany, from 1969 onwards a growing interest also emerged among researchers in Germany in studying more thoroughly the strategic and political aims as well as the individual military-technical plans of the German Naval Command, using the source material that was then accessible. In this context, it is noticeable that research focused on the following points:

- Naval arms policy in Imperial Germany, with the Secretary of the Navy, Grand Admiral Alfred v. Tirpitz, in charge of building up the high seas fleet (Volker Berghahn, Wilhelm Deist);[14]
- The continuity or discontinuity of naval armaments from Emperor William II to Hitler (Jost Dülffer, Werner Rahn, Michael Salewski);[15]

---

[13] Walther Hubatsch, *Der Admiralstab und die obersten Marinebehörden in Deutschland 1848–1945* (Frankfurt/M.: 1958).

[14] For complete bibliographic datas of their publications, see Bird, *German Naval History*, passim., and recently Volker R. Berghahn and Wilhelm Deist, *Rüstung im Zeichen der wilhelminischen Weltpolitik. Grundlegende Dokumente 1890–1914* (Düsseldorf: Droste 1988) and Wilhelm Deist, "Kiel und die Marine im Ersten Weltkrieg," in J. Elvert, J. Jensen, and M. Salewski, eds., *Kiel, die Deutschen und die See* (Stuttgart: Steiner, 1992), pp. 143–54.

[15] For complete bibliographic datas of their publications, see Bird, *German Naval History*, passim., and recently Michael Salewski, "Das maritime Dritte Reich—Ideologie und Wirklichkeit 1933–1945," in Deutsches Marine-Institut and Militärgeschichtliches Forschungsamt, eds., *Die deutsche Flotte im Spannungsfeld der Politik 1848–1985. Vorträge und Diskussionen der 25. Historisch-Taktischen Tagung der Flotte 1985*, Schriftenreihe des Deutschen Marine Instituts, Band 9 (Herford: Mittler, 1985), pp. 113–39; Werner Rahn, "Kriegführung, Politik und Krisen—Die Marine des Deutschen Reiches 1914–1933," *ibid.*, pp. 79–104; M. Salewski, "Deutschland als Seemacht," *Kiel, die Deutschen und die See*, pp. 21–34; Jost Dülffer, "Wilhelm II. und Adolf Hitler. Ein Vergleich ihrer Marinekonzeption," *ibid.*, pp. 49–69.

- The ideological orientation in the Naval Command's strategic and political thinking up to 1945; and the planning and decision-making of the Supreme Naval Command during World War II (Michael Salewski, Gerhard Schreiber, Werner Rahn).[16]

After Volker Berghahn published his seminal book on *Der Tirpitz-Plan* in 1971,[17] a gap still remained in the research on the Imperial Navy which was closed only recently by Michael Epkenhans' study *Die Wilhelminische Flottenrüstung 1908–1914*.[18] On a broad basis of sources, he analyses the phase of naval armament policy which Berghahn had already characterized as a "decline of Tirpitz' original concept." Epkenhans establishes that Tirpitz succeeded until 1914 in keeping his armaments program going despite declining public enthusiasm for the fleet and despite political doubts.

As historians concentrated on the Tirpitz era, two important phases of the Imperial Navy were long neglected: the time before 1890, and World War I. Recently, Jörg Duppler presented a comprehensive analysis of the development of the Navy from 1848 to 1890, which concentrates mainly on naval relations between Germany and Britain.[19] Duppler proves in great detail that since 1848 the Royal Navy, by selling ships and training officers, gave a kind of "development aid" to the fledgling German Navy.

The naval historians' reluctance to take a closer look at war itself has been mentioned before. It is particularly evident for World War I. All the documents are well catalogued and easily accessible in the archives, and they challenge the historian to revise the official version as presented in *Der Krieg zur See 1914–1918*.[20] Even so, in recent years only two historians dealt with questions relating to the war at sea from 1914 to 1918. Bernd Stegemann's doctoral dissertation analyzed naval policy from 1916–1918, mainly concentrating on the interdependence of fleet deployment and submarine warfare.[21] In his Ph.D. dissertation

---

[16] For complete bibliographical datas of their publications, see Bird, *German Naval History, passim.*, and recently Werner Rahn, "Der Seekrieg im Atlantik und Nordmeer," *Der globale Krieg. Die Ausweitung zum Weltkrieg und der Wechsel der Initiative 1941–1943* (Stuttgart: 1990) [= Das Deutsche Reich und der Zweite Weltkrieg, ed. by MGFA, Vol. 6], pp. 275–425. [Paperback edition: *Die Welt im Krieg 1941–1943*, vol. I: *Von Pearl Harbor bis zum Bombenkrieg in Europa* (Frankfurt a.M.: Fischer Taschenbuch Verlag, 1992), pp. 329–496], and W. Rahn, "Strategische Wechselwirkung zwischen Nord- und Ostseekriegführung im 19. und 20. Jahrhundert," *Kiel, die Deutschen und die See*, pp. 89–103.

[17] Volker R. Berghahn, *Der Tirpitz-Plan. Genesis und Verfall einer innenpolitischen Krisenstrategie unter Wilhelm II* (Düsseldorf: Droste, 1971).

[18] Michael Epkenhans, *Die wilhelminische Flottenrüstung 1908–1914. Weltmachtstreben, industrieller Fortschritt, soziale Integration* (Munich: Oldenbourg, 1991) [= Beiträge zur Militärgeschichte, ed. by MGFA, vol. 32]. - Cf. in this context also, Weir, *Building the Kaiser's Navy.*

[19] Jörg Duppler, *Der Juniorpartner. England und die Entwicklung der deutschen Marine 1848–1890*, Schriftenreihe des Deutschen Marine-Instituts, Band 7 (Herford: Mittler, 1986).

[20] *Der Krieg zur See 1914–1918*, ed. by Marinearchiv, by Kriegswissenschaftliche Abteilung der Marine and by Arbeitskreis für Wehrforschung, 22 vols. (Berlin/Frankfurt/M.: 1920–1966).

[21] Bernd Stegemann, *Die deutsche Marinepolitik 1916–1918* (Berlin: 1970).

presented in 1989, Gerhard P. Groß—an Army major!—concentrates entirely on the conduct of the naval war in 1918.[22] A comprehensive study of the Imperial Navy, with particular emphasis on the naval war of 1914–1918, similar to Arthur J. Marder's exemplary five volumes on the Royal Navy, cannot be expected in the foreseeable future.

Even the *Handbuch zur deutschen Militärgeschichte 1648–1939* (six volumes, completed in 1981)[23] makes a point of excluding the individual campaigns and wars. The military, as a means of conducting war, was meant to be eclipsed by the military as a structural part of society.[24] However, the historical process called "war" always influences the thoughts and actions of the military, even in peacetime. It is regrettable that, while this seminal handbook contains an article on the principles of land warfare, a similar chapter on naval warfare was not even attempted.

With regard to the German naval campaign during World War II, and the U-boat campaign in particular, an abundance of widely varying literature is available, ranging from popular general accounts to special studies rich in material that deals with operational and tactical questions regarding the employment of surface units and anti-convoy operations by U-boats. However, there is as yet no comprehensive learned overall account of the naval war compiled on the basis of both German and British files. The World War II series edited by the MGFA entitled *Das Deutsche Reich und der Zweite Weltkrieg*[25] is not comparable in its conceptional approach to corresponding works published in Great Britain by Stephen W. Roskill and in the USA by Samuel Eliot Morison. Thus, for instance, in volume 6, *Der globale Krieg. Die Ausweitung zum Weltkrieg und der Wechsel der Initiative 1941–1943*, the account of the Battle of the Atlantic from the spring of 1941 to May 1943 had to be confined to one hundred fifty printed pages,[26] since this volume with a total length of 1,181 pages was, after all, designed to give an account of everything that happened in the war in Europe, the Mediterranean, the Atlantic and also the Pacific. With his three-volume work, *Die deutsche Seekriegsleitung 1935–1945*, Michael Salewski,[27] too, was not

---

[22] Gerhard P. Groß, *Die Seekriegführung der Kaiserlichen Marine im Jahre 1918* (Frankfurt/M., Bern: Peter Lang, 1989).

[23] For the naval aspects, see Wolfgang Petter, "Deutsche Flottenrüstung von Wallenstein bis Tirpitz" and Jost Dülffer, "Die Reichs- und Kriegsmarine 1918–1939," *Handbuch zur deutschen Militärgeschichte 1648–1939*, ed. by Militärgeschichtliches Forschungsamt, vol. 4 / part VIII (Munich: 1978).

[24] See Wolfgang Petter, "Ein neues Handbuch zur Marinegeschichte," *Marineforum, 53* (1978), pp. 201–3, and the critical comments of Paul Heinsius, Hans-Otto Steinmetz and Thilo Bode, *ibid.*, pp. 236 and 314–15.

[25] Volumes 1–6, to be continued; English translation published by Oxford University Press under the title, *Germany and the Second World War.*

[26] Cf. Werner Rahn, "Der Seekrieg im Atlantik und Nordmeer," *Der globale Krieg*, pp. 275–425.

[27] Michael Salewski, *Die deutsche Seekriegsleitung 1935–1945*, vol.1: *1935–1941* (Frankfurt a.M.: Bernard & Graefe, 1970), vol. 2: *1942–1945* (Munich: 1975), vol. 3: *Denkschriften und Lagebetrachtungen 1938–1944* (Frankfurt a.M.: 1973).

able to study and describe the actual naval war; rather, he concentrates mainly on the events at the heart of the Naval Command, *i.e.*, in the Naval Staff, where the strings were pulled and the decisions taken. With regard to the U-boat war, the interested historian continues to be dependent above all on the numerous works by Jürgen Rohwer.[28] In addition, the memoirs of Erich Raeder and Karl Dönitz, which the two published soon after their release from Spandau, are consulted time and again. English translations followed a few years later. Today we know fairly well how these memoirs came to be written. Raeder's memoirs[29] were for the most part the work of a team of former flag officers led by Erich Förste, who felt particularly attached to their former commander-in-chief. Karl Dönitz,[30] on the other hand, was able to rely on the already-mentioned work by his son-in-law, Günter Hessler, of which the latter had at his disposal a complete copy—either unknown to his British employers or with their tacit permission. At any rate, it later struck the historians in Germany that the U-boat files used by Hessler, and later also quoted by Dönitz, had not been freely accessible to researchers until 1977.[31] It was not until 1978 that they were returned to the Federal Republic of Germany, and they are now in Freiburg where they are available to historians.

In addition, the notes left by the two commanders-in-chief, Raeder and Dönitz, on their conferences with Hitler continue to remain an indispensable source for any research activity into the German Navy during World War II. The edition of these conferences with their numerous annexes contains a lot of source material on all problems of naval warfare and naval armaments, illustrating the Naval Command's struggle for resources and priorities.[32] These conferences were first published in English in 1948 in *Brassey's Naval Annual*. In this version, however, the original texts were abridged in places, and some important annexes to the conferences are also missing. This information is of particular importance to historians from English-speaking countries, since an unaltered reprint of the 1948 edition was published in 1990 without mentioning the missing sections.[33] This reprint unfortunately also contains a preface giving a misleading statement

[28] For complete bibliographical datas of his publications, see Bird, *German Naval History*, passim. Cf. also the recently published new edition of J. Rohwer and G. Hümmelchen, *Chronology of the War at Sea 1939–1945. The Naval History of World War Two* (Annapolis: Naval Institute, 1992).

[29] Erich Raeder, *Mein Leben*, vols. 1 and 2 (Tübingen: Schlichtenmayer, 1956–57), English translation in one volume: *My Life* (Annapolis: Naval Institute Press, 1960). Cf. Salewski, *Seekriegsleitung*, vol. 2, p. 590.

[30] Karl Dönitz, *Memoirs, Ten Years and Twenty Days*, with an introduction and afterword by Jürgen Rohwer (Annapolis, Md.: Naval Institute Press, 1990). Cf. also Dieter Hartwig, "Karl Dönitz - Versuch einer kritischen Würdigung," *Deutsches Schiffahrtsarchiv*, 12 (1989), pp. 133–52.

[31] See the critics of Salewski, *Seekriegsleitung*, vol. 2, p. 276, note 21 and p. 658.

[32] Gerhard Wagner, ed., *Lagevorträge des Oberbefehlshabers der Kriegsmarine vor Hitler 1939–1945*, (Munich: Lehmanns, 1972).

[33] *Fuehrer Conferences on Naval Affairs 1939–1945*, (Annapolis: Naval Institute Press, 1990).

on the genesis of the German original edition of 1972. Michael Salewski, in his comprehensive and fundamental study of the German Naval Staff, was right in pointing out that the topic "German naval armaments" deserved "extensive special treatment."[34] As far as the history of the entire German U-boat construction is concerned, a work by Eberhard Rössler, rich in material, has been available for quite a few years.[35] It is indispensable, above all, concerning technical details of the individual types of U-boats and their variants as well as for problems concerning the mass production of U-boats. In *Das Deutsche Reich und der Zweite Weltkrieg*, the problems of the German war economy are examined primarily at the level of the Wehrmacht High Command and the Reich Ministry of Armaments and Ammunition.[36] The analysis focuses on Army and Luftwaffe armaments. Naval armaments are only touched upon, which means that the special study of German naval armaments during World War II based on the documents, as suggested by Salewski, will continue to remain a desideratum.

Apart from the OKW (German Supreme High Command) War diary,[37] the War Diary of the Naval Staff, Part A, is one of the most important and most comprehensive sources for World War II. Day by day, it documents the situation, the strategic and operational deliberations, and decisions of the naval high command, as it strove assiduously for an adequate role of the naval component within German overall warfare. In 1988, the MGFA began to publish a facsimile edition.[38] It will include a reprint of all sixty-eight volumes, covering a month each, from August-September 1939 to April 1945. In view of the enormous size of this publication, which will run to some 35,000 pages when it is completed, the editors had to cut rigorously their critical apparatus. Their annotations concentrate on clarifying difficult handwritten alterations, notes and inserts as well as on cross-references to other Naval Staff documents. Even so, on average, each volume contains some two hundred footnotes. Even if this does not reach the standard of a comprehensive critical edition, this procedure was the only feasible option if this important source for the history of World War II is to be made available to researchers at large. Forty-four volumes have

---

[34]   Salewski, *Seekriegsleitung*, vol. 1, p. 130, note 98.

[35]   Eberhard Rössler, *The U-boat. The evolution and technical history of German Submarines* (Annapolis: Naval Institute Press, 1981).

[36]   Cf. *Das Deutsche Reich und der Zweite Weltkrieg*, vol. 5, part I: B. Kroener, R.D. Müller, H. Umbreit, *Organisation und Mobilisierung des deutschen Machtbereichs*, part I: *Kriegsverwaltung, Wirtschaft und personelle Ressourcen 1939–1941* (Stuttgart: DVA, 1988), pp. 570–74, 626–30 (Müller) and pp. 966–80 (Kroener). Compare in this context the documentation of Werner Rahn, "Einsatzbereitschaft und Kampfkraft deutscher U-Boote 1942," *Militärgeschichtliche Mitteilungen*, 47 (1990), pp. 73–132.

[37]   P.E. Schramm, ed. *Kriegstagebuch des Oberkommandos der Wehrmacht (Wehrmachtführungsstab) 1940–1945*, vols. 1–4, (Frankfurt a.M.: Bernard & Graefe, 1961–1979).

[38]   Werner Rahn and Gerhard Schreiber with the assistance of Hansjoseph Maierhöfer, eds., *Kriegstagebuch der Seekriegsleitung 1939–1945, Teil A*, vol. 1 (August/September 1939); vol. 44 (April 1943) (Bonn, Herford: Mittler, 1988–93), [to be continued].

been published so far, containing 20,150 pages, covering the period up to April 1943.

In concluding, I should like to point out some gaps in research. So far, there are no comprehensive biographical analyses for either Raeder or Dönitz, nor for the leading admirals of the Imperial Navy, including Tirpitz. For the post-1945 period, there are only very few studies which, based on original sources, cover the origins and development of the two German navies between 1955 and 1990. The three-volume series *Anfänge westdeutscher Sicherheitspolitik 1945–1956*,[39] however, presents first results of ongoing research into the origins and beginnings of the Federal German Navy.

Naval History: The State of Teaching

German universities offer naval history neither as an independent subject nor in specialized courses. As a consequence, the forces are the only organization to teach naval history on various levels of their cadet and officer training programs. The naval cadets receive an instruction in naval history as part of their term with the Naval Academy, Flensburg. The level they are expected to achieve is defined as follows:

> The cadet will be able to describe the development, structure and tasks of German naval forces during the 19th and 20th centuries as well as German strategy and naval strategy during both World Wars. As a future leader of men, he has to be able to instruct his subordinates on the origins and role of the Navy within the Bundeswehr.[40]

During a cadet course, which lasts for four or six months, twenty or thirty hours respectively will usually be allotted to the naval history teacher. He will explain the basic pattern of naval development from 1848 to the present, with particular emphasis on the twentieth century. The naval cadet will be acquainted with the strategic aims and political repercussions of Tirpitz' fleet-building program as well as with the command problems of the World War I German Navy. Another period which receives special attention is the inter-war years and naval warfare 1939–1945.

The Bundesmarine, the Federal German Navy, has been in existence for nearly forty years now, which is longer than the combined lifespan attained by the Reichsmarine and Kriegsmarine from 1919 to 1945. Therefore, it is necessary and legitimate to place particular emphasis on teaching about this

---

[39] Militärgeschichtliches Forschungsamt, ed., *Anfänge westdeutscher Sicherheitspoltik 1945–1956*, vol. 1: Roland G. Foerster *et al.*, *Von der Kapitulation bis zum Pleven-Plan* (Munich: Oldenbourg, 1982); vol. 2: Lutz Köllner *et al.*, *Die EVG-Phase* (Munich: Oldenbourg, 1989); vol. 3: Hans Ehlert *et al.*, *Die NATO -Option* (Munich: Oldenbourg, 1993).

[40] Information from Commander Dr. Dieter Hartwig to the author, May 1993.

period, even more so, since the present navy was founded as a result of the Cold War, which has shaped its development and structure up to 1990.

Since 1958, a large "historical collection" has been available as a valuable teaching aid.[41] In 1976, it was reorganized into the "Naval Historic Training Center," which combines naval history, tradition of the Navy, and teaching. This collection largely resembles a museum, and will be discussed later.

Following their first military training period, the cadets or young officers continue their education at one of the Bundeswehr universities, either in Hamburg or Munich. These universities do offer a course in history, but it is largely unconnected with military or naval history. Since the professors who teach history at these universities are intent on preserving their academic independence, they will not discuss subjects drawn from military history on a regular basis.

After taking his degree, the young officer will return to the Naval Academy for a few months to prepare himself for his first posting in the Navy. At this point, a more thorough naval historical education is envisaged, but experience shows that most officers have lost virtually all previous knowledge they might have acquired in this field, making the job more challenging for teachers.

As part of their continued training, some 10 to 12 percent of every class attend the two-year course for general-admiral staff officers at the Armed Forces General Staff College in Hamburg. During this course, eighty-six hours are scheduled for military and naval history. Here, the intended level of achievement is defined as follows:

> The officer on Admiral Staff Duty should be able to understand the interdependence and mutual influence of political and military leadership. He should understand the influence of the various elements of war on past concepts of warfare and draw conclusions which apply to the present. Based on historical examples, he should be able to follow some basic principles of military commanders.[42]

In this course, particular care is taken that the officer will get to know und understand German and international concepts of naval strategy, of both the nineteenth and twentieth centuries. Selected examples should enable him to realize the nature and the elements of the reality of war. About thirty-five hours, i.e., about 40 percent of the total reserved for the entire discipline, are scheduled for these two fields of naval historical teaching. A special form of academic training at the Armed Forces General Staff College is the requirement that students write a thesis. This will analyze a specified, limited subject and must be written during their stay at the Staff College. The lecturers in military history

---

[41] Jörg Duppler, "Das Wehrgeschichtliche Ausbildungszentrum Flensburg–Mürwik," in Nordseestadt Wilhelmshaven/Der Oberstadtdirektor, ed., *Dokumentation Symposium Deutsches Marine-Museum* (Wilhelmshaven: 1988), pp. 91–5.

[42] Curriculum of Führungsakademie der Bundeswehr for the 34th Admiralstaff Course (information from Commander Dr. Nägler to the author, May 1993).

regularly offer a choice of historical topics, some of which will be researched using original sources. A number of especially qualified papers have been published, indicating the high standards of teaching at the Armed Forces General Staff College.[43]

Beginning in 1957, the German Navy began to develop a new approach in studying its own history. That year, the first Commander-in-Chief Fleet, Rear Admiral Rolf Johannesson, organized the first Historical-Tactical Convention. Since then, it has been held every year, and it is now a standard element of the entire naval officer corps' historical education. Admiral Johannesson's aim was to distance himself from the subjective naval historiography about World War I.[44] He hoped that a critical discussion of the past would teach the officers truth, loyalty, and moral courage, and that they would determine their own position more solidly by a recourse to history and to the federal constitution. One of his successors, Vice Admiral Günter Fromm, summed this up in 1985 in a phrase which can be taken as exemplary for any serious dealing with the past:[45] "Yet, there must be no taboos. What is necessary is rather a permanent effort to come closer to the truth. Only truth, however difficult it may be to attain and to bear, can give us the security of a sound foundation."

Up to 1993, thirty-three conventions have been held, covering a wide variety of subjects.[46] Papers are usually presented by junior officers (commanders and captains are exceptions) from the fleet who are assisted in their preparations by naval historians. The papers presented in some of the conventions have been collected and published as books.[47] The contents and results of the conventions are regularly reported in the monthly naval journal, *Marineforum*. The papers do

[43] Cf. H. Schuur, R. Martens, W. Koehler, *Führungsprobleme der Marine im Zweiten Weltkrieg*, 2nd ed. (Freiburg: Rombach, 1986); Diether Hülsemann, "Die Versorgung des deutschen Kreuzergeschwaders 1914 und ihr Einfluß auf seine Operationen," *Die Bedeutung der Logistik für die militärische Führung von der Antike bis in die neueste Zeit* (Herford, Bonn: Mittler, 1985) [= Vorträge zur Militärgeschichte, vol. 7], pp. 167–209; Uwe Dirks, "Julian S. Corbett und die britische Seekriegführung 1914–1918," *Militärgeschichtliche Mitteilungen*, 37 (1985), pp. 35–50; and Wulf Diercks, "Der Einfluß der Personalsteuerung auf die deutsche Seekriegführung 1914–1918," *Militärgeschichtliches Beiheft zur Europäischen Wehrkunde*, Nr. 1/1988.

[44] Statement of Rear Admiral Rolf Johannesson (Ret.) to the audience in Deutsches Marine Institut, ed., *Der Marineoffizier als Führer im Gefecht. Vorträge auf der Historisch-Taktischen Tagung der Flotte 1983* (Herford: Mittler, 1984), p. 241.

[45] Günter Fromm, "Schlußbemerkungen des Befehlshabers der Flotte," in Deutsches Marine-Institut and Militärgeschichtliches Forschungsamt, eds. *Die deutsche Flotte im Spannungsfeld der Politik 1848–1985. Vorträge und Diskussionen der 25. Historisch-Taktischen Tagung der Flotte 1985*, Schriftenreihe des Deutschen Marine instituts, Bd 9 (Herford: Mittler, 1985), p. 223.

[46] See "Generalthemen der Historisch-Taktischen Tagungen 1957–1985," *ibid.*, pp. 225–7.

[47] Cf., for example, *Bild der russischen und sowjetischen Marine. Vorträge der 5. Historisch-Taktischen Tagung der Flotte, 6.-7- Dezember 1961* (Frankfurt a.M.: Mittler, 1962) [= Beiheft No. 7/8 of Marine Rundschau]; *Die Entwicklung des Flottenkommando. Vorträge der 7. Historisch-Taktischen Tagung der Flotte am 5. und 6.12.1963* (Darmstadt: Wehr und Wissen, 1964); and Deutsches Marine Institut, ed., *Der Einsatz von Seestreitkräften im Dienste der auswärtigen Politik. Vorträge auf der Historisch-Taktischen Tagung der Flotte 1981* (Herford: Mittler, 1983).

not always live up to the standards of the professional historian, but their presentation and the candid, often lively, discussion of subjects relevant to the business of the day usually give testimony of the multiple intellectual talents among the Navy's officer corps. Many an admiral-to-be made his mark when, as a lieutenant, he presented some sharply critical theory in the Naval Academy's Grand Hall, provoking the older generation's opposition.

Maritime History: State of Research and Publications

The field of maritime history extends its range far back into ancient history and covers the central aspects of the age of exploration. A key German language work in this area is the comprehensive multivolume collection of documents covering the history of European expansionism, covering the entire period of European expansionism prior to the age of imperialism.[48] However, the sources have been translated into German only. The first volume covers the period from about 500 A.D. to 1500, i.e., the beginnings of the age of exploration.[49]

The second volume covers the great voyages of exploration from Henry the Navigator in the fifteenth century to the opening up of the Pacific in the eighteenth century.[50] The third volume deals with the origins of the colonial empires from about 1500 through the mid-eighteenth century.[51]

The Deutsches Schiffahrtsmuseum (DSM—German Maritime Museum) at Bremerhaven is the only learned institute in Germany that is exclusively concerned with maritime history. At present, eleven historians and scholars of other branches work in this museum. Their research covers, among others, subjects such as: passenger shipping, merchant shipping, whaling, oceanography, social history of navigation, marine painting, naval industrial archeology.

For a long time, the museum's research was focussed on maritime archeology, which was justified by the finding and restoration of the Hanse Cog of 1380. This aspect will be presented in more detail later on. Another focus of museum work is the social and economic history of navigation. Recent publications by members of the museum's staff deal mostly with problems of social history, such as harbor workers, shipbuilders and the sailors' work.

---

[48] Eberhard Schmitt, ed., *Dokumente zur Geschichte der europäischen Expansion,* 7 vols. (Munich: Beck, 1984 ff.).

[49] Eberhard Schmitt, ed., *Dokumente zur Geschichte der europäischen Expansion,,* vol. 1: *Die mittelalterlichen Ursprünge der europäischen Expansion,* ed. by Charles Verlinden and Eberhard Schmitt with contributions of Hanno Beck et al. (Munich: Beck, 1986).

[50] Eberhard Schmitt, ed., *Dokumente zur Geschichte der europäischen Expansion,* vol. 2: *Die großen Entdeckungen,* ed. by Matthias Meyn et al. (Munich: Beck, 1984).

[51] Eberhard Schmitt, ed., *Dokumente zur Geschichte der europäischen Expansion,* vol. 3: *Der Aufbau der Kolonialreiche,* ed. by Matthias Mey et al. with contributions of Annegret Bollée *et al.* (Munich: Beck, 1986). Vols. 4 through 7 cover economy, trade, and life in the colonies, their role in international politics and the end of the colonial system.

This varied research results in a large number of specialized publications which are listed every year in the museum's annual report. These annual reports are published in the museum's journal, *Deutsches Schiffahrtsarchiv*, which has existed since 1975 and has been published annually since 1980. It is now one of the leading publications on maritime history in the German language. Also, the traditional *Hansische Geschichtsblätter*, which appeared in its 111th annual volume in 1993, contains important contributions to the research of maritime history. Its regular report on publications, called *Schiffahrt und Schiffbau* (Navigation and Shipbuilding), and edited with profound knowledge by the museum's director, Professor Detlef Ellmers, deserves particular attention. Out of the numerous titles published by members of the museum's staff, only a few can be listed here. Arnold Kludas's five-volume *Geschichte der deutschen Passagierschiffahrt* (History of German Passenger Shipping) is by now complete.[52] Lars U. Scholl, a well-known expert in history of German marine painting and economical aspects of maritime history, has published the results of his research in several articles and catalogues.[53] However, there is still no comprehensive history of German merchant shipping. Any interested historian will have to make do with representative volumes whose individual articles offer important summaries of the latest research.[54]

Maritime History: State of Teaching

So far, there are no courses in maritime history in any German university. However, the departments of history in several north German universities regularly offer seminars on subjects that are closely related to maritime history: history of emigration, social history of shipbuilders and sailors. The lecturers will often be staff members of the German Maritime Museum in Bremerhaven or historians who have touched upon questions of shipbuilding and ship design as part of their work on the history of technology.

Maritime and Naval Museums and Collections. Archaeology of Shipping and Private Maritime Collections

Before World War II, Germany had a central institution for the study and display of objects relating to shipping, namely the Museum für Meereskunde

---

[52] Arnold Kludas, *Die Geschichte der deutschen Passagierschiffahrt*, vols. 1–5, (Hamburg: Kabel, 1986–1990).

[53] Lars U. Scholl: *Claus Bergen 1885–1964. Marinemalerei im 20. Jahrhundert* (Bremerhaven: 1982); *Felix Schwormstädt 1870–1938* (Herford: Koehler, 1990) and *Der Marinemaler Hans Peter Jürgens* (Herford: Koehler, 1991); "Shipping Business in Germany in the Nineteenth and Twentieth Centuries," in Tsunehiko Yui and Keiichiro Nakagawa, eds., *Business History of Shipping. Strategy and Structure* (Tokyo: University of Tokyo Press, 1985), pp. 185–213, and "The Harriman-Hamburg-American Line Agreement of June 1920: The Foremost German Shipping Company's Return to the Seas," *Research in Maritime History*, 2 (1992), pp. 349–81. Dr. Scholl presented a paper, "German Maritime Historical Research during the past twenty-five years. A critical survey" at the conference on New Directions in Maritime History (December 1993, Perth-Freemantle, Australia).

[54] Cf., for example, Volker Plagemann, *Übersee. Seefahrt und Seemacht im deutschen Kaiserreich* (Munich: Beck, 1988).

(Museum of Oceanography) in Berlin. During the war, the building and large parts of its collections were destroyed. Only a few pieces survived, and today they are scattered among various collections and museums. Not least, the division of Germany and of her capital Berlin meant that for several decades it was impossible to fill this gap in an appropriate manner.

As a result of the vacuum created by the lack of a central museum, smaller museums in the port towns and cities gained in importance. Thus, today, almost every German port from Emden in the West to Stralsund in the East has a small maritime museum. They often developed from private collections, and today they provide the maritime historian and ship lover with an abundance of material from different eras of maritime history. From the point of view of their location and tasks, they naturally concentrate their collections on local peculiarities and those of the adjacent coastal region.

The city of Wilhelmshaven has been canvassing for a central German Naval Museum since 1988. However, this project did not get beyond its initial stage, i.e., the preparation of a small collection.[55] In 1992, an attempt failed to take over the former naval training vessel, the *Deutschland*, and to set it up as a museum ship.

From among these numerous museums, one museum stands out, which is to be described in greater detail here. This is the Deutsches Schiffahrtsmuseum (German Maritime Museum) in Bremerhaven.[56] The starting point for the foundation of the museum lay in three different spheres:

• When the Bremerhaven Morgenstern Museum moved to new premises in 1961, a maritime section was also opened. In the years that followed, the museum succeeded in acquiring important estates and collections, which today form a major foundation of the German Maritime Museum.

• In 1962, the city of Bremerhaven decided not to fill in the old docks located directly on the Weser but to preserve them as an expanse of water. This created ideal conditions for a subsequent museum harbor, which got its first old ship in 1966.

• The salvage in 1962 of a medieval Hanseatic cog was a pioneer achievment in the archaeology of shipping. Immediately after the ship had been salvaged, funds for its lengthy restoration were also obtained. Thus, there was a major impulse for the establishment of a central German maritime museum. The museum was subsequently founded in 1971 and opened in 1975.

In the museum's charter of foundation, its tasks are described as follows:

---

[55] Nordseestadt Wilhelmshaven/Der Oberstadtdirektor, *Dokumentation Symposium Deutsches Marine-Museum* (Wilhelmshaven: 1988).

[56] Cf. Wolf-Dieter Hoheisel, "Aufgaben und Aufbau des Deutschen Schiffahrtsmuseums," *Hansische Geschichtsblätter*, 91 (1973), pp. 54–7, and *Deutsches Schiffahrtsmuseum '75*, Führer des Deutschen Schiffahrtsmuseums, Nr. 1 (Bremerhaven: 1975), and "Deutsches Schiffahrtsmuseum Bremerhaven," *Museum*, Januar 1/1977 (Braunschweig: Westermann, 1977).

1. To collect historical exhibits, to illustrate and to document German maritime history and its correlations;

2. To conduct academic research into all fields of German maritime history;

3. To use the museum's scientific and technological capabilities at its disposal in order to work for the public on behalf of German maritime history.

In January 1972, the first ships were able to dock in the museum harbor. From 1970 to 1975, the museum's main building was constructed to a design by Hans Scharoun. The concept of this building was to combine systematically arranged exhibits in the building with an open-air collection of museum ships.

One of the major difficulties of maritime history exhibitions is caused by the size of the ships, which precludes the use of originals to illustrate the evolution of ship types. It is necessary to resort to scale models and accept the effect of minimization that this involves. To counterbalance this, the German Maritime Museum has attached particular importance to establishing the relation to the original dimensions—the ships in the Old Docks and on the Weser can be seen from the exhibition. At the same time, these ships, plus a few original-size systems, form the centerpieces of the individual exhibition sections, to which the other exhibits are clearly subordinated. From among the museum ships, I should like to mention only the naval ships: they are a fast patrol boat from the early days of the post-war Bundesmarine and the only surviving Type XXI World War II submarine.[57] The museum includes a separate naval department which displays, *inter alia*, an original type *Seehund* midget submarine of fifteen tons.

The Hanse Cog

Archaeology of shipping and reconstruction is exemplified by the Hanse cog.[58] On 9 October 1962, during dredging work in the Weser river, the wreck of a ship was discovered which, on the basis of numerous symbols on seals, was identified as a medieval Hanseatic cog.[59] This type of ship was not only the regular cargo ship of the early Hanseatic league until well into the fifteenth century, the cog was also the means of early Hanseatic naval warfare. As this wreck had been found by chance, nobody was prepared for salvaging such a ship. However, the rescue of the find had to commence immediately, as the cog was in danger of breaking apart as soon as the supporting masses of sand were

---

[57] Cf., Technikmuseum U–Boot "Wilhelm Bauer." *Kleine Geschichte und Technik der deutschen U–Boote* (Bremerhaven: 1990).

[58] The following part is based on the special journal *Museum*, 1 (1977), pp. 20–24. (This chapter was written by Wolf-Dieter Hoheisel). Cf. also Klaus-Peter Kiedel and Uwe Schnall, *The Hanse Cog of 1380* (Bremerhaven: 1985) and *Die Kogge von Bremen*, vol. 1, Werner Lahn, *Bauteile und Bauablauf*, Schriften des Deutschen Schiffahrtsmuseums, 30 (Hamburg: Kabel, 1987) with 37 plans and 161 illustrations.

[59] See Paul Heinsius, *Das Schiff der hansischen Frühzeit*, 2nd ed. (Cologne and Vienna: Böhlau, 1986).

removed. Eventually, a great effort made it possible to complete most of the salvage operation before the onset of the winter of 1962–63. However, another ten years were to elapse before it was possible to lay down the keel of this Hanseatic ship for a second time, this time in the purpose-built *"Kogge-Haus"* of the German Maritime Museum on 1 November 1972. As nobody knew the exact size and shape of the cog, the restorers had to put the ship back together by assembling some 2,000 pieces. It was one big jigsaw puzzle. They often had to rely on conjectures, which were then checked by using the actual conditions. In the course of their work, the restorers tested new measurement, damp wood bonding, and preservation techniques. The reconstruction of the cog took place in a foggy atmosphere, since otherwise the saturated, almost six-hundred-year-old oak would have shrunk by 25 to 30 percent. Then, a preservation basin had to be constructed around the ship in which the cog is impregnated with a preservation fluid for many years. During this time, the water-soluble preservation agent, polyethylne glycol, slowly penetrates all the components starting from the surface. In the process, the water present in the cells of the wood is gradually replaced by the polywax, which then, during the subsequent drying process, forms a "supporting corset" and prevents shrinkage. This process should be completed in around 10 years. The cog is now the central exhibit of the "Middle Ages" section at the German Maritime Museum.

Once the restoration of the original cog had progressed so far that it was possible to clearly distinguish the design of the ship, the suggestion was made to build an exact reproduction of the cog.[60] It was hoped that tests with this replica under actual sea conditions in the area in which it used to operate, i.e., primarily the North Sea and the Baltic, might answer questions as to the cogs' sail-carrying ability, their seaworthiness, load capacity, navigation, etc.

The replica's length overall is 23 meters, its beam over all is 7.26 meters. When loaded with the maximum cargo of 87 metric tons, the draught is 2.25 meters, giving a displacement of about 120 metric tons. The cog, which was salvaged from the Weser, had been lost in an accident in 1380 while being built. Because none of the rig's original parts were found near the wreck, which would have provided clues to the ship's sail-carrying ability, replicating the rig posed special problems. The rig's reproduction had to be based on old representations; a description by the Italian, Timbotta, dating from 1444 could also be used. Final details such as the sail area of 200 square meters were eventually decided upon after a model had been tried in a wind tunnel.

From 1987 to 1990, two replicas of the cog were built, one in Kiel and another in Bremerhaven. They were meant for two different purposes:

---

[60]   The following description is based on Wolf-Dieter Hoheisel, "A Full-Scale Replica of the Hanse Cog of 1380," *Yearbook of the International Association of Transport Museums*, 15/16 (1988/1989), pp. 26–33. Cf. also Wolf-Dieter Hoheisel, "Rekonstruktion der Bremer Hans-Kogge," *Jahrbuch der Schiffbautechnischen Gesellschaft*, 82 (1988), pp. 223–9.

- The Kiel replica was built as true to the original as possible, to permit a better analysis of the advantages and disadvantages of the medieval structure and its influence on the ship's characteristics. Without an engine or any other aids, it was used to determine exactly how a Bremen cog sailed in the Middle Ages.
- The Bremerhaven replica was built for a different purpose. It was to undertake studies in long-term cruises along the Hanseatic sailing routes in the North Sea and in the Baltic. For safety reasons, an engine and modern navigation aids had to be included to prevent accidents, *e.g.*, on a lee shore. Of course, the city of Bremerhaven also sees visits of this cog to former Hanse cities as good public relations for Bremerhaven and its German Maritime Museum.[61]

In June 1991, the first sailing trials of the Kiel cog commenced.[62] Their results confirmed the prior calculations. Up to wind-force 4–5, the cog could run under full sail, heeling less than 15 degrees. With wind-force 6–7 from nearly abaft, the cog made slightly more than 7 knots. However, during the first trials the cog was unable to beat against the wind. Scientific results of the trials, however, are not expected until 1994–5, and will probably be published in the *Jahrbuch der Schiffbautechnischen Gesellschaft*.

Until 1945, the Museum für Meereskunde (Museum of Oceanography) in Berlin included a large department of naval history. Among other items, it held the first German submarine, the *Brandtaucher,* built by Wilhelm Bauer in 1848.[63] When this museum was destroyed, Germany lost its most valuable exhibits, which had documented naval history.

Before 1990 the German Armed Forces had no central museum of military history which might have included a separate section for naval history. This was for a variety of reasons, not the least being a lack of funds. After reunification in October 1990, the Bundeswehr took over the former East German Army (NVA) Museum of Military History, which had been established in Dresden. At the moment, it looks as if that museum will eventually be the central German museum for military history. It includes a naval department with a number of valuable exhibits and good models. Its showpiece is certainly the *Brandtaucher* which, although very badly damaged during World War II, was rescued from among the ruins of the Museum of Oceanography and later restored.

The best collection documenting naval history can be found in the Naval Historic Training Center of the German Naval Academy at Flensburg. When this collection originated in 1958, its aims were defined as follows:

---

[61] Information from Professor Dr. Detlev Ellmers and Dr. Lars U. Scholl, both of German Maritime Museum, Bremerhaven, to the author, May–September, 1993.

[62] Cf. Wolf-Dieter Hoheisel, "Erste Segelversuche mit dem Kieler Nachbau der Bremer Hanse-Kogge von 1380," *Deutsche Schiffahrt*, 2 (1991), pp. 23–5.

[63] Cf. Klaus Herold, "Der Kieler Brandtaucher. Ergebnisse einer Nachforschung," *Kiel, die Deutschen und die See*, pp. 123–42.

The Historic Collection, as part of the Center of Military History, will illustrate the various epochs of the German naval past to the officer cadets and officers as part of their education, so as to motivate them for their chosen profession as naval officers. Also, it will serve to cultivate naval tradition and to inform the public about Germany's maritime interests, past and present. The exhibition will therefore center on the development and history of naval forces from the end of the 19th century.[64]

Based on a Naval Staff order dated April 1958, the Naval Academy developed a department which was initially called the "Historical Collection." Renamed "Naval Historical Training Center" in 1976, it united naval history, the tradition of the Navy, and teaching into an organic whole, with all three components enjoying equal status.

This collection started from humble beginnings in 1958, and it is not actually a museum. Still, in view of the large number of exhibits, some of which are extremely valuable, it compares favorably with other, similar institutes. Today, it holds some 150 model ships, 350 oil paintings and prints, 300 flags and pennants, 15 busts, 7 figureheads, 25 coats of arms from ships' bows, 80 situation maps, 300 ships' diagrams as well as several thousand photographs depicting individuals, ships, and events. The photographs are often from old albums which have been presented to the collection by former officers and men of the Navy. The collection is mainly used for the instruction and education of the officer cadets. Also, some 6,000 visitors per year, excluding Navy personnel, find it a source of valuable information for their historical interests. The manuscript collection now numbers about 17,000 items, and it is used increasingly by historians, both from Germany and from abroad. Meanwhile, the exhibition has found better accommodation in what used to be the commandant's villa, making it more accessible to outside visitors.

This report on German museums and collections relating to maritime and naval history can by no means be complete; it can only present a selection. However, one private collection has to be mentioned. It has a special position as one of the largest and most important of its kind. Its owner is the publisher and former Chief Executive of Springer Publishing Company, Peter Tamm, in Hamburg.[65] This collection includes not only a special library of about 60,000 volumes, it consists of a vast number of extremely valuable ship models, paintings

---

[64] Jörg Duppler, "Das Wehrgeschichtliche Ausbildungszentrum Flensburg-Mürwik," Dokumentation Symposium Deutsches Marine-Museum, pp. 91–5, and Franz Hahn, "Ein Rundgang durch das Wehrgeschichtliche Ausbildungszentrum," in Deutsches Marine Institut. Conception and Redaction: Dieter Matthei, Jörg Duppler and Karl Heinz Kruse, Marineschule Mürwik (1910–1985), 2nd rev. ed. (Herford: Mittler, 1989), pp. 213–20.

[65] Cf. Heinrich Walle, "Private Sammler maritimer Kunst," in Deutsches Marine Institut and Militärgeschichtliches Forschungsamt, eds., Seefahrt und Geschichte (Herford and Bonn: Mittler, 1986), pp. 220–5, and [without author] "Das Wissenschaftliche Institut für Schiffahrts- und Marinegeschichte," Marineforum, 67 (1992), pp. 426–7.

dating from the sixteenth century to the present, innumerable manuscripts, charts, uniforms, decorations, weapons, and other historic maritime exhibits. The collection is now a part of the private Institute of Maritime and Naval History, which is still in the process of development. Large parts of the collection have time and again enriched major exhibitions elsewhere.

Correlations between Naval and Maritime History

The close relationship between maritime and naval history makes it obvious that there is an interdependence between the two fields of research. Even so, cooperation between historians dealing with maritime and naval history, respectively, has so far been sporadic rather than intensive. As there was always a tension between naval and merchant navigation, this distance is also quite discernible between historians researching naval and maritime history. The much-regretted general tendency of all historians to specialize also contributes to a neglect of subjects which cover more than one narrow field. A number of learned associations exist, but they do not care to improve cooperation. In view of the forthcoming cuts in research grants, cooperation will be more essential than ever if the available monetary and staff resources are to be employed effectively for fundamental naval and maritime research.

Conclusion

It is a basic, and perennial challenge to historians to try and come close to historic truth. Today, the German Navy has both a lively interest in its history and also a special relationship with it. A clear link can be seen between the historical self-perception of its officers and the history of their service. In the past, this link often served only to legitimize and to secure the Navy's own position in its fight for recognition and even for its existence, during a relatively short period. In such situations, there is a danger if historical interest is limited only to the Navy itself and to naval warfare, and too little attention is paid to the "general context, to the subordination of the individual aspect under the varied panorama of historical development."[66]

The various aspects of highly specialized maritime historiography are beset by similar dangers. The commercial success of popular publications as well as the number of visitors attracted to the museums indicate how many people have some historical interest. This continuing interest is a stimulating challenge for the professional historian. We should continue to try and present our findings about past backgrounds and structures in such a way that the message gets across, i.e., in such a way that historical knowledge and sensitivity become a stabilizing factor for a liberal society. And if this calling sounds ponderous enough, we

---

[66] Wilhelm Deist, "Auflösungserscheinungen in Armee und Marine als Voraussetzungen der deutschen Revolution," in MGFA, ed., *Menschenführung in der Marine*, Vorträge zur Militärgeschichte, 2 (Herford and Bonn: Mittler, 1981), p. 37.

should not forget the humorous touch—it always was and always will be a refreshing element of human life.

In 1943, the following story received clearance for publication in Germany:

A circus had been hit during an air raid on Berlin. Two lions escaped and were on the loose without anyone having any idea where they might be.

After two weeks had passed, one of the lions returned ruefully to his cage. He looked worn out and thin and swore to his fellows: "Never again! I'd rather put up with bad horse meat than have to find my own food in Berlin!"

The next day, the other lion came back; proud as anything and fatter than he had ever been before. "Hello! Where have you been?" the others called to him, "what have you been up to?"

"Who me?—I was in Naval Command Headquarters and every day I had an admiral for my supper. But be careful not to tell anyone—no one's noticed yet." And back he ran to the Naval High Command.[67]

To draw an analogy from this story, you could say that after World War II, German naval archives were indeed eaten by British and American historians while German historians, without any access to the original documents, looked worn out and thin for a long time.

★ ★ ★

The collation of this material and its translation into English was generously supported in a variety of ways by a number of colleagues. I am grateful to Colonel (GS) Dr. Roland Foerster and Major Winfried Heinemann, both of the MGFA, as well as to Commander Dr. Dieter Hartwig of the Naval Academy in Flensberg, Lieutenant Commander Dr. Frank Nägler of the Armed Forces Staff College, Hamburg, Professor Dr. Detlev Ellmers and Dr. Lars U. Scholl, both of the German Maritime Museum, Bremerhaven, and Professor John Hattendorf of the Naval War College.

---

67 Peter Ernst Eiffe, *Seemannsgarn. "Splissen und Knoten" zweite Folge. Heitere Marinegeschichten* mit einem Geleitwort des Admiralinspekteurs der Kriegsmarine des Großdeutschen Reiches Großadmiral Raeder (Magdeburg: 1943), pp. 45–6.

13

India

Captain C. Uday Bhaskar, Indian Navy

The study of naval and maritime history offers a curious paradox in the Indian context. For a nation whose recent political history has been inextricably linked with the dictates of sea power and whose maritime history goes back to earliest antiquity—namely to the Mohenjo–Daro–Harappa period (c. 3000–1500 B.C.)—the actual study of naval and maritime subjects in India is modest, to say the least.

History itself, as interpreted in the Western context, is something alien to the Indian psyche. There are various reasons for this trait. At the broad level of civilizations, it is averred that the timelessness of Indian thinking and metaphysics defies the special perch of history. The continuum of time is seen as an endless cycle punctuated by the birth, life, death, and rebirth of the protagonist—be it the individual or the soul—the only perennial entity being the essence of civilization. At a more simplistic level, a casual observer may look at language and deduce that in Hindi, the national language of the country, the word for yesterday and tomorrow is the same, *kal*, thereby diluting the need to preserve the past in a codified and rigorous manner.

Be that as it may, a preliminary survey suggests that, barring the professional naval establishments, there is no dedicated institutional infrastructure for the study of naval and maritime history in India. All the universities in India offer detailed courses in the study of history *per se*, but the division is more traditional in the sense that ancient Indian history, the medieval period, and the British period are some of the broad areas studied. These may be explored further in their political, social, and economic dimensions, but the actual study of military history, with specific reference to the naval and maritime dimension is currently in its infancy.

A wealth of material remains to be excavated. For instance, the linkages between sea power and the political fortunes of the early Indian dynasties—the Satavahanas and the Mauryans—need to be authoritatively analyzed and, in like fashion, specific linkages in maritime commerce, ship-building, and contacts

---

Captain C. Uday Bhaskar, Indian Navy, is currently Senior Fellow at the Institute for Defense Studies and Analyses, New Delhi.

with the rest of the ancient world need to be rigorously examined. Some research at the post-graduate level is now being encouraged in certain universities in India, such as those in Delhi, Calcutta, Bombay, and Madras. A more detailed survey of Indian academia may be warranted at a later stage to fill in the inadvertent omissions of this preliminary report.

Among the service establishments, naval and maritime history receives tangential attention at the Defence Services Staff College, Wellington, Nilgiris, Tamil Nadu, and at the College of Naval Warfare, Bombay, and the National Defence College, Delhi. But none of these three establishments teach the subjects in the pristine, academic sense. In an effort to infuse a historical sense into their respective studies, these colleges correlate naval and maritime history strands with the specific issue or subject being studied. Here, the threshold at which the students come to the college is relevant and this gives one an insight into the manner in which naval and maritime history are woven into the curriculum.

The Defence Services Staff College is the first stepping stone for higher command in the Indian armed forces, and officers enter at the grade of lieutenant commander and its equivalent, major or squadron leader. Here, naval and maritime history are related to specific tactical studies and are undertaken in groups. Campaign studies receive greater attention, and, here again, the correlation is between the principles of war and twentieth century naval battles and campaigns. The Atlantic and Pacific campaigns of World War II are studied in detail, specifically the Battle of Midway, the Normandy landing, along with the Korean War landing at Inchon. More recently, the Falklands campaign and the Gulf War have become logical priorities in the Defence Services Staff College.

In sum, the Defence Services Staff College does not teach maritime or naval history, but it deals with specific historical issues that encompass naval battles at sea or amphibious operations that are taken up in the syndicate and divisional portions of the group study program. Each group makes a final presentation to the entire college, at which stage certain relevant aspects of naval and maritime history are discussed.

The College of Naval Warfare conducts courses for officers at the rank of senior commander or captain. Here also, there is no attempt to teach naval and maritime history. However, in the effort to infuse a historical sense into studies of naval strategy, the discussions on ancient and medieval Indian history include specific aspects of naval and maritime history. This syllabus is still being refined, and I believe that there will be a gradual shift from the political science content to a marked maritime strategy content in the years ahead. Currently, the College of Naval Warfare offers a separate session on the maritime heritage of India and the ancient methods of navigation in these waters. The latter aspect is also receiving attention in the Bombay University.

The National Defence College, New Delhi, is the apex college for the Indian Armed Forces and also has representatives from other nations. Student officers are of brigadier and equivalent rank. Here again, there is no formal teaching of naval and maritime history. However, during this one year–long course at the National Defence College, sea power *per se* is analyzed. The historical perspective, the Indian context, and the colonial paradigm are explored. Guest lecturers are invited to address these subjects and, for the last two years, I have been involved in structuring lectures around these subjects. For example, subject themes, such as "Maritime Rivalry in the Indian Ocean: A Historical Perspective" and "The Impact of Sea-power on the Littoral of the Pacific and Indian Oceans: Prognosis in the Post–Cold War," have evolved to cover all the salient political, economic and military aspects of naval and maritime history.

There is no single intellectual trend or critical theory that is adhered to in the discussions at the above institutions, but there is little doubt that the perspective of the naval and maritime events under study is from that of a non-white, former colony. It is often averred in India that the lack of adequate appreciation about the relevance of sea power by early Indian rulers led to the later colonization of the sub-continent. This theme has been amply dealt with by K.M. Panikkar in his books on the subject and provides the basic intellectual thrust to the current Indian interpretation.[1]

No Indian university offers any specific courses in naval/maritime history *per se*. These subjects are dealt with as part of a larger sub-heading, e.g., in addressing economic history of a period or region, the maritime trade aspects are covered. In like fashion, while naval battles or capabilities receive little individual attention in the universities, references are made to the maritime strand while dealing with the specifics of political history.

While it has not been possible to survey all the Indian universities individually, one has been able to look more closely at the syllabus of the Jawaharlal Nehru University, New Delhi and some of the findings here may be extrapolated to the larger Indian university canvas as a general indicator of the current trend.

For example, one of the courses offered at the post-graduate level in the Center for Historical Studies at the Jawaharlal Nehru University is entitled: "Economic History of India: Trade, Commerce and Industry in India in the 17th and 18th centuries." The subject is treated in the following manner: Structure of Asian trade: 10th-15th centuries; the Portuguese domination of the Indian Ocean in the 16th century; the response of Indian merchants and rulers to Portuguese hegemony; the Dutch rule in intra-Asian trade; Dutch trade in India; the English East India Company; the economy of Gujarat; the Indian merchants and their trading practice; the role and position of merchants in

---

[1]   K.M. Panikkar, *India and the Indian Ocean* (London: George Allen and Unwin, 1962).

economy and society; the Coromandel; the economy of Bengal; and some aspects of technology and industry.[2]

In like fashion, while dealing with medieval Indian history, for instance, the Cholas in the ninth to thirteenth centuries of peninsular India are the subject of a separate course. In this course, the maritime trade practices of the Cholas and their expeditions into Sri Lanka and South East Asia are dealt with as part of the economic and political history of the period.[3]

Further, a course on "Trade Networks in the Indian Ocean: Fifteenth to Eighteenth Centuries" examines the geographical setting of the Indian Ocean, the pre-European concepts, nature and meaning of the Indian Ocean as a world economy, the Indian Ocean trade network before the fifth century, the contribution of European trading companies, the role of China and East Asian countries and ship-building technology.[4]

These illustrative examples from the Jawaharlal Nehru University are symptomatic of the larger trend in Indian academia, wherein there appears to be a lack of any specialization in naval and maritime history *per se*. This is a glaring gap as far as the professional sailor is concerned, and more recently there has been an attempt by the Indian Navy to make a modest contribution in this regard. Naval Headquarters has been encouraging naval historians to research specific subjects, and in the last few years retired Rear Admirals Satyindra Singh[5] and K. Sridharan[6] have made noteworthy contributions.

A small but significant step in creating a national maritime consciousness has been the addition of a naval-maritime wing to the National Museum in New Delhi. Despite the claims to an ancient maritime past that goes back to about 4000–6000 B.C., there was no dedicated maritime museum in India barring the few naval museums outside of Delhi. This lacuna was partially redressed by the addition of this new maritime wing to the National Museum in 1992.

However, there is a need to encourage greater specialist studies in Indian naval and maritime history in the first instance and then attempt an interdisciplinary study of the different strands that, taken collectively, will point to a more holistic understanding of the Indian past.

---

[2]   *Academic Perspectives* (New Delhi: Centre for Historical Studies, Jawaharal Nehru University, 1989), pp. 105, 106.

[3]   *Ibid.*, p. 113.

[4]   *Ibid.*, p. 118.

[5]   Rear Admiral Satyindra Singh, *Under Two Ensigns: The Indian Navy, 1945–50* (New Dehli: Oxford and IBH Publishing Company, 1985); Rear Admiral Satyindra Singh, *Blueprint to Bluewater: The Indian Navy, 1951–65* (New Delhi: Lancer International, 1992).

[6]   Rear Admiral K. Sridharan, *History of the Naval Dockyard Bombay—250 Years, 1735–1985* (Bombay: The Admiral Superintendent, Naval Dockyard, 1989).

14

Ireland

John E. de Courcy Ireland

The independent Irish State was set up in 1922 after centuries of unrest following the definitive English occupation of the island early in the seventeenth century. The Irish had always been a maritime people, and in the two centuries preceding the definitive English occupation, Irish seamen and shipowners were engaged in lively maritime commerce with England and Scotland, Portugal, Spain, France, the Netherlands, Germany, and Scandinavia. There is powerful evidence that as well as a variety of traditional–type vessels, Irish shipowners had ships of the most modern types available in Europe. The Irish sea fisheries were very rich and were frequented by continental as well as Irish fishermen. Some of them were fishing the Grand Banks by the 1550s, and the wealth of these fisheries was one of the reasons for the English government undertaking a final conquest of Ireland later in the sixteenth century.

Being divided into nearly one hundred petty principalities, with about a score of largely autonomous seaport towns and no centralized Irish authority, the Irish people had no navy or naval policy and only rudimentary systems of maritime law. In the past, a remarkable English seaman, Thomas Stucley from Devon, with ambitions to become a power in Ireland, was the first person to realize the strategic importance of Ireland. He presented Philip II of Spain with detailed ideas on the subject of Waterford as an ideal base for Spain to seize to exercise permanent strategic pressure on England. After Philip ignored the advice, Stucley fell out with the government in London and offered his services to Spain. Only Hugh O'Neill, leader in the last phase of resistance to the English invasion, understood the need to create an Irish state with a navy and merchant ships at its disposal.

Very few leaders of the numerous movements that arose in Ireland in the centuries after 1607 showed serious interest in the economic potential of Ireland's geographical situation, if it attained freedom, or in the end, was given independence, in some kind of naval defence forces, nor, indeed, in consideration of means, during a struggle for independence, to try to cope with the fact that the struggle was against the leading sea power in the world. In the final and successful phase of the independence struggle, only one leader, Arthur Griffith, had thought profoundly about the importance of the sea to an independent Ireland, and he died within a few months of the establishment of the new state.

Yet, throughout the centuries of English occupation and despite the imposition of restrictions, particularly on the development of the fisheries, an Irish maritime economy continued to function, given a particular boost by the arrival of maritime Protestant refugees from France in the late seventeenth and eighteenth centuries. Thousands of Irishmen served in the British Navy (probably 15 percent of its personnel were Irish over a long period) and in the merchant navy. Shipbuilding flourished in Ireland and hundreds of Irishmen distinguished themselves at sea in the navies of France, Spain, Portugal, the Netherlands, Austria–Hungary and in at least ten countries on the American continent, North and South.[1]

The state that was set up in 1922 introduced no legislation establishing an Irish merchant fleet; therefore, merchant ships registered in Irish ports continued to fly the British ensign until such legislation in September 1939, and no attempt was made to create a coast defence navy until August of that year.

Maritime history was ignored in the schools and in the universities to the point where, thirty years ago, the head of Ireland's oldest university, a historian, wrote publicly that Ireland had no maritime history or traditions. In the 1930s, with the likelihood of a world war growing closer, isolated individuals, all of whom were later to become active in the Maritime Institute of Ireland set up in 1941 to crusade for the creation of a strong Irish maritime economy and for the revival of Ireland's great maritime tradition, spoke out about the need to operate an Irish merchant navy and coast guard fleet and to revive the almost defunct fishing fleet. When, ten years ago, the Department of Defence archives were opened to the public, I was immediately shown a detailed document, marked Top Secret and evidently left to smoulder quietly in a pigeon hole for half a century, in which two officers of the Irish Army, on instructions from the Chief of Staff, demonstrated clearly what sort of coastal defence navy would be suitable for Ireland. They then reasoned that the provision of such a navy would be of little ultimate value unless a merchant navy and a revived fishing fleet also became part of policy. This document had never before seen the light of day nor awoken the smallest echo in political circles.

The 1939–45 war led to the improvisation of a navy, the establishment of an Irish merchant fleet, and the revival of the fishing fleet, though that did not really start to grow until 1962. Since then it has increased quite phenomenally in size and catching capacity in spite of a variety of problems associated with the over-fishing of Irish waters and the slow growth of the essential research work.

---

[1]   See for example, John de Courcy Ireland, "The Confederate States Navy 1861–1865: The Irish Contribution," *Mariner's Mirror*, 66 (August 1980), pp. 259–63 and "Irish Naval Connections in Brest in the Eighteenth and Ninteenth Centuries," *Irish Sword*, 17 (Summer 1987), pp. 57–60.

From its foundation, the Maritime Institute of Ireland,[2] an independent non-official body, has conceived the teaching of maritime history—general or even Irish—to be one of its absolute priorities. It runs regular lectures and occasional conferences on maritime historical topics, provides lectures for any organization, society, or college that requests one; has published books and pamphlets on both maritime history and actualities; and has since 1946 (though with a break of several years in the late 1960s) published, under different titles, a journal,[3] at first monthly, now quarterly, containing maritime historical information as well as information on maritime activities. The Institute has been able to interest the official radio–television station and several local radio stations in transmitting maritime historical material quite regularly. It has encouraged primary and secondary schools to allow students to specialize on maritime topics, although it has not yet persuaded the state educational authorities to recognize maritime history as a subject. The Institute has helped undergraduate and graduate students at Irish universities and at foreign ones, allowing them to choose maritime topics for degree theses, and it has enabled the Free University of Ireland, set up in Dublin in 1986, to offer annually a course in maritime history. Each of the country's local history societies is invited to study its own local maritime history and to invite a lecturer from the Institute. The Institute helped to found the Military History Society of Ireland in 1949 and has provided lecturers for its annual October–March lecture programme. Institute members have contributed frequently to its prestigious twice-a-year journal, *The Irish Sword*. In 1959 the Institute founded (and operates through volunteers as with all its other work) the non-state subsidized National Maritime Museum of Ireland, which presents a series of lessons on Irish and general maritime and naval history. Schools and learned societies that visit the museum are provided with a guide competent in maritime history.

The museum is affiliated with the International Congress of Maritime Museums and is represented at its triennial conferences. Members of the Institute form the Irish section of the International Conference of Maritime Historians and have provided papers at its conferences, which began in 1975 and are held every five years, as well as at conferences organized by the French and British sections. The Institute has helped in the last five years to persuade the universities at Cork, Limerick, and Belfast in Northern Ireland to consider seriously the introduction, in the next few years, of courses on maritime studies, including maritime history. It has also assisted in the establishment of a local maritime historical research center for Northwestern Ireland at Derry, Northern Ireland. The Institute can also take some credit for the fact that, whereas between 1948 and 1981 only one maritime book was published in Ireland, now three or four

---

[2] The Maritime Institute of Ireland, B. Donnelly, Hon. Sec., Haigh Terrace, Dun Laoghaire, Co. Dublin, Republic of Ireland.

[3] *The Irish Maritime Journal.*

are published annually. Ten books on maritime history published in Ireland in the last twelve years were either written or edited by Institute members.[4]

Outside of the Institute, whose members are all volunteers, Irish maritime history is taught to the cadets at the maritime division of Cork Regional Technical College (formerly the Irish Nautical College) by Captain Brunicardi, a staff member who has also written a history of the Irish Naval Service[5] and whose father, Commander Brunicardi, has written and lectured locally in West Cork on local maritime history.[6]

The officers of the Naval Service[7] receive rather elementary education in the history of their service and some very sketchy international naval and maritime history as part of their training. Occasional arrangements are made for officers, cadets, or seamen to attend lectures by Captain Brunicardi; but, apparently, unless they do courses abroad (at which some have excelled) Irish naval officers are not adequately educated about naval history.

Other than the Institute and its members on the Free University staff, no academics in Ireland teach these subjects, though some good economic historians do deal with aspects of maritime history inevitably (and quite well), and moves are being made for the academics who run the archives at Cork to start propagating maritime history based thereon. Some fishery history is taught at the fine Fisheries Training College, Greencastle, County Donegal.

There is no coordination of Irish maritime studies. The innate and more or less unconscious anti-British bias with which history is generally approached in Ireland tends to be nullified by the fact that outside the Institute maritime history is dealt with in English and from British sources. The periods least covered are probably the medieval, eighteenth, nineteenth, and twentieth centuries. Most help is needed in the post-medieval field in getting at the vast amount of archival material which we know to be available in the National, Cork city, and Northern Ireland archives, and in archives abroad (e.g., France, Britain, Portugal, Spain, the United States and the Netherlands), where Institute members have identified material and done much preliminary work on it. The gulf between naval and general maritime history is not great as presented in Ireland, and it should be possible to prevent its swelling when the study of maritime history in Ireland becomes better organized and less elementary.

A very recent and very welcome development was the Argentine Navy's invitation to the Irish Naval Service to send one of its most promising young Irish officers on a training cruise in the famous Argentine naval sail-training ship,

---

4   Among recent works, see for example, John de Courcy Ireland, *Ireland and the Irish in Maritime History* (Dun Laoghaire: Glendale Press, 1986) and *Ireland's Sea Fisheries: A History* (Dublin: Glendale Press, 1989); Nicholas Rossiter, *Wexford Port: A History* (Wexford: Wexford Council of Trade Unions, 1989).

5   *A History of the Irish Naval Service* (Haulbowline: Naval Base, 1989), 10 pages.

6   For example, Niall Brunicardi, *Haulbowline, Spike and Rocky Islands in Cork Harbour* (Fermoy, n.d.).

7   See Thomas A. Adams, *Irish Naval Service* (Kendal, Cumbria: World Ship Society, 1982).

the *Libertad*. The invitation followed, but may not have been inspired by, a long lecture tour in the autumn of 1993 by the Maritime Institute's research officer, author of the soon-to-be published first English-language biography of the Irishman, William Brown (1777–1857), founder of the Argentine Navy. In 1922, Argentina was the first country to recognize the separate Irish state. Irish Naval Service officers have been trained in Britain, but it is hoped that this first serious contact with another naval tradition may become permanent. Meanwhile, the Irish Navy's ships are kept busy protecting, with their insufficient numbers, Irish and European fishery zones from frequent intruders, varied from time to time with a visit abroad, notably to revictual Irish military units on peace-keeping duty in the eastern Mediterranean basin.

15

Israel

Meir Sas, Nadav Kashtan, and Sarah Arenson

Geographical and historical factors give Israel an important role to play in the contacts between the two seafaring systems, the Red Sea and Indian Ocean on the one hand, the Mediterranean and the Atlantic Ocean on the other.[1] Since the days of King Solomon and his maritime expeditions in the South seas, through the maritime exploits of the Hasmonean Kings and Herod's Caesarea Maritima, to the tragedy of the Great Jewish Revolt against Rome, there was a sound link between the land, the people, and the sea.

After the destruction of the Second Temple, the Talmud and other literary sources point out the continuity of Jewish maritime activity in the diaspora. All through the Middle Ages, and especially under Charlemagne, the Jews carried on a vast maritime, commercial network. They shared in the development of astronomy and cartography prior to the period of the great discoveries, fought Spain along with the Barbary corsairs, and were among the first settlers in the New World.

The rise of the Jewish national movement at the end of the nineteenth century changed radically the situation of the Jewish people. Nevertheless, agriculture took the lead at first, and there was no awareness of the sea until the 1930s. During those years, the first attempts were made to train Jewish mariners at Riga in Latvia and Civitavecchia in Italy.[2] These first attempts were superseded by the Haifa Nautical School of Technology, which later moved to Acre to become the still active Israel Nautical College. In 1936 a new port was built in Tel Aviv, due to the Arab Revolt and the difficulties in using the ports of Jaffa and Haifa.

The British Mandate on the land of Israel (1918–1948) put severe restrictions on Jewish immigration. During those years, especially in the last four years of British rule, illegal immigration by sea, which had already started in the 1930s, took on growing proportions. There are many written works that deal with this period, offering general descriptions and monographs of particular ships and

---

[1] The first portion of this essay is by Dr. Meir Sas of the Israeli Nautical College, Acre. Dr. Sas passed away on 26 July 1993. His two coauthors dedicate this chapter to his memory.

[2] J. Halperin wrote about his experience in his book in Hebrew, *The Renaissance of Jewish Seamanship* (Tel–Aviv: Hadar, 1962).

actions, but due to the authors' general ignorance of conditions at sea, they do not contribute much to the analysis of Jewish, illegal, maritime immigration as a historical phenomenon during this period.

In those years, the prevalent opinion was to strengthen the maritime inclination of the people through the study and revival of old traditions. The first historical essay was by R. Patai and dealt with Biblical and Talmudic times, 700 B.C. to A.D. 700.[3] N. Slouschaz wrote another historical study, centering around Carthage and the Phenico-Punic achievement,[4] and S. Tolkowsky wrote a general history of Jewish involvement in naval affairs.[5]

Since the moment that the State of Israel was declared on 15 May 1948, it started fighting for its existence. The same vessels that had served the immigrants were converted to form the nucleus of the new marine corps of the Israel Defence Forces. The role of the Navy in the Israel War of Independence was summed up by E. Tal[6] in the best work on any of the Israeli Defence Forces' naval operations, which, since then, have been covered only by journalistic essays in various Hebrew language military and naval magazines. The *Encyclopedia of Army and Security* has published one volume dedicated to the Navy, but it consists mainly of pictures accompanied by a short text.[7]

Meir Sas has published many short articles on the history of seafaring and naval affairs, including translations from the classics such as A.T. Mahan's *The Influence of Sea Power upon History*. He has also written a monograph on the history of Acre.[8] As there are no textbooks in Hebrew for the general history of seafaring and sea power, Dr. Sas has compiled several textbooks for high school and naval college students.[9]

Z. Herman is another prolific writer of maritime themes in Hebrew. Most of his books deal with the ancient world,[10] but he has dealt also with modern Jewish commercial shipping.[11] His most recent book deals with the history and challenge of oceanography.[12]

---

[3] R. Patai, *Jewish Seafaring in Ancient Times, a Contribution to the History of Palestinian Culture* (Jerusalem: Mass, 1938) in Hebrew.

[4] N. Slouschaz, *The Book of the Sea* (Tel Aviv: 1948) in Hebrew.

[5] S. Tolkowsky, *They Took to the Sea* (New York: Yoseloff, 1964).

[6] E. Tal, *Naval Operations in the Israeli War of Independence* (Tel Aviv: Ministry of Defence Publications, 1964) in Hebrew.

[7] *Zahal Beheilo* (Tel Aviv: Revivim, 1982) in Hebrew.

[8] Meir Sas, *Maritime Acre* (Acre: Israel Nautical College, 1981) in Hebrew.

[9] Meir Sas, *The Book of the Sea* (Haifa: Renaissance, 1970) and *Oars and Sails* (Jerusalem: Ministry of Education, 1973). His most recent book is *Seapower through the Ages* (Jerusalem: Ministry of Defence Publications, 1991) in Hebrew.

[10] For example, Z. Herman, *Man and the Sea* (Haifa, 1979); *People, Seas and Ships* (Tel Aviv: Massada, 1964) and *Carthage, A Maritime Empire* (Tel Aviv: Massada, 1963) in Hebrew.

[11] Z. Herman, *History of Hebrew Shipping* (Tel Aviv: 1978) in Hebrew.

[12] Z. Herman, *The Depth of the Sea* (Haifa: 1985) in Hebrew.

The Academy of the Hebrew Language has summarized the professional, linguistic innovations that maritime activity has brought to Hebrew.[13]

Haifa University Center for Maritime Studies[14]

The Leon Recanti Center for Maritime Studies at the University of Haifa was established in 1972. Guided by an interdisciplinary concept, the center conducts and promotes research projects which encompass man's activities relating to the sea, bringing to light what was known in the past, man's involvement in the present, and what man can accomplish by using the sea in the future. By combining disciplines, such as history, archaeology, earth sciences, and marine resources, the Center has found a way of bridging between humanities, sciences, and technology. This is reflected in the graduate program of the Department of Maritime Civilizations, initiated by the Center for Maritime Studies in the framework of the Faculty of Humanities.

The Department of Maritime Civilizations offers courses that aim to broaden and deepen the historical, archaeological and geographical knowledge of cultures, people, countries, and coastal settlements whose history and development were or are affected by the sea. Emphasis is placed on maritime activities and interrelations in the Mediterranean and the Red Sea. These courses include subjects such as: history of naval power, coastal and marine archaeology, development of ships in antiquity, navigation and seamanship, ancient harbors, marine ecology and geology.

The National Maritime Museum in Haifa

Founded forty years ago, the National Maritime Museum in Haifa, Israel celebrated the twentieth anniversary of the opening of its current, 1972 purpose–built facility. The Museum grew out of the significant personal collection of Arie L. Ben–Eli, who at the time in 1953 was a lieutenant commander in the Israeli Navy. By the end of the following year, the museum had been turned over to the Haifa Municipality with the full support of the Israel Maritime League. Its first premises were on one floor of the League's building near the port of Haifa. Arie L. Ben–Eli became its first Director.

Soon a familiar pattern emerged. As the collections grew, the facility became overcrowded, while interest and demand grew for a proper museum building that could do justice to the museum's programs. This was finally built and opened in 1972. Named the National Maritime Museum, Haifa, the new museum aimed at establishing itself as the major maritime museum in Israel. It has achieved its goal, while attracting substantial donors along the way.

---

13 *Dictionary of Maritime Terms, Hebrew–English–French–German* (Jerusalem: The Academy of the Hebrew Language, 1970).

14 The following section is by Dr. Nadav Kashtan, Director, of the National Maritime Museum, Haifa.

The overall theme of the museum is the "History of Seafaring," which is presented in two complementary ways: chronologically and through the illumination of specific themes. The chronological approach has four main periods: ancient seafaring, seafaring in the Middle Ages, modern seafaring, and present–day shipping. This history is richly illustrated by artifacts acquired by the museum or donated by collectors. Objects which are relevant to ancient and medieval seafaring have come primarily from underwater archaeological activity. These artifacts include anchors, storage jars, statuettes, terra–cotta oil lamps, and ancient coins. An important core of the museum's collection is a large number of ship models. Sub-themes have also been developed which include: geography, including discoveries and cartography; economics, including maritime trade, types of ships and cargoes; science and engineering, including warships and naval battles; and art and culture, including the development of coastal cities and ports along with the relationships between peoples.

The museum has produced a number of temporary exhibits that have travelled within Israel and abroad. A wide range of educational programs are offered, and a university course on the "Maritime History of Israel in Antiquity" is held in cooperation with Haifa University. The first two Directors, Arie Ben–Eli and Joseph Ringel, created an active publication program and produced several monographs,[15] but most important of all is the scholarly journal *Sefunim*, of which eight volumes have been published since 1966.

The museum has a research library of over 5,500 volumes and subscribes to a number of periodicals. Over 190 periodical titles are represented in the collection.

The current director's goals are to maintain the museum's excellent standing among the world's maritime museums and to continue the development and expansion of its collections and programs. Construction of a new floor of exhibition space is planned. The museum also needs to strengthen its finances and to introduce environmental controls in the entire building.

Maritime Research and Activity in Israel[16]

The following is a list of marine-related institutions and activity centers in Israel:

The National Maritime Museum in Haifa exhibits ancient seafaring from Pharaonic times to the end of the Middle Ages and modern shipping. Special items include The Athlit ram, Jewish ship graffiti, anchors and amphoras

---

[15] A. Ben–Eli, ed., *Ships and Parts of Ships on Ancient Coins* (Haifa: National Maritime Museum, 1975); A. Zemer, *Storage Jars in Ancient Sea Trade* (Haifa: National Maritime Museum, 1977); D. Avrahami, *Eskimo and N.W. Indian Art at the Maritime Museum, Haifa* (Haifa: National Maritime Museum, 1979); and J. Ringel, *Marine Motifs on Ancient Coins* (Haifa: National Maritime Museum, 1984).

[16] The following section was compiled by Mrs. Sarah Arenson, Director of the Man and Sea Society, Israel.

discovered by marine archaeology, Greek Fire containers, figurines of sea-goddesses, and coins with marine symbols. The museum has a fine collection of old maps of the Holy Land and its shores, as well as rare nautical instruments.

The Museum of Illegal Immigration, also in Haifa and adjacent to the National Maritime Museum, is concerned with Jewish seaborne immigration to Israel, mostly between the Second World War and the establishment of the State of Israel.

The National Oceanographic and Limnological Institute in Haifa conducts basic and applied research, mainly in marine geology, biology, and chemistry. It cooperates in international projects such as MAP and other regional plans concerned with marine resources and pollution. It has a branch on the Lake of Galilee and another on the Red Sea, in Eilat. Its publications include annual conference reports and special issues in English.

The Fisheries Research Institute is centered in Haifa, as well, and conducts field research projects in the Eastern Mediterranean and brackish waters along the coast. The Ministry of Agriculture has a central research institute, Vulcani, which is also involved with fishing experimentation. Its publications are in Hebrew.

The Research Institute of Shipping and Aviation is concerned with the planning of ports, the economics of shipping, the welfare of seamen, and weather problems. It is located at Haifa University. Its publications are mostly in English with a few in Hebrew.

Zim Shipping company has its own research unit located in Haifa and publishes its work in Hebrew.

The Technion, Israel Technological Institute, has a naval engineering laboratory, which conducts research in port engineering and the architecture of ships. Its reports are published mostly in English.

The Hyperbaric Medicine Institute (M.R.I) is affiliated with the Navy and situated at the Rambam Hospital in Haifa. It does both basic and applied research in all aspects of physiology and medicine related to the sea, on the surface and underwater, and treats both civil and military cases. Its publications are in English.

The Center for Maritime Studies at Haifa University is occupied with academic and applied research in all fields concerned with man and sea relations, such as marine archaeology, marine biology, and oceanography. There is also a Department for the *History of Maritime Civilizations*, granting the master's degree. Publications in English and Hebrew.

Marine Biology Department at Tel Aviv University is academically active and, together with several other universities in the country, maintains a laboratory in Eilat. Its publications are in English and Hebrew.

The Center for Strategic Research is affiliated with Tel Aviv University and is involved also with naval affairs. Its publications are in Hebrew and English.

The Israeli Defence Forces Navy has an academic historical branch which conducts historical and practical research in naval affairs. Its publications are mostly in Hebrew and with restricted circulation.

In Jerusalem, the government *Geological Institute* has a marine section, which conducts surveys in all Israeli waters.

The Antiquities Authority has a marine section, situated at present in Kibbutz Neve-Yam, South of Haifa. It is concerned with guarding the coasts against damage to the cultural heritage and conducts surveys and salvage excavations as necessary. Its publications are in Hebrew and English.

The Society for the Preservation of Nature in Israel (SPNI) has a network of field-schools, several of which are marine related, such as the ones at Akhziv, Maagan-Michael, and Eilat, as well as Kinrot and Yarkon. It publishes *Eretz* magazine, in English.

The Man and Sea Society of Israel is concerned with educational programs for the youth and the wider public. It has initiated a major TV series, "The Encircled Sea: Mediterranean Maritime Civilization," a British-Israeli joint venture production. Among other projects, there is an innovative high-school program of maritime studies and a summer course, "A Maritime Experience in Israel."

16

Twentieth Century Italy

Brian R. Sullivan

An understanding of the present state of Italian naval and maritime history benefits from a review of the context in which such history has been and is being researched and written. Perhaps most useful for American readers in this regard are some relevant comparisons between Italy and the United States. Such comparisons involve both material and non-material factors.

Perhaps the most significant physical factors involve considerable differences in scale between the United States and Italy. Italy is considerably smaller in terms of territory and population than the United States. Furthermore, their national income makes contemporary Italians somewhat less wealthy on a per capita average than Americans. More relevant is the fact that, while the gap between average individual incomes in the United States and Italy has narrowed considerably in the last twenty years, previously, Americans enjoyed a far higher standard of living, particularly before 1960. Certainly the differences between Italian and American national geography are likely to remain permanent. The Republic of Italy covers 301,000 square kilometers, with a coastline of about 5,000 kilometers long, entirely within the Mediterranean; the territory of the United States is over thirty-one times larger and includes a coastline of almost 20,000 kilometers on the Atlantic, Pacific, and Arctic Oceans and the Gulf of Mexico. In mid-1993, the Italian population reached 58 million, while that of the United States rose to nearly 257 million. In 1991, the American gross domestic product was $5.695 trillion, Italian GDP for that year was about $1.099 trillion. The Italian merchant marine numbers about 1,600 vessels of some 8 million gross tons, while that of the United States counts over 6,300 vessels of nearly 20 million gross tons.[1]

But ratios in favor of the United States are even more imbalanced when navies are compared. Proportionately, the United States has far outspent Italy on defense, even when differences in size of populations and economies are taken into consideration. The following table compares American outlays on defense

1   Central Intelligence Agency, *The World Fact Book 1992* (Washington: 1992), pp. 167–69, 358–60; International Monetary Fund, *International Financial Statistics August 1993* (Washington: 1993), pp. 304, 556.

with Italian defense budgets in the 1985 to 1991 period, each expressed in billions of dollars.

Year	Italy	United States
1985	8.6	245.2
1986	9.8	265.5
1987	13.4	274.0
1988	16.1	282.0
1989	16.7	294.9
1990	19.6	289.8
1991	19.7	262.4

Even with the marked decrease in American defense spending and the doubling of Italian defense spending over the past decade, the Italian government expends far less per capita on its armed forces than does the American government. At present, Americans spend about 5.7 percent of their GNP on defense, Italians about 2.2 percent.[2] These disparities are reflected in the different sizes of the two national navies.

In mid-1993, the United States Navy numbered about 515,000 and the U.S. Marine Corps about 180,000, for a total of roughly 695,000 men and women. In comparison, the Italian Navy and Marine Corps comprised some 54,500 personnel. True, the U.S. Navy is expected to decline from its present strength of 452 ships to about 340 by 1999; the Italian Navy is expected to retain its present strength, thanks to a healthy building and replacement program. However, this will maintain the Italian Navy at only about 60 major warships and support vessels. In addition, the U.S. Navy not only vastly outweighs the Italian Navy in numbers of warships but in size of warships. At present, the U.S. Navy has 23 ships of over 39,000 tons full-load displacement in commission, compared to just two ships of over 9,000 tons in the Italian Navy. Even with the coming decommissioning of a number of the largest American warships and the construction of a second Italian light aircraft carrier and several large destroyers, these differences in scale between the two navies will remain indefinitely.[3]

A glance at the history of the American and Italian navies emphasizes the smaller and less prominent role of the latter in its nation's development. The United States came into existence in 1776 and fought ten major wars over the next 215 years. Its navy took a significant part in every conflict and had a major role in at least seven. Perhaps more important, the American Navy established a highly favorable reputation during the first decades of its existence, as a result of its actions during the Revolution, the Quasi-War with France, the naval campaign against the Barbary Pirates and, most of all, the War of 1812. The

[2] The International Institute for Strategic Studies, *The Military Balance 1986–87* (London: 1986), p. 70; *ibid.: 1987–88*, p. 68; *ibid.: 1988-89*, p. 69; *ibid.: 1989–90*, p. 67; *ibid.: 1990–91*, p. 71; *ibid.: 1991–92*, p. 63; *ibid.: 1992–93*, pp. 17, 49; *The World Factbook 1992*, pp. 169, 360.
[3] Richard Sharpe, ed., *Jane's Fighting Ships 1993–94* (London: 1993), pp. 321–40, 753–802.

exploits of Paul Jones, Biddle, Barry, Truxton, Preble, Bainbridge, Decatur, Hull, Lawrence, Stewart, Perry, and Macdonough and their sailors helped create the worshipful attitude of the American people toward their navy that has sustained its popularity ever since. Equally important for maintaining interest in and support for the U.S. Navy were American naval actions after the early nineteenth century, especially during the Civil War, the Spanish American War and, of course, the Second World War. Such successful campaigns have encouraged a strong interest in American naval history among both the general public and the scholarly community.

The Italian naval tradition offers a rather stark contrast. Following its unification in 1861, Italy engaged in seven major wars in which six involved naval activity but only four in a major way.[4] In contrast with the history of the U.S. Navy, the early decades of the Italian Navy proved extremely difficult. Its first war in 1866, the short mid-summer conflict with Austria, ended in the disastrous Italian naval defeat at Lissa, marred by the incompetence of the Italian commander, Admiral Carlo Persano, and the treachery and cowardice of his subordinates, Admirals Giovanni Battista Albini and Giovanni Vacca. Thereafter, the Italian Navy experienced no significant wartime action until 1911, although draining its impoverished nation of significant resources to little practical end until the turn of the century. While the subsequent history of the Italian Navy offers numerous examples of heroism, Italy's only major victorious naval conflict came to an end in 1918, and its last serious naval conflict ended in humiliation in September 1943 with the surrender of its battle fleet. At the moment of its capitulation in World War II, the Italian Navy enjoyed its all-time maximum size: 259,000 officers and men. In contrast, the United States Navy reached a maximum strength of 3.4 million in 1944–45, joined with a U.S. Marine Corps of 475,000.[5]

These facts help explain Italian political and psychological attitudes toward their navy and merchant marine, as well as the limited degree of general Italian interest in the history of these institutions. In brief, Italians have shown and continue to exhibit far less fascination with their naval and maritime history than do Americans with their own. But the major negative influence on the Italian attitude in these regards—indeed on the Italian attitude toward almost all public institutions—comes from widespread perceptions of the defunct monarchy and of the Fascist regime, culminating in the disasters of 1940–45. Such attitudes

---

[4]   The Italian Navy engaged in considerable action in the Italian–Turkish War of 1911–12; World War I, 1915–18; Italian intervention in the Spanish Civil War, 1936–39; World War II, 1940–43 (as well as providing some naval assistance to the Allies in 1943–45). The Italian Navy fought one losing battle in the war of 1866 with Austria and provided major naval support in the Italian–Ethiopian War of 1935–36, without engaging in hostilities.

[5]   For a survey of Italian naval history, see the relevant portions of Lucio Ceva, *Le forze armate* (Turin: 1981).

have created additional obstacles to the pursuit of naval and maritime history in Italy.

Throughout the first eighty-odd years of Italian unification, despite severe national poverty, the state spent very heavily on its armed forces. Well into the twentieth century, the House of Savoy and the ministers who served it relied on the army to hold together a kingdom whose subjects felt little sense of nationalism. In turn, the royalist officer corps was expected not only to provide internal security but to enhance the prestige of the monarchy and the weak sense of Italian nationalism by waging expansionist wars. In the mid–1880s, with the enthusiastic support of the monarchy, Italy founded an African empire and began a series of foreign wars that were to last until 1943. Naturally, the establishment of an overseas empire stimulated the expansion of the Italian Navy. In the 1860s, spending on the Navy amounted to only 22 percent of spending on the Army. By the 1890s, following the creation of the Italian colonial empire, that percentage had expanded to 39 percent. In the first decade of the twentieth century, thanks to a surge in national industrialization and wealth, spending on the Italian Navy rose to 51 percent of military spending. It remained on roughly that level until the Second World War.[6]

As much as such oppressive military and naval spending burdened the subjects of the Kingdom of Italy, it could be justified to some degree by Italian successes in the Italian-Turkish War of 1911–12 and, especially, the First World War. But the arms spending of the Fascist dictatorship from the mid–twenties onward reached unprecedented levels, crushing the ordinary Italian under an array of ever–mounting direct and indirect taxes. Simultaneously, Italians were bombarded by hysterical militarist and navalist propaganda in support of such spending. Such propaganda efforts included considerable official support for highly subjective naval historical publications and navalist sloganeering at every level of the Italian school system. The argument of national prestige was also enlisted in support of the expansion of the Italian merchant marine, devastated by submarine warfare in the Great War, and the construction of such giant trans-Atlantic ocean liners as *Rex* and *Conte di Savoia*.

The monarchy maintained an attitude of reserve toward some aspects of the Fascist regime and, as a means of self-protection, remained closely associated with the highly royalist officer corps. But the approval of the naval officer corps for the Fascist regime's large program of naval and maritime construction and the bestowal of many monarchist names on the Italian vessels built in the 1920s and 1930s necessarily linked the House of Savoy with Mussolini's navy in the public mind.

---

[6] For statistics on Italian naval spending, see Giorgio Rochat and Giulio Massobrio, *Breve storia dell'esercito italiano dal 1861 al 1943* (Turin: 1978). Despite its title, the book deals with all the Italian armed forces.

By 1940, the Fascist dictatorship had constructed a navy roughly the same size as the French Navy but—due to autarkist economic policies and officially-tolerated corruption—at about twice the expense it should have cost, in a country of approximately half the wealth of France.[7] When these sacrifices were followed by the humiliating Italian naval defeats of 1940–41, the loss of the colonial empire, the destruction of most of the merchant marine, the surrender of the battle fleet to the British in September 1943 and the ruinous war fought up the length of the Italian peninsula in 1943–45, it is no wonder that the Italians abolished their monarchy in 1946 and rejected with disgust the legacies of the Fascist era. Among that baggage was excessive navalism and heavy official support for naval and maritime history. Such attitudes continued to affect very negatively the study of those areas of Italian history for the next several decades. The fact that in the generation after 1945 a certain number of historians who could be described as ex-Fascist or neo-Fascist continued to work in the fields of military and naval history made it difficult for others to write on those subjects and to be judged objectively.[8]

The end of the Cold War, Italy's rise to third in rank among the European economies, and the simultaneous earthquake shaking the Italian political system marks the end of what may be called the post-Fascist period of Italian history. While it is too soon to state with certainty, a greater degree of Italian national assertiveness and of Italian willingness to deploy armed force abroad will probably become evident over the next few decades. In fact, such tendencies have been discernible for the past ten years or so and have stimulated a growing interest in Italian naval and maritime history.[9] The study of such history, long tainted by its unfortunate association with the Fascist regime, has already begun a modest revival since the 1970s. Nonetheless, while these areas of Italian history will almost certainly benefit from growing official and public support in the future, the present state of their study is hardly robust.

---

[7]   For a detailed examination of aspects of corruption in the naval shipbuilding industry under the Fascist regime, see Lucio Ceva and Andrea Curami, *Industria bellica anni trenta. Commesse militari, l'Ansaldo ed altri* (Milan: 1992).

[8]   For an appraisal of the influence of domestic politics on Italian historiography since 1945, see chapter 6, "The eclipse of anti-Fascism in Italy," of R.J.B. Bosworth, *Explaining Auschwitz and Hiroshima. History Writing and the Second World War 1945–1990* (London & New York, 1993).

[9]   One recent example of increased national pride in naval accomplishments is the renaming of two Italian destroyers, completed in 1992–93. The names originally to be given to these ships were *Animoso* and *Ardimentoso*. Before commissioning, however, they were renamed *Luigi Durand de la Penne* and *Francesco Mimbelli*.
       Durand de la Penne was the commander of the two-man guided torpedo that sank HMS *Valiant* in Alexandria harbor in December 1941. Mimbelli commanded the torpedo boat *Lupo*, which engaged three British light cruisers at point-blank range and escaped while escorting a German troop convoy to Crete in May 1941. Mimbelli later led motor torpedo boat flotillas in many legendary actions in the Black Sea and off Sicily against Soviet and British forces. See Marc'Antonio Bragadin, *The Italian Navy in World War II* (Annapolis: 1957), pp. 108–9, 269, 278, 284–6, 301; Callum MacDonald, *The Lost Battle: Crete 1941* (New York: 1993), pp. 237–42; *Jane's Fighting Ships 1993–94*, p. 326.

Within the Italian university system, the teaching of naval and maritime history has been limited recently to only two schools, the Universities of Pisa and Rome, and to two scholars, the highly respected Mariano Gabriele and his student, Alberto Santoni. For many years earlier in this century, the University of Rome had a chair in naval history and policy, held by the illustrious expert on World War I at sea, Camillo Manfroni.[10] After the Second World War, Manfroni was effectively succeeded by Gabriele. However, since Gabriele was and remains a civil servant in the Ministry of Finance, he has been forbidden under Italian law from being an official professor at the University of Rome and has been only an *incaricato* (adjunct). Since such a position within the Italian university system has been abolished recently, it is now legally impossible for Gabriele to go on teaching at the University of Rome. Barring the unexpected, when Santoni eventually retires from the University of Pisa, the teaching of naval and maritime history may well cease there. In fact, officially, Santoni holds a chair in military history and technology and will probably be succeeded by a scholar of land warfare.

The situation within the Italian Navy educational system is slightly better. The Italian Naval Academy at Livorno offers a three-year course in naval history and policy taught by Commander Pier Paolo Raimono. In effect, Raimono has attempted to carry on the work initiated by Camillo Manfroni at the University of Rome. In this effort Raimono collaborates closely with Alberto Santoni, aided by the proximity of the Livorno Academy and the University of Pisa. Raimono is attempting to expand his course to four years. However, most of the subject matter covered by Raimono involves the naval and maritime history of other countries, rather than of Italy.

The Istituto di Guerra Marittima, also located on the grounds of the Italian Naval Academy, is roughly equivalent in purpose and functioning to the U.S. Naval War College. That is, the Istituto di Guerra Marittima offers both a junior and senior course, corresponding to the command and staff college level and the war college level. For these courses, Commander Raimono teaches a one-year course in naval strategy and history, with somewhat greater emphasis on Italian matters than is the case for his courses at the Naval Academy. However, the stress on the above-mentioned course at the Istituto di Guerra Marittima is on naval strategy, rather than history. Raimono has succeeded in getting a number of prominent Italian military and naval historians to give guest lectures at the Italian Naval War College and to expand the teaching of Italian naval history there. However, given the politically sensitive nature of many aspects of of Italian naval history, Raimono has encountered difficulties. In fact, many of his students

---

[10] Manfroni's most significant published works include *La marina militare durante la guerra mondiale* (Bologna: 1923); *I nostri alleati navali* (Milan, 1927); *Storia della Marina italiana durante la guerra mondiale 1915–1918* (Bologna: 1933).

seem to have a greater knowledge of the naval history of Britain or the United States than of their own country.

The schools of the Italian Army and Air Force largely ignore naval history, whether that of Italy or of other nations. The two-year Italian Military Academy at Modena has abolished the teaching of the history of ground, sea, or air warfare. When the graduates of the academy at Modena pass on to the two-year Scuola di Applicazione at Turin, they receive a one-year course in military history that includes a modest naval component. However, this is limited to such points as a passing mention of the battles of Trafalgar, Jutland, or Midway. The Italian Army War College (Scuola di Guerra) at Civitavecchia offers a one-year course in military history. Naval history is covered by an annual conference with lectures by a few naval officers. Neither the Italian Air Force Academy nor the Italian Air War College offers any naval history whatsoever.

Italy has no equivalent of the U.S. Merchant Marine Academy, although it does have a number of government high school-level vocational schools for mariners. The University of Naples offers a program in maritime studies that provides roughly the type of education available in the United States from Kings Point. However, in none of these schools is Italian maritime history taught, except for passing references.

In pleasant contrast to the state of the teaching of naval history is the status of Italian Navy official history. Such history falls under the jurisdiction of the Ufficio Storico della Marina Militare (USMM). The archives and publication service of the USMM are located in Rome, at present under the able direction of Admiral Renato Sicurezza.

The Navy historical archives are undoubtedly the best organized and most accessible of the three Italian services. They are devoted to the history of the Italian Navy since the amalgamation of the Sardinian and Neapolitan Navies in 1861, obviously covering only the age of steam. Utilizing teams of professional archivists and historians, the USMM directorate is completely reorganizing the archive and creating comprehensive finding aids as it progresses through its huge collection of documents. The USMM staff is extremely knowledgeable and very helpful. Probably the only serious criticism that one can make of the USMM archive is its lack of adequate photocopying services.

Two other archives in Rome also contain much material relevant to Italian naval and maritime history. The Archivio Centrale dello Stato in the EUR suburb holds the records of the Naval Ministry, the Merchant Marine Ministry, and also the records of cabinet discussions that sometimes touched on naval matters, Air Ministry records from the Fascist period that occasionally deal with relations with the Navy, and records of the Fascist-era Ministry of Communications that controlled ports and the merchant marine. The archives of the Foreign Ministry are located separately in the Foreign Ministry office and contain diplomatic records of naval and disarmament conferences. Both these archives are quite well ordered and researchers can have access to good finding aids.[11] However, those using such archives must be prepared to deal with the frustrating practices of the Italian bureaucracy, especially those of its lowliest members.

The publications of the USMM are generally well researched and of high quality, although they are devoted almost exclusively to technical and narrative questions. The single most impressive of the USMM publications remains its excellent twenty-three-volume history of the Italian Navy in World War II, *La marina italiana nella Seconda Guerra Mondiale*, published between 1950 and 1988 (including revisions of earlier volumes). The value of this massive work lies in its objectivity, accuracy, thoroughness and honesty of self-appraisal. It stands in striking contrast to the Navy's eight-volume official history of World War I (published under the heavy hand of Fascist censorship in 1935–42), to the Italian Army's official history of its operations and activities in World War II—the earlier volumes of which fall so short of historical objectivity that newer volumes are being produced to supercede the older—and to the Italian Air Force historical effort, which has never even issued an official history of the 1940–45 period that it has been willing to publish.

Much of the credit for the success of the Italian Navy's official history of World War II should go to Admiral Giuseppe Fioravanzo, the director of the USMM at the time of its publication. Admiral Fioravanzo was himself the author of a number of the twenty-three volumes and ensured the adherence of the entire project to the high standards that he laid down. Fioravanzo was ably assisted in the project by its other authors, notably Carlo De Risio, Aldo Cocchia, and P.F. Lupinacci. It is a pleasure to note that Admiral Sicurezza has restored the USMM to that same high level of performance.

Admiral Sicurezza is also president of the Commissione Italiana di Storia Militare, which is in the process of publishing a series of volumes entitled *L'Italia in Guerra*, on the history of Italy in the Second World War. These volumes, one for each year of Italian participation in the conflict, are resulting from annual conferences that began to be held in 1990. Each volume explores topics of considerable depth and breadth, going beyond the operations of the three services to include strategy, diplomacy, civil-military relations, propaganda, industrial production, weapons design and procurement, intelligence, logistics and German-Italian relations.

It is to be hoped that such an approach to official history will be reflected in future USMM publications in general. For too long even its best publications have been rather narrowly focussed. The USMM can be rightly proud of Giovanni Bernardi's massive work, *Il disarmo navale fra le due guerre mondiali* (1975) or Ezio Ferrante's short but excellent *La grande guerra in Adriatico* (1987). Nonetheless, both studies would have benefitted from a greater and more frank

---

[11] For the records of the naval and merchant marine ministries, see *Guida generale degli Archivi di Stato Italiani* (Rome: 1981), vol. 1, pp. 179–93.

analysis of related political and strategic questions. The naval historical office has recently issued a long-awaited monograph on a previously taboo subject: Mario Bargoni, *L'impegno navale italiano durante la Guerra Civile Spagnola (1936–1939)* (1992). In many ways, Bargoni's book is admirable, offering the first complete narrative of Italian naval operations in the Spanish Civil War, revealing many previously unknown facts and offering a candid assessment of the Navy's tactical, operational, and technical weaknesses. However, again there is a disappointing lack of strategic and political discussion and a failure to place Italian naval activities within the broader context of international naval, military, and diplomatic developments.

One hopes for the appearance of USMM publications on the development of Italian naval doctrine, strategic thinking, and warship design akin to such official Italian Army publications as Filippo Stefani, *La storia della dottrina e degli ordinamenti dell'esercito italiano* (1984–85); Ferruccio Botti and Virgilio Ilari, *Il pensiero militare italiano dal primo al secondo dopoguerra* (1985), and Lucio Ceva and Andrea Curami, *La meccanizzazione dell'esercito fino al 1943* (1989). Mariano Gabriele has produced such monographs for the USMM on the earlier years of the Italian Navy: *Le convenzioni navali della Triplice* (1969) and in collaboration with Giuliano Friz (Fritz): *La flotta come strumento di politica nei primi decenni dello stato unitario* (1973), and *La politica navale italiana dal 1885 al 1915* (1984). But there is a serious scholarly need for similar studies on the period of World War I, of Mussolini's expansion of the Italian Navy in the 1920s and 1930s, the naval aspects of the Italian-German alliance, and the Italian Navy as part of NATO's southern flank forces.[12]

Of indisputable merit is the USMM's quarterly *Bollettino d'Archivio dell'Ufficio Storico della Marina Militare*, which has been published since 1987. Each 300 to 400-page issue is divided into two sections. One describes a section of the USMM archives and provides a detailed finding aid, the result of the ongoing reorganization and indexing project. (Eight recent issues provide a complete guide to the archive's holdings related to the Spanish Civil War.) The other section of each *Bollettino* contains fine scholarly articles on various aspects of post-1861 Italian naval history, often accompanied by complete documents.

Of related interest are the historical publications of the official Italian naval journal, *Rivista Marittima*, which are produced under the overall direction of Admirals Vincenzo Pellegrino and Francesco Pascazio. *Rivista Marittima* itself usually contains at least one historical article in each issue. However, such articles are aimed at Italian naval officers in general and are not always of the same high

---

12 However, USMM has published Mariano Gabriele, *Operazione C.3: Malta* (1965) on the strategic and operational planning for the aborted Axis seizure of Malta in mid-1942. Also useful in regard to Italian Navy strategy in World War II is the Italian Army Historical Office publication of the transcripts of the chiefs of staffs discussions during their 1939–43 meetings: Stato Maggiore dell'Esercito, Ufficio Storico, *Verbali delle riunioni tenute dal capo di SM Generale*, 3 vols. (Rome: 1982–85).

scholarly quality as those that appear in the *Bollettino*. On the other hand, one or more times a year, *Rivista Marittima* is accompanied by usually superb historical supplements in the same format as the journal. Among such supplements are Ezio Ferrante's short but illuminating biography, *Il Grande Ammiraglio Paolo Thaon di Revel* (1989), his examination of all-too-neglected subjects, *Il potere marittimo. Evoluzione ideologica in Italia, 1861–1939* (1982), and *Il pensiero strategico navale in Italia* (1988), and Erminio Bagnasco and Achille Rastelli's *Le costruzioni navali italiane per l'estero* (1991).

Beyond official publications, a fair number of Italian books and articles on Italian naval history have appeared since 1945. Most are popular and only a few scholarly; the majority, as might be expected, devoted to the Second World War period. However, recently, publications devoted to naval and maritime history prior to 1915 have appeared in increasing volume. Until the last twenty–five years or so, the general quality of such works was not very high, with the exception of the studies and memoirs of Admirals Alberto Da Zara, Vittorio Tur, Romeo Bernotti, and Angelo Iachino, and the work of Mariano Gabriele.[13] Recently, however, as one sign of the revival of Italian military and naval history, a number of good studies have been published. These include the books and articles of the above-mentioned Alberto Santoni, Lucio Ceva, Andrea Curami, Ezio Ferrante, as well as Walter Polastro, Giorgio Giorgerini, Matteo Pizzigallo and Francesco Mattesini.[14] Admittedly, some twenty or so Italians working in the field is not many. In fact, as an indication of the number of Italians devoted

---

[13] Alberto Da Zara, *Pelle d'ammiraglio* (Milan: 1949); Vittorio Tur, *Plancia ammiraglia*, 3 vols. (Rome: 1958–63); Romeo Bernotti, *Cinquant'anni nella marina militare* (Milan: 1971); idem., *Storia della guerra nel Mediterraneo 1940–43* (Milan: 1960); Angelo Iachino, *La campagna navale di Lissa, 1866* (Milan: 1966); idem., *Le due Sirti* (Milan: 1953); idem., *Gaudo e Matapan* (Milan: 1946); idem., *Il punto su Matapan* (Milan, 1969); idem., *La sorpresa di Matapan* (Milan, 1962); idem., *Tramonto di una grande marina* (Milan, 1959). In addition to Gabriele's works cited elsewhere in this article, noteworthy are his *La politica navale italiana dall'Unità alla vigilia di Lissa* (Milan: 1958) and *Da Marsala allo stretto. Aspetti navali delle campagne di Sicilia* (Milan: 1961).

[14] Among the more important publications of these authors not already cited are: Alberto Santoni, *Il vero traditore. Il ruolo documentato di ULTRA nella guerra del Mediterraneo* (Milan: 1981); idem., *La seconda battaglia della Sirte* (Rome: 1982); idem., *Da Lissa alla Falkland: storia e politica dell'eta contemporanea* (Milan: 1987); idem., "Strategia marittima ed operazioni navali dell'anno 1940" in *L'Italia in guerra, il primo anno—1940* (Rome: n.d. [but 1991]); Francesco Mattesini, *Il giallo di Matapan* (Rome: 1985); idem., *La battaglia di Punto Stilo* (Rome: 1990); Santoni and Mattesini, *La participazione tedesca alla guerra aeronavale nel Mediterraneo* (Rome: 1980); Lucio Ceva, "L'evoluzione dei materiali bellici in Italia" in Ennio Di Nolfo, Romain Rainero and Brunello Vigezzi, eds., *L'Italia e la politica di potenza 1938–1940* (Milan: 1985); Ezio Ferrante, "Un rischi calcolato? Mussolini e gli ammiragli nella gestione della crisi di Corfù" in *Storia delle relazioni internazionali*, no. 2, 1989; idem., "L'ammiraglio Lais, Roosevelt e la 'beffa' delle navi" in *Storia delle relazioni internazionali*, no. 2, 1991; Walter Polastro "La marina militare nel primo dopoguerra, 1918–1925" in *Il Risorgimento* no. 3, 1977; Giorgio Giorgerini, *La battaglia dei convogli in Mediterraneo* (Milan: 1977); idem., "La preparazione e la mobilitazione della Marina italiana nel giugno 1940" in *L'Italia in guerra, il primo anno—1940* (Rome: n.d. [but 1991]); idem., "Il problema dei convogli e la guerra per mare" in *L'Italia in guerra, il secondo anno—1941* (Gaeta, 1992); Matteo Pizzigallo, "L'Italia alla conferenza di Washington (1921–1922)" in *Storia e Politica* July–September and October–December 1975.

to naval and maritime history of all kinds, the International Naval Research Organization lists only about seventy–five Italian members.

However, one other group of Italians deserve to be mentioned as enthusiasts of Italian naval and maritime history: the Associazione Italiana di Documentazione Marittima e Navale (AIDMEN) and the Associazione Navemodellisti Bolognesi. Together, these organizations number about 250 members and are devoted to preserving photographs of ships and original builder's plans, building models, and publishing books and articles on ship designs. Prominent among these passionate experts are the famous Aldo Fraccaroli, as well as Erminio Bagnasco, Giorgio Giorgerini, Augusto Nani, Franco Gay, Elio Andò, Achille Rastelli and Gino Galuppini, each of whom has written one or more books on merchant or naval ship design, construction or armament.[15] All these men have aided USMM over the years in its superb publications devoted to the specifications of Italian naval vessels and have authored many of them. Such work constitutes more the raw material for naval and maritime history rather than the heart of such studies, but it deserves mention for the painstaking care that has gone into its creation. Italian research and publication on ship design—perhaps reflecting Italian superiority in design of all kinds—is of particularly high quality.

Italian maritime history has been advanced by an extensive series of excellent publications subsidized by the Istituto per la Ricostruzione Industriale (IRI), the government holding agency created by the Fascist regime in 1933, which still plays a huge role in the Italian economy. IRI also maintains an extensive and well-ordered archive in Rome devoted to the history of Italian industry, especially the state-sponsored naval armaments, steel and shipbuilding industries, and the government-supported Italian ports. In contrast to the publications of the USMM, IRI's volumes have been devoted to Italian shipyards, ports, maritime and naval industries, and seaborne commerce from the end of the Napoleonic period to the present. V. Marchese, Mariano Gabriele, Fulvio Babudieri, and L.A. Pagano have all produced volumes notable for their detail, accuracy and careful research.[16] Equally excellent private scholarship on the history of the

---

15 Aldo Fraccaroli, *Italian Warships of World War I* (London: 1970); idem., *Italian Warships of World War II* (London: 1968); Erminio Bagnasco, *Submarines of World War Two* (London: 1977); idem., *Le armi delle navi italiane nella seconda guerra mondiale* (Parma: 1978); Erminio Bagnasco and Elio Andò, *Navi e marinai italiani nella seconda guerra mondiale* (Parma: 1977); Erminio Bagnasco and Mark Grossman, *Italian Battleships of World War Two* (Missoula, Mont.: 1986); Erminio Bagnasco and Achille Rastelli, *Le costruzioni navali italiane per l'estero* (Rome: 1991); Giorgio Giorgerini and Augusto Nani, *Gli incrociatori italiani 1861–1964* (Rome: 1964); idem., *Le navi di linea italiane 1861–1961* (Rome: 1962); Franco Gay with Elio Andò and Franco Bargoni, *Orizzonte mare. Navi italiane nella seconda guerra mondiale*, 14 vols. (Rome: 1972–79); Franco and Valerio Gay, *The Cruiser Bartolomeo Colleoni* (London & Annapolis, 1987); Gino Galuppini, *Guida alle navi d'Italia. La marina da guerra dal 1861 ad oggi* (Milan: 1982).

16 V. Marchese, *L'industria armatoriale italiana dal 1815 al 1859* (Rome: 1955); idem., *L'industria ligure delle costruzioni navali dal 1815 al 1859* (Rome: 1957); idem., *Il porto di Genova dal 1818 al 1891* (Rome: 1959); Mariano Gabriele, *L'industria armatoriale nei territori dello stato pontificio dal 1815 al 1880* (Rome: 1961); idem., *L'industria delle costruzioni navali nei territori dello stato pontificio dal 1815 al 1880* Rome,

Italian merchant marine, shipbuilding, maritime law and, of particular, Italian ports was pioneered by Arturo Assante after the First World War.[17] More recently, such work has been continued and expanded (to include studies of the seafarers' union and maritime law, among other subjects) by Vito Dante Flore, Tomaso Gropallo, Francesco Ogliari, Ennio Poleggi, Guglielmo Salotti, Pasquale B. Trizio, and Ludovica De Courten.[18] Thanks in particular to the work of Gabriele in the area of Italian maritime history, there has been an unusual and happy integration of naval and maritime history in Italy. Whatever other criticism can be fairly leveled at IRI, its support of such scholarship deserves high praise.

Outside of Italy, few historians have paid much attention to that country's naval and maritime history. What work has been done has been almost exclusively limited to the period from the Italian–Turkish War to the end of World War II and often in the context of Italian naval activities in alliance with or in conflict with other powers. Paul G. Halpern deserves special mention for his studies of the Mediterranean naval situation from 1908 to 1918.[19] Other Americans include MacGregor Knox, James Sadkovich and the author.[20] Also,

1961); idem., *I porti dello stato pontificio dal 1815 al 1880* (Rome: 1963); Fulvio Babudieri, *L'industria armatoriale di Trieste e della regione giulia dal 1815 al 1918* (Rome: 1966); idem., *I porti di Trieste e della regione giulia dal 1815 al 1918* (Rome: 1967); L.A. Pagano, *L'industria armatoriale siciliana dal 1816 al 1880* (Rome: 1966).

[17] Arturo Assante, *Il porto di Napoli* (Naples: 1938); idem., *La funzione mediterranea del porto di Napoli* (Naples: 1941).

[18] Vito Dante Flore, *L'industria dei trasporti marittimi in Italia, 1860–1943* (Rome: 1970); idem., *L'inserimento nei mercati internazionali* (Rome: 1973); idem., *Le emergenze nazionali* (Rome, 1973); Tomaso Gropallo, *Navi a vapore ed armamento italiano dal 1818 ai nostri giorni* (Milan: 1976); Francesco Ogliari, *Trasporti marittimi di linea*, 7 vols. (Milan: 1975–87); Ennio Poleggi, *Porto di Genova: Storia e attualità* (Genoa: 1977); Guglielmo Salotti, *Giuseppe Giulietti: il sindicato dei marittimi dal 1910 al 1953* (Rome: 1982); Pasquale B. Trizio, *La marineria a vapore del Levante d'Italia 1876–1932* (Bari: 1983); Ludovica De Courten, *La Marina mercantile italiana nella politica di espansione, 1860–1914: industria, finanza e trasporti marittimi* (Rome: 1989).

[19] Paul G. Halpern, *The Mediterranean Naval Situation, 1908–1914* (Cambridge, Mass.: 1971); idem., *The Naval War in the Mediterranean, 1914–1918* (London: 1987).

[20] MacGregor Knox, *Mussolini Unleashed 1939–1941. Politics and Strategy in Fascist Italy's Last War* (New York: 1982); idem., "The Italian Armed Forces, 1940–3" in Allan R. Millett and Williamson Murray, eds., *Military Effectiveness*, vol. III, *The Second World War* (Boston: 1988); James Sadkovich, "Aircraft Carriers and the Mediterranean: Rethinking the Obvious " in *Aerospace Historian*, December 1987; idem., "Re-evaluating Who Won the Italo–British Naval Conflict, 1940–42" in *European History Quarterly* October 1988: idem., "The Italian Navy in World War II: 1940–1943" in Sadkovich, ed., *Reevaluating Major Naval Combatants of World War II* (Westport, Ct.: 1990); Brian R. Sullivan, "Prisoner in the Mediterranean: The Evolution and Execution of Italian Maritime Strategy, 1919–1942" in William B. Cogar, ed., *Naval History. The Seventh Symposium of the U.S. Naval Academy* (Wilmington, Del.: 1988); idem., "A Fleet in Being: The Rise and Fall of Italian Sea Power, 1861–1943" in *The International History Review*, February 1988; idem., "The Italian Armed Forces, 1918–1940" in Millett and Murray, op. cit., vol. II, *The Interwar Period*; idem., "The Strategy of the Decisive Weight: Italy, 1882–1922" in Williamson Murray, Alvin H. Bernstein, and MacGregor Knox, eds., *The Making of Strategy* (New York, 1993); "Italian Naval Power and the Washington Disarmament Conference of 1921–1922" in *Diplomacy & Statecraft*, Fall 1993.

the French Pierre Barjot, Jean Savant, and Raymond De Belot stand out for their work several decades ago on the naval aspects of the Second World War in the Mediterranean.[21] The Germans, Michael Salewski, Walter Baum, and most of all, Gerhard Schreiber deserve praise for their more recent studies, as do Josef Schroder and Jürgen Rohwer for their more specialized research.[22] In the area of Italian ship design and construction, Siegfried Breyer, Robert O. Dulin, Jr., and William H. Garzke, Jr., have published outstanding work.[23]

This brief survey of the state of Italian naval and maritime history indicates that much work in the field remains for the future, particularly in naval history. To begin with, there is no truly adequate history of the Italian Navy. Fioravanzo's *La marina militare nel suo primo secolo di vita 1861–1961* (Rome, 1961) and Giuliano Colliva's *Uomini e navi nella storia della marina militare italiana* (Milan, 1971) are the best available. But neither are sufficiently detailed nor analytical, nor based on primary research, nor on extensive use of foreign sources. Both are also outdated, even in regard to recent Italian publication in the field.

Scholarly biography, until recently, has not been emphasized in any area of Italian history. This is certainly true in regard to Italian naval history. Carlo Persano, Simone de Saint-Bon, Benedetto Brin, Augusto Riboty, Carlo Mirabello, Vittorio Cuniberti, Giovanni Bettolo, Giovanni Sechi, Luigi di Savoia, Paolo Thaon di Revel, Alfredo Acton, Costanzo Ciano, Umberto Pugliese, Giuseppe Sirianni, Domenico Cavagnari, Arturo Riccardi, Angelo Iachino, Inigo Campioni, and Romeo Bernotti all deserve modern, detached biographies. Ezio Ferrante has written a short study of Brin[24] and the previously mentioned brief biography of Thaon di Revel. Recently, Aldo Santini has published a biography of Costanzo Ciano that covers his naval career to some extent.[25] Otherwise, with the exception of the short, although generally excellent, sketches and bibliographies that have appeared in the forty–odd volumes

---

[21] Pierre Barjot and Jean Savant, *Histoire mondiale de la Marine* (Paris: 1961); Raymond De Belot, *La guerra aeronavale nel Mediterraneo 1939–1945* (Milan: 1971).

[22] Michael Salewski, *Die deutsche Seekriegsleitung 1935–1945*, 3 vols. (Frankfurt am Main & Munich, 1970–75); Walter Baum, *Der Krieg der "Achsenmächte" im Mittelmeer-Raum. Die "Strategie" der Diktatoren* (Ottingen, Zurich & Frankfurt am Main: 1973); Gerhard Schreiber, "Italien im machtpolitischen Kalkul der deutschen Marinefuhrung 1919 bis 1945" in *Quellen und Forschungen aus italienischen Archiven und Bibliotheken*, no. 62, 1982; idem., *Revisionismus und Weltmachtstreben. Marinefuhrung und deutsch-italienische Beziehungen 1919 bis 1944* (Stuttgart: 1978); idem., "Die Seeschlacht von Matapan" in *Marineforum*, no. 50, 1975; Gerhard Schreiber et al., *Das Deutsche Reich in der Zweite Weltkrieg*, vol. 3, *Der Mittelmeerraum und Südosteuropa: Von der 'non belligeranza' Italiens bis zum Kriegseintritt ver Vereinigten Staaten* (Stuttgart: 1984); Josef Schroder, "Weicholds Plane zur Aktivierung der Seekriegfuhrung im Jahre 1943" in *Wehrwissenschaftliche Rundschau*, no. 19, 1969; Jürgen Rohwer, *Axis Submarine Successes 1939–1945* (Annapolis: 1983).

[23] Siegfried Breyer, *Battleships and Battle Cruisers 1905–1970* (Garden City, N.Y.: 1973); William H. Garzke, Jr. and Robert O. Dulin, Jr., *Battleships. Axis and Neutral Battleships in World War II* (Annapolis: 1985).

[24] Ezio Ferrante, *Benedetto Brin e la questione marittima italiana 1866–1898* Rome, 1983).

[25] Aldo Santini, *Costanzo Ciano, il ganascia del fascismo* (Milan: 1993).

of the far from completed *Dizionario Biografico degli Italiani* (Rome, 1960–)(up to the "Ds" so far) and the even shorter entries by MacGregor Knox and the author in Philip V. Cannistraro's *Historical Dictionary of Fascist Italy* (Greenport, Ct.: 1982), all the above-mentioned major Italian naval figures lack objective studies of their lives.

A third aspect of Italian naval history that has been neglected is the period since 1945. Given the Italian political situation described above, this is to be expected. Bernardi's monograph for the USMM on the naval aspects and consequences of the 1947 peace treaty, the latter parts of Admiral Franco Maugeri's two books of memoirs, Enea Cerquetti's Marxist analysis of the Italian armed forces, 1945–1975, and Elizabeth MacIntosh's unpublished doctoral dissertation on Italian naval arms sales and foreign policy, 1949–89, are the only major works known to the author.[26] The revelations that have emerged in recent months about the degree of corruption that has tainted relations between the Italian government and private industry will probably expand to Italian shipyards and naval armaments firms. If true, this would present yet another impediment to the study of recent Italian naval history.

For those interested in seeing Italian naval history, Venice provides its excellent Museo Storico Navale. The museum is only a short walk from St Mark's cathedral and illustrates the naval history of both Venice and of modern Italy.

The gaps in Italian naval and maritime historiography have been mentioned above. The most serious appears to be the near-total neglect of the teaching of naval and maritime history in Italian universities. Given Italy's re-emergence as a major power in the Mediterranean region, the Balkans, and in the European Community, and given the likely diminution of American naval power in the waters surrounding Italy, it is very much in the interest of Italian democracy that Italy's citizens understand such aspects of their nation's history. Over the last dozen years, Italian naval forces have returned to taking a major role in Italy's foreign policy, making operational deployments to the Suez Canal and the Red Sea, to the waters off Lebanon, Libya and Somalia, to the Persian Gulf and to the coastlines of Albania and Croatia. Given the turbulence in North and East Africa, the Middle East, and Eastern Europe, such Italian naval operations seem likely to increase in future. Italy's citizens seem on the brink of remaking their nation's politics and of creating a new, far more accountable system of government. While it is presumptuous for a non-Italian to so state, to make wise

---

[26] Giovanni Bernardi, *La marina, gli armistizi e il trattato di pace, settembre 1943-dicembre 1951* (Rome: 1979); Franco Maugeri, *From the Ashes of Disgrace* (New York: 1948); idem., *Ricordi di un marinaio. La Marina italiana dai primi del Novecento al secondo dopoguerra nelle memorie di uno dei suoi capi* (Milan: 1980); Enea Cerquetti, *Le forze armate italiane dal 1945 al 1975* (Milan: 1975); Elizabeth MacIntosh, "Italy: Defense Industries and the Arms Trade, 1949–1989," Ph.D. dissertation, University of Edinburgh, 1989.

decisions about their national security, it would be best for Italians to have a far better knowledge of their naval and maritime past and present.[27]

―――――――――
[27] In the writing of this article, the author has relied heavily on two publications of the *Centro Interuniversitario di Studi e Ricerche Storico-Militare* of the Universities of Padua, Pisa, and Turin: *La storiografia militare italiana negli ultimi venti anni* (Milan: 1985) and *Bibliografia italiana di storia e studi militari 1960–1984* (Milan: 1987). In addition, he wishes to express his gratitude for help from his friends Lucio Ceva, Willard C. Frank, Jr., and Paul G. Halpern.

Comments on Brian Sullivan's "Twentieth Century Italy"

James J. Sadkovich

Dr. Sullivan has presented an excellent paper on those Italian archives, authors, and publications that are concerned with contemporary naval and maritime history. He has raised a number of issues, including the question of whether the Italian peninsula's naval and maritime history is synonymous with twentieth-century Italy's naval and maritime history or should it also include those of the maritime republics of the late medieval and early modern periods as well as those of the pre-*Risorgimento* navies of Naples, Sardinia, Venice, and Tuscany.[1]

Italians have certainly been preoccupied with the role of the *Regia Marina* since unification, and they have debated its performance during the Fascist *ventennio* and World War II in numerous books and articles, including such popular histories as those by Arrigo Petacco and Gianni Rocca. That Rocca's book, *Fucilate gli ammiragli* [*Shoot the Admirals*] was published in 1987 and reissued in 1990 as one of Monadadori's popular Oscar Storia series indicates that there is a large public for such offerings, and its title, like that of Di Sambuy's *Match pari fra due grandi flotte* [*Drawn Match between Two Great Fleets*], hints at the polemical nature of the historiography on World War II. The publication over the past two decades of a large number of technical and scholarly studies on World War II and the fascist era by both academics and former naval officers demonstrates that if the Italians have not adopted a "worshipful attitude" toward their navy, they certainly are interested in recent naval history.[2]

At the same time, there is also an interest in ancient and early modern naval and maritime history, and there appears to be a public for books on such subjects as

---

[1] This essay is an expanded version of the remarks that I made during the Conference on Naval and Maritime Affairs and contains a number of observations that I neglected to make in June. I have tried to retain the spirit of my comments, while including bibliographic information and interpretive comments precluded in an oral presentation. Both Dr. Sullivan and I concentrated on contemporary naval and maritime history, much to the distress of Dr. Hervé Coutau–Bégarie, who correctly observed that Italian naval and maritime history extends far beyond the twentieth century. I have therefore alluded to works on the medieval and modern period as well. The bibliographic notes are not comprehensive, but are intended to serve as a guide to recent publications, many of which have excellent bibliographies.

[2] Gianni Rocca, *Fucilate gli ammiragli: la tragedia della Marina italiana nella seconda guerra mondiale* (Milan: Mondadori, 1987, 1990) and *La battaglia di Matapan* (Milan: Mondadori, 1985); and Arrigo Petacco, *Le battaglie navali del Mediterraneo nella seconda guerra mondiale* (Milan: Mondadori, 1977). The interest in recent naval history has tended, perhaps properly, to blur the lines between amateur enthusiast and professional historian and to move popular and academic history closer together.

maritime archaeology and folklore.[3] There are also strong regional and local organizations, such as the Centro Veneto per le Ricerche Storiche, which launched a new journal, *Ricerche Venete*, in December 1989, and the University of Genoa's *Istituto di Medievistica*, which has published a number of studies on Genoa and Liguria, including a series of volumes that deal with everything from early modern business women (*donne d'affari*), to deserters, pirates, foreign affairs, and Genoese colonies in the Black Sea.[4] The Institute has also published a number of studies dealing with the history of Liguria, among them Laura Balletto's interesting collection of essays on piracy, fishing, and port operations.[5]

It is therefore no surprise that the Italians have continued their tradition of publishing popular and scholarly works on maritime centers such as Ancona,[6] Carrara,[7] Florence and Tuscany,[8] Genoa,[9] Manfredonia,[10]

---

[3]   For example, Attilio Della Porta, *Marina di Vietri: Storia, vicende, folklore* (Cava dei Tirreni: Arti Grafiche Palumbo & Esposito, 1984); Peter Throckmorton, *Atlante di archeologia subacquea: la storia raccontata dal mare: dall'Oddissea di Omero al Titanic* (Novara: Istituto Geografico De Agostini, 1988); Anna Maria Crinò's edition of Petruccio Ubaldini, *La disfatta della flotta spagnola, 1588: due commentari autobiografi inediti* (Florence: L. S. Olschki, 1988). Also see Elizabeth Bostwick Shuey, *Etruscan Maritime Activity in the Western Mediterranean c. 800–400 B.C.: An Archaeological Perspective on Historical Interpretations* (Ph.D., University of California at Santa Barbara, 1982). For the importance of archaeology to Italians during the early 1900s, see Maria Petricoli, *Archaeologia e Mare Nostrum* (Rome: Valerio Leri, 1990).

[4]   Istituto di Medievistica, *Miscellanea di storia ligure*, vols. I and IV (Genoa: 1958, 1966), vols. II and III (Milan: 1961, 1963); *Miscellanea di storia ligure in onore di Giorgio Falco*, (Milan: 1962 and 1966); *Miscellanea di studi storici* (Genoa: 1969); *Miscellanea di storia italiana e mediterranea per Nino Lamboglia* (Genoa: 1978); *Miscellanea di storia savonese* (Genoa: 1978). The *Centro per la Storia della Tecnica del Consiglio Nazionale delle Ricerche (Sezione 4)*, has published *Studi di storia navale* (1975).

[5]   Laura Balletto, *Genova nel Duecento: uomini nel porto e uomini sul mare* (Genoa: 1983) is volume 36 of the Institute's Collana storica di fonti e studi. Also see her *Battista de Luco mercante genovese del secolo XV e il suo cartulario* (Genoa: 1979), and *Mercanti pirati e corsari nei mari della Corsica* (Genoa: 1978). Among the more recent publications by the Institute are G. Airaldi, *Studi e documenti su Genova e l'oltremare* (Genoa: 1974); M. L. Balletto, *Navi e navigazione a Genova nel quattrocento. La "Cabella marinariorum" (1482–1491)* (Genoa: 1973); and G. Forcheri, *Navi e navigazione a Genoa nel Trecento. Il "Liber Gazarie"* (Genoa: 1974).

[6]   Alberto Caracciolo, *Le port franc d'Ancône: Croissance et impasse d'un milieu marchand su XVIIIe siècle* (Paris: SEVPEN, 1965), and *Francesco Trionfi: capitulista e magnate d'Ancona* (Milan: Giuffrè, 1962).

[7]   Antonio Bernieri, *Il porto di Carrara* (Genova: Sagep, 1983), a volume in the Collana I Manufatti series.

[8]   The recent works by Cesare Ciano, footnote 81, below, and Camillo Manfroni's early study, *La marina militare del granducato mediceo* (Rome: Forzani & C., 1895).

[9]   Mario Bottaro, *Genova 1892 e le celebrazioni colombiane* (Genoa: F. Pirella, 1984); Georg Caro, *Genova e la supremazia sul Mediterraneo, 1257–1311* (Genoa: Società Ligure di Storia Patria, 1974); Giovanni Forcheri, *Navi e navigazione e Genova nel Trecento*, op. cit., Antonino Ronco, *Genova tra Massena e Bonaparte: storia della Repubblica ligure, il 1800* (Genoa: Sagep, 1988). Also B. Z. Kedar, *Mercanti in crisi a Genoa e Venezia nel '300* (Rome: 1981), and Camillo Manfroni, *Banco di Genova* (Genoa: A. Donath, 1911); and Anita Ginella Capini, Enrica L. Aronica, and Maria G. Buscaglia, eds., *Immagini di vita tra terra e mare: la Foce in età moderna e contemporanea, 1500–1900: mostra storico–documentaria* (Genoa: Azione Cattolica S. Zita, 1984), an exhibition held in Genoa from 31 May to 8 June 1984.

[10]   Vincenzo Gennaro Valente, *Manfredonia: Storia della città di Manfredi* (Rome: Manzella, 1986).

Massa,[11] Messina,[12] Milan,[13] Naples,[14] Sardinia,[15] Taranto,[16] Trieste,[17] and Venice.[18] Genoa hosted two international congresses on maritime history over the last decade,[19] Ancona held a conference on Zara and other Yugoslav cities,[20] and even Lake Como has its historians.[21] Authors such as Gino Galuppini,[22] Marc'Antonio Bragadin,[23] Ezio

---

[11] Stefano Giampaoli, *Vita di sabbie e d'acque: il litorale di Massa, 1500–1900* (Massa: Palazzo di S. Elisabetta, 1984).

[12] R. Battaglia, *Mercanti e imprenditori in una città marittima. Il caso di Messina* (Milan: Giuffrè, 1992).

[13] Milan functioned as an inland port, whose superb canals made it a major commercial center. Giuseppe Codara, *I navigli della vecchia Milano* (1977). For a general history, Domenico Sella, *Il Ducato di Milano dal 1535 al 1796* (Turin: UTET, 1984).

[14] Among the many works on Naples and Sicily, Antonio Calabria, *The Cost of Empire: The Finances of the Kingdom of Naples in the Time of Spanish Rule* (New York: Cambridge Univ. Press, 1991).

[15] Giorlamo Sotgiu, *Storia della Sardegna sabauda, 1720–1847* (Rome: Laterza, 1984).

[16] Giacinto Peluso, *Taranto, 1919–1953: una città, un monumento: cronaca, fatti, personaggi* (Taranto: Mandese, 1984); Giuseppe Mataluno, "Cenni storici sull'arsenale M. M. di Taranto," *Rivista marittima* (1986).

[17] For example, Fulvio Babudieri's many works, e.g., *Industrie, commerci e navigazione a Trieste e nella regione Giulia dall'inizio del Settecento ai primi anni del Novecento* (Milan: Giuffrè, 1982), *La funzione dell'emporio marittimo di Trieste nell'ambito della Monarchia absburgica nell'Ottocento* (Milan: 1980), *Il porto di Trieste nel quadro della politica absburgica dell'Ottocento* (Innsbruck, 1977), *I porti di Trieste e della regione Giulia dal 1815 al 1918* (Rome: 1965), *L'industria armatoriale di Trieste e della regione Giulia dal 1815 al 1918* (Rome, 1964), and *La nascita dell'emporio commerciale e marittimo di Trieste* (Genoa: 1964). Also Spiridione P. Nicolaidi, *La presenza greca a Trieste* (Triest: B & MM Fachin, 1990); Gottfried von Banfield, *L'aquila di Trieste: l'ultimo cavaliere di Maria Teresa narra la propria vita* (Triest: LINT, 1984) (originally published in German as *Der Adler von Triest: der letzte Maria-Theresien-Ritter erzahlt sein Leben* (1984).

[18] For example, the late Roberto Cessi's *Venezia ducale* (Venice: Deputazione di Storia Patria per la Venezia, 1963), *Studi sul Risorgimento nel Veneto* (Padua: Liviana, 1965), and *Storia della Repubblica di Venezia* (Milan/Messina: G. Principato, 1968); and Armando Lodolini's, *Le repubbliche del mare* (Rome: Ente per la Diffusione e l'Educazione Storica, 1967), part of the Biblioteca di Storia Patria series. Also Thomas F. Madden's recent dissertation, *Enrico Dandolo: His Life, His Family, and His Venice before the Fourth Crusade* (Ph.D., University of Illinois at Urbana–Champaign, 1993); Frederic Chapin Lane's classic history, *Venice. A Maritime Republic* (Baltimore: Johns Hopkins Univ. Press, 1973), published in Italy as *Storia di Venezia* (1978), vol. 137 of the Biblioteca di Cultura Storica. Lane's bibliography is still useful.

[19] Raffaele Belvederi, ed., *Atti del congresso internazionale di studi storici. Rapporti Genova—Mediterraneo—Atlantico nell'età moderna* (Genoa: Prima Cooperativa Grafica, 1982).

[20] S. Anselmi, ed., *Sette città jugo–slave tra Medioevo e Ottocento* (Ancona: Quaderni di Proposte e ricerche, 1991). The "seminario" was held in September 1989 and focused on a number of cities, including Zara.

[21] *L'idea del lago: un paesaggio ridefinito, 1861–1914* (Milan: G. Mazzotta, 1984), was published on the occasion of an exhibition on Lake Como.

[22] In addition to *Guida alle navi d'Italia dal 1861 a oggi* (Milan: Mondadori 1982), Gino Galuppini has published *La bandiera tricolore nella Marina sarda* (Rome: Ufficio Storico della Marina Militare, 1987), "La scuola per i sottufficiali della marina borbonica," *Rivista marittima* (1985), and "Lo schnorchel è una invenzione italiana," *Rivista marittima* (1975).

[23] Marc'Antonio Bragadin's *Le repubbliche marinare* (Milan: Mondadori, 1974) is a popular, illustrated history of Venice, Pisa, Genova, and other maritime republics prior to Venice's capitulation to Napoleon in 1797. It has neither bibliography nor notes, but does have a definite nationalist bias that credits the Italian republics with writing "many of the most luminous chapters" of human history, notes that Europe is indebted to Venice for repelling the Turks and insists that the spirit of the early modern republics lives on in today's Italian mariners.

Ferrente,[24] and Lamberto Radogna,[25] have dealt with the Bourbon and Sardinian navies of the eighteenth and nineteenth centuries as well as those of the early modern maritime republics of Venice, Genova, and Pisa and the modern Italian Navy.[26]

But if early modern history is fairly robust, my impression, perhaps skewed by my own research, still is that contemporary naval history dominates Italian bookstores and that since 1945 relatively little has been done on the nineteenth and early twentieth centuries.[27] To the best of my knowledge, there is no organization comparable to the Italian Naval League, which popularized naval affairs from 1897 to the 1920s, although the Historical Office of the Italian Navy has done a great deal to keep naval and maritime history before the Italian public.[28] Such studies by historians, as those by Caracciolo on early modern capitalism in Ancona and by Babudieri on the shipbuilding industry in Triest, are notable, but more is needed on the development of maritime industries, ship design, and maritime law, and it is reassuring to know that IRI is sponsoring

---

[24] In addition to *Benedetto Brin e questione marittima italiana, 1866–1898* (Rome: Rivista Marittima, 1983) and *La sconfitta navale di Lissa* (Rome: Vito Bianco, 1985)., Ezio Ferrente has published "Romanze navali e guerre ipotetiche nel secolo XIX," *Informazioni parlamentari difesa* (1982), "August Vittorio Vecchj: lugotenente di vascello e storico della Marina," *Rivista marittima* (1972).

[25] Lamberto Radogna, *Cronistoria delle unità di guerra delle marine preunitarie* (Rome: Ufficio Storica della Marina Militare, 1981). This is an extremely useful listing of the ships of the various Italian navies prior to unification.

[26] Also Carlo Zaghi, *P. S. Mancini, l'Africa e il problema del Mediterraneo 1884–1885)* (Rome: Casini, 1955); and the numerous articles published in *Rivista marittima*, including Augusto De Toro, "La squadra austriaca prima e dopo Lissa: interessanti elementi da due immagini fotografiche," (1987); Nunzia Esposito Elefante, "La marina Sarda nella guerra di Crimea" (1986); Antonio Formicola and Claudio Romano. "L'industria navale nel regno delle due Sicilie sotto Ferdinando II" (1986), and "1860: Marina borbonica ultimo atto" (1984); Giovanni Macchi, "La marina italiana a Creta in una operazione multinazionale di fine ottocento," (1985); Arturo Marcheggiano, "Le operazioni navali italiane nella prima guerra di indipendenza (1848–49)" (1984).

[27] For example, Ferruccio Botti's articles in *Rivista marittima*: "Esercito e armata navale nel pensiero militare 'terrestre' dalla fine del secolo XIX all'inizio della prima guerra mondiale" (1987), "La 'correlazione terrestre marittima': un precedente italiano dell'attuale cooperazione interforce all'inizio del secolo XX" (1987), and "Aviazione navale in Italia agli inizi del secolo i un raffronto con le intuizioni precorritrici di Clement Ader" (1986). Botti has also published on armored forces and military doctrine with Nicola Pignato and Vicenzo Ilari. Also see Luigi Romani, *D'Annunzio e il mare* (Rome: Rivista Marittima, 1988) and Timothy W. Childs, *Mediterranean Imbroglio: The Diplomatic Origins of Modern Libya (The Diplomacy of the Belligerents during the Italo-Turkish War, 1911–1912)* (Ph.D., Georgetown University, 1982).

[28] The Lega Navale Italiana published an illustrated periodical, *La lega naval* (Florence, 1897–98, La Spezia, 1898–1901, Rome, 1901–19), as well as a number of studies on naval and maritime affairs. For example, the patriotic *The Adriatic Avenged: The Apotheosis of Nazario Sauro* (Rome: E. Armani, 1917) and *La marina italiana nella guerra mondiale, 1915–1918* (Rome: 1920). The League also published the *Album marinaresco* (Rome: 1914), as well as Luigi Castagna, *Dizionari Marnaro* (Rome: LNI, 1955) and Giuseppe di Maceo, *La battaglia di Lepanto e il mare di Gaeta* (Gaeta: Tipografia Salemne, 1930). For the League's official history, Angiolo Ponti, *Venticinque anni di vita della Lega navale italiana (1899–1924)* (Rome: LNI, 1924).

studies on maritime industries and commerce.[29] I agree with Dr. Sullivan that a great deal also needs to be done on the Italo-Turkish war of 1911–12 and World War I, both significant, if neglected, victories for the Italian Navy that were crucial to its development and affected the evolution of such naval weapons as MTBs, pioneered as Mas (*Motoscafi antisommergibili*) by the Italians.[30] Nor is there an abundant biographical literature on those who shaped and implemented Italian naval policy.[31] And even many official histories are now out of date.[32]

---

[29] Above for Babudieri and Caracciolo. The recent study that Dr. Sullivan has cited by Lucio Ceva and Andrea Curami has interesting data on naval weaponry and the scandal at Ansaldo in the 1930s; see *Industria bellica anni Trenta* (Milan: Franco Angeli, 1992). Also Michele Nones, "L'industria militare in Liguria da 1945 al 1975." *Storia contemporanea* (1986); Maria Ottolino, *Commercio e iniziativa marittima in Puglia, 1876–1914: la Società di navigazione a vapore Puglia* (1981); Donato Riccesi (1956–), *Gustavo Pulitzer Finali: il disegno della nave: allestimenti interni, 1925–1967* (1985); Valerio Staccioli, "Il linguaggio architettonico nel disegno della nave passeggeri: I. Dai transatlantici di Brunel agli anni venti." "II. Dagli anni trenta ai nostri giorni," *Rivista marittima* (1987). Also see Francesco La Saponara, *The Shipping Industry and Statistical Information in Italy: A Survey* (1986). For maritime law Riniero Zeno, *Storia del diritto marittimo italiano nel Mediterraneo* (Milan: Giuffrè, 1946), vol. 3 of the series Fondazione Vittorio Scialoia per gli Studi Giuridici and *Documenti per la storia del diritto marittimo nei secoli XIII e XIV* (1970/1936), vol. 4 of the series Documenti e Studi per la Storia del Commercio e del Diritto Commerciale Italiano; and Luigi Benvenuti, *La frontiera marina* (Padua: CEDAM, 1988), who examines the concept of territorial waters.

[30] Most of the studies on these topics are dated, e.g., Adolfo Balliano and Giuseppe Soavi, *L'Italia sul mare nella grande guerra* (Turin: Successore Loescher Ermanno, 1934); Capitano di Fregata Roncagli, *Guerra italo–turca. I. Dalle origini al decreto di sovranità su la Libia* (Milan: Hoepli, 1937); and Camillo Manfroni's works, *Guerra Italo–turca (1911–1912). Cronistoria delle operazioni navali* (Milan: Hoepli, 1918–26), which is the official history of the war; *Tripoli nella storia marinara d'Italia* (Padua: Drucker, 1911); *L'Italia nelle vicende marinare della tripolitania* (Intra/Verbania: A. Airoldi, 1935/1942); *Marina e aviazione italiane nella guerra mondiale* (Milan: F. Vallardi, 1937); and *Storia della marina italiana durante la guerra mondiale, 1914–1918* (Bologna: Zanichelli, 1923).

[31] Among the more recent works on early twentieth–century naval history are the two works Dr. Sullivan has cited by Paul Halpern, and E. Europoli, "La lega navale italiana," *Rivista marittima* (1980). Among the works that are now dated are those by Adolfo Balliano and Camillo Manfroni; Guido Po, *Il grande ammiraglio Paolo Thaon di Revel* (Turin: Lattes, 1936); Ettore Bravetta, *La grande guerra sul mare*, 2 vols. (Milan: Mondadori, 1925); Bernardo Melli, *La guerra italo–turca* (Rome: E. Voghere, 1914); Whitney Warren, *The Role of the Italian Navy in the Great War: A Lecture Given at the Colony Club, New York, 22 January 1920* (New York, 1920/microfilm); and A. Thomazi, *La guerre navale dans l'Adriatique* (Paris: Payot, 1927); and *La guerre navale dans la Méditerranée* (Paris: Payot, 1929).

[32] Most of the early histories tended to fall within the category of pamphlets and apologies more than scholarly analysis. *La Marina italiana* (Rome: Ministero della Marina, 1918), was only eleven pages long; *La marina italiana nella guerra mondiale, 1915–1918* (Rome: Ufficio Storico dello Stato Maggiore della Marina, 1920), only 84 pages; and *The Italian Navy in the World War 1915–1918. Facts and Figures* (Rome: Ufficio Storico della Regia Marina Italiana, 1927) was a defense of Italian naval operations during the war. Also see G. Almagià and A. Zoli, *La marina italiana nella grande guerra. I. Vigilia d'armi sul mare* (Florence: Vallecchi, 1935), published by the Office of the Chief of Staff of the Royal Italian Navy's Historical Section (Ufficio Storica dello Stato Maggiore della Regia Marina Italiana); and *Storia della campagne oceaniche della regia marina* (Rome: Ufficio Storico della Stato Maggiore della Regia Marina Italiana, 1936, 1960), 4 vols.

On the other hand, since the 1940s there has been a continual outpouring of literature on the fascist era, often of a polemical nature. Why this is so is not clear, but it certainly is due partially to the impression that the Italian fleet was largely intact when it surrendered in 1943, because it had elected to stay in port rather than fight during the war. But if a handful of cruisers and most battleships survived the war, few smaller vessels did so, because they played the major role in a war that was characterized by convoy, not fleet, operations. Nonetheless, the polemical conflagration that touched off efforts to assign blame for the apparent failure of the Navy to perform well during the war has been fuelled by the difficulty of reconciling antifascist postwar politics with a patriotism that was compromised by fascism during the *Ventennio*. As a result, there is a massive literature on World War II and the fascist era, and a great many historians have contributed to it.[33]

Among the better known are Erminio Bagnasco,[34] Franco Bargoni,[35] Giovanni Bernardi,[36] Marc'Antonio Bragadin,[37] Carlo De Risio,[38] Vittorio Di Sambuy,[39]

[33] For example, Achille Rastelli, "Il naviglio mercantile requisito nella storia della marina militare," *Rivista marittima* (1984); Ernesto Giuriati, "Storia e tradimento," *Rivista marittima* (1981); Gino Jori, "La crittologia nelle operazioni navali in Mediterraneo (1940–1943)," *Rivista marittima* (1982); Nino Bixio Lo Martire, *Navi e bugie* (1983); Gianni Padoan, *La guerra nel Mediterraneo* (Bologna: Capitol, 1978); and Dobrillo Dupuis, *La flotta bianca: le navi ospedale italiane nel secondo conflitto mondiale* (Milan: Mursia, 1978). Also Renzo De Felice, *Mussolini l'alleato. I. L'Italia in guerra 1940–1943. II. Crisi e agonia del regime* (Turin: Einaudi, 1990), 2 vols., who discusses the Navy's role; Salvatore Minardi, *Italia e Francia alla conferenza navale di Londra del 1930* (1989); and Rosaria Quartararo, "Imperial Defence in the Mediterranean on the Eve of the Ethiopian Crisis (July–October 1935)," *Historical Journal* (1977).

[34] Erminio Bagnasco collaborated with Elio Andò on *Navi e marinai italiani nella seconda guerra mondiale* (Parma: Ermanno Albertelli, 1977/1981), and with Marco Spertini on *I mezzi d'assalto della X* MAS, 1940–1945* (Parma: Ermanno Albertelli, 1991). On his own has published a number of studies, including *Le armi delle navi italiane nella seconda guerra mondiale* (Parma: Ermanno Albertelli, 1978); *Italian Battleships of World War II: A Pictorial History* (1986); *La portaerei nella marina italiana. Idee, progetti e realizzioni dalle origini a oggi* (Rome: Rivista Marittima, 1989); *Submarines of World War Two* (Annapolis: USNIP, 1977); "Navi incorporate nella Marina italiana durante la seconda guerra mondiale." *Rivista marittima* (1961); *I M.A.S. e le motosiluranti italiane, 1906–1968* (Rome: Ufficio Storico della Marina Militare, 1969).

[35] Franco Bargoni, *L'impegno navale italiano durante la Guerra civile spagnola (1936–1939)* (Rome: Ufficio Storico della Marina Militare, 1992); *Corazzate italiane classi Duilio–Italia–Ruggiero di Lauria, entrate in servizio fra il 1880 e il 1892* (Rome: Ateneo e Bizzarri, 1978); and *Le prime navi di linea della marina italiana (1861–1880)* (Rome: Bizzarri, 1976).

[36] Giovanni Bernardi, *La Marina, gli armistizi e il trattato di pace: settembre 1943—dicembre 1951* (Rome: Ufficio Storico della Marina Militare, 1979); and *Il disarmo navale tra le due guerre mondiali, 1919–1939* (Rome: Ufficio Storico della Marina Militare, 1975); "La dibattuta questione della parità navale tra Italia e Francia nel periodo tra le due guerre mondiali," *Revue internationale d'histoire militaire* (1978).

[37] Marc Antonio Bragadin, *Il dramma della marina italiana, 1940–1945* (Milan: Mondadori, 1982), and *The Italian Navy in World War II* (Annapolis: USNIP, 1957, 1980). Both works are slightly revised reissues of earlier studies.

[38] Carlo De Risio, *Navi di ferro, teste di legno: la marina italiana, ieri e oggi* (Rome: Ciarrapico, 1976).

[39] Vittorio Di Sambuy, *Match pari tra due grande flotte. Mediterraneo, 1940–1942* (Milan: Mursia, 1976); and "Un segreto svelato—il segreto 'Ultra'," *Rivista marittima* (1976).

Mariano Gabriele,[40] Giorgio Giorgerini,[41] Tullio Marcon,[42] Francesco Mattesini,[43] Riccardo Nassigh,[44] Sergio Nesi,[45] and Alberto Santoni.[46] Although the fascist period is relatively narrow and early approaches were often in the nature of reciprocal reproaches, a rather wide spectrum of approaches has evolved, while a keen interest in such elite units as the San Marco marine division and the X Mas has remained high.[47] Bagnasco, Di Sambuy, Mattesini, Nassigh,

[40] Mariano Gabriele, *Operazione C/3: Malta* (Rome: Ufficio Storico della Marina Militare, 1965, 1990); "La guerre des convois entre l'Italie et l'Afrique du nord," in Comité d'Histoire de la 2e Guerre Mondiale, *La guerre en Méditerranée, 1939–1945. Actes du colloque International tenu Paris du 8 au 11 avril 1969* (Paris: Editions du Centre National de la Recherche Scientifique, 1971). He has also written on other periods, e.g., *La flotta come strumento di politica nei primi decenni dello stato unitario italiano* (Rome: Ufficio Storico della Marina Militare, 1973); *La politica navale italiana dal 1885 al 1915* (Rome: Ufficio Storico della Marina Militare, 1982); "La politica navale italiana alla vigilia del primo conflitto mondiale," *Rivista marittima* (May 1965): pp. 15–32; "La convenzione navale italo–franco–britannica del 10 maggio 1915," *Nuova antologia* (April–May 1965): pp. 483–502, 69–84.

[41] Giorgio Giorgerini, *La battaglia dei convogli in Mediterraneo* (Milan: Mursia, 1977); *Da Matapan al Golfo Persico: la Marina militare italiana dal fascismo alla Repubblica* (Milan: Mursia, 1989); *Almanaco storico delle navi militari italiane: la Marina e le sue navi dal 1861 al 1975* (Rome: Ufficio Storico della Marina Militare, 1978); "The Role of Malta in Italian Naval Operations, 1940–43," in *New Aspects of Naval History* (Annapolis: U.S. Naval Institute Press, 1985); and with Aldo Nani, *Le navi d'Italia. I. Le navi di linea italiane, 1961–1969* (Rome: Ufficio Storico della Marina Militare, 1969), *Gli incrociatori italiani, 1861–1975* (Rome: Ufficio Storico della Marina Militare, 1976), and *Almanacco storico delle navi militari d'Italia, 1861–1975* (Rome: Ufficio Storico della Marina Militare, 1980).

[42] Tullio Marcon, "Operazione Malta due ovvero il rispetto del nemico," *Rivista marittima* (1976); *Ali marine: gli osservatori della Regia Marina nella seconda guerra mondiale* (Milan: Mursia, 1978).

[43] Francesco Mattesini, *La battaglia aeronavale di mezzo agosto* (Rome: Edizioni dell'Ateneo, 1986); *Il giallo di Matapan. Revisione di giudizi* (Rome: Edizioni dell'Ateneo, 1985); *La battaglia di Punta Stilo* (Rome: Ufficio Storico della Marina Militare, 1990); *I sommergibili di Betasom 1940–1943* (Rome: Ufficio Storico della Marina Militare, on press); "Navi da guerra e mercantili della Gran Bretagna e nazioni alleate affondate e danneggiate in Mediterraneo (10 giugno 1940—5 maggio 1945)" *Archivio Storico Marina*. XI (9); "I retroscena inediti del mancato intervento delle navi di superficie italiane nella battaglia di mezzo agosto 1942," *Il Giornale d'Italia* (5 January 1984); "La battaglia aeronavale di mezzo agosto," *Aeronautica: mensile dell'aviazione italiana* (1985), nos. 8, 9, 10, 11.

[44] Riccardo Nassigh, *Guerra negli abissi. I sommergibili italiani nel secondo conflitto mondiale* (Milan: Mursia, 1971); *Operazione mezzo agosto.* (Milan: Mursia, 1976).

[45] Sergio Nesi, *Decima flottiglia nostra: i mezzi d'assalto della Marina italiana al sud e al nord dopo l'armistizio* (Milan: Mursia, 1986).

[46] As Dr. Sullivan has noted, Alberto Santoni has published a number of important works on contemporary naval history, especially *Il vero traditore: il ruolo documentato di ULTRA nella guerra del Mediterraneo* (Milan: Mursia, 1981). He has also collaborated with Theodor Fuchs on "Der Einfluss von 'ULTRA' auf den Krieg im Mittelmeer," *Marine Rundschau* (1981); and with Francesco Mattesini on *La partecipazione tedesca alla guerra aeronavale nel Mediterraneo (1940–1945)* (Rome: Edizioni dell'Ateneo e Bizzarri, 1980).

[47] The official history has a volume on the X Mas, which was popularized by Julio Valerio Borghese, *Sea Devils* (Chicago: Henry Regnery, 1954). Among the recent publications on the unit is the excellent volume by Bagnasco and Spertini, and Ricciotti Lazzero, *La decima Mas* (Milan: Rizzoli, 1984). Also see Pieramedeo Baldrati, *San Marco. . .San Marco. . .Storia di una divisione* (Milan: San Marco Infantry Division, 1989); Guido Bonavicini, *Decima Marinai! Decima comandante! La fanteria di marina, 1943–45* (Milan: Mursia, 1988); and Aurelio Scardaccione, *Il delfino dorato: in guerra sui sommergibili* (Fasano: Schena, 1988), a diary by a former submariner.

Nesi, and Santoni have generally focused on the technical and operational aspects of naval affairs; Bargoni, Bernardi, and Gabriele have been more concerned with policy and diplomacy; and Giorgerini and Bragadin have written synthetic works on the Italian Navy. In short, there are a great many Italians who are currently working on naval and maritime topics.[48] While the number of foreign scholars is much smaller, as Dr. Sullivan notes, many, such as Germany's Gerhard Schreiber, have made contributions to the field.[49]

Recent naval history thus seems to be thriving; and if some chaff remains, that is the price the Italians pay to stimulate interest in the subject. The firms of Mursia, Rizzoli, and Mondadori may not always publish scholarly studies, but they provide a valuable service by issuing memoirs and popular studies that keep the public interested in naval and maritime history, while Edizioni dell'Ateneo e Bizzarri and Ermanno Albertelli focus on a more restricted audience interested in the nuts and bolts of naval history.

In short, while there are undoubtedly enormous differences between the United States and Italy, I am not sure that Italians are less enthused with their naval history than we are with ours; and if ground forces played a much greater part in Italian development than naval forces, that was also true of the United States, save in the Caribbean, where our Navy and Marines consolidated an informal empire against weak forces, and in the Pacific, where a combination of naval and air secured victory in the early 1940s. Our Navy is certainly larger than the Italian Navy, and it is better publicized in this country,[50] where

---

[48] I am indebted to Admiral Renato Sicurezza, who currently heads the Italian Navy's Historical Office and to Admiral Francesco Pascazio, the former editor of *Rivista Marittima*, for their generous help in identifying those Italian historians who are currently working in the contemporary era; to Professor Domenico Sella for his suggestions regarding the early modern period; to Professor Alberto Santoni for his courteous and informative reply to my inquiries; and to Admiral Carlo Gottardi, for his interest. Among those who are currently writing on contemporary history are Vittorio Barbati, Franco Bargoni, Colonel Ferruccio Botti, Admiral Alfredo Brauzzi, Augusto De Toro, Admiral Luigi Donini, Admiral Antonio Flamigni, Antoni Formicola, Aldo Fraccaroli, Professor Mariano Gabriele, Commandante Franco Gay, Admiral Gino Galuppini, Giorgio Giorgerini, Admiral Carlo Gottardi, Tullio Marcon, Francesco Mattesini, Riccardo Nassigh, Franco Puddu, Admiral Luigi Romani, Claudio Romano, Professor Alberto Santoni, and Admiral Pietro Zancardi.

[49] See Gerhard Schreiber, "Italien im machtpolitischen Kalkül der deutschen Marineführung 1919 bis 1945," in *Quellen und Forschungen aus italienischen Archiven und Bibliotheken* (Tübingen: Istituto Storico Germanico in Roma, 1982) vol. 62; "Les structures stratégiques de la conduite de la guerre italo–allemande au cours de la deuxième guerre mondiale" *RHDGM* (1980); "Sul teatro mediterraneo nella seconda guerra mondiale: inediti punti di vista della marina germanica del tempo." *Rivista marittima* (1987). Also see Josef Schröder, "Les prétensions allemands à la direction militaire du théâtre italien d'opérations en 1943" *RHDGM* (1974).

[50] Given that the United States has five times the population of Italy and is considerably wealthier, the disparities between the two states diminish or disappear. Multiplying Italy's budget by five, one gets an annual outlay of $120 billion, not $24 billion, about a third of the US budget of $290 billion; the adjusted size of the Italian navy is 275,000, about half that of the USN; and the number of ships about 300, comparable to the 340 that Dr. Sullivan projects for the USN. Indeed, the adjusted merchant figures yield 8,000 Italian ships displacing 40 million GRT, compared to 1,600 American vessels displacing 8 million. It is also worth noting that while there is a considerable public for works on the Navy in the United States, there is not a large market for histories of such maritime organizations as the Coast Guard and merchant marine.

only a handful of academics have devoted any attention to Italian naval matters over the past twenty years.[51] But that is to be expected, given our preoccupation with superpowers.

Whether "the major negative influence" on Italian attitudes toward the Navy, merchant marine and public institutions in general have derived from "widespread perceptions of the defunct monarchy and of the Fascist regime" is debatable, although there is no doubt that during the 1950s the Italians had nothing comparable to America's *Victory at Sea* to extol their Navy, and a spate of critical works, such as Antonio Trizzino's *Navi e poltrone*, censured the Italian Navy as so inept as to be treasonous.[52]

But such attitudes predated Mussolini's era and seem to be rooted in the problems that accompanied the creation of a unitary Italian state, including the monarchy's emargination of Mazzini and its "betrayal" of Garibaldi, the South's resistance to Piedmontese rule, and the influence of socialism, syndicalism, and anarchism in areas as diverse as Puglia, the Romagna, Lombardy, and Sicily. A great many Italians thus came to view the armed forces as repressive, and Italy's failure to realize an African empire disillusioned the more patriotic, even if it stimulated Enrico Corridoni and the ANI to clamor for even more spending on overseas expansion and eventually led Mussolini to discern and exploit the political advantages of the concept of an Italian "proletarian" nation. In other words, if the Fascist regime disillusioned many Italians, the liberal Italian state had already alienated many others. Since 1945, pugnacious and partisan media have helped to keep political debate lively and censorious in Italy, whereas in the United States the mass media have usually fallen into line behind government efforts to glorify its military and naval exploits. And, as noted above, the difficulties of reconciling postwar antifascism with a patriotism and navalism tainted by their association with the fascist regime has created a climate in which polemics flourish.

---

[51] Brian Sullivan, "A Fleet in Being: The Rise and Fall of Italian Sea Power, 1861–1943," *The International History Review* (1988); and Marco Rimanelli, *The "Least of the Powers": Italy's Foreign, Security, and Naval Policy in the Quest for Mediterranean Pre-eminence, 1860s–1989*, (Ph.D, Johns Hopkins Univ., 1989). Bernard MacGregor Knox, *Mussolini Unleashed, 1939–1941. Politics and Strategy in Fascist Italy's Last War* (Cambridge: UP, 1982), also deals with naval matters in his survey of Italy's war effort. Jack Greene is an aficionado of naval history and his *Mare nostrum: The War in the Mediterranean* (Watsonville, Calif.: Typesetting, etc., 1990) is a useful compilation of data, all the more so because few academic studies have been published in this country. Also see James J. Sadkovich, *The Italian Navy in World War II* (Westport, Conn.: Greenwood, 1994); "The Italian Navy," in *Reevaluating Major Naval Combatants of World War II* (Westport, Conn.: Greenwood, 1990); "Aircraft Carriers and the Mediterranean, 1940–1943: Rethinking the Obvious," *Aerospace Historian* (1987); and "Re-evaluating Who Won the Italo-British Naval Conflict, 1940–42," *European History Quarterly* (1988).

[52] Antonio Trizzino, *Navi e poltrone* (Milan: Longanesi, 1966). From 1945 into the 1960s, American films exalted our victory in the war, but in Italy such fare as *Città aperta* and *Bicycle Thief* reflected a resigned weariness with the whole subject of war, as Fellini and others created a pacifist postmodern world.

Yet I do not think that one can simply dismiss the fascist era and its naval and maritime achievements. It seems to me that the success of the fascist campaigns in Africa and the prestige conferred on Italy by its trans-Atlantic liners more than offset earlier defeats. The *Rex*'s brief appearance in Fellini's *Amarcord* underlined the effect on the Italian psyche of such spending, even if in retrospect the achievements proved as illusory as the ship's illuminated outline on a summer night.[53] The defeat of 1943 was unquestionably a major blow to the Italians, but there were no decisive defeats in 1940–41, except in the minds of Allied wartime propagandists and some postwar historians, and after 1945 the Italians had no choice but to reject those "legacies of the Fascist era" not approved by the Allies.[54] But if the neo-fascists have been reduced to a fringe group in postwar Italy, the referendum mounted by the Radical Party in 1977 reminded everyone that their legacy included the penal code and IRI, both integral parts of the postwar liberal regime.

Italy's excessive navalism and heavy official support for naval and maritime history prior to 1945 was fairly typical of great powers, and its more moderate military pretensions since then characteristic of such former imperial powers as Britain. There were a number of ex-fascist or neo-fascist historians in the postwar era who tried to refurbish the fascist *ventennio*, but the greatest impact on the historiography of the war has been that of such naval officers as Angelo Iachino, Marc'Antonio Bragadin, and Giuseppe Fioravanzo, who had served in the "fascist" navy and sought to set the record straight by challenging an Allied wartime propaganda that was anything but objective.[55]

[53] Although the fascist media were hardly objective, I think it still a safe assumption that many Italians shared the pride in Italy's naval achievements expressed in such articles as Domenico Cavagnari, "La Marina dell'Italia fascista." *Rassegna italiana* (1938).

[54] Of course, prior to 1943, the fascist regime issued its own propaganda, e.g., Vincio Araldi, *Marinai d'Italia sulle vie della gloria* (Bologna: Cantelli, 1942); Marc'Antonio Bragadin, *Vittoria sui mari di Roma, 15 giugno XX (1942)* (Verona: Mondadori, 1942); Vittorio Calvino, *La guardia del mare: l'aviazione da ricognizione marittima* (Rome: Editoriale Aeronautica, 1942); Giuseppe Fioravanzo, *Il Mediterraneo, centro strategico del mondo* (Verona: Mondadori, 1943); Vittorio G. Rossi, *La guerra dei marinai* (Milan: Bompiani, 1941); Ministero della Marina, *Amanecer heroico en el Mediterráneo: dos torpederos contro una escuadra británica. La épica empresa de los torpederos "Circe y Vega"* (Milan: 1941), and *Appello al mare* (Rome: Tipografia Novissima, 1940).

[55] Aldo Cocchia and Giuseppe Fioravanzo, who oversaw the writing of the first official monographs on the Navy, were both members of the fascist navy, the one a war hero, the other a serious theorist. A prolific writer, Fioravanzo wrote on theory in the 1930s, composed propaganda during the 1940s, and was instrumental in issuing the Italian official histories in the 1950s, e.g., *Manuale teorico–pratico di cinematica aero-navale e d'impiego delle unità in combattimento* (Livorno: Accademia Navale, 1930), *La guerra sul mare e la guerra integrale* (Turin: Enrico Schioppo, 1931), 2 vols, *Basi navali nel mondo* (Milano: Istituto per gli studi di politica internazionale, 1936), *History of Naval Tactical Thought* (Annapolis, Md: USNIP, 1979), *Il Mediterraneo, centro strategico del mondo* (Verona: Mondadori, 1943). Iachino published a number of books and articles, e.g., *Le due Sirti* (Milan: Mondadori, 1953), *Gaudo e Matapan. Storia di un'operazione della guerra navale nel Mediterraneo, 27–28–29 marzo 1941* (Milan: Mondadori, 1946), *Operazione mezzo giugno. Episodi dell'ultima guerra sul mare* (Milan: Monadadori, 1955), *Il punto su Matapan* (Milan: Mondadori, 1969), and *Tramonto di una grande marina* (Milan: Mondadori, 1959). See above for Bragadin, and the official histories for Aldo Cocchia, as well as "Il peso strategico di Malta fu veramente determinante?" *Rivista marittima* (1964). Virgilio Spigai also published on the war, e.g., "Italian Naval Assault Craft in Two World Wars." United States Naval Institute Press (1965); and V. Spigai and L. D. De la Penne, "The Italian Attack on the Alexandria Naval Base." United States Naval Institute Press (1956).

Dr. Sullivan's observations regarding the Italian university system are not encouraging, but essentially the same could be said of our own system, with the caveat that ours is so much bigger than the Italian's that it can accommodate a few more professors in fields such as naval and maritime history. Like Camillo Manfroni, Mariano Gabriele has been crucial to the development of Italian naval history, and Alberto Santoni has written a number of valuable works, including his work on Ultra and the study he co-authored with Francesco Mattesini on German participation in the Mediterranean during World War II. But as valuable as Santoni's contributions have been, like those of Mattesini, they tend to be pointedly revisionist and critical of the performance of the Italian armed forces, while on occasion appearing to rationalize German failures in the Mediterranean theater. It thus seems that polemics are an unavoidable part of doing contemporary Italian naval history.

Professor Raimono's efforts to continue Manfroni's work at the Naval Academy at Livorno are laudatory, as are the activities of the Istituto di Guerra Marittima. But I would be curious to know what sorts of "difficulties" Raimono has encountered and wonder if the acquaintance of his students with Anglo–American naval history is more a function of the number of works published on the subject than of "the politically sensitive nature of Italian naval history."

That the other service academies ignore naval history is to be expected, although it seems a shame that there has been no effort to coordinate at least air and naval studies, especially since historians like Nino Arena and Nicola Malizia have written works that include both areas and there is no question that to fully understand the war in the Mediterranean between 1940 and 1945 it is necessary to integrate naval and air actions.[56] In this regard, it is worth noting that the publications of the Italian Foreign Ministry and the Italian army are useful to those doing naval history.[57]

The holdings of the Naval Archives, the State Archives (Archivio Centrale dello Stato), and the Foreign Ministry's Archives (Archivio Storico del Ministero

---

[56] Nino Arena, *Bandiera di combattimento: Storia della Marina militare italiana (1925–1945)* (Rome: CEN, 1974), 2 vols., and *La regia aeronautica, 1939–1943* (Rome: Ufficio Storico dello Stato Maggiore Aeronautica, 1981–1984); and Nicola Malizia, *Inferno su Malta. La più lunga battaglia aeronavale della second guerra mondiale* (Milan: Mursia, 1976), and with Christopher Shores, and Brian Cull, *Malta: The Hurricane Years, 1940–1941* (London: Grub Street, 1987), and *Malta: The Spitfire Year, 1942* (London: Grubb Street, 1991).

[57] The Army is in the process of publishing the General Staff's war diary, and its volumes on the minutes (verbali) of the meetings held by Comando Supremo during the war are indispensable. See Ufficio Storico dell'Esercito, *Diario storico del Comando Supremo* [Antonello Biagini, Fernando Frattolillo] (Rome: 1986), Vol. I-III, and *Verbali delle riunioni tenute dal capo di Stato Maggiore Generale* (Rome: 1985), Vols. I-III. For the Foreign Ministry, Ministero degli Affari Esteri, Commissione per la pubblicazione dei documenti diplomatici, *I documenti diplomatici italiani*. Ottava serie, 1935–39 (Rome: 1952, 1953), Vols. XII, XIII; Nona serie, 1939–43. (Rome, 1957–1988), Vols. I-VIII. Also see Istituto Centrale di Statistica del Regno d'Italia, *Compendio statistico italiano, 1939–1942*, (Rome, 1939–42) Vols. XIII-XVI, and *Sommario di statistiche storiche italiane, 1861–1958* (Rome: 1958).

degli Affari Esteri) are useful to anyone working in naval history, and the helpfulness of their personnel is well known. It is also noteworthy, as Dr. Sullivan stresses, that only the Navy has published solid monographs of World War II. Although I am not as critical of the Army's publications as he is, there is no question that the Air Force has lagged behind the other services, and despite its length, even Arena's recent work is not a great improvement on earlier studies by Santoro and Licheri.[58] However, the recent publication of two volumes of Superaereo's directives should help to fill in gaps in our knowledge of the air-naval war during 1940.[59]

Admiral Sicurezza's efforts to reorder the MM's archives and to bring together contributions by established historians on strategy, diplomacy, and other aspects of naval and maritime history are laudatory. But long-range activities are also needed, as well as support for historians new to the field, especially given that while maritime history can disguise itself as social or economic history, naval history suffers from the same sort of emargination within the academic community as diplomatic, political, and military history. And if it is unreasonable to expect naval historians to become postmodernists, it seems equally unrealistic to expect that traditional ways of doing naval history will retain a large audience. Yet those of us writing on contemporary naval affairs seem mired in yesterday's polemics and content with an approach that seems increasingly dated and irrelevant, and I can personally attest to how difficult it is to shake off traditional approaches and find a way out of the polemical maze, which I still regularly wander.

Although service histories may be expected to have a narrow focus and a certain bias because of institutional restraints, Dr. Sullivan's praise for the high standards maintained by the Italian Navy's historical office is not misplaced. Bernardi's works are exceptionally well-done analyses of diplomatic matters and the

---

[58] Arena, *op. cit.*; Giuseppe Santoro, *L'aeronautica italiana nella seconda guerra mondiale* (Milan: Edizioni Esse, 1957), 2 vols., and Sebastiano Licheri, *L'arma aerea italiana nella seconda guerra mondiale, 10 giugno 1940—8 settembre 1943* (Milan: Mursia, 1976). Also Mario Angelozzi and Ubaldo Bernini, *Il problema aeronavale italiano* (Livorno: Belforte, 1981); M. Circi and A. Guglielmetti, *Gli attuali reparti A.M. della aviazione per la marina. Note storiche dal 1926 al 1972* (Rome: Grafica Veant, 1977); Carlo Unia, *Storia degli aerosiluranti italiani* (Rome: Bizzarri, 1974); Corrado Ricci, *Il corpo aereo italiano (CAI) sul fronte della Manica (1940–1941)* (Rome: Ufficio Storico dell'Aeronautica Militare, 1980); Corrado Ricci and Christopher E. Shores, *La guerra aerea in Africa Orientale, 1940–41* (Rome: Ufficio Storico dell'Aeronautica Militare, 1979); and Vincenzo Lioy, *L'Italia in Africa. Serie Storico–Militare. Vol. III. L'opera dell'Aeronautica* (Rome: Ministero degli Affari Esteri, 1964). Lioy has also written two early works on the Italian air force and operations during the war, *Elementi storici nell'Aeronautica Italiana* (Nisida: Accademia Aeronautica, 1960), and *Gloria senza allori* (Rome: Failli, 1953). Others, like Giulio Lazzati, have contributed to the literature on air operations, *e.g.*, his *Stormi d'Italia. Storia dell'aviazione militare italiana* (Milan: Mursia, 1975). Also see Guido Bonavicini, *Carlo Gaffioni e gli aerosiluranti italiani* (Milan: Cavallotti, 1987), and Andrea Curami and Giancarello Garello, "L'aviazione ausiliaria per la Regia Marina fra le due guerre (1923–1940)," *Rivista marittima* (1985).

[59] Franco Mattesini and M. Cermelli, eds., *Le direttive tecnico-operative di Superaereo* (Rome: Stato Maggiore Aeronatuica/Ufficio Storico, 1992), 2 vols.

Italian official histories in general are of a very high quality that compares favorably with the best that has been done by Italian, British, and American academics.[60] On the other hand, more detailed monographs on the evolution of the Italian Navy, recruitment, contracting, and the formulation of naval policy would be welcome.[61]

The publications mentioned by Dr. Sullivan, from the *Bollettino d'archivio dell'ufficio storico della marina militare* to *Rivista marittima* are extremely useful, and the organizations he mentions (Associazione italiana di documentazione marittime e navale and Associazione navemodellisti bolognesi) have helped to stimulate interest in naval affairs and provided some of the raw stuff of naval history, as anyone who has used the publications on naval ships and weaponry by Aldo Fraccaroli and Erminio Bagnasco can attest. And it is reassuring to know that a fascist institution, IRI (Istituto per la ricostruzione industriale) is funding scholarly studies on naval and maritime history.

Dr. Sullivan is also correct to note that we do not have enough biographies of Italian naval and maritime personalities, that there is no comprehensive study of the Italian Navy, and that the post–1945 development of the Navy has been ignored. However, I am not as convinced as he is that it is necessary to teach naval history in order to make good citizens out of Italians, given that the popularity of naval history in this country has not appreciably increased the sophistication with which the average American reacts to domestic and foreign crises.

There are a few observations I would like to add to those made by Dr. Sullivan, whose paper I found both interesting and informative, and whose acquaintance with Italian archives and historians I can only envy. Indeed, that is my first observation—while there are relatively few Italians working in naval

[60]   The data in the twenty-two volumes of the Italian Navy's World War II series is both abundant and comprehensive, with everything from details on the losses of merchant and naval shipping to convoy operations, naval battles, technical development, and command structures. The Navy's seven-volume series on naval vessels contain extremely useful data on the technical aspects of classes and individual ships, complete with operational summaries. See *La marina Italiana nella seconda guerra mondiale* (Rome: Ufficio Storico della Marina Militare, 1952–present), 22 vols., and *Le navi d'Italia* (Rome: Ufficio Storico della Marina Militare, 1969–present), 8 vols. Among those who collaborated on the historical series were Giuseppe Fioravanzo (series editor and various volumes), Mario Peruzzi (hospital ships, 1956), Aldo Cocchia (convoy operations, 1958–76), P. F. Lupinacci (Mines, 1968, and Albania and Aegean operations, 1972), U. Mori Ubaldini (submarines, 1976), M. Bertini (submarines, 1968, 1972), Carlo De Risio (X Mas and blockade runners, 1972), and V. Rauber (ASW, 1978). The series dealing with ships was compiled by Giorgio Giorgerini and Augusto Nani (battleships, 1969; cruisers, 1976; and an almanac, 1980); P. M. Pollina (torpedo boats, 1974), and with Mario Bertini (submarines, 1971); G. Fioravanzo, P. M. Pollina, G. Riccardi, and F. Gnifetti (destroyers, 1971); E. Bargoni (scouts, frigates, and corvettes, 1974); and Erminio Bagnasco (Mas and Ms, 1969).

[61]   Fioravanzo's slim volume on naval tactics was a good beginning, and Ezio Ferrente's history of Italian perceptions of the Mediterranean is unusual in its stress on ideas rather than facts. Ezio Ferrante, *Il Mediterranean nella coscienza nazionale* (Rome: Rivista Marittima, 1987); and Giuseppe Fioravanzo, *A History of Naval Tactical Thought*, op. cit. Fioravanzo has published a number of theoretical works, including *Basi navali nel mondo*, op. cit.

and maritime history, there are even fewer Americans, in large part owing to problems obtaining funding. There is, to the best of my knowledge, no easy way for scholars in this country to obtain grants to use Italian naval and maritime archives, and our priorities, especially in an age that flaunts its commitment to "diversity," should include ways to encourage the American academic community to support the study of such "marginal" subjects as naval history and to encourage an interest in such "minor" powers as Italy. In this country, Dr. Sullivan rightly mentions only a handful of scholars in the field: MacGregor Knox, who focuses on political and diplomatic questions; Halpern, whose studies on the Mediterranean were published in 1971 and 1987; and the two of us, who have published a handful of articles on contemporary Italian naval history. Nor has there been a rush to do Italian naval and maritime history recently. Still, there are a number of Americans, for the most part recent Ph.D.s, who have dealt with naval and maritime topics, among them Marco Rimanelli, who finished a two–volume dissertation at Johns Hopkins on Italian naval policy, and Timothy W. Childs, whose 1982 dissertation dealt with the diplomacy of the Italo-Turkish war.[62] There are also a number of Americans who have written on subjects that involve Italian naval history, such as the siege of Malta.[63]

Yet even a brief glance at the annual bibliographies put out by the Society for Italian Historical Studies is enough to confirm the impression that naval and maritime studies have become more marginal in this country as social history has become more dominant. Non-academics like Jack Greene, whose interest in tactics and whose careful compilation of orders of battle are very useful to us academic types, are fascinated by naval history, but our colleagues seem not to be, unless naval and maritime history is viewed in another context. Benjamin Arbel therefore highlighted the social aspects of Venetian trade in the fifteenth century,[64] Mark John Angelos discussed the role of women of twelfth–century Genoa's commerce,[65] Robert Davis discussed the workers of the Venetian arsenal, and Richard Jackson, Mediterranean seamen.[66] Irene Katele has taken

---

[62] Timothy Childs, *Mediterranean Imbroglio: The Diplomatic Origins of Modern Libya (The Diplomacy of the Belligerents during the Italo-Turkish War, 1911–1912)* op. cit.; and Marco Rimanelli, *The "Least of the Powers" Italy's Foreign Security and Naval Policy in the Quest for Mediterranean Pre-eminence, 1860s–1989,* op. cit. While the works of Salewski, Breyer, and Dulin are useful, they are not primarily concerned with the Italian war effort in the Mediterranean. Those by Barjot, de Belot, Baum, Weichold, Ruge, and others are more directly focused on the Mediterranean theater, but many are now dated, others rather biased by the participation of the authors in the war.

[63] Charles A Jellison, *Besieged. The World War II Ordeal of Malta, 1940–42* (New England: 1987); Dora Alves, "The Resupply of Malta in World War II," *Naval War College Review* (1980); and Rowena Reed, "Central Mediterranean Sea Control and the North African Campaigns, 1940–1942" *Naval War College Review* (1984).

[64] Benjamin Arbel, "Venetian Trade in Fifteenth Century Acre: The Letters of Francesco Bevilaqua (1471–72)," *Asian and African Studies* (1988).

[65] Mark John Angelos, *Genoese Women, Family Business Practices, and Maritime Commerce, 115-1216* (Ph.D., Univ. of Illinois at Urbana–Champaigne, 1992).

[66] Robert C. Davis, *Shipbuilders of the Venetian Arsenal: Workers and Workplace in the Preindustrial City* (Baltimore:

another look at piracy in the late middle ages, [67] Catherine Bracewell has studied the Uskoks of Senj,[68] and Ilona Klein reexamined the Order of Santo Stefano.[69] In effect, early modern naval and maritime historians seem to have resolved the problem of how to make the subject germane, whether it is looking at technique (shipbuilding, contracts, organization) or recasting naval history as social, cultural, or gender history.[70] Such studies as that by Augusta Molinari on sanitary conditions aboard ships carrying emigrants show that the same approach can work for contemporary history.[71] At this point, one can even hope to publish in such unlikely places as *Asian and African Studies*, rather than in the handful of journals and with the few publishers who will consider studies of twentieth-century Italian naval history. Yet, on the whole, in this country there are relatively few secure outlets for studies on Italian naval and maritime topics.[72]

If finding a place to publish can be frustrating in the United States, where relatively few journals and publishers concern themselves with Italian naval and maritime affairs, there is still a fairly wide choice of publications and publishers to choose from, whether one is writing on the early modern period or dealing with more contemporary questions. For example, *Storia e politica* published Francesco Lefebvre d'Ovidio's studies on the London naval conference and Italian and British naval policy in the 1930s,[73] *Storia contemporanea* published Luigi Castioni's essay on the development of Italian radar,[74] the *Revue de l'occident musulman et de la Méditerranée*

Johns Hopkins, 1991). Also Richard Paul Jackson, "*Ma misi me per l'alto mare aperto.*" *Mediterranean Seamen during the Medieval Commercial Revolution* (Ph.D., Yale, 1992).

[67] Irene Birute Katele, *Captains and Corsairs: Venice and Piracy, 1261–1381 (Maritime, Pirates, Naval, Military, Medieval)* (Ph.D., Univ. of Illinois at Urbana–Champaign, 1986). Like Angelos and Madden, Katele did her work under Donald E. Queller.

[68] Catherine Wendy Bracewell, *The Uskoks of Senj: Piracy, Banditry, and Holy War in the Sixteenth–Century Adriatic* (Ithaca: Cornell Univ. Press, 1992).

[69] Ilona Klein, *The Order of Santo Stefano in the Levant: An Unpublished Account of a Voyage in 1627* (Berkeley: Univ. of California Press, 1990). Also see Giuseppe Gino Guarnieri, *I Cavalieri di Santo Stefano nella storia della Marina italiana (1562–1859)* (1960), and *L'ordine di Santo Stefano nei suoi aspetti organizzativi interni e navali sotto il Gran Magistero Lorenese* (1965).

[70] For example, Brian Pullen's *Rich and Poor in Renaissance Venice* (Oxford: Blackwell, 1971) and his more recent *The Jews of Europe and the Inquisition of Venice, 1560–1670* (Oxford: Blackwell, 1983), a social history of a maritime port, but strictly speaking neither a maritime nor a naval history, save in the sense that any history of a port could be defined as maritime.

[71] Augusta Molinari, *Le navi di lazzaro: aspetti sanitari dell'emigrazione transoceanica italiana: il viaggio per mare* (Milan: Angeli, 1988).

[72] Although not concerned with naval and maritime history, of some interest is Jonathan Morris, "Italian Journals: A User's Guide," *Contemporary European History* (1992).

[73] Francesco Lefebvre d'Ovidio, "Politica e strategia britannica nel Mediterraneo, 1936–1939," *Storia e politica* (1978); "L'Italia e la conferenza navale di Londra del 1930," *Storia e politica* (1978).

[74] Luigi Carillo Castioni, "I radar industriali italiani. Ricerche, ricordi, considerazioni per una loro storia." *Storia contemporanea* (1987). *Rivista marittima* had published a series of articles on radar by Ugo Tiberio, but Castioni's was the first systematic treatment of the subject. See Ugo Tiberio, Ugo, "Cenni sull'opera della Marina italiana nel campo radiotecnico durante la guerra, 1940–1945," "Un ricedisturbatore antiradar italiano del 1942," and "Ricordo del primo radar navale italiano," *Rivista marittima* (1948, 1976, 1976).

printed Salvatore Bono's article on buying Turkish slaves for papal galleys,[75] and the Centre de recherches sur l'evolution de la vie rurale issued Marie-Claude Dionnet's study on the Abruzzi.[76]

Judging from recent publications in early modern maritime and naval history, it would seem that the subject is doing relatively well in Italy. In addition to local and regional histories, such as those noted above, there are a number of studies on the early modern and late medieval periods. Franco Gay has published numerous works on Venetian history,[77] Gino Benvenuti contributed 300 pages on the maritime republics to the Quest'Italia series,[78] Raffaella Brunetti and Lorenza Mazzino have written a popular history of Genoa's naval leaders,[79] Pierangelo Campodonico has published works on Genovese mariners in the middle ages and the Renaissance,[80] and Cesare Ciano has written excellent monographs on Medicean maritime history.[81] A number of works deal with shipbuilding, and a good deal has been written on the arsenal at Venice.[82] There are also works on the Venetian

---

[75] Salvatore Bono, "Achat d'eclaves turcs pour les galleres pontificales (xvie—xviii siecles)," *Revue de l'occident musulman et de la Méditeranée* (1985).

[76] Marie–Claude Dionnet, *L'Abruzze maritime: un mezzogiorno en evolution* (Pisa: Biblioteca del Bollettino Storico Pisano, 1986). Also see Terence K. Hopkins and Immanuel Wallerstein, "Capitalism and the Incorporation of New Zones into the World Economy," *Review* (Fernand Braudel Center) (1987).

[77] For example, Franco Gay, "Fantasticherie galleggianti, splendori e ricchezze delle feste acquatiche veneziane," *Rivista marittima* (1982); "Port Louis, un museo navale nuovo, Una proposta per l'Arsenale di Venezia," *Rivista marittima* (1976); "La campagna navale del 1810–1811 in Adriatico," *Rivista Marittima* (1977); and *Le navi della Marina Militare italiana* (Rome: Salomone, 1977).

[78] Gino Benvenuti, *Le repubbliche marinare: Amalfi, Pisa, Genova e Venezia: la nascità, le vittorie, le lotte e il tramonto delle gloriose città-stato che dal Medioevo al XVIII secolo dominarono il Mediterraneo* (1989). Also the late Angelo Iachino's *Le marine italiane nella battaglia di Lepanto* (1971), a 48–page volume published by the Accademia nazionale dei Lincei.

[79] Raffaella Brunetti and Lorenza Mazzino, *Guerre e guerrieri genovesi* (Genoa: D'Amore Editore, 1989). Also see Giuseppe Gavotti, *Battaglie navali della Repubblica di Genova* (1990).

[80] Pierangelo Campodonico, *Navi e marinari genovesi nell'età di Cristoforo Colombo* (Genova: Edizioni Colombo, 1991), and *La marineria genovese dal medioevo all'unità d'Italia* (1991).

[81] Cesare Ciano, *I primi Medici e il mare: note sulla politica marinara toscana da Cosimo I a Ferdinando I* (Pisa: Pacini, 1980), and *La sanità marittima nell'età medicea* (Pisa: Bollettino Storico Pisano, 1976).

[82] Franco Gay, *Le costruzioni navali nell'Arsenale di Venezia* (Rome: Rivista Marittima, 1989); Guglielmo Zanelli, *L'Arsenale di Venezia* (Venice: Centro Internazionale della Grafica di Venezia, 1991); Ugo Pizzarello, *Pietre e legni dell'arsenale di Venezia* (Venice: Cooperativa editoriale l'altra Riva, 1988); Giorgio Bellavistis, *L'Arsenale di Venezia* (Venice: Marsilio Editore, 1983); Romano Chirvi, Franco Gay, Maurizio Crovato, Guglielmo Zanelli, *L'Arsenale dei Veneziani* (Venice: Filippi Editore, 1983); Frederic C. Lane, *Navires et constructeurs à Venise pendant la Renaissance* (Paris: École Pratique des Hautes Ètudes, 1965); Cesare August Levi, *Navi da guerra costruite nell'Arsenale di Venezia dal 1664 al 1896* (Venice: A. Forni, 1983), a reissue of an 1892 study; and Renato Fadda, "L'Arsenale di Venezia," *Edilizia Militare* (1983); Frederic C. Lane, *Navires et constructeurs à Venise pendant la Renaissance* (Paris: SEVPEN, 1965); and Bruno Caizzi, *Industria e commercio della Repubblica Veneta nel xviii secolo* (Milan: banca Commerciale Italiana, 1965). Also see Giuseppe Mataluno, "Cenni storici sull'arsenale M. M. di Taranto" *Rivista marittima* (1986), and *La Spezia e l'Arsenale M.M: mostra storica 1860–1960, 3–21 agosto 1960, Palazzo degli Studi, Piazza Verdi: catalogo* (1961); and Domenico Sella, *Commerci e industrie a Venezia nel secolo XVII* (Venice: Istituto per la Collaborazione Culturale, 1961).

gondola and galley,[83] Mario Murino has examined early maritime law,[84] and Giorgio Silvini has analyzed the role of Venice and Portugal in the spice trade.[85] There are also, as noted earlier, general surveys and local and regional histories of ports such as Triest and maritime provinces like Liguria that run the gamut from scholarly monographs of notarial contracts to broad popular surveys spanning centuries.[86]

There are also a large number of museums and local maritime archives in Italy, and as Dr. Sullivan has noted, the Universities of Pisa and Rome offer naval courses, and the University of Naples has a department of maritime sciences.[87] Among the better known museums are the Museo Storico Navale Venezia,[88] La Spezia's Museo Tecnico Navale[89] and Genoa's Museo Navale.[90] Italians have been a maritime people for centuries, and there are still numerous organizations in Italy that concern themselves with naval and maritime affairs.[91]

---

[83] Graziella Chiesa Buttazzi, *Venezia e la sua gondola* (Milan: Görlich, 1974); Gabriella Cargasacchi, Neve, *La gondola* (Venice: Arsenale Cooperativa Editoriale, 1975); and Giorgio Crovato, Maurizio Crovato, and Luigi Divari, *Barche della laguna di Venezia* (Venice: Arsenale Cooperatrice Editrice, 1980); Guglielmo Zanelli, Silvio Testa, Quirino del Brazolo, *Squeraroli e squeri* (Venice: Ente Gondola, 1986); and Giovanbattista Rubin de Cervin Albrizzi, *Bateau e Batellerie de Venise* (Lausanne: Edita, 1978).

[84] Mario Murino, *Andar per mare nel Medioevo: le antiche consuetudini marittime italiane* (Chieti: Vecchio Faggio Editore, 1988). Also see Riniero Zeno, *Storia del diritto marittimo italiano nel Mediterraneo* (Milan: Giuffrè, 1946), and G. Cassandro, "La formazione del diritto marittimo veneziano," *Annali di storia del diritto* (Milan: Giuffrè, 1968–69).

[85] Giorgio Silvini, *Venezia e Portogallo sulla via delle spezie (1498–1517)* (Treviso: TET, 1982).

[86] For example, Franco Gay, *Le navi della Marina militare italiana* (Rome: Salomone, 1978); and with Elio Andò and Frano Bargoni, *Orizzonte mare: il naviglio militare italiano dal 1861 alla 2ª guerra mondiale* (Rome: Bizzarri, 1976), cited by Dr. Sullivan. Also the late Armando Lodolini's heavily illustrated *Le repubbliche del mare* (Rome: Ente per la Diffusione e l'Educazione Storica, 1967).

[87] The University of Naples has a Dipartimento Scienze Marittime, and the University of Pisa offers courses on naval history.

[88] The museum is located at Riva degli Schiavoni 2148, 30100 Venezia, and its current curator is Admiral Carlo Gottardi, who has discussed some of its holdings in his "La Sala svedese del Museo storico navale di Venezia," *Rivista marittima* (1986).

[89] La Spezia's Museum is operated by the Marina Militare and is located on the Piazza Chiodo, 19100 La Spezia.

[90] Genoa's Museo Navale is administered by the Servizio Beni Culturali and is located in the Villa Doria on Piazza Bonavino, 16156 Genoa–Pegli. Also, Mario Marzari, "Il museo della marineria di Cesenatico," *Rivista marittima* (1986) 119(5); *Mostra navale italiana* (Genoa, Italy: 1982), 669 pp.; and *Mostra navale italian* (1986); *Velieri di Camogli: la quadreria del Museo marinaro "Gio Bono Ferrari"* (1981).

Other museums include (ship models) Museo delle Navi, Via Zamboni 33, 40126 Bologna; Museo Storico Navale, Campo S. Biagio 2148, Via degli Schiavoni, 30122 Venice; (Roman Ships) Museo delle Navi, 00049 Nemi; (fishing) Civico Museo del Mare, Via di Campo Marazio 5, 34123 Trieste; (flags) Museo Sacrario delle Bandiere della Marina Militare, Vittoriano, Rome; (models, relics, navigation equipment) Civico Museo Navale Didattico, Via San Vittore 21, 20123 Milan; (collection on Amalfi's role as a maritime republic) Museo Civico, Piazza Municipo, 84011 Amalfi. There is also a naval museum at Imperia.

[91] Among these are the Centro di Studi sulla Storia della Tecnica at the University of Genoa's Istituto di Storia Moderna e Contemporanea, Via Balbia 6, 16126 Genoa; the Instituti Policattedra di Ingegneria Navale dell' Univesrsità di Genova, Via Montanello, 16145 Genova; the Associazione Italiana di Diritto

As noted above, there are relatively few monographs on the *Risorgimento*, and, like Nunzia Elefante's article on the Sardinian navy in 1986 or the pieces by Antonio Formicola and Claudio Romano on the Bourbon navy, they seem to focus more on the navies of Italian states than on maritime matters.[92] Moreover, aside from Ferrante's study of Thaon di Revel, there are few biographies and relatively little recent work on the early twentieth century.[93] But the lack of biographies does not mean that Italy has had no naval heroes. Although such traditional heroes as Andrea Doria spring most easily to mind, there are a number of major and minor twentieth-century naval figures, some of whom have written memoirs or autobiographies,[94] including Romeo Bernotti,[95] Mario De Monte,[96] Oscar di Giamberardino,[97] Angelo Iachino,[98] Franco Maugeri,[99] Vittorio Tur,[100] Alfredo Viglieri,[101] and Alberto Da

Marittimo in Rome, Via Po 1, Palazzo Assitalia; the Istituto Nazionale per Studied Esperienze di Architettura Navale, Via Corrado Segre 60, 00146 Rome; the Istituto Italiano per gli Studi Storici, Via Benedetto Croce 12, 80134 Naples; The Instituto di Studi Adriatici, 1364–A Riva 7 Martiri, 30122 Venice; and the Istituto per gli Studi di Politica Internazionale, Palazzo Clerici, Via Clerici 5, 20121 Milan.

[92] Nunzia Esposito Elefante, "La marina Sarda nella guerra di Crimea," *Rivista marittima* (1986); Antonio Formicola, and Claudio Romano, "L'industria navale nel regno delle due Sicilie sotto Ferdinando II," *Rivista marittima* (1986), and "1860: Marina borbonica ultimo atto," *Rivista marittima* (1984). Also see *La marina militare italiana nel 1848* (Rome: Ufficio Storico della Marina Militare, 1948); Giovanni Macchi, "La marina italiana a Creta in una operazione multinazionale di fine ottocento," *Rivista marittima* (1985); Arturo Marcheggiano, Arturo, "Le operazioni navali italiane nella prima guerra di indipendenza (1848–49)," *Rivista marittima* (1984); Sante Romiti, *Le marine militari italiane nel Risorgimento, 1748–1861* (1950); and Franco Micali Baratelli, *La marina militare italiana nella vita nazionale (1860–1914)* (1983).

[93] For recent biographies, Paolo Luigi, *Andrea Doria* (Milan: Editoriale Nuova, 1984). Among earlier biographies are Robert Sabatino Lopez, *Genova marinara nel Duecento. Benedetto Zaccaria, ammiraglio e mercante* (Genoa: 1933), Vol. 17 of the Biblioteca storica Principato series; Alberto Tenenti, *Cristoforo Da Canal: la marine venitienne avant Lepante* (1962); and Mario Battaglieri, *La politica navale del conte di Cavour* (1942). And, of course, there are a great many works in Italian and English on Columbus, including Kirpatrick Sale's critical *The Conquest of Paradise: Christopher Columbus and the Columbian Legacy* (New York: Knopf, 1990).

[94] For the minor, Alessandro Caldara, *Quelli di sottocastello: cronaca di guerra, 1940–1943* (Milan: Mursia, 1978); and Dino Selmi, *Marò, li ricordi di guerra sul mare, 1940-1943* (Pisa: Giardini, 1977).

[95] Romeo Bernotti, *Cinquant'anni nella Marina militare* (Milan: Mursia, 1972); *Storia della guerra in Mediterraneo, 1940–1943* (Rome: 1960).

[96] Mario De Monte, *Uomini ombra. Ricordi di un addetto al servizio segreto navale, 1939–1943* (Rome: Nuova Editoriale Marinara Italiana, 1955). Also see Giovanni Roccardi, *Gioco d'ala* (Rome: Trevi, 1981).

[97] Oscar Di Giamberardino, *La marina nella tragedia nazionale* (Rome: Danesi in via Margutta, 1947); and *La politica bellica nella tragedia nazionale* (Rome: Polin, 1945).

[98] See Dr. Sullivan's paper and footnote 55, above, for Iachino's works.

[99] Franco Maugeri, *From the Ashes of Disgrace* (New York: Reynal & Hitchcock, 1948); *Ricordi di un marinaio: la Marina italiana dai primi del Novecento al secondo dopoguerra nelle memorie di uno dei suoi capi* (Milan: Mursia, 1980).

[100] Vittorio Tur, *Plancia ammiraglio* (Rome: Edizioni moderne, 1958).

[101] Alfredo Viglieri, *In mare, in terra, in cielo. Vicende di pace e di guerra (1915–1945)* (Milan: Mursia, 1977).

Zara.[102] That more biographies are not being done is probably due to the association of such figures as Costanzo Ciano and Gabriele D'Annunzio with the fascist regime[103] and the tendency of the Italian services to credit units, such as the X Mas, rather than commanders, like Julio Borghese, with spectacular performances—a tendency that has also created the impression that Italy had no aces during World War II.[104]

But while I am not particularly pessimistic with regard to Italy, I am less sanguine when contemplating the future of Italian naval and maritime studies in this country. Not only does it appear that most Americans, including academics, have little interest in the field, but if the Pentagon's budget is cut, surely one of the first things to go, aside from low-level personnel, will be the historians. It thus might be worth considering ways in which to stimulate interest in naval and maritime studies, and by extension, military, diplomatic, and political history, because all of these suffer from the same diseases—the hegemony of social history within academics and the general indifference to things Italian among the general public, which includes publishers and editors.[105] Finding a niche in the curriculum can thus be as difficult as finding a publisher in this country.

One way to promote naval and maritime history is, of course, to recast it as social history by rejecting Mahan and embracing Braudel.[106] This, I think, will

---

[102] Alberto da Zara, *Pelle d'ammiraglio* (Milan: Le Scie, 1949).

[103] Ciano and D'Annunzio thus tend to be thought of as subjects for studies on "fascism," not on naval or maritime history, and it is reassuring to know that there is a recent biography on Costanzo Ciano. For example, Gioacchino Volpe, *Gabriele D'Annunzio: L'italiano, il politico, il combattente* (Rome: Volpe, 1981); Giovanni Rizzo, *D'Annunzio e Mussolini: la verità sui loro rapporti* (Rocco San Casciano: F. Cappelli, 1960); or Ludovico Domenico, *Gli aviatori italiani del bombardamento nella guerra 1915–1918* (Rome: Ufficio Storico Aeronautica Militare, 1980), which stresses D'Annunzio impact on air operations, and Giovanni Battista Giuriati, *Con D'Annunzio e Millo in difesa dell'Adriatico* (Florence: Sansoni, 1954). Franco Cordova and Michael Ledeen therefore both treated D'Annunzio and the occupation of Fiume in 1919–20 as "political" subjects. Similarly, even though he headed the seamen's union, Giuseppe Giulietti has acquired a political aura; see his biography, *Pax Mundi* (Naples: Rispoli, 1945).

[104] For an example of the tendency to deal with the unit, Maurizio Circi, *30° stormo idrovolanti. Note storiche dal 1931 al 1974* (Rome: Ufficio Storico Aeronautica Militare/Bizzarri, 1974); Antonio Duma, *Quelli del cavallino rampante. Storia del 4° stormo caccia* (Rome: Ateneo, 1981); Nino Arena, *50° stormo d'assalto* (Modena: STEM, 1979); Alberto Borgiotti, *97° gruppo autonomo bombardamento a tuffo 1940–1941: Sicilia, Balcani, Africa Settentrionale* (Rome: Ateneo & Bizzarri). Also Junio Valerio Borghese, *Sea Devils*, op. cit., also wrote a history of his unit rather than an autobiography.

[105] This certainly has been my experience. Evidently books on Italy, whether on prostitution in the Renaissance or nineteenth–century military policy, do not sell well in this country. As one editor of a major publishing house, both of which shall remain anonymous, wrote me regarding a manuscript on the Italian Navy during World War II, "surely the obsession with Germany is a correct one" because "Anglo–Italian clashes" were "thoroughly unimportant" in the "Battle of the Atlantic."

[106] For example, Alvarez Javier Guillamón, "Congreso histórico: ciudad y mar en la edad moderna," *Contrastes* (Spain) (1985), describes a September 1984 conference in Cartagena that focussed on (1) geographical framework and urban development, (2) demography and socioprofessional structures, (3) economic bases and productive factors, (4) market and commercial relations, (5) institutional and military aspects, and (6) maritime science and techniques. Or one could follow the example of David A. Cappell,

occur in the field of contemporary naval studies as it has in the field of early modern naval and maritime history. Such a shift in emphasis would undoubtedly be healthy because it would expand the horizons of those of us who dabble in naval and maritime history as well as those of our colleagues who do not. But while such a shift will be relatively easy for Italian historians, who are close to archival sources, it will be more difficult for those of us who survive by using published sources, at least until a solid foundation of published documents and monographs on naval and maritime history is available.

Another way to promote naval and maritime history is to do colonial and transnational studies. But this will be difficult, since one of the characteristics of naval histories is that they tend to be parochial, and too often hyperbolically patriotic, which is certainly one of the reasons that the field is not taken seriously by many historians.[107] Yet in the case of Italian navies, such an approach makes considerable sense, since the essence of Italian naval and maritime history is its diversity and the interaction of the navies of Italian states over the centuries with each other and with surrounding naval forces, whether Barbary corsairs, Dalmatian *Uskoks* and the Turkish fleet in the early modern period; the French fleet and the Austrian navy during the Napoleonic wars and the *Risorgimento*; or the British and Austrian fleet during this century.[108]

By its very nature, naval and maritime history is part of an international political, economic, social, and diplomatic history, and it should not be contained within narrow national boundaries but connected to the wider world. Dragan ivojinovi has done this for the Dalmatian littoral by focusing on topics as diverse as the role of naval officers in the Adriatic during the unsettled period of 1918–21 and the relations between Dubrovnik and the American colonies in the late 1700s.[109] Indeed, cities such as Dubrovnik–Ragusa, Rijeka–Fiume, Split–

"Shipboard Relations between Pacific Island Women and Euroamerican Men, 1767–1887," *Journal of Pacific History* (1992), and write on such topics as "madamismo" in Italian East African ports and aboard Italian ships.

[107] For example, the exaggeration of the role played by British submarines in the Adriatic during World War I in Paul Kemp and Peter Jung, "Five Broken Down B Boats: British Submarine Operations in the Northern Adriatic, 1915–1917," *Warship International* (1989).

[108] For example, Gligor Stanojevi, *Senjski Uskoci* (Belgrade: Vojnoizdavaki Zavod, 1973); and Alberto Tenenti, *Piracy and the Decline of Venice, 1580–1615* (London: Longman, 1967), originally published as *Venezia e i corsari, 1580–1615* (Bari: Laterza, 1961); and Giulio Giacchero, *Pirati barbareschi, schiavi e galeotti nella storia e nella leggenda ligure* (1970), a volume in the Scaffaletto Genovese series. Tenenti dealt with Uskoks, Barbary Corsairs, and English, Spanish, Maltese and Florentine pirates. Unfortunately, the tendency is to draw a line through the middle of the Adriatic and treat one side as Italian, the other as eastern European, e.g., Apostolos E. Vacalopoulos, Constantinos D. Svolopoulos, and Béla K. Király, eds., *Southeast European Maritime Commerce and Naval Policies from the Mid–Eighteenth Century to 1914* (Boulder: Columbia Univ. Press, 1988), vol. 23 of the War and Society in East Central Europe series. The volume discusses the British, French, Austrian, and even American navies, and policy in the Adriatic and on the Danube, but Italy is largely ignored.

[109] Dragan ivojinovi, *Amerika revolucija i dubrovaka republika, 1763–1790* (Belgrade: Prosveta, 1976), and "The United States and its Unknown Role in the Adriatic Conflicts of 1918–21" (1989), Occasional Paper, East European Program, European Institute, n. 15.

Spalato, Zadar–Zara, Pola–Pula, and Šibenik–Sebenico are as integral to Italian history as Trst–Triest, Venice, or Bari, and the Adriatic is as international a sea as the Tyrrhennian, Ionian, or Mediterranean.[110] Although the tendency is to see the Adriatic as dividing Italy from eastern Europe, it is clear that the sea unites the Italian to the Balkan peninsula, and authors as diverse as Paolo Alatri and Bernard Stulli have dealt with the connection in one context or another.[111]

To the extent that the Adriatic, Tyrrhenian, Black, and Red Seas are extensions of the Mediterranean, Italian naval and maritime history forms an integral part of Italian colonial and imperial history. In a sense, Austrian, Italian, French, and Balkan history—whether Turkish, Yugoslav, Greek, or Albanian— are therefore complementary.[112] But while there are studies ranging from the expansion of the early maritime empires into the Black sea to the role played by the Italian Navy in colonial expansion in Africa in this century, there is a great deal that can still be done. For example, to the best of my knowledge, there are no comprehensive histories of the Adriatic or Tyrrhenian seas that would integrate a variety of approaches over time, as Braudel did almost a half-century ago for the Mediterranean.[113]

Finally, let me note that while relatively few publishers and journals take a consistent interest in naval and maritime history, there are a number of journals

[110] For the Adriatic, its cities, and its fleets, see Lawrence Thomas Sondhaus, *Austria and the Adriatic: The Development of Habsburg Maritime Policy, 1797–1866* (Ph.D., University of Virginia, 1986); Lothar Höbelt, "Die Marine," *Habsburgermonarchie 1848–1918* (1987); Karl Gogg, *Österreichs Kriegsmarine, 1848–1918* (Salzburg: Verlag das Berland-Buch, 1967); Roberto Cessi, *La Repubblica di Venezia e il problema adriatico* (Naples: 1953); Bariša Kreki, *Dubrovnik et le Levant au Moyen Âge* (Paris: Mouton, 1961), and *Dubrovnik in the 14th and 15th Centuries* (Norman, Okla.: Univ. of Oklahoma Press, 1972).

[111] Paolo Alatri, *Nitti, D'Annunzio e la questione adriatica* (Milan: Feltrinelli, 1959), and Bernard Stulli, "Talijanski historiografija i jadranska irredentizam," *Hrvatski Zbornik* (1954). Also see Milan Marjanovi, *Borba za Jadran, 1914–1946: Iredenta i imperializam* (Split: 1953); Vjekoslav Maštrovi, *Kako je svršena okupacija Zadra 1918. godina* (Zadar: 1951); and Berislav Viskovi, "Ratna 1943. Godina kao presuda forza bitke za Jadran," *Vojnoistoriski Glasnik* (1984); Ferdo ulinovi, *Rijeka drava* (Zagreb, 1953).

[112] For example, Kenneth M. Setton, *Venice, Austria, and the Turks in the Seventeenth Century* (Philadelphia: American Philosophical Society, 1991); or Juliette Bessis, *La Méditerranée fasciste: l'Italie mussolinienne et la Tunisie* (Pairs: Éditions Karthala, 1981). Although neither of these is a naval history, the interaction of the Mediterranean states makes a transnational approach natural for maritime and naval history.

[113] The Italian Foreign Ministry's Comitato per la documentazione dell'opera dell'Italia in Africa sponsored a series of studies on the work of the Italian services overseas, including that by Giuseppe Fioravanzo and Guido Viti on the navy, *L'Italia in Africa. Serie Storico-militare. Vol. II. L'opera della marina (1868–1943)* (Rome: Istituto Poligrafico dello Stato, 1959). But the work is now rather dated. Among works on the subject, see Vittorio Giglio and Angelo Ravenni, *Le guerre coloniali d'Italia* (Milan: Francesco Vallardi, 1942); Luigi Goglia, "Sulla politica coloniale fascista," *Storia contemporanea* (1988); and E. S. Zevakin and A. Penko, "Ricerche sulla storia delle colonie genovesi nel Caucaso occidentale nei secoli XIII-XIV," in *Miscellanea di Studi Storici* (Genoa: Istituto di Medievistica, 1969), vol. I. There have been a great number of works published on Italy's colonial policy over the past fifteen to twenty years, but they have tended to focus on land operations, economics, and diplomacy rather than maritime or naval matters, even though the Navy played a crucial role in the Italian conquests of Libya in 1911–12 and Ethiopia in 1935–6.

that will publish works on naval and maritime history. In Italy, *Rivista marittima*, *Bollettino d'Archivio dell'Ufficio Storico della Marina Militare*, *Panorama Difesa*, *Storia Militare*, and *Rivista Italiana Difesa* regularly publish articles dealing with naval and maritime history, technique, and current policy,[114] as do such organizations as Genoa's Istituto Medievistica.[115] Storia contemporanea, Storia e politica, Archivio Storico Italiano, Nuova Rivista Storica, Rivista Storica Italiana, Quaderni Stefaniani,[116] and Rassegna Storica della Liguria have also published essays on naval and maritime history. In this country, aside from the *Naval War College Review* and the United States Naval Institute Press, there are few outlets for naval historians, although, as with major publishers, major journals will publish articles on maritime and naval history.[117] In Italy, a handful of editorial houses publish the bulk of the books on maritime and naval history, among them Ermanno Albertelli, who publishes Bagnasco and others; Mursia, which has published Giorgerini; and Edizioni dell'Ateneo e Bizzarri, which publishes a variety of air-naval studies. In this country a major press, such as Johns Hopkins, might issue a work like that by Davis on early modern maritime history, but they shy away from works on World War II Italian naval history, leaving only Greenwood and a few publishing houses in England, like Frank Cass.[118]

What is needed, it seems to me, is some way to provide more outlets for articles on naval and maritime history that are not associated with a service institute, and to create an organization that would provide a network for those of us interested in the area, even if we teach in such places as Hattiesburg, Mississippi where merely keeping up with the literature is an impossible task and where beauty pageants, the NFL draft, and the Dixie League are of much more immediate interest to most people than naval and maritime history.

---

[114] See Ezio Ferrente, *La Rivista Marittima dalla fondazione ai nostri giorni. La storia, gli autori, le idee* (Rome: Rivista Marittima, 1986). My thanks to Admiral Pascazio and Professor Alberto Santoni for calling my attention to these publications, some of which Dr. Sullivan has also mentioned.

[115] Or the Deputazione di Storia Patria per le Venezie, which publishes the *Archivio Veneto*.

[116] For example, Cesare Ciano, "Considerazioni sulla disciplina a bordo delle navi mediterranee nel XVII secolo," (1987); Franco Gay, "L'Arsenale di Venezia," (1984). *Quaderni Stefaniani* is published in Pisa.

[117] *Contemporary European History*, the *Journal of Strategic Studies*, and the *Journal of Contemporary History*, the *Journal of Modern History*, *Economic History Review*, and the *Journal of European Economic History* also have published pieces on Italian naval or maritime history. Other possible outlets include, but are not limited to journals such as the *Mediterranean Historical Review*, *War & Society*, *Revue internationale d'histoire militaire*, *Aeronautica: mensile dell'aviazione italiana*, *Marine Rundschau*, *Revue d'histoire de la deuxième guerre mondiale et des conflits contemporains*, *Archivio storico marina*, and *The Mariner's Mirror*.

[118] Among other editorial houses that have published works on Italian naval history are Biblioteca del Bollettino Storico Pisano (Pisa) and Istituto di Medievistica (Genoa); Harvard Univ. Press; and the Istituto Storico Germanico in Roma. But only the Istituto di Medievistica in Genoa has a large list of titles, which include the works of Laura Balletto.

17

Japan

Mark R. Peattie and David C. Evans

Fifty years ago Alexander Kiralfy, writing about Japanese naval thought, asserted that the Japanese "lack interest in waters which do not directly concern them."[1] Allowing for a certain degree of wartime ignorance and prejudice about the Japanese enemy which he displayed in the article, Kiralfy had a point. For reasons that have to do with geography and history, Japan's maritime interests throughout its history have been mostly limited to its home waters and to those of the northeast Asian littoral. Only for one brief period, 1940–1945, did those interests stretch as far as the mid-Pacific, southeast Asia, and the eastern Indian Ocean.

This regional focus, or "continental strategy," as Clark Reynolds would have it, has meant that modern Japanese naval thought has been subjective, rather than objective, concerned with the specific application of the principles of sea power to the Japanese case, rather than with the study of sea power as a general historical phenomenon about which broad judgments can be drawn. Even the most erudite of Japan's modern naval thinkers, Satō Tetsutarō, sometimes mistakenly referred to as the "Japanese Mahan," framed his arguments solely for a Japanese audience. While the evidence on which he rested his ponderous and somewhat mystical *On the History of Imperial Defense* (1908) was drawn from examples of the naval and maritime history of the West, his theoretical point of reference was exclusively Japanese. Those lesser Japanese naval writers who followed after Satō in the 1920s and 1930s were even more subjective in their concerns. In the decade immediately prior to the Pacific War, Japanese naval thought, expounded by civilians as well as naval professionals, was essentially directed toward the mobilization and increase of Japanese naval power and the defeat of the American naval enemy.

General State of the Field in Postwar Japan

Given its outcome, it is not surprising that the Pacific War did nothing to broaden the Japanese perspective on naval matters and, indeed, in one sense

---

[1] Alexander Kiralfy, "Japanese Naval Strategy," in Edward Earle *et al.*, eds., *Makers of Modern Strategy: Military Thought from Machiavelli to Hitler* (New Jersey: Princeton Univ. Press, 1943), pp. 457–84.

further narrowed its focus on national concerns. Certainly, any discussion of the state of naval history in postwar Japan must begin with the impact of the Pacific War on that nation. Not only did that conflict shape the view of the Japanese public toward the subject of military history in general, but the nation's defeat in that war and the Imperial Japanese Navy's role in it have shaped the concerns of those who have been most active in thinking and writing about naval history.

To begin with, for decades after its conclusion there was a general turning away from the rationale for the Pacific War by the majority of the Japanese people. Civilian scholars, indifferent if not hostile to operational history, sought explanations for Japan's defeat in the nation's pre-war political, economic, and social systems. Those who were concerned with the Navy's operational history were those former officers who had served in the Navy. But there were inhibitions to writing about it publicly, even for those naval professionals, for the undeniable fact was that the history of the Japanese Navy ended badly. Whatever the early triumphs of the Imperial Japanese Navy, its humiliating demise cast a pall of gloom over its story. In the United States, following naval victory on two oceans, there were hundreds of thousands of Navy veterans who looked forward to reading about the triumphant campaigns in which they had taken part. In Japan, a large portion of the potential audience rested at the bottom of the ocean and that portion which survived wished largely to forget the trauma of war. In the early postwar years, moreover, the existence of the war crimes tribunals undoubtedly had a chilling effect on the publications and pronouncements of anyone who had held a responsible position in either of the two services during the war.

Nevertheless, in the first decades after the war, a small group of former Japanese naval officers did begin sifting through the ashes of defeat to study the pre-war navy, seeking answers as to how and why it played a leading role in the initiation of the war, and how and why it was defeated in the end. With the establishment of the War History Office in 1955 as part of the Japanese Defense Agency, their central effort, along with that of a number of former Imperial Army officers, was channeled into participation in the research and writing of what eventually became the official *Senshi sōsho*, (War History Series), more than one hundred volumes recounting the activities of both services in the China and Pacific wars. Over the course of time, building on their work on the *Senshi sōsho*, through books and articles they wrote as individuals, a number of these former Navy men-turned historian—Normura Minoru and Seukuni Masao, to name two of the most prominent—came to enjoy a solid reputation in the field for their firsthand knowledge and for their professional integrity. Other former Navy officers not connected with the project have produced important works on the war: Chihaya Masataka has written on strategy, Ōi Atsushi on antisubmarine warfare, and Torisu Kennosuke on submarine operations. It has been by the hands of these men that such operational history of the Japanese Navy as exists has been preserved since 1945. On the whole, their work has been highly informative and often usefully analytical. But to much of the academic community in postwar Japan, their writings have lacked intellectual rigor, their subject matter has been seen as irrelevant, and they have been regarded, sometimes unfairly, as apologists for the old navy.

In any event, what has distinguished the work of these men from that of their counterparts in the West has been the absence of personal controversy among themselves and of any open professional debate as to the principal naval campaigns of the war or as to the reputations of the foremost naval commanders who conducted them (some of whom were their direct superiors). In part this may be due to the Navy's traditional reputation as the silent service, but more importantly, perhaps, to the Japanese cultural tradition which does not encourage the open airing of disputes or assaults on the reputations and character of individuals. Nor does it permit a Japanese, no matter how highly placed, to claim achievements for himself, a fact that explains the absence of any real naval autobiographies of the free-wheeling, now-I-can-tell-it variety known in the West. Those autobiographies which do exist are often simply records of long interviews conducted at the behest of disciples. There are, of course, dozens of detailed biographies, often being the product of committees composed of the admirers of the naval figure in question; they too often concentrate on externals and the inconsequential.

Though in the immediate postwar decades the academic community itself, by and large, continued to avoid naval history as a suspect field, established scholars (political scientists and international relations specialists for the most part) and front-rank publishing houses touched upon naval matters in a number of major publications. The collections of primary sources like the Documents on Modern History [*Gendai shi shiryō*] (1962–70) and analytical histories such as *The Road to the Pacific War* [*Taiheiyō sensō e no michi*] (1962–63) contained a wealth of information on the Navy and served as departure points for a myriad of more specialized studies on the role of the Navy in the modernization of Japan and in the origins of the Pacific War.

In the past several decades, moreover, younger academics, educated after the war and thus with no particular bias for or against the pre-war Navy, have begun to enter the field. Many have furthered the study of the Navy's involvement in the origins of the Pacific War, though their perspective is almost entirely that of international relations, domestic politics, or foreign policy. Asada Sadao of Doshisha University, publishing in both Japanese and English, has established himself as the world's authority on Japan's role in the interwar naval treaty system. Itō Takashi of Tokyo University has done important work on the Navy's actions in politics. Ikeda Kiyoshi of Tōhoku University has produced a survey history and a set of critical essays on the old Navy. Others have sought to broaden the study of the Navy in the Pacific War into such non-operational topics as the character and impact of the Navy's administration of those occupied areas assigned to the Navy in Southeast Asia. Still others have sought to push back the study of their nation's naval history to the Meiji (1868–1912) and Taisho (1912–1926) periods, illuminating new aspects of the Navy's history: finances, statutes, personnel policies, education, institutions, and other topics which reflect, to a certain extent, the "new military history" so much in vogue in the West.

The quality of these nonoperational studies is generally good. Yet, what still characterizes almost all the study of naval history in postwar Japan, either by former naval personnel or by civilian scholars, is that which characterized it before the war: its subjective quality, its absolute absorption in the Japanese case. Still lacking is any major work in Japanese which has attempted to provide observations on sea power with global, rather than just national, implications, or any major work that has made wide use of primary sources for a study of the naval history of any Western nation (although articles appear on such topics from time to time), or any that has sought to place Japanese naval thought and history in a comparative context. Until such studies appear, Japanese naval history, for all its intrinsic interest *and* importance, will remain isolated by language and by narrowness of perspective, a monologue in what should be a dialogue.

The public attitude toward Japan's naval past has been ambivalent to say the least. On the one hand, books and magazines for the layman relay masses of information on the old Imperial Navy, its ships, its planes, and especially its exploits during the Pacific War. Some years ago, model kits of the super-battleship *Yamato* were among the top sellers in Japanese toy stores, and a recent NHK (government) television documentary series on the Pacific War, which featured the major naval engagements in the Pacific, 1941–1945, drew a wide audience. On the other hand, any governmental efforts to promote public respect or reverence for Japan's military past can be expected to meet stout public resistance, particularly from the political left, as witnessed by the heated protests over the occasional visits by the Emperor and various Japanese prime ministers to Yasukuni Shrine, dedicated to the spirits of Japan's military dead. Indeed, the general public acceptance of the present Maritime Defense Force, like the other Defense Forces, rests upon the assumption that it is qualitatively different from its hugely more prestigious Imperial predecessor.[2] A third element, the most

---

[2]   In this connection, the authors recall that, on a visit to the First Service School of the Maritime Self-Defense Force at Etajima (the site of the prewar Academy) in 1985, they stopped in to view the naval museum and were surprised to see at the top of the grand stairway leading into the building a triptych of portraits: Tōgo Heihachirō, Horatio Nelson, and John Paul Jones. Later, when asked what sort of message the last portrait was intended to convey to aspiring young Japanese naval cadets, the superintendent of the Service School replied somewhat vaguely that it was the duty of the Self-Defense Force to instill "a spirit of internationalism" in its graduates. Clearly, it meant that, while Tōgo was sufficiently removed in time to be an acceptable icon to postwar Japanese naval officers, and while the addition of Nelson's portrait paid tribute to British tutelage of the Japanese Navy in its infancy, the

conservative band in the Japanese political spectrum, further complicates public attitudes toward Japanese naval history. Though small in numbers, its power to influence scholarly discourse on military matters is out of proportion to its size. While this influence is difficult to gauge with any accuracy, it does appear to limit research into topics deemed too delicate, such as the relationship of the Imperial family to the pre-war Navy, or too revered, such as the reputation of Admiral Tōgo, to be appropriate subjects for unrestricted scrutiny and discussion. The authors have been told by younger Japanese naval historians on more than one occasion that foreign researchers are able to write about the Imperial Navy in ways that would not be possible for them. Such assertions do not in any way imply that contemporary Japanese naval historians have maintained anything less than the highest professional standards in their work, but they do indicate that Japanese researchers are obliged to be a bit more guarded in their judgments and in their choice of subjects than are their counterparts in the West.

Institutions Promoting the Study of Naval History

The principal element of the Japanese government involved in promoting the study of naval history in Japan is the Japanese Defense Agency, both through its instruction at the various service academies (see below) and through the research activities of the Military History Department (Senshi-bu, which succeeded the War History Office) of the National Institute for Defense Studies. Since the completion of the Senshi sōsho series, the mission of the Department has broadened to include research on military and naval history in general, though the thrust of its studies is largely related to Japan and the rest of Asia. Though the faculty of the department contributes to scholarly journals outside the Defense Agency, the purpose of the department is essentially the training and education of members of the Japanese Defense Forces.

More specifically devoted to the promotion of studies on the former Imperial Navy is the Japanese Navy History Preservation Association (Kaigun Rekishi Hozonkai), a semi-governmental foundation affiliated with the Defense Agency. At present, the main efforts of the association are directed toward the compilation of a ten-to-twelve volume narrative history, with substantial appendices, of the Imperial Navy.

Two private institutions promote the study of naval history to varying degrees. The larger of these, the Military History Society (Gunjishi Gakkai), was founded in 1955 to bring together both scholars and military professionals interested in furthering the study of military history in general. While the focus of its interest is largely that of land warfare, its regularly published journal, *Military History*

---

inclusion of any Japanese commanders from the Pacific War, such as Yamamoto Isoroku, Ozawa Jisaburō, or Nagumo Chūichi, could only create an image problem for the Self-Defense Force. Far safer to honor an American naval hero whose combat experience had nothing to do with Japan and whose reputation, in any event, was largely unknown to the Japanese.

[*Gunjishi*] occasionally carries articles of naval interest. It is a sign of the slowly increasing respectability of military history among Japanese academic circles that the Society was admitted as a member of the Science Council of Japan in 1984. A smaller institution, The Navy Library (Kaigun Bunko) in Tokyo, is devoted entirely to the study of Japanese naval history and its regularly published journal, *Navy History Research* [*Kaigunshi Kenkyū*], presents articles almost exclusively focused on the Imperial Navy and largely based on materials possessed by the Library.

Resource Collections and Basic Sources

The library of the Military History Department of the National Institute for Defense Studies is a major resource for the study of Japanese military and naval history, housing as it does some 25,000 books, 48,000 maps, and 146,000 documents, of which 33,000 deal with naval matters. The library is essentially closed to the public, though limited access is available on a selected basis. The Kaigun Bunko, with approximately 30,000 volumes, is somewhat smaller but similarly valuable. Public access to the collection is similarly limited and granted selectively. The National Diet Library also has a good number of important naval works, though these do not comprise a major consolidated collection, nor is there a specialist in naval history on the library staff.

One of the principal difficulties in the study of Japan's modern naval history is the dearth of primary sources, at least in comparison to those available in major archives in the United States and Western Europe. There are a number of reasons for this state of affairs, but none is as critical as the wholesale destruction of files and documents by the Japanese military services and civilian government in the several days after the Japanese surrender which ended the Pacific War. It is regrettable, but inevitable, therefore, that there are numerous issues of major importance concerning the Japanese Navy and its plans and operations in the China and Pacific wars that will never be resolved or which will be understood incompletely because of the absence of adequate documentation. Of course, a significant portion of the Navy's records did escape destruction and the compilers of the 106–volume *Senshi sōsho*, published from 1966 to 1980 by the Asagumo Shimbunsha, have exploited these, supplementing them wherever possible with diaries and interviews with former Imperial Army and Navy officers.

The thirty-three volumes of the Senshi sōsho, which are devoted to naval matters, therefore, comprise the most detailed, most complete, and most authoritative record of the Navy's plans, operations, organization, weaponry, strategy and tactics from 1937 to 1945. One can scarcely research any topic within these categories as they relate to the Imperial Navy without consulting the relevant volumes of the series. Nevertheless the collection not only suffers from the usual debilities of official history, but presents a number of problems to the serious researcher. A practical difficulty is that the series, like most Japanese scholarly works, includes neither an overall index nor indexes for any of the individual volumes. More serious is the lack of any interpretive or critical approach to the subjects treated. This is due partly to the fact that the hundred or more compilers of the series, most of them former members of the Imperial armed forces, were reluctant to critique the actions of the major commanders, most of whom were deceased and many of whom were their own superior officers. More importantly, most of those involved in this huge effort in research and writing were untrained in historical inquiry and thus frequently became absorbed in accumulating enormous detail without being able to stand back and ask larger questions of the material which came under their hands, believing, perhaps, that great masses of fact would naturally and inevitably yield the truth. A final and curious defect in the series is the frequent and unfortunate redundancy from volume to volume whereby campaigns and operations are given in exhaustive detail from the standpoints of both services, a ghostly echo of the traditional rivalry between the Imperial Army and Navy, which reached dangerous levels during the Pacific War.

The *Senshi sōsho* comprise only the largest and best known of the published collections which deal, *inter alia*, with the Japanese Navy. While even a partial listing of the histories on specialized naval topics is impossible to provide here, by way of example we note the *History of Naval Organization* [*Kaigun seido enkaku*], originally produced by the Navy Ministry in the 1930s and reissued in twenty-six volumes by Hara Shobō (1971–72); the four–volume History of Japanese Naval Aviation [*Nihon kaigun kōkūshi*], published in 1969 and compiled by veterans of the Japanese naval air service: the *History of Shipbuilding in the Showa period* [*Showa zosenshi shi*], a two–volume work published in 1977, of which the second volume is devoted to naval construction from the mid–1920s onward; the two–volume study of the Japanese Navy's use of naval fuels [*Nihon kaigun nenryōshi shi*], published in 1972; and the Showa period social and economic history collection of Navy Ministry materials [*Showa shakai keizaishi shūsei: Kaigunsho shiryo*], which is now being published by the Daitō Bunka Daigaku Tōyō Kenkyujo and contains some important naval documents not found elsewhere. When it is completed in 1995, the multivolume history of the Imperial Navy by the Hozonkai, mentioned earlier, will undoubtedly be a major resource. Finally, we should mention the existence of a number of important diaries of leading figures in the prewar and wartime Japanese Navy, including those of Katō Kanji, Ishikawa Shingo, Fujii Shigeru, Takagi Sōkichi, Nagumo Chūichi, and Ugaki Matome, the last of these having recently appeared in an English translation.

With very few exceptions, this material remains untranslated and thus inaccessible to those researchers who cannot read Japanese. But gradually, as the number of Western-trained Japanese scholars in the field increases, along with the number of Western naval historians possessed of Japanese language facility, we in the West will gain a more sophisticated understanding of Japanese naval history.

Instruction in Naval History

Formal study of naval history in Japan is confined to the educational institutions of the Defense Agency.

At the Defense Academy, cadets aiming at a commission in the Japanese Maritime Self-Defense Force (JMSDF) take several courses that include naval affairs, for example, "Technology and War," "Western Military History" and "Contemporary Military History." Naval history is the exclusive focus of one course, "History of Naval War." A prospectus, echoing Mahan—who enjoys a high reputation seemingly undiminished by time and change among JMSDF officers[3]—states that it "examines the influence of sea power on the rise and fall of states." Instructors of this course are normally senior JMSDF officers who have done a stint as scholars of naval history at the National Institute for Defense Studies. In recent years, all have been active scholars. Toyama Saburō, a Pacific War veteran and rear admiral, JMSDF (ret.), published an exhaustive study of the battles of the Russo–Japanese War and several other books of naval battle history. Nomura Minoru, already mentioned in connection with the *Senshi sōsho*, wrote on the Navy's role in the politics of the prewar period and many other subjects. Hirama Yōichi, the current Professor of Maritime Defense Studies, has published on the Japanese Navy in World War I, the influence of Sun Tzu on naval thinking, and other topics.

At the JMSDF Staff School, lieutenants and lieutenant commanders take part in seminars on strategic affairs and national security matters. Their work often involves naval history, and they often publish their work in the Staff School journal, *Waves* [*Hatō*], though their studies are often of a narrow technical nature.

Maritime History

This area of scholarship, in the words of a knowledgeable Japanese informant, is "at a low ebb." Why this should be so is difficult to understand, particularly given Japan's current position as one of the world's leaders in maritime commerce. One reason may be that the professional schools and colleges run by the government, at which maritime history might be pursued, have a strictly technical and practical curriculum that excludes such "soft" subjects as history. This is true of the Maritime Safety (coast guard) Academy, the Marine Technical

---

3   Hirama Yōichi's recent article, "The influence of A.T. Mahan on the Japanese navy" (A.T. Mahan ga Nihon kaigun ni ataeta eikyō), *Seiji keizai shigaku*, no. 320 (February 1993), pp. 29–48, documents the continuing popularity of Mahan, who is "still revered as the god of sea power." The most recent Japanese translation of *The Influence of Sea Power upon History* appeared in 1984. Its editor, Kitamura Ken'ichi, admiral, JMSDF, Ret., said in an interview with one of the authors (10 June 1986) that Mahan was still valid for today provided proper allowance was made for technological advances since Mahan's time.

College, the Tokyo Merchant Marine Academy, the Tokyo College of Fishery and the Kobe Merchant Marine Academy. The Tokyo Merchant Marine Academy sponsors the Japan Nautical Association, which publishes *Seafaring* [*Kōkai*], but its articles are almost all on technical subjects.

For many years a private organization, the Japan Maritime History Association has published a well-respected journal, *Studies in Maritime History* [*Kaijishi kenkyū*]. Recently, however, the organization has suffered from lack of funding. Further, it shares the parochialism of the naval history establishment in Japan by concentrating on Japanese maritime history, primarily that of the early and medieval periods.

One slim hope for maritime history in Japan would seem to be the example of the just-married Crown Prince. While at Oxford, Naruhito studied medieval river traffic on the Thames.

18

Republic of Korea

Kim Ill Sang

Ancient Korea was closely tied to the Chinese Empire, and for the people of Korea, China represented the external world almost exclusively. As a result, Koreans viewed the Korean peninsula as an appendage of the Asian continent rather than as a separate entity poised on the sea. Given this landward focus, ancient Koreans were not concerned with naval and maritime affairs. This, however, does not mean that there was no maritime activity or sea transportation. It has, in fact, been demonstrated that intercoastal sea communication existed, although limited, as early as 4000 B.C. One example of this activity is the body of comb-pattern earthen wares which have been excavated all along the Korean peninsula coastline.

The Kokuryo (37-66 B.C.), Shila (57-935 B.C.) and Paekche (18-660 B.C.) empires were all deeply entwined with the Chinese Empire. All three empires maintained important and close political and economic relations with the Chinese. At the same time, however, these empires failed to develop strong naval forces, so their military systems were designed to meet land-based threats rather than those from the sea. It is not surprising, then, that Japanese sea pirates frequently encroached upon the southern coast of Korea in those lean years of the Three Empires.

In 1592, Toyotomi, then Emperor of Japan, decided to invade the Korean peninsula with the intent of changing the international balance of power which, until then, had been a hierarchy in terms of power and influence with China at the top, Korea in the middle, and Japan at the bottom. In the end, the Shila Empire unified the peninsula through the advantage provided by their control over the Han River, which facilitated communications with China. After unification, a significant development in Korean maritime history was brought about by Bo-Ko Chang in A.D. 828. He became a base commander of Wan-Do, an island off the southern coast, after serving in the Chinese Army as a general. With the security Chang provided on that strategic island, Shilla was able to achieve economic growth through international trade and destroy the pirate menace.

In 1231, the Mongols invaded the Koryo dynasty. The King of Koryo resisted the usurpation for 30 years by taking refuge on Kwang-Hwa Island. The Mongols never completely dominated Korea and, after 30 years conflict, they made peace. A number of important factors made this long resistance possible. First, Kwang-Hwa island was isolated by the sea and strongly fortified. Additionally, the Koreans built combatant vessels of various sizes, some with cannon aboard, to enhance the island's defense. Finally, thousands of Koreans were on the islands, providing the manpower base to continue the resistance.

It is interesting to note that, in the process of the peace negotiations, the Mongols asked the Koryos to join them in a combined forces to invade Japan. The Koreans agreed to this request. Two joint invasion operations failed, however, because of bad weather, which the Japanese called Kami-Kaze (God's Wind). The first joint invasion force of 1274 consisted of 20,000 Mongol-Chinese and 5,400 Koryos in 900 ships built in Koryo. In 1281, the second joint invading forces totalled 40,000 men with more than 4,000 ships.

This mission's failure led the Japanese to believe that Koryo and the Mongols were militarily weak. Japanese pirates then increased their encroachment of the southern part of Koryo in the fourteenth century. By the end of the Koryo dynasty, Japanese pirates had become quite powerful. Koreans living on the coastlines began to move inland, and the Korean government had difficulty protecting seaborne commerce. This created many problems for Korea. For instance, the ancient Korean taxation system was primarily monetary, but an important part involved assessments in grain (mostly rice) for government use. Typically, the local authorities shipped the grain to the authorities at the Imperial Palace by sea. The sea pirates, however, interdicted this trade and contributed to the decline of the Koryo dynasty's power. In fact, the failure of the two joint invasion operations and the suspension in shipping tax grain were the two most important events that led to the Koryo dynasty's collapse.

The early fifteenth century witnessed a number of significant changes for Korean maritime affairs. In 1408, the Lee dynasty consolidated a naval force, as the number of vessels increased from 412 to 597, and the number of the sailors increased to 49,000. In 1413, the Koryo dynasty invented the turtle ship. In 1415, 10,000 guns were manufactured.

In 1592, Toyotomi's Japanese invading forces attacked Pusan and then advanced toward Seoul. However, Admiral Soon-Shin Lee recovered control of the entire southern part of the sea basin, and swept the enemy from the southern part of the coastline except for the Pusan area. Admiral Lee fought many sea battles against the Japanese and won every engagement. During the Japanese invasion of Korea, the most important sea battles were fought at San-Han Myung-Yang and No-Ryang. Admiral Lee was killed in the battle of No-Ryang, but in doing so he saved the Lee dynasty, in a manner similar to that of Nelson, who achieved his victory over the French and Spanish at Trafalgar three hundred years later.

By the nineteenth century, a policy of isolation was firmly entrenched in both Japan and Korea. In 1853-54, a U.S. naval squadron under command of Commodore Perry took an aggressive attitude toward Japan with regard to opening that country's ports for trade. Japan, in the end, accepted an open door policy.

In Korea however, the "open door" came with greater difficulty. In 1866, an American merchantman, the *General Sherman*, was burnt by Pyong-Yang officials in Tae-Dong River. The Americans protested this incident on Kwang-Hwa island, and a military engagement between the Korean garrison forces and five U.S. naval ships ensued.

In 1875, Japan took coercive action toward Korea in much the same way as Admiral Perry had done to Japan before. The Korean peninsula was soon occupied by Japan, and an open door policy was adopted under Japanese "guidance."

Japan completed the colonization of the Korean peninsula following her victory over China in the Sino-Japanese War of 1894. In 1904, Japan soundly defeated the Russian Navy in the Russo-Japanese War. One of the most important reasons for this important victory was the Japanese occupation of the Chinhae Bay of Korea. Later, Japan started building a naval base at that location. This Japanese decision is significant because it later turned out to be one of the critical naval bases supporting Japanese military operations in the Pacific during World War II.

Today, the geopolitical position of Korea is similar to that of 1890-1910 in Alfred T. Mahan's terms. It occupies a strategically central position. Korea's strategic importance as a peninsula surrounded by the four major powers, U.S., Russia, China, Japan, has remained significant even in the post-Cold War period.

It is unfortunate that most Korean universities and colleges do not cover the naval and maritime history, with the exception of the Naval War College. Most of them consider naval and maritime history only in connection with other, independent aspects of the nation's history.

The Naval War College does cover the history of war at sea, naval tactical and strategic thought in the context of sea power and history of sea power.

The Naval Academy, on the other hand, has a system similar to civilian universities and consists of departments of various engineering, management, oceanography and international relations. The department of international relations is divided into international politics and military history. The school curriculum does provide a history of sea war in the third year of study. The National Defense College and its post-graduate school cover the history of sea power the and tactical and strategic thought of the great leadership.

Naval and maritime history is also considered in other courses as follows:

The Korea Maritime University provides post-graduate education in Maritime Industry and the College of Science provides degrees in maritime and social science.

The Mokpo Merchant Marine Junior college has departments in navigation, engineering, and communication.

The National Fisheries University of Pusan has colleges of sciences, engineering, humanities-social science, as well as a post-graduate school of industry.

The Che Ju National University consists of colleges of humanities, law, economic-commercial, agriculture, oceanography, natural science and engineering.

Editor's note: Very little writing on Korean naval and maritime history is available in English, but see the references in various volumes of *The Cambridge History of Japan* (Cambridge: Univ. Press, various years); G.M. Hagerman, "Lord of the Title Boats," U.S. Naval Institute Proceedings 93 (1967), pp. 67–75; Edward D. Rockstein, "Maritime Trade and Japanese Pirates: Chinese and Korean Responses in Ming Times"; *Asian Pacific Quarterly of Cultural and Social Affairs.* vol. 5, no. 2 (no year given), pp 10–19, and Sang-woon Jeon, *Science and Technology in Korea: Traditional Instruments and Techniques* (Cambridge: MIT Press, 1974).

On U.S. naval affairs, see Frederick C. Drake, *The Empire of the Seas: A Biography of Rear Admiral Robert Wilson Shufeldt, USN* (Honolulu: Univ. of Hawaii Press, 1984), chapters 13-14: "The Opening of Korea, 1881–1882," and the Korean War (1950–53) sources listed in Barbara A. Lynch and John E. Vajda, *United States Naval History: A Bibliography* (Washington: Naval Historical Center, 1993), p. 74.

Professor Kim is Chairman of the Maritime Policy and Strategic Studies Department of the Korean Naval War College. He is a 1957 graduate of the Korean Naval Academy, and a captain (retired) in the Korean Navy (ROK).

19
The Netherlands

Jaap R. Bruijn

Historians always look back. That is their profession. Naval and maritime historians are no exception to that rule, and the same is certainly true for historiographers. Hence, there is a feeling of being completely at sea when asked to write an outline of the *present* status of naval and maritime history in the Netherlands. While the present status has its history, which is worthwhile telling, there is a reason for feeling hesitant about the subject: the suggested dichotomy between naval and maritime history. In the Netherlands, that dichotomy is nonexistent. For this reason, the Dutch historiography which I will now examine refers only to sea history or to maritime history.

The Founding Period: A Private Interest

During the seventeenth century, the contemporary was aware of the importance of the Dutch activities at sea. A surprisingly high number of books were published about the exploits at sea, which were always assured of wide readership and were often reprinted. The discovery of the sea route to Asia and the subsequent voyages of the East India Company were treated by I. Commelin in 1645.[1] The year before, in 1644, a director of the West India Company, J. de Laet, published the history of his company, year-by-year, based on archival sources.[2] The biographies of at least three admirals were written soon after their deaths. G. Brandt's *Life of Admiral De Ruyter*, containing data drawn from the admiral's papers and letters, became famous.[3] Books on less spectacular topics such as the whaling industry and the mechanisms of the Amsterdam staple market were published as well.[4] More or less the same happened in the

---

[1] I. Commelin, *Begin ende voortgangh van de Nederlantsche geoctroyeerde Oost-Indische Compagnie*, 2 vols. (Amsterdam: 1645).

[2] J. de Laet, *Historie ofte jaerlijck verhael van de verrichtinghen der geoctroyeerde West-Indische Compagnie* (Leiden: 1644).

[3] G. Brandt, *Het leven en bedrijf van den heere Michiel de Ruiter* (Amsterdam: 1687). Further, A. Montanus, *Het leven en bedrijf van den doorluchtigen zeeheldt Johan van Galen* (Amsterdam: 1654) and n.n., *Leven en bedrijf van den vermaarden zeeheld Cornelis Tromp* (Amsterdam/Haarlem: 1692).

[4] C.G. Zorgdrager, *Bloeijende opkomst der aloude en hedendaagsche Groenlandsche visscherij* (The Hague: 1727) and J. le Moine de l'Espine and J. le Long, *Den Koophandel van Amsterdam* (Amsterdam: 1719; 3rd ed.).

shipbuilding industry.[5] Most of these works that were written by interested contemporaries can to a great extent be considered the entirety of history books written until the nineteenth century when a survey study of the history of the Dutch at sea was published. It was written by the head of the General State Archive, J.C. de Jonge and entitled *The History of Dutch Marine Affairs*, in ten volumes, published between 1833 and 1848. Marine affairs, according to De Jonge, were the 'faits et gestes' of the navy.[6] This connotation stayed alive for more than a century and was used by later historians as well; the most famous example is J.E. Elias' *Sketches from the History of our Marine Affairs*, six volumes dealing with the Eighty Years' War (1568–1648), published between 1916 and 1930.[7] Marine affairs were naval affairs. Other 'wet' matters were considered different and belonged, though not explicitly, to the field of economic history.

De Jonge's study was and still is a landmark. It describes in great detail the naval activities from the sixteenth to the early nineteenth century and is based upon original material, much of which was burned in a fire in the Ministry of the Navy in 1844; hence, the study's irreplacable value. Around 1870 de Jonge's work was followed by that of J.J. Backer Dirks. A teacher of naval history at the Royal Naval College of the Dutch Navy, he devoted four volumes to the Dutch Navy and included its exploits in the East Indies up to his own time; he created a still useful, though old-fashioned reference book.[8]

During the same period the study of "non-naval" marine affairs was encouraged by competitions held by learned societies, which resulted in two excellent books on the history of early Dutch whaling and the fishing industry. The prize winners were a young lawyer, later an archivist, S. Muller Fzn, and an economist, later a professor, A. Beaujon.[9] A remarkable event in 1874 was the opening of a maritime museum in a yacht club at Rotterdam. The heart of the exposition was a collection of about two hundred models of nineteenth-century ships. The underlying idea was to stimulate the public's interest in seafaring in general. The display was in chronological order and it dealt with the mercantile marine, the navy, and fishing.[10]

New developments took place in the first three decades of the twentieth century when several naval officers, secondary schoolteachers, and a few private

---

[5] N. Witsen, *Aeloude en hedendaegsche scheepsbouw en bestier* (Amsterdam: 1671) and C. van IJk, *De Nederlandsche scheepsbouwkonst opengestelt* (Amsterdam: 1697).

[6] J.C. de Jonge, *Geschiedenis van het Nederlandsche zeewezen*, 10 vols. (The Hague: 1833–1848); also the annotated second edition in 5 vols. (Haarlem: 1858–1862).

[7] J.E. Elias, *Schetsen uit de geschiedenis van ons zeewezen*, 6 vols. (The Hague: 1916–1930).

[8] J.J. Backer Dirks, *De Nederlandsche zeemagt in hare verschillende tijdperken geschetst*, 4 vols. (Rotterdam: 1865–1876).

[9] S. Muller Fzn, *Geschiedenis der Noordsche Compagnie* (Utrecht: 1874) and A. Beaujon, *Overzicht der geschiedenis van de Nederlandsche zeevisscherijen* (Leiden: 1885).

[10] L.M. Akveld, "De Watersport-Prins," in Ph.M. Bosscher a.o., *Prins Hendrik de Zeevaarder* (Naarden: 1975), pp. 91–107.

scholars took a keen interest in the naval side of the Dutch Golden Age (seventeenth century) and in the discoveries of the Arctic and in the East. These people, who came to know each other, published and joined forces in founding the Linschoten Society in 1908 and the Scheepvaartmuseum at Amsterdam in 1916. Like the Hakluyt Society, the Linschoten Society started editing original descriptions of sea and land voyages—in practice, nearly always late sixteenth and early seventeenth-century sea voyages—producing a new volume each year. The only person who looked at the social aspects of seafaring was the archivist J. de Hullu. He wrote a substantial number of handsome articles on life on board Dutch East Indiamen in the seventeenth and eighteenth centuries. Until the 1970s he would remain an exception.[11]

Academic Recognition

During the Interbellum, the leading person was the retired naval officer J.C.M. Warnsinck. He published several well-written monographs, based upon good historical insight and archival research in combination with nautical knowledge. His great interest was in admirals, naval campaigns and battles. He also made sea history, as it was then called, academically fashionable. Professor P.J. Blok, prominent historian of the University of Leiden, obtained Warnsinck's advise about his biography of Admiral De Ruyter, published in 1928. Academic recognition was realized in 1933. In that year the Royal Academy of Sciences founded the Committee for Sea History, with Warnsinck as its secretary, who also became an unsalaried university lecturer at the University of Amsterdam, and four years later at Leiden too. In 1939 at the Univerity at Utrecht, a special chair for the history of marine affairs was created for him.[12]

The Committee for Sea History was very active and was instrumental in getting several good monographs published, amongst which were a few Ph.D. theses. Only two exceptions challenged the then unwritten rule that the topics deal with seventeenth-century naval history. The publications of the foreigner, C.R. Boxer, strengthened this trend.[13] During the years of the German occupation, 1940–45, books on naval history of the seventeenth century were popular. The same was true for studies on the early period of the Dutch presence in Asia. The history of fishing or overseas trade, let alone social or institutional aspects of marine affairs, were hardly studied.[14]

---

[11] J.R. Bruijn and J. Lucassen, eds., *Op de schepen der Oost-Indische Compagnie. Vijf artikelen van J. de Hullu* (Groningen: 1980).

[12] For a short sketch of Warnsinck and also J.E. Elias, see: *Biografisch Woordenboek van Nederland*, vol. I (The Hague: 1979) and vol. II (The Hague: 1985).

[13] On C.R. Boxer, see the introduction to the third Dutch editon of his *The Dutch Seaborne Empire: Het profijt van de macht* (Amsterdam: 1988).

[14] For example: J.H. Kernkamp, *De handel op den vijand 1572–1609*, 2 vols. (Utrecht: 1931–1934); M. Simon Thomas, *Onze IJslandvaarders in de 17e en 18e eeuw* (Amsterdam: 1935) and, though older, J.E. Elias, *Het voorspel van den Eersten Engelschen oorlog*, 2 vols. (The Hague: 1920).

Warnsinck died in 1943, but academic recognition of sea history was soon continued. In 1946 the university at Leiden appointed former naval officer and professional historian T.H. Milo, professor of colonial history and the history of marine affairs. Milo's Ph.D. topic had broken with the seventeenth-century tradition. It dealt with a Dutch naval expedition during the French Revolution-ary wars.[15] Milo focussed his research interest on two projects: 1) the edition of documents on late sixteenth-century naval administration and campaigns, and 2) a study of the Dutch Navy during World War II. Meanwhile a few of Warnsinck's students continued publishing. Abroad, Boxer was joined by C. Wilson in his interest in Dutch history. The Dane, K. Glamann, was the first (foreign) student who did serious research into Dutch trade with Asia in the seventeenth and eighteenth centuries.[16]

A Difficult Period (c. 1955–1975)

The future looked bright for sea history during the early fifties. There were, however, symptoms of gloom. Milo's lectures always attracted a reasonable number of students, but very few of them started research of their own. Both of Milo's two projects failed. In 1960, after his sudden death, no obvious successor was available. His chair was abolished. The Committee for Sea History of the Royal Academy of Sciences had no manuscripts suitable for publication. Volume 13 appeared in 1955, and it would be fifteen years, before volume 14 was published. Up till then, publication of yearbooks and special exhibitions had stimulated directors and staff of the two great museums at Rotterdam and Amsterdam to jot down the results of their investigations. That custom lapsed into disuse.

In 1961 two former students of Warnsinck, R.E.J. Weber and Miss A.M.P. Mollema, who were worried about the status of sea history, founded the Nederlandse Vereniging voor Zeegeschiedenis (Dutch Society for Sea History). At the start they collected sixty members. A newsletter was published. The new society also acted as a national subcommittee of the recently founded Commission Internationale d'Histoire Maritime.

The society was well and enthusiastically received, and its membership increased rapidly. Nevertheless, the situation remained difficult. The great majority of the members only took an amateur's interest in the past, though in their professional life they were often actively involved in the shipping busi-nesses. Those members seldom published, and professional sea historians were scarce indeed. Despite this handicap, the newsletter slowly increased in scope

---

[15] T.H. Milo, *De geheime onderhandelingen tusschen de Bataafsche en Fransche Republieken van 1795 tot 1797 in verband met de expeditie van schout bij nacht E. Lucas naar de Kaap de Goede Hoop* (Den Helder: 1942). On Milo see *Biografisch Woordenboek van Nederland*, vol. IV (The Hague: 1994).

[16] C. Wilson, *Profit and power; a study of England and the Dutch wars* (London: 1957) and K. Glamann, *Dutch-Asiatic trade 1620–1740* (The Hague: 1958).

and quality of content. The variety of topics became vast. And, not in vain, at its inaugural meeting the society stipulated that sea history was more than naval history.[17] Dutch historians in general took a growing interest in economic and social aspects of centuries other than the seventeenth. That line was followed by the society and its biannual publication.

Although the time period of sea history that was being studied was broadened, naval and maritime history were artificially separated in 1972. The tables, however were now reversed. In that year, the Historical-Scientific Commission of the Royal Academy of Sciences began an investigation into the status of historical research. It proclaimed sea history a field of its own, dealing with social and economic aspects of seafaring. Naval history was attached to military history, and the historical department of the Navy, founded in 1946, was considered its main representative.[18]

Revitalization (c. 1975–present)

De Jonge's interpretation of marine matters as identical with naval matters definitely belonged to the past. And in the mid and late seventies some important developments took place, which resulted in a revitalization of the study of sea history as a natural entity.

Perhaps all-important were the conception, writing and publication of a four-volume *Maritime History of the Low Countries* between 1974 and 1978.[19] All volumes had the same structure, and the dividing lines for periods were innovative: c. 1585, c. 1680, and c. 1850–70. The approach was thematic. Each volume started with chapters on ships and shipbuilding, ports, shipowning, seafarers, and navigation. Next came the operational chapters on the five different Dutch branches of seafaring: the mercantile marine in Europe and outside Europe (mainly Asia and the Americas), fishing, whaling, and the Navy. An annotated bibliography was added to each chapter. Lacunae were indicated. Right from the beginning it was obvious that such a book could be written only by a team of authors. To prevent delays in time, no author was asked for more than two chapters; thirty-seven authors committed themselves. Most of them got to know each other, and this often proved fruitful in later days. All chapters in a volume were read in draft by all authors contributing to that volume. *The Maritime History of the Low Countries* was well received and several thousand of the four-volume set were sold, to the delight of the publisher as well as the authors.

The new handbook, which included the Netherlands as well as Belgium, made any idea about a dichotomy between naval and maritime history obsolete.

---

17   *Mededelingen Nederlandse Vereniging voor Zeegeschiedenis*, vol. 1 (1961), p. 6.

18   *Rapport over de huidige stand en toekomstige planning van het wetenschappelijk onderzoek der Nederlandse geschiedenis* (Amsterdam: 1974), pp. 7, 33–5 and 126–38.

19   *Maritieme Geschiedenis der Nederlanden*, 4 vols. (Bussum: 1976–78).

The five branches of seafaring have their common base in the chapters on ships, seamen, navigation, and administrators. Only their operations are different, having their own characteristics. Since that time the teaching of maritime history has been structured along this concept.

A second development in the seventies occurred at the universities. The democratization of the Dutch society made an academic education possible for larger sections of the population. The enrollment of students overall increased enormously, as it did in the departments of history. Lectures and research seminars in sea or maritime history at the university at Leiden also got their share of this students' boom. At Leiden, a lectureship in maritime history had been created in 1968, followed by a readership in 1977, and three years later converted into a chair. From 1978, a steady stream of completed Ph.D. theses in maritime history began to flow.[20]

A third development was the growing internationalization of the study of maritime history. The International Commission for Maritime History (the French name disappeared when M. Mollat's initiative became widely accepted) held a conference every five years, bringing together scholars from different countries. Their attention always focussed on one well-prepared theme. Also, general trends in the study of history at-large could no longer escape the maritime historian's notice. Smaller international meetings became popular, where staff members of universities, research institutes, and museums discussed one special topic or period. The International Commission for Maritime Museums and its meetings also stimulated wider cooperation.

Factor number four in revitalizing the world of Dutch maritime historians was the Dutch Society for Maritime History. Its membership increased vastly and reached about five hundred around 1980. But its journal, in particular, became the vehicle for an exchange of research products. The original newsletter was transformed into a proper journal with articles, book reviews, and a bibliography. In 1982 the name was changed from *Communications* to *Journal for Maritime History*.[21] The bibliography had become so vast and elaborate that journals abroad republished sections of it.

Summing up the main trends of the past fifteen to twenty years, one can observe, firstly, that the four-volume *Maritime History of the Low Countries* functions as a book of reference and a starting point for most research. Secondly, more students of maritime history with an academic background are now available. Thirdly, Dutch maritime historians actively participate in international

---

[20]   One of the first students was Frank J.A. Broeze, who in 1971 was invited to start a course in maritime history at the University of Western Australia (Nedlands). His Ph.D. degree was awarded at Leiden in 1978. The author of this article was appointed to the Leiden-positions.

[21]   *Mededelingen Nederlandse Vereniging voor Zeegeschiedenis* vol. 1–27 (1961–73) quarto, vols. 28–43 (1974–81) octavo; *Tijdschrift voor Zeegeschiedenis* vols. 1 (1982) in two issues per year (vol. 13, first issue has just been published).

organizations and meetings, and fourthly, the *Journal* is being offered so many manuscripts that its editorial board can be very selective. Special issues have become possible.

The Present Organizational Status

Those who are interested in maritime history in the Netherlands, one might safely say, are members of the Dutch Society. At present, about 650 members are registered. The *Journal* is considering three issues per year. The financial means have grown. Publishers' advertisements and flyers are holding the costs down.

The wide range of maritime museums—the two great ones at Rotterdam and Amsterdam plus a variety of specialized or regional ones—all restrict themselves firstly to the preservation and exposition of artifacts of all kinds. For the major museums, which are highly dependent on state or municipal funds as well as activities that raise sponsorships, increasing the number of visitors to museums has become top priority. Sometimes an occasional lecture is organized in relation to a special exhibition. Museum publications are rare indeed, though the Shipping Museum at Amsterdam has re-established its former tradition of publishing a yearbook with object-related articles. The regional museum at Sneek in Friesland never abandoned that good tradition and is, incidentally, not afraid to publish an M.A. thesis or an article of wider importance.[22] The libraries in the museums also keep manuscripts and regularly attract research students. By and large, however, one must say that Dutch maritime museums do not function as active centers of research.

As to the actual teaching of naval, and nowadays maritime, history, the Royal Naval College at Den Helder has the oldest tradition. All naval cadets must take a short course in history. This same requirement existed in the nineteenth century, though naval battles then did not have to compete with social structures. Teaching the history is a part-time job and in the past seldom fulfilled by one person for a long period. The most renowned teacher was Backer Dirks, the author of the nineteenth century handbook. A well-known teacher in the sixties and seventies was Ph.M. Bosscher, who finally wrote a three-volume history of the Dutch Navy in the second World War, the work his former professor, T.H. Milo, had only started.[23] In 1980 the position of naval history at the college was strenghtened by the appointment of G. Teitler as professor of strategic studies. His main research interest being in the strategic position of the Navy in the former Dutch East Indies.

J.C.M. Warnsinck's appointment at the universities at Amsterdam, Leiden, and Utrecht in the thirties only had a sequence at Leiden with a chair in maritime

---

22 *Jaarboek Fries Scheepvaartmuseum en Oudheidkamer.* See for example, G. Groenhof, "De N.V. Friesche Kofscheepsrederij (1839–1859)," in *Jaarboek* 1989, pp. 46–115.

23 Ph.M. Bosscher, *De Koninklijke Marine in de Tweede Wereldoorlog*, 3 vols. (Franeker: 1984–1990).

or sea history. No other university created facilities for teaching maritime history. In 1992, however, F.J.A.M. Meijer, senior lecturer in ancient history, was appointed extra-ordinary professor of the Maritime History and Archaeology of Classical Antiquity at the university of Amsterdam. To my knowledge Meijer is the first professor combining history and archaeology in teaching and research.[24]

The academic staff for maritime history at Leiden university includes one full professor and a half-time senior lecturer, F.S. Gaastra, and a few research students. The teaching is at several levels and is always optional for students. An introductory lecture course is in two parts, one dealing with the seventeenth and eighteenth centuries, the other with the modern time, each for two hours during twelve weeks. Point of reference for this course is the *Maritime History of the Low Countries*, but the scope is also international: British, American, and German aspects are treated as well. A short introduction into archival work is also included in the course (often the reading of early modern ship logs), plus visits to two maritime museums to discuss museum policy with staff members. An oral exam based upon the course work and some additional reading completes this course. The number of students per part differs annually, but is mainly in the range of ten to twenty. Each year there are also thematic classes, often given by research students. Such a class studies the literature and printed sources on one general theme as, for instance, the modernization of the nineteenth-century navy, mutinies, passenger transport or naval administration in the sixteenth century. These classes take two weekly hours during twelve weeks, and the student must write a paper. Research is done in special seminars, one or two per year. A seminar is twenty-four weeks long. The main body of the research material has to be investigated in the archives; research papers always bring new information. The themes vary greatly, from the Dutch whaling industry after the Second World War and the shipping policy of the Dutch Trading Company (NHM) to the careers of East India captains and the lives of fishermen's wives. The number of participants is always between eight and sixteen. A lecture course of twelve weeks on a broad theme was begun in 1989, and it is open to students as well as to interested people from outside the university.

Individual research work is done for the M.A. thesis and the Ph.D. degree. The topic is the student's choice or as advised by the staff. The M.A. thesis is supposed to take at least six months and is the last piece of work before leaving the university. Work for the Ph.D. degree does not require enrollment and is done either in one's private time or in the scarce position of research student for which one has to apply. The supervision is on on a personal but regular basis, though groups of Ph.D. students meet together in bimonthly sessions; about

---

[24] F.J.A.M. Meijer, *Een duik in een zee van bronnen. Oude Geschiedenis vanaf de bodem van de Middellandse Zee*, inaugural address 30 March 1993 (Amsterdam: 1993); see Warnsinck, note 12.

twenty dissertations are in preparation, a few even abroad. The topics deal with the sixteenth to the twentieth centuries.

The research potential can be divided into three categories. The greater part of original research is from the Ph.D. students and from the staff members at Den Helder, Leiden and some other universities. Next is the group of amateur maritime historians who devote their leisure time to their favorite topics. They are not very numerous, but the share of those with an academic background is increasing. There is, however, a third, not yet mentioned category of researchers: the academic staff of the department of Maritime(!) History at The Hague. This department of the Naval Staff of the Ministry of Defense is committed to stimulating research and publications on the Navy, publishing its own in first instance. Though the production has not yet been particularly impressive, the department's potential promises well.

This gets us straight on to the last organizational aspect: the publishing facilities. In 1985 the Department of Maritime History at The Hague substantially enhanced these facilities by starting the publication of a series of books called *Contributions to Dutch Naval History*.[25] Volume 6 was published in 1992. In 1972 the Committee for Sea History of the Royal Academy of Sciences resumed its publications. Volume 18 appeared in 1990. The Linschoten Society never stopped its activities and continues editing descriptions of sea and land travels: volume 92 in 1993. Even more important is the interest in maritime history demonstrated by several publishing houses, an interest that tends to shift from one house to another over the course of time. In the seventies De Boer Maritiem was a prolific publisher, but was forced to give it up. In the eighties, other smaller ones took over: De Bataafsche Leeuw, Walburg Press, Van Wijnen and Verloren, for example. They have published many a Ph.D thesis as a monograph. Modern equipment and the heigtened birth of one-man publishing houses has facilitated the printing of manuscripts—an asset for young scholars who want to have their dissertations published.

Production and Trends

The days of naval campaigns and discoveries as the most favored topics in maritime historiography have long gone. The study of maritime history now figures in the study of history as an academic discipline. Therefore, it is regularly being influenced by new ideas about the relevant approaches of the past. Economic, social and institutional aspects are studied as well as mental and technical ones. Statistics are common features in many publications. These aspects also permeate the publications of some amateur historians.

The production over, say, the past twenty years has been carefully registered in the extensive bibliography in each issue of the *Communications* (later the *Journal*

---

25   The Dutch name is: *Bijdragen tot de Nederlandse Marinegeschiedenis.*

for Maritime History of the Dutch Society). Dutch titles are intermingled with foreign ones. A quantitative approach to the production is feasible, but I rather prefer to point out the main trends of the publications, which cover the early modern and modern periods evenly. The sixteenth century and the Middle Ages have received less attention than later periods.

The general themes which cross the ages and trades are ships, ports, navigation and seamen. As to ships, there were hardly any typically Dutch, apart from the fluyts. Hence the focus in Dutch publications is more on shipbuilding: ship carpenters' guilds by R.W. Unger, the East India Company dockyard at Amsterdam by J. Gawronski, nineteenth century-naval engineers and innovations by J.M. Dirkzwager and A.A. Lemmers.[26] Shipbuilding was also an important industrial activity in the late nineteenth and twentieth century. Most shipyards have now gone. Their rise and fall have been studied neither for the industry as a whole nor for any of the main yards. Some archives have been saved from destruction. The demise of the major shipyards around 1980 has been investigated by a parliamentary commission and has produced huge files of documentation, on government interference in particular. Financial problems in the 1980s surrounding the construction of submarines had the same very attractive opportunity for historians.[27] As to the Navy, the history of their dockyards from the late sixteenth century to the present day is mainly a blank.

Ports and port cities have not been studied intensely. C.M. Lesger set a fine standard in 1990. He studied Hoorn in the early modern times, regarding this port city as part of a network and central location system. J.P. Sigmond published a handsome survey of the planning and digging of smaller and greater harbors from the sixteenth to eighteenth centuries. For ports in the modern period, some studies of a different nature have become available; for instance, two monographs on post-Second World War labor relations in the port of Rotterdam and the cooperation between international liner shipping, stevedoring, and road haulage industry at Rotterdam in the container era. Two articles deal with Rotterdam's tariff policy and Amsterdam's efforts to invest in its infrastructure before World War II.[28] Social and financial aspects of seamen's lives in port cities were also

---

[26] R.W. Unger, *Dutch Shipbuilding before 1800* (Assen/Amsterdam: 1978); J. Gawronski's book on wrecks of East Indiamen and shipbuilding at Amsterdam in the 1740s will be published in 1994; J.M. Dirkzwager, *Dr. B.J. Tideman 1834–1883. Grondlegger van de moderne scheepsbouw in Nederland* (Leiden: 1970) and some recent articles from his hand in the *Tijdschrift voor Zeegeschiedenis*; A.A. Lemmers is preparing a Ph.D. thesis based on the huge collection of late 18th and 19th century naval models and instruments, kept in the Rijksmuseum at Amsterdam.

[27] *Enquête Rijn-Schelde-Verolme (RSV)*, Tweede Kamer, vergaderjaar 1984–1985, 17817, no. 16. *Het Walrusproject. Besluitvorming en uitvoering*, Algemene Rekenkamer September 1985.

[28] C.M. Lesger, *Hoorn als stedelijk knooppunt. Stedensystemen tijdens de late middeleeuwen en vroeg moderne tijd* (Hilversum: 1990); J.P. Sigmond, *Nederlandse zeehavens tussen 1500 en 1800* (Amsterdam: 1989); E. Nijhof, "*Gezien de dreigende onrust in de haven. . . .*" *De ontwikkeling van de arbeidsverhoudingen in de Rotterdamse haven 1945–1965* (Amsterdam: 1988); H. van Driel, *Samenwerking in haven en vervoer in het containertijdperk* (Rotterdam: 1990); A.H. Flierman, "'This much too high retribution.' Municipal

touched upon.[29] The evolution and transformation of modern port cities, as entities has not yet been tackled.

The art of navigation, the education of it, the maps and the instruments have been carefully studied by C.A. Davids, G.G. Schilder, and W.F.J. Mörzer Bruyns; their results have been widely published. The main developments and many details are now known for the early modern period, not only for European and Atlantic waters, but also for the Indian Ocean. Navigational education during the nineteenth and twentieth centuries was the theme of a special issue of the *Journal* in 1985. Elly Decker introduced research into the influence of astronomers on the development of navigation technology.[30] This side of maritime history during the modern period requires specialized knowledge.

The fourth and last general theme regards the seamen, popular since the 1970s. It was started in the eighteenth century with studies of naval and East Indian personnel. It was mainly quantitative: total numbers, geographical origins, and wages. Pay and muster rolls provided the information. Not only the officer, but also the common seaman was of interest.[31] The relevant chapters of the *Maritime History of the Low Countries* presented estimates of the labor force employed by all seafaring branches. In the early eighties, studies of a more qualitative nature began to be published. It is likely that a reissue of J. de Hullu's innovating articles on life on board East Indiamen had a stimulating effect. Davids wrote about music and songs on board sailing vessels, mutinies were studied, and P.C. van Royen published a book on the social side of the mercantile marine around 1700.[32] Seamen's unions also came into the picture and the same is true of social

---

harbour fees and the competiviness of the port of Rotterdam 1900–1940," and M. Wagenaar, "Amsterdam harbour between 1850" and "1940: from national focus to regional prop," both in L.M. Akveld and J.R. Bruijn (eds.), *Shipping Companies and Authorities in th 19th and 20th Centuries* (The Hague: 1989), pp. 87–106 and 107–24 resp.

29 M.A. van Alphen, "The Female Side of Dutch Shipping: Financial Bonds of Seamen Ashore in the 17th and 18th Centuries," in J.R. Bruijn and W.F.J. Mörzer Bruyns, eds., *Anglo-Dutch Marine Relations 1700–1850* (Amsterdam-Leiden: 1991), pp. 125–32; J.R. Bruijn, "Seamen in Dutch Ports: c. 1700–c. 1914," in *Mariner's Mirror*, 65 (1979), pp. 327–38.

30 The most important publication is C.A. Davids, *Zeewezen en wetenschap. De wetenschap en de ontwikkeling van de navigatietechniek in Nederland tussen 1585 en 1815* (Amsterdam-Dieren: 1986), an extensive bibliography included. For later publications see the *Journal*'s bibliography. Further, E. Dekker, "Frederik Kaiser en zijn pogingen tot hervorming van 'Het sterrekundig deel van onze zeevaart,'" in A. de Knecht-van Eekelen and G. Vanpaemel, eds., *Met zicht op zee. Zeewetenschappelijk onderzoek in de Lage Langen na 1800* (Amsterdam: 1990), pp. 23–41.

31 J.R. Bruijn, "Dutch Men-of-War: Those on board c. 1700–1750," in *Acta Historiae Neerlandicae: Studies on the History of the Netherlands*, vol. 7 (The Hague: 1974), pp. 88–121; idem, "De personeelsbehoefte van de VOC overzee en aan boord, bezien in Aziatisch en Nederlands perspectief," in *Bijdragen in Mededelingen Geschiedenis der Nederlanden* 91, 1976, pp. 218–48; for a correction, see K.L. van Schouwenburg's articles in *Tijdschrift voor Zeegeschiedenis* 7 (1988), pp. 76–93 and 8 (1989), pp. 179–86.

32 C.A. Davids, *Wat lijdt den zeeman al verdriet: Het Nederlandse zeemanslied in de zeiltijd (1600–1900)* (The Hague: 1980); P.C. van Royen, *Zeevarenden op de koopvaardijvloot omstreeks 1700* (Amsterdam: 1987); J.R. Bruijn and E.S. van Eyck van Heslinga, *Muitery. Oproer en berechting op schepen van de VOC* (Haarlem: 1980). For de Hullu, see note 11.

legislation. The medical side did not escape the maritime historian's attention either.[33] Research into a number of detailed aspects is making good progress. Time is almost ripe for overview monographs for each branch of seafaring. One thing, indeed, has become clear: the background of seamen differed with each branch. A seaman did not switch between the Navy and the mercantile marine, as was the case for his British colleagues. The traditional influx of foreign labor on Dutch ships made the situation even more complex. The theme of seamen suits an international comparitive approach: numbers, level of wages, and movement of labor.

Coming now to the five different branches of seafaring, one can establish that two have been studied intensively in the recent past: the whaling trade and the East India Company (in Dutch: VOC). The Dutch played a prominent role in early whaling in the Arctic. At its peak (1721), nearly 260 ships were involved. The South-African economic historian C. de Jong wrote a good, though not easily accessible survey of two centuries of Dutch whaling (the 17th and 18th). A.M. van der Woude integrated the whaling industry into the social, economic and demographic structure of the northern part of the province of Holland. P. Dekker studied the careers of several masters of whaling vessels. Innovative, because of its multi-disciplinary approach, is L. Hacquebord's study of the first Dutch whaling activities and settlements on Svalbard in the first part of the seventeenth century. He puts the numbers of vessels involved into the right perspective and proves that new patterns in whaling were caused by climatical changes. F.J.A. Broeze has demonstrated why the Dutch failed to participate in nineteenth-century whaling in the Southern Hemisphere. The post-World War II activities in the Antarctic have also been studied.[34] Further whaling research will probably serve only to refine the available knowledge.[35]

The story of research into the VOC is an interesting one. In the sixties, Dutch society in general did not want to be reminded of its colonial past in Asia. Colonial history was out of date. In the early seventies, however, interest in the maritime aspects of the VOC was regenerated by the university at Leiden[36] and

---

[33] J.M.W. Binneveld and F.S. Gaastra, "Organisatie en conflict van een vergeten groep," in *Economisch-en Sociaal-Historisch Jaarboek* 35 (1972), pp. 303–23; J.R. Bruijn, "Marinevakbonden tussen wereldoorlog en muiterij (1914–1933)," in *Tijdschrift voor Zeegeschiedenis* 9 (1990), pp. 135–57; A.E. Leuftink, *Harde heelmeesters: Zeelieden en hun dokters in de 18e eeuw* (Zutphen: 1991).

[34] C. de Jong, *De geschiedenis van de oude Nederlandse walvisvaart*, 3 vols. (Pretoria: 1972–1979); A.M. van der Woude, *Het Noorderkwartier* (Wageningen: 1972); F.J.A. Broeze, "Whaling in the Southern Oceans. The Dutch Quest for Southern Whaling in the Nineteenth Century," in *Economisch- en Sociaal-Historisch Jaarboek* 40 (1977), pp. 66–112; W.J.J. Boot, *De Nederlandsche Maatschappij voor de Walvischvaart* (Amsterdam: 1987); J.R. Bruijn, "De Nederlandse Maatschappij voor de Walvisvaart, 1946–1967," in *Economisch- en Sociaal-Historisch Jaarboek* 48 (1985), pp. 233–57. For Dekker's articles see the bibliography of the *Communications* between 1970 and 1979.

[35] A study on Dutch whaling in Davis Strait is prepared by J.R. Leinenga (University at Groningen).

[36] J.R. Bruijn, F.S. Gaastra and I. Schöffer, *Dutch-Asiatic Shipping in the 17th and 18th Centuries*, 3 vols. (The Hague: 1979–1987). C.R. Boxer's *The Dutch seaborne Empire 1600–1800* (London: 1965) was

the discovery of some shipwrecks. New insight about frequency of sailings, numbers of people on board and those who died, and duration of the voyages even reached the newspapers. It made the VOC fashionable, which then also became an item for museums. Replica's of East Indiamen were constructed. Reports of the discovery of more wrecks and the auction of their cargoes sometimes reached the world press.[37] Recently it was decided that the VOC will be boosted as a cultural and tourist asset of the Netherlands! Meanwhile, historical research continues and is resulting in a number of Ph.D. theses and books.[38] F.S. Gaastra is the expert at large on the history of the VOC.[39] The overall picture of the maritime aspects is now considered to be complete, apart from the intra-Asian shipping and trade of the company. A second generation of Ph.D. students is well on its way, dealing with more detailed topics like the transport of mail, medical care, the effects of malaria, and social life on board. The maritime activities have also been put in a wider, comparative context.[40]

Of the three remaining branches of seafaring, the fisheries have been studied the least. H.A.H. Kranenburg's analysis of the early modern herring and cod fishery of 1946 has not been matched by the study of other kinds of fishery.[41] There are, of course, a number of popular or local publications, but from a scholarly point of view the catch is small. The early period has hardly been dealt with. Promising, however, is a forthcoming book on the fisheries in the Meuse estuary in the first half of the seventeenth century.[42] The economic and social aspects of the modern period (c. 1860–1940) have been given a bit more attention. A new development is the interest taken by cultural-antropologists in seafaring communities.[43]

---

translated and had several reprints.

[37] P. Marsden, *The Wreck of the Amsterdam* (London: 1974); C.J.A. Jörg, *The Geldermalsen. History and Porcelain* (Groningen: 1986); J. Gawronski a.o., *Hollandia Compendium. A Contribution to the History, Archeology, Classification and Lexicography of a 150-foot Dutch East Indiaman, 1740–1750* (Amsterdam: 1992).

[38] F.S. Gaastra, *Bewind en beleid by de VOC 1672–1702* (Zutphen: 1989); E.S. van Eyck van Heslinga, *Van Compagnie naar koopvaardij. De scheepvaartverbindingen van de Bataafse Republiek met de koloniën in Azië 1795–1806* (Amsterdam: 1988) and I.G. Dillo, *De nadagen van de Verenigde Oostindische Compagnie 1783–1795. Schepen en zeevarenden* (Amsterdam: 1992).

[39] F.S. Gaastra, *De geschiedenis van de VOC*, first edition Bussum: 1982, second Zutphen: 1992). A short survey in English is E.M. Jacobs, *In pursuit of pepper and tea. The story of the Dutch East India Company* (Zutphen-Amsterdam: 1991). The inventory of the Company's archive was printed in 1992.

[40] J.R. Bruijn and F.S. Gaastra, eds., *Ships, Sailors and Spices. East India Companies and their Shipping in the 16th, 17th and 18th Centuries* (Amsterdam: 1993).

[41] H.A.H. Kranenburg, *De zeevisscherij van Holland in den tijd der Republiek* (Amsterdam: 1946).

[42] R.D. van der Vlis, "Friese haringvisserij in de zeventiende en achttiende eeuw," in *It Beaken* 50 (1988), pp. 345–62; R.T.H. Willemsen, *Enkhuizen tijdens de Republiek* (Hilversum: 1988), chapter II. A.P. van Vliet's study will be published in 1994.

[43] See the special issue "Holland en de Visserij" of *Holland, Regionaal Historisch Tijdschrift* 16 (1984). For the communities see R. van Ginkel, *Elk vist op zijn tij. Een Zeeuwse maritieme gemeenschap, Yerseke 1870–1914* (Zutphen: 1991) and his study of Texel, *Tussen Scylla en Charybdis* (Amsterdam: 1993).

Much more research has been done into the mercantile marine. A comprehensive survey, however, of the different European trades in the early modern period is not available and is difficult to write. No register like that of British shipping has ever existed; shipownership and the exploitation of ships can only be studied per single ship. There is no equal to Ralph Davis' *The Rise of the English shipping Industry in the Seventeenth and Eighteenth Centuries* (1962). One book, however, explains lucidly the practice of shipownership at the end of the early modern period. That is F.J.A. Broeze's *De Stad Schiedam*, complete with the texts of many documents.[44] It has been estimated that about 1,750 ships were used in the seventeenth century and about 1,500 in the eighteenth century. Other estimates provide the number of seamen employed in the European trades at around the year 1700.[45] The best studied trade is the Russian, apart from the Baltic which can always rely on the Sound Toll Registers. The other trades are hardly known in general or in detail.[46] As to Dutch shipping in the Atlantic Ocean, the slave trade is covered by J. Postma's already classic survey. Research on eighteenth century African and Caribbean trade is in progress. The biggest shipowner and merchant in the early nineteenth century, Anthony van Hoboken, has found his biographer.[47] Privateering belongs to warfare as well as to commercial shipping. Its size and its economic, legal, and administrative aspects have been studied in detail for the War of the Spanish Succession and more generally for the Second and Third Anglo-Dutch Wars. Sources are there for other wars, the Eighty Years' War in particular.[48]

For the later periods of steam navigation and other means of ship propulsion, a variety of studies have been published, but there has been no survey. The one ship company had almost completely disappeared and the incorporated companies came into existence. If one needs a survey of all major and middle-sized companies, chapters 6 and 7 in the *Maritime History of the Low Countries*, volume

[44] F.J.A. Broeze, *De Stad Schiedam. De Schiedamsche Scheepsreederij en de Nederlandse vaart op Oost-Indië omstreeks 1840* (The Hague: 1978).

[45] Van Royen, *Zeevarenden op de Koopvaardijvloot om streeks 1700.*

[46] J.V.T. Knoppers, *Dutch Trade with Russia from the Time of Peter I to Alexander I. A Quantitative Study in Eighteenth Century Shipping*, 3 vols. (Montreal: 1976) and P. de Buck, "De Russische uitvoer uit Archangel naar Amsterdam in het begin van de achttiende eeuw (1703 en 1709)," in *Economisch- en Sociaal-Historisch Jaarboek* 51 (1988), pp. 126–93. Further studies by De Buck and J.Th. Lindblad and other authors in three bundles: *The Interactions of Amsterdam and Antwerp with the Baltic region, 1400–1800* (Leiden: 1983), W.G. Heeres a.o., *From Dunkirk to Danzig. Shipping and Trade in the North Sea and the Baltic, 1350–1850* (Hilversum: 1988) and J.Ph.S. Lemmink and J.S.A.M. van Koningsbrugge, *Baltic Affairs. Relations between the Netherlands and North-Eastern Europe 1500–1800* (Nijmegen: 1990). A whole survey of Dutch trade is, of course, J.I. Israel's, *Dutch Primacy in World Trade 1585–1740* (Oxford: 1989).

[47] J.M. Postma, *The Dutch in the Atlantic Slave Trade, 1600–1815* (Cambridge: 1990); B. Oosterwijk, *Koning van de Koopvaart: Anthony van Hoboken, 1756–1850* (Rotterdam: 1983).

[48] J.Th.H. Verhees-Van Meer, *De Zeeuwse Kaapvaart tijdens de Spaanse Successie oorlog, 1702–1713* (Middelburg: 1986); J.R. Bruijn, "Dutch Privateering during the Second and Third Anglo-Dutch Wars," in *The Low Countries History Yearbook 1978: Acta Historiae Neerlandicae* 11 (1979), pp. 79–93.

4, will help as well as B. Oosterwijk's, *Op één koers* for the more recent decades. At the level of the one single company, J.N.F.M. à Campo's study of the Royal Packet Company in the East Indies is voluminous but brilliant. He combines the study of the development of a network of liner services within the archipelago and with the outside world, foreign competition, and colonial state formation into one book. There is also a many-sided book on the Zeeland Company, dealing with cargo and passenger traffic between Holland and Britain; a comparable study is available for the Rotterdamsche Lloyd around 1900.[49] Further research in this field would be welcome. Diaries or memoirs in printed form from captains of the shipping industry are very rare indeed. Most valuable are the diaries of Ernst Heldring covering the first four decades of the twentieth century. The memoirs of D.A. Delprat for some later decades are rather disappointing, still keeping his own council. The Royal Shipowners' Association, the expression of the need amongst shipowners of closer cooperation in their relations with trade unions and the increasing numbers of national and international rules, has been studied.[50] A new approach of the shipping industry is the financing of the Rotterdam maritime sector after World War II. Traditional is Bezemer's study in three volumes of the role and fate of the mercantile marine in that war. The hinterland is vital for the Dutch economy. The transportation of goods over the rivers has received attention for only the nineteenth century.[51]

As to the Navy, there are two modern surveys, one for the early modern and the other for modern times. Not only the 'faits et gestes,' but also the naval administration, officers, crews, and ships are treated, though in a different degree of detail.[52] The focus on battles and campaigns has gone. Only one article was dedicated to the fighting tactics during the Anglo-Dutch Wars, other studies are more interested in strategical and tactical planning of the defense of the East Indies in the nineteenth and twentieth centuries.[53] By and large, however, one

---

[49] B. Oosterwijk, *Op één koers. Nedlloyd* (Rotterdam: 1988); J.N.F.M. à Campo, *Koninklijke Paketvaart Maatschappij. Stoomvaart en staatsvorming in de Indonesische archipel 1888–1914* (Hilversum: 1992); P.W. Klein and J.R. Bruijn, eds., *Honderd jaar Engelandvaart. Stoomvaart Maatschappij Zeeland. Koninklijke Nederlandsche Postvaart nv, 1875–1975* (Bussum: 1975); F. de Goey, ed., *Vaart op Insulinde. Uit de beginjaren der Rotterdamsche Lloyd NV, 1883–1914* (Rotterdam: 1991). For a recent merger see H. van Driel, *Een verenigde Nederlandse scheepvaart. De fusie tussen Nedlloyd en KNSM in 1980–1981, een bedrijfshistorische analyse* (Rotterdam: 1988).

[50] J. de Vries, ed., *Herinneringen en dagboek van Ernst Heldring 1871–1954*, 3 vols. (Utrecht: 1970); D.A. Delprat, *De reeder schrijft zijn journaal* (The Hague: 1983); A.H. Flierman, *"Het centrale punt in de reederswereld." De Koninklijke Nederlandse Redersvereniging. Vijfenzeventig jaar ondernemingsorganisatie in de zeevaart* (Bussum: 1984).

[51] P.Th. van Laar, *Financieringsgedrag in de Rotterdamse maritieme sector 1945–1960* (Amsterdam: 1991); K.W.L. Bezemer, *Geschiedenis van de Nederlandse Koopvaardij in de Tweede Wereldoorlog*, 3 vols. (Amsterdam: 1986–1990); H.P.H. Nusteling, *De Rijnvaart in het tijdperk van stoom en steenkool, 1831–1914* (Amsterdam: 1974).

[52] J.R. Bruijn, *The Dutch Navy of the Seventeenth and Eighteenth Centuries* (Columbia, S.C.: 1993); G.J.A. Raven, ed., *De Kroon op het anker: 175 jaar Koninklijke Marine [1813–1993]* (Amsterdam: 1988).

[53] R.E.J. Weber, "The Introduction of the Single Line Ahead as a Battle Formation by the Dutch.

observes that most attention has been given to the twentieth century. The research policy of the historical branch of the Navy has been successful. The role of the Navy in the Second World War has been described, as well as many naval activities in the period after 1945.[54] The equivalent of the American Waves are at present being studied. The relations between Navy and society have been analyzed as to the failed introduction of a Navy law in 1923 and a spectacular mutiny in 1933.[55] The early modern period has been given a comparatively less generous share of attention. Some biographies of naval officers have been published—most extensive is one of Admiral J.H. van Kinsbergen. There is, of course, more: a study of the Dutch naval side of the Glorious Revolution of 1688, for example, and not to be forgotten, a nice analysis of the phenomenon of the Sea Beggars around 1570.[56]

One can easily describe the lacunae and research opportunities in naval history. Naval finances have not yet been placed in a wider context. The structure of the naval administration needs more attention as well as the study of some important administrators. The same is true of the officers' corps as such. The leading scientific role of naval officers in the eighteenth and nineteenth centuries is quite remarkable. Several technical innovations were then instigated by the Navy. The structure and development of a naval base like Amsterdam, Flushing, and Den Helder in particular, have not yet been dealt with. In some of these directions research is already in progress.

A Balance

When comparing the past fifteen to twenty years with the period after the Second World War, the balance in all respects is more favorable for the recent span of time. The amount of publications is greater and more varied in kind and topic. In general, all the fashionable points of view in history are present: from political to social and cliometric. Maritime history books are reviewed in the

1665–1666," in *Mariner's Mirror* 73 (1987), pp. 5–19; G. Teitler, *Anatomie van de Indische defensie. Scenario's, plannen, beleid 1892–1920* (Amsterdam: 1988); G. Teitler, *De strijd om de slagkruisers* (Amsterdam: 1984); G. Jungslager, *Recht zo die gaat. De maritiem-strategische doelstellingen terzake van de verdediging van Nederlands-Indië in de jaren twintig* (The Hague: 1991). Teitler is the most productive author in this field. To keep in touch with his publications requires careful consultation of the bibliography in the *Tijdschrift voor Zeegeschiedenis*, to which I refer for most other naval history books and articles.

[54] Ph.M. Bosscher, *De Koninklijke Marine in de Tweede Wereldoorlog*. See also J.J.A. Wijn, ed., *Tussen vloot en politiek: 100 jaar marinestaf 1886–1986* (Amsterdam: 1986).

[55] H.J.G. Beunders, *Weg met de Vlootwet! De maritieme bewapeningspolitiek van het kabinet-Ruys de Beerenbrouck en het succesvolle verzet daartegen in 1923* (Bergen: 1984); J.C.H. Blom, *De muiterij op de Zeven Provinciën. Reacties en gevolgen in Nederland* (Bussum: 1975).

[56] A. van der Kuijl, *De Glorieuze overtocht. De expeditie van Willem III naar Engeland in 1688* (Amsterdam: 1988); J.C.A. de Meij, *De Watergeuzen en de Nederlanden, 1568–1572* (Amsterdam: 1972); R.B. Prud'homme van Reine, *Jan Hendrik van Kinsbergen (1735–1819): admiraal en filantroop* (Amsterdam: 1990).

leading historical journals and also in national newspapers and magazines. The *Journal of Maritime History* shows quality and is not lacking manuscripts submitted for publication. A difference between naval and maritime history does not exist. Ideology is an unknown word and does not permeate any kind of debate. The three academic staff members of the historical department of the Navy have a scholarly past in maritime history, if one uses this term in the American connotation!

The present group of maritime historians is bigger than ever before. The staffs of museums have been enlarged, in Amsterdam and Rotterdam in particular; their output in the shape of scientific publications, however, is small. There are no more than a total of six to seven historians attached to universities, the naval academy, the naval historical department; although that is certainly a number that would be unbelievably high for earlier generations. Their scholarly output is considerable. One may fear a growing discrepancy between museum and academic institutions in this respect. The aims of the present policy of the ministry of culture, to which most museums belong (and not to that of education), is to reach the general public in an effort to have well-visited exhibitions. The best that one can hope for at the moment is the preservation of good library and research facilities. Gratifying is the fact that a considerable number of Ph.D. students are involved in maritime history, broadening the group of scholarly trained maritime historians.

Plans for research do exist, but only on a small scale. In general, the personal preference for a subject is decisive. The interest of the established scholars is regularly guided away from their own research by (inter)national conferences and commemorations of events of national historic importance. At times one is inclined to think of a superabundance of those events. Dutch maritime historians, as far as I have observed, bear a fair share of that burden. They do not do research into non-Dutch topics, though well aware of foreign publications. It was a long time before they published in a language other than Dutch, but several books and articles are now available in English. International contacts have boosted this trend.

Periods and aspects which have lacked attention belong to the later Middle Ages, the sixteenth century, and plus the fisheries. A survey of the mercantile marine would be welcome. The results of the excavation of shipwrecks should be better incorporated in historical research. New information can be expected from the archive of the Zeeland auditor's office for the early modern period which is presently being inventoried and from the files of the nineteenth century Dutch Trading Company (NHM). The soon to be introduced "twenty year-rule" for governmental and local administration records (instead of closing them for fifty years) will offer greater opportunities for contemporary research. There is sufficient vitality amongst young and older Dutch maritime historians to exploit both the forthcoming and the already existing opportunities.

20

New Zealand

Ian McGibbon and Gavin McLean

As an island state in a vast ocean, New Zealand has always had a strong relationship with the sea. It was colonized by people who sailed long distances across the ocean, first, Polynesians who began arriving more than a thousand years ago, and later Europeans, mainly from the British Isles, for whom the voyage to the antipodes was often one of months-long hardship and deprivation. The economy which these people developed was—and remains—uniquely dependent on seaborne trade. New Zealanders have traditionally been conscious, moreover, that any direct threat to their security must come from across the sea. The importance of New Zealand's maritime environment has been enhanced by the resource management measures associated with the establishment of exclusive economic zones. New Zealand's zone, proclaimed in 1978, is one of the largest in the world.

At times, New Zealanders have been inspired by visions of maritime greatness. This was especially so during the heyday of the British Empire, when British naval and maritime predominance seemed part of the natural order. Some saw New Zealand, in time, emulating its British mentor. William Massey, the imperialist-minded Prime Minister from 1912 to 1925, for example, was apt to proclaim New Zealand's future naval greatness. That these aspirations have gone largely unfulfilled is less surprising than that New Zealanders have tended increasingly to take for granted the sea and its importance to their well-being.

New Zealand's economy has been characterized by its supply of a narrow range of unprocessed primary products to markets that are a great distance from its shores. At first, wool held pride of place, but the introduction of refrigerated ships in the 1880s allowed a diversification of the nature, if not the direction, of New Zealand's overseas trade. The ability to transport meat and dairy products to the other side of the world helped transform the pattern of farming in New Zealand. While the direction of its trade has shifted as the assured British market has disappeared, New Zealand remains as dependent in 1993 upon the free flow of its produce across the seas as it did in 1893. Because of its limited industrial base, it was—and is—equally dependent upon the import by sea of a great range of commodities and goods.

New Zealanders were, from an early stage, engaged in a range of maritime activities, including shipbuilding, though inevitably on a small scale. Shipping companies were founded by enterprising capitalists, usually with the backing of British capital. Two companies were especially important—the New Zealand Shipping Company established in Christchurch in 1873 and the Union Steam Ship Company established in Dunedin in 1875. The former competed on the United Kingdom–New Zealand route, while the latter came to dominate the New Zealand coastal and inter-colonial shipping scene. Both were taken over by the British P&O group during the First World War. Small, locally based companies continued to operate in a coastal role in the first three-quarters of this century. The fishing industry in New Zealand was generally small scale and at a subsistence level until the late 1970s when the establishment of the exclusive economic zone brought new attention to local fishing resources. Fishing's importance to the New Zealand economy has been greatly enhanced in the last twenty years.

The vital importance of New Zealand's sea trade routes ensured that maritime activities would play a significant role in its affairs, even if ownership of the shipping lines upon which it depended lay outside New Zealand hands. The rapid turnaround of shipping demanded attention to port facilities and cargo handling. Periodically union activities on the waterfront have caused major disruptions, notably in 1890, 1913, and 1951. Governments, conscious of the adverse economic impact of the resulting hiatus in cargo flow, have often reacted strongly during such disputes. In 1951, even troops were deployed on the waterfront to work the cargo ships. More recently, attention has been focused on resource management. The need to monitor and control the operations of foreign fishing vessels has placed the spotlight on New Zealand maritime policing capacity, primarily the responsibility of the Royal New Zealand Navy.

For more than a century, the British connection dominated New Zealand's naval activities even more completely than it did general maritime activities. The Royal Navy was deeply involved in New Zealand's establishment as a colony of the British Empire. It was Captain James Cook, RN, who took possession of the country on behalf of the British Crown, and another British naval officer, Captain William Hobson, RN, who not only signed the Treaty of Waitangi with Maori chiefs in 1840 but also became the new colony's first governor. British naval vessels were involved in operations in New Zealand during the conflict over land issues of the 1860s. Moreover, New Zealanders regarded the Royal Navy as their shield against invasion or attack by potential external enemies and as an essential protector of the trade routes upon which they depended for their economic well-being. When that shield was threatened, they were prepared to make financial contributions to its sustenance, culminating in the gift of a battle cruiser to the Royal Navy in 1909 as well as financial contributions towards the construction of the Singapore Naval Base between the world wars.

Within this framework, a small New Zealand naval force emerged, initially as a Division of the Royal Navy. Established in 1913, the New Zealand Naval Forces were heavily dependent on the Royal Navy for both ships and personnel. This reliance had not been significantly lessened when, in 1941, the New Zealand Division was reconstituted as the Royal New Zealand Navy. The provision of British officers for senior and technical posts remained of vital importance to the viability of the force for another twenty years. British influence within the RNZN's higher command was also considerable, with the last British officer not leaving the New Zealand Naval Board until 1966.

Since cutting the painter with the Royal Navy, the RNZN has survived with difficulty. Whereas in the early days New Zealand borrowed warships from the Royal Navy, paying only for their maintenance and upkeep, the RNZN today is faced with the capital charges of replacing warships. This has caused political problems, which were especially evident when New Zealand and Australia in the late 1980s developed a joint project to build a series of frigates for their navies. By participating in the construction of the so-called ANZAC frigates, New Zealand is deriving spin-off economic benefits. In particular, its languishing shipbuilding industry has been given a shot in the arm. Nevertheless, opposition within New Zealand has been substantial. Lulled by their sense of isolation from the world's trouble spots, many New Zealanders no longer consider their country's naval defence a significant problem, requiring prudent long-term planning and diversion of resources from other, socially oriented activities. Two vessels only are scheduled at present, with options on two more unlikely to be exercised in New Zealand's straitened circumstances.

While New Zealanders remain chary of expenditure on naval defence in peacetime, they have responded with alacrity to calls to arms this century. New Zealand's naval involvement in the First World War was limited to its newly acquired cruiser HMS *Philomel*, which operated in the Red Sea area for three years until being decommissioned in 1917. A number of New Zealanders served in a variety of Royal Navy vessels, one of them winning the Victoria Cross for his exploits. New Zealand's "gift" warship, HMS *New Zealand*, took part in all the major encounters of the British and German battle fleets during the First World War. In the Second World War, this pattern was repeated, though on a much larger scale. One of New Zealand's cruisers, HMS *Achilles*, had early action when it took part in the Battle of the River Plate. New Zealand ships were active in the Pacific War. Moreover, New Zealanders participated in every facet of the naval war aboard British ships. The Second World War also gave a boost to shipbuilding in New Zealand, with small craft being built for the British, United States, and New Zealand navies.

Given this background, maritime and naval history might have been expected to attract significant academic attention. That this has not been the case is a reflection of both the smallness of New Zealand's scholarly establishment and the fact that social themes hold the field in New Zealand history at present, with inevitable effect on the composition and interests of university history departments. Maritime history gets limited attention from a few academics in the universities as part of more general courses, especially in economic history. There is a School of Maritime Studies at the Otago Polytechnic in Dunedin, but its skills-based course is designed to meet the practical needs of an expanding deep-sea fishing industry rather than academic enquiry.

There are only a few individuals specializing in maritime history. Gavin McLean, the New Zealand Historic Places Trust's historian, has been conspicuous in recent years, producing ground-breaking work on the business of shipping in New Zealand and a series of books on maritime themes, but his interest is necessarily limited by his other duties. Some other scholars publish on maritime-related themes from time to time. For example, Simon Ville, until recently a member of Auckland University's Economic History Department, but now in Australia, has recently published a study of New Zealand's coastal shipping.[1] Gordon Boyce of Victoria University of Wellington's Economic History Department is working on aspects of the Furness Withy Group. Other maritime subjects to engage scholarly attention have included Polynesian voyaging, the early European exploration of the Pacific and whaling. The staging of New Zealand's first maritime history conference in 1992 provided a boost to scholarly interest, and this will be reinforced by the decision of the Stout Research Centre at Victoria University of Wellington to devote its 1993 conference to the theme of "The Sea."

Despite the lack of academic interest, there is a vast secondary literature on New Zealand's maritime history, though much of it is of indifferent quality. Most books deal with company histories and fleet lists. Prolific writers from the past have included S.D. Waters, J. O'C. Ross and A.A. Kirk. The most active writers today are David Johnston, whose *Maritime History of New Zealand*[2] is a key document, and Gavin McLean, whose works include *Canterbury Coasters*,[3] *Richardsons of Napier*[4] and *The Southern Octopus: The Rise of a Shipping Empire*.[5]

Other themes to have received attention include port histories. The majority are commissioned works, with Otago leading the way with two major scholarly

[1]   Simon Ville, "The Coastal Trade of New Zealand Prior to World War One," *New Zealand Journal of History*, vol. 27, no. 1 (1993).

[2]   David Johnston, *Maritime History of New Zealand* (Auckland: David Bateman/Collins, 1989).

[3]   Gavin McLean, *Canterbury Coasters* (Wellington: NZ Ship & Marine Society, 1987).

[4]   Gavin McLean, *Richardsons of Napier* (Wellington: NZ Ship & Marine Society, 1989).

[5]   Gavin McLean, *The Southern Octopus: The Rise of a Shipping Empire* (Wellington: NZ Ship & Marine Society and Wellington Harbour Board Maritime Museum, 1990).

histories: A.H. McLintock, *The Port of Otago*[6] and Gavin McLean, *Otago Harbour: Currents of Controversy.*[7] Lyttelton and Oamaru are well served by W.H. Scotter, *A History of Port Lyttelton*[8] and Gavin McLean, *Oamaru Harbour,*[9] respectively. Production of port histories peaked in the late 1970s and early 1980s, although updated accounts of Napier and Nelson harbors have recently appeared.

There is an extensive literature on migration. The publication of migrants' diaries began last century and has gained its second wind with an upsurge of interest in genealogy in recent decades. Sir Henry Brett's *White Wings*[10] remains a key document. Charlotte Macdonald's *A Woman of Good Character*[11] is a rare example of a scholarly publication in this field.

Shipwrecks are a major theme. An updated version of C.W. Ingram and P.O. Wheatley's 1936 *Shipwrecks and Maritime Disasters*[12] is still in print. Academic writers have also shown intermittent interest in waterfront labour in recent decades. Little has yet been written on Maori craft, though this deficiency is currently being remedied.

The pattern of naval history in New Zealand is similar. No tertiary institutions offer courses in naval history. The nearest approach to such treatment is coverage of naval aspects within a course on New Zealand defence run on an extramural (off-campus) basis by Massey University. There is no naval academy which might provide a focus for such activity. Because of the smallness of its naval establishment, New Zealand has traditionally sent its young officers to schools in Britain and Australia.

If maritime history has a tenuous place in scholarly interests, naval history is virtually ignored by the scholarly community. There is consequently no historiographical debate. In recent times, Ian McGibbon, Senior Historian in the Historical Branch, Department of Internal Affairs, has been alone in the field. Although unable to devote himself full time to the subject, he is currently working on the naval aspect of New Zealand's involvement in the Korean War.

While there is no ongoing tertiary-based work on New Zealand's naval history, a small body of literature does exist. A starting point is S.D. Waters's *Royal New Zealand Navy*[13] in the official war history. It provides in-depth coverage of RNZN operations and the activities of New Zealanders with the Royal Navy during the Second World War. Ian McGibbon, in his *Blue-water*

6   A.H. McLintock, *The Port of Otago* (Dunedin: Otago Harbour Board, 1951).

7   Gavin McLean, *Otago Harbour: Currents of Controversy* (Dunedin: Otago Harbour Board, 1985).

8   W.H. Scotter, *A History of Port Lyttelton* (Christchurch: Lyttelton Harbour Board, 1968).

9   Gavin McLean, *Oamaru Harbour* (Palmerston North: Dunmore Press, 1982).

10   Sir Henry Brett, *White Wings*, 2 volumes (Auckland: Brett Publishing Company, 1924 and 1928).

11   Charlotte Macdonald, *A Woman of Good Character* (Wellington: Allen & Unwin, 1991).

12   C.W. Ingram and P.O Wheatley, *Shipwrecks and Maritime Disasters* (Auckland: Beckett Publishing, 1990).

13   S.D. Waters, *Royal New Zealand Navy* (Wellington: War History Branch, 1956).

Rationale, The Naval Defence of New Zealand 1914–1942,[14] sought to place these operations in a strategical context, while outlining the development of the New Zealand Division of the Royal Navy. Naval policy was also covered by W. David McIntyre in his *New Zealand Prepares for War, Defence Policy 1919–39.*[15] More recently, in his *The Path to Gallipoli, Defending New Zealand 1840–1915,*[16] Ian McGibbon has further examined the origins of New Zealand's naval policy leading to the payment of subsidies to the Royal Navy and the creation of the New Zealand Naval Forces in 1913. He has also given attention to the naval relationship between Australia and New Zealand.[17] Among the areas awaiting scholarly treatment are the Royal Navy in New Zealand and the New Zealand Naval Forces.

For the time being, naval history seems likely to remain largely the preserve of enthusiastic amateur historians and antiquarians. They will add to an extensive antiquarian literature on naval activities. T.D. Taylor's *New Zealand's Naval Story*[18] leads the field, providing much useful information about naval visits to New Zealand in particular. More recently, R.J. McDougall, in his *New Zealand Naval Vessels,*[19] has exhaustively catalogued the ships of the RNZN and its antecedents. Among other recent works of a non-academic nature are accounts of New Zealand's wartime cruisers by Jack S. Harker,[20] two largely pictorial histories by Grant Howard,[21] and a brief account of the Royal Navy in New Zealand and a study of the hydrographic branch by Rear Admiral John O'C. Ross.[22]

In the absence of interest among tertiary institutions, museums will continue to play a key role in promoting New Zealand's naval and maritime heritage. There are three of primary importance. At the RNZN Naval Base at Devonport, Auckland, the Royal New Zealand Naval Museum will soon assume a higher

---

[14] Ian McGibbon, *Blue-water Rationale, The Naval Defence of New Zealand 1914–1942,* (Wellington: Government Printing Office, 1981).

[15] W. David McIntyre, *New Zealand Prepares for War, Defence Policy, 1919–39* (Christchurch: University of Canterbury Press, 1988).

[16] Ian McGibbon, *The Path to Gallipoli, Defending New Zealand 1840–1915* (Wellington: GP Books, 1991).

[17] Ian McGibbon, "Australian-New Zealand Naval Relations," in T.R. Frame, J.V.P. Goldrick and P.D. Jones, eds., *Reflections on the RAN* (Kenthurst NSW: Kangaroo Press, 1991).

[18] T.D. Taylor, *New Zealand's Naval Story* (Wellington: A.H. & A.W. Reed Ltd, 1948).

[19] R.J. McDougall, *New Zealand Naval Vessels* (Wellington: GP Books, 1989).

[20] Jack S. Harker, *HMNZS Achilles* (Auckland: Collins, 1980); *Well Done Leander* (Auckland: Collins, 1971); *HMNZS Gambia* (Wellington: Moana Press Ltd, 1989); *Almost HMNZS Neptune* (Wellington: Moana Press Ltd, 1991).

[21] Grant Howard, *The Navy in New Zealand, An Illustrated History* (Wellington: A.H. & A.W. Reed, 1981); Grant Howard, *Portrait of the Royal New Zealand Navy, A Fiftieth Anniversary Celebration* (Wellington: Grantham House, 1991).

[22] J.O'C. Ross, *The White Ensign in New Zealand* (Wellington: A.H. & A.W. Reed, 1967); *This Stern Coast* (Wellington: A.H. & A.W. Reed, 1969).

profile when a planned new building is completed. Its growing collection of material will provide a basis for future research. Particularly useful will be an ongoing series of oral history interviews with former naval personnel, being conducted by the present director.

The country's premier maritime museum is the Wellington Maritime Museum and Gallery on Wellington's Queen's Wharf. Founded by the former Wellington Harbour Board in the early 1970s, it holds the country's largest collection of maritime archives, photographs, and models. Merchant shipping is its specialty. It hosted the maritime history conference in 1992. A newsletter, *Leading Light*, is published.

The Auckland Maritime Museum was formed in the late 1980s. Its large multi-million dollar complex will open at Auckland's Hobson Wharf in August 1993. The museum will be less of a research centre than its Wellington counterpart and will specialize in small craft and Polynesian/Maori vessels. It will operate a fleet of approximately forty authentic and replica craft and will franchise shops designed to keep alive traditional crafts such as sailmaking and boat-building. The museum's quarterly journal, *Bearings*, has a wide general circulation.

In addition, there is a small maritime museum at Bluff, Southland, which was expanded in 1992, and museums at Port Chalmers and Lyttelton are maritime-dominated. The new Museum of New Zealand will be devoting space and resources to the history of Polynesian and Maori voyaging and watercraft.

Several societies have been formed to restore veteran craft. The Paeroa Maritime Park has a collection of small coasters and former RNZN craft, but is less active than it was a decade ago. At Picton, the Edwin Fox Society is planning to restore the *Edwin Fox*, the world's last East Indiaman. At Wanganui, a historical society has recovered a paddle steamer for restoration. Private individuals have restored several trading schooners and scows. Shiplovers' societies also provide a maritime-focused network. Founded in 1949, the New Zealand Ship and Marine Society has branches in Wellington, New Plymouth, and Napier and publishes a quarterly journal, *New Zealand Marine News*. The Auckland Maritime Society and Otago Maritime Society service their respective areas.

Where to from here? There appears little prospect of early change to the pattern described above, wherein maritime and naval history is mostly the preserve of non-professionals. Previous generations of New Zealanders were forcibly reminded of their country's dependence on the sea during the world wars. Such concerns have not been of overriding importance in the late twentieth century. In the absence of some new disruption of New Zealand's trading links, or some shift in strategic outlook which might reawaken a sense of vulnerability, it is likely that academic interest will remain limited, and that personal rather than institutional influences will remain the main driving force in maritime and naval studies in New Zealand.

21
Norway

Captain Tore Prytz Dahl, Royal Norwegian Navy

In the wake of the unification of Norway under one king, a defence system was created that included all the coastal districts. This system, called the *leidang*, was based on earlier local defence arrangements. The coastal districts were divided into *skipreder*, and each *skiprede* was to build, equip, and maintain a longship of a certain size. From about the year 950, the *leidang*-system included all Norway. The defence system represented a cornerstone in the formation and protection of the Norwegian realm which included approximately the present Norwegian area of land as well as Iceland, Greenland, the Faroe Islands, the Shetland Isles, the Orkneys, the Hebrides, and the Isle of Man. The *leidang* was an efficient system for about 250 years. Then new, more costly types of ships were introduced in the seafaring countries around the North Sea. The Norwegian realm, sparsely populated and ruled by kings in possession of very limited resources, came increasingly under foreign influence and fell apart.

The story of *leidang* has been of great interest to military as well as civilian historians. In 1951, the Norwegian naval high command marked the millennium of the *leidang* with a publication.[1] The book was based on contributions from military and naval historians, Colonel G.P. Harbitz, Commodore S. Oppegård, and Commander Rolf Scheen, with the advisory help of civilian historians.

With the Treaty of Kalmar in 1397, the three northern countries, Denmark, Norway, and Sweden, entered a union under one king.[2] A century later, in 1523, the Swedes succeeded in breaking out of the union, while Norway steadily became more closely knitted with Denmark. From the Danish rulers' point of view, the ideal thing was to regard Norwegian territory simply as "a part of Denmark." In practical policy, however, this proved to be impossible due to the size of the Norwegian population and resources compared with the might of the Danish colonial power.

Captain Tore Prytz Dahl, Royal Norwegian Navy, is Senior lecturer in naval history at the Norwegian Naval Academy (Sjøkrigsskolen), N-5034 Ytre Laksevåg.

[1] G.P. Harbitz, S. Oppegård, Rolf Scheen, *Den norske leidangen* (Oslo: 1951).

[2] Gottfrid Carlsson, *Medeltidens nordiska unionstanke* (Stockholm: 1945).

The period of Danish dominance, which lasted for about 400 years, from 1397 to 1814, is traditionally treated by Norwegian historians in a rather nationalistic way, with great emphasis on the emergence of new Norwegian institutions.[3] This trend in Norwegian historical ideology has been significant for the status of Norwegian naval history as opposed to the country's military history. During the reign of King Hans (1483–1513), a combined Danish–Norwegian navy was created with its main base in Copenhagen.[4] The primary task of this navy was to protect and dominate the sea routes in the Baltic.[5] In this area, both Sweden and Denmark had large economic interests at stake. During the century between 1620 and 1720, the heyday of this common Danish–Norwegian navy, about two-thirds of the seamen and many of its officers were of Norwegian descent.[6]

In 1628, however, a new Norwegian army came into being by royal decree.[7] This army, called the "*legdshaer*," was based on conscription in the rural areas. For practical reasons, the new army was, to a great extent, administered in Norway, with its high command in the capital, Christiania, and different administrative arrangements in rural districts. The new army became an important factor in Norwegian national growth. It had, for instance, the very first institutions of higher education in the country. At the same time, the Norwegian Army in the wars against an expansive Sweden in the last half of the seventeenth century and the beginning of the eighteenth, fought mainly on, and defended, Norwegian soil. In that way, the Army became well known in the country, while as a rule, the common navy operated out of its main base in Copenhagen for equally important, but not so well-known or well-appreciated operations in distant Baltic waters. Emphasized by the nationalistic trend in Norwegian historical writing, this contributed to the pronounced military tradition in Norway. Traditional Norwegian history tends to be rather narrowminded,[8] nationalistically, but there are a few exceptions to this, for instance the work of Commodore Olav Bergersen and Commander Rolf Scheen, who have tried to stress the great Norwegian share in the achievements of the common Danish-Norwegian Navy. Traditional writing has tended to overemphasize the importance of the operations of the *legdshaer* and, to some extent, discounting or even omitting the deeds of the Navy.[9]

The Napoleonic wars brought the Danish-Norwegian union to an end. After the bombardment of Copenhagen in 1807 and the British capture of the seagoing

[3] Ottar Dahl, *Norsk historieforskning i det 19. og 20. århundre* (Oslo: 1959).

[4] Kay Jungersen, *Danmarks Søkrigshistorie* (København: 1945) pp. 51–2.

[5] O. Eidem and O. Lütken, *Vor Sømagts Historie* (Kristiania and København: 1906) p. 182.

[6] Axel Coldevin, *Vårt folks historie*, vol V (Oslo: 1963) pp. 163–67.

[7] *Ibid.* pp. 158–63.

[8] Niles P. Vigeland, *Norge på havet*, 2 volumes (Oslo: 1953–54).

[9] Forsvarets Krigshistoriske Avdeling, *Forsvarets rolle i Norges historie* (Oslo: 1965), pp. 7–20.

portion of the combined Danish–Norwegian Navy, the two countries, allied with Napoleon, entered an unhappy war with Great Britain. The outcome of the war brought Norway into a union partnership with Sweden in 1814. However, the Norwegian–Swedish union was more restrictive than the earlier connection with Denmark: primarily a common king and joint foreign policy.[10] After the Napoleonic wars, the new Norwegian state was in fact bankrupt.[11] For the new Norwegian Navy, the sad economic picture implied unrealized plans for a new seagoing fleet. At the same time, based on experience from the war, most Norwegians thought that the waters along our extended coasts were dominated, as well as protected, by the Royal Navy. With the exception of spasmodic naval efforts in the wake of the Crimean War and in the last decade before the breakup of the union with Sweden, 1895–1905, the Army dominated Norwegian national defence.[12]

After a peaceful restoration of an independent kingdom of Norway in 1905, Norwegian defence policy was dominated by fear of Swedish plans for revenge. With the long land frontier between the two countries, this naturally resulted in an augmentation of the Army and, to a large extent, neglect of the Navy. A late awakening to the dangerous aspects of the Anglo–German naval race before 1914 produced very few material results in our Navy.[13] During World War I Norway remained neutral, but with steadily increasing pro-allied sentiment, not least because of the sufferings of thousands of Norwegian sailors caused by the German war against shipping.[14] However, during the war the Norwegian Navy guarded national waters on neutrality patrol, and the seas outside territorial waters were protected by the Royal Navy.[15] The dominance of the Royal Navy in adjacent waters remained a prevailing belief in Norwegian naval and political circles up to the German invasion in 1940. This conception had a decisive influence on our small defence effort during the interwar years.[16]

After a stumbling start, the Norwegian Army fought against the German invaders for two months in 1940, rather inefficiently supported by French and British troops.[17] In connection with the withdrawal of Allied forces from Norway in the beginning of June 1940 (the principal cause was the collapse in France), an armistice was signed between the German and Norwegian military high commands. The Norwegian king and government, however,

---

[10] Knut Mykland, *Norges historie*, vol. 9 (Oslo: 1977), pp. 145–55, pp. 425–76.

[11] Francis Sejersted, *Norges historie*, vol. 10 (Oslo: 1978), pp. 32–65.

[12] Article by Tore Prytz Dahl in Roald Gjelsten, ed., *Verktøy for fred* (Oslo: 1993), pp. 58–66.

[13] *Ibid.* pp. 66–8.

[14] Olav Riste, *Forsvar og nøytralitet under 1. verdenskrig* (Oslo: 1965).

[15] Olav Riset, *The neutral ally* (Oslo: 1965).

[16] Nils Ørvik, *Sikkerhetspolitikken 1920–1939*, 2 volumes (Oslo: 1960–61).

[17] Odd Lindbäck-Larsen, *Krigen i Norge 1940* (Oslo: 1965).

fled to England to continue the war from abroad.[18] The armistice affected the Army in particular, while naval vessels, destroyers, patrol vessels and a submarine sailed for the British Isles. A few naval planes succeeded in reaching the British shores as well. While it was rightly considered impossible to muster a sufficient number of soldiers to form new army divisions abroad, naval officers and pilots were in demand to join the new Norwegian armed forces in Great Britain. Therefore, during the government's exile in Great Britain, the Norwegian Navy was the largest service, and the Navy and Air Force participated in a great number of operations along with British forces. The small Norwegian Army on British soil, however, was to a great extent held in reserve by our political authorities for use in a possible campaign to liberate Norway. Luckily, the Germans in Norway capitulated as a result of defeats outside our country.[19]

After the war, a special historical branch was established in the Norwegian Defence Staff. The members of the historical branch had their background chiefly from service academies; only a few of the members came from civilian universities, for instance Professor Nils Ørvik, who had studied at the universities of Oslo and Wisconsin.[20] The main task of the historical branch was to clarify the background and the events of Norwegian participation in World War II. Consequently, Army historians treated the Norwegian Army's operations during the war. In Particular, they treated in great detail the two months of war in Norway in 1940.[21] The Air Force had their histories as well,[22] and last but not least, the operations of the Royal Norwegian Navy during the period of neutrality and in conditions of war, have been dealt with by Commander E.A. Steen.[23] In the beginning of the eighties, the historical branch was disbanded in the belief that its work was completed. At present, no special unit exists for the treatment of historical topics in the Norwegian armed forces, with the exception of the work done by the Museum of Defence in Oslo and its subdivisions: the Norwegian Home Front Museum, the Air Force museum in Bodø, the Naval Museum in Horten, and a small centre of defence studies in Oslo, led since 1980 by Professor Olav Riste.[24]

The Norwegian Museum of Defence has, until recently, been directed by officers with an Army background. The last military director resigned in protest against the transfer of the Air Force museum from Gardemoen near Oslo to Bodø in northern Norway. The new director, Rolf Scheen, the first director of the Museum of Defence with a non-military background, is an archaeologist in

---

18 Halvdan Koht, *Norway, neutral and invaded* (London: 1941).

19 Forsvarets Krigshistoriske Avdelning, *Forsvarets rolle i Norges historie* (Oslo: 1965), pp. 37–50.

20 *Norges Statskalender 1951* (Oslo: 1951), p. 1086.

21 Forsvarets Krigshistoriske Avdelning, *Krigen i Norge i 1940*, Ca. 15 volumes (Oslo: 1952–1965).

22 Fredrik Meyer, *Haerens og Marinens flyvåpen 1912-1945* (Oslo: 1973).

23 Erik Anker Steen, *Norges Sjøkrig 1940–45*, 7 volumes (Oslo: 1954–1963).

24 *Norges Statskalender 1993* (Oslo: 1993), pp. 141, 174.

his mid-forties.[25] Rolf Scheen's pronounced goal is to improve the cooperation with civilian bodies. The new director judges his museum as one of the biggest in the country and aims at making the institution a center for competent research in matters concerning Norwegian defence forces.[26] At present, with few exceptions, the majority of the museum's personnel have a military background. In the same way the Naval Museum at Horten, the main naval base of Norway until the 1960s, has a director educated at the Norwegian naval academy.[27]

The teaching of Norwegian naval history, with the exception of occasional museum lectures, is done almost exclusively by the Norwegian naval academy in Bergen. At the academy, all the students, regardless of specialization, attend courses in naval history. The executive branch students, however, have the most extensive syllabus. The prescribed texts in Norwegian naval history are prepared mainly at the academy.[28] Thanks to the efforts of Captain K.E. Kvam, who was the lecturer in naval history during the first decades after World War II, naval officers were selected as future teachers and prepared for their profession through M.A. theses in naval history in addition to their general education at the naval academy. In that way, since the middle of the sixties, the teachers in naval history have possessed professional naval knowledge in combination with a passed examination for a university degree in history.[29] In addition to Norwegian naval history, international naval history is also taught. The students at the Norwegian naval academy are expected to graduate with a fairly good insight into the naval history of the United States, Great Britain, Russia, France, Germany, and Japan as well. To that end, the Potter and Nimitz text book, *Sea Power,* is highly valued.[30]

Maritime History

The field of maritime history can be defined widely to include both the history of the merchant fleet as well as that of the Navy. Traditionally in Norway, however, there is a division between the study of naval affairs and non-military, maritime history.[31] A merchant fleet is an important constituent of sea power, since its protection provides the Navy with a rationale. The resources of the merchant marine (hulls, sailors, and expertise) can support naval strength to a considerable degree. However, civilian and naval types of maritime power do not necessarily sail together, and that is clearly the case in Norway. First and

---

25   *Forsvarets Forum*, 19 (1992).

26   *Ibid.*, 21 (1992).

27   *Norges Statskalender 1993* (Oslo: 1993), p. 141.

28   Norwegian Naval Academy, Education plans 1993, (SKUP-3).

29   K. Kvam, *Beretning om den norske sjøkrigsskoles virksomhet 1817–1967* (Oslo: 1967), pp. 584, 629.

30   Norwegian Naval Academy, Education plans 1993, (SKUP-3).

31   Helge W. Nordvik: "Norwegian Maritime Historical Research during the past twenty years: A Critical Survey," *Sjøfartshistorisk Arbok 1990* (Bergen: 1991), p. 241.

foremost, the Norwegian Navy is a coastal one,[32] while the Norwegian merchant fleet ranks among the foremost in the field of international transportation across the oceans.[33]

The last century of Norwegian political independence in the Middle Ages, saw a steady increase in the Hanseatic cities' participation in Norway's foreign trade, eventually dominating it.[34] Not until the great economic expansion in the Netherlands by the turn of the sixteenth century did Norwegian economic life experience a substantial change for the better.[35] Norway's forests proved to be one of her most important resources, with timber being exported to the Netherlands and to other countries in Western Europe such as England and Scotland. To a great extent, this trade was carried out on Dutch keels. The blooming of the Dutch economy led thousands of Norwegians, especially from southern Norway, to emigrate to the Netherlands. Norwegians served in the Dutch Navy as well as on Dutch merchantmen. The Dutch served as our teachers in naval and maritime matters since these specialties, to a large extent, had sunk into oblivion in Norway after the Middle Ages.

England struck a serious blow against the Dutch carrying trade to English ports by the Navigation Act of 1651. However, by the exclusion of Dutch merchantmen from the timber trade between Norway and England, Norwegian ships were given an advantage, giving the Norwegian merchant fleet many favourable years at the turn of the seventeenth century. These conditions also prevailed in the 1750s and later during the American War of Independence and in the first decade of the French Revolutionary War.[36] During these periods, Denmark–Norway enjoyed a profitable neutrality.[37]

The battle in the roadstead of Copenhagen in 1801, and especially the British bombardment of Copenhagen in 1807 and the taking away of the better part of the Danish–Norwegian Navy, however, brought the countries into the turmoil of the Napoleonic wars, and a war against the mistress of the seas, Great Britain. The British blockade brought disaster to the Norwegian merchant fleet. Since free transportation by sea was of vital importance for Norway, some parts of the country even experienced famine when the sea routes were interrupted.[38]

After the union with Sweden in 1814 and the restoration of peace, British protectionism put obstacles in the way of Norwegian maritime expansion, for instance the favoring of Canadian instead of Norwegian timber.[39] The abolition of the British

---

[32] Geoffrey Till, *Modern Sea Power*, vol. 1 (London: 1987), pp. 12–3.

[33] *Statistical Yearbook of Norway 1992* (Oslo: 1992), p. 460.

[34] Ole Jørgen Benedictow, *Norges historie*, vol. 5 (Oslo: 1977), pp. 207–8, 232–39.

[35] Axel Coldevin, *Vårt folks historie*, vol. 5 (Oslo: 1963), pp. 87-90.

[36] *Ibid.*, pp. 348–51.

[37] *Ibid.*, pp. 407–16.

[38] Knut Mykland, *Norges historie*, vol. 9 (Oslo: 1977), pp. 145–55.

[39] Bernt A. Nissen, *Vårt folks historie*, vol. 6 (Oslo: 1964), p. 129.

Navigation Act in 1849, however, was of the greatest importance for the growth of the Norwegian merchant fleet.[40]

During the 1850s, Norwegian shipping expanded dramatically in the overseas trades. Sailings between foreign ports, without Norwegian ports of call, became customary. Norway was able to maintain competitive advantage by paying low wages to the sailors and using second-hand ships. At the same time, the conditions of life in the Norwegian coastal districts produced sailors well adapted to the seafaring life.

The upward trend for Norwegian shipping continued, with a few setbacks, into the present century. By the beginning of the twentieth century, Norway's merchant fleet ranked number four after Great Britain, Germany, and the United States. Before 1914, most shipowners had managed the transition to steam, and Norwegian shipyards mastered the new technology.[41]

The merchant fleet of neutral Norway was highly affected by World War I; however, due to political sympathy for the Allied cause, common economic interests, and Allied pressure, the Norwegian policy became definitely pro-Allied. In the final years of the war, the largest part of the merchant fleet was engaged in British transport, although at very high expense. Nearly half (49.6 percent) of the pre-war fleet was lost. About 900 ships were sunk due to war-related causes, and nearly 2,000 sailors perished.[42]

After the war, the development of Norwegian liner trades continued, hand in hand with the reconstruction of the fleet. The difficult market was met by modernization—for instance a change from steam to motor. At the same time, new, more specialized trades were developed, most importantly the tanker trade. In 1921, tonnage reached the pre-war level. With the exception of a few setbacks, the expansion of the merchant fleet went on throughout the inter-war years.[43] By the outbreak of World War II, Norwegian merchant tonnage had doubled to 4.9 million G.R.T. and ranked fourth after Japan. Before 1914, during the previous period of great expansion, growth had taken place through the procurement of cheap, old ships. During the inter-war years, the competitive ability was maintained by sailing vessels that, in technical terms, were the best of ships. In 1939, 70 percent of the fleet used motor propulsion, and 20 percent of the world's tanker tonnage was Norwegian.

After the German attack in 1940, about 16 percent of the Norwegian ships, the "home fleet," came under German control. The rest of the fleet, about 4 million tons, remained under the control of the legal Norwegian government.[44] By decision in cabinet, the Norwegian merchant fleet was placed under

---

[40] Hans Try, *Norges historie*, vol. 11 (Oslo: 1979), pp. 116–53.

[41] Per Fuglum, *Norges historie*, vol. 12 (Oslo: 1978), pp. 234–52.

[42] Chr. A.R. Christensen, *Vårt folks historie*, vol. 8, (Oslo: 1961), pp. 66–83).

[43] Edvard Bull, *Norges historie*, vol. 13 (Oslo: 1979), pp. 59–68.

[44] Niels P. Vigeland, *Norge på havet*, vol. 2 (Oslo: 1954), p. 582.

governmental control for the duration of the war.[45] In that way, "The Norwegian Shipping and Trade Mission," usually abridged to NORTRASHIP, was born. NORTRASHIP, with its estimated 1,000 ships and 25,000 sailors, was the most valuable asset of the Norwegian government in exile. The income from NORTRASHIP made the government economically independent during its forced stay in Great Britain.[46] At the same time, the Norwegian merchant fleet was Norway's greatest contribution to the Allied victory. For instance, in the period "when Great Britain stood alone," nearly 50 percent of the vital oil-transports came to Britain on Norwegian keels.[47] As during World War I, the cost was grim: 2.7 million tons, 47 percent of the fleet, was lost and about 4,000 Norwegian sailors died.[48]

Within five years after the end of World War II, the Norwegian merchant fleet had reached its pre-war level. All through the fifties and sixties, the fleet had a remarkable growth, reaching 25 million tons in the middle of the seventies. In that decade, however, the merchant fleet experienced a downward economic trend and felt the negative consequences of the higher Norwegian costs of operation. Competition from ships registered under "flags of convenience," with lower taxes and far less social costs, elucidated the competitive disadvantages that the post-war Norwegian welfare state implied for international shipping.[49] The result was a pronounced downward trend in the Norwegian tonnage of shipping. Not until the creation of the Norwegian International Ship's Register (NIS) in 1987 was the decline halted, perhaps temporarily. By the end of 1992, the size of the Norwegian merchant fleet was about 23 million G.R.T. Of this total, 21,769 million tons was in the NIS.[50]

After this very short survey of Norwegian maritime history, what is the present state of naval and maritime history in Norway? Maritime finds from antiquity and the Middle Ages are regulated by law. The Chief of Inspectorate of Ancient Monuments and Historic Buildings [Riksantikvar] has country-wide authority. As for archeological finds, the country is divided between the University of Oslo and the Norwegian Maritime Museum in Oslo, the Archaeological Museum, and the Maritime Museum in Stavanger, the University of Bergen and the Maritime Museum in Bergen, the University of Trondheim and the Museum at the University of Tromsø. According to Norwegian law, maritime finds from the modern period, if they are more than one-hundred years old, belong to the Norwegian state when private ownership is impossible to establish. The respon-

---

[45] Ibid., p. 579.

[46] Chr. A.R. Christensen, Vårt folks historie, vol. 9 (Oslo: 1961), pp. 422–23.

[47] Niels P. Vigeland, Norge på havet, vol. 2 (Oslo: 1954), p. 582.

[48] Ibid., p. 609.

[49] Edvard Bull, Norges historie, vol. 14 (Oslo: 1979), pp. 197–203.

[50] Central Bureau of Statistics of Norway, Monthly Bulletin of Statistics, 1/1993 (Oslo: 1993).

sibility for material of this category is divided in the same way among the above mentioned institutions.[51]

As for maritime history in the modern period, it has been maintained that fascinating ships, sailors, and personalities always tend to win in the competition with structures, strategies, and politics.[52] In a somewhat exaggerated reaction to this issue, primarily to the book on *The History of Norwegian Shipping up to 1914*,[53] Professor Johan Schreiner published his study of Norwegian shipping in the period 1914–1920. In his preface, Professor Schreiner explicitly stated that his book contained no pictures of ships or portraits and no accounts of ships and men. Instead, Schreiner concentrated on the new problems created by the war and the shipping boom of the period.[54]

The history of the individual shipping firms, quantitatively the most common type of maritime history in Norway, has largely been written through commissioned assignments to journalists and "popular" writers. Fortunately, however, there are several exceptions to this fact. Some research is being done in this area, but it is usually done outside the universities, because Norwegian professional historians generally have concentrated their research on Norwegian political history, especially the emergence of the new state after 1814 and the creation of the modern welfare state.[55] The most prominent institutions that have dealt with maritime history in the shape of scientific research published in books and well-edited yearbooks are the maritime museums of Oslo and Bergen, both of which are led by professional historians. Bård Kolltveit is the director at the Norwegian Maritime Museum and Dr. Atle Thowsen is at the Maritime Museum in Bergen.[56] The foundation of the "Norwegian Research Fund for Maritime History" at the Bergen Maritime Museum in 1971 is an attempt to turn the tide in favor of scientific research in the field of Norwegian maritime history, but its resources are very limited. Consequently, the foundation can support only a few research workers per year. Although some progress has taken place, the negative trend has not been changed permanently. During the two decades leading up to the 1990s, some twenty master of arts theses in maritime history have been written at Norwegian universities. In the same period, only three doctoral theses in maritime history have been defended at Norwegian academic institutions.[57]

---

[51] Lov om kulturminner av. 9. juni 1978, Lovendring av 3. juli 1992.

[52] Helge W. Nordvik, "Norwegian Maritime Historical Research during the past twenty years: A Critical Survey," *Sjøfartshistorisk Årbok 1990* (Bergen: 1991), p. 242.

[53] Jac. S. Worm-Muller, Ed., *Den norske sjøfarts historie fra de aeldste tider til vore dage*, 3 volumes (Kristiania-Oslo, 1923–51).

[54] Preface to Johan Schreiner, *Norsk skipsfart under krig og høykonjunktur 1914–1920* (Oslo 1963).

[55] Ottar Dahl, *Norsk historieforskning i det 19, og 20. århundre* (Oslo: 1959), pp. 268–71.

[56] Universitetet i Bergen, *Årsmelding 1968-69* (Bergen: 1970), p. 133; *Hvem er Hvem* (Oslo: 1984), p. 419.

[57] Helge W. Nordvik, "Norwegian Maritime Historical Research," *Sjøfartshistorisk Årbok 1990*

Among the most important works published recently is Commander Jon Rustung Hegland's account of the NORTRASHIP Fleet.[58] This well-documented account studies the activities of 1,081 ships and about 25,000 seamen. Based on primary sources, Hegland used maritime statutory declarations, actions reports from naval gunners aboard the ships, the Admiralty's War Diary, NORTRASHIP's records of losses, Norwegian naval documents, as well as some British and German printed documents. Although Hegland only treated the economic and administrative aspects when they are important for the overall view, the very comprehensive works of Lauritz Pettersen, Bjørn L. Basberg, Guri Hjeltnes, and Atle Thowsen on *The Merchant Navy at War* have more completely elucidated these aspects.[59]

These works are good examples of the complementary research done by naval and civilian historians. To a certain extent, the two groups may be said to be mutually prejudiced, with naval men writing oversimplified explanations of complex historical causes and effects, while civilian historians tend to give amateur treatment to naval and military problems.

In the future, one may hope that the goal of the new director of the Norwegian Museum of Defence, to improve contact between civilian and military research establishments, may help to bridge the existing gulf between Norwegian maritime and naval history.

(Bergen: 1991), pp. 243, 248, 256; Atle Thowsen, "Norsk sjøfartshistorie—periferi eller sentrum i norsk historieforskning?" *Sjøfartshistorisk Årbok 1972* (Bergen: 1973), p. 38, (Summary in English).

[58] Jon Rustung Hegland, *Nortraships Flåte*, 2 volumes (Oslo: 1976).

[59] Atle Thowsen, *Handelsflåten i krig 1939–1945*, vol. 1; Bjørn L. Basberg, *Handelsflåten i krig 1939–1945*, vol. 2; Guri Hjeltnes, *Handelsflåten i krig 1939–1945*, vols. 3 & 4; Lauritz Pettersen, *Handelsflåten i krig 1939–1945*, vol. 5 (Oslo: 1992–1995).

22

Pakistan

Commodore S.Z. Shamsie, Pakistan Navy, Retired

Pakistan came into existence on 14 August 1947. Prior to that date there was only one well-established maritime institution in what was to become Pakistan, that being the Karachi Port Trust. It was on that same day in August that the Royal Pakistan Navy was born, with its ships being allocated from the old Royal Indian Navy.[1]

The region has a long-standing relationship with the sea. Two small islands near the mainland in Karachi harbour contain a thriving shipbuilding industry which, for many years, has been focused on building dhows. Even today, these indigenous boats ply the Arabian and Red Seas, the Persian Gulf, as well as other areas. Now equipped with diesel engines, the dhows are able to operate in nearly all weather conditions. They also carry a surprising amount of cargo, as little space is devoted to comfort, and crews are small.

The infancy of the Pakistan Navy was difficult, given the chronic lack of financial resources, manpower, and expertise. It took time to create these new institutions, and it was not until the 1950s that substantive growth appeared. Two important facilities were developed during that time frame: the Royal Pakistan Navy Dockyard and, near it on West Wharf, the Karachi Shipyard and Engineering Works.

Although the subject of a naval academy and a marine academy had been discussed as early as 1948, nothing significant happened for several years. The Cadet Training School was started in HMPS *Himalaya* (the training complex) on Manora Island in the early 1950s. The Naval Academy was commissioned at another location on the island in 1957. The Pakistan Marine Academy was eventually set up in 1961 in East Pakistan, near Chittagong. After East Pakistan became Bangladesh in 1971, temporary accommodation for the Marine Academy was found in Karachi. Construction of a new Academy, not far from Sandspit Beach, was started in 1976. That institution is now under control of the Ports and Shipping Wing.[2]

---

[1] A general history of the development of the Pakistan Navy is provided in the official history, titled the *Story of the Pakistan Navy 1947–1972*, (Karachi: Elite Publishers, Ltd., 1991); See also, Herbert Feldman, *Karachi Through a Hundred Years; the Centenary History of the Karachi Chamber of Commerce and Industry, 1860–1960* (Karachi: Pakistan Branch, Oxford Univ. Press, 1970).

[2] This information, and that which follows about the Pakistani National Shipping Corporation, the Academy, the Coast Guard, and Port Qasim, was obtained from official Naval Headquarters Records

The Ports and Shipping Wing was established in Karachi at the end of 1961, under a director general who held the rank of commodore. He was assisted by two directors who were naval officers. Although it initially functioned under the Ministry of Defence, the Wing was later transferred to the Ministry of Communications.

The National Shipping Corporation was established in the public sector by the government to ensure better operation and development of shipping in Pakistan. The first ship was purchased in 1964, and by 1971 the number had increased to thirty-two. From its inception this corporation has been led by a naval officer.

The concept of a coast guard, initiated by the Navy, was developed as a seagoing force for the protection of national marine resources, patrolling coastal waters, anti-smuggling and assistance to merchantmen. It had been assumed that this was a natural function of the Navy. The proposal to establish a coast guard bumbled through the meandering channels of bureaucracy and emerged, having suffered a significant metamorphosis, as a land-based, ancillary force to assist the local police and Customs agencies.

The Karachi Shipyard and Engineering Works (KSEW) proved to be an unprofitable industry. With high overhead and labour unrest it was not competitive. After a Presidential Order, it was taken over by the Ministry of Defence and placed, in 1970, under the charge of a naval officer.

Discussions were also held on the subject of creating another port to ease the burden on Karachi. The intent was that it be close so that transportation of goods from the north would be enhanced. Finally, it was decided that both the steel mill (which was to be set up with the help of the USSR) and the new port should be located at Pipri, which is close to Karachi while just to the south of it. That port was named after the man who conquered Sindh in 711; Port Mohammad Bin Qasim.

The Department of Hydrography was established in 1948 with the assistance of an officer from the Royal Australian Navy. A continuous demand by the Navy for scientific information about the marine environment led to the formation in 1958 of the National Committee for Oceanographic Research (NCOR). This organization was chaired by the Hydrographer of the Navy. The Pakistan Navy took part in the International Indian Ocean Expedition (1962–65) and generated much interest in the region. UNESCO organized training schemes for naval personnel, and equipment was donated by a number of countries, including the United States.

The Ministry of Technology was established in 1978. The Navy played a significant role in the establishment of the National Institute of Oceanography, (NIO) as the Committee for Oeanographic Research was the primary advisory

and Naval Archives and from the Office of the Director, General Ports and Shipping.

body for the development of that organization. That institute was set up in Karachi in 1981, with the aim of initiating oceanic research and exploiting marine resources.

The Navy further extended its research and training facilities. Close cooperation with the Pakistan Navy led to an increase in the activities of the National Institute of Oceanography. For instance, the need for tidal data from the United Kingdom was eliminated through the introduction of tidal predictions in Pakistan. In addition, coastal protection works were commenced. The Institute also arranges special lectures for the Navy and other organizations. The Institute's Director was appointed Vice Chairman of the Inter-governmental Oceanographic Commission For UNESCO, in Paris 1989–93.[3]

The need for an oceanographic research vessel had been felt for some time, and approval had been pending for some time. Continued pressure by the Navy and National Institute of Oceanography ultimately lead to action and, in 1982, a research vessel was launched. This Oceanographic vessel was commissioned and named *Behr Paima* in 1983. It is under the administrative control of the Ministry of Communications, while naval personnel man it.

Two Pakistan research expeditions have been undertaken to the Antarctic. The first was from 12 December 1990 to 1 March 1991. An Antarctic station was established and named after the founder of our nation: Jinnah. On the second expedition, the ship left Karachi on 27 December 1992 and returned on 11 March 1993. There were twenty scientists, thirteen naval officers, eleven Army officers and one Air Force observer. Jinnah Station 2 and Iqbal Observatory were established on the ice shelf, while detailed scientific research was carried out in the surrounding waters.[4]

In addition, an oceanographic ship was chartered by the Ministry of Technology for National Insitute of Oceanography and expeditions were organized and led by the Pakistan Navy. Scientists from the Institute and other institutions carried out extensive research on the ice shelf and adjacent waters, with the Navy and Army providing assistance.

As mentioned earlier, the Navy initiated a case for the establishment of the Coast Guard which, unfortunately, became a para-miliary unit. The situtation was reconsidered in order to redress that error, and the Coast Guard was reconstituted in 1986 to perform its originally assigned functions. This organization is now called the Maritime Security Agency. It is currently manned by naval personnel and was started with ships allocated by the Navy.

Some years ago, a body called the Foundation for Development through Moral Revival was formed as a non-profit making public charity trust by retired

---

3   Information about general oceanographic developments was obtained by interview with the former Director of the National Institute of Oceanography.

4   Specific data for the 1992 expedition was provided in an interview with the naval officer directly in charge of the 1992 expedition.

Vice Admiral Choudri, who was the first Pakistan naval officer to become the commander in chief. His purpose was to call together various intellectuals and persons interested in discussing matters of national importance. At a later stage, a maritime studies group was formed, as attention was focused on maritime subjects. Admiral Choudri has developed an abiding interest in maritime matters and has actively supported them on every suitable occasion. Last year, the decision was made to expand its activities and form an independent research body. It has now been named the Pakistan Institute of Maritime Affairs (PIMA). Its charter encompasses many aspects of maritime history, including merchant ships, shipbuilding, ship repairs, ports, fisheries, offshore activity, pollution and hinterland infrastructure.

The Pakistan Navy is also in the process of building a museum, to be named the Pakistan Maritime Museum. This museum will include display rooms, a laboratory, a historic reference section, and a library. Construction is scheduled to be completed in 1994.

Most maritime institutions are under the control of the Ministry of Communications. All of them have published articles on their activities on special occasions. A book was published on the occasion of the centennial of the Karachi Port Trust in 1980. A souvenir magazine was produced by the Pakistan Marine Academy, providing a brief history, an account of its activities, and the courses held subsequent to the aid provided by Japan.

Given that our country is very young, the histories are very limited as well. In 1997, when we celebrate the 50th anniversary of our Independence, all these institutions will publish special issues to commemorate the event. When considered together, they will comprise our maritime history.

There is, however, another aspect of Pakistani maritime history which also warrants a certain amount of attention. Specifically, the Muslims did much productive work in that regard between the eighth and fifteenth centuries. Though books and articles that touch on the maritime aspect have been written in the past, many of them are in Arabic or Turkish. A fair amount was also written by the English during their rule in India. But the impression is that not enough has been written in the Urdu language (the language of Pakistan) or in English. While a few articles have appeared from time to time in newspapers and periodicals on navigation, astronomy, ship construction, and charts, and instruments for navigation, research in this area deserves greater attention and resources. In general, books on maritime history are not readily available to the public.

Considering our ethos, our people's thoughts are focused landward, particularly to the north. Very little happened at sea during the rule of the Moghuls, and the small navy which existed for a short period of time remained in the eastern part of the subcontinent. Historically, the only person who understood the importance of the sea and the Navy was Tippu Sultan, and his advice went unheeded. Today, paradoxically, most naval personnel are recruited from the north. But, in general, there is little interest in maritime affairs.

In fact, the word maritime has a different connotation to most students in this country. In the universities, there are few students who have shown interest in the subject, though some have displayed an interest in the Muslim history in the period A.D. 700–1500. In the recent past, some Sindh students have been keen to study the history of old Sindh as a maritime province, going back as far as the time of Moenjo Daro, and the Indus Valley civilization. Some books in the Sindhi language are available. An effort has been made to encourage the University of Karachi to create a Department of Maritime History.

Naval history is taught, on a limited scale, in the Naval Academy at the Navy Staff College. Certain aspects are taught in the Army and Air Force Staff Colleges and in the National Defence College.

The intellectual atmosphere in Pakistan was vitiated some years ago. There are, however, faint signs that interest in intellectual subjects may be revived in the future, but this will come only slowly. Significant interest in maritime affairs is not likely to develop soon. In 1992, an international seminar was held in Lahore on the achievements of the Muslims, including the maritime sphere, in order to generate interest. Many experts came from abroad. That seminar did generate some interest. But, without concerted follow-up, that interest is also likely to wane.

The Institute of Maritime Affairs held a seminar in Islamabad in 1992, and planned to hold another in Lahore in May 1993, to raise the consciousness of maritime issues for those who are generally far removed from the sea. Political events forced them to postpone the seminar which was to be held in Islamabad in March 1994. The institute's objective was, and is, to make the maximum possible contribution as a non-political, non-governmental organization, inter alia, through study/research and development, in as many of the maritime subjects as resources permit. They also hope, wherever possible, to help other organizations engaged in similar work in the interest of the country.

The Pakistan Maritime Museum will probably assume the task of producing the maritime history of the country. One of the functions of a maritime museum is to make people aware of their maritime heritage. In this case, it will be entrusted with the task of writing notes on the achievements of the Muslims. Any assistance which can be provided from other sources will certainly be deeply appreciated.

As mentioned earlier, while there has been a slight resurgence of interest recently in the achievements of the Muslims, there is inadequate intellectual interest presently in the maritime sphere. Just the same, an effort to record maritime history is underway. A modest start in this process was made by the publication of the *Story of the Pakistan Navy*, which was referenced earlier in this article. That book provides the first reference to our extended maritime history.

23

Peru

Commander Jorge Ortiz, Peruvian Navy

The sea has always been an important factor in Peruvian life. It played a decisive role in the formation of Andean culture and in the evolution of the colonial world, and it has remained just as important throughout our modern history as well. However, for many different reasons, Peruvians remained outside this important process. Historically, Peru has remained an observer, while foreigners exploited one of the richest seas of the world, laying adjacent to her coast (for example, the use of the whaling grounds off the northern coast of Peru by the British and North Americans in the late eighteenth and early nineteenth centuries, and the development of the important guano trade in the last century).

A possible explanation for this situation is the tremendous influence that the Andes have exerted on Peruvian life. It was in the sierra that the most important cultures flourished, exploiting the great diversity of ecological niches. After the Europeans arrived in the sixteenth century, enormous mineral resources located in the mountains became the base for the Spanish colonial economy in the New World. Nonetheless, maritime routes were the only feasible means for the export of gold and silver taken from the Andes. That exploration moved the Peruvian economy increasingly away from agriculture and towards mining. That trend continues today.

This condition restricted Peruvian maritime activity to insignificant fishing communities and to a small number of maritime entrepreneurs, ship owners and seamen. The vast majority of these people were concerned only with their own businesses. Very few of them played an active role in politics, or devoted themselves to developing an awareness in the Peruvian community of the importance of the sea to the national well-being.

This article is intended to explain why maritime and naval history are nearly absent in the Peruvian academic world and are not being offered as courses or seminars in any Peruvian university. In fact, aside from some valuable and pioneering research done in the late nineteenth century, maritime history was, in the past, largely confined to an adjunct status to naval history. That history was, in the main, produced by naval officers. Taking this situation into account, and with the intent of renewing maritime and naval history, a group of naval officers and historians took upon themselves the task of writing a Peruvian maritime history nearly thirty years ago.

A few years later, with the firm support of the Peruvian Navy, this group formed the Peruvian Institute of Maritime History, (Instituto de Estudios Histórico-Maritimos del Perú) and published a large collection of books under the general title, *Historia Marítima del Perú*. This collection, covering Peru's maritime past, from prehispanic times to the twentieth century, already numbers twenty volumes, and three other volumes are in work.[1]

The functions of the Institute are complemented by the Navy itself through its historical service. However, despite its formal intentions to promote maritime history, the Institute has devoted a considerable amount of its effort to naval history, not only because it forms an important part of maritime history, but also because the Institute is directed by retired naval officers. Apart from the Institute and the Navy, and closely linked to both, there are a small number of historians and other scholars who do research in maritime or naval history themes. As already suggested, though, while there are historians who have written about maritime and naval topics, it cannot, in general, be said that they are truly naval or maritime historians. The exception, perhaps, is Commander Fernando Romero Pintado, who holds a Ph.D. in history, but whose advanced age has limited his involvement in academic activities during the last few years.

Taking all of this into consideration, the Peruvian Institute of Maritime Studies has encouraged and supported some naval officers to take up maritime historical studies. Furthermore, efforts have been made to attract young historians and researchers to maritime themes. Several young naval officers studied at the Faculty of Arts at the Universidat Católica del Perú and have become professional historians. One of the first to accept this challenge was the author of this short essay who, along with some other young historians and researchers, devoted his studies to topics of the sea. In both cases, there have been some initial successes. In the near future at least, a small cadre of trained maritime and naval historians will be working in the areas that maritime and naval history encompass.

Some reference should also be made to the dissemination or publication of maritime and/or naval themes. While no seminars or courses on maritime or naval history are currently being given in the universities, they are being offered, although with some difficulty, at the Instituto de Estudios Histórico-Marítima del Perú, as well as by the Navy itself. In the last few years the following courses have been offered:

- Naval War College (Escuela Superior de Guerra Naval). Between 1988 and 1991 a course was offered in Maritime Identity. Since 1992, it has been replaced by three seminars: Historical Analysis of Peruvian Naval Campaigns, A History of War at Sea, and History of the Navy.

---

[1]   *Historia Marítima del Peru (Lima: Instituto de Estudios Histórico-Maritimas del Peru, 1972–).*

- Peruvian Naval Academy (Escuela Naval del Perú) provides a course on the History of the Navy.

- Institute for the Study of Peruvian Maritime History (Instituto de Estudios Histórico-Marítimos del Perú). In 1992, a course in maritime history was begun which was designed to give students a general overview of maritime topics. That course had three parts: a) evolution of ships, b) history of war at sea, and c) general maritime history.

The first course mentioned above, the maritime identity, was given by this author to the Captain's Course. The objective was to present a general overview of Peruvian maritime history, emphasizing the way it helped to build our national identity. Among the points covered were the importance of the sea to the prehistoric settlement of Peru; the myths and legends that shed light on this reality; and prehispanic navigation as a fundamental element in the production of food as well as in the pursuit of commerce. Reviewing the colonial period, the importance of Callao in the maritime commerce of the South Sea was emphasized, not only during the time of the annual fleets in the sixteenth and seventeenth centuries, but also during the epoch of the special license ships in the eighteenth and early nineteenth centuries. Furthermore, we directed the students' attention to the nascent interest in Peru which was awakened by the exploitation of marine resources. These activities included whale hunting at the end of the eighteenth century, which was later replaced by the great guano boom of the nineteenth century, and by the lucrative fishing industry, especially of anchovies, in the twentieth century. Peru became the world's leading producer of fish products in the 1950s.

The seminar covering the analysis of Peruvian naval campaigns is given by several retired admirals and includes three campaigns: Independence (1818–1826), the war with Chile (1879–1880), and the war with Ecuador (1941). Two other seminars are directed by this author, which are efforts to provide lieutenant commanders and commanders with an overview of the evolution of war at sea and of the Peruvian Navy itself. This course on naval history, given in the Naval Academy, has not been taught regularly in the last few years, and for this reason will not be analyzed fully. In 1992, the professor for the course, a retired commander, died and was replaced by his assistant, a young civilian historian.

The course of maritime history, mentioned above, offers a common base for researchers who work on maritime and naval themes. It should be noted that no similar course has ever been given in the country. As a result, in the past every researcher approached the topic with his own understanding of what was naval and what was maritime, but often with little understanding of the big picture and how the two fields meshed. So, for example, we not only try to present general ideas on the evolution of naval ships, but also emphasize points on worldwide maritime and naval history as well.

Having already mentioned the work carried out by the Instituto de Estudios Histórico-Maritimos del Perú in reference to the development of maritime studies, its organization and editorial efforts should be presented as well. The Institute is a private enterprise, strongly linked to the Navy, but independent in all its activities. It is made up of forty members, half of them naval officers, and the other half academics of diverse disciplines, including historians, diplomats, biologists, etc. Its principal endeavor, *The Maritime History of Peru* [*Historia Marítima del Perú*] which, as previously noted, is the primary resource for those who wish to become acquainted with the maritime and naval history of Peru. In addition, they have published more than a dozen other titles, and a reputable journal is issued, although on a somewhat irregular basis.

On the other hand, the Navy itself carries out and promotes historical research through the Direccion de Intereses Maritimos, which administers the Navy Museum and the Historic Archives of the Navy, and which contains documents dating from the beginnings of the nineteenth century. Another important archive for study of Peruvian and South American maritime and naval history is the National Archive, with documentation dating to the sixteenth century. The Navy has an editorial fund that has published almost thirty titles in the last few years, not all of which are on strictly naval history topics.

Apart from these two institutions, other works are being or have been produced which touch on maritime or naval themes. One of these is a thesis currently in preparation for presentation to the Catholic University, and another is the collected works of Dr. Maria Rostworowsky de Diez Canseco, published by the Institute of Peruvian Studies, which deals with the Peruvian coast in the Late Prehispanic Period.[2]

Finally, it should be noted that, given the importance of the Peruvian viceregal period, there are more than a few works, published outside Peru, which deal with maritime or naval aspects of the period.[3]

Naturally, one institution is not capable of handling all these works. Nonetheless, there is a concerted effort to establish links among all those who are interested in these topics. This effort was reinforced in 1991, with the First Symposium of Ibero-American Maritime Studies of Peru. One of the major achievements was the establishment of a permanent secretariat, and Chile as well

---

[2] María Rostworowsky de Diez Canseco, *Costa peruana prehispánica* (Lima: Instituto de Estudios peruanos, 1989) 2nd ed.; *Recursos naturales renovables y pesca, siglos XVI y XVII* (Lima: Instituto de Estudios Peruanos, 1981).

[3] Pablo E. Pérez-Mallaifna y Bibiano Torres Ramírez, *La Armada del Mar del Sur* (Sevilla: Escuela de Estudios Hispano-Americanos de Sevilla, 1987). Peter T. Bradley, *The Lure of Peru. Maritime Intrusion into the South Sea, 1598–1701* (London: The Macmillan Press: 1989). Peter T. Bradley, "The ships of the Armada of the Viceroyalty of Peru in the Seventeenth Century" in *The Mariner's Mirror*, 79 (1993), pp. 393-402. Hugo O'Donell, *El Viaje a Chiloé de José de Moraleda (1787–1790)* (Madrid: Editorial Naval, 1990).

as Argentina and Brazil agreed to host successive symposia in 1993, 1995, and 1999, respectively.

It is probably too early to speak of intellectual tendencies in the fields of maritime and naval history, as interest in academic circles has not been applied consistently over a prolonged period of time to demonstrate such trends or tendencies.

The War of the Pacific (1879–1884), which Peru and Bolivia lost to Chile, endowed the Navy with its most famous heroes. This, combined with the fact that the war proved traumatic for the nation, has been primarily responsible for so much of Peruvian naval and maritime history being devoted to that war and that epoch in general. Only in recent times have several works highlighted other aspects of Peru's rich and diverse maritime and naval past.

In this category, that being the periods least treated but also quite important, the one spanning the end of the eighteenth and the beginnings of the nineteenth centuries should be noted. It was the period between the authorization of the entrance of British and North American whalers and the war for national independence.[4] A methodical study is also needed on the Spanish South Sea Fleet, whose existence spanned almost two centuries (between 1579 and 1750). Some work on the topic exists, but much more needs to be known about this important colonial entity. Present day Peruvian maritime communities also need study. One can still find some prehispanic customs and artifacts (such as rafts) in a number of small fishing villages and ports. It is also necessary to research boats in general. In Peru, many immigrants settled on the coast in the past two centuries and many of the boats presently in use by fisherman reflect the influence of these immigrants. Another theme that should be dealt with urgently is the conquest of the Amazon, a process begun in the sixteenth century via the river system. This began to be systematized with the participation of the Navy after 1864.

As noted above, Peruvian historical studies deal largely with naval topics. Works on maritime themes, if they are attempted, face lack of incentives in the academic world. It is worth mentioning that while the Navy, through the Instituto de Estudios Histórico-Maritimos and through its own historic division, supports and develops historic studies,the same does not occur among the diverse elements that make up the maritime world of our nation.

In sum, Peruvian maritime history is very rich, given its diversity and the long relationship that Peruvians have had with the sea. In the case of naval history, it is equally abundant, having begun in the sixteenth century with the formation of the South Seas Fleet. All this information has been gathered and reviewed by

---

[4]   Jorge Ortiz, *El Vicealmirante Martin Jorge Guise Wright (1780–1828)* (Lima: Dirección de Intereses Maritimos, 1993). Jorge Ortiz and Alicia Castafieda, *Diccionario biográfico maritimo peruano* (Lima: Dirección de Intereses Marítimos, 1993). Jorge Ortiz, "Peru and the British Naval Station (1809–1839)," Ph. D. Thesis, St. Andrews University, Scotland, 1994.

the Institute of Historic-Maritime Studies of Peru, however, much research remains to be done in this field.

24

Poland

Jerzy Litwin
and
Commander Dr. Wincenty Karawajczyk, Polish Navy

Maritime History[1]

S tudies of the history of shipping and the Navy, which have been conducted in Poland over the past seventy-five years, have been strictly related to the country's political situation. During that period, the country's political-economic doctrines have undergone three radical changes. As a result, with each change, the authorities intensified demands to have at their disposal syntheses of particular fragments of Poland's history. These were utilized, more or less, for pertinent educational purposes, but also for specific propaganda activities, conducted in the name of the politics of the state at the time.

The first such period embraced the years 1918–1947, that is, from the regaining of Poland's independence after 123 years of annexation by Russia, Prussia, and Austria at the end of the eighteenth century. This period also included the Second World War and the post-war struggles for independence conducted by the Polish underground. The second period lasted from 1948 to the spring of 1989, when Poland was ruled by a communist government whose policies were imposed by U.S.S.R. authorities. The third period began in the spring of 1989 when, after the agreement of the so-called "round table," the communist authorities handed over power in Poland, agreeing to its being taken over by the forces which produced the social uprising in 1980, known by the name "Solidarity."

Polish Maritime History in Outline. The oldest written sources telling of the riparian navigation of the Slavic peoples date to the sixth century A.D. The northern borders of the Slavic lands stretched along the Baltic coast from the region known today as Lubeck in the west, to the mouth of the Vistula in the east.[2]

The people living adjacent to the western Slavs called them Wends. This point is brought to light in a description by Wulfstan, a ninth century Anglo-

---

[1]   This section is written by Dr. Jerzy Litwin, Deputy Director of the Polish Maritime Museum, Gdańsk.

[2]   Władysław Filipowiak, *Wolin - Vineta* (Rostock-Stralsund: 1986); Władysław Filipowiak, "Początki

Saxon traveller, who claims to have had the Wendic lands off his starboard bow during the entire voyage from Hedeby (Haithabu) to Truso. From Gdańsk Bay he sailed up the Vistula which, as he pointed out, was the natural frontier between the Wends and the "Old" Prussians.[3]

To meet their transportation, communication, and fishery needs, the riparian Slavs produced rafts and logboats and, if the necessity arose, larger craft as well. It was probably in the seventh century that the Slavs first ventured out into the open sea.[4] To sail in safety there required appropriately constructed craft. This usually involved increasing the ships' freeboards by attaching single planks to them, or sets of two or more overlapping planks.

In the larger boats, the dugout part of the ship's bottom was of no great significance, and in time it came to be left as a semicircular beam: the keel. By the end of the ninth century, keels had become T-shaped in cross-section.[5] Dugout keels in small boats persisted on the south coast of the Baltic until the beginning of the twentieth century.[6]

Ancient Slavic boatbuilding reached its peak of development in the tenth though the twelfth centuries, when large plank-built boats made quite long commercial voyages.[7] The Western Slavs also sent fleets to wage war against the Vikings.[8] Many wrecks and parts of Slavic vessels from this period have been discovered not only along the southern shores of the Baltic but also in Denmark. Sweden, and Germany.[9]

Slavic boats of the ninth through the twelfth centuries had a number of characteristic structural features. They were made of oak. In silhouette they resembled Viking ships, but their cross-sections were different. Their bottoms were flat and, even though they were made from overlapping planks; the 10-30

zeglugi słowiańskiej u ujścia Odry," *Studia nad etnogeneza Słowian i kultura Europy wczesnośredniowiecznej*, vol. 2 (Wrocław-Warszawa-Kraków-Gdańsk-Łódź: 1988); Witold Hensel, *Słowiańszczyzna wczesnośredniowieczna* (Warszawa: 1965); Jozef Kostrzewski, *Pradzieje Pomorza* (Wrocław-Warszawa-Kraków: 1966); Zdenek Vana, *Swiat dawnych Słowian* (Praha: 1985).

[3] Niels Lund, *Two Voyagers at the Court of King Alfred* (York: 1984), p. 22-30.

[4] W. Hensel, *ibid.*

[5] Przemysław Smolarek, *Studia nad szkutnictwem Pomorza Gdańskiego w X-XIII w.* (Gdańsk: 1969); Przemysław Smolarek, "Szkutnictwo Pomorza Gdańskiego we wczesnym sredniowieczu," *Historia budownictwa okrętowego na Wybrzezu Gdańskim*, ed. E. Cieślak (Gdańsk: 1972).

[6] Wolfgang Rudolph, *Handbuch der volkstumlichen Boote im ostlichen Niederdeutschland* (Berlin: 1966); Wolfgang Rudolph, *Inshore Fishing Craft of the Southern Baltic from Holstein to Curonia* (London: 1974).

[7] Władysław Łega, *Obraz gospodarczy Pomorza Gdańskiego w XII i XIII wieku* (Poznań: 1949); P. Smolarek, *ibid.*

[8] Krystyna Pieradzka, *Walki Słowian na Bałtyku w X-XII wieku* (Warszawa: 1953).

[9] Detlev Ellmers, *Fruhmittelalterliche Handelsschiffahrt in Mittel- und Nordeuropa* (Neumunster: 1984); P. Herfert, *Ralswiek ein frühgeschichtlicher Seehandels platz auf der Insel Rugen* (Greifswald: 1982); Jan Skamby Madsen, *Danish-wendische Beziehungen am Schluss des 11. Jahrhunderts vom Fund einer Schiffswerft bei Fribrodre A auf Falster aus beleuchtet, Bistum Roskilde und Rugen* (Roskilde: 1987); K.W. Struve, "Ein slawisches Schiffswrack aus der Eckernforder Bucht," *Offa* (1978); "Kazimierz Slaski, Slawische Schiffe des westlichen Ostseeraumes," *Offa* (1978).

millimeter diameter pegs used to hold the structural elements together proved to be an entirely satisfactory substitute for nails.[10]

The East Baltic Slavonic tribes, which belonged to Poland from the end of the tenth century, continued to expand maritime economy within the boundaries of the Piast monarchy, which in the tenth and eleventh centuries organized the state of Poland. At the end of the twelfth century, Poland was divided into a number of principalities. One of them, Masovia, experienced problems with its strong neighbor to the west, Prussia. Masovia's Prince Konrad, in 1226, invited the Teutonic Order Knights to fight with them against Prussia. These newcomers very soon established their own state on Prussian territory, and at the beginning of the fourteenth century they, in turn, invaded Gdańsk. With that act Poland lost her access to the Baltic.[11]

Two points stand out in fifteenth century Poland: her economic growth and her struggle for supremacy with the Teutonic Order.[12] Settlement in coastal towns was increasing, which helped to foster trade with foreign centres. By then, goods were being carried mostly by ship. As early as the fourteenth century, inland towns were making their contribution to the country's export drive. A variety of goods were shipped downriver to the coast on rafts, large logboats, or other craft.[13]

Cogs and holks were vessels frequently used in medieval sea transport. Their designs had generally become more sophisticated, but they differed from one another in detail. Cogs became common on the Baltic shores in the thirteenth century and, although probably originating in the Frisian Islands, they were also built in Gdańsk and Elbląg. Cogs had flat, flush bottoms and clinker-built sides, closely resembling Vistula ships in these design features. Holks, which were usually larger than cogs, became common in the fifteenth century and were traditionally built on a keel, like boats, by means of the shell technique.[14]

River navigation on the Vistula reached its zenith in the sixteenth through eighteenth centuries, when thousands of ships and rafts sailed down to Gdańsk and Elbląg and then, laden with overseas goods, plied back upstream to their points of origin. Products of farm and forest, minerals and goods in transit, were all shipped down the Vistula and its tributaries.[15]

---

[10] Smolarek, see note 5; Tadeusz Delimat, "O genezie łodzi klepkowych na Pomorzu," *Lud*, 42 (1956); Jerzy Litwin, "Szkutnictwio i zegluga," *Z dziejów techniki w dawnej Polsce* (Warszawa: 1992); K. Slaski, *ibidem*.

[11] Edmund Cieślak, *Historia Gdańska*, I (Gdańsk: 1978).

[12] Marian Biskup and Gerard Labuda, *Dzieje Zakonu Krzyzackiego w Prusach* (Gdańsk: 1988).

[13] Aleksander Gieysztor, "Wisła w średniowieczu," *Wisła, monografia rzeki*, ed. A. Piskozub (Warszawa: 1982); Stanisław Gierszewski, *Wisła w dziejach Polski* (Gdańsk: 1982); Przemysław Smolarek, "Types of Vistula Ships in the 17th and 18th Centuries," *Yearbook of the International Association of Transport Museums*, 8 (Gdańsk: 1981).

[14] Jerzy Litwin, *Some Remarks Concerning Medieval Ship Construction* (Malta: 1989); and *From Studies on Gdańsk and Elbląg Ship-building and Shipping in the 13th–15th Centuries* (Malta: 1991).

[15] Jan W. Gan, *Z dziejów zeglugi śródlądowej w Polsce* (Warszawa: 1978); Sebastian F. Klonowic, *Flis, to*

The szkuta was the largest vessel that shipped goods on the Vistula. A szkuta could be up to 38 meters long, 8.5 meters wide, and was capable of taking 100 tons of cargo on board.

A great opportunity to create a Polish navy arose in 1570 when the Polish king, Zigismund August, brought two experts from Venice and entrusted the construction of a galleon at Elbląg. This brought a new type of warship to the Baltic.[16] We know how the ship was built from surviving expenditure records.[17] Construction of the galleon began in June 1570. Ready for launching a year later, the ship was completed in 1572. However, she was not armed and never entered service, owing to the premature death of King Zigismund August.[18]

While Zigismund August failed in his effort to establish a navy, the Polish kings of the Vasa dynasty enjoyed greater success in that field in the first half of the seventeenth century. King Zygmunt III created a fighting fleet for which five ships were built at Gdańsk in 1605–6. Poland's naval successes included a victory over the Swedish fleet in 1627 in the Battle of Oliwa, which took place in Gdańsk Bay. During this battle the Swedish warship *Solen* was sunk, while another, the *Tigern*, was captured.[19]

In 1641–43, King Wladislaw IV's fleet was scrapped. The consequence of this was that for the next three hundred years the rulers of Poland, for a variety of reasons, turned their backs to the sea.[20] At the same time, from the mid-seventeenth century onwards, the policies of Gdańsk, which had become rich acting as the middleman in Polish-European trade, led to a standstill in the local shipbuilding industry.[21]

Although Poland had never been a major producer of oceangoing ships, she was a major supplier of raw materials to foreign shipbuilders through the end of the nineteenth century; timber (beams, planks, and masting) was shipped to the sea ports, where it was resold, principally to Holland and Britain. Up to the

---

jest spuszczanie statków Wisła i inszymi rzekami do niej przypadającymi (Warszawa: first edition 1595); Stanisław Kutrzeba, *Wisła w historii gospodarczej dawnej Rzeczypospolitej Polskiej* (Warszawa: 1922); J.M. Małecki, "Wisła w okresie od pokoju toruńskiego do pokoju oliwskiego," *Wisła, monografia rzeki*, ed. A. Piskozub (Warszawa: 1982); H. Obuchowska-Pysiowa, *Handel wiślany w pierwszej połowie XVII wieku* (Wrocław: 1964); Krystyna Waligórska, "Konstrukcje statków pływających po Sanie i Wiśle w XVIII w," *Kwartalnik Historii Kultury Materialnej*, vol. 8, no. 2.

[16] Mieczysław Boczar, *Galeona Zygmunta Augusta* (Wrocław-Warszawa-Kraków-Gdańsk: 1973); Jerzy Litwin, "The First Polish Galleon and its Construction Register from 1570-1572," *Carvel Construction Technique*, Oxbow Monograph 12 (Oxford: 1991).

[17] Adam Kleczkowski, *Regestr budowy galeony* (Kraków: 1915).

[18] M. Boczar, *ibid.*; J. Litwin, "First Polish Galleon."

[19] Witold Hubert, "Bitwa pod Oliwą," *Przegląd Historyczno-Wojskowy*, vol. 1 (Warszawa: 1929); Stanisław Bodniak, *Związek floty i obrona wybrzeża w wojnie Zygmunta III z Karolem IX* (Poznań: 1930); Kazimierz Lepszy, *Dzieje floty polskiej*, (Gdańsk-Bydgoszcz-Szczecin: 1947); Eugeniusz Koczorowski, *Bitwa Pod Oliwą* (Gdynia: 1968).

[20] K. Lepszy, *ibid.*

[21] Edmund Cieślak, *Historia Gdańska*, vol. I-III (Gdańsk: 1978; 1982; 1993).

eighteenth century, the materials specification for ships-of-the-line built in British yards expressly required 4 to 4 1/2 inch-thick oaken planks from Gdańsk.[22]

Steam power, which revolutionised industry in Western Europe at the turn of the eighteenth century, also had an effect on inland shipping. The first river and canal steamships made their appearance, making transport on those waterways more efficient.

Moreover, companies operating steamships came into existence despite the fact that the powers partitioning Poland were wilfully neglecting the country's waterways. The pioneers in this respect were Piotr Steinkeller and Konstanty Wolicki, who established a shipping company in 1825–27.[23] In 1827 they imported two ships from England, the *Victory* and the *Książę Ksawery*. Unfortunately, both ships were sunk during the November Insurrection of 1830.[24] In 1840–42, Steinkeller bought two new ships, again in England, intended for passenger transport in the Warsaw area.[25]

The most successful steamship company operating on the Vistula at that time was the "Steamship Company on the Navigable Rivers of the Kingdom, Count Zamoyski et Companie," founded in 1848 with the assistance of French capital provided by Eduard Guibert.[26] In 1849, this firm had ten lighters with two steamboats to move them (the *Prince de Varsovie* and the *Vistule*), both built at Nantes in 1847. Eduard Guibert was also the managing director of the company until 1852. Additional ships were built for this company in Poland, most of them at the Steamship Workshops, founded in 1851 in Solec, a suburb of Warsaw. The company's operations ended as a result of the restrictions imposed by the tsarist authorities after the January Insurrection of 1863. Count A. Zamoyski was also deported and his estate confiscated. In 1871 the company was formally dissolved and the ships sold.[27]

Towards the end of the nineteenth century, passenger travel by boat became very popular, not only as a means of getting from one place to another, but also as a form of recreation. Many pleasure steamers were built at Solec (Warsaw), Włocławek and Kraków. M. Fajans' company was the leader in this field.[28]

After the First World War, inland navigation was reactivated under Polish auspices. The leading companies operating on the Vistula were the Polish

[22] John Charnock, *An History of Marine Architecture* (London: 1800); John Fincham, *An Outline in Ship Building* (London: 1852); James Dodds and James Moore, *Building the Wooden Fighting Ship* (London: 1984).

[23] Witold Arkuszewski, *Wiślane statki pasażerskie XIX i XX wieku* (Gdańsk: 1973).

[24] *Ibid.*

[25] *Ibid.*

[26] *Ibid.*

[27] *Ibid.*

[28] *Ibid.*

Navigation Company of Kraków, the Polish River Navigation "Vistula" of Warsaw, and Lloyd of Bydgoszcz.

From 1918 to 1939 inland Polish shipyards prospered. Among their achievements were the large passenger ships, *Polska* and *Francja*, built in 1925, and the *Bajka* built at Solec in 1927. The largest vessel of all was the *Bałtyk*, built at the Gdańsk yard in 1928.[29] Other yards produced smaller ships and lighters. They also received orders for specialised craft. Particularly profitable for the shipyards were vessels supplied to the Polish Navy for the Vistula and Pinsk flotillas, and those supplied to the customs and frontier guards at Gdynia. The Zieleniewski yard in Kraków built a series of monitors. The Navy's own yards at Pińsk and Modlin built armed cutters and minelayers, and the Modlin yard built the first sea-going ship for the modern Polish Navy, the *Jaskółka*.

As well as fostering the growth of inland navigation, Polish authorities in that period emphasized the organisation of a sea-going fleet. Among the most important undertakings of that period were the construction of a modern port at Gdynia and the formation of a navy and a merchant fleet. The Higher Naval School was founded to train future ship's officers, and a nationwide association, the Maritime League, was brought into existence to disseminate information about and to organise activities dealing with the sea among the populace in general and among young people in particular.

At that time, France was very active in helping establish Poland's maritime activities. It was in France that Poland purchased her first modern warships, destroyers, and submarines, as well as a series of cargo ships, popularly known as "Frenchmen," many of which were still in service after 1945.

One tremendous achievement on the part of the organisers of the Polish maritime economy was the founding of a shipyard at Gdynia, where construction of sea-going vessels developed rapidly. Unfortunately, this healthy progress was interrupted by the outbreak of the Second World War.

After the war, cleanup operations got under way in the ports and shipyards along Poland's devastated, but now very much longer, coast. Harbours and shipyards were rebuilt. A system of maritime education came into being, and specialist design offices were established.

The industrialization of Poland undertaken after the war has also effected the dynamic development in the shipbuilding industry which was, until 1989, the pride of Poland's maritime economy. Even today, following the recent political and economical changes, the shipbuilding industry seems well positioned to be a dominant force in the Polish economy.

The Study and Preservation of Polish Maritime History. Compared to other European literature on naval and shipping history, Polish research publi-

---

[29] *Ibid.*

cations remain rather modest. The reason for this state of affairs is that systematic studies on these questions, as well as ship and boat-building, and fishers, started relatively late. This was due to a large extent to the country's unstable political situation prior to 1918 and to the prolonged lack of access to the sea, which precluded the development of more important maritime traditions.

Characteristic of the post–1918 period was the positively enthusiastic interest in maritime matters demonstrated by the whole population. This followed the award to Poland of a land corridor to the sea by the Treaty of Versailles. This, in connection with access to the seaport of Gdańsk (which had been given the status of a free city), led to the development of a maritime economy. A social organization, most frequently known as the Maritime League, was also established.

The first popular maritime publications also appeared. These offered articles on the Slavs' struggles on the Baltic, the times of King Zygmunt August, the founder of the Maritime Commission, and the only naval victory—the Battle of Oliwa, in 1627. The results of studies were also published by such historians as S. Bodniak,[30] A. Czołowski,[31] W. Hubert,[32] W. Konopczyński,[33] and others. Of particular importance in these considerations is the work of K. Lepszy, whose crowning study was *The History of the Polish Fleet.*[34]

Traditional fishery and small boat-building was primarily the subject of interest to ethnographers. Unfortunately, these subjects did not constitute a specific concerted area of study but, rather, just a fragmented body of papers presenting the material culture of the people inhabitating Poland at the time. Of a dozen or so papers, that by K. Moszyński, "The Popular Culture of the Slavs,"[35] was of particular importance. It was an attempt to present the basic types of Slavonic floating structures, including rafts and canoes.

With regard to linguistic studies concerning aquatic occupations, B. Slaski's *Fishery-Nautical and Boat-building Dictionary* remains a good source of information when studying earlier boat-building.[36]

Information on research and publications concerning shipping, shipbuilding, navies, fishery, rafting and boat-building was substantially supplemented by periodicals published at the beginning of the twentieth century. An important

[30] Stanisław Bodniak, *Związek floty i obrona wybrzeza w wojnie Zygmunta III z Karolem IX* (Poznań: 1930); "Morze w głosach opinii dawnej Rzeczpospolitej," *Rocznik Gdański*, vol. IV (Gdańsk: 1931); "Sprawy morskie w 'Księgach Hetmańskich' Sarnickiego," *Rocznik Gdański*, vol. XII (Gdańsk: 1938).

[31] Aleksander Czolowski, *Marynarka w. Polsce (Lwów: 1922).*

[32] Witold Hubert, "Próba tworzenia marynarki wojennej podczas powstania 1863-64," *Przegląd Morski*, vol. 2, no. 4 (1929); "Bitwa pod Oliwą," *Przegląd Historyczno-Wojskowy* (1937).

[33] Władysław Konopczynski, *Polska polityka bałtycka* (Poznań: 1930).

[34] Kazimierz Lepszy, "Strażnicy morza Stefana Batorego," *Rocznik Gdański*, vol. 7 (Gdańsk: 1933); Kazimierz Lepszy, *Dzieje floty polskiej* (Gdańsk-Bydgoszcz-Szczecin: 1947).

[35] Kazimierz Moszyński, *Kultura ludowa Słowian*, vol. 1; *Kultura materialna* (Kraków: 1929).

[36] Bolesław Slaski, *Słownik rybacko-zeglarski i szkutniczy* (Poznań: 1930).

popularizing role here was played by *The Sea* [*Morze*] and *The Maritime Review* [*Przegląd Morski*] concerning naval matters; *The Technical Review* [*Przegląd Techniczny*], which was devoted to industry, including shipyard questions; *Fishery Review* [*Przegląd Rybacki*], which was dedicated to fishermen; *The People* [*Lud*], *The Land* [*Ziemia*] and *The Vistula* [*Wisła*], which were designed for a wider circle of readers. There were also a whole series of weeklies containing articles on maritime subjects.

During that period efforts were also made to establish museums of a maritime character. This was not an easy task, as Poland's maritime traditions were not as extensive as those of many other European countries. The first attempts to establish such institutions were taken up in the 1930s, when a private maritime museum was organized in Warsaw and a fishery museum in the small fishing village of Dębki. Neither of these survived the ravages of the war. Numerous relics from other museums and private collections also met the same fate.

Despite the tremendous enthusiasm to learn about and propagate maritime matters in Poland in the years 1918–1947, no comprehensive system of professional studies and education in the field of historical-maritime problems could be established. Only the staff of the Baltic Institute conducted studies on Poland's maritime history, although there was also a fairly large group of scholars who took up sporadic studies in this field. That group managed to create the climate for the propagating of maritime history in postwar times.

The period following the Second World War, particularly in the years 1945-1947 was, for Poles, a period of continued struggle to regain independence. The Yalta Conference of 1945 had bound the future of the nation, oppressed by the six years of war, to a treaty of unreserved subordination to Soviet Russia, which was imposed by force. This struggle was carried out with considerable effort throughout Poland. Diplomatic steps were taken up in allied countries but, in view of the declining political force of Polish emigre circles, these efforts failed to achieve expected results. Thus, after 1948, following the wiping out of the patriotic groups throughout the country, Poland became totally subordinate to the Soviet Union.

The consequences of this situation became apparent in all spheres of learning, including history, the fields of studies, and dissemination of knowledge of the history of the Polish nation, as well as its modest maritime history. All of these were conducted, particularly until 1956, in the new communist spirit. It became customary to avoid, or hold back information regarding the country's economic achievements of the pre-war time when, for over a dozen years, Poland had managed to establish genuine bases for a versatile maritime economy. It was also not advisable to glorify the Navy's combat achievements during the 1939-1945 period, when it was on active service with the Western allied fleets. Perfidious communist authorities generated political trials based on false accusations against war heroes who continued to serve as officers during the Stalinist rule of terror

(1949–1953). These acts of repression included Navy men, and resulted in the sentencing of several outstanding officers for (unproven) espionage. The sentences included the death penalty.

Later, the Polish Navy, thanks to the dedicated, professional attitude of its officers, refused to participate in the suppression of the so-called social protests which took place with particular intensity in 1956, 1970, and 1981. Thanks to this, it earned the respect and friendship of the Polish society.

Generally speaking, the achievements in the organization of the maritime economy in Poland in 1948-1989 were considerable. Not only were the commercial and fishing port complexes established, but shipowning firms were developed and shipyards organized. An extensive system of education for this field of the economy began to function, beginning with basic vocational studies and leading to specialized, postgradate work. Several schools, particularly the Gdańsk and Szczecin technical universities, as well as other universities and merchant navy academies in the towns previously mentioned, promoted hundreds of graduates each year. The Navy could also boast of its own university-level academies.

In the field of propagation of maritime culture and history, as well as the conservation of nautical relics, Poland's achievements were the most distinctly manifested of all the countries in the "Eastern Block."

Attempts to found a maritime museum in Poland were made just as soon as hostilities ceased, and, in fact, the first such museum was set up in Szczecin in 1946. Unfortunately, this museum was subordinated to the Museum of Western Pomerania in 1950, where, to this day, it functions as the Maritime Department of the National Museum in Szczecin. Despite its subordinate status it continues to play an important part in the preservation of historical nautical objects and in encouraging townspeople to visit its attractive maritime exhibition. That exhibition is housed in a building apart from the main body of the museum and comprises, among other things, the wrecks of three early medieval Slavic boats and other artifacts illustrating the maritime traditions of the western Slavs. The museum has a varied collection of ship's fittings, many of which are from the ship *Poznań*, one of the "Frenchmen" mentioned earlier.

The second museum to be established in Poland was the Naval Museum, established in 1953, which can today boast of approximately ten million visitors. It has no dedicated, permanent display ship, but the destroyer *Błyskawica*, built in Great Britain in 1936, has been on display since 1976. Following successful adaptations to its new purpose, substantial exhibition space was gained. This was improved by a special passageway made through the turbine and steam boiler rooms.

An important achievement of the museum employees is the permanent exhibition of armaments. Thanks to this, it has been possible to safeguard several examples of what are now relics of armaments used at sea in the twentieth century. It warrants mention here that the experience in keeping a ship as an exhibit afloat was gained by the museum in the years 1960-1975 when another worthy veteran of World War II, built in France in 1928, the destroyer *Burza*, was opened to the public. Unfortunately, such exploitation was the reason for the ship finally being scrapped.

A significant achievement on the part of the scientific staff of the Naval Museum, is the publishing of the *Historical Bulletin* [*Biuletyn Historyczny*]. The twelfth edition appeared in 1992. Such publications present articles concerning various aspects of naval history.

The Naval Museum is not the only entity that accumulates relics and disseminates information on questions of war at sea. A considerable role is played by the fourteen halls of tradition found in the particular barracks, which constitute local historical centres not only for the sailors, but also for local communities. Among these, the most interesting exhibitions and collections are accommodated at Gdynia-Oksywie and Hel, where one of the exhibits is the Coast Guard cutter *Batory*, built in Poland before the war. In October 1939, the *Batory* managed to break through the German blockade and reach neutral Sweden. One commendable tradition is the custom of naming new naval vessels after units previously famous for their active service. For example, a third Polish submarine now bears the famous name of *Orzeł* (*Eagle*).

The Polish Navy also conducts several cultural-educational activities. An example of this is the organizing of numerous training-propaganda voyages for young people and teachers. Within the framework of training activities, salvage vessels traditionally cooperate with the Gdańsk Maritime Museum, providing assistance in the search for and exploration of shipwrecks.

A third museum dealing with the sea is the Oceanographic Museum and Aquarium in Gdynia. As a part of the Sea Fisheries Institute, it has discharged its statutory responsibilities in strict accordance with its original charter. Only recently has it begun to develop broader interests, such as the study of the ethnography of fisheries.

The leading museum of this kind in Poland, however, is the Central Maritime Museum in Gdańsk, established in 1960 and financed by the Ministry of Culture and Art. Considering the country's remaining economic difficulties, Gdańsk's Maritime Museum has become a museum giant in the last thirty years, employing a staff of about 250. In the same way, it constitutes the centre of Polish nautological studies and provides protection for these types of relics. Through the staff's efforts, it has been possible to purchase and adapt two historical sea-going ships: the sail-training frigate *Dar Pomorza*, and the first coal-ore carrier to be built entirely in Poland after the last war, the S.S. *Sołdek*. The museum also possesses a large collection of traditional inland and sea-going craft, both from Poland and from elsewhere in the world.

The Museum's continually expanding premises are already extensive: the unique port crane on the Motława river in the old city of Gdańsk; a group of three port granaries and a building taken over from the city's former power station on the opposite bank of the Motława; a branch museum in Hel, displaying exhibits from the history of fisheries; and a branch in Tczew, the museum of the Vistula River. The Central Maritime Museum also has a large conservation laboratory specialising in the preservation of artifacts recovered form the seabed. It merits mention that the museum initiated in 1965 the first regular underwater archaeological research in Poland. It has had its own ship for these purposes since 1973. The permanent exhibitions at the museum have become very much more diverse as a result of the exploration of the numerous wrecks lying around and on the bed of Gdańsk Bay.

Having organised a historical monument conservation service, the Polish Maritime Museum has taken on the responsibility of curator of all nautical objects of historical interest in the whole of Poland. As a result, the museum has also developed extensive programmes of ethnological, underwater, and land-based archaeological investigations.

The Central Maritime Museum attaches considerable attention to educational activities, offering, among other things, systematic classes for groups of school children. It also conducts lectures and practical workshops for archaeology students from the universities of Toruń and Warsaw.

A number of societies have been important in assisting the Polish Maritime Museum fulfil its statutory obligations. These include the Friends of the Polish Maritime Museum, who have made an important contirbution towards the founding and expansion of this institution; the Friends of the *Dar Pomorza*, who are raising funds for the construction of a dry dock for this ship; and the Friends of the S.S. *Sołdek*, through whose efforts this vessel was adapted to museum purposes.

A few other museums in Poland are involved in the protection of maritime heritage. Among them is the Toruń Museum of Ethnography, with its extensive exhibition of traditional fisheries in Poland. This is yet another institution playing its part in the conservation of objects of nautical interest. It has a collection of Vistula craft dating from the early twentieth century. A number of other museums each have several boats and dugouts. In all, there are some thirty traditional boats in Polish museums (not counting the maritime museums) as well as nearly 150 dugouts, mostly obtained from archaeological excavations.

Company museums have also played an important part in preserving Poland's cultural-industrial heritage. The idea of creating such museums was born in the early days of communism in Poland. Their purpose was to collect documents and artifacts illustrating the achievements of that era. Today, in the wake of major political and economic change, these museums face serious difficulties. Still, their collections illustrate an important era that has come to an end and are of significant historical value. Two companies with such museums are shipyards: The Gdynia Shipyard, known as the Paris Commune yard before 1990, which, besides its own museum, has managed to preserve and exhibit on it premises the first ship it ever built there in 1930. The Gdansk Shipyard Museum has by far the largest display area, much of which is now devoted to the birth of the social movement, known to the world today as "Solidarity."

Apart from direct steps taken to safeguard material nautological relics, various scientific institutions and societies play an important part in popularizing and promoting that role. Thus, those conducting their activities in Gdańsk include the Institute of Pomeranian History and Maritime Affairs, the Baltic Institute, and the Maritime Institute. Additionally, the University of Gdańsk is becoming more and more "maritime" in character, boasting a huge library with a significant maritime profile. For several years now, an Institute of Ocean Technology has been in existence, but there are no lectures provided in the history of this field. Toruń University, in contrast, has an active faculty of Underwater Archaeology.

The scientific societies boast a considerable contribution to the study and propagation of maritime history in Poland. The Gdańsk Scientific Society, whose members include scholars from various fields, including a considerable group of historians interested in maritime problems, is a force with substantial potential. Its achievements include several books on Gdańsk's maritime history, shipbuilding and shipping. Another such association is the Polish Nautological Society, located at Gdynia. Its trademark is the quarterly *Nautologia*, which has appeared, uninterrupted, for twenty-eight years. While considering the various societies, mention must also be made of the Brotherhood of Submarine Lovers, memberships of which include former crew members of such ships, among others.

Recently, the "Cutter Brotherhood" has become very active. This is a society whose aim is the preservation and proper operation of craft that have become rare or have been withdrawn from service.

Poland's return to democracy in 1989 is clearly reflected in her domestic politics. The outcome of this change includes elimination of publication censorship, which has allowed impartial study of naval history to reappear. One example of this is the intensification of studies on the inland Pińsk flotilla. That unit was the only formation of the Polish Navy to participate in operations against the Soviet armies which invaded Poland without declaring war in September, 1939. We still await the results of these and other studies.

Several new steps have recently been taken in respect of the protection and popularisation of Poland's maritime heritage. Not all can boast visible effects today, but it is expected that there will be continued increase in interest in naval history and the protection of such relics in the future. This was supported by the establishment in 1991 of twelve Regional Centres of Studies and Preservation of Built Environment. Among these, Gdańsk's centre has been entrusted with an additional specialization: the study and protection of our waterside cultural heritage. The Gdańsk centre also collects documents and evidence of relics of technology connected with the shipbuilding industry and shipping.

One expression of this new outlook on our heritage is the call for a conference devoted to the protection of relics of industrial heritage. This conference, to be held at Gdansk Technical University in 1999, will devote the sessions to the protection of the maritime heritage and will be held at the Central Maritime Museum in Gdansk.

There is hope, therefore, that the combined activities of all these groups will ensure the continued growth of interest in the protection of maritime heritage and, particularly, the completest possible preservation of artifacts, inluding traditional craft which, because of their physical characteristics and condition, present serious technical problems.

Naval History[37]

In Poland, there is a distinct division between maritime and naval history, as well as a significant absence of works considering their relationship. Naval history is regarded as a sub-discipline of military history which, in turn, is considered a part of general history. This makes it a subject of special interest to the Polish Navy and Army. The vast majority of books and articles on Polish naval history have been published by naval officers or other researchers connected with the armed forces, since they have had better access to documents kept in military archives than their civilian colleagues. Access to source materials plays an important role, particularly in writing contemporary history on the Polish Navy.

There are now in the Polish armed forces three principal institutions interested in naval history: the Institute of Military History in Warsaw, the Naval Museum in Gdynia, the Institute of Humanities at the Naval Academy in Gdynia.

The Institute of Military History conducts research in all branches of military history, including naval history. The most famous naval historian at the Institute is, in my opinion, Captain W. Dyskant, an assistant professor. Dyskant has written several books and many articles on the history of the Polish Navy up to 1939, with an emphasis on the history of river flotillas. It is appropriate to note that doctoral students of the field of naval history from all over Poland may defend their theses at the Institute and, if successful, earn their degrees in military history.

The Naval Museum in Gdynia is busy collecting all kinds of items related to the past and present history of the Polish Navy, including Polish and foreign publications. The Museum has a large collection of diaries, memoirs, accounts and reports produced by officers and seamen who took part in World War II,

---

[37] This section has been written by Commander Wincenty Karawajczyk, Polish Navy. Dr. Karawajczyk is assigned to the Polish Naval Museum in Gdynia.

as well as many personal documents and keepsakes presented by members of naval personnel or their families. The Museum has two distinct parts: the museum ship *Błyskawica*, and an open-air exhibit of naval armaments. It warrants mention here that the staff of the Naval Museum is engaged in publishing the *Historical Bulletin* [*Biuletyn Historyczny*], which has produced thirteen issues thus far. All Polish naval historians may publish articles in this bulletin. At present, Commander Dr. Z. Wojciechowski is director of the Naval Museum.

The Naval Academy's Institute of the Humanities, part of which is the Department of Naval History, plays a leading role in studies and teaching of Polish naval history. The staff is headed by Captain J. Przybylski, an assistant professor and a prominent Polish naval historian. The Department of Naval History is conducting research on the development of the Polish Navy during its most interesting period: 1918–1989. Its staff prepares doctoral and habilitation theses which include the main results of this research. These theses are, in most cases, defended at the Institute of Military History in Warsaw.

The Department of Naval History is presently engaged in writing a monograph on the Polish Navy and its role in coastal defense through the years 1918–1989. This effort should appear in print in 1996. It is worthwhile to emphasize that, in preparation of this monograph, not only have professional historians from the Institute of the Humanities taken part, but also economists who study economic problems within the Navy in that period, teachers, who examine the process of education and training of naval officers and seamen, and sociologists, who study social aspects of the Navy.

Captain J. Przybylski's research concentrates on the postwar development of the Polish Navy. He also conducts a seminar in naval history for doctoral candidates. His students prepare theses on the organization, tasks, development, training, and armament of various parts of the Polish naval forces for the years 1918–1989. They have contributed significantly to the development of the previously mentioned monograph. Under Captain Przybylski's leadership, the Institute of the Humanities has organized many symposia in the field of naval history.

Apart from naval historians working for military institutions, there is a small group of academic historians, dispersed in a few universities, who are also interested in naval matters. Most of them are located at the University of Gdańsk (for example, Professors C. Ciesielski, Z. Machaliński and S. Ordon are part of the faculty there). A fair number of writers producing popular books about the Polish Navy and its role in war at sea should also be mentioned. Among them, E. Kosiarz and J. Pertek deserve special attention. Many valuable publications on the history of the Polish Navy have also been authored by "researchers living abroad." Most of them were originally members of the Polish Navy who did not return to Poland after the dissolution of Polish naval forces in Great Britain in 1947. They have had excellent access to original documents from World War

II. S. Piaskowski from the older generation, and M. Kułakowski from the younger, both conducting their studies in Canada, are the most eminent authors in this category, and are cited in later footnotes.

With regard to the teaching of naval history, only the Polish Navy demonstrates a great interest. Except for the Naval Academy in Gdynia, this subject is not taught at any university in Poland. The Academy has two courses in naval history that midshipmen must study: the history of the Polish Navy, and the history of the art of naval warfare. Each course is composed of sixty hours of lectures and seminars and must be taken by students during the fourth year of study. The course, on the history of the Polish Navy, examines the antecedents, origins and development of the Polish naval forces in both their national and international setting. Special attention is paid to the Polish fleet between the fifteenth and seventeenth centuries and to the period after 1918, when Poland regained its independence. The Last seventy-five years are divided into three main time frames: (1) the Navy of the Second Republic, 1918–1939; (2) the Polish Navy in World War II and in the postwar period in Great Britain, 1939–1947; and (3) the Navy of the Polish People's Republic, 1945–1989.

The second course examines the development of maritime strategy and tactics from ancient to modern times. It is made up of three parts; first is the art of naval war from the age of rowing fleets through World War I; second is the art of naval warfare in World War II; and, third, the development of the art of naval warfare after World War II. The focus is on tactical analysis of actions carried out by surface ships and submarines against shipping lanes, and on the ways and means of conducting anti-surface and anti-submarine warfare in the two World Wars.

The academic staff for teaching naval history at the Naval Academy includes one professor and three lecturers, all of whom possess Ph.D. degrees in Military History.

Not only prospective naval officers, but also ordinary seamen (conscripts), are introduced to naval history in the Polish Navy. During the so-called "patriotic education" they take an eighteen-hour course entitled "Tradition and the present day of the Polish arms at sea." This course includes such topics as Polish arms at sea before 1918, the Polish Navy in the years 1918–1939, combat operations of the Polish Navy in World War II, and the Polish Navy in the years 1945–1990. Commanding officers at company or ship's department level perform all teaching duties in this course.

The Naval Museum is not involved in the regular teaching process, but it plays an important role in popularizing and protecting our naval heritage.

It must be emphasized that there is no organization in Poland that coordinates and brings together the various studies in naval history. Each institution has its own research program. Individual historians choose problems for studies in accordance with their personal preferences. At times, plans for research are made only in a small way, as in the Department of Naval History at the Naval Academy, where the academic staff has focused its efforts on the comprehensive study of the Polish Navy in the years 1918–1989. There is no doubt that Polish naval historians, in order to be more effective, need a proper, underlying platform to develop a common research scheme.

Polish naval tradition goes back to the period between the fifteenth and eighteenth centuries, when Polish kings made several attempts, some of them successful, to organize a fleet in order to protect the coast and seaborne trade. Unfortunately, at the end of eighteenth century, Poland lost its independence and for many decades could only dream about naval affairs. Hopes revived in 1918, when Poland again became independent. On 28 November 1918, Marshal Piłsudski, the Polish head of state, issued a decree bringing the Polish Navy into being. After the outbreak of World War II, the Polish Navy moved to Great Britain, and it was the only branch of the Polish armed forces that fought against Nazi Germany and its allies from the very beginning to the very end of that war. That navy was officially dissolved in March 1947.

When Poland was liberated from Nazi occupation, reconstruction of another navy, brought into being by the order of the commander-in-chief of the Polish Army on 7 July 1945, was undertaken. So, for almost two years, there were actually two Polish navies in existance; one in Great Britain and the other in Poland, subordinate to the Soviet Union. That is why the Polish Navy, which operated in conjunction with the British during World War II, did not return to Poland as an entity. More than 85 percent of its personnel, totalling over 4,000 men, remained in Great Britain, the United States, France, Canada, and Australia. The current Polish Navy is building on the traditions of both the prewar and postwar navies.

Most naval historians in Poland have placed most of their research emphasis on combat actions and on where Polish Navy ships served during World War II, rather than on any other problems or periods of Polish naval history. Curiously enough, the majority of comprehensive books on the role of the Polish Navy in the Second World War have been produced by popular marine writers like E. Kosiarz and J. Pertek, rather than by professional historians.[38] Their works have been very well received by the younger generation. Among the numerous works devoted to World War II, there are a considerable number of studies made by professional historians as well. For example, A. Rzepniewski and R. Witowski, among others, have carefully examined the efforts of Polish seamen in the defense of the Polish coast in September 1939, and later on the side of the Allies.[39] Some diaries and memoirs published by naval officers taking part in

[38] E. Kosiarz, *Flota Białego Orła* (Gdańsk: 1980); E. Kosiarz, *Od pierwszej do ostatniej salwy* (Warszawa: 1973); J. Pertek, *Mała flota wielka duchem* (Poznań: 1989); J. Pertek, *Wielkie dni małej floty* (Poznań: 1967); W. Kosianowski, ed., *Polska Marynarka Wojenna od pierwszej do ostatniej salwy w drugiej wojnie światowej. Album pamiątkowy* (Rome: 1947).

[39] A. Rzepniewski, *Obrona Wybrzeża w 1939 roku na tle rozwoju marynarki wojennej Polski i Niemiec* (Warszawa: 1970); R. Witkowski, "Udział Polskiej Marynarki Wojenne j w drugiej wojnie światowej," *40 lat Ludowego Wojska Polskiego* (Warszawa: 1984); A. Jaskowski, *Kampania norweska* (Glasgow: 1944).

World War II supplement a vast literature in this field. Most valuable are the diaries of B. Romanowski, B. Karnicki, W. Kon and J. Kłossowski.[40] Thus, the role of the Polish Navy in the war against the Kriegsmarine is one of the best explored and most fully described areas of Polish naval history.

Studies of the 1918–1939 Polish Navy have also been undertaken quite frequently. Although no elaborate, scientific description of that period has thus far been completed, many interesting monographs on particular subjects have been produced. For example, C. Ciesielski wrote about the Polish fleet in the Baltic, and about naval education in Poland between the two World Wars.[41] W. Dyskant made a thorough analysis of river flotillas in Polish war plans,[42] S. Ordon described legal and economic problems of the Polish Navy,[43] S. Rozwadowski touched upon the history of naval air division,[44] and R. Witowski showed the role of the naval base of Hel in the defense of the coast.[45] Some authors have attempted to present a comprehensive vision of the Polish Navy during that period as well. Chronicles by S. Piaskowski, and two volumes of M. Kuałkowski's monograph are among the best known works written with such intentions.[46]

After World War II, having discovered new original materials, many naval historians focused their efforts on the era between the fifteenth and eighteenth centuries. The privateer fleets attracted much attention and were described in works authored by K. Lepszy, M. Biskup, E. Koczorowski, and J. Trzoska among others.[47]

With regard to the history of the People's Navy (the naval forces in Poland in the years 1945–1989)—that is becoming an increasingly interesting subject of thorough studies, although archival materials for the last twenty-five years are still unavailable. Articles and books published by W. Radziszewski deal with the first period of the People's Navy.[48] Recent periods have been explored by J.

---

[40] B. Romanowski, *Torpeda w celu* (Warszawa: 1985); B. Karnicki, *Marynarski worek wspomnień* (Warszawa: 1987); W. Kon, *Atlantyckie patrole* (Warszawa: 1958); J. Kłossowski, *Wspomnienia z Marynarki Wojennej* (Warszawa: 1970).

[41] C. Ciesielski, *Polska flota wojenna na Bałtyku w latach 1920–1939 na tle bałtyckich flot wojennych* (Gdańsk: 1985); C. Ciesielski, *Szkolnictwo Marynarki Wojennej w II Rzeczypospolitej* (Warszawa: 1974).

[42] W. Dyskant, *Flotylle rzeczne w planach i działaniach wojennych II Rzeczypospolitej* (Warszawa: 1991).

[43] S. Ordon, *Polska Marynarka Wojenna w latach 1918–1939. Problemy prawne i ekonomiczne* (Gdynia: 1966).

[44] J. Rozwadowski, *Morski Dywizjon Lotniczy 1918–1939* (Albany: 1973).

[45] R. Witkowski, *Hel na straży Wybrzeża 1920–1939* (Warszawa: 1974).

[46] M. Kułakowski, *Marynarka Wojenna Polski Odrodzonej* (Toronto: 1988), vols I-II; S.M. Piaskowski, *Kroniki Polskiej Marynarki Wojennej 1918–1946* (Albany: 1983–1990), vols. I-III.

[47] K. Lepszy, *Dzieje floty polskiej* (Gdańsk-Bydgoszcz-Szczecin: 1947); M. Biskup, *Gdańska flota kaperska w okresie wojny trzynastoletniej 1454–1466* (Gdańsk: 1953); E. Koczorowski, *Flota polska w latach 1587–1632* (Warszawa: 1973); E. Koczorowski, *Bitwa pod Oliwą* (Gdynia: 1968); J. Trzoska, *Kaprzy króla Augusta Mocnego 1716–1721* (Gdańsk: 1993); Z. Ciećkowski, *Kaprowie króla Kazimierza* (Gdynia: 1968); M. Krwawicz, *Marynarkę Wojenną i obrona polskiego wybrzeża w dawnych wiekach* (Warszawa: 1961).

[48] W. Radziszewski, "Powstanie i rozwój Marynarki Wojennej PRL (Zarys historyczny)," *Dzieje oręża*

Przybylski who, in my opinion, is the most competent researcher in this field. His doctoral thesis covered the development of the Polish Navy between 1949 and 1956,[49] while his work, which qualified him as an assistant professor, deals with more recent times.[50] It is worth mentioning that in 1992 J. Przybylski, together with C. Ciesielski and W. Pater, produced the most comprehensive work on the history of the Polish Navy for the years 1918–1980.[51] Apart from such fundamental works, a great number of detailed studies on the above subject have been published in the *Maritime Review* [*Przegląd Morski*], the *Historical Bulletin* [*Biuletyn Historyczny*], the *Review of Military History* [*Wojskowy Przegląd Historyczny*] and other journals. The most important of them were recounted by Z. Waśko and R. Witkowski in their article about the state of research on the People's Navy.[52]

Historians of the Polish Navy have written not only on the main periods of its development but also on some particular problems. Unfortunately, not all essential problems have been touched upon so far. Among the best examined and described are studies of famous Polish men-of-war, such as the *Błyskawica, Burza, Grom, Wicher*, and *Orzeł*.[53] The history of Polish submarines in the years 1926-1969, published by C. Rudzki should also be included in this group of works.[54]

Another question, relatively well explored, is the education of Polish naval officers. The period between two World Wars was thoroughly researched by C. Ciesielski,[55] while the postwar period was studied by W. Białek and T. Struniewski.[56] A special 70th anniversary issue of the *Przegląd Morski* (September 1992) was devoted entirely to Polish naval education.

Other problems have not been investigated so comprehensively. As a result, we experience numerous lacunae and other weaknesses in Polish naval history. From this long list, at least a few should be mentioned. For instance, the

---

polskiego na morzu (Gdynia: 1961); W. Radziszewski, *XXX lat marynarki wojennej PRL* (Warszawa: 1975); W. Radziszewski, *Marynarka Wojenna w latache 1945–1949* (Gdańsk: 1976).

[49] J. Przybylski, *Rozwój Marynarki Wojennej i jej rola w obronie Wybrzeza w latach 1949–1956* (Warszawa: 1979).

[50] J. Przybylski, *Marynarka Wojenna PRL w latach 1956–1980* (studium historyczno-wojskowe) (Gdynia: 1988).

[51] C. Ciesielski, W. Pater, J. Przybylski, *Polska Marynarka Wojenna 1918–1980* (Warszawa: 1992.

[52] Z. Waśko, R. Witkowski, "Próba oceny stanu badań historii Marynarki Wojennej PRL," *Przegląd Morski*, 1980, no. 9.

[53] W. Szczerkowski, ORP "Błyskawica" (Gdańsk: 1970); J. Marczak, *Niszczyciel* "Błyskawica" (Warszawa: 1970); J. Marczak, *Kontrtorpedowiec* "Burza" (Warszawa: 1970); R. Mielczarek, ORP "Grom." Zarys dziejów (Gdańsk: 1970); J. Pertek, *Niszczyciele* "Grom" i "Błyskawica" (Gdańsk: 1969); J. Pertek, *Niszczyciele* "Wicher" i "Burza" (Gdańsk: 1971); J. Pertek, "Burza" - *weteran atlantyckich szlaków* (Gdynia: 1965); J. Pertek, *Dzieje ORP* "Orzeł" (Gdańsk: 1972).

[54] C. Rudzki, *Polskie okręty podwodne 1926–1969* (Warszawa: 1985).

[55] C. Ciesielski, *Szkolnictwo Marynarki Wojennej w II Rzeczypospolitej* (Warszawa: 1974).

[56] W. Białek, T. Struniewski, *Wyższa Szkoła Marynarki Wojennej imienia Bohaterów Westerplatte* (Warszawa: 1978).

development of naval aviation has not been sufficiently covered. There are only two important publications from a scholarly point of view: one dealing with prewar times[57] and the other with postwar times.[58] In addition, economic and legal aspects of the Navy have not attracted much attention. So far, only one naval historian, S. Ordon, has considered this subject. In the 1960s he wrote two remarkable books devoted to the period between 1918 and 1939.[59] Furthermore, the history of ports and naval bases has been almost completely ignored. Apart from one of R. Witkowski's publications relating to the Hel naval base in the years 1920–1939,[60] there is virtually no literature in this field.

One of the serious drawbacks of Polish naval historiography has been lack of a "Mahanian" school, or even individual researchers thinking like A.T. Mahan. Such a situation can be understood to a certain degree because Poland never intended to become a sea power. It is much more difficult to understand, however, why Mahan's works are almost unknown in Poland. None of them, for instance, have even been translated into Polish.

International naval history issues have often been evaluated by Polish authors. I note, for example, E. Kosiarz, J. Lipiński, and J. Pertek.[61] In most cases, however, their publications have not been based on their own sound studies, but rather on the research of foreign naval historians. Very few publications have been dedicated to the art of naval war, strategy, and fighting tactics. Those authored by W. Glinski and R. Pietraszkiewicz are the most valuable.[62]

Since World War II, ideology and politics have been very important to Polish naval history. Under the communist regime a few topics, such as brotherhood in arms, and friendship and cooperation between fleets of socialist countries in the Baltic, were particularly well received. Others, on the other hand, were prohibited; for example, the role of the Polish Navy in the war against Soviet Russia in 1920 and in September 1939, or the oppression of prewar naval officers in the postwar period. Sweeping political changes in Central and Eastern Europe from 1989 on have, to some extent, affected the development of naval history in Poland. There are no longer forbidden themes or problems for scientific

---

[57] J. Rozwadowski, *Morski Dywizjon Lotniczy 1918–1939* (Albany: 1973).

[58] Z. Misztal, "Poczatki Lotnictwa Marynarki Wojennej," *Rocznik Ośrodka Nauk Społecznych i Wojskowych Marynarki Wojennej*, no. 5 (1975).

[59] S. Ordon, *Kampania wrześniowa 1939 r. na morzu w świetle prawa miedzynarodowego* (Gdynia: 1963); S. Ordon, *Polska Marynarka Wojenna w. latach 1918–1939. Problemy prawne i ekonomiczne* (Gdynia: 1966).

[60] R. Witkowski, *Hel na strazy Wybrzeża 1920–1939* (Warszawa: 1974).

[61] E. Kosiarz, *Wojna na Bałtyku 1939* (Gdańsk: 1988); E. Kosiarz, *Wojna na morzach i oceanach 1939–1945* (Gdańsk: 1988); J. Lipinski, *Druga wojna swiatowa na norzu* (Gdańsk: 1976); J. Pertek, *Od Reichsmarine do Bundesmarine 1918–1965* (Poznań: 1966).

[62] W. Glinski, *Morski operacje desantowe w drugiej wojnie swiatowej* (Gdańsk: 1969); H. Pietraszkiewicz, "Rozwój polskiej morskiej myśli wojskowej w latach 1945–1969," *Rocznik Ośrodka Nauk Społecznych i Wojskowych Marynarki Wojennej*, no. 5 (1970); E. Kosiarz, L. Ratajczak, "Taktyka 'wilczych stad' niemieckich okretów podwodnych," *Przegląd Morski*, no. 10 (1958).

research, but that does not mean that the current political situation has no impact on naval history. Sometimes one can come away with the impression that some historians investigate particular problems, not because they are important, but because they have been prohibited for a long time. In the war against Soviet Russia in 1920, for example, the Polish Navy played an altogether insignificant role. Only about one hundred seamen took part in the fighting on land, as there were no actions at sea. Still, a number of historians have devoted research to this subject, while there are many considerably more important topics to explore.

To sum up these remarks on the state of naval history in Poland, I must point out, in the first place, that there exists a wide gulf between the study of military affairs on the seas and of non-military maritime history; additionally, naval history is taught exclusively in the Navy, mainly at the Naval Academy, and research in this field is being done primarily by historians employed by military institutions; furthermore, most researchers have concentrated on military operations of the Polish Navy while other topics have been to some extent neglected. Also of concern is that there is no organization or journal that brings the studies in naval history together; and, finally, ideology and politics have shaped, to a certain degree, the debates about naval history, mostly by creating demands for investigation into specific problems.

25
Portugal

Commander J.A. Rodrigues Pereira, Portuguese Navy

The geographical position of Portugal, at the southwestern extremity of the European continent, has placed it, throughout history, astride important sea routes. The territory of Portugal, which includes several parallel river systems with good havens and ports, permits easy penetration of the country's interior by ships and has led the various populations to pursue maritime activities, sometimes as a complement to their terrestrial ones.

The Portuguese Navy evolved from the twelfth century and attained, through judicious legislative measures, a great development by the fourteenth century. At the beginning of the fifteenth century, under the guiding hands of the maritime bourgeoisie and the Military Order of Christ,[1] the nation became conscious of its maritime capabilities and launched the enterprise of maritime discoveries. In the space of about one century, this endeavor gave the Portuguese extensive knowledge of two thirds of the surface of the world and produced an immense maritime empire.[2] Using, for the first time, innovative strategic concepts that would later be adopted by other nations, Portugal succeeded in obtaining for a time a command of the seas, which are written about today by many respected naval strategists.

Portugal is definitively connected with the sea. Its maritime history has played a significant role in the development of some of the most important chapters of the world's history: its maritime achievement, its ships and seamen, its caravels and carracks that voyaged over "seas that had never been previously navigated;"[3] the transportation and supply of military expeditions; and seaborne trade and fishing. The importance of leaving this rich history of our maritime and military accomplishments to future generations was recognized very early by responsible national leaders.

---

[1] The Military Order of Christ replaced the Templars, who had previously been predominant in Portugal.

[2] Passing through many vicissitudes, and suffering various amputations, this maritime-colonial empire would last until 1975.

[3] Luis de Camões, *The Lusiads* (1655: reprint, with introduction by Geoffrey Bullough, Cartendale: Southern Illinois University Press, 1964). For a broad general overview in English of early Portuguese maritime history, see the essays by Charles Verlinden and George Winius in Hattendorf, ed., *An Introduction to Maritime History: The Age of Discovery* (Malabar, Fla.: Krieger Publishing, 1995).

We can say that the history of the Portuguese Navy began with the scribes of the sixteenth century carracks and with the chroniclers of the realm who left us detailed accounts of Portuguese voyages, and military and naval actions, particularly those that took place in the Orient and Africa. Although this was done in a style that was very characteristic of that age, we find in them a comprehensive account of Portuguese maritime activities in the fifteenth and sixteenth centuries.

In 1835 the first attempt to write a systematic study of our maritime history appeared in the *Annals of the Portuguese Navy*, Royal Academy of Sciences. However, whether due to the possibility that the original author had not finished his work, or that it was lost, only the part that covers the years of 1140-1640 has been preserved, and that deals only with the events that took place in the Atlantic Ocean.

The end of the nineteenth century and beginning of the twentieth witnessed the appearance of numerous scattered studies of our maritime history. The majority of these were produced by illustrious naval officers.

In the 1930s, when the commemorations of the eighth centenary of the founding of Portugal and the third centenary of the restoration of Independence were taking place,[4] The Clube Militar Naval[5] promoted the writing of a history of the Portuguese Navy, the absence of which was felt by all. This project, which emerged from an organizing commission presided over by Commander Fontoura da Costa, was divided into six parts,[6] and sub-divided into chapters.[7] Unfortunately, only the first volume, covering the period 1140–1385, was eventually published.

In the 1960s, when the great commemoration of the fifth centenary of the death of Prince Henry[8] took place, the absence of a comprehensive naval history was once again made a prominent issue. At that time an important work of maritime historiography was published, containing a repository of all the known Portuguese nautical charts of the fifteenth to the seventeenth centuries.[9]

On 5 March 1969, a Ministry of the Navy decree led to a group of studies of maritime history. These proved to be the embryo of the present Academia de Marinha, created in 1978, which presently comprises over one hundred members. The Academia includes some of the most dedicated and zealous inves-

---

[4] Between 1580 and 1640, Portugal and Spain were united under a dualist monarchy.

[5] A Club of naval officers founded at the end of the nineteenth century.

[6] The Periods that were to be covered were 1) from the founding of the nation to the battle of Aljubarrota (1140–1385); 2) The dynasty of Aviz (1385–1580); 3) The Philippine dynasty (1580–1640); 4) The dynasty of Bragança (until 1820); and 5) the Constitutional Monarchy and the Republic (1820–1926).

[7] Each period was intended to focus on administration, personnel, materials, and operations.

[8] The Master of the Military Order of Christ, and the great stimulator of the Portuguese discoveries.

[9] Armando Cortesão and Avelino Teixeira da Mota, *Portugaliae Monumenta Cartographica* (Lisboa: Comissão Executiva das Comemorancões da V Centenaria da Marte do Infante D. Henrique, 1960).

tigators of maritime history, although it must be recognized that other exceptional workers in the same field exist outside that fine organization, as well.

At a time when Portugal is commemorating the centennials of its most important maritime voyages and discoveries,[10] the Academia de Marinha has now undertaken the task of publishing a history of the Navy. The intent of this project is to recognize in a significant manner, the transition from past to future. After having made an analysis of previous attempts, and their planning, the decision was made to produce a profound and well-documented work that could be consulted by serious scholars and investigators, and one which would serve as a fundamental source for study and investigation. According to the elaborated plan, the work would be divided into periods, materials, parts and chapters, with each period being designated a tome and containing the necessary number of volumes based on the development of the parts and the required chapters. A first estimate suggested that the complete work would consist of thirty-three tomes in about one hundred volumes. The theses would be coordinated by a scientific commission of seven members, who would select the authors and make a preliminary evaluation of their proposed work so as to ensure compliance with the defined directives.

The work is to be divided into six periods, according to the following distribution:

1) From the beginning of the nation to the beginning of expansion (1140–1415).

2) From the conquest of Ceuta to the death of D. João II (1415–1484).

3) From the reign of D. Manuel I to the invasion by the Duke of Alba (1484–1580).

4) From the Philippine period until the end of the War of Restoration (1580–1669).

5) The period of absolute monarchy (1669–1820).

6) The period of constitutional governments (after 1820).

Each period consists of generically equal parts comprising the following subject areas in general:
- Ships, seamen, the art of navigation, and war at sea.
- Men, doctrines, organization, and legislation.
- Voyages and naval operations.
- The passage to India.
- Ports and maritime trade.

---

[10] Those being the Cape of Good Hope (1487), the maritime route to India (1487–1488), Brazil (1500), and the arrival in Japan (1543).

Maritime history was first taught in the Naval Academy in 1864, with the aim of providing "a brief and simple presentation of facts, some development of outstanding events and a very brief synthesis of the various periods."[11] A course of naval history is currently being taught at the Naval Academy to give the students a perspective of the development of naval power throughout history, its use by the peoples who possessed it, and its consequences for the political structure of the world. At the same time, it emphasizes the Portuguese maritime position.[12]

The following themes, dedicated exclusively to the History of the Portuguese Navy, are also explored:
- The Portuguese Navy from the eleventh to the fourteenth century;
- Portuguese discoveries and expansion in the fifteenth century;
- The Portuguese maritime empire in the sixteenth century;
- The Evolution of cartography and Nautical Science;
- The Portuguese Navy in the seventeenth and eighteenth centuries;
- The Portuguese Navy in the nineteenth century: technical evolution and occupation of the coasts of the continent of Africa.
- The Portuguese Navy in the twentieth century: participation in World War I, NATO and the war in Africa.

The Higher Institute of Naval Warfare also teaches some facts about our maritime history, but only from the strategic point of view.

Courses at several Portuguese universities teach maritime history in the programs leading to degrees in history, but under different names; for example, the history of the expansion versus the history of the discoveries. The Lisbon Faculty of Letters even has a course that is designated the History of the Portuguese Navy.[13] There is, in the Faculty of Letters of the University of Oporto, a Centre of Historical Studies which is dedicated to study of the country's traditional vessels in their historical and archaeological context. The Luis de Camões University also has a discipline on naval archaeology included in its curriculum.[14]

The Faculty of Social and Human Sciences of the Universidade Nova de Lisboa awards a master's degree in the History of the Portuguese discoveries and Expansion, with a specific area of study in Portuguese maritime activities during the fifteenth and sixteenth centuries. The Faculty of Letters of the classical University of Lisbon awards a master's degree in Modern History, for the study

---

[11] Vicente Almeida d'Eça, *Lipcaes historia maritima geral* (Lisboa: Imprensa Nacional, 1895).

[12] The author taught at the Naval Academy from 1982 to 1988, and collaborated in the elaboration of the present study programme.

[13] Faculty of Letters of the Lisbon Classical University, Faculty of Letters of the University of Coimbra, Faculty of Letters of the University of Oporto, Faculty of Social and Human Sciences of the Universidade Nova de Lisboa, University of Evora, University of the Minho, and University of the Azores, these being all teaching establishments of the State.

[14] Luis de Camões University is a private institution.

of the Maritime Discoveries, and conducts seminars on nautical science and cartography. Other, recently created, Portuguese universities give courses in military history, which naturally includes the naval aspects of the conflicts in which Portugal has been involved.

There is also the Maritime Museum in Lisbon which is a dependency of the Portuguese Navy. It is dedicated to the study, gathering, and presentation of elements related to Portuguese maritime activities. Its director enjoys the collaboration of a consultative technical commission of eight members who are specialists in various fields and who support the Museum with their studies and investigation.[15] The Museum also provide replies to consultations requested from abroad. There are, in addition, about ten small regional museums in Portugal, dedicated to local maritime affairs, regional craft, and fishing activities.

The period of maritime discoveries and Portuguese expansion (fifteenth and sixteenth centuries) is the period best studied, albeit with a few lapses,[16] because it belongs to the most important period of Portuguese history, when Portugal was a great maritime power and when significant developments in nautical science and cartography occurred.

On the contrary, the least studied period is the eighteenth and nineteenth centuries, when there was a progressive reduction in the importance of the nation in international affairs, primarily as a consequence of the decline in Portuguese naval power.[17]

Students of our maritime history have been predominantly naval officers. Thus, those aspects of it which are connected with military activities are logically more developed than those linked to civilian ones. However, there are also other dedicated investigators who have made studies of our merchant marine, regional or traditional vessels (history and archaeology), and fishing activities. In some parts of northern Portugal, these have special characteristics since they are, at times, associated with agricultural pursuits.

The lack of a comprehensive history of the Portuguese Navy is a serious lapse in national historiography, and one which must be corrected. The Portuguese people, and the rest of the world, need to understand what our seafarers did and how they lived—from the anonymous sailors of the medieval galleys, to those who have collaborated recently with the United Nations in the embargoes placed on Iraq and Serbia—so that other cultures that presently possess maritime power will not forget that it was Portugal that pioneered those ocean voyages that made it possible for it to "give new worlds to the world."[18]

---

[15] The Director is an active naval officer.

[16] Specifically in the fields of strategy and naval shipbuilding.

[17] The Napoleonic wars and Liberal wars are stressed here, particularly from the perspective of naval power.

[18] Luis de Camões, *The Lusiads*.

26

Singapore

Malcolm H. Murfett[1]

It is rather paradoxical to think that the Republic of Singapore, which owes a great deal of its phenomenal commercial success to its close involvement with the sea, has still to develop more than a token appreciation of the roots of its maritime and naval history.[2]

Little is done on the island, for example, in an academic sense, to further the cause of either of these branches of Singapore's local history. No courses on these themes are offered at its two universities (the National University of Singapore (NUS) and the Nanyang Technological University (NTU), or at the Singapore Command and Staff College (SCSC) at Seletar Base. Apart from a few lectures devoted to the ideas and influence of Mahan, Corbett, and Richmond in the strategic studies course offerings at NUS and SCSC, there is little attempt to cover international naval history in a systematic way at either of these institutions. Although specific naval topics, such as the Anglo-German naval armaments race, the Washington Conference and the Singapore Strategy, do find their way onto existing regional-based courses at NUS, and the war at sea is studied as part of a much broader military component within its history department, the fact remains that naval issues appear more as an accompaniment rather than a core of these academic courses. Maritime history fares little better in comparison. Several lectures by Associate Professor Ng Chin Keong are devoted to the development of Chinese maritime trade as part of a third year B.A. general degree course on the Economic and Social History of Modern China at NUS, but there is little else on the existing slate of courses that takes account of maritime subjects.[3]

Fortunately, some element of change is likely in light of the modularization of curricula that both the NUS and NTU are planning to introduce at the

---

[1]   Senior Lecturer in British and European History, National University of Singapore.

[2]   In some senses, the irony is greater still since in the recent past Singapore has not only become the world's busiest port, but also has been actively expanding its relatively small but modern, well-equipped, naval fleet.

[3]   Ng Chin Keong is best known for his admirable book, *Trade and Society: The Amoy Network on the China Coast 1683–1735* (Singapore: Singapore Univ. Press, 1983), on the maritime trade of Fukien. His book is a revised version of his award winning Ph.D. thesis at the Australian National University in Canberra.

beginning of the 1994–95 academic year. It is highly probable that a postgraduate course in International Naval History will be launched at the NUS by the author of this article at the earliest opportunity after 1994, and the likelihood is that once the Singapore Armed Forces Training Institute (SAFTI) is expanded and upgraded into a military academy in 1995, it will be better able to offer a greater variety of naval topics for its students than is possible at the present time. On the maritime front at the NUS, Associate Professor Ng Chin Keong is intending to introduce a postgraduate level course on the Maritime History of China from the Twelfth Century to the Fall of the Ch'ng Dynasty, but apart from this new offering, nothing else is planned for the immediate future. Clearly, much more could be done than is being tackled at present, particularly in the sphere of Southeast Asian economic history and on specific issues such as piracy, which have a contemporary relevance in Southeast Asian waters.

While the development of Singapore's maritime trade and its management by the Port of Singapore Authority does receive some attention from the staff of both the Geography and Economics Departments at the NUS and NTU, a far more rigorous set of practical and technical training courses are offered to school leavers at the well-equipped Singapore Polytechnic and Ngee Ann Polytechnic. At the Singapore Polytechnic, which has a marine simulator on the premises, diploma courses are offered in marine engineering, maritime transport, and nautical studies, whereas Ngee Ann Polytechnic provides a diploma course in shipbuilding and offshore engineering.

Of those academics currently working in the area of maritime studies at the tertiary level in Singapore, arguably, the best known is Associate Professor Chia Lin Sien of the Geography Department of NUS. Amongst his many research publications are articles on container port development, ship-generated marine pollution, navigational, resource, and environmental impacts upon the Straits of Malacca and Singapore; and a chapter on "The Port of Singapore" in the magisterial volume edited by Kernial Singh Sandhu and Paul Wheatley entitled *Management of Success: The Moulding of Modern Singapore*.[4]

C. Northcote Parkinson was among the first of the academics in Singapore to write about maritime and naval affairs. As Raffles Professor of History at the

---

[4] Chia Lin Sien, "The Port of Singapore" in Kernial Singh Sandhu and Paul Wheatley, eds., *Management of Success: The Moulding of Modern Singapore* (Singapore: ISEAS, 1989), pp. 314–36.

A selection of Chia's prolific output is provided below:

"Ship-Generated Marine Pollution Issues in Southeast Asia," a conference paper presented to the SEAPOL *International Conference on the Implementation of the Law of the Sea Convention in the 1990s: Marine Environmental Protection and Other Issues*, Denpasar, Bali, Indonesia, 28–30 May 1990, pp. 264–303; "Container Port Development in Asean: Shaping up for the Future," *Shipper's Times*, vol. 11(2), 1991, pp. 2–6; "The Strait of Malacca and Singapore; navigational, resource environmental considerations," in Chia Lin Sien & Colin McAndrews eds., *Southeast Asian Seas: Frontiers for Development* (Singapore: McGraw Hill, 1981), pp. 239–66; "Transportation of Oil in the Strait of Malacca and potential Marine Pollution," in P.R. Burbridge, Koesoebiono, H. Dirschl & B. Patton eds., *Coastal Zone Management in the Strait of Malacca* (Halifax, Nova Scotia: Dalhousie Univ. Press, 1988), pp. 165–78.

University of Malaya, Singapore, in 1950–58, Parkinson published several books, including his famous book on naval administration, *Parkinson's Law*,[5] as well as more regionally oriented books, such as *War in the Eastern Seas, 1793–1815*,[6] and *British Intervention in Malaya, 1867–1877*.[7] After the university changed its name, Kenneth G. Tregonning became Head of the Department of History at the University of Singapore (Uni of S) and wrote *Home Port Singapore: A History of Straits Steamship Company Limited 1890–1965*,[8] while he was still working in the republic. His successor as Raffles Professor, Wong Lin Ken, a distinguished economic historian in his own right, was the author of the standard work on Singapore's early nineteenth century trade.[9] He felt that Singapore's unique geostrategic position—lying as it does between the Indian and Pacific Oceans—deserved a more comprehensive study of this equatorial island's place in the scheme of things than had been attempted hitherto. His exploratory findings, which were published for the first time as an article,[10] merely whetted the appetite for more. Sadly, his untimely death in February 1983 robbed the academic community of the fruits of his ongoing research on this fascinating subject. Following on from Wong's work on trade, Ambassador Chiang Hai Ding published his doctoral thesis from the Australian National University, *A History of Straits Settlement Foreign Trade, 1870–1915*.[11]

Despite the relative paucity of local academicians working in the realm of maritime history, Singapore's close relationship with the sea has continued to exert quite an appeal for a fair number of tertiary students in the past. Over the years there has been no shortage of honours degree dissertations (known as Academic Exercises) and masters' theses devoted to maritime affairs. A selection of the more interesting is provided in the appendix at the end of this chapter.

Outside the realm of the academic world, the Port of Singapore Authority (PSA) does have an educational function to perform and one which it discharges responsibly. Apart from holding regional conferences and seminars on a host of specialist maritime subjects from bunkering to container traffic,

---

[5]   C. Northcote Parkinson, *Parkinson's Law and Other Studies in Administration* (Boston: Houghton, Mifflin, 1957).

[6]   C. Northcote Parkinson, *War in the Eastern Seas, 1793–1815* (London: Allen and Unwin, 1954).

[7]   C. Northcote Parkinson, *British Intervention in Malaya, 1867–1877*, Malayan Historical Studies (Singapore and Kuala Lumpur: University of Malaya Press, 1960). Although much of this deals with the Royal Navy, it is a written only from the Colonial Office papers, not the Admiralty papers.

[8]   Kenneth G. Tregonning, *Home Port Singapore: A History of Straits Steamship Company Limited 1890-1965* (Singapore: Oxford Univ. Press, 1967).

[9]   Wong Lin Ken, "The Trade of Singapore, 1819–69," *Journal of the Malaysian Branch, Royal Asiatic Society*, vol. xxxiii, part 4, no. 192 (December 1960), pp. 1–315.

[10] Wong Lin Ken, "The Strategic Significance of Singapore in Modern History" *Commentary*, (the Journal of the NUS Society), vol. 5, no. 2 (1981), pp. 3–16.

[11] Chiang Hai Ding, *A History of Straits Settlements Foreign Trade, 1870–1915*. Memoirs of the National Museum, no. 6 (Singapore: National Museum, 1978).

the PSA encourages members of its executive team to undertake postgraduate courses overseas in business management. In addition, the PSA also does its best not only to cater to the demands of MBA students from a wide range of Singaporean and foreign business schools and trade missions, but also services requests from secondary school students in the republic who wish to work on various port-related projects. It has recently established a new computerized library at the Singapore Port Institute in Maritime Square with an array of specialist books and reports, microfilm resources, a reasonable file of press clippings from the early 1970s onwards, numerous trade periodicals, and the proceedings of the many conferences and seminars the PSA has held on maritime subjects in the past two decades. Furthermore, the PSA also publishes its own monthly in-house staff magazine, *Port View*, and assists in the production of the annual factual handbook, *Singapore Port & Shipping*, which is actually published by Charter Pacific Publications of Victoria, Australia. Being an important element in Singapore's commercial development, the PSA naturally takes its economic role very seriously and is justifiably proud of its record of achievement in the maritime world. Its buoyant and polished self-image is reflected in the two elegant pictorial studies which it has commissioned in the past decade. Both of the quasi-coffee table variety, *Singapore: Portrait of a Port*[12] and *A Port's Story: A Nation's Success*,[13] are expensively produced books that look good and provide a clue to the unabashed professionalism of the PSA. Eric Alfred, the former curator of the PSA–sponsored Maritime Museum, also wrote and compiled an interesting sixteen-page illustrated booklet, *Singapore Port History*,[14] which does much to complement Chris Yap's text in *A Port's Story: A Nation's Success*.

Apart from its publications, the PSA has also endeavoured in the past to bring Singapore's success as a modern port to the attention of the general public through the medium of its Maritime Museum sited on the offshore island of Sentosa. Unfortunately, the static display items, faded photographs, and unexciting textual commentaries on the growth of Singapore's maritime trade and port are not calculated to appeal to the younger generation. In addition, no lectures, seminars, or conferences on maritime subjects are held on the premises, and the Museum does not have a manuscript collection or a library or resource centre for research purposes. It has produced a few, well-written, information sheets on various aspects of Singapore's seafaring tradition, but these are not readily available to any but the most inquisitive or persistent visitor. It is, therefore, difficult to imagine that the Maritime Museum will be able to attract large numbers of appreciative and enthusiastic visitors to its various galleries without a large infusion of money, a change of location, and the introduction of a much more interactive set of items than it has at present. As the Maritime

---

[12] Port of Singapore Authority, *Singapore: Portrait of a Port* (Singapore: MPH Magazines (S) Pte, 1984).

[13] Port of Singapore Authority, *A Port's Story: A Nation's Success* (Singapore: Times Editions, 1990).

[14] Eric Alfred, *Singapore Port History* (Singapore: 1987).

Museum's long-term future on Sentosa is far from certain, the PSA is understandably reluctant to provide it with the investment it so badly needs. This lack of funds ensures that regardless of how committed its staff may be, the Maritime Museum looks destined to remain a sad and unsatisfactory relic on a holiday island given over to leisure and entertainment on a grand scale. Its future may also be compromised to some extent by the anticipated success of the so-called Singapore Maritime Showcase—a multimillion-dollar development on the waterfront by the World Trade Centre on the main island of Singapore. This high-tech, multimedia attraction—a celebration of Singapore's global port status—will be roughly 5,000 square feet in surface area when the exhibition is completed and opened to the public by the end of 1993. If it proves to be as successful as the PSA imagines it will be, the death knell is likely to sound for the Maritime Museum on Sentosa. Should that happen, the PSA may try to house some of the more interesting artifacts from the Maritime Museum, such as the racing jongs, outrigger canoes, and keeled boats (*Kolek Sauh, Kolek Selat, Kolek Chiau,* and *Pomehai*), in the large foyer of the PSA head office in Alexandra Road on the main island of Singapore.

Shipping companies who have played their part in the development of Singapore's maritime trade, such as the Keppel Corporation and Neptune Orient Lines (NOL), have also recently felt the necessity to commission histories of their past deeds. Although NOL has already produced an earlier slim account of its corporate history, it decided against releasing *Only Yesterday: The Story of Neptune Orient Lines 1969–1983* into the public domain. Now it has decided to commission Dr. Grace Low, the Head of the History Department at NTU, to prepare an updated version for publication in 1994.[15] Keppel's plans for a corporate history are still shrouded in mystery despite the planned launch in late September 1993 of Richard Lim's, *Tough Men, Bold Visions—The Story of Keppel.* Although it is expected to have a print run of 11,000, Lim's book on one of Singapore's flagship companies is unlikely at this stage to be sold to the general public and appears to be reserved for the exclusive use of customers and staff only.[16]

Singapore's controversial (some would describe it as infamous) military legacy, wrapped up as it is with the fate of the British Empire, has never failed to attract the attention of a host of historians from all over the world ever since the island fortress fell to the outnumbered troops of the Imperial Japanese Army on 15 February 1942. Apart from the military historians who have sought a convincing explanation for this allied débâcle, other diplomatic and international scholars moved into the arena in the hope of placing Singapore's surrender into a wider

---

[15] Dr. Low has just completed a manuscript on the development of the port of Jurong (located on the western coast of Singapore) which she is hoping to publish in 1994.

[16] Richard Lim, *Tough Men, Bold Visions—The Story of Keppel* (Singapore: Keppel Corp., 1993), 141 pp.

context of Britain's spectacular fall from grace on the world's stage in the twentieth century. As a result, research work on British military involvement with Singapore developed into one of the historical growth areas in the 1970s and early 80s without much help from any of the island's academics. Interestingly enough, much of this work was concerned with unravelling the so-called "Singapore Naval Strategy." William Roger Louis's, *British Strategy in the Far East 1919–1939*,[17] may be seen as opening up the field for others to exploit in the years that followed. W. David McIntyre went much further in exploring a purely naval theme in his *The Rise and Fall of the Singapore Naval Base*,[18] as did James Lord Neidpath in *The Singapore Naval Base and the Defence of Britain's Eastern Empire 1919–1941*.[19] Paul Haggie's, *Britannia at Bay*,[20] Ian Hamill's, *The Strategic Illusion*,[21] Peter Lowe's, *Great Britain and the Origins of the Pacific War*[22] and Malcolm H. Murfett's, *Fool-proof Relations*,[23] all managed to add something to the naval story of what S. Woodburn Kirby was to describe as "the greatest national humiliation suffered by Britain since Yorktown."[24] After losing some of its research topicality for a few years, the "Singapore Strategy" has resurfaced once more in the vanguard of the republican movement in Australia. David Day's, *The Great Betrayal: Britain, Australia and the Onset of the Pacific War*,[25] led the way and the Rt. Hon. Paul Keating, the Australian Prime Minister, joined in the fray with a series of outspoken remarks about the iniquities of the British military and government in allowing the island of Singapore to fall to the Japanese in 1942. Malcolm Murfett wrote an answer to these charges.[26] While not going as far as Day and Keating in their scathing denunciations of the perfidious British, his article is critical of what he sees as both British and Australian wishful thinking as far as Singapore was concerned during the inter-war period.

Given the high level of interest in Singapore's part in British naval history up to 1942, the fact that its immediate postwar role is usually passed over in silence,

---

[17] William Roger Louis, *British Strategy in the Far East 1919–1939* (Oxford: Clarendon Press, 1971).

[18] W. David McIntyre, *The Rise and Fall of the Singapore Naval Base* (London: Macmillan, 1979).

[19] James Lord Neidpath, *The Singapore Naval Base and the Defence of Britain's Eastern Empire 1919–1941* (Oxford: Clarendon Press, 1981).

[20] Paul Haggie, *Britannia at Bay: The Defence of the British Empire Against Japan, 1931–1941* (Oxford: Clarendon Press, 1981).

[21] Ian Hamill, *The Strategic Illusion: The Singapore Strategy and the Defence of Australia and New Zealand, 1919–1942* (Singapore: Singapore Univ. Press, 1981).

[22] Peter Lowe, *Great Britain and the Origins of the Pacific War* (Oxford: Clarendon Press, 1977).

[23] Malcolm Murfett, *Fool-proof Relations: The Search for Anglo-American Naval Cooperation during the Chamberlain Years, 1937–1940* (Singapore: Singapore Univ. Press, 1984).

[24] S. Woodburn Kirby, *Singapore: The Chain of Disaster* (London and New York : Macmillan, 1971), p. xiii.

[25] David Day, *The Great Betrayal: Britain, Australia and the Onset of the Pacific War* (New York: W.W. Norton, 1989).

[26] Malcolm Murfett, " Living in the Past: A Critical Re-examination of the Singapore Naval Strategy, 1918-1941 " *War & Society*, vol. 11, no. 1 (May 1993), pp. 73–103.

or in a few sentences at most, looks a little odd and requires some investigation. Sadly, it is all too explicable since it results largely from the deficiencies in the primary source material covering this topic. All of the authors who have published works on British defence policy east of Suez in the post–1945 period have, for example, been denied access to more than a mere fragmentary record of the deliberations of the extremely important regional policy-making committee in Southeast Asia known as the British Defence Coordination Committee (Far East). This mixed civil-military review body was chaired by the Commissioner-General Malcolm MacDonald and included the regional Chiefs of Staff from all three British armed services based at the Far East Station in Singapore. It was in virtually constant communication with the Chiefs of Staff and the Joint Planning Section in London, as is witnessed by the large number of references to the COSSEA and SEACOS cables which litter the Ministry of Defence files for the immediate post–1947 period. Its work embraced review studies and military appreciations which were sent to both departmental and Cabinet sources in Whitehall. Unfortunately, the British government has embargoed all the files relating to the work of this committee under Section 3(4) of the Public Records Act 1958 and steadfastly refuses to relent and release this information into the public domain. As a result, scholarship on the Singaporean end of the British defence story east of Suez in the post-war period has been sparse, although Toni Schönnenberger did try to do justice to this theme in his book.[27] Unfortunately, little scholarly activity on this topic followed in his wake. After vainly pursuing the British government for clearance to use the British Defence Coordination Committee (Far East) papers throughout the decade of the 1980s, Malcolm Murfett finally decided in 1992 to write up the research project on Singapore's role in British naval defence of the Far East, which he had been working on for a number of years.[28]

Complaints about the lack of access to the British records may also be advanced in the case of the Singaporean National Archives. Although Singapore has officially adopted a twenty-five-year rule for its public records, there are two notable departmental exceptions to this rule, namely, the Ministry of Defence and the Ministry of Home Affairs. Neither of these departments are required by the government to lodge their official records with the National Archives, and both will remain independently responsible for all their documents in the years to come. Presumably, therefore, public access to these primary sources will be severely restricted. Even those departments and statutory boards that are required by law to send their primary source material to the National Archives have somehow managed to circumvent the ruling and retain their most important and confidential files. Moreover, they have even imposed a restricted access on

---

[27] Toni Schönnenberger, *Der britische Rückzug aus Singapore 1945–1976* (Zurich: Atlantis Verlag, 1981).

[28] Malcolm Murfett, *In Jeopardy: The Royal Navy and the Role of Singapore in British Far Eastern Defence Policy, 1945–51* (Kuala Lumpur: Oxford Univ. Press, 1994).

those papers which they have been willing to pass to the National Archives. Applications from researchers for approval to examine these records in the National Archives will be handled on a strictly case-by-case basis. Although it is not specifically stated, one may infer that Singaporean nationals are more likely than foreign scholars to get what access may be granted to these records in the years to come. It is a moot point, of course, whether or not the individual public bodies will ever trust the National Archives sufficiently to handle their most sensitive material. An additional problem is posed by the fact that some of the statutory boards may not have established a file registry as yet—the PSA is a prime example—an administrative omission that will vastly complicate the process of anyone using these official records for research purposes in the future. Moreover, before the bulk of these files are turned over to the National Archives, the individual ministries and statutory boards will have to evaluate all this material and decide on what ought to be released for public inspection, or that which must be embargoed for a specific number of years—or even indefinitely. Once this stage has been completed, and before the public records of the Republic of Singapore can be made available to *bona fide* scholars, the staff of the National Archives will have to compile a number of reference ledgers that list by name and number all the individual files which these public bodies have passed to the National Archives for its safeguarding. If these are not sufficient reasons for pessimistic concern, the fact is that the National Archives desperately needs a purpose-built building to house its permanent records. Its present building—an old, labyrinthine structure, which it shares with the Oral History Archive and other assorted ventures—is thoroughly unsuitable on a number of grounds. Apart from its somewhat dilapidated appearance, the Hill Street building is neither secure nor large enough to act as a repository for all the official Singaporean records generated since 1959, nor is it equipped to serve as a modern search-room for scholars and interested members of the general public to consult those public records that it possesses. Its Oral History Archive (OHA) has some considerable potential, but its catalogue is hardly user-friendly and provides insufficient information to potential researchers about the contents of the taped interviews or personal reminiscences which form the bulk of the OHA's stock of material.

Of the documents that are open in the National Archives and relate to naval and maritime history, there are five War Office files drawn from the WO 32 and WO 106 classifications (originating in date between 1924–1939 on the subject of the Singapore Naval Base); thirty-nine documents are to be found in the CO 273 series on a range of different naval and maritime subjects, and an index of Straits Settlements records for the years 1890–1946 is also available. It should be noted, however, that all this archival material and much else, besides, in the Ministry of Defence (DEFE) and Foreign Office General Correspondence

(FO 371) files can be consulted in the Public Records Office at Kew Gardens in London.

Owing to the highly sensitive nature of its work, the Ministry of Defence (Mindef) in Singapore is officially exempt from observing the twenty-five-year rule on the release of its departmental papers. According to the staff of the Military Heritage Branch at Mindef's new headquarters at Bukit Gombak, the likelihood is that non-military personnel will not be granted permission to examine its confidential files at any time in the foreseeable future. If such a ruling is likely to apply to local researchers, it stands to reason that foreigners will not have the faintest chance of gaining access to Mindef's files for many years to come. Research possibilities into aspects of the history of the Republic of Singapore Navy (RSN) are, therefore, very limited and largely dependent upon the information the RSN wishes to yield to the general public in the com-memorative volumes which the Naval Archives produces from time to time. *The Republic of Singapore Navy*[29] is one such volume—a slim thirty-page affair replete with colourful snapshots capturing the essence of an active and demand-ing service. It does not seek to be a scholarly tome, but looks and reads as though it were designed as part of a recruitment campaign to sell the merits of the RSN to the youth of the island.[30] *The Pointer*, the journal of the Singapore Armed Forces (SAF), can also be relied upon to publish uncontentious pieces on the RSN from time to time. Far more important than either of these sources of information is the ongoing research project on the history of the RSN, which was set in motion in the early 1990s by Teo Chee Hean, the then Commander of the RSN. Lieutenant Colonel Lim Kwong Hoon, a trained historian with a master's from Duke University, was asked to begin the task before he took early retirement from the service. According to Lieutenant Colonel Lim, he had finished a chapter on the Confrontation period (1963–65), written up a proposed outline for a thirteen-chapter manuscript covering the entire history of the Singaporean fleet and had found source references for many of the individual topics which he thought should be included in this work before he left the RSN in 1992. One may assume that the project will continue to be advanced through the work of other naval officers until the complete history of the RSN is concluded. Whether this manuscript will be published or merely used as an in-service information tool for RSN personnel is far from clear at this stage.

Despite its silence on this matter, the RSN is nonetheless keen to provide the general public with what it describes as "a showcase of the RSN's Heritage" through the establishment of the Naval Museum which was opened at RSS *Panglima*—the School of Naval Training—in Sembawang Camp on 22 June 1987 by Lieutenant General Winston Choo, Chief of General Staff on the SAF.

29 *The Republic of Singapore Navy* (Singapore: RSN Archives, 1988).

30 See also the Singapore Naval Archives booklet, *Pictorial History of Brani Naval Base: Republic of Singapore Navy* (Singapore: 1987).

Unfortunately, it has neither a library nor an archive of its own, nor is it used as a centre for lectures, seminars, or conferences on the RSN's historical development. Far from being a research facility, the Naval Museum is designed as a visual experience. On display are a range of interesting artifacts (including such items as the mine-sweeping hammer, a decompression chamber, and a host of naval guns) that have been collected over the years by S.W.O. Wee Cheng Leong, the part-time curator of the Naval Museum. Despite the fact that S.W.O. Wee has done a good job in gathering display items to reflect the history of the RSN, the Naval Museum lacks a certain sophistication and is chronically underfunded. Its very existence may be an encouraging step in the right direction, but unless the RSN has a change of heart and decides to upgrade its facilities, it looks destined to remain a small amateur venture rather than a glamorous professional attraction.

On the whole, therefore, the record of maritime and naval history in Singapore today is mixed. While, admittedly, some work is being done on both subjects, research on a whole range of interesting contemporary topics—especially for the post–1959 period—is full of potential pitfalls even for those trusted and empowered to undertake this work on behalf of the Singaporean authorities. By the same token, foreign scholars who wish to work on these topics in Singapore face an even more daunting challenge. If they are denied access to archival sources (a reasonable assumption in the circumstances!), they will almost certainly be forced to rely upon conducting oral interviews and scouring the pages of the local English-language daily newspapers, *The Straits Times and Business Times*, together with those quality journals, such as *The Economist, Asia Wall Street Journal* and the *Far East Economic Review*, in an effort to stitch together what, under the circumstances, cannot be anything more than an incomplete story. Unless the government relaxes its rules on the freedom of information, and major companies follow suit—an unlikely scenario—quality research work on Singaporean maritime and naval subjects in the modern era will remain regrettably compromised. This is particularly unfortunate since there are lessons for others to learn from Singapore's postwar experience. At this stage, however, debate on various aspects of Singapore's maritime and naval past remains muted—a casualty, one imagines, of the prevailing belief that history is somehow irrelevant at a time when a nation is in active pursuit of commercial success and material prosperity. For these reasons the unusual paradox mentioned in the opening paragraph looks likely to remain ironically valid for many years to come.

Bibliographical Appendix

Economics and Statistics Department (University of Singapore and National University of Singapore)

Unpublished Academic Exercises:

Chou Sook May, "Marine Resources and Tourism: The Case of Singapore" (1986)

Kaur, Pirtpal, "Pricing of Services at Telok Ayer Basin" (1973)

Kuek Eng Chyne (Anthony), "Development of Coastal Shipping in Singapore" (1971)

Lee Fou Yoong, "A Manpower Study of the PSA Operations Division" (1973)

Lee Tuan Penh (Michael J.), "The Port of Singapore" (1969)

Leong Mun Keong, "Shippers and Agents in Singapore's Coastal Trade" (1971)

Loh Fong Kwee (Daniel), "Concentration in the Shipbuilding and Repairing Industry in Singapore" (1971)

Ng Chee Keong, "The Effects of the Free Trade Zone or the Entrepot Trade of Singapore" (1973)

Oh Kim Wee, "Flags of Convenience: Practice and Implications for Singapore" (1977)

Sze Toh Kok Leang, "A Study of Cargo Handling in Singapore in Singapore's Coastal Shipping" (1971)

Yeo, Annie, "The Structure of Singapore Shipping Industry" (1973)

Geography Department (University of Singapore and National University of Singapore)

Unpublished Academic Exercises:

Chia Beng Hock (Alan), "The Malacca Straits: A Study in Political Geography" (1986)

Kalyanam, Ganesh s/o R., "Container Port Development in ASEAN" (1990)

Lee Kai Yin, "South Asian Shipping and its Links with Singapore" (1989)

Teo Kiew Ting (Mary Celine), "The development of the port of Singapore 1819-1959" (1962)

Wee Siew Sun, "The port of Singapore—postwar development of its physical facilities" (1977)

History Department (University of Singapore and National University of Singapore)

Unpublished Academic Exercises:

Richard Cheong, "The Singapore Naval Base, a local history" (1983)

Chiang Ming Shun, "Military Defences and Threat Perceptions in Nineteenth Century Singapore" (1992)

R.D. Jansen, "The idea of Singapore as a Naval Base & the abandonment of that idea 1885-1905 (1954)"

Bhajan Singh, "The Defence of Singapore from 1902 to the Washington Conference" (1975)

E. Wong, "The Singapore Harbour Board 1913-1941 (1961)"

Yeo Piah Woon, "The Singapore Harbour Board 1946-57 (1975)"

History Department

Master of Arts Thesis:
George Bogaars, "The Tanjong Pagar Dock Co." (1952)

Political Science Department (National University of Singapore)

Unpublished Academic Exercises:
Kuldip Singh, "Implications for security in Southeast Asia of the 1982 Convention on the Law of the Sea" (1985).

27

South Africa

C.I. Hamilton[1]

To most South Africans, the sea is the hidden frontier. There are so many who appear to regard it as nothing more than a pleasing background to a holiday, or perhaps a source of vicarious excitement when a storm endangers ships off the coast. This indifference is striking, given the strong maritime elements present in the country's geography, history, and economy. Maritime studies have inevitably suffered, and to a degree not to be found in other countries known to this author. The circumstances peculiar to South Africa will be addressed after a survey of what is taught there and its current state of research.

A suitable beginning is maritime archaeology, because it offers a striking example of South Africa's uninterest in its maritime heritage. There are nearly three thousand recorded wrecks off the coast of South Africa, dating from the sixteenth century; but scarcely any of these have been properly investigated. There is a telling contrast here with another "new country," Australia, where there are few wrecks, but much research. It is encouraging, however, that interest has been increasing lately. Admittedly, some of the growing interest in wrecks is from scuba-looters, and there are increasing complaints about their selfish depredations, but there are also private divers who are putting their energies and enthusiasm at the disposal of institutions. Museums have also become more active in the area. Those in ports, notably the Local History Museum, Durban; the East London Museum; the Port Elizabeth Museum and the Natal Museum in Pietermaritzburg, and to a lesser extent the Bredasdorp Museum, tend to have good collections of artefacts from wrecks, look to extend them and, where

[1] Dr. C.I. Hamilton is a member of the Department of History, University of the Witwatersrand, Republic of South Africa.

Acknowledgenment: I wish to thank all those who responded to my requests for information about maritime studies in South Africa, though I am obliged in particular to the generous help of Commander W.M. Bisset, Dr. L. van Sittert, Miss H. Van Niekerk (Transport Economics, University of Stellenbosch), and Drs B. Werz. Of course, only the author can be held responsible for his opinions. I also owe much to those who suggested (with perfect politeness, apart from one oddity) a degree of surprise that members of their departments should be thought to have anything to do with the sea: such replies set the context to the chapter.

The references given are almost entirely limited to work undertaken in the last twenty years. It is not exhaustive; notably, short reports and undergraduate theses have been excluded; but it is hoped that at least the great majority of recent significant work has been included.

possible, study them and publish results.[2] The South Africa Cultural Museum in Cape Town has a Maritime Archaeology Unit, though at present it has only one member, and the Local History Museum, Durban, hopes soon to make a similar appointment. These museums are also much concerned with educating the public in regard to salvage.

University interest in the subject has grown somewhat, but is still more limited. There is no specialist department in the country, but in 1988 a trained maritime archaeologist was appointed to the Archaeology Department at the University of Cape Town (UCT).[3] The departmental courses reflect this, perhaps most interestingly in the one on maritime traffic around the African coast from about 1500 to 1800, dealing, *inter alia*, with shipboard life and contacts with indigenous peoples. Moreover, joint student projects have been arranged with surveying, oceanography, chemistry, marine law and marine geo-science. With regard to research, one must note the work on the wrecked V.O.C. vessel

---

[2]   C. Auret and T. Maggs [Natal Museum], "The Great Ship São Bento: Remains from a mid-sixteenth century Portuguese wreck on the Pondoland Coast," *Annals of the Natal Museum*, 25, 1 (1982), pp. 1–39.

G. Bell-Cross [Curator, the Provincial Museum, Mossel Bay], "The Occurrence of Cornelian and Agate Beads at Shipwreck Sites on the Southern African Coast," *The Coelacanth*, 25, 1 (1987) pp. 20–32.

Bell-Cross, "Portuguese Shipwrecks and Identification of their Sites," in E. Axelson, ed., *Dias and his Successors*, (Cape Town: Saayman & Weber, 1988), pp. 47–80.

T. Maggs, "The Great Galleon São João: Remains from a mid-sixteenth century wreck on the Natal South Coast," *Annals of the Natal Museum*, 26, 1 (1984), pp. 173-86.

B.R. Stuckenberg [Director, Natal Museum], research on the *Santiago* wreck is far advanced and publication is planned.

G.N. Vernon [East London Museum], "Oriental Blue and White Porcelain Sherds at Shipwreck Sites between the Fish and Kei Rivers," *The Coelacanth*, 25, 1 (1987), pp. 15–19.

On also the human consequences of wrecks, see:

G. Bell-Cross, "A brief Maritime History of the Coast between the Kei and Fish Rivers," *The Coelacanth*, 20, 2 (1982), pp. 27–39, and 21, 1 (1983), pp. 7–12.

J.M. Costello [East London Museum], "S.S. Umzimvubu," *The Coelacanth*, 24, 2 (1986), pp. 6–15.

D.A. Webb and K. Stripp [East London Museum], "Wrecked Twice in one Voyage. The Experiences of an Eastern Cape Merchant," *The Coelacanth*, 26, 1 (1988), pp. 35–47.

J. S. Bennie [Port Elizabeth Museum], M.A. research on the *Amsterdam*.

For an enthusiastic account of a non-professional survey of a wreck, see Allan Kayle, *Salvage of the Birkenhead* (Johannesburg: Southern Book Publishers, 1990).

[3]   B.E.J.S. Werz [Archaeology, UCT], "Saving a Fragment of the Underwater Heritage; a Multi-Faceted Approach," *CABO: Yearbook of the Historical Society of Cape Town*, 4, 4 (1989), pp. 13–18.

Werz, "A Preliminary Step to Protect South Africa's Undersea Heritage," *IJNA*, 19, 4, (1990), pp. 335–38.

Werz, "The Excavation of the *Oosterland* in Table Bay: the first Systematic Exercise in Maritime Archaeology in Southern Africa," *South African Journal of Science*, 88, 2 (1992), pp. 85–90.

Werz, "Tafelbaai gee sy geheime prys. 'n Histories-argeologiese ondersoek van die VOC-skip *Oosterland*," *Huguenot Society of South Africa Bulletin*, 29 (1992), pp. 54–61.

Werz, "Maritiem argeologiese ondersoeke in 'n Suid-Afrikaanse konteks: doelstelling, metode en pratyk," *Tydskrif vir Geesteswetenskappe*, 33, 1 (1993), pp. 20-6.

D. Miller, J. Lee-Thorp, & B. Werz, "Amber in Archaeological Contexts in South Africa," *The South African Gemmologist*, 7, 2 (1993), pp. 4–8.

Werz and U.A. Seemann, "Organic Materials from Wet Archaeological Sites: the Conservation of Waterlogged Wood," *The South African Archaeological Bulletin*, 48(1993), pp. 37–41.

Oosterland, the first scientific underwater excavation in South Africa. In the same general context, one ought to mention the Maritime Law Institutes at the Universities of Natal, Durban (ND) and UCT, and the Department of Public Law at UCT, not so much because the two former offer courses of inevitable historical maritime significance (more striking in the case of UCT), but because there are researchers at all three studying jurisdiction in coastal waters (which is crucial to control of wrecks) as well as other matters of interest to maritime historians.[4]

One area in which there has long been interest is port development and the urban history of ports. Here, too, the port musuems are engaged, not just at the level of organizing exhibits and exhibitions, but occasionally also publication.[5] One museum unmentioned so far, Simon's Town Museum, has its own historical society, which regularly publishes articles on the local history of the town in its *Bulletin,* and some years ago published a solid and well-illustrated volume of research work.[6] (This is separate from the new Simon's Town Naval Museum, in the Dockyard.)

---

[4]   Professor Devine, (Institute of Maritime Law, UCT), was good enough to send me the following list of relevant publications of himself and his colleagues:

D.J. Devine and G. Erasmus, "International Environmental Law," chapter 9 of M.A. Rabie, *et al., Environmental Management in South Africa* (Cape Town: Juta, 1982), pp. 155–79.

Devine, "The Cape's False Bay: a Possible Haven for Ships in Distress," *SAYIL,* 16 (1990–91), pp. 81–91.

J.I. Glazewski, "The Admiralty Reserve—an Historical Anachronism or a Bonus for Conservation in the Coastal Zone," *Acta Juridica,* (1986), pp. 193–201.

Glazewski, "The International Law of the Sea," *Marine Science and Technology in South Africa,* (1990), pp. 12–13.

Glazewski & M.A. Rabie, "The Evolution of Public Policy with regard to the Environment: a Legal Perspective over the last Fifty Years," *S.A. Journal of Science,* 86 (1990), pp. 413–19.

Glazewski, "The Regulation of Whaling in International and South African Law," *SAYIL,* 16 (1990–91), pp. 61–80.

Glazewski, A. Dodson, and H. Smith, "Tightening Up the Law" in M. Ramphele, con. ed. with C. McDowell, *Restoring the Land: Environment and Change in Post–Apartheid South Africa,* (London: The Panos Institute, 1991), pp. 139–54.

Glazewski, J. Gurney, and J. Kirkley, "Offshore Minerals," in M.A. Rabie, *et al., Environmental Management,* pp. 380–416.

Glazewski, A. Heydorn, and B. Glavovic, "The Coastal Zone," in M. A. Rabie, pp. 669–89.

One should note, too, B.L. Allen, *Coastal State Control over the Historical Wrecks Situation on the Continental Shelf as Defined in Article 76 of the Law of the Sea Convention 1982,* M.A., Public Law, UCT, 1991; and H. Staniland (Institute of Maritime Law, ND), is working on Admiralty Court jurisdiction over salvage and wreck claims.

[5]   G.N. Vernon, [East London Museum], "From Sail to Ro-Ro: the Story of a River Port," *The Coelacanth,* 19, 1 (1981), pp. 5–10.

See also M. Parkes and V.M. Williams, *Knysna the Forgotten Port. The Maritime Story,* (Knysna: EMU, 1988).

[6]   B.B. Brock and B.G. Brock, in close collaboration with H.C. Willis, *Historical Simon's Town. Vignettes, Reminiscences and Illustrations of the Harbour and Community from the Days of the Dutch East India Co. and of the Royal Navy at the Cape of its Administrators, Personalities and Buildings, with Special Notes on Shipwrecks and Navigation,* published on behalf of the Simon's Town Historical Society (Cape Town: A.A. Balkema, 1976).

However, it is the universities that take the lead in studying the history of ports, although there appear to be no courses with a strong enough historical and maritime element to qualify for inclusion here. The Architecture Department at the University of Port Elizabeth, however, is considering a course on shipbuilding and urban development. On the other hand, at the research level there is much activity; a number of masters and even doctoral theses have been written since the Second World War and more are in hand, with consequent publications, not just in history departments but also economics, architecture, and geography.[7] The approaches vary, but even where the ultimate aim is to write a contemporary study, at least some historical context is given; inevitably, though, it is the history departments where port research is most relevant to this survey. The UCT department is predominant, having issued several volumes of working papers over the past years on various aspects of Cape Town's past and members of the staff have also published independently on the subject.[8] A three-year project is now under way to write the history of the "mother city."

However, once one looks beyond work on the ports and the shoreline, far less research activity is to be found.[9] Seamen, shipping, fishing, and exploration

---

[7]   D.P. De Beer, "A Study of the Utilisation of East London Harbour and its Relative Importance in the South African Import and Export Trade to 1975," doctoral thesis, University of Rhodes, 1979.

H.R. Fitchett [Architecture, Witwatersrand], doctorate research on early architecture at the Cape under the VOC, 1652–1710.

E.J. Inggs [Ec. History, University of South Africa], "Liverpool of the Cape: Port Elizabeth Harbour Development, 1820–70," M.A., Economics & Ec History, University of Rhodes, 1984.

A.B. Lumby [Economics, ND], and I. H. McLean, "The Economy and the Development of the Port of Durban," in B. Guest and J.M. Sellars, eds., *Receded Tides of Empire: Aspects of the Economic and Social History of Natal–Zululand since 1910* (Pietermaritzburg: Natal Univ. Press, in press). § D.W. Rush, "Aspects of the Growth of Trade and the Development of Ports in the Cape Colony, 1795–1882," M.A., Economics, University of Cape Town, 1972.

H.E. Soonike, "The Development of the Port and Harbour of Table Bay with Special Reference to the Period 1825–1848," M.A., History, UCT, 1974.

K.P.T. Tankard [History, University of Rhodes, East London] "East London. The Creation and Development of a Frontier Community, 1835–1873," M.A., University of Rhodes, 1985.

Tankard, "The Development of East London through Four Decades of Municipal Control," doctoral thesis, University of Rhodes, 1990.

Tankard, "Strangulation of a Port: East London, 1847–1873," *Contree*, 23 (March 1988), pp. 5ff.

L.J. Twyman (Heydenrych), [History, University of South Africa], *Durban Harbour in the History of Natal, 1845–1900*, doctoral thesis, University of South Africa, 1986.

Twyman, "Port Natal Harbour, c1850-1897," in B. Guest and J. M. Sellars, eds., *Enterprise and Exploitation in a Victorian Colony: Aspects of the Economic and Social History of Colonial Natal*, (Pietermaritzburg: Univ. of Natal Press, 1985), pp. 17–45.

Twyman, "Port Natal Harbour and the Colonial Politics of Natal," *Historia*, 36, 2(1991), pp. 5–16.

Twyman, "The First Harbour Works at Port Natal—the Role of John Milne, 1849–1857," *The Civil Engineer in South Africa*, 1993.

[8]   C. Saunders [History, UCT], *et al.*, *Studies in the History of Cape Town*, 5 vols. (Cape Town: Centre for African Studies, UCT, 1980+).

[9]   Recently a volume has been published about the Cape (in the sumptuous Brenthurst series) of wider maritime significance: (the late) M. Boucher and N. Penn [History, UCT], eds., *Britain at the Cape 1795 to 1803* (Johannesburg: Brenthurst, 1992). For more information on publications about the history of

attract relatively little attention. Take the case of the last. One thinks of the activities of the Van Riebeeck Society, which since 1918 has been publishing editions of historical documents, many of them of maritime importance.[10] One thinks as well of Professor E. Axelson, famous for the discovery and uncovering of the Dias cross at Kwaaihoek in 1937–8, and author since then of numerous works on Portuguese navigation.[11] He was also the prime mover behind the commemoration in 1988 of the Dias voyage, when the replica caravel, *Bartolomeu Dias*, built in Portugal, sailed to South Africa. (The replica is now at Mossel Bay.) He is both a leading figure in the country and a nearly isolated one.[12] Seamen, shipping and fishing however, do not have someone of Professor Axelson's eminence, though there are a number of researchers,[13] and there is a Whale Research Unit at the University of Pretoria

Cape Town, and confirmation about the emphasis on the *terra firma*, see C. Saunders, ed., and T. Strauss, comp., *Cape Town and the Cape Peninsula, 1806+: A Working Bibliography*, (Cape Town: Centre for African Studies, UCT, 1989).

[10] Recent relevant publications are:

M.D. Nash, ed., *The Last Voyage of the* Guardian. *Lieutenant Riou, Commander 1798–1791*, Van Riebeeck Society, Second Series no. 20 (Cape Town: 1990).

Randolphe Vigne ed., *Guillaume Chenu de Chalezac, the "French Boy." The narrative of his experiences as a Huguenot refugee, as a castaway among the Xhosa, his rescue with the Stavenisse survivors by the Centaurus, his services at the Cape and return to Europe, 1686–9*, Van Riebeeck Society, Second Series no. 22, (Cape Town, 1993).

[11] E. Axelson [History, UCT], *Portuguese in South–East Africa, 1600–1700*, (Johannesburg: Witwatersrand Univ. Press, 1960).

Axelson, *Portuguese in South-East Africa: 1488–1600* (Cape Town: Struik, 1973).

Axelson, *Congo to Cape: Early Portuguese Explorers* (London: Faber, 1973).

Axelson, *Portugal and the Scramble for Africa, 1875–1891* (Johannesburg, Witwatersrand Univ. Press, 1967).

Axelson, E.N. Katz, and E.C. Tabler, *Baines on the Zambesi, 1858–1859* (Johannesburg: Brenthurst, 1982).

Axelson, "Recent Identifications of Portuguese Wrecks on the South African coast, especially of the *São Gonçalo* (1630), and the *Sacramento* and *Atalaia* (1647)," *II Seminário Internacional de História Indo-Portuguesa, Actas* (Lisbon: 1985), pp. 41–61.

Axelson, "The Dias Voyage, 1487–1488: Toponymy and Padrões," *Revista da Universidade de Coimbra*, XXXIV (1988), pp. 29–55.

See also note 2.

[12] See E. Axelson, *Early Portuguese Explorers of Southern Africa*, Camões Annual Lecture, no 2, 1981, at the University of the Witwatersrand; and "The Voyages of Bartolomeu Dias 1487–88 and of the *Bartolomeu Dias* 1987–88," *Congresso Internacional Bartolomeu Dias e a sua Época, Actas*, Volume II, *Navegações na segunda Metade do Século XV* (Porto: 1989), pp. 106–9.

Commodore N.R. Guy is currently editing a volume *Charting and Navigation in Southern Africa*, with a significant historical bias, to be published under the auspices of the Hydrographic Office. Despite her base just outside South Africa, perhaps one ought also to mention J. Kinahan, [Curator of Historical Archaeology, State Museum of Namibia], *By Command of their Lordships. The Exploration of the Namibian Coast by the Royal Navy, 1795–1895*, (Windhoek: Namibia Archaeological Trust, 1992).

[13] **a. Seamen:**

M.C. Kitshoff [Church History, University of Zululand], currently researching on Mission and Ministry to Seamen in S.A.

(although housed in the South Africa Museum) with some historical interests.[14] With regard to courses involving shipping and fishing, one can point to those in maritime economics in the Transport Economics Department at the University of Stellenbosch, which go up to honours' level and beyond, though the historical element is comparatively small, at least at the lower levels.

Looking to other topics, there is a research project to compile a *catalogue raisonné* of the William Fehr collection at Rust-en-Vreugd, Tichiu nowal art. This is particularly interesting because it is a group effort—one, moreover, that involves the cooperation of members of the Art History Department at UCT as

C.I. Hamilton [History, Witwatersrand], "Seamen and Crime at the Cape, c1850–1880," *The International Journal of Maritime History*, 1, 2, (December 1989), pp. 1–35.

b. Shipping:

E.A.G. Clark, presently at work on British merchants and the establishment of new ports and trades in the Cape of Good Hope, 1795–1840. Education, University of Rhodes.

P. Dickinson [Ec. History, Witwatersrand], "Smith's Coasters: the Shipping Interests of C.G. Smith, 1889–1966," *The South African Journal of Economic History*, 3, 1 (1988), pp. 20–32.

N.P. Fawcett, M.A. research on shipping in the Eastern Mediterranean in the first millennium B.C., Semitiese Tale, University of Stellenbosch.

B.D. Ingpen, *South African Merchant Ships. An Illustrated Recent History of Coasters, Colliers, Containerships, Tugs & Other Vessels* (Cape Town: S.S. Balkema, 1979).

Ingpen, "The Coastwise Shipping Industry of Southern Africa—A Study in Transportation Geography," M.A. thesis, Geography, UCT, 1983.

A.L. Müller (Economics, University of Port Elizabeth], "Coastal Shipping and the Early Development of the Southern Cape," *Contree* (July 1985), pp. 10–15.

V.E. Solomon [former Ec. Hist, Witwatersrand, now S.A. Treasury], "The South African Shipping Question, 1886–1914," doctoral thesis, History, University of Rhodes, 1979. (Published 1982 by the Historical Publications Society.)

Solomon, "The Freight Rates crisis of 1907," *Journal of Natal and Zulu History*, 4 (1981), pp. 39–48. Dr. Solomon is presently working on a biography of Sir Donald Currie.

c. Fishing:

K. Cadle, "The Response of a Coloured Fishing Community to their Marine Resource Base," M.A. thesis, School of Environmental Studies, UCT, 1983.

A. Kirkaldy, "The Sea is in our Blood: Community and Craft in Kalk Bay, 1880–1939," master's thesis, History, UCT, 1988.

T. Quinlan, "Line Fishing in Kalk Bay: An Account of a Marginal Livelihood in a Developing Industrial Environment," M.A. thesis, Soc. Anth., UCT, 1981.

L. van Sittert [Oral History Project, UCT].

"Labour, Capital, and the State in the St. Helena Bay fisheries, c1856–c1956," doctoral thesis, History, UCT, 1992.

Van Sittert, "Making Like America: the Industrialisation of the St Helena Bay Fisheries c1936–1956," *Journal of Southern African Studies* (September 1993).

Van Sittert, "'More in the Breach than the Observance': Crayfish, Conservation and Capitalism, 1890–1939," *Environmental History Review*, forthcoming. Dr. van Sittert also has several other papers in preparation, and his work is particularly interesting in drawing on both oral and archival sources.

[14] P.B. Best, [South African Museum], "Seals and Sealing in South and South West Africa," *S.A. Shipping News and Fishing Ind. Rev.*, 28 (1973), pp. 49, 51, 53, 55, 57.

Best and P.D. Shaughnessy. "An Independent Account of Captain Benjamin Morrell's Sealing Voyage to the South West Coast of Africa in the *Antarctic*, 1828–29," *Fish. Bull. S. A.*, 12 (1979), pp. 1–19.

Best, "Sperm Whale Stock Assessments and the Relevance of Historical Whaling Records," *Rep. Int.*

well as staff of the collection.[15] It certainly contrasts with the general pattern of maritime studies research in the country, much of which is a matter of individual work carried on in relative isolation, often little known outside the sheltering institution.

However, one category of maritime studies has not yet been spoken of at all: the history of war navies, or naval history proper. It has been left aside until now, because in South Africa it is very largely confined to one institution outside the universities. This is not to say that there is no naval history carried on at the universities, but there is little of it, only a handful of researchers carrying on individual work.[16] There are also two courses that have a considerable naval history element: the honours course offered by the Strategic Studies Centre at the University of South Africa, and the History of Diplomacy course occasionally offered by the International Studies Unit at the University of Rhodes. Outside the universities, some amateur historians have performed sterling work, above all Wilhelm Grütter, who in one book openly raised some interesting (if

Whal. Comn. (Special Issue 5), 1983, pp. 41-55.

Best & G.J.B. Ross, "Catches of Right Whales from shove-based establishments in Southern Africa, 1792-1975," *ibid* (Special Issue, 10), 1986, pp. 275-89.

Best, "Estimates of the landed Catch of Right (and other whalebone) whales in the American fishery, 1805-1909," *U.S. Fish. Bull.*, 85 (1987), pp. 403-18.

Best, "Right Whales (Eubalaena australis) at Tristan da Cunha—a Clue to the 'Non-Recovery' of Depleted Stocks?" *Biol. Cons.,* 1988, 46, pp. 23–51.

Best and G.J.B. Ross, "Whales and Whaling," in *Oceans of Life off Southern Africa*, Vlaeberg Publishers, Cape Town, 1989, pp. 315–38.

Best, "The 1925 catch of Right Whales off Angola," *Rep. Int. Whal. Comn.,* 40 (1990), pp. 381–82.

C. de Jong, (Ec. History, University of South Africa, "Walvisvangst bij Kaap de Goede Hoop tijdens de Bataafse Republiek," *Historia*, 12, 2, (September 1967), pp. 171–98.

[15] a. History of Art: M. Godby, S. Klopper, M. Stevenson.

   b. William Fehr collection: L. Melzer, B. Cole.

[16] E.A. Biggs, M. A. research on the development of traditions and customs in the S.A.N. Afrikaanse Kultuurgeskiedenis, University Stellenbosch.

   E. and F. Bradlow, (respectively History, UCT, and Chairman, Van Riebeeck Society, Witwatersrand *Here Comes the Alabama*, (Cape Town: A.A. Balkema, 1958).

   G. Burford, M.A. research on Seapower and the Second Gulf War. I.R., Wits.

   D.F.S. Fourie (Strategic Studies, UNISA), studying problems of doctrine for the navies of middle to minor powers.

   C.I. Hamilton, "Naval Hagiography and the Naval Hero," *The Historical Journal*, University of South Africa 23,2 (1980), pp. 381–98.

   Hamilton, *Anglo–French Naval Rivalry 1840–1870* (London: Oxford Univ. Press, 1993).

   D.B. Saddington (Classics, Witwatersrand), "Praefecti classis, orae maritimae and ripae of the Second Triumvirate and the Early Empire," *Jahrbuch des Romish-Germanischen Zentralmuseums Mainz*, XXXV, (1992), pp. 299–313.

   Saddington, "The origin, and character, of the Provincial Fleets of the Early Roman Empire," *Proceedings of the XVth International Congress of Roman Frontier Studies*, ed. V.A. Maxfield and M.J. Dobson, (Exeter: 1991), pp. 413–8.

   Saddington, "The origin and nature of the German and British fleets," *Britannia*, XXI (1990), pp. 223–32.

embarrassing) questions about the recent history of the South African Navy, notably concerning the Afrikanerization of the force in the 1950s.[17] Otherwise, naval history in the country is essentially the province of the South African Navy.

Naval history has only a small role in the courses at the Gordon's Bay college for midshipmen, but is significant at the Muizenberg staff college: one of the four modules at the latter is largely historical in nature. The colleges' staffs are principally responsible for the teaching, but Commander W.M. Bisset, the senior staff officer at the Simon's Town Naval Museum, gives an illustrated survey of S.A. naval history, principally with the intention of fostering *esprit de corps*. And at Muizenberg, Professor D.F.S. Fourie of the Strategic Studies Centre at the University of South Africa gives lectures on strategy and revolution.

At Saldanha Bay is the tri-service academy, which (in association with the University of Stellenbosch) offers a bachelor's degree in military science. Students may take military history as one of their majors and spend some time on a topic in naval history. The potential for concentration is all the greater at honours' level.

Naval officers are also encouraged, where feasible, to take research degrees; few are relevant to this survey, though one officer has just completed an M.A. at Randse Afrikaans Universiteit on the recent history of missile-carrying vessels.[18] Some officers, retired as well as active, also undertake non-degree research and publication. Unfortunately, Union War Histories are no longer being written; the organization was discontinued in 1961, in part as an economy measure, though some hitherto unpublished chapters appeared recently in *Navy News* and *Militaria*.[19] But there is at least a small historical section of the South African Defence Force, although not at present engaged with any specifically naval project.

The survey has already suggested not just a general inadequacy but also some specific weaknesses. First, there is the "patchiness" of coverage of subjects and periods. Particularly noticeable is the way that interest declines markedly with increased distance from the shore; if coastal shipping and fishing arouse little enough attention, the maritime history of other nations is usually ignored, at least outside the naval colleges. There is also a certain narrowness of approach discernable in the universities, to be observed in South Africa as elsewhere: the barriers of the discipline often appear to be the barriers to inquiry; this is certainly apparent in the history departments. It does not seem wholly accidental that

---

[17] *A Name among Sea Faring Men. A History of the Training Ship* General Botha (Cape Town: The T.B.F. Davis Memorial Sailing Fund, 1973).

[18] Lt. Commander L.T. Potgieter. In Afrikaans; restricted circulation.

[19] By (the late) Commander H.R. Gordon-Cumming, "The Loss of HMSAS *Parktown*," *Navy News*, September 1992, pp. 5f. *Militaria*, S.A. Navy Anniversary Issue, 22, 1 (1992). On pp. 51f of the latter, Gordon-Cumming expresses a strong opinion about the poor understanding shown at the S.A. Ministry of Defence about sea power and the role of a navy. He was discussing an early period, but later officers might well find the statement still has some pertinence.

Professor Couzens' life of Trader Horn, undeniably the best recent local work in maritime studies, and generous in its multidisciplinary approach, came from an African Studies Centre (Witwatersrand) and not a history department.[20]

But the most obvious point to be picked out from the survey is the few links between institutions, notably between the universities and the South African Navy. In part, this is because of long-standing mutual suspicion that is common enough in other countries, but is particularly sharp in South Africa where politics have long had a severe effect upon maritime studies. Many academics identify all the armed forces with apartheid tyranny, and many officers believe that at least the English-speaking universities are radical hotbeds. Each side has had its misconceptions: the one, failing to notice the outward-looking, even liberal strand implicit in naval policy making, and the other, confusing opposition to vicious stupidity with attempted revolution. And naval history has suffered. If one looks at what has been published in recent years, ignoring the works of anecdote or piety or nostalgia, a too-common tendency is found towards unadorned factual accounts. One looks back with regret to the last of the Union War History volumes, *War in the Southern Oceans*,[21] with its insight, telling detail (a most valuable comparative element), and even some humour. But that was written in more accommodating days. It is pleasant to note that the S.A.D.F. historical section is currently attempting to develop military history through approaching the universities to sponsor projects and encourage more use of the

20 T. Couzens, *Tramp Royal. The True Story of Trader Horn with such of his Philosophy as is the gift of Age and Experience learned in his Quest from Joss House to Doss House and in which appear severally Cannibals and Pyrates, Gorillas and Lynchings with a guest appearance by Greta Garbo as well as numerous other adventures of a Remarkable Nature*, (Johannesburg: Ravan Press and Witwatersrand Univ. Press, 1992).

Other interesting works of maritime significance from outside the history departments, so far unmentioned, are:

J. Hilton, (Classics, ND), "Azania—Some Etymological Considerations," *Acta Classica*, XXXV (1992), pp. 151–59.

Hilton, "Peoples of Azania," *Scholia*, ns, 2 (1993), pp. 3–16.

M.H. Lategan, M.A. research on autobiographical literature with special reference to the writings of single-handed sailors, English, University of the Orange Free State.

H.P. Maltz, M.A. research on myth in the novels of Herman Melville, a study of the function of the myths of Eden, the Golden Age and Hero and Dragon in *Typee*, *Moby Dick*, and *Billy Budd, Sailor*, English, ND.

R. Laverde (International Studies Unit, University of Rhodes), *Development, Pursuit and Maintenance of the South African Antarctic Policy: 1926–1988*, M.A., 1990.

A. Vos (English, ND), presently researching on the relationship between myth, literature, and history, in connection with the schooner *Mazeppa*.

B. Warner (Astronomy, UCT), presently researching on the early history of the Cape Observatory. Professor Warner is also contributing a chapter to the Guy volume (see note 12) concerning the role of astronomers in the history of navigation in southern waters.

21 By L.C.F. Turner, H.R. Gordon-Cumming, and J.E. Betzler (Cape Town: Oxford Univ. Press, 1961). Also worthy of note are *South Africa's Navy: the First Fifty Years* (Cape Town: W.J. Flesch, 1973), by the late J.C. Goosen (this incorporates work by the late Commander Gordon-Cumming. It was also published in an Afrikaans version), and *Sailor Women, Swans: A History of the South African Women's Auxiliary Naval Service, 1943–49* (Simon's Town: Simon's Town Swans History Publication Fund, 1986).

Pretoria military archives' still largely unexploited resources, although—and perhaps this is in itself indicative—the section has put forward no naval history topics.

Politics have to be considered in another way as well. Given the fractured state of maritime studies within the country, there were no serious interior debates that politics could sharpen. But politics could work from the outside to encourage uninterest or even aversion towards the subject as a whole. The sea has been politically suspect to most of the peoples of the country. Evil came from over the sea, according to the different viewpoints, taking the form of Dutch settlers, or English ones, or capitalism, or godless communism, or sanctions. Furthermore, politics encouraged South African historians to look inwards, to study the trekkers fleeing from English imperialism or, more recently, to study those previously historically disfranchised. As one of my correspondents commented, it can seem almost perverse today for a South African historian to work on anything other than the history of the oppressed majority. The politics of race and domination are usually the major theme, even in ostensibly maritime research.[22]

It is easy to over-generalize about the country. One must allow that it is the heartland which remains most indifferent to the sea. A news item about it might reach the front pages at the coast, only to be relegated to the inside of a Johannesburg newspaper. At the coast one can find excitement about some maritime events, such as the raising of a sunken cannon. It is also there that one can expect to find numbers of maritime enthusiasts, such as the Friends Association of the Local History Museum, Durban, or the engagingly obsessive "ship-spotters" who publish their sightings in the Cape Town journal, *Flotsam and Jetsam*, now more enthusiastic than ever since there is no longer any need to disguise the identity of certain ships that appear in South African ports. It is also the coastal branches of the Navy League that have tended to be the most active.[23] However, both heartland and rimland have suffered alike from two recent forces inimical to maritime studies—sanctions and depression. The former was instrumental in choking the two-way relationship that encouraged some to look towards the sea. When one can see only turned backs on another shore, the response is also to turn

---

[22] Slavery is usually dealt with only in its shore-based manifestations. But there is one researcher working on the maritime slave trade:

G. Campbell (Ec. History, Witwatersrand): "Madagascar and the Slave Trade, 1810–1895," *Journal of African History*, XXII (1981), pp. 203–27.

Campbell, "The East African Slave Trade, 1861–1895: the 'Southern Complex,'" *International Journal of African Historical Studies*, XXII, 1 (1989), pp. 1–27.

Campbell, "Madagascar and Mozambique in the Slave Trade of the Western Indian Ocean, 1800–1861," in W.G. Clarence–Smith ed., *The Economics of the Indian Ocean Slave Trade in the Nineteenth Century* (London: Frank Cass, 1989), pp. 166–93.

Campbell, "Disease, Cattle, and Slaves: the Development of Trade between Natal and Madagascar, 1875–1904," *African Economic History*, XIX(1990–91), pp. 105–33.

[23] The S.A. Navy League remains vigorous overall, in large part because the naval cadet corps operates under its auspices. For the League, and a brief history of the cadet corps by the League's Federal Secretary, Captain D. Brown, plus numerous other details about the sea and S.A., see the current Navy League's *Mariner's Diary*, published by Walker-Ramus Trading Co. (Pty) Ltd, Durban.

away. Significantly, the recent permission for South Africa to participate in commemorating the Battle of the Atlantic immediately led, even in Johannesburg, to richly nostalgic newpaper articles about the war at sea.

Sanctions also deepened the depression, which has been a powerful factor affecting all levels of maritime studies. The lack of money has been bedeviling the universities, forcing severe reductions and a concentration on core subjects rather than something that can be described with dangerous ambiguity as "peripheral." It has affected the museums, where many artefacts cannot be given proper storage let alone the treatment vital to their preservation. The Navy has been forced "to cut fat" and rationalize. And bodies such as the Maritime Institute, at Durban, which offers courses in maritime trade and transport, have been forced to focus on narrowly vocational training, cutting away any historical context.

But there are a few hopeful signs. The central grant-giving body, the Human Sciences Research Council, is improving its data base, so perhaps the present difficulty in gathering information about maritime research will be mitigated. Moreover, an attempt is being made to formulate a maritime policy for the country. Three conferences have been held, attended by academics, museum staffs, naval officers, and others, and a drafted policy is about to be sent to the cabinet. The main aim is to coordinate the various coastal maritime agencies, and there are implications *inter alia* for fishing, customs, air-sea rescue, tourism, and salvage.[24]

The significant aspect of that attempt is the way it has been pushed through by a comparatively small number of people, led by B.C. Floor, lately of the University of Stellenbosch, but now the head of a private agency. This is typical of the country. The shortage of the highly trained, and the narrowness of the elites, means that individual expertise and energy can achieve results that would not be expected in Western societies, at least when the correct contacts have been made. One thinks also of Vice-Admiral G. Syndercombe, former Chief of the Navy, who acts as a universal armature, linking together many of the maritime organizations in the country. Or there is Drs B. Werz, the maritime archaeologist at The University of Cape Town, in the midst of a coming together of the Navy and the National Monuments Council (itself an important organization and responsible for coordinating salvage work).[25] This grouping articulated "Operation Sea Eagle," a survey of the shipwrecks around Robben Island, followed by a general management plan for the area,

---

[24] The papers are available as a bound volume from the National Maritime Policy Committee, University of Stellenbosch.

[25] Dr. J. Deacon has the general supervisory role: see her "Protection of Historical Shipwrecks through the National Monuments Act," given at the Third National Maritime Conference, at Durban, in March 1993 (see note 24); and "Conservation of Historical Shipwrecks: A Need for Cooperation," *Information Bulletin. Council for the Environment*, no. 9 (August 1993), pp. 8–11.

one that may lay a basis for the future rational exploitation of the island for leisure as well as research.[26]

Of course, such schemes depend for their ultimate success upon political stability, economic prosperity, and—crucially—the attitudes of the coming government. As yet, those attitudes remain uncertain. From what some A.N.C. representatives have said, one might have cause for pessimism about maritime studies, for instance in the calls for researchers to concentrate on the history of the black majority, which would largely mean a history of the soil and of struggle. But there are also reasons for optimism, as in the suggestion that South Africa should follow the U.S. example and set up a National Endowment fund with only a relatively light control over subjects of research, though duplication of effort is to be avoided. Moreover, the A.N.C. is actively discussing the subject of fishing, something the Nationalists tended to avoid. A conference in March 1993 in Cape Town, organized by the South African Institute of International Affairs (Cape) and the Institute for Defence Policy, also suggested that the A.N.C. has some sympathy towards the Navy and sees a significant future for it.[27] These are only straws in the wind, but one has to agree with supporters of the fishing industry and at least some officers in the Navy who think that the future holds promise for them, if only because it cannot be worse than the past. In a mood of cautious optimism, one might well say the same about maritime studies in South Africa.

---

[26] B.E.J.S. Werz and J. Deacon, *Operation Sea Eagle: Final Report on a Survey of Shipwrecks around Robben Island* (Cape Town: National Monuments Council, pending).

[27] Some of the papers and comments were printed in the *South African Defence Review*, 10 (1993), issued by the Institute for Defence Policy, Halfway House (Midrand), S.A. 1685. I am grateful to Dr. J. Cilliers for letting me have a copy of the issue.

28

Spain

Carla Rahn Phillips

S pain's relationship with the sea goes back as far as recorded history, when mariners from Carthage, Greece, and Rome established settlements of their seaborne empires on the Iberian peninsula. Muslims from North Africa invaded Spain by sea in the eighth century, and again in the twelfth century, and naval engagements marked important phases in the Christian reconquest of the peninsula in the late Middle Ages. During the sixteenth and seventeenth centuries, Castile governed a vast worldwide empire, held together by maritime trade and communication and defended by an impressive naval establishment. Seaborne trade and defense loomed large in Spanish affairs as long as the empire lasted—that is, until the late nineteenth century—although with inevitable shifts of emphasis after most of Spanish America became independent. The twentieth century presented a different set of challenges, as the civilian shipbuilding industry eclipsed the naval establishment.

This essay surveys the historiography of Spanish naval and maritime affairs over the past ninety years or so, during which time virtually every aspect of Spain's long relationship with the sea has been discussed in print. Bibliographic aids, such as listings of books and articles published during the twentieth century, yielded 1,328 items. Although they seem to represent a valid sampling of the field, undoubtedly many items eluded me.[1] The most serious deficiency in my search is that I was able to deal only superficially with the enormous output of the *Revista General de Marina (RGM)*, founded in 1877. The *RGM* was published regularly except for a hiatus during the Spanish Civil War; in over 115 years of existence, nearly 10,800 articles on a wide range of topics have appeared in its pages. A conference in 1990 focused on the *RGM* and its impact on the field of naval and maritime history. Ten short papers analyzing the journal's contents since its foundation were prepared for that conference and appeared in print as part of the monographic series published by the Institute of Naval History and

---

[1] Lawrence Mott, a graduate student in history at the University of Minnesota, served as my research assistant on this project, assembling the references and entering them on the bibliographic program Pro-Cite. I can provide the computer files for the bibliography on WordPerfect 5.0 to any interested parties. Send a diskette (3.5 or 5.25 in.) and a self-addressed stamped mailer to Prof. Carla Rahn Phillips, Department of History, University of Minnesota, Minneapolis, MN 55455.

Culture (Instituto de Historia y Cultura Naval).[2] Because the full run of the *RGM* was not available to me, I relied primarily on indirect analyses such as these to characterize the journal's output. I also used a computerized index of key-words in the titles of *RGM* articles, prepared by a researcher at the Consejo Superior de Investigaciones Científicas in Madrid.[3] In the discussion that follows, I have included material from the *RGM* wherever possible, but I cannot pretend to have analyzed its contents as thoroughly as they deserve.

Judging from that index and from an unsystematic survey of articles, the *RGM* seems to deal more heavily with naval history than with maritime history, as those distinctions are commonly used, though its range is too broad to define in simple terms. Moreover, in publications of all sorts, distinctions between naval and maritime history have little relevance in Spain. Many books and articles deal with all aspects of Spanish seaborne experience, and journals regularly publish a variety of articles that defy rigid labels. Moreover, books about naval and maritime history are regularly reviewed in national newspapers, as well as in scholarly periodicals; in other words, the field is not marginalized as it is in some countries.

The authors who publish in Spanish naval and maritime history are—not surprisingly—mostly Spanish. Of the publications I surveyed in detail, nearly 80 percent were written by Spaniards, and the foreign authors generally focused on matters concerning their home countries. For example, the ill-fated armed fleet, or *armada*, that Spain sent against England in 1588 inspired a predictable interest among English authors, and the naval actions of the 1898 Spanish–American war attracted a number of authors from the United States. Very few non-Spaniards have published on broader Spanish nautical topics, however, and *some* detailed research by non-Spaniards is not likely ever to be published. I have in mind here the international fraternity and sorority of treasure hunters who have leafed through countless documents looking for clues to sunken treasure from Spain's Atlantic and Pacific fleets, and whose interests are more pecuniary than scholarly.

Among the Spanish authors my survey turned up, the vast majority are male, many of them serving in the Spanish Navy. That is predictable, given the nature of the topic. Several extraordinary scholars and naval officers in the nineteenth century provided ideal models. Martín Fernández Navarrete and Cesáreo Fernández Duro each published numerous works of their own research, as well as editing multivolume series of documents related to Spanish naval and maritime

---

[2] "La Revista General de Marina y su Proyección histórica," *Cuadernos monográficos del Instituto de Historia y Cultura Naval*, no. 10 (Madrid: 1990).

[3] Fernando Alonso Castellanos, "Indización de la Revista General de Marina mediante un sistema automático: El índice rotado de títulos. Utilidades," *Cuadernos monográficos del Instituto de Historia y Cultura Naval*, no. 10 (Madrid: 1990), pp. 57–68. The author analyzed key words in the titles of nearly 11,000 articles. A listing of words mentioned fifteen or more times is included in that article.

history.[4] They were followed in the twentieth century by Julio Guillén Tato and José María Martínez-Hidalgo Terán, to name only the most distinguished of the generation that began to publish in the middle of this century.[5] The tradition continues with Ricardo Cerezo Martínez and José Cervera Pery, each noteworthy for publications on themes that span several centuries, and a score of other naval officers who are also naval and maritime historians.

Members of the military establishment are by no means the only Spaniards publishing in the field, however. A small minority of the authors currently active seems to have no direct connection with the Navy and was trained in regular history doctoral programs in various Spanish universities. Others studied nautical archaeology, a relatively new field everywhere, whose practitioners are not necessarily part of the naval establishment in Spain. Federico Foerster Laures is the most noteworthy Spaniard publishing in this field; his articles regularly appear in English in the *International Journal of Nautical Archaeology*, where they find a wide audience.

Somewhat unexpectedly, a few Spanish women have also published on naval and maritime history. Spanish naval archives—in the last several decades at least—have been staffed in large measure by women. Some of them come from naval families, and it is quite natural for them to work for the ministry and to publish on nautical themes. Others are university-trained professional archivists who happen to specialize in naval and maritime archives. Ana María Vigón Sánchez served as Director of the General Marine Archive (Archivo General de la Marina) in the Naval Museum (Museo Naval) in Madrid for many years. The Museo Naval houses a prominent research collection of documents as well as ship models and other artifacts. Currently, María Dolores Higueras Rodríguez and María Luisa Martín-Merás head research sections at the Museo Naval and publish regularly on naval and maritime history. The significant presence of women might be typical of the naval history establishment in other countries as well, although I have not made a study of the matter.

The 1,328 publications in my survey showed a sharply defined pattern of distribution over time, with an enormous increase from the 1970s onward. The number of publications began very modestly, with twenty to forty books and articles per decade from 1900 to 1930. Despite the disruptions of the Spanish Civil War (1936–39) and World War II (1939–45), however, I noted nearly fifty publications in the 1930s and nearly one hundred in the 1940s. The number of publications stayed at an average of nearly one hundred per decade in the 1950s and 1960s as well, but the 1970s marked an increase to one hundred forty-one publications. During the 1980s, nearly six hundred books and articles

---

4   Fernández Duro was the subject of an issue of the *Cuadernos monográficos del Instituto de Historia y Cultura Naval*, no. 6 (Madrid: 1990).

5   Even Admiral Luis Carrero Blanco, for several decades the principal adviser of General Francisco Franco, published several extended works on naval history.

were published about Spanish naval and maritime history, and the upward trend seems to be continuing in the 1990s. The 10,800 titles from the *Revista General de Marina* would probably change the temporal distribution somewhat, although the same impulses inspired publications in the field as a whole. Moreover, although my search captured recent publications much more easily than older ones, the sharp increase of activity shown for the 1980s seems to be real rather than a statistical illusion.

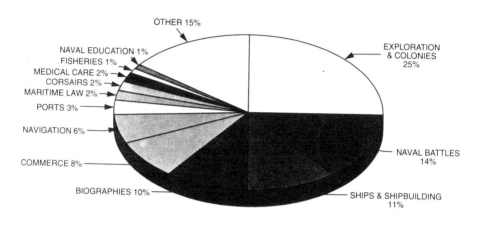

SPANISH NAVAL AND MARITIME HISTORY
FREQUENCY OF TOPICS

OTHER 15%

NAVAL EDUCATION 1%
FISHERIES 1%
MEDICAL CARE 2%
CORSAIRS 2%
MARITIME LAW 2%

PORTS 3%

NAVIGATION 6%

COMMERCE 8%

BIOGRAPHIES 10%

EXPLORATION & COLONIES 25%

NAVAL BATTLES 14%

SHIPS & SHIPBUILDING 11%

THE TOTAL NUMBER OF PUBLICATIONS IS 1,328, MANY OF WHICH DEALT WITH MORE THAN ONE TOPIC. THE CHART REPRESENTS ONLY THE MOST FREQUENT THEMES.

The *Revista de Historia Naval*, founded by the Instituto de Historia y Cultura Naval in 1983, responded to the growing interest in the field by adding another venue for publication. Both the *Revista de Historia Naval* and the *Revista General de Marina* sponsor additional publications on a diversity of themes as well. The topics covered by the field in any given decade show a wide variety, but the anniversaries of historical events with a nautical dimension attract particular interest.

The books and articles in my detailed survey of 1,328 publications were characterized by topic and chronological period. The largest cluster of topics—fully one-quarter—concerned voyages of exploration and the maritime links connecting Spain with its overseas empire. By contrast, the key-words in titles published in the *RGM* suggest that Spanish exploration figures much less prominently in that journal than in the field as a whole. This is probably due to the *RGM*'s emphasis on modern maritime topics rather than historical ones. A similar example emerges from publications about physical ships. In my survey, over 11 percent of the books and articles dealt with shipbuilding, repair, wrecks, and the lives of individual ships, heavily weighted toward the period before the nineteenth century. In article titles in the *RGM*, nearly 14 percent of the key words concerned ships and shipbuilding, but with a decided bias toward modern times. In other words, there were hundreds of references to aircraft carriers, submarines, cruisers, and other modern vessels. By contrast, caravels, galleons, galleys, and other historical ship types of importance do not appear in the published index of key words at all, because they fall beneath the threshold for inclusion.

Naval battles accounted for about 14 percent of the titles in my survey, and about 10 percent of the key words in the *RGM*. Biographies of famous mariners and naval strategists also figure prominently in the field as a whole. Matters relating to Spanish commerce and the merchant marine account for over 8 percent of my surveyed publications, but for a much smaller proportion of articles in the *RGM*. Other matters that have attracted notable attention include navigation, ports, maritime law, piracy and privateering, medical care, nautical education, and fisheries. Because no Spanish river is navigable very far from the coast, inland navigation forms no part of the field. Taken as a whole, Spanish naval and maritime history reflects the broader patterns of Spanish history and interests in Europe and around the world. Therefore, it makes sense to discuss the published work according to the chronological periods covered.

Very little has been published in Spain about ancient nautical history, and much of that has concerned Greek and Roman shipwrecks near the Spanish coast rather than topics specifically Spanish. Similarly, the early medieval centuries and the period of Muslim domination in Spain have attracted little attention, presumably because the most important historical developments in that period occurred on land. The late medieval period has been somewhat better served; I noted twenty-nine publications dealing with the tenth through the fourteenth centuries. The largely land-based Reconquest of the Iberian Peninsula from the Muslims dominates Spain's late-medieval historiography. Nonetheless, visual evidence of ships in illustrated devotional works and architectural embellishments provides a range of hull types and nautical equipment for historians to interpret. Modern scholars have only just begun to mine these riches. The documentary record for the Atlantic fleets of the medieval kingdom of Castile and for the Mediterranean fleets of the eastern regions of Catalonia and Valencia in the kingdom of Aragon have begun to attract scholarly attention as well. They may soon provide important insights into the evolution of European ship design in the era of the Crusades.

The number of scholarly publications about nautical matters in the fifteenth century nearly doubles that for all previous periods. The fifteenth century is usually considered part of the Middle Ages, yet it contained developments such as the consolidation of large territorial monarchies in Europe that heralded the early modern age. The late fifteenth century also witnessed the first persistent efforts by Europeans to explore the African coastline and to conquer and colonize various groups of Atlantic islands.

Not surprisingly, books and articles about Christopher Columbus overwhelmingly dominate works on the fifteenth century—one hundred one of the one hundred forty-five publications in my survey for the century as a whole. Also, predictably, the majority appeared in years centered around 1942 and 1992, the 450th and 500th anniversaries of his first voyage across the Atlantic. The *Revista General de Marina* also published extensively on Columbus. Most of the publications about Columbus are much more concerned with his life and the consequences of his voyages than with his ships or his methods of navigation. Nonetheless, nautical matters occupy a sizeable percentage of the publications. Many authors have tried to estimate the tonnages and configurations of Columbus's ships over the past century, and replicas have been designed, built, and sailed in attempts to bring them back to life. It is not clear, however, that we are any closer to knowing their characteristics now than we were in 1892. The documentary and pictorial record is simply too sparse to help us much, and the craftsmen's traditions that produced the original ships are all but lost in the modern world. Fortunately, underwater archaeology may eventually analyze enough shipwrecks from the early years of European global exploration to suggest believable configurations, not only for Columbus's ships but also for other Spanish ship types in the late medieval period.

Scholars concerned with the fifteenth century have also focussed on the art and science of navigation. Modern methods of celestial navigation were pioneered by Portuguese and Spanish mariners and refined as they confronted the challenges of sailing far from shore in unfamiliar parts of the globe. One of the liveliest controversies surrounding Columbus concerns his first landfall in the Western Hemisphere, a matter intimately related to his navigational track across the Atlantic and in the waters of the Caribbean. An extraordinary amount of effort has been expended in exploring this mystery, most of it by non-Spaniards. A team of researchers at *National Geographic* in November of 1986 claimed to have solved the matter by computerized analysis of Columbus's log of his 1492 voyage—or, rather, of the only existing version of that log, an abstract by Friar Bartolomé de las Casas, prepared several decades after Columbus's death. Many scholars, including several Spanish experts on navigation, greeted the *National Geographic*'s findings with marked skepticism. The Columbian Quincentenary produced several new editions of the abstracted log, yet the text itself is so questionable that any definitive replication of Columbus's course remains unlikely.

Books and articles in whole or in part about the sixteenth century accounted for over a quarter of the 1,328 items surveyed for this study—some 373 in all. During the sixteenth century Spain reached the peak of its power, with an extensive empire in Europe, a large and growing colonial empire in the Western

SPANISH NAVAL AND MARITIME HISTORY
FREQUENCY OF FIFTEENTH CENTURY TOPICS

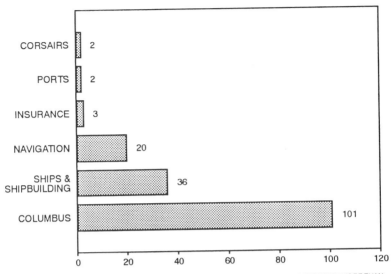

THE TOTAL NUMBER OF PUBLICATIONS IS 145, MANY OF WHICH DEALT WITH MORE THAN ONE TOPIC. THE BAR CHART REPRESENTS ONLY THE MOST FREQUENT THEMES.

FREQUENCY OF SIXTEENTH CENTURY TOPICS

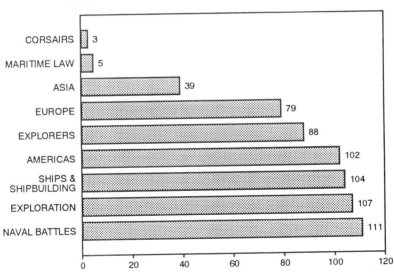

THE TOTAL NUMBER OF PUBLICATIONS IS 373, MANY OF WHICH DEALT WITH MORE THAN ONE TOPIC. THE BAR CHART REPRESENTS ONLY THE MOST FREQUENT THEMES.

Hemisphere, and outposts in Asia as well. As the dominant Roman Catholic power in Europe, Spain also bore the brunt of defending Catholicism in Europe after the Protestant Reformation began in 1517, and from external enemies in the Islamic Ottoman Empire and its North African tributaries and allies. The Ottomans had captured the Christian stronghold of Constantinople in 1453 and remained on the offensive against the eastern borders of Christian Europe, as well as in the Mediterranean.

The defense of Catholicism can be said to have dominated Spanish foreign policy during the first half of the sixteenth century. Naval operations such as the campaigns to capture and hold Tunis and Goleta on the North African coast in the 1530s were part of the struggle waged against the Islamic world by Charles I, the king of Spain who also served as Holy Roman Emperor with the title Charles V. Even Charles' perennial wars against Catholic France had a religious dimension once the French allied with the Ottomans in 1536. The naval and maritime aspects of these wars in the early sixteenth century have attracted some scholarly attention, but not as much as one would expect.

Dynastic politics in Europe and abroad shaped Spain's national policies throughout the 1500s, but maritime and global concerns came to the fore in the last half of the century, during the reign of Philip II. Historians have written about the Spanish naval expedition against Djerba in 1560 and about Philip II's efforts to reinforce Spanish *presidios* in North Africa, policies that aimed to secure the Western Mediterranean against Muslim pirates and privateers allied with the Ottomans. The Christian and Islamic powers confronted one another definitively in 1571 at the battle of Lepanto in the Gulf of Corinth. Spain provided the majority of ships and men for the Christian fleet, with smaller contingents from the papacy and the Republic of Venice. Spain also provided the commander-in-chief, in the person of Don Juan of Austria, half-brother of Philip II. The great Christian victory at Lepanto was commemorated with lavish celebrations all over Europe and long remained a symbol of Christianity's response to the loss of Constantinople. Because of its psychological importance, Lepanto also generated a wealth of commemorative engravings and paintings, providing precious visual evidence for maritime historians.

Lepanto has continued to attract the interest of scholars in this century, especially during the four-hundredth anniversary of the battle in 1971. Ten publications in my survey were devoted entirely to Lepanto, and numerous others dealt with it in conjunction with other naval engagements in the Mediterranean. Although the battle itself settled nothing decisively, it marked a turning point in the struggle between the Ottoman and Spanish empires. After Lepanto, the Ottomans turned to more pressing matters on their eastern land frontier with Persia, and Philip II turned toward northern Europe, where rebellion in the Netherlands and worsening relations with England threatened Spain's grip on its European possessions.

Naval actions during the early phase of the Netherlands rebellion have not figured prominently in writings about the late sixteenth century, though the Spanish convoys of men and money through the channel appear in all the general histories of that conflict. By contrast, the fleet sent by Spain against England in 1588 has attracted an extraordinary amount of attention, primarily from writers in England and Spain. Although the Great Armada, as the Spanish called it, has long held a prominent place in sixteenth-century naval scholarship, the four-hundredth anniversary of that fleet in 1988 produced a floodtide of publications, over 23 percent of all sixteenth-century themes. A series of international conferences in 1988 brought Spanish and English scholars together to reconsider various aspects of the armada campaign, moving the debate away from simpleminded nationalism toward a deepened understanding of the ships, armament, men, and tactics involved. A number of distinguished publications resulted from those conferences, as well as a wealth of other serious work. For example, the Instituto de Historia y Cultura Naval in Madrid sponsored a series of monographs on the armada in its many aspects: ships, medical care, political concerns, armaments, tactics, and so on. Regrettably, 1988 was also marked by publication of the inevitable drivel that often accompanies important anniversaries.

One of the primary reasons that Philip II decided to launch the Great Armada had its origins far from Europe, in the Spanish empire in the Western Hemisphere. To the extent that English privateers threatened Spanish control of that empire, they threatened a major source of tax revenue for the crown, and a much larger source of profits for Spanish merchants. Publications dealing with maritime aspects of the American empire accounted for over 27 percent of the total publications on the sixteenth century.

Spanish scholars have also shown a keen interest in the numerous voyages of exploration by their countrymen in the late sixteenth century, especially in the vast Pacific Ocean. Books and articles on the Pacific, Asia, and Spain's outpost in the Philippines account for over 10 percent of the publications in my survey dealing with the sixteenth century. The *Revista General de Marina* also published many titles dealing with discovery (22 percent) and the Pacific (25 percent), though not necessarily all on the sixteenth century.

Predictably, famous expeditions such as Ferdinand Magellan's circumnavigation of the globe in 1519–22 have attracted greater attention than more obscure voyages. Pedro Sarmiento de Gamboa,—navigator, natural philosopher, poet, and tireless explorer of the Pacific in the late sixteenth century—formed the subject of several full-fledged biographies and a half dozen articles, and many other explorers inspired at least one author. Samuel Eliot Morison, John H. Parry, and other historians of European exploration dealt with many of these voyages in the 1950s, but the next generation of historians turned to other topics. Only recently has global exploration resumed its role as an active field for scholarly investigation. Overall, the range of exploratory voyages has been fairly well covered by Spanish authors, especially in the concerted effort at publication spawned by the Columbian Quincentenary. The Spanish government endorsed numerous series of publications starting in the 1980s that edited explorers' accounts of their voyages and provided scholarly analyses of them.

The Netherlands rebellion, the Spanish empire, and further voyages of exploration have also piqued the interest of scholars publishing on maritime aspects of the seventeenth century. The first decade of that century, marked by a new king and the winding down of Spain's conflicts with France, England, and the Netherlands, has often been seen as a static period in maritime affairs. Scholars are just beginning to realize that a decade and more of peace allowed the government of Philip III to sponsor debate on the ideal sizes and configurations of ships for the Atlantic run. The regulations of 1607, 1613, and 1618 established measurements for shipbuilders to follow, in effect forcing private industry to produce ships that would be suitable for the government to commandeer and rent in wartime. Spanish governments in the early seventeenth century also promoted advances in salvage technology. Pedro de Ledesma's beautifully illustrated manuscript on that topic in 1623 recently appeared in facsimile in a limited edition.

The Netherlands rebellion resumed in 1621 after a twelve-years' truce, forming one phase in The Thirty Years' War from 1618 to 1648. In its various phases, the war used up Spanish men, money, and ships at an alarming rate. Stretching its resources to the limit, the Spanish government frequently sent ill-manned and poorly supplied fleets into battle, relying on the courage and self-respect of commanders and men to overcome adversity. Surprisingly, they often succeeded in defiance of the odds, which only encouraged the government to demand more and supply less.

Some distinguished commanders such as Antonio de Oquendo have found their biographers, but most of his colleagues remain little known outside the Spanish naval establishment. Only eight biographies of prominent figures surfaced in publications about the seventeenth century compared to thirty-two such biographies for the sixteenth century, although brief histories of individual commanders appear in studies devoted to broader issues of seventeenth-century war and politics. This neglect may simply reflect a distaste for dealing with Spain's loss of power; Spanish archives contain ample documentation for a more extensive collection of biographies, if only scholars seek it out.

The conflicts subsumed under the heading of the Thirty Years' War broke Spain's power in Europe. Incessant warfare on land and sea coincided disastrously with a steep decline in Spain's internal economy and in revenues from the empire in the middle third of the seventeenth century. Given the circumstances, it is astonishing that Spain held on to as much as it did, including the American empire. With the peace treaties of 1648, the Netherlands officially won its independence from Spain. With the Peace of the Pyrenees in 1659, Spain and France disengaged and France emerged from their century and a half of intermittent warfare as the dominant power in Europe. Louis XIV of France, the great-grandson of Philip II of Spain, also held one of the strongest claims to the Spanish throne itself, in case the Spanish Habsburg line died out. Just as interest in England and the Netherlands featured prominently in publications about the sixteenth century, interest in France increased in publications about the seventeenth century.

Spain's American colonies and exploration and colonization in the Pacific and Asia held a prominant place among seventeenth-century topics. Of the one hundred thirty publications dealing with that century in my survey, fifty-six (43 percent) concerned the Americas, and another two dozen or so dealt with exploration. Their focus could be as narrow as the voyage of a single obscure mariner or as broad as the geopolitical strategies pursued by Spain in the Pacific. The continued interest in global topics serves as a reminder that, whereas Spain had slipped to second-rank status in Europe by the end of the seventeenth century, it was still the foremost colonial power abroad, by a large margin.

Spanish ship design changed little in the seventeenth century after the activity of the early years. The galleon continued to be the workhorse of the Atlantic fleets, and vessel size edged upward as the century progressed. A series of wars in the last three decades of the 1600s, provoked by French aggression, sapped the waning strength of Spain's navy, but the country nonetheless maintained fleets to protect commercial voyages to America. Spain's internal economy and its American trade showed unmistakable signs of recovery by 1680. It is likely that this revival encouraged renewed attention to Spain's fleets on the part of the government. The recent discovery of an important manuscript on ship design by Antonio de Gaztañeta, from the end of the century, is already generating more interest in Spanish naval architecture.

At the start of the eighteenth century, the Bourbon dynasty of France inherited the Spanish throne when the Habsburgs died out. The change was not welcomed by other European countries, however, which waged the War of the Spanish Succession (1701–1713) in an attempt to block Bourbon power. Land engagements during the war of succession have attracted much more attention than naval battles, though British grand strategy has inspired one thorough treatment by John Hattendorf. On the Bourbon side, Spain bore the brunt of the limited action at sea, as France had a very small navy, and Spain also had to protect its overseas colonies from English incursions. The strains of war and the simultaneous restructuring of the Spanish bureaucracy by the Bourbon government of Philip V meant that even major naval engagements were documented erratically. After more than a decade of struggle, the Bourbons kept the Spanish throne, but at the cost of virtually all Spain's remaining territory in Italy and the Mediterranean, plus Gibraltar on Spanish soil.

SPANISH NAVAL AND MARITIME HISTORY
FREQUENCY OF SEVENTEENTH CENTURY TOPICS

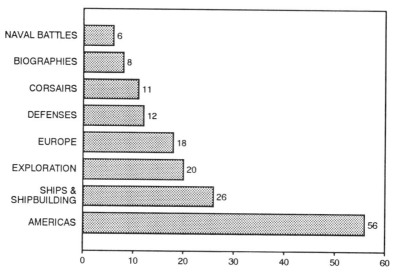

THE TOTAL NUMBER OF PUBLICATIONS IS 130, MANY OF WHICH DEALT WITH MORE THAN ONE TOPIC. THE BAR CHART REPRESENTS ONLY THE MOST FREQUENT THEMES.

FREQUENCY OF EIGHTEENTH CENTURY TOPICS

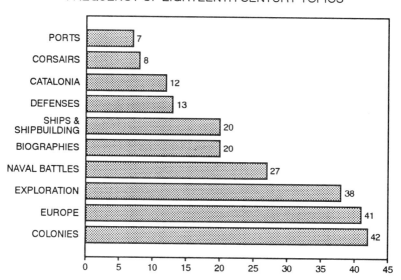

THE TOTAL NUMBER OF PUBLICATIONS IS 206, MANY OF WHICH DEALT WITH MORE THAN ONE TOPIC. THE BAR CHART REPRESENTS ONLY THE MOST FREQUENT THEMES.

Once the Bourbons settled in, during the reigns of Ferdinand VI (1746–59) and Charles III (1759–88), they pursued a vigorous policy of administrative reform that included a revival of the navy. The monarchy and a succession of extraordinarily able ministers found their efforts aided by demographic and economic growth that spanned most of the eighteenth century. Within Europe, England mounted increasing challenges to the power of France, while Spain aimed to protect its empire and enhance its fortunes by turning the rivalry of its neighbors to advantage. More often than not, Bourbon Spain allied with Bourbon France in a series of so-called "family pacts." The reason for this stance was less dynastic loyalty, however, and more a realization that England posed the more serious danger to Spanish America. Books and articles about England account for nearly 12 percent of the historiography of Spain's eighteenth century naval and maritime history; publications about France account for nearly 8 percent. As an ally of France, Spain participated in the maritime wars of the mid-eighteenth century and aided the North American colonies rebelling against England after 1776, inspired in part by the vain hope of regaining control of Gibraltar. Several articles deal with each of these conflicts and with noted Spanish commanders.

Imperial concerns outside Europe loomed large in Spanish naval policies during the eighteenth century, which is reflected in published scholarship. The defense of Spain's American colonies continued to claim government resources, and the much-vaunted "Bourbon reforms" of colonial administration aimed in part to foment seaborne commerce. All of these initiatives have attracted scholarly interest.

Spanish voyages of exploration also gained a new impetus under the Bourbon dynasty, and thirty-eight publications in my survey reflect that activity. Voyages in the Pacific figured in thirty-three (16 percent) of the publications dealing with the eighteenth century. Prominent among those voyages were the expeditions of Alessandro Malaspina, an Italian sailing for Spain, in 1789–94. In 1989, spurred by the bicentenary of Malaspina's expedition, authors of seventeen publications examined its various aspects. Much of the impetus behind Malaspina's voyage was scientific—to study and illustrate the flora and fauna encountered in diverse regions. The expedition's sojourn on the northwest coast of North America had an important geopolitical focus as well, to pursue Spain's interests from San Francisco to the Aleutian Islands against rival English and Russian claimants. Unfortunately, the expedition began in the same year that Bourbon France erupted in revolution and returned to find Spain involved in war against the revolutionary French regime. The subsequent chaos in Spain's administration ensured that the lengthy documentation and exquisite illustrations generated by the Malaspina expedition were largely forgotten. Thanks to the bicentenary, they have finally come to light.

The nineteenth century began disastrously for Spain and its navy. After a brief flirtation with the anti-French coalition in 1792–95, Spain returned to alliance with France and was drawn into the Napoleonic wars that followed. Although individual ships and crews performed well, the Spanish fleet as a whole was ill-prepared to face Britain and its allies. The Spanish Navy was effectively destroyed at the Battle of Trafalgar in 1805, an engagement that featured in twelve of the one hundred seventy-two books and articles about the nineteenth century.

Worse was yet to come, as Napoleon sent his armies into Spain, bamboozled the Bourbon king Charles IV into abdicating in his favor, and then appointed his brother Joseph Bonaparte as king of Spain. With the Bourbon royal family in exile in France, and no effective central leadership against the Bonapartes, the people of Spain organized their own government from the bottom up and launched a crusade to oust the French invaders. Unaided, they dealt Napoleon's armies their first defeat, and thus attracted the help of the British-led coalition. As the war proceeded, and Joseph Bonaparte tried to govern in Madrid, Spanish patriots met in Cádiz in the name of the exiled Bourbons and wrote a constitution to govern the country after Bourbon rule was restored. Eventually the allies defeated Napoleon's forces in Spain and throughout the rest of Europe.

Spain's struggle for and against the French during the revolutionary epoch resulted in catastrophe, not only for the Navy at Trafalgar, but for the internal economy and the American empire as well. No sooner had the Bourbon monarchy been restored under Ferdinand VII than Spain's American colonies, one after another, declared their independence, after over three centuries of colonial rule. Virtually without a navy, and with the government still in disarray, Spain lost most of its American empire by 1824. The large viceroyalties that had governed nearly fifteen million people in the late eighteenth century were split into sixteen republics that undertook the difficult task of governing themselves.

Most of the twenty-nine publications dealing with the Americas in the nineteenth century concern one aspect or another of the colonial wars of independence. Not surprisingly, most of the officer corps in the navies formed by the new American republics had begun their careers in Spanish service. With their loss, the Spanish faced yet another obstacle to rebuilding after the Napoleonic era.

Within Spain, government ministers formulated a variety of plans to restore the Navy, but they proved largely ineffectual during the first half of the nineteenth century. With most of the empire gone, the Navy could not claim to be a top priority any longer, and the government of Ferdinand VII lacked the will and the resources to accomplish much. Civil War erupted after Ferdinand's death in 1833, between supporters of a continued constitutional monarchy and those who favored a return to absolutism and a tight alliance between the crown and the Catholic Church. The triumph of the constitutionalists in 1839 led to

SPANISH NAVAL AND MARITIME HISTORY
FREQUENCY OF NINETEENTH CENTURY TOPICS

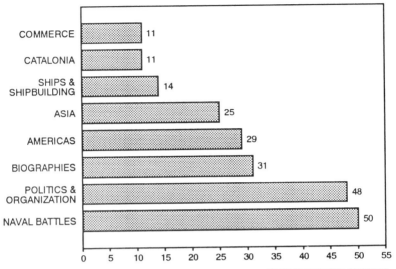

THE TOTAL NUMBER OF PUBLICATIONS IS 172, MANY OF WHICH DEALT WITH MORE THAN ONE TOPIC. THE BAR CHART REPRESENTS ONLY THE MOST FREQUENT THEMES.

FREQUENCY OF TWENTIETH CENTURY TOPICS

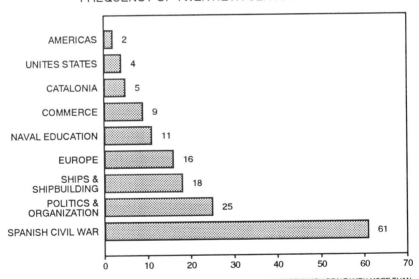

THE TOTAL NUMBER OF PUBLICATIONS IS 128, MANY OF WHICH DEALT WITH MORE THAN ONE TOPIC. THE BAR CHART REPRESENTS ONLY THE MOST FREQUENT THEMES.

several decades of fairly stable government, though elections were largely irrelevant to the process. Through largely bloodless military coups, the right and left wings of the constitutionalists succeeded one another as advisers to Queen Isabel II.

Naval reform began in earnest in 1847–51, with the administration of the Marqués de Molina. His plans were aided by the quickening pace of the Spanish economy, which was increasing in population and agricultural output, as well as gradually industrializing. Encouraged by this growth and by the recovery of the navy, the Spanish government engaged in several naval expeditions around the globe in the 1850s and 1860s. Spanish fleets traveled to Morocco and to Cochin China (Vietnam), they engaged in a brief unsuccessful naval war against three South American republics, and they embarked on a joint expedition with the French to Mexico in the early 1860s, while the United States was embroiled in Civil War. Scholars have examined these activities in print, even though nineteenth-century events pale in comparison with Spanish global voyaging in previous centuries.

A dozen publications about the nineteenth century dealt with naval architecture, centered around the shift from the age of sail to the age of steam. From the first steamship in 1817 through the rest of the century, designers worked with new materials and new specifications, as the naval administration tried to remedy a shortage of engineers and machinists needed to crew the new ships. Chronic governmental disarray during the late nineteenth century hindered the work of naval reformers and architects, however. Isabel II had been forced into exile in 1868 by a military conspiracy, and for the next several years a succession of monarchist and republican governments attempted unsuccessfully to consolidate their rule. The period of experimentation ended in 1875 with the restoration of the Bourbons in the person of Alfonso XII, Isabel's eldest son.

Although several capable ministers formulated plans for a large-scale program of naval construction in the 1870s and 1880s, political in-fighting within the government nullified their efforts. A plan proposed in 1887 had better success, although its original aims had to be scaled back to match the financial and political realities of the times. In the last decade of the nineteenth century, increasing strife caused by clashes between government forces and increasingly militant labor organizations created a high degree of tension within the Spanish state. In that atmosphere, a major naval construction program was simply not feasible, although some ships were built for both the Navy and for the merchant marine. The merchant fleet was owned by several large private companies, including the Transatlantic Company founded in 1850. Together these companies played a major role in maintaining commercial ties between Spain and the remnants of its overseas empire in the nineteenth century. The centenary of the Transatlantic Company in 1950 resulted in several articles analyzing its organization, successes, and failures over the long term.

Spain managed to hold on to Cuba and Puerto Rico with great effort during the early decades of the nineteenth century and also retain the Philippines. In 1898 those colonies rebelled, providing a pretext for the United States to intervene. The ensuing Spanish-American War found the Spanish Navy unprepared. Major defeats at Santiago Bay in Cuba and Cavite in the Philippines led to Spain's being stripped of its remaining colonies. Publications about Cuba, Puerto Rico, and the Philippines in the nineteenth century focus on that war, its antecedents, its battles, and its aftermath. The war itself generated thirty-nine publications in my survey, most of them analyzing the reasons for Spain's defeat.

The national anguish at Spain's final loss of empire in 1898 spawned a generation of novelists, poets, and essayists who explored the national psyche in a passionate outpouring of self-criticism and a quest for renewal. This so-called "Generation of '98" had its governmental counterparts, as well, in civil servants and in the person of King Alfonso XIII. During the first decade of the new century the Navy languished, widely blamed for the defeat of 1898. Spurred by the need to supervise an unstable situation in Morocco, however, and by the increasing sophistication of Europe's premier navies in England and Germany, the Spanish government adopted a far-reaching plan of naval reform in 1908. Enthusiastically supported by Alfonso XIII, naval reform made considerable progress, especially as Spain arrived at a modern level of industrialization and managed to stay out of World War I.

During the nineteenth century, Army officers had often intervened in politics, protraying themselves as the guarantors of the liberal constitutional monarchy. Bloodless takeovers by one faction of the Army or another had shifted the emphasis of the government on a half dozen or more occasions. Against the rising tide of left-wing demands for worker representation in the late nineteenth century, the Army seemed to see itself as the preserver of stability against the fractious divisions of civilian politicians. The Navy largely absented itself from these confrontations, concentrating on its own priorities.

The Spanish armed services as a whole underwent significant professionalization in the late nineteenth and early twentieth centuries, and the Army in particular became more conservative. When the Army intervened once again in politics in 1922, General Miguel Primo de Rivera took power for himself, with the acquiescence of King Alfonso XIII, rather than working through civilian politicians. He used his dictatorial powers to bolster the economy and to coerce the political left and right into cooperating with his national program, modeled on the corporate fascism of Mussolini's Italy.

The Navy concentrated on rebuilding its strength and modernizing the structure and training of its officers, following the initiative launched in 1908, with an additional program of naval construction in 1915. The Navy recovered much of its prestige in military culture, attracting a higher class of officers and staying apart from political concerns. Publications about the early twentieth century focus on naval education, naval architecture, shipbuilding, and the merchant marine. Very few publications even allude to the Army's takeover of the government under Primo de Rivera.

The king withdrew his support from Primo in 1930, but Primo's dictatorship had discredited the monarchy and civilian politicians as well as the Army. In 1931 municipal elections favored republican candidates so strongly that Alfonso XIII abandoned the field and went into exile. Civilian politicians, largely on the left of the political spectrum, organized the Second Republic, wrote a new constitution, and tried to consolidate a stable government. Instead, they managed to alienate a broad range of opinion from center to right, as well as irritating the left by cautious approaches to social and economic reform. The republic descended into chaos as rebellions of the left and of the right brought down a succession of governments between 1932 and 1936.

Street violence by both extremes of the political spectrum inspired factions of the Army to launch a major coup in July of 1936. Rather than submit, the elected Republican government determined to fight back, arming civilian militias. The Civil War that ensued in 1936–39 would convulse Spain and engage the rest of Europe in an ongoing debate about the merits of intervention. Hitler's Germany and Mussolini's Italy openly aided the Army's rebellion. The Soviet Union and Mexico openly aided the Republic. Everyone else watched as Spain tore itself apart.

The Spanish naval high command generally backed the Army's insurgency, though many ordinary sailors tried to rally to the Republic's defense. Sailors at the southeastern naval base in Cartagena mutinied, murdered many officers, and commandeered dozens of ships, which became the navy of the Republic. They then steamed for the Strait of Gibraltar to prevent the Army's insurgents from ferrying troops from Morocco. The uprising would have failed before it began, had it not been for the airborne support of Germany and Italy. Naval matters in the Spanish Civil War emerge in the historiography as the most compelling topics among all twentieth-century themes. Whether authors deal with individual ships and their commanders, with actions at sea, or with other themes, the Civil War accounts for nearly half of the one hundred twenty-eight publications about the twentieth century.

From this brief survey it is clear that Spanish naval and maritime history has followed the agenda established by Spanish history in general, rather than defining a set of topics from within. Some of the topical distribution of publications is predictable and logical. Exploration and matters related to Spain's overseas empire loom large in publications about the several centuries wherein the empire flourished; then they fade precipitously. Other topics, despite their continuing importance and a wealth of documentation, ebb and flow as appendages to other concerns. For example, the history of ship design is only sporadically considered in the published literature, surfacing in periods or around events that are judged important for other reasons. Sixteenth century ship design is fairly well known because the sixteenth century defined the peak of Spanish power in Europe and abroad. Seventeenth century ship design has been neglected because Spain's loss of hegemony has attracted less attention.

Although I have not examined naval and maritime historiography systematically for other countries, I suspect that the pattern I have found for Spain is typical. To a certain extent, naval and maritime themes cannot and should not be considered separately from their broader historical contexts. The history of the sea, broadly conceived, is of necessity also the history of the land and can best be understood as part of a larger whole. Yet naval and maritime history also needs to have definitions of its own and priorities for research independent of general history. How can we establish valid comparisons among nations if the published work about a given period is abundant for the dominant country and sparse for the rest? Without such comparisons, it is difficult to see how naval and maritime history can progress beyond the narrow and often nationalistic concerns that have defined it in the past.

29

Sweden

Jan Glete

By strong tradition, Swedish naval and maritime history is divided into what the two words imply: the history of the Swedish Navy and the history of the Swedish maritime community: maritime trade, seafaring, shipowning, shipbuilding, and fishing. This tradition is to a considerable extent based on the realities of naval and maritime history itself. The Swedish Navy has had, over the centuries, fewer connections with general maritime life than many other navies. The Navy has been closely associated with the expansion, defence, and decline of Sweden's Baltic empire and, in the nineteenth and twentieth centuries, with Swedish anti-invasion planning and coastal defence. Trade warfare has been of less importance and the connections between naval seamen and mercantile sailors weaker than in most navies.

The bulk of our present stock of written Swedish naval history was published from the late nineteenth century up to the 1940s. The last major work of this type was a five-volume study of the Navy's central administration, written partly by academic historians and published between 1950 and 1983. Most of it was produced by sea officers or others connected with the Navy. Few of these works were official history, but much of the research was sponsored by the Navy. To their credit, some of these naval historians, even in the late nineteenth century, put great emphasis on naval administration, personnel and finance, rather than concentrating on naval operations, as most naval historians in other countries did in this period. There was no strong "Mahanian" or "blue water" school in Swedish naval historiography. Most authors stressed the interdependence between naval and land warfare in the Baltic area rather than the independent importance of sea power. There was, however, a certain bias in favor of the battle fleet compared to the archipelago fleet. This had much to do with the intense nineteenth century political debate about Swedish naval doctrine: a navy for the open sea or only for the archipelagoes? The debate about the role of the Navy in twentieth century strategic planning also influenced the naval historians. As long as most sea officers wished to have ships with heavy guns and armor, naval historians often tried to derive lessons from the past which showed the importance of big ships with heavy guns.

These studies are still useful, but, as they are fifty to one hundred years old, inevitably much of the research is now dated. Today, the descendants of Navy-sponsored historical research are found in the activities of the Military History Department at the Swedish Staff and War College of the Armed Forces (Militärhögskolan or MHS) in Stockholm. In recent decades, the naval side of this activity has been very limited and concentrated on the twentieth century. The school also favors integrated studies which cover the armed forces as a whole, and much twentieth century Swedish naval history is to be found in studies of defense policy as a whole. The possibly last major research project about older history sponsored by MHS is a multi-volume work about Sweden's wars in the Baltic area from 1655 to 1660. It is perhaps typical of the present lack of interest in Sweden in writing operational naval history that the volume about sea warfare in this period was entrusted to a Danish historian, Finn Askgaard.[1]

Historical research about the armed forces is also to some extent government-sponsored through the Delegation for Military Historical Research (Delegationen för militärhistorisk forskning). This organization gives at least partial financial support to several research projects; it supports conferences and it distributes grants for the printing of books. However, it has no coordinating responsibility for military and naval history.

Academic interest in naval history has been limited, although rather more has been written about defense policy and wars, where the Navy is treated usually as a junior partner to the Swedish Army. A pioneering study in its day was the doctoral dissertation of Oscar Nikula in 1933.[2] The author, a Swedish-speaking Finnish historian, wrote about the large Swedish eighteenth century archipelago fleet. More recent studies are about the Navy during the Second World War by Åke Holmquist,[3] the debate about future coast defence armoured ships before World War I by Anders Sandström,[4] and the interplay between politicians and sea officers as experts in the debate about the structure of the Navy from 1918 to 1939 by Anders Berge.[5] Within a project about military professionalization, the present author has undertaken a study of the change of Swedish naval doctrine during the nineteenth century,[6] while Lars Niléhn[7] wrote about the early development of the Swedish Naval Staff College.

[1]   Finn Askgaard, *Kampen om östersjön på Carl X Gustafs tld: Ett bidrag till nordisk sjökrighistoria* (Stockholm: Militärhistoriska förlaget, 1974).

[2]   Oscar Nikula, *Svenska skärgårdsflottan 1756–1791* (Helsingfors: Samfundet Ehrensvärd Seura, 1933).

[3]   Åke Holmquist, *Flottans beredskap 1938–1940* (Stockholm: Allmänna Förlaget, 1972).

[4]   Anders Sandström, *Pansarfartyg åt Sveriges flotta: En studie om flottan och striden om F-båten 1906–1909*, (Stockholm: Sjöhistoriska museet, 1984).

[5]   Anders Berge, *Sakkunskap och politisk rationalitet: Den svenska flottan och pansarfartygsfrågan 1918–1939* (Stockholm: Almqvist & Wiksell International, 1987).

[6]   Jan Glete, *Kustförsvar och teknisk omvandling: Teknik, doktriner och organisation inom svenskt kustförsvar 1850–1880* (Stockholm: Militärhistoriska Förlaget, 1985).

[7]   Lars Niléhn, *Vägen till erkännande: Militär professionalisering och tillkomsten av en svensk sjökrigshögskola* (Stockholm: Militärhistoriska Förlaget, 1986).

Older periods of naval history are still being investigated, although with limited resources. The present author has made a study of Swedish sixteenth century warships and their connections to naval policy and the developing technology.[8] Nils-Åke Villstrand, a Finnish historian, has made a minor, but important, study of the Navy's recruitment of sailors during the seventeenth century.[9] I have also written the naval chapter in a recent study of the Swedish-Russian war of 1788–1790, one of the few studies about older history recently undertaken by the Military History Department.[10] Furthermore, the Karlskronavarvet Company, formerly the main naval dockyard, is sponsoring a two–volume study about its history from 1680 to the present day (1993). This work is being undertaken by several historians and it concentrates on the relations between the yard and the maintenance of the Navy.[11]

The author of this essay has also published his research in international naval history. The intent is to analyze naval shipbuilding and its long-term development as part of the state-building process from the sixteenth to the nineteenth century; it was published in a two-volume work in 1993.[12]

Except for some very elementary education given to future sea officers, naval history is not taught in Sweden. Officers taking courses at MHS, the Staff College, may study naval history as a special subject and prepare papers on historical subjects, but there are no regular courses. No university teaches naval history as a special subject.

The interest among sea officers about naval history is not dead, and the history of naval technology provokes public interest. In recent years a naval engineer, Curt Borgenstam, has edited, together with several co-authors, illustrated books about Swedish twentieth century warships.[13] Captain Bertil Åhlund has published two studies about Swedish naval policy from the late nineteenth century to the Second World War.[14] Part of this research has been sponsored by the Royal Swedish Academy of Naval Science (Kungliga Örlogsmannasällskapet),

---

8 Jan Glete, "Svenska örlogsfartyg 1521-1560: Flottans upbyggnad under ett tekniskt brytningsskede," *Forum Navale*, 30 (1976), pp. 5–74; 31 (1977), pp. 23–119.

9 Nils-Erik Villstrand, "Manskap och sjöfolk inom den svenska örlogsflottan 1617–1644," *Historisk Tidskrift för Finland*, 1 (1986).

10 Jan Glete, "Kriget till sjöss 1788–1790," in Gunnar Artéus, ed., *Gustav III:s ryska krig* (Stockholm: Probus, 1992).

11 Erik Norberg, ed., *Karlskronavarvts historia*, 2 vols. (Karlskrona: Karlskronavarvet AB, 1993).

12 Jan Glete, *Navies and Nations: Warships, Navies and State Building in Europe and America, 1500–1860*, 2 vols. (Stockholm: Almqvist & Wiksell International, 1993).

13 Curt Borgenstam & Bo Nyman, *Motortorpedbåt: En Krönika i ord och bild om "Havets flygande brigad,"* (Mjölby: BM-förlaget, 1981), Curt Borgenstam & Bo Nyman, *Attack till sjöss: Med svenska flottans torpedbåtar i 100 år* (Karlskrona: CB Marinlitteratur, 1985), Curt Borgenstam et al., *Jagare: Med svenska flottans jagare under 60 år* (Västra Frölunda: CB Marinlitteratur, 1989).

14 Bertil Åhlund, *Från vanmakt till sjömakt: Oscariansk sjöförsvarspolitik 1872–1905* (Karlskrona: Kungliga örlogsmannasällskapet, 1989), Bertil Åhlund, *Svensk maritim säkerhetspolitik 1905–1939* (Karlskrona: Marinlitteraturföreningen, 1992).

an organization of sea officers founded in 1771, which recently has tried to raise interest in the naval aspects of the history of the Baltic area. The sweeping political changes in this area from 1989 onward has, to some extent, increased the public interest in Baltic history.

Maritime history, as such, is hardly a coherent tradition in Sweden. There is considerable study of economic history with maritime connections: maritime trade, the development of the mercantile marine and shipbuilding. Among recent works, one may mention Steffan Högberg's study of the eighteenth century Swedish maritime trade,[15] the same author's biography of the twentieth century shipowner Axel Ax:son Johnson (1990)[16] and Åke Sandström's study of Stockholm's maritime trade during the first half of the seventeenth century.[17] Swedish–Dutch maritime trade in the eighteenth century has been treated with econometric methods by J. Thomas Lindblad, a Swedish historian working in the Netherlands.[18] Nineteenth century Swedish shipbuilding has been studied from an economic perspective by Sven A. Björkenstam.[19]

The late nineteenth and twentieth century Swedish shipbuilding industry, its companies, economic conditions, subcontractors and trade unions, has been the subject of several studies. Jan Kuuse, Kent Olsson, Bo Stråth and Tommy Svensson, and Jan Bohlin have given a comprehensive survey of this industry, which from its heyday up to the 1970s, was one of the largest producers of mercantile shipping in the world.[20] These studies put a strong emphasis on the labor market conditions in the industry. Bo Stråth has also undertaken a comparative study of the decline of the European shipbuilding industry in recent decades.[21]

Apart from studies written by academic historians, Sweden also has a fair amount of writers producing popular books about ships and shipping, especially

---

[15] Staffen Höberg, *Utrikeshandel och sjöfart på 1700-talet: Stapelvaror i svensk export och import 1738–1808* (Stockholm: Bonniers, 1969).

[16] Staffan Höberg, *Generalkonsuln: Axel Ax:son Johnson som företagare* (Stockholm: Norstedts, 1990).

[17] Åke Sandström, *Mellan Torneå och Amsterdam: En undersökning av Stockholms roll som förmedlare av varor i regional - och utrikeshandel 1600–1650.* Stockholmsmonografier, vol. 102 (Stockholm: Stockholms Universitet, 1990).

[18] J. Thomas Lindblad, *Sweden's Trade with the Dutch Republic, 1738–1795* (Assen: 1982).

[19] Sven A. Björkenstam, *Svenskt skeppsbyggeri under 1800–talet: Marknad och produktion* (Göteborg: Ekonomisk-historiska institutionen vid Göteborgs universitet, 1989).

[20] Kent Olsson, *Från pansarbåtsvarv till tankfartygsvarv: De svenska storvarvens utveckling till exportindustri 1880-1936,* (Göteborg: Svenska Varv AB, 1983); Thommy Svensson, *Från ackord till månadslön: En studie av lönepolitiken, fackföreningarna och rationaliseringarna inom svensk varvsindustri under 1900-talet* (Göteborg: Svenska Varv AB, 1983); Bo Stråth, *Varvsarbetare i TVÅ varvsstäder: En historisk studie av verkstadsklubbarna vid varven i Göteborg och Malmö* (Göteborg: Svenska Varv AB, 1983); Jan Kuuse, *Varven och underleverantörerna: Förändringar i fartygsbyggandets industriella länkeffekter* (Kungälv: Svenska Varv AB, 1983); Jan Bohlin, *Svensk varvsindustri 1920–1975: Lönsamhet, finansiering och arbetsmarknad* (Göteborg, Ekonomisk-historiska institutionen vid Göteborgs universitet, 1989).

[21] Bo Stråth, *The Politics of Deindustrialisation: The Contraction of the west European Shipbuilding Industry* (London: Croom Helm, 1987).

sailing merchantmen and early steamers. Several such studies have the character of local history, covering a certain area of the long Swedish coast. There are few monographs about Swedish shipping companies, but, the one hundred-year jubilee of the Johnson shipping group in 1990[22] produced two books of this character, one about the ships and one about the company.

Maritime history as a special subject is not taught at Swedish universities or other institutions. This is not to be taken as a total lack of interest in maritime questions, but "maritime" is not identified as a coherent historical subject. It is rather divided into various economic and social subjects which have asserted a stronger position in the Swedish academic world.

History is, however, not the only academic discipline involved in the study of the naval and maritime past. In Scandinavia, archaeology and ethnology have strong traditions in these spheres of interest and, through the museums, primarily the Swedish National Maritime Museum (Statens Sjöhistorika Muséer), Stockholm, these disciplines have a considerable institutional base. In 1956, underwater archaeology was much stimulated by the discovery of the *Wasa* (1628). Through its salvage and restoration, Swedish archaeologists developed considerable skill in this special field. Since the 1980s, the Sjöhistoriska Muséer has cooperated with the Department of Archaeology at Stockholm University in a research and education program in nautical archaeology. This program, which includes education up to the Ph.D. level, is led by Carl Olof Cederlund, who wrote his dissertation[23] about carvel-built wrecks known to exist in the Baltic Sea. Two other major archaeological studies—based on interpretations rather than excavations are those of Sibylla Haasum and Björn Varenius.[24] Both concentrate upon the Viking period, about 1,000 years ago.

The raising and excavation of *Wasa* offered a unique opportunity to study the sculptural ornamentation of a large seventeenth century warship. Hans Soop took advantage of this opportunity and wrote a major study of these sculptures as his dissertation in the History of Arts.[25] Björn Landström, the internationally well-known maritime artist has given his analysis of the design and construction of *Wasa* in a book with his usual high-quality illustrations.[26]

Maritime ethnology is an important subject in all of Scandinavia, covering both the near past of maritime history and long traditions in ship– and boat-

---

[22] Sören Larsson & Jaak Saving, *Nordstjernan: The Inside Story, 1890–1990* (Stockholm: Norstedts, 1990), Torsten Rinman, *The Johnson Line, 1890–1990* (Goteborg: Rinman & Lindén, 1990).

[23] Carl-Olof Cederlund, *The Old Wrecks of the Baltic Sea: Archaeological recording of the wrecks of carvel-built ships*. BAR Internaitonal Series, no 186 (Oxford, 1983).

[24] Sibylla Haasum, *Vikingatidens segling och navigation* (Stockholm: Theses and papers in North European Archaeology, 1974), Björn Varenius, *Det nordiska skeppet: Teknologi och samhällsstrategi i vikingatid och medeltid* Stockholm Studies in Archaeology, 10 (Stockholm: Stockholm Universitet, 1992).

[25] Hans Soop, *The Power and the Glory: The Sculptures of the Warship Wasa* (Stockholm: Almqvist & Wiksell International, 1986).

[26] Björn Landström, *The Royal Warship Wasa* (Stockholm: Interpublishing, 1988).

building. Olof Hasslöf, an internationally known Swedish ethnologist, did much to develop this tradition. In recent years, doctoral dissertations and other major studies, covering a wide range of subjects, have been produced: deep sea sailors (Knut Weibust, 1969), a coastal area in change 1800–1970 (Orvar Löfgren, 1977), fishing (Lars Skotte, 1981), nineteenth century countryside shipowners (Kerstin G:son Berg, 1984), harbor workers in Gothenburg and a shipyard.[27] The Sjöhistoriska Museet has a department for ethnological studies, and research reports are published regularly. In spite of this considerable research activity, maritime ethnology is nowhere taught as a special subject and the theories and methods used are the same as in ethnology in general.

As we have seen, with the exception of archaeology and a limited amount of staff college teaching, there is no regular teaching of naval and maritime history in Sweden. Maritime history is a part of history, economic history, ethnology, and archaeology, and methods and theories common to these academic disciplines are used. Naval history is part of political history, archaeology, and (to a very limited extent) the training of officers. Books about naval and maritime history are read in courses of more general subjects, such as trade and defence policy. Scholars with naval and maritime interests are conducting research into their subjects with the expectation that they will be evaluated in comparison with studies of entirely different subjects.

The result is that such studies often are well connected with Swedish history in general. The intellectual trends are the same as in the historical disciplines in general. On the other hand the naval and maritime studies are little connected with each other or with international debate in the same field. Naval history is not used in debates about defence policy, nor is it possible today to detect any systematic bias due to contemporary debate in naval historiography. Although ideology and political issues have for a long time been more or less dead in this field of research, an exception is developing: in the 1980s and early 1990s several incidents, or supposed incidents, where foreign submarines were reported in Swedish territorial waters, became major foreign policy problems and are now evolving into a controversial, historical debate.

There is no organization that holds responsibility for coordinating naval and maritime history on an academic level. The Statens Sjöhistoriska muséer has considerable activity in ethnology and archaeology—in the latter subject in cooperation with Stockholm University—but it undertakes no comparable research activity in history. This museum also has the largest collections of books

---

[27] Knut Weibust, *Deep Sea Sailors: A Study in Maritime Ethnology* (Stockholm: Nordiska museet, 1969), Orvar Löfgren, *Fångstmän i industrisamhället: en halländsk kustbygds omvandling 1800–1970* (Lund: Liber, 1977), Lars Skotte, *Slutfiskat* (Stockholm: Akademilitteratur, 1981), Kerstin G:son Berg, *Redare i Roslagen: Segelfartygsrederier och deras verksamhet i gamla Vätö socken* (Stockholm: Nordiska museet, 1984), Anders Björklund, *Hamens arbetare: En etnologisk undersökning av stuveriarbetet i Göteborg* (Stockholm: Nordiska museet, 1984), Magnus Wikdahl, *Varvets tid: Arbetarliv och kulturell förändring i en skeppsbyggarstad* (Stockholm: Gidlund, 1992).

and journals in naval and maritime history, and it has published bibliographies covering Swedish literature. The lack of coordination may have drawbacks, but from a qualitative point of view, it is an advantage that historians interested in naval and maritime subjects regard themselves primarily as historians and avoid isolation into a special group. There is no Swedish journal of maritime history. The yearbooks of the naval and maritime museums in Stockholm, Karlskrona, and Gothenburg publish historical articles as does *Forum Navale*, the yearly publication of The Society for Sea History (Sjöhistoriska Samfundet). The latter was founded in 1939 and, over the years, has published several important papers in naval and maritime history, but it has no resources for undertaking research of its own.

Finally, which periods and subjects are well covered and which require further research? Sweden has a long naval and maritime tradition with vast archival sources and a large amount of surviving artifacts above and under water. The rather small population makes it difficult to cover all these potential fields of research. In naval history, the old historiography remains as a foundation covering all periods and aspects, but most of this research is ripe for reinterpretations and expansion. Recruitment and training of sailors, the development of the corps of sea officers, the social conditions in the Navy, the connections between policy and administration and naval technology are especially tempting fields for more research for *all* periods. The same applies to the economic history of the Navy: finance, the supply of timber, iron, sails and hemp, the dockyard activities. Operational history up to about 1650, the period of Swedish expansion in the Baltic, has also been neglected. This was an era of many naval operations—blockades, amphibious operations, logistic support of the army—but few battles, and it attracted little attention from traditional naval historiography, which puts its emphasis on battle fleet operations.

The state of Swedish maritime history displays a more scattered picture. Shipping and maritime trade have been most extensively treated for the eighteenth century, while other periods are rather neglected compared to other fields of economic history. The modern Swedish shipbuilding industry is well covered, while shipbuilding as an economic phenomenon before the late nineteenth century is much neglected. Social conditions for Swedish seamen before the period studied by ethnologists are almost forgotten, especially compared to the considerable interest shown to workers in the shipbuilding industry and to harbor workers.

Swedish naval and maritime history is not neglected compared to other fields of Swedish history, but naval history has, from an academic point of view, been a small part of a field of research where the Army has dominated. Most of the literature about warfare and the armed forces are dominated by the studies on the Swedish Army, which was so important during the period 1560–1721. The technical questions are often important in naval history, but such questions have seldom been tempting fields of research for academic historians. This may be a further reason for a comparative neglect of naval history. Maritime history is, like most modern economic and social history dominated by quantifications—a fully justified emphasis considering that Sweden generally has a good supply of quantitative sources. The drawback from a maritime point of view is that historians seldom attempt to put maritime life in the centre of research. For more recent periods, ethnological research fills this gap, but older periods are simply neglected. Looking upon the problem from a more positive view, we may conclude that naval and maritime history belongs to the underexplored and promising fields of future research for Swedish historians.

30

Chinese Maritime History in Taiwan

Vice Admiral Liu Ta-tsai, ROCN, Retired
and
Wang Chia-chien[1]

China is a country with an exceptional history and ancient origins. The Yellow River area was its birthplace. It was over five thousand years ago that the Chinese people established civilization—one based primarily on agriculture. The Loess plateau region symbolizes this traditional and ancient Chinese culture.

For thousands of years, Chinese culture valued agriculture more than commerce. As an agricultural society, it was inclined to be conservative and isolationist; the Chinese people are accustomed to staying where they are and have a strong affinity for the land. Thus, the development of Chinese culture has been land-oriented, nearly to the exclusion of seafaring development.

Just the same, China is located on the western shore of the Pacific Ocean; it has a vast territory, abundant resources, a warm climate and a long and winding coastline. Thus, it commands a superior position for development of sea power. History also shows that there has been a relationship between the Chinese people and the ocean, albeit limited, for more than three thousand years.

Even in medieval times, China was renowned for its shipbuilding and navigation techniques, which were actually far more advanced than Western countries for that period. During that time, China's maritime trade expanded significantly, and relations with foreign countries were very close. However, after seven naval expeditions by Zheng He in the fifteenth century, China's maritime activities were suspended. Why China did not become a maritime super power continues to puzzle Western historians of maritime affairs.[2]

Given China's extensive history, many maritime activities of the ancient Chinese people have been recorded. Modern Chinese history reflects the fact

---

[1] Vice Admiral Liu Ta-tsai is currently Senior Research Fellow at the Society for Strategic Studies, Taipei; Professor Wang Chia-chien is with the Department of History at the National Taiwan Normal University.

The editor is grateful to Professor Arthur Waldron for his assistance with some of the footnotes to this essay.

[2] Geoffrey Till, *Maritime Strategy and the Nuclear Age* (New York: St. Martin's Press, 1982), p. 4.

that China's maritime development is closely tied to the rise and decline of the various dynasties that have ruled the country.

The records of Chinese maritime history support study in a variety of topics, such as the development of shipbuilding and nautical technology, ocean transportation, maritime trade, maritime expeditions, and overseas emigration and exploitation, to name a few. Hence, there is a broad base of Chinese maritime history for scholars to explore. Chinese historians, including scholars from both sides of the Taiwan Straits, have undertaken detailed research, and fruitful results have already been obtained.

The television program, "River Elegy," shown in mainland China in 1988, had a great impact on the minds of Chinese people, both at home and abroad. This program provided them an opportunity to ponder and explore the history created by the Chinese continental and maritime culture. The broadcast literally caused a sensation throughout the Chinese mainland. When the book was finally published in Taiwan, it was the best selling book there for nearly a year.[3]

River Elegy was written by a group of scholars in mainland China, and describes their meditations over the maritime history of China. Their motive was to arouse the maritime consciousness of the Chinese society, while calling for the Chinese people to face and march toward the vast, blue ocean.

China's Maritime Civilization

As noted earlier, China is not only a continental nation, but it is also bound to the sea. Early in the "Emperor Huang Di" period, the maritime industry of building wooden boats had already evolved in China. In the "Spring and Autumn" and the "Warring State" periods (771–221 B.C.), feudal states along the coast of the continent were constantly bickering or making war upon each other, employing their individual boat forces to do so. However, influenced by the vastness of the land, and feudal tendencies of kings with their wild ambition for annexing territory, the focus of interest remained continental.[4]

Over the last several thousand years, foreign aggression toward China often came overland, from the north. The Great Wall, one of the great architectural feats in world history, was originally designed and built to protect against these northern invaders. It is correct to say that the Great Wall symbolizes ancient China's powerful and prosperous strength. However, the perception of China as a landlocked culture is reinforced by the Wall and has emphasized

---

[3]   Su Hsiao-k'ang and Wang Lu-hsiang, *He shang* (Taipei: Feng-yün, Shih-tai, Chin-feng ch'u-pan gong-ssu lien-he ch'u-pan, 1988). Su-Hsiao-k'ang and Wang Lu-hsiang, *Deathsong of the River: A Reader's Guide to the Chinese TV series Heshang*. Introduced and annotated by Richard W. Bodman and Pin P. Wan (Ithaca, N.Y.: East Asia Program, Cornell University, 1991).

[4]   Ts'ao Pao-chien and Kuo Fu-wen, *Meditation in Face of the Pacific Ocean—A Revived Perception of the Ocean and National Defense* (Beijing: Defense Univ. Press, 1989), p. 133.

the evolution of Chinese history, to a great degree, on purely continental issues. This has seriously undermined the understanding of China's maritime culture.[5]

Nevertheless, ancient China's technique in shipbuilding and navigation were extremely advanced. British scholar Joseph Needham produced a comparative research of the nautical technology of ancient China and the West. In this book, he stated, "As far as many ship building and navigation theories are concerned, the West fell behind China by several centuries. With regard to operation of a rudder, the West lagged behind China by four centuries and to the utilization of the compass by about one century."[6]

Early on, before the Han Dynasty (202 B.C.–A.D. 220), China had built a "Silk Road" at sea, which brought economic prosperity to ancient china and propagated the advanced Chinese culture to the West.[7]

According to historical documentation, there were three great inventions in China: paper, powder, and the compass. They provided a superiority in shipbuilding and navigation to the ancient Chinese navies. In the Yuan Dynasty (1279–1367), several expeditions to Southeast Asia, Java, and Japan were recorded. Although these expeditions ultimately failed, they did prove the superior technology of the Chinese Navy.

In the Ming Dynasty (1368–1644), China's greatest navigator, Zheng He, conducted seven expeditions to the Indian Ocean. They were the most brilliant achievements in the maritime history of China. However, after Zheng died, the Ming government imposed restrictions on maritime navigation. Thereafter, China's leadership in the world of maritime affairs suffered a disastrous decline.[8]

China's Maritime History

As previously noted, nautical technology in ancient China was well developed, allowing China to become one of the earliest ancient countries possessing a naval force. The "Silk Road," predating the Han Dynasty, has already been mentioned. Following the Tang Dynasty (618–907), the Silk Road on land was closed by wars. It was at that time that the maritime Silk Road entered its golden age. With the Sung (960–1279) and Yuan (1279–1386) Dynasties, China's maritime transportation entered its most prosperous period. Maritime trade became the country's major financial source. During this period, Chinese ships nearly monopolized the entire sea lane from China to the Indian Ocean. In addition to trade, China's ships greatly stimulated the communication, development, and integration of the ancient Chinese, Indian, and Arab civilizations, as well as other Western and Pacific cultures.[9]

---

5   Ibid., p. 164.

6   Joseph Needham, Science and Civilisation in China, Vol. 4: "Nautical Technology," p. 484.

7   Ts'ao Pau-chien and Kuo Fu-wen, Mediation, p. 132.

8   Chang Wei and Hsü Hua, The Rise and Fall of Sea Power (Beijing: Ocean Publishing Co., 1991), pp. 40–2.

9   Ts'ao Pao-chien and Kuo Fu-wen, Mediation, pp. 136–7.

China's navigation was at its zenith in the early Ming Dynasty. Seven expeditions and goodwill missions, led by Zheng He, to the countries along the South China Sea and the Indian Ocean preceded the grand discovery of world geography during the fifteenth and sixteenth centuries.

For twenty-eight years, from 1405 to 1433, Zheng He led a goodwill fleet southward from the Pacific Ocean to the Indian Ocean, the Red Sea, and to the farthest eastern African coast. Such an accomplishment was unprecedented. Zheng He's navigation feat preceded Christopher Columbus's discovery of the New World by 87 years, Vasco Da Gama's transit past the Cape of Good Hope to India by 92 years, and antedated Ferdinand Magellan's circumnavigation of the world by 114 years. He surely deserved recognition for such a great geographical discovery. The impact on the politics, economy and culture of the countries along the South China Sea and the Indian Ocean of Zheng He's missions has been clearly recorded in the histories of those regions. It was a prelude to the most glorious achievement in China's maritime history.[10]

Since Zheng He's expedition imposed a tremendous financial burden on the government, it came to be considered a flawed policy. The government of the Ming Dynasty, therefore, returned the policy of isolationism and ordered that construction of big ships be stopped. Even the files of Zheng He's expedition were burned. Large-scale overseas navigation in China ceased.

Throughout the Qing Dynasty (1644–1912), pirates pillaged Chinese coastal provinces. Resistance to the Qing Dynasty remained strong in southeastern China along the coast. The Qing Dynasty, therefore, also adopted policies prohibiting navigation and other activities of maritime trade in order to isolate China from the outside world.[11] Only after the European Industrial Revolution did the influence of the West become overwhelming, forcing China to end this policy.

In every conflict with the Western powers (the Opium War, the Sino–French War, the Sino–Japanese War, and the seizure of Beijing by the joint forces of the eight Western powers) China met defeat. The effect of this series of defeats was that China became a miserable, semi-colony of the Western powers. This loss of Chinese sovereignty and dignity was a direct result of its lack of sea power.

Modern Maritime China

After World War II China was split into two political entities. In 1949 the government of the Republic of China (ROC) moved to Taiwan, and mainland

---

[10] Chang Wei and Hsü Hua, *Sea*, p. 41.

[11] A British Army major, George Henry Mason, travelled to China at the end of the eighteenth century. Out of curiosity, he recorded what China looked like to him. To depict vividly the Chinese acrobatics and dramatic costumes, he hired a Chinese painter. Additionally, Major Mason also adopted the works of a British painter, William Alexander, who had travelled along the Grand Canal from north to south; George Henry Mason and William Alexander, *Views of 18th Century China* (1804 and 1805; reprint New York: Portland House, 1988). In the eyes of those British who saw the illustrations and had no idea of this oriental country, China was a mysterious, but rather civilized country. The book has recently been translated into Chinese.

China fell into the hands of the Chinese communists. The two sides adopted and practiced two completely different maritime strategies.

Taiwan, surrounded by the sea, adopted an island-oriented economic system. Its economic development and national framework are closely related to its maritime environment. Taiwan's economic miracle is a maritime-oriented model which has enabled Taiwan to transform from a backward, agricultural society to a newly developed, industrial nation.

Throughout Chinese history, Taiwan's people have been a maritime society, using the surrounding oceans to make their fortunes and accomplish great achievements. Now, Taiwan serves as the example for mainland China to follow as that country develops for the future.

The Chinese mainland, under the cloak of socialism, largely ignored the ocean, becoming an introverted and isolated society in the process. Fortunately, at the beginning of the 1980s, mainland China adopted a more open policy, developing a coastal economy and working on reforms. It moved toward a market economy and even publicly expressed the slogan: "learn economic experience from Taiwan." After more than a decade of efforts, mainland China's economic reform has made substantial progress.

Currently, a trilateral "Greater Chinese Economic Ring" is taking shape. This is a great cooperative effort of Chinese people, both in the homeland and abroad. At the same time, mainland China's economic reform has accelerated. Its sea power development and naval expansion has earned the serious concern of other countries worldwide. In particular, neighboring countries in Asia and the Pacific worry that mainland China will soon become a great maritime power.

During the current period of growth and change, many observers hope that a democratic and open China, possessing a market economy and maritime strengths, will be a strong and rich country contributing to the stability and prosperity of the region in the twenty-first century.

Studies in Maritime History

Despite its continental tendencies, the evolution of Chinese history is closely related to maritime activities. In order to foster the study of Chinese maritime history, the Sun Yat-sen Institute for Social Sciences and Philosophy, led by Dr. Mai Chao-cheng, has regularly gathered scholars interested in this respect to exchange viewpoints. It also holds symposia on the history of Chinese maritime developments biannually to promote systematic academic researches.[12] There are three main reasons for this.

First, China is a continental as well as an oceanic nation. In the past, local scholars made substantial research relevant to the former. The symposia are recognition that the latter has not received the attention it warrants.

---

[12] Academia Sinica, *Proceedings*, Studies in Maritime Development in Chinese History, vol. 1 (Taipei: Academia Sinica, Sun Yat-sen Institute for Social Science and Philosophy, 1984), p. 1.

Second, the boom of maritime navigation and colonialism advocated by the Western nations since the fifteenth century brought forth changes in all civilizations affected by the intersection of China with other cultures. Therefore, the scholar of traditional Chinese maritime history must realize just how far-reaching the impact of western nations has been on Chinese culture and maritime history.

Third, the successful reclamation and cultivation of Taiwan by the Han people not only sets a good example, but also reflects the historical evidence that the Chinese have the capacity for oceanic exploration. The study of Taiwan's history can contribute to an understanding of the developmental process of the Han society and provide a historical tracing for the burgeoning maritime society in Taiwan today.

Based upon the aforementioned reasons, the Institute has gathered a number of domestic historians in this field to promote these research programs. So far, the number of participants has increased annually, and the quality of essays has also become much more refined. It has, therefore, received close attention from the academic circles, both at home and abroad.[13]

1990 was the one hundredth anniversary of the first publication of Admiral Mahan's well-known work, *The Influence of Sea Power Upon History*. It was also the 150th anniversary of the Opium War. Therefore, 1990 was a particularly important year to Chinese naval officers. When considering modern history, it becomes apparent that the Opium War was the prelude to a series of disasters that befell China. Therefore, in order to revive the memory of the Opium War, to review Admiral Mahan's thoughts on sea power, to recall the historical lessons learned from past failures, and to facilitate the correct recognition of sea power, Admirals Ko Tung-hwa and Liu Ta-tsai established a Chinese Sea Power Research Workshop, officially titled "The 21st Century Sea Power Seminar."[14]

The first conference, held in the Republic of China, combined local scholars with experts from all relevant academic areas to produce research on sea power. It produced an emphatic response and received immediate attention from a variety of scholarly circles.

The second conference, held in July of 1992, stressed the review of maritime strategy as well as a review of and consideration of the perspectives on the future development of Chinese naval power. It, too, was characterized as a very successful and fruitful academic activity by the gathered military and civilian scholars and experts. The two communities worked together to engender exchange and to discuss current or prospective issues regarding Chinese sea power.

---

[13]   *Ibid.*, vol. 4, ed. Wu Chien-hsiung, (Taipei: Academia Sinica, Sun Yat-sen Institute for Social Science and Philosophy, 1991), pp. 1–7.

[14]   *Proceedings*, First Seminar on the 21st Century Sea Power, (Taipei: Naval Academic Press, 1991), pp. 1–3.

Both conferences were supported by the shipping industry and by the Foundation of the United World Chinese Commercial Bank. This support serves to confirm that the study of Chinese sea power has earned a broadening and important interest.[15]

In addition, as the Sino-Japanese War of 1894–1895 approaches its one hundredth anniversary, the local historical circle has already engaged in preparations to convene an international academic seminar which will be held by the National Taiwan Normal University. The main subjects of the seminar will be a discussion of the Sino-Japanese War of 1894–1895 and its influence on Chinese history as well as its historical significance and lessons learned.

It is understood that this seminar has already received many sponsors and assistance across the board. In addition, since both the People's Republic of China and the Republic of China in Taiwan have actively prepared for the convention, it appears that a significant seminar may be in the offing.

Because of its diversity, Chinese maritime history offers many subjects for study. Among them are foreign trade, foreign relations, overseas immigration and exploitation, and overseas Chinese societies. Developments in these areas have had an important impact on modern Chinese history. Many scholars in Taiwan have undertaken professional studies in a variety of subjects. Study efforts in mainland China may be even more extensive. A sampling of Taiwanese scholars provides the following:

In naval history, for instance, Professor Pau Tzun-peng, the former curator of National Historical Museum, is a noted author on Chinese naval history. Rear Admiral (retired) Cheng T'ien-chieh and Captain (retired) Chao Mei-ching, are co-authors of *Sino-Japanese War (1894–1895) and Li Hung-chang*. Another is Wang Chia-chien, professor of history at the National Taiwan Norman University and author of the *Anthology of Chinese Modern Naval History*. He is also the author of a series of articles on Chinese naval history.[16] Dr. Ma You-huan, a professor of oriental language and literature at the University of Hawaii in the United States has authored a series of studies regarding Chinese naval history.

In the field of maritime history, Mr. Wu Hsiang-hsiang, a former professor of history at the National Taiwan University, is making many contributions to the study of modern Chinese maritime history. Professor Tsao Yung-he, a scholar versed in the Dutch language, enjoys a solid reputation in historical circles for his specialized study in Taiwan maritime history and related writings. Dr. Chang Pin-tsun, a research fellow of the Chung Shan Social Science Institute of Academia Sinica, is the author of a series of articles concerning his specialized study in

---

[15] Naval Academic Monthly, *Proceedings*, Second seminar on the 21st Century Sea Power, (Taipei: Naval Academic Monthly, 1992), pp. 1–3.

[16] For example, Wang Chia-chien, "Li Hung-Chang and the Peiyang Navy," *Chinese Studies in History*, 25 (1991), pp. 52–66.

modern maritime trade.[17] Additionally, Chu Te-lan, an assistant researcher at the Chung Shan Social Science Institute of Academia Sinica, has authored a series of writings relating to his specialized study in Sino-Japanese maritime trade.

Formal Naval and Maritime History Courses

There are courses regarding naval and maritime history at the Naval Command and General Staff College, the Armed Forces University and the ROC Naval Academy. Additionally, courses in the history of warfare at sea are also given at the War College and Naval Command and General Staff College, as well as the Armed Forces University. Those courses include instructions in ancient Chinese sea battles, studies on the Sino-Japanese War, the Falkland Islands War, and the Persian Gulf War. All lecturers for the courses are active duty military and naval officers.

Modern Chinese history is closely related to maritime history. Although the departments of history in our universities have no specific maritime history course, "Modern Chinese History" is a required course and provides a substantial introduction to maritime history.

Museums

The Naval Historical Museum, located on the campus of the Chinese Naval Academy at Tso-ying harbor in southern Taiwan, is a three-story building decorated with an artistic and systematic design for its collection and exhibition of naval relics. The elaborate planning for the presentation of these artifacts of modern Chinese naval history are particularly conspicuous according to the stages of development. The rich and varied collections of naval relics, particularly the huge number of historical files and records dating from the Qing Dynasty to the early days of the ROC, are of great value to historical research. This museum both helps students understand Chinese naval history and facilitate the implementation of esprit de corps.

The Tamkang University established the first domestic maritime museum in Taiwan to assist the development of marine education. Mr. Rong-fa Chang, Chairman of the Board of Trustees of Evergreen Marine Corporation, not only contributed to the funding of its construction but also provided equipment, books, and documents on navigation and marine engineering for exhibit. Based on the meticulous planning and design of Dr. Tien-fu Lin, the founder and honorary chairman of the board, construction was completed smoothly. Dr. Lin is well known in this country and was engaged in the shipping business in his

---

[17] Chang Pin-tsun, "Chinese Maritime Trade: The Case of Sixteenth-Century Fu-chien (Fukien)" Ph.D. dissertation, Princeton University, 1983; "The Evolution of Chinese Thought on Maritime Foreign Trade from the Sixteenth to the Eighteenth Century," *International Journal of Maritime History* 1(1989), pp. 51–64; "Maritime China in Historical Perspective," *International Journal of Maritime History*, 4 (1992), pp. 239–255.

early years. It is particularly commendable that during the preparation stage of the maritime museum, Dr. Lin travelled around the world to collect various models of sailing ships and combatants for its exhibits.

The Tamkang Maritime Museum is a five-story, ship-shaped building. The first two floors display model ships, the third floor houses a library, and an audio-video room for maritime science books and relics as well. The fourth floor is a bridge house exhibiting diversified navigation equipment.

The maritime museum is a non-profit organization, open to the public free of charge in an attempt to promote maritime education. Besides welcoming visitors, it engages in marine data collection and research and also has undertaken extensive exchanges with maritime museums around the world to gain experience and develop its academic position to a world class level.[18]

---

[18] Tamkang University, *The Convergence of the Ships*, (Taipei County: Tamkang University, Maritime Museum, 1992), p. 2.

31

The State of American Maritime History in the 1990s

Benjamin W. Labaree

In a paper of this sort, it is best to open with a definition of its scope. By "American maritime history," I mean the teaching, writing, or exhibiting of matters pertaining to American maritime, but not naval, history. By "American" I mean that which pertains in some fashion to the territory, both before and after its independence, that became the United States. I should also make clear that the paper considers only work being done *in* the United States (taught, published, or exhibited here). Under "maritime" I have included such land-based activities as inland waterways and seaports. These are difficult limitations at best, particularly for a maritime historian. We are here, after all, to bring our disparate interests together—naval and maritime; national and oceanic; political, economic, and social; academic, archival, and curatorial. The sea connects everything, as Gaddis Smith has observed, and it is difficult to draw rigid lines.

Teaching

Historians are well used to taking a running start to their subject, and so "The State of American Maritime History in the 1990s" very much depends on what has been happening, and in this case, also what has not been happening, over the last decade or so. We shall begin with the most difficult part of the subject: the teaching of American maritime history in the United States today. To look at the worst of it first, the American Historical Association's *Directory of History Departments*[1] shows only sixteen faculty members at American institutions who describe themselves as American maritime historians. We know and admire the maritime work of at least a dozen Americanists who do not describe themselves in the field, and we can add several medieval historians or Europeanists, like Tim Runyan and Tony Busch, who are also active in American maritime history. And then there are the broad-gauged navalists such as Clark Reynolds, Ken

---

[1] Robert B. Townshend, ed., *Directory of History Departments and Organizations in the United States and Canada, 1991–92*, 17th ed. (Washington, DC: American Historical Association Institutional Services Program), 1991. Of course one cannot know whether *Directory* information is provided by the scholars themselves in every instance.

Hagan, and Craig Symonds, who work both sides of our street. Furthermore, not all institutions are listed in the *Directory*, and in the excitement of reading five hundred pages of names I probably missed a few. Yet, taking all of these matters into consideration, we must still conclude that there are no more than, say, thirty American maritime historians on the faculties of our colleges and universities today. Add naval specialists and that number might double.

The purpose of this search was to get a rough idea of how many university-level courses in American maritime history might be offered in the United States each year. Many of these professors do not teach the subject at all; others offer such a course once every two or three years, Gaddis Smith at Yale, for example; still others get to teach their specialty only at off-campus programs. There are, fortunately, two or three such opportunities. Williams College co-sponsors with Mystic Seaport Museum an undergraduate Program in American Maritime Studies. Since its beginning in 1977, nearly seven hundred undergraduates have taken that subject in the unequalled setting of one of our leading maritime museums. The Sea Education Association in Woods Hole, Massachusetts, offers a somewhat similar course. And the Frank C. Munson Institute, also at Mystic Seaport, has been teaching American Maritime History on the graduate level every summer since 1955. Munson alumni are now represented in universities and maritime museums throughout the country. But by whatever reckoning, it is not easy for any American student interested in pursuing the subject to do so in the United States.

The biggest setback in the teaching of maritime history has been at the one American university that actually has an endowed chair in the field. In 1947 Mr. and Mrs. William H. Gardiner gave Harvard University the then princely sum of $250,000 to endow a chair in "Oceanic History and Affairs." Robert Greenhalgh Albion was appointed its first occupant, and he was followed at retirement by John H. Parry. It was for the hundreds of students who took this course, incidentally, that Albion prepared the first comprehensive annotated bibliography of books in English relating to naval and maritime history. Since Parry's untimely death in 1982, however, Harvard has failed to fill this important chair, and the best opportunity for American graduate students to prepare in this field has been lost.

To close this section on a happier note let us turn to East Carolina University. Here is located the largest collection of maritime historians and archaeologists in the States. Offering a broad array of maritime-related courses, including extensive underwater research (a field sadly neglected in this country), East Carolina may soon become our first and only institution to offer a Ph.D. in the field. Others could do so as well, like Brown University with the splendid resources of the John Carter Brown Library (JCB) on campus. Director Norman Fiering of the JCB and John Hattendorf of the Naval War College have teamed up to co-sponsor at Brown a summer maritime studies program under the auspices of the National Endowment for the Humanities.

The *teaching* of American maritime history, then, remains an undeveloped field, so undeveloped in fact that no one should at present encourage graduate students to enter the job market *primarily* as maritime historians. Rather, they should follow the example of Bob Albion, originally a historian of the British Empire—or Gaddis Smith, an American diplomatic historian, or Ted Sloan, a historian of American business and technology—and pursue at the outset a mainstream position, sneaking a maritime history course into the catalog when only eager students are looking. Concerning the graduate level, far more important than our struggling to establish entire Ph.D. degree programs in maritime history at various universities is to offer the subject as an ancillary field in as many graduate schools as possible.[2] Unless more American universities do so, the men and women who will become our future faculty members will not have the opportunity to study the subject, and the number of courses offered will continue to dwindle.

Publication

Fortunately, the next section of this report presents a more positive picture. In the last decade or so, the *publication* of works in American maritime history has continued apace, both in quantity and quality. As compiler of a supplement[3] to Albion's bibliography of naval and maritime history,[4] I can vouch for the quantity—over two thousand for the years 1971–1986. While the great majority of these volumes concerns naval matters or the maritime history of nations other than the United States, over the past decade or so hundreds of first-rate books and articles have enhanced our knowledge and understanding of America's maritime past. There follows some of the more important works that have appeared in the past decade or so, arranged under a number of subject headings and chosen to demonstrate the breadth of range within those headings. Brief comments suggest their particular contributions. In the first group are books on more traditional subjects.

Ships, Shipbuilding, and Shipping. George F. Bass, the eminent marine archaeologist at Texas A&M University, has provided an excellent place to begin the study of vessels that have sailed in American waters in his *Ships and Shipwrecks*

---

2   This position may seem unnecessarily self-limited by those readers from institutions where graduate work is more narrowly specialized than in the United States.

3   Benjamin W. Labaree, comp. *A Supplement 1971–1986 to Robert G. Albion's Naval & Maritime History: An Annotated Bibliography* (Mystic, Conn.: Mystic Seaport Museum for the Munson Institute of American Maritime Studies, 1988).

4   Robert Greenhalgh Albion, comp. *Naval & Maritime History: An Annotated Bibliography*. 4th ed. rev. and expanded (Mystic, Conn.: The Marine Historical Association for the Munson Institute of American Maritime History, 1972).

of the Americas.[5] One of the nation's premier shipbuilding regions, Connecticut's Mystic River is the subject of William N. Peterson's *"Mystic Built,"*[6] a book that is particularly noteworthy for the way in which the author integrates shipbuilding activities into the community as a whole. In *Steam and the Sea,*[7] Paul Johnston gives us a well-written and handsomely illustrated book to accompany the Peabody Museum's exhibit on the origins and development of steam in American coastal waters and transoceanic routes. Virginia S. Wood's *Live Oaking*[8] is the definitive study of how timber from the live oak forests of the American south was procured for mercantile and naval shipbuilding. The eleven essays comprising Robert A. Kilmarx, ed., *America's Maritime Legacy*[9] provide a much-needed update of J.G.B. Hutchins' *American Maritime Industries,* published in 1941. In each of these works, as in all good books about ships *per se,* vessels are shown to be the carefully wrought products of designers and builders and are the means to some further end, be it commerce, fishing, science, or whatever, rather than merely ends in themselves.

Discovery and Exploration. Daniel Boorstin provides a sweeping introduction to the expansion of Europe in *The Discoverers,*[10] the overarching theme of which is the intellectual progress that opened up "the world we now view from the literate West." One of the most exciting books in this category must certainly be Alfred W. Crosby's *The Biological Expansion of Europe,*[11] an expansion of the theme first set forth twenty years ago in his *Columbian Exchange,*[12] showing how European disease, animals, and plants contributed to the conquest of the native populations in the world's temperate zones. "Maritime History?" one might ask. Certainly, for Crosby's work explores the paradoxical role of the sea in human affairs, isolating peoples from one another for centuries and then carrying foreign diseases into their society. The

---

[5]　George F. Bass, *Ships and Shipwrecks of the Americas: A History based on Underwater Archaeology* (London: Thames and Hudson, 1988).

[6]　William N. Peterson, *"Mystic Built:" Ships and Shipyards of the Mystic River, Connecticut, 1784–1919* (Mystic, Conn.: Mystic Seaport Museum, 1989).

[7]　Paul Johnston, *Steam and the Sea* (Salem, Mass.: Peabody Museum, 1983).

[8]　Virginia S. Wood, *Live Oaking: Southern Timber for Tall Ships* (Boston: Northeastern Univ. Press, 1981).

[9]　Robert A. Kilmarx, ed., *America's Maritime Legacy: A History of the U.S. Merchant Marine and Shipbuilding Industry since Colonial Times* (Boulder, Colo.: Westview, 1979).

[10]　Daniel Boorstin, *The Discoverers* (New York: Random, 1983).

[11]　Alfred W. Crosby, *The Biological Expansion of Europe, 900–1900* (New York: Cambridge Univ. Press, 1986).

[12]　Alfred W. Crosby, *The Columbian Exchange: Biological and Cultural Consequences of 1492* (Westport, Conn.: Greenwood Publishing, 1972).

best of the many works commemorating the Columbian quincentenary are William D. Phillips and Carla Rahn Phillips, *The Worlds of Christopher Columbus*[13] and Felipe Fernandez-Armesto's *Columbus*.[14] More specialized essays on the history of North American discovery and exploration are edited in a useful volume by Stanley H. Palmer and Dennis Reinhartz.[15] Two recent works give us contrasting insights into American exploration of the nineteenth century. In *Icebound*[16] Leonard Guttridge makes the tragedy of a failed polar expedition into a fascinating study of leadership. *Voyage to the Southern Ocean*,[17] on the other hand, is an ably edited collection of letters by a participant in the highly successful Wilkes Expedition.

Whaling and Fishing. A perennially popular subject for American maritime writers is whaling, and to a lesser extent commercial fishing. The past decade has brought several significant additions to this literature. Robert L. Webb[18] and John Bockstoce[19] add much to our understanding of the whaling industry by taking their readers into new waters. In *Down on T-Wharf*,[20] Andrew German's excellent text accompanies a superb collection of photographs and reminds us of how the New England fishing industry used to be. In contrast, William Warner's study of Atlantic deepwater fishing,[21] though ten years old, nevertheless foretells in timely fashion the decline in both coastal and offshore fishing that has only recently brought drastic action by both U.S. and Canadian authorities. The outstanding book in this general category is Briton Cooper Busch's remarkable history of sealing.[22] It is the first definitive study of this highly charged subject and offers both the commercial and environmental points of view fair hearings.

Commerce and Shipping. Surely, one might think, there can be little new to be said about maritime trade and commerce, and yet each year increasing

---

13 William D. Phillips and Carla Rahn Phillips, *The Worlds of Christopher Columbus* (Cambridge: Cambridge Univ. Press, 1992).

14 Felipe Fernandez-Armesto, *Columbus* (New York: Oxford Univ. Press, 1991).

15 Stanley H. Palmer and Dennis Reinhartz, *Essays on the History of North American Discovery and Exploration* (College Station: Texas A&M Univ. Press, 1988).

16 Leonard Guttridge, *Icebound: The Jeannette Expedition's Quest for the North Pole* (Annapolis: Naval Institute Press, 1986).

17 Anne Hoffman Cleaver and Jeffrey Stann, eds., *Voyage to the Southern Ocean: The Letters of Lieutenant William Reynolds from the U.S. Exploring Expedition, 1838–1842* (Annapolis: Naval Institute Press, 1988).

18 Robert L. Webb, *On the Northwest: Commercial Whaling in the Pacific Northwest, 1790–1967* (Vancouver: Univ. of British Columbia Press, 1988).

19 John Bockstoce, *Whales, Ice, and Men: The History of Whaling in the Western Arctic* (Seattle: Univ. of Washington Press, 1986).

20 Andrew German, *Down on T-Wharf: The Boston Fisheries as Seen through the Photographs of Henry D. Fisher* (Mystic, Conn.: Mystic Seaport Museum, 1982).

21 William W. Warner, *Distant Water: The Fate of the North Atlantic Fisherman* (Boston: Little, Brown, 1983).

22 Briton Cooper Busch, *The War Against the Seals: A History of the North American Seal Fishery* (Kingston and Montreal: McGill–Queen's Univ. Press, 1985).

numbers of books and articles probe still unexplored aspects of this most fundamental theme in maritime history. The challenge here is to choose from among hundreds of recent works five or six that give us new perspectives on this old subject, that show commerce as an activity with consequences that reach far beyond the economic bottom line. Here we must begin with Philip D. Curtin's *Cross-Cultural Trade in World History*,[23] which concentrates on both maritime and overland commerce as a vehicle of culture through many parts of the world. At the other end of the scale is the study of Irish-American trade by Thomas M. Truxes.[24] Richard Johnson[25] has used the career of Bostonian John Nelson to explain the commercial and political relations between New England and New France at the end of the seventeenth century. Finally, on a totally different scale is the business history of the American President Lines by John Niven,[26] which places the operation of this important transpacific company into the broad context of maritime policy.

Here is perhaps the best place to note the most recent attempt to put into one volume a maritime history of the United States, this one by the late Jack Bauer.[27] Its strength lies in the author's knowledgeable treatment of America's inland waterways and their integration into the maritime world beyond our coasts. Coastal shipping and the fisheries are also well treated. Unfortunately, Bauer's handling of the topic of overseas commerce after the Civil War is marred by his mounting distress over the decline of American-flag shipping.

★ ★ ★

The past decade of scholarly works in maritime history would be noteworthy enough on the strength of the foregoing works. But what has made the past ten years particularly exciting is the abundance of new work in less conventional aspects of the field. Let us turn now to this second group.

Seaports. One must begin somewhere, and so we will start on dry land, with some of the books that have illuminated our understanding of seaports. Beginning in New England, Christine L. Heyrman's excellent study of Gloucester and Marblehead[28] examines the culture of these two fishing communities as it related

[23] Philip D. Curtin, *Cross-Cultural Trade in World History* (London: Cambridge Univ. Press, 1984).
[24] Thomas M. Truxes, *Irish-American Trade, 1660–1783* (New York: Cambridge Univ. Press, 1988).
[25] Richard Johnson, *John Nelson, Merchant Adventurer: A Life Between Empires* (New York: Oxford Univ. Press, 1991).
[26] John Niven, *The American President Lines and Its Forebears, 1848–1984: From Paddlewheelers to Containerships* (Newark: Univ. of Delaware Press, 1986).
[27] Jack Bauer, *A Maritime History of the United States: The Role of America's Seas and Waterways* (Charleston: Univ. of South Carolina Press, 1988).
[28] Christine L. Heyrman, *Commerce and Culture: The Maritime Communities of Colonial Massachusetts, 1690–1750* (New York: W.W. Norton, 1984).

to their commercial activities. In contrast, the planning and development of New York's waterfront over the course of three centuries is the subject of Ann Buttenwiser's *Manhattan Water-Bound*,[29] while Philip C.F. Smith[30] has made extensive use of maps, lithographs, and photographs to demonstrate that Philadelphia was and remains a major port city. New Orleans, of all major American ports perhaps the most neglected by maritime historians, has been the focus of several recent studies, the most comprehensive of which is Eric Arensen's *Waterfront Workers of New Orleans*.[31] The author considers such topics as the relationship between blacks who worked the waterfront and the larger black community, and the effects of race relations on the unions. Another overlooked seaport, Portland, Oregon, is the subject of a study by E. Kimbark MacColl.[32] Bruce Nelson's *Workers on the Waterfront*[33] focuses on the 1930s and gives particular attention to west coast ports. In *Atlantic Port Cities*,[34] Franklin W. Knight and Peggy K. Liss have edited the papers of a 1986 conference that took as its point of departure Jacob Price's essay of 1974 entitled "Economic Function and the Growth of American Port Towns in the Eighteenth Century."[35] Despite the title of the conference essays, however, the book focuses almost exclusively on Latin America and Caribbean ports.

Inland Waterways. Until recently American maritime historians have largely ignored the Great Lakes and other inland waterways that have carried a large portion of this nation's produce to the seaports from which it was ultimately exported. Now, however, we have in addition to Jack Bauer's *Maritime History of the United States* mentioned above, a number of studies that focus on American canals and riverways and the men who served them. Michael Allen's *Western Rivermen, 1763-1861*[36] is a case in point. The author explains how and why the men who operated the flatboats and rafts became romanticized by a rapidly industrializing nation. Further downstream Harry P. Owens has studied the effect of steam on the transportation of cotton in the Yazoo-Mississippi

29 Ann Buttenwiser, *Manhattan WaterBound: Planning and Developing Manhattan's Waterfront from the Seventeenth Century to the Present* (New York: New York Univ. Press, 1987).

30 Philip C.F. Smith, *Philadelphia on the River* (Pennsylvania: Philadelphia Maritime Museum, 1986).

31 Eric Arensen, *Waterfront Workers of New Orleans: Race, Class, and Politics, 1863–1923* (New York: Oxford Univ. Press, 1991).

32 E. Kimbark MacColl, *Merchants, Money, and Power: The Portland Establishment, 1843–1913* (Portland, Ore.: Georgian, 1988).

33 Bruce Nelson, *Workers on the Waterfront: Seamen, Longshoremen, and Unionism in the 1930s* (Urbana: Univ. of Illinois Press, 1988).

34 Franklin W. Knight and Peggy K. Liss, *Atlantic Port Cities: Economy, Culture, and Society in the Atlantic World, 1650-1850* (Knoxville: Univ. of Tennessee Press, 1991).

35 Jacob Price, "Economic Function and the Growth of American Port Towns in the Eighteenth Century" in *Perspectives in American History*, vol. VIII, pp. 123–86.

36 Michael Allen, *Western Rivermen, 1763–1861: Ohio and Mississippi Boatmen and the Myth of the Alligator Horse* (Baton Rouge: Louisiana State Univ. Press, 1990).

delta.[37] Of broader scope is *Western River Transportation*,[38] by Erik Haites and others, who put their subject into the context of national policy. Robert Shaw has given us two useful books, a comprehensive study of the Erie Canal[39] and a fresh history of the canal era itself in *Canals for a Nation*.[40]

Immigration. After a long hiatus, American historians are once again writing about immigration, and several of the recent works on this subject give at least some attention to the oceanic crossing itself. Thus David Cressy's "*Coming Over*"[41] includes a perceptive chapter on the passage to America. Farley Grubb has published his important research concerning immigration into colonial Philadelphia in three articles,[42] and A. Roger Ekirch's *Bound for America*[43] focuses on the transportation of British convicts into the mainland colonies. Although not literally about immigration, James P. Delgado's *To California by Sea*[44] gives us not only a readable account of the sea passage to the gold fields, but also a first-rate history of San Francisco's early years as a seaport. One could not close this section without mentioning Bernard Bailyn's splendid study, *Voyaging to the West*,[45] although it is perhaps less concerned with the maritime aspects of his subject than the title might suggest.

Seamen, Women, and Members of Ethnic Minorities. It is clear to the most casual observer that the most significant innovation in the writing of American maritime history in the past decade or so has been the increasing number of younger scholars who have focused their research on the lives of

---

[37] Harry P. Owens, *Steamboats and the Cotton Economy: River Trade in the Yazoo-Mississippi Delta* (Jackson: Univ. of Mississippi Press, 1990).

[38] Erik F. Haites, James Mak, and Gary Walton, *Western River Transportation: The Era of Early Internal Development, 1810–1860* (Baltimore: Johns Hopkins Univ. Press, 1990).

[39] Robert Shaw, *Erie Water West: A History of the Erie Canal, 1792–1854* (Lexington: Univ. of Kentucky Press, 1990).

[40] Robert Shaw, *Canals for a Nation: The Canal Era in the United States 1790–1860* (Lexington: Univ. of Kentucky Press, 1991).

[41] David Cressy, "*Coming Over:*" *Migration and Communication Between England and New England in the Seventeenth Century* (New York: Cambridge Univ. Press, 1987).

[42] Farley Grubb, "British Immigration into Philadelphia: The Reconstruction of Ship Passenger Lists from May 1772 to October 1773," *Pennsylvania History*, vol. 55 (1988), pp. 118–41; Farley Grubb, "The Market Structure of Shipping German Immigrants to Philadelphia," *Pennsylvania Magazine of History and Biography*, vol. 111 (1987), pp. 27-48; and Farley Grubb, "Morbidity and Mortality on the North Atlantic Passage: Eighteenth Century German Immigration," *Journal of Interdisciplinary History*, vol. 17 (1987), pp. 565–85.

[43] A. Roger Ekirch, *Bound for America: The Transportation of British Convicts to the Colonies, 1718–1775*, (New York: Oxford Univ. Press, 1987).

[44] James P. Delgado, *To California by Sea: A Maritime History of the California Gold Rush* (Columbia: Univ. of South Carolina Press, 1990).

[45] Bernard Bailyn, *Voyaging to the West: A Passage in the Peopling of America on the Eve of the Revolution* (New York: Knopf, 1986).

ordinary mariners, including those belonging to ethnic minorities, and on the role of women in this maritime society. It is premature to proclaim, as Marcus Rediker has done, that their work constitutes a "New Maritime History," for consensus among them has not yet advanced beyond a shared subject-matter. Yet it is encouraging to note how often they discuss their work together, at conferences, in "roundtable articles," and in collaborative books. These scholars also work across international boundaries, bringing to life the dictum that "the sea is one," to which most of their elders have given little more than lip service. Indeed, even to discuss this subject from a "Canadian," "American," "British," or "Scandinavian" point of view seems unnatural. Like most "new" work, the writings of this generation have been influenced by several precedents, most notably Ralph Davis's *The Rise of the English Shipping Industry* (1962)[46] and Jesse Lemisch's "Jack Tar in the Streets"(1968).[47]

Let us begin with seamen in general and therefore with Margaret S. Creighton's *Dog Watch and Liberty Days*.[48] Written as the catalogue to accompany an exhibit the author arranged for the Peabody Museum, *Dog Watch* is based largely on research done for her dissertation.[49] Creighton provides through text and illustration an unembellished glimpse into the lives of ordinary sailors. More specialized is Daniel F. Vickers' "Nantucket Whalemen in the Deep-Sea Fishery,"[50] in which he places mariners into the broader context of the general labor force. In "Physical and Social Profiles of Early American Seafarers, 1812–1815,"[51] Ira Dye provides us with invaluable information gleaned from British Admiralty records of American prisoners. The best known and most controversial of recent studies of maritime society is Marcus Rediker's *Between the Devil and the Deep Blue Sea*.[52] Here the author attempts to show that the common seamen of the mid-eighteenth century in fact constituted a proletariat. This is not the place to catalogue the critiques other scholars (younger and older

---

[46] Ralph Davis, *The Rise of the English Shipping Industry in the Seventeenth and Eighteenth Centuries* (London: Macmillan, 1963).

[47] Jesse Lemisch, "Jack Tar in the Streets: Merchant Seamen in the Politics of Revolutionary America," *William and Mary Quarterly*, 3rd ser. 25 (1968), pp. 371–80.

[48] Margaret S. Creighton, *Dog Watch and Liberty Days: Seafaring Life in the Nineteenth Century* (Salem, Mass.: Peabody Museum, 1982).

[49] Margaret S. Creighton, "The Private Life of Jack Tar: Sailors at Sea in the Nineteenth Century," Ph.D. diss., Boston Univ., 1985).

[50] Daniel F. Vickers, "Nantucket Whalemen in the Deep-Sea Fishery: The Changing Anatomy of an Early American Labor Force," *Journal of American History*, 72 (1985), pp. 277–96. This article is largely based on sections of the author's "Maritime Labor in Colonial Massachusetts: A Case Study of the Essex County Cod Fishery and Whaling Industry of Nantucket, 1630–1775" (Ph.D. diss., Princeton Univ., 1981).

[51] Ira Dye, "Physical and Social Profiles of Early American Seafarers, 1812–1815," in Colin Howell and Richard Twomey, eds., *Jack Tar in History: Essays in the History of Maritime Life and Labour* (Fredricton: Acadiensis Press, 1991), pp. 220–35.

[52] Marcus Rediker, *Between the Devil and the Deep Blue Sea: Merchant Seamen, Pirates, and the Anglo-American Maritime World, 1700–1750* (Massachusetts: Cambridge Univ. Press, 1987).

alike) have made of Rediker's book, but all would agree that he has stimulated our thinking as no other maritime scholar in recent years. With co-author Peter Linebaugh, Rediker has expanded his challenging interpretation in "The Many-Headed Hydra."[53]

One segment of American seamen as a topic that has attracted attention from both older and younger historians is the role of blacks and members of other ethnic minorities in the maritime workforce. Martha S. Putney's *Black Sailors*[54] and James B. Farr's *Black Odyssey*[55] are worthy efforts to get at a difficult subject. More thorough in both concept and research is Jeffrey Bolster's prize-winning article "To Feel Like a Man."[56] Judging from the article, we eagerly await the author's forthcoming book on the subject. Meanwhile, in his biography of Captain Paul Cuffe, *Rise to be a People*,[57] Thomas D. Lamont shows that not all black mariners were condemned to a life in the fo'c'sle. Briton Cooper Busch has given us a glimpse into the lives of another ethnic minority in "Cape Verdeans in the American Whaling and Sealing Industry, 1850–1900."[58]

One of the first of the younger historians to have considered the role of women in the maritime community is Julia C. Bonham. Fifteen years ago she published the results of her work at Mystic Seaport Museum's Munson Institute and Brown University as "Feminist and Victorian: The Paradox of the American Seafaring Woman of the Nineteenth Century."[59] Since that time scholars have broadened the scope of this topic through an increasing number of articles. Among the most ambitious are two by Lisa Norling, "Contrary Dependencies: Whaling Agents and Whalemen's Families, 1830–1870"[60] and "the Sentimentalization of American Seafaring,"[61] and a particularly strong synthesizing essay by Margaret S. Creighton, "Women and Men in American Whaling, 1830–

---

[53] Peter Linebaugh and Marcus Rediker, "The Many Headed Hydra: Sailors, Slaves, and the Atlantic Working Class in the Eighteenth Century," *Journal of Historical Sociology*. 3 (1990), pp. 225–52. This article has been reprinted in Howell and Twomey, eds., *Jack Tar in History*, pp. 11–36.

[54] Martha S. Putney, *Black Sailors: Afro-American Merchant Seamen and Whalemen Prior to the Civil War* (Westport, Conn.: Greenwood Press, 1987).

[55] James B. Farr, *Black Odyssey: The Seafaring Tradition of Afro-Americans* (New York: Lang, 1989).

[56] Jeffrey Bolster, "To Feel like a Man: Black Seamen in the Northern States, 1800–1860," *Journal of American History*, vol 76. 1990, pp. 1173–99, based on research done for Bolster's "African-American Seamen: Race, Seafaring Work, and Atlantic Maritime Culture, 1750-1860" (Ph.D. diss., Johns Hopkins Univ., 1992).

[57] Thomas D. Lamont, *Rise to be a People: A Biography of Paul Cuffe* (Urbana: Univ. of Illinois Press, 1986).

[58] Briton Cooper Busch, "Cape Verdeans in the American Whaling and Sealing Industry, 1850–1900," *American Neptune*, 45 (1985), pp. 104–16.

[59] Julia C. Bonham, "Feminist and Victorian: The Paradox of the American Seafaring Woman of the Nineteenth Century," *American Neptune*, vol. 37 (1977), pp. 203–18.

[60] Lisa Norling, "Contrary Dependencies: Whaling Agents and Whalemen's Families, 1830–1870," *Log of Mystic Seaport*, vol. 42 (1990), pp. 3–12.

[61] Lisa Norling, " The Sentimentalization of American Seafaring: The Case of the New England Whale Fishery, 1790–1870 " in Howell and Twomey, eds., *Jack Tar in History*, pp. 164–78.

1870."[62] Noteworthy among the others are Caroline Mosely's "Images of Young Women in Nineteenth Century Songs of the Sea"[63] and Joan Druett's "More Decency and Order: Women and Whalemen in the Pacific."[64] Most recently Ms. Druett has provided an award-winning edition of the American Mary Brewster's journals.[65] Focusing on a more recent period is Amy Kesselman's monograph, *Fleeting Opportunities*, about women shipyard workers during World War II.[66] Charlene J. Allison *et al.* have studied the growing role of women in the Northwest fisheries.[67] Numerous other memoirs of sea-going women have been published in the last decade or so, including Jane Balano's *Log of the Skipper's Wife*[68] and Julia FreeHand's edition of the memoirs of Captain Sumner Drinkwater and his wife Alice.[69]

In closing this section I should like to reiterate a point I made at its outset. Compared to the *teaching* of American maritime history, the *publication* of books and articles in the field seems to remain numerically quite strong, perhaps one hundred or so a year. And yet a quick survey of the *American Neptune* during the five-year period 1988-1992 shows that only fifty-eight (35.8 percent) of the one hundred sixty-two books reviewed there concern American *maritime* history (distinct from naval), with another thirty (18.8 percent) on European maritime subjects. In contrast, sixty-three works on American and European *naval* history account for 38.9 percent of the total. In one sense these figures reflect how broadly interpreted the phrase maritime history is, and how successful the efforts of the *Neptune* editors have been in reaching beyond national boundaries.

Museums

Before we conclude that America's maritime past is disappearing as rapidly as its deepwater mercantile fleet, let us turn to, and close with, the bright spot on

[62] Margaret S. Creighton, "Women and Men in American Whaling, 1830-1870," *International Journal of Maritime History*, vol. 4 (1992), pp. 195–218.

[63] Caroline Mosely, "Images of Young Women in Nineteenth Century Songs of the Sea," *Log of Mystic Seaport*, vol. 35 (1984), pp. 132–39.

[64] Joan Druett, "More Decency and Order: Women and Whalemen in the Pacific," *Log of Mystic Seaport*, vol. 39 (1987), pp. 65–74.

[65] Joan Druett, *"She was a Sister Sailor": The Whaling Journals of Mary Brewster, 1845–1851* (Mystic, Conn.: Mystic Seaport Museum, 1992). Properly speaking, Ms. Druett's book should not be listed here because she is a New Zealander, but Mary Brewster was an American, her journal is in the library of Mystic Seaport Museum library, and the book was also published by Mystic in its American Maritime Library series. Recently the North American Society for Oceanic History recognized *"She was a Sister Sailor"* as the best non-naval book of nautical history published in 1992.

[66] Amy Kesselman, *Fleeting Opportunities: Women Shipyard Workers in Portland and Vancouver during World War II and Reconversion* (Albany: State Univ. of New York Press, 1990).

[67] Charlene J. Allison, Sue-Ellen Jacobs, and Mary A. Porter, *Winds of Change: Women in Northwest Commercial Fishing* (Seattle: Univ. of Washington Press, 1989).

[68] James W. Balano, ed., *The Log of the Skipper's Wife* (Camden, Maine: Down East Books, 1979).

[69] Julia Freehand, *A Seafaring Legacy: The Photographs, Diaries, Letters, and Memorabilia of a Maine Sea Captain (Sumner Drinkwater and his Wife [Alice Drinkwater]) 1859–1908* (New York: Random House, 1981).

the scene: America's maritime museums. With few exceptions, these institutions are private and not for profit. Most of them are dependent on endowments, gifts, and membership dues instead of government subsidies for their support. Most of them have increasingly come to rely on such sources as sales at retail stores, program charges, and admissions fees. For this reason, whatever activities might attract tourists and other visitors—chowder festivals, Fourth of July celebrations, popcorn and ice cream vendors, horse-and-buggy rides—get serious attention by the management.

But there is an upside to this unfortunate aspect as well. To some extent the need to attract visitors accounts for what maritime museums in America are most noted—the number and quality of preserved vessels they have in the water. Each year hundreds of thousands of people climb aboard, walk the decks, and go below "tall ships" (as the ad-writers love to call them) from Mystic Seaport's nineteenth-century whaleship *Charles W. Morgan*, or South Street Seaport's Cape Horner *Peking*, Galveston's bark *Elissa*, or San Diego's *Star of India*, to note but four out of a score or more such museum ships. Still more scores of vessels are preserved on dry land or under cover. The vessel should not be romanticized as the be-all and end-all of maritime history, but as a means of educating the public about our maritime past, an invitation to inspect a historic vessel firsthand is hard to beat. On the other hand, inviting upwards of a half-million people to tramp all over your last wooden whaleship is hardly the best way to preserve it! To the non-seagoing public, however, these vessels do not interpret themselves very well, and no amount of labeling "martingales," "crojacks," and "fo'c'sles" will help. Not surprisingly, therefore, the effort to explain these exhibits to the visitor takes up a large share of the budget and leaves staff members of American museums with far less time for research and writing than have their colleagues elsewhere.

With this generalized introduction, we should look at what is happening at some of our best maritime museums, because if this history is to survive in America, it will depend largely on these institutions, not on our universities. To demonstrate some of the ways these institutions in widely separated parts of the country carry out their goals, the following institutions were chosen from a group of fifteen or so whose staff responded to a recent questionnaire concerning their activities.

At the Hawaii Maritime Center in Honolulu, forty-five exhibits cover Hawaii's maritime heritage from precontact to the present. Its most recent special exhibit focused on the Japanese attack on Pearl Harbor. In addition to numerous public lectures throughout the year, the Maritime Center sponsors an annual conference on maritime history and underwater archaeology. Its most active educational program brings 3,000 school children to the museum *each month* to plot the track of the Museum's Polynesian voyaging canoe. It is now building a second canoe of traditional materials to retrace the route of Hawaii's original settlers without the aid of modern instruments. The Museum's total annual visitation is about 100,000.

Near the mouth of the Columbia River, in Astoria, Oregon, the Columbia River Maritime Museum focuses on fur trade and exploration of the Northwest coast, fishing, and river navigation. The West Coast's last working lightship, *Columbia*, is now moored at the museum and open to visitors. The Museum's most recent special exhibits have been "Marine Art of the Pacific Northwest" and "This Noble River: Robert Grey and the Columbia." Four special projects collectively called the "Year of the Fisherman" received the Award of Merit from the American Association of State and Local History in 1990. School groups are admitted without charge throughout the year, and Astoria's community college offers a course on Columbia River Maritime History. Other state and regional universities co-sponsor additional lectures and research throughout the year. The Museum publishes a quarterly magazine, *Quarterdeck*, featuring scholarly articles for its 2,000-plus members and has an annual visitation of just under 100,000.

The Mariners Museum at Newport News, Virginia, is one of the nation's largest such institutions, perhaps best known for its research library and archives, which includes a superb collection of nearly 500,000 photographs. The Museum's Chesapeake Bay Gallery, opened in 1989, displays hundreds of artifacts, photographs, and maps relating to that important inland sea. The work of William Francis Gibbs, designer of the Liberty ship and the S.S. *United States*, among many other commercial and naval vessels, is commemorated in another new gallery. The Mariners Museum sponsors a scholarly lecture series, as well as a graduate course in Maritime Geography through the University of Virginia. More than 20,000 school children particpate in classes and other educational programs at the museum each year. Annual visitation is just under 100,000.

Just up the Bay on Maryland's Eastern Shore at St. Michael's, the Chesapeake Bay Maritime Museum has recently added to its fine collection of workboats several vessels including the river tug *Delaware*. A new permanent exhibit, "Mechanical Power," traces two centuries of change in the use of engines for propulsion and deckwork and as such is a rarity among institutions that glorify the age of sail. One educational program, "Bay Heritage Day," really *prepares* 5th graders to get the most out of their class visit. Middle-schoolers can spend an overnight tending to the Hooper Strait Lighthouse, now moved to the Museum grounds. About 85,000 people visit the Chesapeake Bay Maritime Museum each year.

New York's South Street Seaport Museum, unlike its sister institutions, was actually begun to save from the wrecking ball the historic maritime district it now occupies. While restoring buildings, the staff started collecting artifacts of New York's maritime past, an effort enhanced by the acquisition of the 4,000-piece Seaman's Bank for Savings collection of paintings, prints, and models. One of its most recent special exhibits, "Hammer and Hand," tells the history of the New York's maritime trades, as does its quarterly journal, *Seaport*. Over the next two years the museum will be sending out four traveling exhibits and will begin sponsoring a regular symposium on maritime art. In addition to the restoration work it has done along the waterfront, the museum also has preserved in the water the iron-hulled *Wavertree* and the big four-masted bark *Peking*. Another of its vessels, the schooner *Pioneer*, built in 1885, offers daytime sail training excursions for local school children, who can also spend an overnight on board the *Peking*. Altogether 27,000 school children particpate in the Museum program, out a total visitation of nearly 500,000.

Perhaps America's finest maritime institution is Mystic Seaport Museum. The Museum's collections of watercraft now number four hundred fifty, with a dozen vessels in the water, including the whaleship *Charles W. Morgan*, the Danish training ship *Joseph Conrad* (ex-*George Stage*), and the Gloucester fishing schooner *L.A. Dunton*, all of which are open to the public. The Blunt White Library's collection of manuscripts grows steadily each year, along with the necessary monographs and periodicals to support ongoing research. The oral history division has taped over two hundred interviews with fishermen, mariners, shipwrights, and others and nearly one hundred scholarly lectures delivered at the Museum. Represented in the ships plans division is the work of numerous marine architects from both Atlantic and Pacific seaboards.

Until the recent recession, 70,000 school children visited Mystic each year (about half that number still do). Annual conferences on such topics as yachting history, small craft, and sea music attract hundreds of scholars and enthusiasts. As mentioned earlier, Mystic Seaport cosponsors an undergraduate program in maritime studies with Williams College and since 1955 has offered its own graduate-level courses to which public school teachers are particularly welcome. Outreach programs send teacher institutes, theatrical productions, and maritime artifacts to area schools. Through the generosity of a local family, the museum awards several Paul Cuffe Fellowships each year to encourage research in the history of mariners of native American or African descent. The undergraduate Williams College—Mystic Seaport program offers young scholars the Albion Fellowship for teaching maritime history to the program's students.

The Publications department puts the Museum's best foot forward to thousands of scholars and general readers. In addition to its quarterly journal, *The Log*, the Museum keeps more than fifty books in print, from John F. Leavitt's beautifully crafted *Wake of the Coasters (1970)* to the latest book, *Classic Small Craft You Can Build (1993)* by the dean of American wooden boatbuilders, John Gardiner (age 87). In between are such works as Andrew German's *Down on T-Wharf*, Tony Busch's *Master of Desolation*, and Joan Druett's "*She was a Sister Sailor*." John Rogers' *Origins of Sea Terms* and Douglas L. Stein's *American Maritime Documents* are just two of the useful guides recently published by the museum. Mystic's average annual attendance over the past five years stands at about 450,000, and its activities are supported by more than 20,000 members.

The contributions of our maritime museums are impressive. Collectively, they offer as many accredited courses in one or another aspect of American Maritime History as do our universities. Through museums, several hundred thousands of school children are made aware of our nation's maritime past, along with millions of adults. Counting the maritime museums that are too small to belong to The Council of American Maritime Museums (CAMM), there are upwards of seventy-five such institutions in the country. Because they provide the primary line of contact between the public and our maritime past, whatever we can do to improve them will in the long run serve the efforts of us all.

Conclusion

Looking back over the state of American maritime history today brings us to several conclusions.

First, the sea is one, and it *does* connect us all, as so many of us have observed in our research and writings. Maritime history is therefore an *inter*-national subject and therefore a difficult one to fit into our compartmentalized departments of history.

Second, maritime history is popular. Enrollments in the few courses we do offer, attendance at museums, special exhibits, and tall ship extravaganzas all demonstrate this fact. But in some academic circles popularity is the kiss of death. The Munson Institute is occasionally criticized for making its courses available to public school teachers and museum staff members, many of whom have more modest academic backgrounds than one finds in our graduate schools. We must improve our standards without jeopardizing our accessibility.

Third, we must be careful that our overuse of nautical terminology in our work does not become mere jargon for its own sake. We must resist criticizing newcomers to our field for not having been aloft in a howling gale or knowing the difference between tacking and wearing ship.[70] There are now more important aspects to our subject than shiphandling.

Fourth, we must put people back into our history, especially the men and women of the maritime labor force who, while hardly a proletariat, are nevertheless an all-important element in the equation. If we ourselves are not interested in the social and cultural aspects of our topics, we should at least give encouragement through fellowships and other forms of recognition to those who are.

Finally, we must bring the two fields of naval and maritime history closer together. Albion began that effort more than sixty years ago, first with his courses at Princeton and later at Harvard and the Munson Institute, and since 1951 with

---

[70] Recent reviews of Barbara Tuchman's *The First Salute* and Marcus Rediker's *Between the Devil and the Deep Blue Sea* do just that.

his bibliography, still called a *Naval and Maritime* bibliography. This volume gives all of us the opportunity to renew that effort. Let us now get to work.

32

Mahan Plus One Hundred
The Current State of American Naval History

Kenneth J. Hagan and Mark R. Shulman

The logos of the U.S. Naval Academy and the Naval War College feature the three-pronged trident of Neptune, an apt icon for the three principal manifestations of naval history in the United States: teaching, museums, and publication. The current state of health of each of these endeavors varies markedly. The teaching of naval history at colleges and universities is uneven at best, with historians often forced to subsume naval history under other subjects in courses with broader orientations. Naval museums, by contrast, are a thriving industry, although the future of some of them is under a cloud. Most surprisingly, in light of the absence of firm support from academic institutions, naval history today is an extremely vigorous outlet for scholarly and popular writing.

This essay attempts to substantiate the assertions just made. In doing so, it examines several subsidiary and related topics, such as archival depositories, libraries, and bibliographies. The conclusions are meant to be cautionary, not pessimistic.

Teaching

Military and naval history emerged as distinct subdisciplines in the late nineteenth century. Since that time they have been consistently marginalized or ignored by history departments. In the early twentieth century, studies of war, once a prominent feature of the profession, gradually disappeared from university and college curricula. By 1935–1936, a survey of the thirty leading universities found no such courses, aside from ROTC offerings. Even at the height of Cold War paranoia in 1954, only thirty-seven of four hundred ninety-three surveyed departments were offering any military history courses.[1] A few select departments

---

[1] The surveys are reported in John Bowditch, "War and the Historian," H. Stuart Hughes, ed., *Teachers of History: Essays in Honor of Laurence Bradford Packard* (Ithaca, N.Y.: Cornell University Press, 1954), pp. 322–3; Richard C. Brown, *The Teaching of Military History in Colleges and Universities of the United States,* Historical Studies, no. 124 (Maxwell Air Force Base, Ala.: U.S. Air Force Historical Division, Research Studies Institute, Air University, 1955). See also, Paul M. Kennedy, "The Fall and Rise of Military History," *Military History Quarterly* 3, no. 2 (Winter 1991), pp. 8–12; and Louis Morton, "The Historian and the Study of War," *The Mississippi Valley Historical Review* 18, no. 4 (1962): pp. 599–613.

(e.g., Princeton, Dartmouth, and Yale) engaged trained historians to teach military history to ROTC students, but the rest surrendered their responsibility to active-duty officers with little or no historical training.

In the late 1960s and early 1970s, dissent over the war in Southeast Asia drove ROTC from many campuses. A modest revival of interest in military history began in the 1980s as collegiate anger over Vietnam faded and as President Ronald Reagan began the last military buildup of the Cold War. But the resurrection of military history was incremental, and the college and university offerings most often broadly incorporated the study of naval history or sea power into that of war as a whole. The teaching of naval history as a special offering has remained highly restricted.

Most teaching of United States naval history is done in government educational institutions, specifically the National Defense University (NDU), the Naval Academy (USNA), the Naval War College (NWC), and the Naval Reserve Officers Training Corps units (NROTC). The NDU has long offered an elective course on naval strategy, or on "The American Way of War at Sea," which proceeds chronologically and emphasizes the interaction between national policy and naval strategy. It attracts about a dozen students per semester.[2] A similar elective is also taught with some regularity at the Army War College in Carlisle, Pennsylvania.

Since its founding in 1884, the Naval War College has regarded naval history as an essential element in a curriculum designed to educate mid-career officers for staff positions and high command. Early presidents Stephen B. Luce, Alfred T. Mahan, French E. Chadwick, and William L. Rodgers made significant written contributions to naval history while encouraging their students to seek lessons for the future by studying the past.

Today, there is no explicit course on naval history at the NWC, but the subject is emphasized in other ways. In terms of research, the college maintains an excellent book collection in naval history and a growing collection of personal papers and oral histories. The research arm of the NWC, the Center for Naval Warfare Studies, provides a chair for the college's principal expert in naval history: the Ernest J. King Professor of Maritime History, a position held since 1984 by John B. Hattendorf.[3] The occupant is required to conduct research, write about a wide range of naval historical issues, and establish contacts with other scholars in the field. Finally, the NWC maintains the Alfred Thayer Mahan

---

[2] George E. Thibault taught this course for several years, followed by Captain W.S. Johnson, upon whose retirement the NDU hired on a temporary basis H. P. Willmott.

[3] The King Chair was established at the suggestion of Admiral Raymond A. Spruance and was successively held by such eminent visiting historians as John H. Kemble, James A. Field, Jr., Theodore Ropp, Harry L. Coles, Raymond G. O'Connor, Stephen E. Ambrose, and Martin Blumenson. In 1974, the King Chair became a long-term civilian faculty position with the six year appointment of Philip A. Crowl, followed a decade later by the present incumbent.

Chair of Maritime Strategy, now occupied by George W. Baer, who has just completed a history of twentieth-century American sea power.[4] While the graduate level curriculum of the NWC does not provide formal courses on naval or maritime history, these subjects continue to permeate two core course offerings in strategy and policy and in joint operations. The first employs roughly a dozen civilian specialists in diplomatic, military or naval history, political science, and international relations who use the case study method for the critical analysis of strategy. The faculty and students scrutinize the Peloponnesian War, the Second Punic War, the American Revolution, the French Revolutionary and Napoleonic Wars, the American Civil War, the wars of German unification, the Russo-Japanese War, the First and Second World Wars, the Chinese Civil War, the Korean War, the Vietnam War, and many of the military and naval events of the Cold War. The Joint Operations Course also includes a number of case studies, including: the Nazi German invasion of Norway; the Atlantic campaign of World War II; the Pacific war battles of Midway, Guadalcanal, the Philippine Sea, and Leyte Gulf; and the recent *Achille Lauro* incident, the Falklands/Malvinas War and the Gulf War. In a somewhat catholic approach, the course examines the naval theories of Sir Julian S. Corbett, Alfred T. Mahan, Herbert F. Rosinski, and Joseph C. Wylie, the analytical studies of Ken Booth and James Cable, and selected issues of international maritime law.[5] The breadth and sophistication of these offerings permit the Naval War College to award a master of arts degree in National Security Affairs to its graduates.

The Navy's undergraduate degree-granting institution, the U.S. Naval Academy, records a somewhat different but not too encouraging experience with naval history. Since World War II the academy has consistently offered a one or two-semester course in the field. Until the mid-1970s, this offering was the legendary "sea power" course shaped by Professor E.B. Potter and formatted according to *Sea Power: A Naval History*, a book he co-edited with Admiral Chester W. Nimitz.[6] The course and the book took up the subject with the

---

4   Baer, *One Hundred Years of Sea Power: The U.S. Navy, 1890–1990* (California: Stanford Univ. Press, 1994).

5   For Corbett, see John B. Hattendorf, ed., *Mahan is Not Enough: The Proceedings of the Corbett-Richmond Conference* (Newport, R.I.: Naval War College Press, 1993); for Mahan, see John B. Hattendorf, ed., *The Influence of History on Mahan* (Newport, R.I.: Naval War College Press, 1991). Representative works of the other authors include: Rosinski, *The Development of Naval Thought*, ed., B. Mitchell Simpson III (Newport, RI: Naval War College Press, 1977); Wylie, *Military Strategy: A General Theory of Power Control* (Annapolis: Naval Institute Press, 1989); Cable, *Diplomacy at Sea* (London: Macmillan, 1985); Booth, *Law, Force and Diplomacy at Sea* (Boston: Allen & Unwin, 1985), and *Navies and Foreign Policy* (New York: Crane Russak & Co., 1977).
The Naval Institute Press is cited hereafter as NIP.

6   E.B. Potter and Chester W. Nimitz, eds., *Sea Power: A Naval History* (Englewood Cliffs, N.J.: Prentice-Hall, 1960). There was an earlier version; Potter, ed., *The United States and World Sea Power* (Englewood Cliffs, N.J.: Prentice-Hall, 1955).

Greeks and Romans but rushed rapidly to the golden age of the U.S. Navy—the vast operations of the Pacific campaign of World War II. Many well-known naval historians taught the course, including the prolific Paolo E. Coletta, Robert W. Daly, Clark G. Reynolds, Robert Seager II, and Gerald E. Wheeler.[7] It was a required course, and it is invariably remembered with strong feelings by former midshipmen.

Since the mid-1970s the history department of the academy has offered a quite different one-semester required course in the "American Naval Heritage." As the title suggests, this course focuses very heavily on American naval history. It stresses the interrelationship between U.S. national policy and U.S. naval strategy and operations. Among the nationally known naval historians who have contributed to this course are James C. Bradford, William B. Cogar, Paolo E. Coletta, Kenneth J. Hagan, Frederick S. Harrod, Michael T. Isenberg, Robert W. Love, Jack Sweetman, and Craig L. Symonds.[8] Innumerable officer-instructors have also taught the course, the most recognizable of whom is the widely respected historian of the Marine Corps, Merrill L. Bartlett.[9]

For the foreseeable future, the American Naval Heritage course will remain securely in place as a staple of the history department, but the department itself has demonstrated an erosion of interest in naval history in the last decade. It has rather consistently failed to replace departing naval historians with new ones, choosing instead to broaden itself with faculty specializing in other subsets of the discipline. This ecumenical thrust is understandable, but it has created a staffing crisis. The course on the American Naval Heritage is offered to 1,000 midshipmen per year

---

[7] Coletta, *Admiral Bradley A. Fiske and the American Navy* (Lawrence, Kans.: Regents Press of Kansas, 1979), and *A Selected and Annotated Bibliography of American Naval History* (Lanham, Md: Univ. Press of America, 1988); Daly, *How the Merrimac Won* (New York: Crowell, 1957); Reynolds, *The Fast Carriers: The Forging of an Air Navy* (New York: McGraw-Hill, 1968; Annapolis: NIP, 1992), and *Command of the Sea* (New York: Morrow, 1974); Seager, *Alfred Thayer Mahan: The Man and his Letters* (Annapolis: NIP, 1977); Wheeler, *Prelude to Pearl Harbor* (Columbia, Mo: Univ. of Missouri Press, 1963).

[8] See Bradford, ed., *Crucible of Empire: The Spanish–American War and its Aftermath* (Annapolis: NIP, 1993), *Admirals of the New Steel Navy: Makers of the American Naval Tradition, 1880–1930* (Annapolis: NIP, 1990), *Captains of the Old Steam Navy: Makers of the American Naval Tradition, 1840–1880* (Annapolis: NIP, 1986), and *Command under Sail: Makers of the American Naval Tradition, 1775–1850* (Annapolis: NIP, 1988); Cogar, *Dictionary of Admirals of the United States Navy*, vol. 1, 1862–1900; vol. 2, 1901–1918 (Annapolis: NIP, 1989, 1991); Coletta, ed., *American Secretaries of the Navy*, vol. 1, 1775–1913; vol. 2, 1913–1972 (Annapolis: NIP, 1980); Hagan, *American Gunboat Diplomacy and the Old Navy, 1877–1889* (Westport, Conn.: Greenwood Press, 1973); Harrod, *Manning the New Navy: The Development of a Modern Naval Enlisted Force, 1899–1940* (Westport, Conn.: Greenwood Press, 1978); Isenberg, *Shield of the Republic: The United States in an Era of Cold War and Violent Peace*, vol. 1, 1945–1962 (New York: St. Martin's Press, 1993); Love, *History of the U.S. Navy*, vol. 1, 1775–1941; vol. 2, 1942–1991 (Harrisburg, Pa: Stackpole Press, 1992); Sweetman, *The Landing at Veracruz* (Annapolis: NIP, 1968), *The U.S. Naval Academy: An Illustrated History* (Annapolis: NIP, 1979), and *American Naval History: An Illustrated Chronology* (Annapolis: NIP, 1991); and Symonds, *Navalists and Antinavalists The Naval Policy Debate in The United States, 1785–1827* (Newark, Del.: Univ. of Delaware Press, 1980).

[9] Bartlett, *Lejeune: A Marine's Life* (Columbia: Univ. of South Carolina Press, 1991); ed., *Assault from the Sea: Essays on the History of Amphibious Warfare* (Annapolis: NIP, 1983).

and is taught in small sections of no more than twenty-five students each, for a total of forty sections per year. The four practicing naval historians currently in the department can reasonably cover only sixteen of these, leaving a shortfall of twenty-four sections, or six hundred midshipmen to be taught by non-specialists or officers.

At Annapolis, the 1970s were marked by the introduction of a series of biennial conferences in naval history, and in this respect the support of the department and academy for naval history remains as strong as ever. Directed by Robert R. Love, Jr., the Eleventh Naval History Symposium was held in Annapolis in October, 1993. With an emphasis on World War II, it attracted scholars from all over the world, including delegations from Argentina, Australia, Austria, Canada, Chile, Denmark, Finland, France, Germany, Great Britain, Italy, Japan, Peru, Poland, and Russia. Selected papers from the gathering will be published within two years, as has been the tradition.[10]

The largest program for teaching naval history in the U.S. remains that of the Naval Reserve Officers Training Corps (NROTC). Currently there are about fifty-five college-level NROTC units which "service" a total of about two hundred colleges and universities. For the last seventeen years, Naval Academy Professor Kenneth J. Hagan has served as advisor for the NROTC course entitled "Sea Power and Maritime Affairs."[11] Required in most units, it derives its content and structure from the American Naval Heritage course at the U.S. Naval Academy.

In preparation for teaching the course, junior Navy and Marine Corps officers fresh from the fleet attend a two-week instructors' seminar where Professor Hagan suggests teaching techniques, analyzes the content of the course, and distributes a highly detailed curriculum guide with lesson plans. The officers respond with enthusiasm and gain a sense of confidence, but they nonetheless remain underprepared for teaching a rigorous history course at the college level. This is one of the reasons that very few colleges grant academic credit for the course, despite its Annapolis pedigree.

The future for "Sea Power and Maritime Affairs" is not entirely rosy. The Navy Department has resolved to reduce the number of NROTC units nationally, even though NROTC is demonstrably more cost-effective in producing commissioned officers than is the Naval Academy. An estimated twelve units are scheduled to be decommissioned in the near future, and this means that there will be twelve fewer offerings of the course.

---

[10] The most recent proceedings in print is Jack Sweetman, ed., *New Interpretations in Naval History: Selected Papers from the Tenth Naval History Symposium, Held at the United States Naval Academy, 11–13 September 1991* (Annapolis: NIP, 1993).

[11] For the NROTC format, see Hagan, ed., *In Peace and War: Interpretations of American Naval History, 1774–1984*, 2d ed. (Westport, Conn.: Greenwood Press, 1984).

★ ★ ★

American naval historians traditionally have taught in subjects other than the history of the United States Navy. Harold H. Sprout of Princeton was trained as a political scientist, not as a historian. With his wife as co-author, he published a major synthesis, *The Rise of American Naval Power* in 1939, and he helped establish Princeton's Woodrow Wilson Center of International Relations in 1950. In the early 1960s, he directed a doctoral dissertation on the modern British Navy written by Navy Commander William J. Crowe, Jr., who later became chairman of the Joint Chiefs of Staff under Ronald Reagan and ambassador to Great Britain under President Bill Clinton.[12]

Closer to Clio, if not to the daily teaching of naval history, was Samuel Eliot Morison. He spent a professional lifetime teaching surveys and American colonial history at Harvard University, even though he had distinguished himself in naval history with biographies of John Paul Jones and Matthew C. Perry, and with the 15-volume official history of the Navy in World War II. The fate of teaching mainly outside their specialty in naval history also befell such notable scholars as Raymond G. O'Connor and Gerald E. Wheeler in the 1950s. Similarly, the field's current dean, William R. Braisted, served three decades as a professor of Far Eastern History at the University of Texas.[13]

Today the list of naval historians who are not regularly teaching naval history is depressingly long. Stephen E. Pelz teaches diplomatic history at the University of Massachusetts. Peter D. Karsten has turned to the study of constitutional history at the University of Pittsburgh. Roger Dingman teaches Far Eastern history at the University of Southern California. James R. Reckner specializes in the Vietnam War at Texas Tech University. Allan R. Millett of Ohio State University has written extensively on the Marine Corps and on military affairs, but he does not teach naval history.[14]

---

[12] Harold and Margaret Sprout, *The Rise of American Naval Power, 1776–1918* (New Jersey: Princeton Univ. Press, 1939; Annapolis: NIP, 1990). Crowe's strategic viewpoint can be seen in "The Policy Roots of the Modern Royal Navy, 1946–1963," (Ph.D. diss., Princeton Univ., 1965), and most recently in his memoir, *The Line of Fire: From Washington to the Gulf* (New York: Simon & Schuster, 1993). For an early homage to the Sprouts, see Gordon C. O'Gara, *Theodore Roosevelt and the Rise of the Modern Navy* (New Jersey: Princeton Univ. Press, 1943; New York: Greenwood Press, 1969).

[13] For a Morison sampler, see *History of United States Naval Operations in World War II*, 15 vols. (Boston: Little, Brown, 1947–63), *John Paul Jones: A Sailor's Biography* (Boston: Little, Brown, 1959; Annapolis: NIP, 1989), and *"Old Bruin:" Commodore Matthew C. Perry, 1794–1858* (Boston: Little Brown, 1967). For the others, see O'Connor, *Origins of the American Navy: Sea Power in the Colonies and the New Nation* (Lanham, Md.: Univ. Press of America, 1994); Wheeler, *Prelude to Pearl Harbor: The United States Navy and the Far East, 1921-1931* (Columbia: Univ. of Missouri Press, 1963); and Braisted, *United States Navy in the Pacific, 1897–1909*, and *United States Navy in the Pacific, 1909–1922* (Austin: Univ. of Texas Press, 1958, 1971).

[14] Pelz, *Race to Pearl Harbor: The Failure of the Second London Naval Conference and the Onset of World War II* (Cambridge, Mass.: Harvard Univ. Press, 1974); Karsten, *The Naval Aristocracy: The Golden Age*

Much the same can be said of Carl Boyd at Old Dominion University, Jeffrey M. Dorwart of the University of Delaware, William M. Fowler, Jr. at Northeastern University, William M. McBride at James Madison University, Clark G. Reynolds at the College of Charleston, Alex Roland at Duke University, David Syrett at the City University of New York, Spencer Tucker at Texas Christian University, Richard W. Turk at Allegheny College, Jonathan Utley at the University of Tennessee, Charles J. Weeks, Jr. at Southern College of Technology, and the recently retired David F. Long at the University of New Hampshire.[15] Harold D. Langley teaches occasional courses in diplomatic and military history at Catholic University, but his principal professional position is with the Smithsonian Institution, as was the case with Philip K. Lundeberg and the late Roger Pineau, both protégés of Samuel Eliot Morison.[16] In a category all his own is Professor Raimondo Luraghi of the University of Genoa, Italy who has completed a manuscript on the history of the Confederate States Navy for publication in the United States.

Although the teaching of naval history remains on the margin at most private and public colleges and universities, there are several institutions where new programs have emerged and assumed central pedagogical roles. The pacesetter is the concentration in Maritime History and Underwater Research at East Carolina University (ECU), a two-year curriculum leading to a master of arts degree in history. Established in 1981 by historian William N. Still, Jr. and

of Annapolis and the Emergence of Modern American Navalism (New York: Free Press, 1972); Dingman, Power in the Pacific: The Origins of Naval Arms Limitation, 1914–1922 (Illinois: Univ. of Chicago Press, 1976); Reckner, Teddy Roosevelt's Great White Fleet (Annapolis: NIP, 1988); Millett, Semper Fidelis: The History of the United States Marine Corps, 2d ed. (New York: Free Press, 1991).

15 Boyd and Akihiko Yoshida, The Japanese Submarine Force and World War II (Annapolis: NIP, forthcoming); Dorwart, The Office of Naval Intelligence: The Birth of America's First Intelligence Agency, 1865-1918 (Annapolis: NIP, 1979), and Conflict of Duty: The U.S. Navy's Intelligence Dilemma, 1919–1945 (Annapolis: NIP, 1983); Fowler, Rebels Under Sail: The American Navy During the Revolution (New York: Scribner, 1976), Jack Tars and Commodores: The American Navy, 1783-1815 (Boston: Houghton Mifflin, 1984), and Under Two Flags: The American Navy in the Civil War (New York: Norton, 1990); McBride, Goodnight Officially: The Pacific War Letters of a Destroyer Sailor (Boulder, Colo.: Westview Press, 1994); Reynolds, The Fast Carriers: The Forging of an Air Navy (New York: McGraw-Hill, 1968; Annapolis: NIP, 1992); Roland, Underwater Warfare in the Age of Sail (Bloomington: Indiana Univ. Press, 1978); Syrett, The Royal Navy in American Waters, 1775–1783 (Brookfield, Vt.: Gower Publishing Co., 1989); Tucker, Arming the Fleet: U.S. Navy Ordnance in the Muzzle-Loading Era (Annapolis: NIP, 1989), and The Jeffersonian Gunboat Navy (Columbia: Univ. of South Carolina Press, 1993); Turk, The Ambiguous Relationship: Theodore Roosevelt and Alfred Thayer Mahan (New York: Greenwood Press, 1987); Utley, An American Battleship at Peace and War: The U.S.S. Tennessee (Lawrence, Kans.: Univ. Press of Kansas, 1991); Weeks, An American Naval Diplomat in Revolutionary Russia (Annapolis: NIP, 1993); and Long, Gold Braid and Foreign Relations: Diplomatic Activities of U.S. Naval Officers (Annapolis: NIP, 1988).

16 Langley, Social Reform in the United States Navy, 1798–1862 (Urbana: Univ. of Illinois Press, 1967), and A Medical History of the United States Navy, 1794–1842 (Baltimore: Johns Hopkins Univ. Press, 1994); Lundeberg, The Continental Gunboat Philadelphia and the Northern Campaign of 1776 (Washington: Smithsonian Institution Press, 1966); Pineau, ed., The Japan Expedition, 1852–1854: The Personal Journal of Commodore Matthew C. Perry (Washington: Smithsonian Institution Press, 1968).

underwater archaeologist Gordon P. Watts, the ECU endeavor blends the research methodologies of underwater archaeology and history to paint a clearer picture of the maritime past. ECU's rich and divergent course offerings include "Sea Power: 480 BC to the Present," a survey of the nature of warfare at sea and its changing role in eras of peace and war. East Carolina's most notable archaeological successes have been in relation to the Civil War. Starting with the discovery of the USS *Monitor* off Cape Hatteras and the vessel's designation as a national maritime sanctuary, ECU scholars have documented the USS *Southfield*, the Union transport *Maple Leaf*, and the Confederate blockade-runner *Mary Celestia*. ECU archaeologists have also joined peers in the National Park Service and the Naval Historical Center to investigate and where possible preserve the CSS *Gaines*, the USS *Philippi*, and the USS *Tecumseh*—all sunken relics of the Civil War lying on the bottom of Mobile Bay. In association with French experts and with William S. Dudley of the Naval Historical Center, Professor Still and his crew are investigating the remains of the famed Confederate raider *Alabama*, sunk off Cherbourg, France, in 1864.

The published historical scholarship on American naval topics by ECU scholars is chronologically and topically broad, ranging from Carl E. Swanson, *Predators and Prizes: American Privateering and Imperial Warfare, 1739–1948* to Michael A. Palmer, *On Course to Desert Storm: The U.S. Navy and the Persian Gulf*.[17] These ECU authors and other scholars are fortunate to have established a close working relationship with the University of South Carolina Press, now an excellent outlet for historical monographs.

Beyond ECU, the University of Alabama has long sponsored naval history in the person of three teaching scholars: Robert E. Johnson, recently retired; Ronald H. Spector, briefly; and since 1993, John F. Beeler, who specializes in the Royal Navy.[18] Spector moved to George Washington University to direct an international studies center, but he does occasionally offer a course on world naval history since the 1600s.

Sharply focused on U.S. naval history is Texas A & M University, where James C. Bradford attracts a large audience to his course on the subject. In Philadelphia, Temple University recently opened a Center for the Study of Force and Diplomacy, with David A. Rosenberg teaching naval history. At Yale

---

[17] Swanson, *Predators and Prizes* (Columbia: Univ. of South Carolina Press, 1991); Palmer, *On Course to Desert Storm: The U.S. Navy and the Persian Gulf*, Contributions to Naval History Series, No. 5 (Washington: U.S. Gov't. Print. Off., 1992). See also Palmer, *Guardians of the Gulf* (New York: The Free Press, 1992), and William N. Still, Jr., *American Sea Power in the Old World* (Westport, Conn.: Greenwood Press, 1980).

[18] Johnson, *Far China Station: The U.S. Navy in Asian Waters, 1800–1898* (Annapolis: NIP, 1979), and *Bering Sea Escort: Life Aboard A Coast Guard Cutter in World War II* (Annapolis: NIP, 1992); Spector, *Professors of War: The Naval War College and the Development of the Naval Profession* (Newport, R.I.: Naval War College Press, 1977), and *Eagle Against the Sun: The American War with Japan* (New York: The Free Press, 1985); Beeler, "Steaming Erratically towards the *Dreadnought*: The British Navy in the Era of Gladstone and Disraeli" (Ph.D. diss., University of Illinois, 1991).

University since the early 1980s, American military and naval history has been covered by term appointments.[19] More significantly, at Yale in 1983, Paul M. Kennedy inaugurated the J. Richardson Dilworth Chair of International and Diplomatic History, and in 1989, Sir Michael Howard became the Robert A. Lovett Professor of Military and Naval History. The Lovett professorship passed to Geoffrey Parker four years later.[20] By contrast with Yale, some major university centers of military and strategic studies have no appointments or courses specifically in naval history; witness Harvard's Center for International Affairs as well as that university's long vacant Gardiner Chair of Oceanic History and Affairs. At Stanford University, the Raymond A. Spruance Chair, named for the World War II admiral, is traditionally occupied by a military historian specializing in Clausewitz.

★ ★ ★

The absence of university centers dedicated to the study of naval history explains why so many doctoral dissertations have been written under the direction of specialists in fields other than naval history. The experience of the two authors of this essay is illustrative. Separated by a generation in age and time of doctoral work, neither author was directed by a naval historian. The diplomatic historian Charles S. Campbell, Jr., was Kenneth Hagan's mentor. Mark Shulman's dissertation was directed by Richard Abrams, a political historian. A doctoral dissertation currently in process (retired naval Captain Peter Swartz's study of the Cold War navy) is being directed by Warner R. Schilling at Columbia. While Schilling's own dissertation was an able essay on naval history, it was never published and he has not continued to work in the field.[21] A salient exception to the portrait of doctoral sponsorship just painted is Jon T. Sumida's energetic direction of doctoral dissertations at the University of Maryland, but his field is primarily British naval history, not the history of the United States Navy.[22]

---

19 Harold E. Selesky taught these courses from 1983 until 1991, followed by Mark R. Shulman.

20 Of the three professors holding endowed chairs, only Paul Kennedy has written widely in naval history. See *The Rise and Fall of British Naval Mastery* (New York: Scribner, 1976).

21 Schilling, "Admirals and Foreign Policy, 1913–1919" (Ph.D. diss., Yale University, 1953), photocopy of typescript (Ann Arbor: Univ. Microfilms, 1970).

22 Other American historians of European sea power include: Daniel Baugh, *British Naval Administration in the Age of Walpole* (New Jersey: Princeton Univ. Press, 1965), Professor of History at Cornell University; Volker Berghahn, *Der Tirpitz-Plan* (Dusseldorf: Droste, 1971), Professor of History at Brown University; John T. Guilmartin, *Gunpowder and Galleys* (New York: Cambridge Univ. Press, 1974), Professor of History at Ohio State University; Paul Halpern, *The Naval War in the Mediterranean, 1914–1918* (Annapolis: NIP, 1987), Professor of History at the University of Florida; Jon T. Sumida, *In Defense of Naval Supremacy: Finance, Technology and British Naval Policy, 1889–1914* (Boston: Unwin Hyman, 1989), Associate Professor at the University of Maryland.

★ ★ ★

While it is not a teaching organization, the Naval Historical Center in Washington, D.C. is vital to the national dissemination of historical information about the Navy. The Center employs approximately twenty-five naval historians, a greater number than any other organization in the United States. These professionals write monographs and reference works, edit and publish historical documents, record oral histories, organize scholarly conferences, sponsor underwater archaeological investigations, and contribute to the Navy's museums. Some of them teach courses on American naval history as adjunct faculty at colleges and universities in the Washington area.

The Naval Historical Center is presided over by the Director of Naval History. Prior to July 1986, this position was occupied by a retired naval officer, usually an admiral. Since then, two civilian scholars have held the post: Ronald H. Spector (1986–1989), followed by the present incumbent, Dean C. Allard. The director's headquarters at the Naval Historical Center is located in the Navy Yard at Washington, D.C.[23] The Marine Corps Historical Center is adjacent to the Navy's.

Museums

Most training in U.S. naval history is done by colleges or governmental organizations, but the Mystic Seaport Museum in Connecticut is noteworthy for its long-standing dedication to educating the American public about the history of the sea. In particular, the Munson Institute at Mystic conducts a graduate-level summer program on American maritime studies. Benjamin W. Labaree, William F. Fowler, John B. Hattendorf, Jeffrey Safford and Edward W. Sloan are those who today continue the Mystic tradition of teaching, which was established by the late Harvard Professor Robert G. Albion.

In addition to Mystic, other museums from time to time organize educational programs on American naval history. In the spring of 1994, for example, the Smithsonian Institution joined with the U.S. Naval Academy Museum to offer a three-day seminar on the history of warfare in the age of sail, a concentrated schedule of lectures and discussions directed by faculty of the history department of the Naval Academy at Annapolis.

★ ★ ★

---

[23] The Naval Historical Center is located at the Washington Navy Yard, at M and 9th streets. It is divided into several branches. Phone numbers for these branches are as follows (all are 202–433): Contemporary History, 3891; Curator, 2220; Early History, 2364; Naval Aviation, 4355/8; Navy Art Gallery, 3815; Library, 3172; Photographic Section, 2765; Senior Historian, 7230; and Ships' Histories, 2891.

The Naval Academy Museum is one of twelve naval museums scattered at bases and installations across the United States. The U.S. Marine Corps runs one official museum in the Washington Navy Yard and another at Quantico, Virginia. This Navy-Marine Corps total of fourteen compares with seventy in the Department of the Army, one in the U.S. Air Force, and one for the Coast Guard.

The twelve museums of the Department of the Navy fall under the general administrative umbrella of the Director of Naval History. He exercises immediate supervision over only the Navy Museum in the Washington Navy Yard. Stimulated by former Secretary of the Navy John F. Lehman, Jr., and dynamically directed by Oscar P. Fitzgerald, this museum has made tremendous progress in the last fifteen years. It conducts outstanding educational programs, displays works by leading contemporary naval artists, and maintains the largest World War II exhibit in the country. Its renovated Civil War exhibit contains remnants from David G. Farragut's flagship, the USS *Hartford*.

The Navy's oldest official museum is the one at the Naval Academy in Annapolis, Maryland. Dating back to 1845, the museum presently is housed in Preble Hall, which was constructed in 1939 and expanded in 1962 with the sponsorship of the Naval Academy Athletic Association and the U.S. Naval Institute, both non-governmental institutions. The museum's collection features artifacts and artwork as varied as midshipmen's class rings, memorabilia from Matthew C. Perry's nineteenth-century expedition to Japan, paintings of Columbus's voyages and Commodore Edward Preble's bombardment of Tripoli in 1804, and the table on which the Japanese surrender was signed aboard the battleship *Missouri* in 1945. Across the "Yard" from Preble Hall, in the basement of the Naval Academy Chapel, the museum is responsible for the crypt containing the body of John Paul Jones, perhaps the most popular site for visitors to the Academy.

The Naval Academy Museum experienced a period of revitalization in the early 1990s. Under the directorship of Professor Kenneth J. Hagan (1990–1993), it expanded in scope and assumed much greater importance for the study of naval history by midshipmen, scholars, and the general public. In January, 1993, it opened the new Class of 1951 Gallery of Ships, which for the first time properly houses the phenomenal Henry Huddleston Rogers Collection of wooden dockyard and bone models built in the age of sail.

In October 1993, the museum loaned $3.5 million worth of artifacts to Hamburg, Germany, for a brief but extensive exhibition on maritime and naval history entitled ART MARITIM '93. With an attendance of over 25,000 people, this was the largest overseas exhibit ever mounted by any U.S. Navy museum.

The Naval Academy Museum is also the repository of the Beverley R. Robinson Collection of historic naval aquatints, messotints, engravings, and lithographs. Fully endowed to perpetually honor the donor, the collection now includes over 6,000 originals, many dating from the eighteenth and early nineteenth centuries, before the advent of photography. Prints from this precious source for the study of European and American naval history have been reproduced in a carefully documented catalog and on a 12-inch video disk. The disk contains a total of 19,000 images relating to naval history generally and to the Naval Academy in particular.

The largest official Navy museum is the National Naval Aviation Museum at Naval Air Station Pensacola, Florida. It ranks as the largest by virtue of the size of its artifacts and the enthusiasm of its supporters, many of whom are naval aviators. The museum currently is undergoing rapid growth funded by the aviation industry, naval aviation buffs, foundation grants, and the million dollars in revenues that its gift shop generates annually. When completed, the five-module museum will overshadow the Smithsonian's Air and Space Museum.

Pensacola already dwarfs the Naval Air Test and Evaluation Museum at the Naval Air Warfare Center, Patuxent River, Maryland. Founded in 1978, the Patuxent museum tells the hair-raising story of testing and evaluating naval aircraft. The collection includes many actual aircraft, and a trainer for the F-4 Phantom allows visitors to sit in the simulated cockpit of a Navy fighter.

With over a million visitors per year, the historic frigate *Constitution* in the Charlestown Navy Yard near Boston tops the Navy Department museums in annual attendance. Nearby, the Submarine Force Museum at Groton, Connecticut has made great strides since the mooring of the USS *Nautilus* at the back door of its new facility. It now ranks among the top five museums in New England in terms of attendance. More modest is the nearby Naval War College Museum, which focuses on the Naval War College, the naval and maritime heritage of Newport, Rhode Island, and the seafaring tradition of the people of Narragansett Bay.

Far to the south, the Hampton Roads Naval Museum is expanding into a new facility in the commercial center of Norfolk, Virginia. Devoted to the naval and maritime heritage of the Norfolk region, the exhibitions are chronologically and topically organized to maximize their pedagogical potential. This expansion is a success story which the National Endowment for the Humanities declined to finance, a regrettable commentary on the difficulty of winning support from the NEH or the National Endowment for the Arts for projects connected with the federal government.

In Athens, Georgia, the Naval Supply Corps Museum, established in 1974, serves also as an archives. The Museum traces the development and growth of the Supply Corps using models of auxiliary ships, uniforms, equipment, and a diverse collection of objects. It also houses a collection of technical manuals, cookbooks, and documentary material related to the Supply Corps School in Athens.

The Navy maintains three West Coast museums. The comprehensive Naval Undersea Museum is located at the Naval Undersea Warfare Center, Keyport, Washington. It covers twentieth-century technology as applied to the world beneath the sea, including warfare, exploration, and exploitation of resources on the ocean bed. The Civil Engineer Corps–Seabee Museum at Port Hueneme, California commemorates the achievements of the Naval Construction Force (Seabees) and the Navy's Civil Engineer Corps. In San Francisco Bay, the Treasure Island Museum was founded during the American Bicentennial to promote knowledge of naval, Marine Corps, and Coast Guard activities in the Pacific basin. The future of this small museum is clouded by the uncertainty over base closures accompanying the Navy's "downsizing" in the 1990s.

★ ★ ★

The Smithsonian Institution in Washington, D.C., provides coverage on naval history and occasionally promotes the topic through special travelling exhibitions. In the past twenty-five years two major naval exhibitions have been mounted. "The Japan Expedition of Commodore Matthew C. Perry" in 1964 and "The Magnificent Voyagers: The U.S. Exploring Expedition of 1838–1842" in 1986 were both held in the National Museum of Natural History, with the latter also travelling to other museums. In 1994 the Museum of American History is sending an exhibition on American culture to Japan, to include artifacts relating to Commodore Perry's expedition borrowed from the Naval Academy Museum.

The apparent vigor of the Smithsonian Institution in the field of naval history masks an unfortunate structural malady. The Museum of American History, presumably the preferred locus for exhibits on American naval history, does not contain the Smithsonian's walk-through of a simulated World War II aircraft carrier. That popular eye-grabber, which enables the public to watch film-strips of carrier operations from the vantage points of the ship's skipper and "air boss," is situated in the Air and Space Museum across the Mall from the Museum of American History.

More ominous is the Museum of American History's consistent retrenchment of support for naval history during the last two decades. Administratively subordinated to military history, the naval specialty has lost curatorial time, exhibit space, and research fellowships. There is now only one curator of naval history and little prospect of replacement when he retires. A pool of irreplaceable expertise has evaporated because the Smithsonian hierarchy lacks interest in the history of the United States Navy.[24]

---

[24] For a comprehensive view, see Philip K. Lundeberg, "Military Museums," John E. Jessup, Jr., ed., *Encyclopedia of the American Military*, 3 vols. (New York: Macmillan, 1994).

★ ★ ★

In the private arena, one highly important organization is the Historic Naval Ships Association of North America, which assists in the preservation of sixty-seven former U.S. Navy vessels, including four aircraft carriers, four battleships, two cruisers, ten destroyers, one destroyer escort, twenty-four submarines, four wooden ships, and other smaller types such as minesweepers and PT boats. More than seven million people boarded these vessels in 1990, and in the same year, their operating budgets reached $21.5 million. Besides the ships themselves, some of these centers contain elaborate exhibits on board the ships or in nearby shore facilities. Some have extensive educational programs, among the most effective of which are overnight youth encampments with lectures, tours, and films.

Certain exhibitions deserve special note. The Second World War carrier USS *Intrepid* is one of the most popular tourist attractions in New York City. Battleship Cove in Fall River, Massachusetts, has an outstanding collection of ships, including the USS *Massachusetts*. And finally, the National Park Service maintains the emotionally wrenching USS *Arizona* Memorial in Pearl Harbor— one of the most highly visited of the national parks.

Many submarines have been saved and converted into museums because they are smaller and therefore easier and less expensive to maintain than most warships. For this reason, several submarines are located far from the ocean, perhaps most dramatically the captured German *U-505* in Chicago. At the other end of the spectrum are the aircraft carriers, notably the USS *Yorktown* (CV-10) in Charleston, South Carolina, where hull maintenance in a semi-tropical climate is a fiscal nightmare.

The historic naval ships of World War II were saved in part because so many thousands of their crew members came to share a sense of nostalgia for the exciting times of wartime shipboard life. What will become of these ships once the veterans of World War II are gone is a major concern to those maintaining and operating them today as museums.

State aid may be one answer; it has rescued two important relics of earlier eras. In 1988, the U.S. brig *Niagara*, one of Commodore Oliver Hazard Perry's flagships in 1813, was rebuilt at Erie, Pennsylvania, and now is used as an official promotional vessel for the state of Pennsylvania. Similarly, the battleship *Texas*, the only survivor of service in both world wars, was rescued by the state of Texas a few years ago when its veterans' support group became minuscule. The *Texas* recently underwent an overhaul valued in excess of $21 million.

Two other masterpieces have been less fortunate. Commodore George Dewey's 1898 flagship, the cruiser *Olympia* at Philadelphia, and the sailing warship USS *Constellation* at Baltimore—both beguiling historical specimens—have suffered devastating periods of neglect. They could sink at their piers because they have no natural national constituency of concerned individuals to rescue them.

The Historic Naval Ships Association is attempting to alert Congress to the plight of these ships and win appropriations for their repair in the years ahead. One innovative idea is to use funds obtained from the scrapping of less historic ships in the Navy's inventory to maintain the wooden *Constellation*, the U.S. destroyer *Kidd*, the diesel submarine USS *Cod*, the nuclear-powered USS *Nautilus*, and others.

★ ★ ★

Two non-government museums fall into a special category and are essential sites for people interested in the Normandy invasion of 6 June 1944. The First Division Museum on the Cantigny estate in Wheaton, Illinois, contains a remarkable recreation of a portion of the Normandy beach as it was on D-day. In New Orleans, the Eisenhower Center is planning a large D-day museum, with groundbreaking scheduled for the fiftieth anniversary of history's most massive amphibious landing. Both sites deserve all the popularity they will receive in the future.

Archives, Manuscript Collections, and Libraries

American naval studies traditionally have focused heavily on strategy and operations and have been based almost solely upon government documents, mostly from within the Department of the Navy or the Defense Department. A stunning variety of resources used by social and cultural historians remains virtually untapped by naval historians: the popular press; records on immigration, health, and voting; television and movie portrayals; propaganda; advertising; and even sermons. Historians of the United States Navy have also neglected such trans- or non-national agencies as the United Nations, NATO, and the Red Cross—each of which holds keys to the American naval experience. These resources belong to all historians and will not be surveyed here, but one set of records external to the Navy must be mentioned.

Reports from U.S. consuls and consulates are extremely useful for studies of overseas naval operations and the category of cruising known as "showing the flag," or "gunboat diplomacy." Most consular records have been accessioned by the National Archives, and many have been microfilmed as part of Record Groups 59 and 84. In addition, many consuls kept priceless letterbooks that have found their way into other depositories. The Special Collections Division of the Naval Academy Library, for example, contains the letterbooks of Richard B. Jones and Moses Young pertaining to U.S. relations with North Africa at the time of the Barbary Wars. Among the issues they discuss are Great Britain's claims to two Tripolitan prize ships taken by the U.S. Navy. This is an essential dimension to the proper analysis of nineteenth-century U.S. naval strategy and operations.

Three types of archival sources directly applicable to United States naval history present themselves for special consideration: those concerning construction plans and blueprints, operational records, and the documents of high-level decision making. The accessibility of each category of records varies. Plans, blueprints, and ship-building folders have been preserved to a considerable extent and are available to scholars at the National Archives Cartographic Office, located at the new National Archives building at the University of Maryland.

The records of the technical bureaus that did so much to shape the Navy's physical elements beginning in 1842—BuOrd, BuShips, BuAer, etc.—are available, but pose a problem of access. Post-1941 bureau files are stored at the National Archives Federal Records Center in Suitland, Maryland, but locating the documents relevant to any particular study is an uncertain and frustrating exercise. One way to get at some of this material for the twentieth century is to study the records of the General Board of the Navy, which have been published on microfilm by Scholarly Resources.[25]

Records of operations, including ships' logs, war diaries, and action reports, are relatively easy to access at the National Archives. For greater convenience, Scholarly Resources of Wilmington, Delaware, has microfilmed most of the material pertaining to the nineteenth-century Navy.

The third category of archival naval records, covering policy and high-level decision making, is difficult to save and recover, and eventually to declassify. Since World War II, especially, decisions regarding naval strategy and policy have been made by numerous bodies, and there is no national standard for storage and accessibility of interagency documents. Among the bodies that tackle strategic questions are such sensitive offices as those of the State Department, the Joint Chiefs of Staff, the National Security Council, the National Security Agency, the Central Intelligence Agency, and the President. Partly because of interagency "turf wars" and partly because of valid concerns about preserving state secrets, these records present a myriad of challenges to the naval historian. One helpful technique is to desert Washington, D.C. in favor of the presidential libraries, which often contain a great deal of relevant interagency material.

It is important to recall that many momentous decisions were made at the "CinC" level, that is, by commanders of joint commands, or of fleets far distant from Washington. Often the decisions were conveyed over message traffic. The Navy messages are preserved in the Operational Archives of the Naval Historical Center, but accessibility is restricted by security-classification considerations.[26]

---

[25] *Hearings Before the General Board of the Navy, 1917–50* (Wilmington, Del.: Scholarly Resources, 1983), microfilm, 15 reels.

[26] For more on these issues, see David Alan Rosenberg, "Process: The Realities of Formulating Modern

The impediment of security classification affects a broad range of the Navy's Cold War archives. For all intents and purposes, systematic declassification of Navy records halted in 1982 with the declassification of most of the Korean War files. Review of some accessioned records of special interest to the Naval Historical Center and the Naval Intelligence Command continued after 1982. In general, however, there now exists a forty-year spread (1953–1993) of needlessly classified and hence inaccessible materials.

This regrettable situation requires remedy through issuance of a new declassification executive order and implementing directives. The emphasis should be placed on the release of information, as in President Richard M. Nixon's E.O. 11652, rather than on security, as in President Ronald Reagan's E.O. 12356. The Clinton administration ought to address questions of what should be classified and for how long, as well as the possibility of bulk declassification of Cold War-era materials. Hopefully, a new and liberal executive order would emerge from such a reexamination of policy.

★ ★ ★

The National Archives will accession the World War II operations and planning records from the Naval Historical Center and the Marine Corps Historical Office in 1995. In that same year, these and all other military and diplomatic records dating back to 1941 will be moved to the new National Archives building on the campus of the University of Maryland at College Park. For the first time, one repository will house the major documentary resources on the politico-military policies, decisions, and actions of World War II and after. This is a major accomplishment and will alleviate hours of tiresome travel between various repositories scattered around Washington.

The National Capitol contains valuable manuscript collections, although the personal records of leading naval figures will always remain somewhat scattered. Many important papers assembled by the Naval Historical Foundation have been deposited with the Library of Congress Manuscript Division in the Madison Building. As an aid to locating this collection and others, the Naval Historical Center publishes *U.S. Naval History Sources in the United States*. A more comprehensive guide is the *National Union Catalogue of Manuscript Collections*.[27]

The Naval Historical Center at the Washington Navy Yard is presently making efforts to collect papers, including those of Admirals Arleigh A. Burke, Elmo R. Zumwalt, Jr., and Arthur W. Radford, as well as those of recent chiefs

---

Naval Strategy," in James Goldrick and John B. Hattendorf, eds., *Mahan is Not Enough: The Proceedings of a Conference on the Works of Sir Julian Corbett and Admiral Sir Herbert Richmond* (Newport, R.I.: Naval War College Press, 1993), 14, 15, *inter alia*.

27 *U.S. Naval History Sources in the United States* (Washington: Naval History Division, 1979); *The National Union Catalog of Manuscript Collections* (Washington: Library of Congress, 1959–61).

of naval operations (CNOs) Carlisle A.H. Trost, James D. Watkins, and Frank B. Kelso. The most recent collections will remain classified for years. But they bring up the question as to whether there ought to be an American equivalent of the successful British Naval Records Society to encourage the collection and study of the papers of men and women below the top tier of the Navy. The American Naval History Society has been defunct since World War I and the Naval Historical Foundation, which did so much to create the manuscript collection deposited in the Library of Congress, has not demonstrated marked energy in preserving papers in recent years.

Outside Washington, manuscript collections of special importance to U.S. naval history are found at the Naval Academy and the Naval War College. Among the more significant individual papers in the War College's Historical Collection are those of Admirals Stephen B. Luce, A. T. Mahan, Ernest J. King, Harris Laning, William V. Pratt, and Raymond A. Spruance.[28] Fragments of personal records can be found in the Naval Academy Museum and in the Special Collections Division of the Nimitz Library at the Naval Academy. Elsewhere, East Carolina, Duke, Yale, Harvard, Brown, the New York Public Library, and the Hoover Institution at Stanford University have notable manuscript collections, as do the hometown presidential libraries administered by the National Archives.

★ ★ ★

Two invaluable oral history programs must not be overlooked by serious scholars seeking insights into the mind-sets of the men and women who made policy and strategy, even though their recollections must be somewhat discounted because of the inevitable impact of hindsight on memory. One is conducted by the Naval Historical Center in Washington, D.C. and the other by the U.S. Naval Institute in Annapolis.

Begun in 1969 and currently directed by Paul Stillwell, the Naval Institute Oral History Program has amassed a library of one hundred ninety bound volumes of transcripts. Most of the oral histories cover an individual's entire career, but some concentrate on specialized topics, such as early WAVES officers, the first black naval officers, and the Normandy invasion of June 1944. The volumes are available to the researcher at the Naval Institute's headquarters in Annapolis, Maryland, and through rental or purchase.[29]

---

[28] See Evelyn M. Cherpak, *A Guide to Archives, Manuscripts and Oral Histories in the Naval Historical Collection* (Newport: Naval War College, 1991).

[29] For the oral histories at the Naval Historical Center, see Edward J. Marolda, et al., eds., *Oral History Collection in the Operational Archives, Naval Historical Center* (Washington: Naval Historical Center, 1983); those at the Naval Institute are cumulatively listed in "U.S. Naval Institute Oral History Collection: Catalog of Transcripts" (Annapolis: NIP, 1993–1994).

For two accessible oral histories, see Paul Stillwell, ed., *The Golden Thirteen: Recollections of the First*

The Oral History Program is an adjunct of the Naval Institute's Library Services and Photo Archives, a research center administered by Mary Beth Straight. This reference collection consists of 4,500 books, indexed back copies of the U.S. Naval Institute *Proceedings* and *Naval History*, and more than 400,000 photographic images.

★ ★ ★

One of the nation's two best libraries for the study of naval history is the Nimitz Library of the U.S. Naval Academy in Annapolis, Maryland. The other one is the Navy Department Library at the Naval Historical Center in Washington, D.C. These two repositories house virtually every book ever written on the topic of U.S. naval history.

As part of the Naval Academy, the Nimitz Library relies on year-end funding to supplement its book budget. Without this special but wildly fluctuating allocation of funds, the library's periodicals' purchases—devoted mostly to science and engineering—would soon exceed 70 percent of the library's materials' budget. As a result of this erratic allocations system, the library's book purchases have declined sharply, from 10,000 titles in fiscal year 1992 to slightly more than 6,000 in fiscal year 1993. This decline practically guarantees that the core collection in naval history, so painstakingly gathered by dedicated faculty and librarians in the one hundred fifty years of the Naval Academy's existence, will cease to stand as an infallible source of books for scholars and midshipmen.[30]

Published Collections

Published collections of personal papers and correspondence are of considerable use to the historian. Foremost of these is *The Letters and Papers of Alfred Thayer Mahan*, edited by Robert Seager II and Doris D. Maguire.[31] Also useful are the *New American State Papers, Naval Series*; microfilm editions of the papers of John Paul Jones, Samuel DuPont, and John Ericsson; the diaries of Josephus Daniels; the correspondence of Theodore Roosevelt and Henry Cabot Lodge; the writings of Stephen B. Luce; and the various impressive collections of presidential papers.[32]

Black Naval Officers (Annapolis: NIP, 1993), and ed., *Assault on Normandy: First-Person Accounts from the Sea Services* (Annapolis: NIP, 1994).

[30] For a dated but comprehensive listing of depositories relevant to this section, see Dean C. Allard, et al., *U.S. Naval History Sources in the United States* (Washington: Naval History Division, 1979).

[31] Seager and Maguire, eds., *The Letters and Papers of Alfred Thayer Mahan*, vol. 1, 1847–1889; vol. 2, 1890–1901; vol. 3, 1902–1914 (Annapolis: NIP, 1975).

[32] *The New American State Papers, Naval Series*, ed., K. Jack Bauer (Wilmington, Del.: Scholarly Resources, 1981); *The Papers of John Paul Jones*, microform edition, ed., James C. Bradford (Alexandria, Va.: Chadwyck-Healey, 1986); *Official Dispatches and Letters of Rear Admiral DuPont, U.S. Navy: 1846–48, 1861–63* (Wilmington, Del.: Press of Ferris Bros., Printers, 1883; Ann Arbor, Mich.: University Microfilm International, 1986); *The Papers of John Ericsson*, microfilm edition, Esther

Following the rise of the modern American Navy in the 1880s, the Navy Department made several serious efforts to collect relevant historical books and documents for historians. James Russell Soley created the Office of Library and Naval War Records (in 1915 the name was reversed) and was given funds to start publishing the documentary series, *Official Records of the Union and Confederate Navies in the War of the Rebellion* (1894–1922).[33] This series was followed by those on the Quasi– and Barbary Wars at the suggestion of President and former Assistant Secretary of the Navy Franklin D. Roosevelt. This type of project continues with the ongoing publication of the records of the Revolutionary and 1812 wars—an enterprise based on documents that FDR himself found in the State, War and Navy Building.[34] When these projects are eventually completed, decisions must be made concerning the future of such documentary editing. Given the sheer volume of collections from subsequent wars, perhaps only representative selections should be collected, using as a model Ronald H. Spector's *Listening to the Enemy*.[35]

Bibliography

Bibliography has always been a thriving form of publication in U.S. naval history. Each essay in Kenneth J. Hagan's *In Peace and War: Interpretations of American Naval History, 1775–1984* provides a thoughtful bibliography, as do the individual chapters of Allan R. Millett and Peter Maslowski, *For the Common Defense*—the most widely used college textbook of American military history—and of Millett's *Semper Fidelis*. The most important volumes specifically dedicated to bibliography are: Robert G. Albion, *Naval and Maritime History: An Annotated Bibliography*; Charles T. Harbeck, *A Contribution to the Bibliography of the History*

Chilstrom Meixner, project director (Philadelphia: American Swedish Historical Foundation, 1970); *The Cabinet Diaries of Josephus Daniels*, ed., E. D. Cronon (Lincoln: Univ. of Nebraska Press, 1963); *Selections from the Correspondence of Theodore Roosevelt and Henry Cabot Lodge* (New York: Charles Scribner's & Sons, 1925); *The Writings of Stephen B. Luce*, ed., John D. Hayes and John B. Hattendorf (Newport R.I.: Naval War College Press, 1975); *The Letters of Theodore Roosevelt*, eds., Elting E. Morison and John M. Blum (Cambridge, Mass.: Harvard Univ. Press, 1951–54).

For a general overview, see John B. Hattendorf, "Purpose and Contribution in Editing Naval Documents," in *Editing Naval Documents* (Washington: Naval Historical Center, 1984), pp. 43–61.

[33] *Official Records of the Union and Confederate Navies in the War of the Rebellion*, 30 vols. (Washington: U.S. Govt. Print. Off., 1894–1922).

[34] William B. Clark and William J. Morgan, eds., *Naval Documents of the American Revolution: 1774–1777*, 9 vols. (Washington: Naval Historical Center, 1964–1980); *Naval Documents Related to the Quasi-War Between the United States and France: Naval Operations from February 1797 to October 1798*, 7 vols. (Washington: U.S. Govt. Print. Off., 1935–1938); and *Naval Documents Related to the United States Wars with the Barbary Powers: Naval Operations Including Diplomatic Background from 1785 through 1807*, 6 vols. (Washington: U.S. Govt. Print. Off., 1939–1944).

[35] William S. Dudley, ed., *The Naval War of 1812: A Documentary History*, vol. 1, 1912; vol. 2, 1913 (Washington: U.S. Govt. Print. Off., 1985, 1992); Ronald H. Spector, *Listening to the Enemy: Key Documents on the Role of Communications Intelligence in the War with Japan* (Wilmington, Del.: Scholarly Resources, 1988).

of the United States Navy; Benjamin W. Labaree, *A Supplement (1971–1986) to Robert G. Albion's Naval and Maritime History: An Annotated Bibliography*; Robin D. S. Higham, *A Guide to Sources of United States Military History*; Paolo E. Coletta, *A Bibliography of American Naval History* and *A Selected and Annotated Bibliography of American Naval History*; Myron J. Smith's multi-volume bibliographies, *The American Navy* and *World War II at Sea*; and the Naval Historical Center's *United States Naval History: A Bibliography*.[36]

More particular bibliographies include: John C. Fredricksen, *Free Trade and Sailors' Rights: A Bibliography of the War of 1812*; John B. Hattendorf and Lynn C. Hattendorf, *A Bibliography of the Works of Alfred Thayer Mahan*; John D. Hayes and John B. Hattendorf, *The Writings of Stephen B. Luce*; and Edward J. Marolda and James Lesher, *A Bibliography of the United States Navy and the Conflict in Southeast Asia, 1950–1975*.[37]

The *Journal of Military History* (formerly *Military Affairs*) publishes fine annual bibliographies on military history by subject, including books, collections, articles, and dissertations. The *JMH* also publishes book reviews—the critical means of keeping bibliographically current—as do *The American Neptune*, *Naval War College Review*, and the U.S. Naval Institute *Proceedings*, and its new offshoot, *Naval History*.

Immeasurably valuable for beginning to comprehend the tortured history of women in the Navy and in the military generally is a bibliographical essay, "Women in the Military," by the historian D'Ann Campbell. Campbell's working premise touches the Navy directly: "The infamous 'Tailhook' incident

---

36 Hagan, *In Peace and War: Interpretations of American Naval History, 1775–1984* (Westport, Conn.: Greenwood Press, 1984); Millett and Maslowski, *For the Common Defense* (New York: Free Press, 1984); Albion, *Naval and Maritime History: An Annotated Bibliography* (Mystic, Conn.: The Marine Historical Assoc., 1955, 1963, 1972); Harbeck, comp., *A Contribution to the Bibliography of the United States Navy* (Cambridge, Mass.: Harvard Univ. Press, 1906); Labaree, *A Supplement (1971–1986) to Robert G. Albion's Naval and Maritime History: An Annotated Bibliography*, 4th ed. (Mystic, Conn.: Mystic Seaport Museum, 1988); Higham, ed., *A Guide to Sources of United States Military History* (Hamden: Archon Books, 1975), also, three supplements covering five years each, Higham and Mrozek, eds. (Hamden, Conn.: Archon Books, 1981–1993); Coletta, *A Bibliography of American Naval History* (Lanham, Md.: Univ. Press of America, 1981), and *A Selected and Annotated Bibliography of American Naval History* (Lanham, Md.: Univ. Press of America, 1988); Smith, *The American Navy, 1789–1941: A Bibliography*, 5 vols. (Metuchen, N.J.: Scarecrow Press, 1972–1974), *World War II at Sea: A Bibliography of Sources in English*, 3 vols. (Metuchen, N.J.: Scarecrow Press, 1974–1990), and *United States Naval History: A Bibliography*, Naval History Bibliographies, no. 1, 7th ed., revised by Barbara A. Lynch and John E. Vajda (Washington: Naval Historical Center, 1993). See also Dean L. Mawdsley, *Cruise Books of the United States Navy in World War II: A Bibliography*, Naval History Bibliographies, no. 2 (Washington: Naval Historical Center, 1993).

37 Fredricksen, *Free Trade and Sailors' Rights: A Bibliography of the War of 1812* (Westport, Conn.: Greenwood Press, 1985); J. Hattendorf and L. Hattendorf, comps., *A Bibliography of the Works of Alfred Thayer Mahan* (Newport, R.I.: Naval War College Press, 1986); Hayes and Hattendorf, eds., *The Writings of Stephen B. Luce* (Newport, R.I.: Naval War College Press, 1975); and Marolda and Lesher, comps., *A Bibliography of the United States Navy and the Conflict in Southeast Asia, 1950–1975* (Washington: U.S. Govt. Print. Off., 1991).

and cover-up of 1991–1992 has spotlighted the problem of sexual harassment in military culture."[38] The strong implications of this assertion may partially explain why the Naval Historical Center is contracting for a comprehensive monograph on the history of women in the naval service, a project that will take several years to complete.

The Historiography of the United States Navy

Naval history in the United States is as old as the Navy itself, with origins in accounts of the Revolutionary, Quasi- and Barbary Wars. The first large body of writing appeared soon after the now-famous frigate actions of the young American Navy in the War of 1812. Heroes and martyrs of these early wars provided most of the subjects for battle narratives tending toward hagiology.[39] Nonetheless, there were contemporaneous efforts at institutional history by Benjamin Folsom, Thomas Clark, Isaac Bailey, and Abel Bowen.[40] In a period of relatively low literacy rates, naval history in the early national period also included an impressive body of paintings and published engravings.

Nearly three decades after the War of 1812, James Fenimore Cooper challenged the prevailing eulogistic interpretation of Commodore Oliver Hazard Perry and opened a rancorous debate about American naval policy with his controversial *History of the Navy of the United States of America*.[41] By then the service was deeply imbued with a heroic history, one personified by the Perry family that already had third-generation officers in the Navy.[42] George Bancroft joined in the Perrys' defense. As the pre-eminent historian of mid-nineteenth century America, Bancroft hastened the demise of Cooper's brand of historical objectivity by promoting an enduring tradition

---

[38] Campbell, "Women in the Military," *Choice*, vol. 31 (September 1993): pp. 63–70.

[39] For an example, see Alexander Slidell Mackenzie, *The Life of Paul Jones* (Boston: Hilliard, Gray, & Co., 1841).

[40] Folsom, *A Compilation of Biographical Sketches of Distinguished Officers in the American Navy* (Newburyport, Mass.: n.p., 1814), which included Washington Irving's "Commodore Oliver Hazard Perry;" Clark, *Sketches of the Naval History of the United States, from the Commencement of the Revolutionary War to the Present Time* (Philadelphia: M. Carey, 1813); Bailey, *American Naval Biography* (Providence, R.I.: H. Mann and Co., 1815); and Bowen, *The Naval Monument* (Boston: A. Bowen, 1816).

[41] Cooper, *History of the Navy of the United States of America* (London: R. Bentley, 1839). His account of the Battle of Lake Erie (1813) reopened a feud over credit and blame for the great victory. For the controversy, see Cooper, *The Battle of Lake Erie: or, Answers to Messrs. Burges, Duer, and Mackenzie* (Coopertown, N.Y.: H.E. Phinney, 1843); Robert Emmet Long, *James Fenimore Cooper* (New York: Continuum, 1990); and David Curtis Skaggs, "James Fenimore Cooper and the Battle of Lake Erie: Historical Veracity and Political Correctness" (paper presented at the Eleventh Naval History Symposium, U.S. Naval Academy, Annapolis, Md., 1993).

[42] See Morison, *"Old Bruin:" Commodore Matthew C. Perry 1794–1858* (Boston: Little, Brown & Co., 1967), pp. 447–9. Much of the historiography of the U.S. Navy is covered in Hagan, "Bibliographical Essay," *This People's Navy: The Making of American Sea Power* (New York: Free Press, 1991), pp. 391–411; and in Shulman, "The Influence of History Upon Sea Power: The Navalist Reinterpretation of the War of 1812," *Journal of Military History* (April 1992),: pp. 183–205.

of heroic patriotic nationalism.[43] Bancroft also brought note to the Navy Department when, as Secretary of the Navy, he founded the Naval Academy at Annapolis in 1845, an institution designed to instruct in the technical requirements of the profession while also inculcating the chauvinism of nineteenth-century military culture.

The Civil War turned the nation's interest in military history to the operations, heroes, and villains of the land war. The only significant early volumes on the naval aspects of the war were written by two naval officers, Daniel Ammen and Alfred Thayer Mahan, and a civilian employee of the Navy, James R. Soley.[44] The Navy Department ultimately did what it could to facilitate a broader scholarship with the compilation of the multi-volume *Official Records of the Union and Confederate Navies*.[45]

With the construction of the first steel-hulled warships in the early 1880s, a new breed of politically savvy historians began to search for guidelines from American naval history to encourage the creation of a modern strategy. The young Theodore Roosevelt took the lead in 1882 with his book, *The Naval War of 1812*, but several other historians soon discovered invaluable admonitions about the importance of sea power to American security in that remote conflict.[46] Soon after the opening of the Naval War College at Newport in 1884, these lessons were sanctified as timeless laws by the new lecturer in naval history—Captain Alfred Thayer Mahan.

Mahan's successive studies on sea power and history forever changed the way the nation would regard navies and, indeed, how the Navy would regard itself. His notions on the concentration of force, massed sea battles à la Trafalgar, and the importance of maintaining a battle fleet to insure international status would dominate the service and American naval historiography throughout the twentieth century.[47]

---

[43] Oliver Dyer, *The Battle of Lake Erie and Miscellaneous Papers: The Life and Writings of George Bancroft* (New York: R. Bonner's Sons, 1891; Ann Arbor, Mich: University Microfilm International, 1976), 1 reel.

[44] Ammen, *The Atlantic Coast* (New York: Charles Scribner's Sons, 1883; Wilmington, N.C.: Broadfoot Publishing Co., 1989); Mahan, *The Gulf and Inland Waters* (New York: Charles Scribner's Sons, 1883; Freeport, N.Y.: Books for Libraries Press, 1970); and James R. Soley, *The Blockade and the Cruisers* (New York: Charles Scribner's Sons, 1883; New York: J. Brussel, 1959).

[45] *Official Records of the Union and Confederate Navies in the War of the Rebellion* (Washington: U.S. Govt. Print. Off., 1894–1922).

[46] Roosevelt, *The Naval War of 1812* (New York: G. P. Putnam's Sons, 1882; Annapolis: NIP, 1987). See also James Barnes, *Naval Actions of the War of 1812* (New York: Harper & Bros., 1896); and Rossiter Johnson, *A History of the War of 1812–1815* (New York: Dodd, Mead, & Co., 1882).

[47] Mahan, *The Influence of Sea Power upon History, 1660–1783* (Boston: Little, Brown & Co., 1890), *The Influence of Sea Power upon the French Revolution and Empire, 1783–1812* (Boston: Little, Brown & Co., 1892), and *Sea Power and its Relations to the War of 1812* (Boston: Little Brown & Co., 1905). The literature on Mahan virtually dominates the non-operational history of the United States Navy. See especially, Seager and Maguire, eds., *The Letters and Papers of Alfred Thayer Mahan*, vol. 1, 1847–1889; vol. 2, 1890–1901; vol. 3, 1902–1914 (Annapolis: NIP, 1975), and Seager's "warts and all" biography,

The most persuasive and articulate naval spokesman for this viewpoint was retired Captain Dudley W. Knox, who published *A History of the United States Navy* during the debates over rearmament in the 1930s.[48] Outside the Navy, the Mahanian torch was brightly carried by Harold and Margaret Sprout, whose *The Rise of American Naval Power* remained a standard interpretation from 1939 until the 1960s.[49] Challenges to this intellectual hegemony were few and diverse, featuring primarily George T. Davis and the noted economic determinist, Charles A. Beard.[50]

Mahan's critics and supporters were writing with an eye to the coming war, and indeed, the lessons of sea power soon appeared to be vindicated by the staggering American naval victories in the Atlantic and Pacific in 1942–1945. This, at least, was the viewpoint of the late Harvard Professor Samuel Eliot Morison who oversaw the monumental fifteen-volume official *History of United States Naval Operations in World War II*.[51] After the conclusion of the war, Morison and Mahan were indirectly institutionalized in the required text at the U.S. Naval Academy, E.B. Potter's *Sea Power: A Naval History*.[52]

Among the leading successors to the Mahan-Morison navalist interpretation was Bernard Brodie, who completed his first book, *Sea Power in the Machine Age*, just in time to start studying the changing strategic environment of the postwar world. His subsequent works adapted the lessons of the history of sea power to

---

Alfred Thayer Mahan: The Man and His Letters (Annapolis: NIP, 1977). For the influence of Mahan, see Hagan, *This People's Navy: The Making of American Sea Power* (New York: Free Press, 1991); Shulman, *Navalism and the Emergence of American Sea Power, 1882–1893*, (Annapolis: NIP, 1995); Hattendorf, ed., *The Influence of History on Mahan* (Newport, R.I.: Naval War College Press, 1992); Hattendorf, B. Mitchell Simpson, and John R. Wadleigh, eds., *Sailors and Scholars: The Centennial History of the U.S. Naval War College* (Newport, R.I.: Naval War College Press, 1984); Potter and Nimitz, eds., *Sea Power: A Naval History* (Englewood Cliffs, N.J.: Prentice-Hall, 1960); also, Potter, ed., *Sea Power: A Naval History*, 2d ed. (Annapolis: NIP, 1981); and William D. Puleston, *The Life and Work of Captain Alfred Thayer Mahan* (New Haven, Conn.: Yale Univ. Press, 1939). It should also be noted that an enthusiastic following has long existed for "popular" naval histories such as those by J. Willis Abbot, William Bell Clark, and Fletcher Pratt.

[48] 48. Knox, *A History of the United States Navy* (New York: G.P. Putnam's Sons, 1936, 1948).

[49] Sprout and Sprout, *The Rise of American Naval Power, 1776–1918* (New Jersey: Princeton Univ. Press, 1939; Annapolis: NIP, 1990). See also, Charles Oscar Paullin, *The Navy and the American Revolution* (Cleveland: Burrows Brothers, 1906), and *Diplomatic Negotiations of American Naval Officers* (Baltimore: The Johns Hopkins Univ. Press, 1912; Gloucester, Mass.: P. Smith, 1967). Paullin was the first professionally trained American naval historian. The Sprouts drew upon his essays, which appeared in the U.S. Naval Institute *Proceedings* early in the twentieth century.

[50] Davis, *A Navy Second to None: The Development of Modern American Naval Policy* (New Haven, Conn.: Yale Univ. Press, 1940). Davis was a New Haven school teacher who took a Yale Ph.D. and then disappeared from the field. Beard, *The Navy: Defense of Portent?* (New York: Harper & Bros., 1932). One of the foremost scholars of his day, Beard wrote widely in history, first from Columbia University and then from the New School For Social Research.

[51] Morison, *History of United States Naval Operations in World War II*, 15 vols. (Boston: Little, Brown & Co., 1947–1963).

[52] Potter and Nimitz, eds., *Sea Power: A Naval History* (Englewood Cliffs, N.J.: Prentice-Hall, 1960); also Potter, ed., *The United States and World Sea Power* (Englewood Cliffs, N.J.: Prentice-Hall, 1955).

nuclear strategy and established the standard of discourse for this popular new Cold War field.[53] Beard and Davis, on the other hand, found no successors until the dissolution of consensus associated with the Vietnam-era debates over empire, strategy, policy, and politics.

In the 1960s, historians of the "New Left" became a potent force in the reinterpretation of American diplomatic and naval history. Many of them were schooled in the tradition of the University of Wisconsin's "Progressive Historians," and in particular by William Appleman Williams, who ironically was a World War II graduate of the U.S. Naval Academy.[54] These younger scholars, soon dubbed "revisionists," quickly focused upon businessmen's pressure for overseas investments and trade as the source—and the Navy as the tool—of American aggression, especially in the late nineteenth century. Firing the first shots in nearly a generation, Walter LaFeber, not himself trained by Williams, wrote suggestively in *The New Empire* of the Navy secretary who oversaw the authorization of America's first true battleships: "In preparing the United States to occupy this 'seat of empire,' [Benjamin F.] Tracy had few equals."[55]

LaFeber's work, as well as the contemporaneous political debates over "America's Empire," sparked a remarkable new industry of tightly focused works examining the nonoperational aspects of the Navy. The studies include James C. Bradford, *Makers of the American Naval Tradition*, an edited series of naval biographies in three volumes thus far; Richard D. Challener, *Admirals, Generals, and American Foreign Policy*; Benjamin F. Cooling, *Benjamin Franklin Tracy*; Vincent Davis, *The Admirals Lobby*; Jeffery M. Dorwart, *The Office of Naval Intelligence* and *Conflict of Duty*; Frederick C. Drake, *The Empire of the Seas*; James A. Field, Jr., *From Gibraltar to the Middle East: America and the Mediterranean World, 1776–1882*; J.A.S. Grenville and George B. Young, *Politics, Strategy, and American Diplomacy*; Kenneth J. Hagan, *American Gunboat Diplomacy and the Old Navy, 1877–1889*; Frederick S. Harrod, *Manning the New Navy: The Development of a Modern Enlisted Force, 1899–1940*; Walter R. Herrick, *The American Naval Revolution*; Peter D. Karsten, *The Naval Aristocracy*; Harold D. Langley, *Social Reform in the United States Navy, 1798–1862*; Christopher McKee, *A Gentlemanly and Honorable Profession: The Creation of the U.S. Naval Officer Corps, 1794–1815*; Robert L. O'Connell, *Sacred Vessels: The Cult of the Battleship and the Rise of the U.S. Navy*; Ronald H. Spector, *Professors of War*; and Craig L. Symonds, *Navalists and Antinavalists*.[56] These important volumes signified the emergence of a new

---

[53] Brodie, *Sea Power in the Machine Age* (New Jersey: Princeton Univ. Press, 1943), and *The Absolute Weapon* (New Jersey: Princeton Univ. Press, 1946). For a gathering of naval historians of the 1950s and early 1960s, see Richard A. von Doenhoff, ed., *Versatile Guardian: Research in Naval History*, National Archives Conferences, vol. 14 (Washington: Howard Univ. Press, 1979).

[54] Williams, *The Tragedy of American Diplomacy* (Cleveland: World Publishing Co., 1959).

[55] LaFeber, *The New Empire: An Interpretation of American Expansion, 1860–1898* (Ithaca, N.Y.: Cornell Univ. Press, 1963), 127.

[56] Bradford, ed., *Admirals of the New Steel Navy: Makers of the American Naval Tradition, 1880–1930*

generation of historians dedicated to furthering a critical understanding of naval history.

To a considerable extent, the new naval historians were scrutinizing the late nineteenth-century origins of the modern American Navy. They and several others soon moved forward. In 1981 the diplomatic historian David F. Trask published a thoughtful reappraisal of all aspects of the Spanish American War of 1898, including strategy and leadership. Inevitably, he resurrected the hoary topic of who deserved credit for the naval victory in Santiago de Cuba on 3 July 1898: Rear Admiral William T. Sampson, who was in overall command, or Winfield Scott Schley, the tactical commander?[57] Trask also published a definitive study of U.S. naval preparations and operations during the First World War, joining a debate about the relative merit of battleships and convoys originally opened by the brilliant commander of U.S. naval forces in European waters, William Sowden Sims, in his Pulitzer Prize-winning book, *The Victory at Sea.*[58]

(Annapolis: NIP, 1990), *Captains of the Old Steam Navy: Makers of the American Naval Tradition, 1840–1880* (Annapolis: NIP, 1986), and *Command under Sail: Makers of the American Naval Tradition 1775–1850* (Annapolis: NIP, 1988); Challener, *Admirals, Generals, and American Foreign Policy, 1898–1914* (New Jersey: Princeton Univ. Press, 1973); Cooling, *Benjamin Franklin Tracy: Father of the Modern American Fighting Navy* (Hamden, Conn.: Archon Books, 1973); Davis, *Postwar Defense Policy and the U.S. Navy, 1943–1946* (Chapel Hill: Univ. of North Carolina Press, 1966), and *The Admirals Lobby* (Chapel Hill: Univ. of North Carolina Press, 1967); Dorwart, *The Office of Naval Intelligence: The Birth of America's First Intelligence Agency, 1865–1918* (Annapolis: NIP, 1979), and *Conflict of Duty: The U.S. Navy's Intelligence Dilemma, 1919–1945* (Annapolis: NIP, 1983); Drake, *The Empire of the Seas: A Biography of Rear Admiral Robert Wilson Shufeldt, USN* (Honolulu: Univ. of Hawaii Press, 1984); Field, *From Gibraltar to the Middle East: America and the Mediterranean World, 1776–1882* (Chicago: Imprint Publications, 1991); Grenville and Young, *Politics, Strategy, and American Diplomacy: Studies in Foreign Policy, 1873–1917* (New Haven, Conn.: Yale Univ. Press, 1966); Hagan, *American Gunboat Diplomacy and the Old Navy, 1877–1899* (Westport, Conn.: Greenwood Press, 1973); Harrod, *Manning the New Navy: The Development of a Modern Enlisted Force, 1899–1940* (Westport, Conn.: Greenwood Press, 1978); Herrick, *The American Naval Revolution* (Baton Rouge: Louisiana State Univ. Press, 1966); Karsten, *The Naval Aristocracy: The Golden Age of Annapolis and the Emergence of Modern American Navalism* (New York: Free Press, 1972); Langley, *Social Reform in the United States Navy, 1798–1862* (Urbana: Univ. of Illinois Press, 1967); McKee, *A Gentlemanly and Honorable Profession: The Creation of the U.S. Naval Officer Corps, 1794-1815* (Annapolis: NIP, 1991); O'Connell, *Sacred Vessels: The Cult of the Battleship and the Rise of the U.S. Navy* (Boulder, Colo.: Westview Press, 1991); Spector, *Professors of War: The Naval War College and the Development of the Naval Profession* (Newport, R.I.: Naval War College Press, 1977); and Symonds, *Navalists and Antinavalists: The Naval Policy Debate in the United States:* (Newark, Del.: Univ. of Delaware Press, 1980).

[57] Trask, *The War With Spain in 1898* (New York: Macmillan, 1981), and the analysis continued in James C. Bradford, ed., *Crucible of Empire: The Spanish American War & its Aftermath* (Annapolis: Naval Institute Press, 1993). For another endless controversy about the war, see Hyman G. Rickover, *How the Battleship Maine was Destroyed* (Washington: Naval History Division, 1976).

[58] Trask, *Captains and Cabinets: Anglo-American Naval Relations, 1917–1918* (Columbia: Univ. of Missouri Press, 1972); and Sims, with Burton J. Hendrick, *The Victory At Sea* (Garden City, N.Y.: Doubleday, Page & Co., 1920). See also, Trask, *The United States in the Supreme War Council: American War Aims and Inter-Allied Strategy, 1917–1918* (Middletown, Conn.: Wesleyan Univ. Press, 1961), and *The AEF and Coalition Warmaking, 1917–1918* (Lawrence: University Press of Kansas, 1993).

Even as they negotiated the terms of the German surrender at the Paris conference in 1918–1919, the Anglo-American naval partners fell out over the postwar naval force structure, thus setting the stage for the Washington Conference on the Limitation of Armaments of 1921–1922. The U.S. Navy's uncompromisingly hostile reaction to that conference set the tone for the conservative, pro-Mahanian historiography of the interwar years epitomized by the works of Captain Dudley W. Knox. A generation later, Thomas H. Buckley and William R. Braisted analyzed the epochal meeting with unparalleled fairness and clarity.[59]

While Trask and Braisted were dissecting the Navy of the early twentieth century, Ronald H. Spector was leaping from the formative years of the "new navy" of steam and steel to a keenly analytical study of the American war against Japan, 1941–1945. His searching book, *Eagle Against the Sun*, puts the nostalgically glamorous battles of the Pacific war and the possibly decisive American submarine campaign against Japanese shipping into proper balance. He has been joined by Dan van der Vat, an English scholar whose comprehensive study of the Pacific war suggests a more influential role for air power than has previously been conceded. Van der Vat had earlier analyzed the Battle of the Atlantic from a non-Mahanian perspective.[60]

★ ★ ★

The story of the United States Navy in the Cold War remains largely untold, although scholars are beginning to chip away at the iceberg. The two earliest analyses were the studies of naval politics and strategy by Vincent Davis in the 1960s. Next came a pioneering monograph, *Nuclear Navy, 1946–1962*, which appeared in 1974 and was written by two historians of the Atomic Energy

---

[59] Buckley, *The United States and the Washington Conference, 1921–1922* (Knoxville: Univ. of Tennessee Press, 1970); Braisted, *The United States Navy in the Pacific, 1909–1922* (Austin: Univ. of Texas Press, 1971).

[60] Spector, *Eagle Against the Sun* (New York: Free Press, 1985); and van der Vat, *The Atlantic Campaign: World War II's Great Struggle at Sea* (New York: Harper & Row, 1988), and *The Pacific Campaign: World War II, The U.S.–Japanese Naval War, 1941–1945* (New York: Simon & Schuster, 1991).

See also H.P. Willmott, *The Barrier and the Javelin: Japanese and Allied Pacific Strategies, February to June 1942* (Annapolis: NIP, 1983), and *Empires in the Balance: Japanese and Allied Pacific Strategies to April 1942* (Annapolis: NIP, 1982); Clark M. Reynolds, *The Fast Carriers: The Forging of an Air Navy* (New York: McGraw-Hill, 1968), and *Admiral John Towers: The Struggle for Naval Air Supremacy* (Annapolis: NIP, 1991). Clay Blair, *Silent Victory* (Philadelphia: J.P. Lippincott, 1975) corrects oversights of the Morison project arising from its not having been privy to the ULTRA secrets. The debate continues to be fought by some of the original actors. For the debates, books, and players, see Roger Pineau, review of *Pearl Harbor: Final Judgement* by Henry Clausen and Bruce Lee (New York: Crown, 1992) in U.S. Naval Institute *Proceedings* (July 1993), pp. 98–9.

The documentary point of departure for balancing the American surface, subsurface, and air campaigns is United States, Strategic Bombing Survey, *The United States Strategic Bombing Survey*, 10 vols. (New York: Garland, 1976).

Commission, Richard G. Hewlett and Francis Duncan. Dean C. Allard, Floyd D. Kennedy, Jr., and Lawrence J. Korb continued the Cold War examination four years later with essays in *In Peace and War*, edited by Kenneth J. Hagan.[61] For some time, retired Navy Captain Peter M. Swartz has been writing a doctoral dissertation on the Navy of the early Cold War. At the Naval Historical Center, Edward J. Marolda is sparking research and publication as head of the Contemporary History Branch.[62] One of his former subordinates, Michael A. Palmer, has published *Origins of the Maritime Strategy: American Naval Strategy in the First Postwar Decade* and two monographs on the Navy in the Persian Gulf.[63] The second volume of Robert W. Love's *History of the U.S. Navy* has an extensive dissection of the Navy since 1945. But the hands-down leader in the race at the moment is the Naval Academy's Michael T. Isenberg, who has just issued the first of a monumental two-volume analysis of the Cold War Navy.[64] The views of Isenberg, Love, Palmer, and Swartz differ fundamentally from the revisionist interpretation in Kenneth J. Hagan, *This People's Navy: The Making of American Sea Power*.[65] This wide disparity of interpretation promises an intense historiographical debate about sea power in the Cold War, especially as scholars begin to exploit the previously sealed archives of the former Soviet Union.

Until very recently, the "new military history" had not yielded a complete history of the U.S. Navy. The 1948 edition of Captain Dudley Knox's *A History*

[61] Davis, *Postwar Defense Policy and the U.S. Navy, 1943–1946* (Chapel Hill: The Univ. of North Carolina Press, 1966), and *The Admirals Lobby* (Chapel Hill: The Univ. of North Carolina Press, 1967); Hewlett and Duncan, *Nuclear Navy, 1946–1962* (Illinois: The Univ. of Chicago Press, 1967); Hagan, ed., *In Peace and War: Interpretations of American Naval History, 1775–1984*, 2d ed. (Westport, Conn.: Greenwood Press, 1984), pp. 290–370.

[62] Marolda's own work concentrates on the Vietnam War: Marolda, comp., *A Bibliography of the United States Navy and Conflict in Southeast Asia* (Washington: Contemporary History Branch, Naval Historical Center, 1991), and Marolda, ed., *Operation End Sweep: A History of Minesweeping Operations in North Vietnam* (Washington: Naval Historical Center, 1993). For the output of Marolda's staff and a comprehensive listing of other works on the Navy in the Cold War, see Barbara A. Lynch and John E. Vajda, 7th ed. rev., *United States Naval History: A Bibliography* (Washington: Naval Historical Center, 1993), pp. 70–9.

[63] Palmer, *Origins of the Maritime Strategy: The Development of American Naval Strategy, 1945–1955* (Washington: Naval Historical Center, 1988; Annapolis: NIP, 1990); *On Course to Desert Storm: The U.S. Navy and the Persian Gulf*, Contributions to Naval History Series, no. 5 (Washington: Naval Historical Center, 1992); and *Guardians of the Gulf: A History of America's Expanding Role in the Persian Gulf, 1883–1992* (New York: Free Press, 1992). For a contrasting view, see especially Jeffrey Record, *Hollow Victory: A Contrary View of the Gulf War* (Washington: Brassey's (US), 1993), pp. 116–7.

[64] Love, *History of the U.S. Navy, 1942–1991*, vol. 2 (Harrisburg, Pa.: Stackpole Books, 1992), pp. 278–837; Isenberg, *Shield of the Republic: The United States in an Era of Cold War and Violent Peace*, vol. 1, 1945–1962 (New York: St. Martin's Press, 1993).

[65] Hagan, *This People's Navy: The Making of American Sea Power* (New York: Free Press, 1991), pp. 333–87.

of the United States Navy remained a standard summary, often supplemented with E.B. Potter's *Sea Power: A Naval History,* or the Sprouts' *Rise of American Naval Power.*[66] But in the last decade, six major syntheses have appeared, giving the reader a choice of interpretations: George W. Baer, *One Hundred Years of Sea Power: The United States Navy, 1890–1990*; Captain Edward L. Beach, *The United States Navy: 200 Years*; Kenneth J. Hagan, *This People's Navy: The Making of American Sea Power*; Stephen Howarth, *To Shining Sea: A History of the United States Navy, 1775–1991*; Robert W. Love, Jr., *History of the U.S. Navy*; and Nathan Miller, *The U.S. Navy: A History.*[67] To some extent, each of these books attempts "to chronicle and explain the high politics of American naval history."[68]

Also healthy is the list of "big books" which place the American naval experience in a wider historical context. Foremost among recent contributions in this line are: Martin van Creveld, *Technology and War: From 2000 B.C. to the Present*; John Keegan, *The Price of Admiralty*; Robert O'Connell, *Of Arms and Men: A History of War, Weapons, and Aggression;* and Paul M. Kennedy, *Rise and Fall of the Great Powers: Economic Change and Military Conflict from 1500 to 2000.*[69] It should be noted that fictional accounts of naval history have never done better than now, with Patrick O'Brian's salty tales of warfare in the age of Nelson and the techno-thrillers of Tom Clancy and Stephen Coonts leading the pack.[70]

---

66 Knox, *A History of the United States Navy* (New York: G.P. Putnam's Sons, 1936, 1948); Potter, ed., *Sea Power: A Naval History,* 2d ed. (Annapolis: NIP, 1981); Sprout and Sprout, *The Rise of American Naval Power, 1776–1918* (New Jersey: Princeton Univ. Press, 1939; Annapolis: NIP, 1990).

The last comprehensive synthesis by a member of the old guard was Edwin B. Hooper, *United States Naval Power in a Changing World* (New York: Praeger, 1988).

While historians disagree widely on a definition of new military history, it would almost certainly have to be written by a professionally trained historian rather than a career officer. It might also be characterized as less teleological ("the Rise and Rise". . .), or as giving less credence to notions of America's unique mission or righteousness.

67 Baer, *One Hundred Years of Sea Power: The United States Navy, 1890–1990* (California: Stanford Univ. Press, 1994); Beach, *The United States Navy: 200 Years* (New York: H. Holt, 1986); Hagan, *This People's Navy: The Making of American Sea Power* (New York: Free Press, 1991); Howarth, *To Shining Sea: A History of the United States Navy, 1775–1991* (New York: Random House, 1991); Love, *History of the U.S. Navy*, vol. 1, 1775–1941; vol. 2, 1942–1991 (Harrisburg, Pa.: Stackpole Press, 1992); and Miller, *The U.S. Navy* (New York: Quill, 1990).

68 Robert W. Love, Jr., introduction to *History of the U.S. Navy: 1775–1941*, vol. 1 (Harrisburg, Pa.: Stackpole Books, 1992), xi.

69 Van Creveld, *Technology and War: From 2000 B.C. to the Present* (New York: Free Press, 1989); Keegan, *The Price of the Admiralty: The Evolution of Naval Warfare* (New York: Viking, 1988); O'Connell, *Of Arms and Men: A History of War, Weapons, and Aggression* (New York: Oxford Univ. Press, 1989), also *Sacred Vessels: The Cult of the Battleship and the Rise of the U.S. Navy* (Boulder, Colo.: Westview Press, 1991); and Kennedy, *The Rise and Fall of the Great Powers: Economic Change and Military Conflict from 1500 to 2000* (New York: Random House, 1987).

70 O'Brian, *The Ionian Mission* (New York: W.W. Norton, 1992), and *Master and Commander* (1970; New York: W.W. Norton, 1990); Clancy, *The Hunt for Red October* (Annapolis: NIP, 1984), and *Red Storm Rising* (New York: G.P. Putnam's Sons, 1986); and Coonts, *Flight of the Intruder* (Annapolis: NIP, 1986), and *The Final Flight* (New York: Doubleday, 1988).

★ ★ ★

Historically, the Navy has been the most technologically sophisticated of the American armed services. Its historiography reflects this reality, despite the marked indifference of academic historians. Notwithstanding Jonathan G. Utley's new social history of the battleship USS *Tennessee*, American naval hardware traditionally has been the domain of specialists not holding permanent university or college positions.[71] Frank M. Bennett, for example, was chief engineer of the Navy. Howard I. Chapelle, author of the monumental *History of the American Sailing Navy*, was professionally associated with the Smithsonian Institution. One of his scholarly successors is Jean Boudriot of France, author of the scrupulously accurate *John Paul Jones and the Bonhomme Richard: A Reconstruction of the Ship and an Account of the Battle with HMS Serapis.*[72]

Within today's community of technically oriented naval historians, it is the physicist Norman Friedman who has made the most indelible mark with his studies of ships and ordnance. Sometimes assisted by the naval intelligence specialist A. David Baker III, Friedman has added a ponderous depth of technical material on types and designs of "gray-hulled" American fighting ships. A competitor, free-lance writer Norman Polmar, shows a genius for blending hard technical data with operational aspects of the history of weapons systems. At the Naval Academy Museum, Ship Model Curator Robert F. Sumrall specializes in the histories of certain classes of American warships, his favorite being battleships. Another biographer of battleships, Paul Stillwell, is on the staff of the U.S. Naval Institute.[73]

---

[71] Utley, *An American Battleship at Peace and War: The U.S.S. Tennessee* (Lawrence, Kans.: Univ. Press of Kansas, 1991).

[72] Bennett, *The Steam Navy of the United States: A History of the Growth of the Steam Vessel of War in the U.S. Navy, and of the Naval Engineer Corps* (Pittsburgh: Press of W.T. Nicholson, 1896); Chapelle, *History of the American Sailing Navy* (New York: W.W. Norton, 1949); Boudriot, *John Paul Jones and the Bonhomme Richard: A Reconstruction of the Ship and an Account of the Battle with HMS Serapis*, trans., David H. Roberts (Annapolis: NIP, 1987).

[73] Friedman, *U.S. Aircraft Carriers: An Illustrated Design History* (Annapolis: NIP, 1983), *U.S. Cruisers: An Illustrated Design History* (Annapolis: NIP, 1984), *U.S. Destroyers: An Illustrated Design History* (Annapolis: NIP, 1982), *U.S. Small Combatants: An Illustrated Design History* (Annapolis: NIP, 1987), *U.S. Submarines: An Illustrated Design History* (Annapolis: NIP, 1994), *Naval Radar* (Annapolis: NIP, 1981), *U.S. Naval Weapons* (Annapolis: NIP, 1985), and *World Naval Weapons Systems*, 2d ed. (Annapolis: NIP, 1992); Baker, illus., *U.S. Aircraft Carriers* (Annapolis: NIP, 1983 and *The Aircraft Carrier Intrepid* (Annapolis: NIP, 1982); Polmar, *The Ships and Aircraft of the U.S. Fleet*, 15 editions (Annapolis: NIP, 1978-1992); Alan Raven, *Fletcher-Class Destroyers* (Annapolis: NIP, 1986), *Essex-Class Carriers* (Annapolis: NIP, 1988); Sumrall, *Iowa Class Battleships: Their Design, Weapons, and Equipment* (Annapolis: NIP, 1988), *Summer-Gearing Class Destroyers: Their Design, Weapons, and Equipment* (Annapolis: NIP, forthcoming), *Ship's Data Series*, 12 vols. (Annapolis: Leeward Publications, 1973–1979), and *Warship's Data Series*, 5 vols. (Missoula, Mont.: Pictorial Histories, 1985–1990); and Stillwell, *Battleship Arizona: An Illustrated History* (Annapolis: NIP, 1991), and *Battleship New Jersey: An Illustrated History* (Annapolis: NIP, 1986).

Gary E. Weir, the leading historical analyst of the technology of American submarines, previously taught at the U.S. Naval Academy, but today he is on the staff of the Naval Historical Center. A colleague, Tamara M. Melia, broke new ground with a history of U.S. naval mine countermeasures. Much earlier, the Ships' History Branch and a team of naval reservists produced the chronological biography of almost every American warship, the *Dictionary of American Naval Fighting Ships*. This extremely valuable multivolume encyclopedia should be used in conjunction with the two volumes of ships' histories prepared by K. Jack Bauer.[74]

With a few exceptions, the burgeoning analyses of naval technology have not been matched by a flowering of new studies in logistics and administration.[75] Older works continue to be the standards. Duncan S. Ballantine's *U.S. Naval Logistics in the Second World* remains virtually unchallenged, as does A. Hunter Dupree's, *Science in the Federal Government* and Robert G. Albion's *Makers of Naval Policy, 1798–1947* — a volume which had been quashed for many years as reflecting unfavorably upon its subject.[76]

In many ways, scholars interested in the human aspects of the field dominate American naval historiography. Nowhere is their triumph more evident than in the field of biography. The long section on biographies and memoirs in the

[74] Weir, *Building American Submarines, 1914–1940*, Contributions to Naval History, no. 3 (Washington: Naval Historical Center, 1991), and *Forged in War: The Naval-Industrial Complex and American Submarine Construction, 1940–1961* (Washington: Naval Historical Center, 1993); Melia, *Damn the Torpedoes: A Short History of U.S. Naval Mine Countermeasures, 1777–1991*, Contributions to Naval History Series, no. 4 (Washington: Naval Historical Center, 1991); *Dictionary of American Naval Fighting Ships*, 8 vols. (Washington: U.S. Govt. Print. Off., 1964–1981); K. Jack Bauer and Stephen S. Roberts, *Register of Ships of the U.S. Navy, 1775–1990* (Westport, Conn.: Greenwood Press, 1991); and Bauer, *Ships of the Navy, 1775–1969* (Troy, N.Y.: Rensselaer Polytechnic Institute, 1970).

Weir now has some high-powered competition in Tom Clancy, *Submarine: A Guided Tour from Inside a Nuclear Warship* (New York: Berkley Books, 1993).

[75] For one new study, see Thomas Hone, *Power and Change: The Administrative History of the Office of the Chief of Naval Operations, 1946-1986* (Washington: Navy Historical Center, 1989).

[76] Ballantine, *U.S. Naval Logistics in the Second World War* (New Jersey: Princeton Univ. Press, 1947); A. Hunter Dupree, *Science in the Federal Government: A History of Policies and Activities to 1940* (Cambridge, Mass.: The Belknap Press of Harvard Univ. Press, 1957); Albion, *Makers of Naval Policy, 1798–1947*, Rowena Reed, ed. (Annapolis: NIP, 1980).

For more on administration, see Julius A. Furer, *Administration of the Navy in World War II* (Washington: U.S. Govt. Print. Off., 1959); Charles O. Paullin, *History of Naval Administration* (Annapolis: NIP, 1968); and Robert W. Neeser, *Statistical and Chronological History of the United States Navy, 1775–1907*, 2 vols. (New York: n.p., 1909; New York: B. Franklin, 1970).

For more on logistics, see Robert H. Connery, *The Navy and Industrial Mobilization* (New Jersey: Princeton Univ. Press, 1951); Worrall Reed Carter, *Beans, Bullets, and Black Oil: The Story of Fleet Logistics Afloat in the Pacific During World War II* (Washington: Department of the Navy, 1953); and Carter with Elmer E. Duvall, *Ships, Salvage, and Sinews of War: The Story of Fleet Logistics Afloat in Atlantic and Mediterranean Waters During World War II* (Washington: Department of the Navy, 1954).

Naval Historical Center's *United States Naval History: A Bibliography* attests to the fascination exerted on writers by the men and women who made American naval history.[77] A perusal of the listings shows that conservative, often uncritical interpretations of wartime leaders predominate. But there is also a resilient interest in officers whose most notable contributions lay outside the seas of glory, such as the new biography of the naval diplomat, Vice Admiral Newton A. McCully, by Charles J. Weeks, Jr.[78] And even the revisionists can take comfort in the existence of essays like Robert W. Love's "Fighting a Global War," an incisive criticism of the strategy of Admiral Ernest J. King, and books like Frederick S. Harrod's *Manning the New Navy: The Development of a Modern Enlisted Force, 1899–1940*, Peter D. Karsten, *The Naval Aristocracy: The Golden Age of Annapolis and the Emergence of Modern American Navalism*, and Arnold A. Rogow, *James Forrestal: The Study of Personality, Politics, and Policy.*[79] This short list means the challenge and opportunity exist for the critical biographers of the late twentieth century.

★ ★ ★

Finally, the U.S. Marine Corps, a branch of the Navy always treated as a separate operational and administrative entity, now has a definitive history in Allan R. Millett's *Semper Fidelis: The History of the United States Marine Corps.* Several recent works also contribute significantly to the Marines' historiography: Merrill L. Bartlett, *Lejeune: A Marine's Life, 1867–1942;* John W. Dower, *War Without Mercy: Race and Power in the Pacific War;* Craig Cameron, *American Samurai: Myth, Imagination, and the Conduct of Battle in the First Marine Division, 1941–1951;* and Timothy Moy, "Hitting the Beaches and Bombing the Cities: Doctrine and Technology of Two New Militaries."[80]

---

[77]   *United States Naval History: A Bibliography*, Naval History Bibliographies, no. 1, 7th ed., revised by Barbara A. Lynch and John E. Vajda (Washington: Naval Historical Center, 1993).

[78]   Weeks, *An American Naval Diplomat in Revolutionary Russia* (Annapolis: NIP, 1993).

[79]   Love, "Fighting a Global War," In *Peace and War: Interpretations of American Naval History, 1775–1984*, 2d ed. (Westport, Conn.: Greenwood Press, 1984), pp. 263-89; Harrod, *Manning the New Navy: The Development of a Modern Enlisted Force, 1899–1940* (Westport, Conn.: Greenwood Press, 1978); Karsten, *The Naval Aristocracy: The Golden Age of Annapolis and the Emergence of Modern American Navalism* (New York: Free Press, 1972); and Rogow, *James Forrestal: A Study of Personality, Politics, and Policy* (New York: Macmillan, 1963).

For Forrestal, see Robert G. Albion and Robert H. Connery, *Forrestal and the Navy* (New York: Columbia Univ. Press, 1962); and Townsend Hoopes and Douglas Brinkley, *Driven Patriot: The Life and Times of James Forrestal* (New York: Knopf, 1992).

[80]   Millett, *Semper Fidelis: The History of the United States Marine Corps*, 2d ed. (New York: Free Press, 1991); Bartlett, *Lejeune: A Marine's Life, 1867–1942* (Columbia: Univ. of South Carolina Press, 1991); Dower, *War Without Mercy: Race and Power in the Pacific War* (New York: Pantheon Books, 1986); Cameron, *American Samurai: Myth, Imagination, and the Conduct of Battle in the First Marine Division, 1941–1993* (New York: Cambridge Univ. Press, 1993); and Moy, "Hitting the Beaches and Bombing the Cities: Doctrine and Technology of Two New Militaries" (Ph.D. diss., University of California,

★ ★ ★

This section ends with mention of a well-known paradox: much of the armed maritime history of the United States involves a service other than the United States Navy—the U.S. Coast Guard. No attempt has been made here to discuss that important historiography, but the starting point is the work of Robert L. Scheina, formerly the Coast Guard's official historian and now a professor at the Industrial College of the Armed Forces.[81]

Outlets for Writing

Naval history is flourishing as a written art form because many publishers are willing to bring out books for a rather limited market. The larger commercial houses that have had success with broadly conceived books include The Free Press, Charles Scribner's & Sons, Random House, and St. Martin's. The leading academic and quasi-academic presses that regularly publish monographs in American naval history are Greenwood, University of South Carolina, University of Kansas, and Westview. Three potent but highly specialized outfits concentrate almost exclusively on the history of naval technology: Brassey's (U.S.), Conway Maritime Press, and Jane's. Brassey's is especially important to watch because in 1993 it sailed into uncharted waters with *Crossed Currents: Navy Women from World War I to Tailhook*, by Jean Ebbert and Mary-Beth Hall.[82] Lastly, two quite different specialty presses always bear watching for new titles in naval history: Nautical & Aviation Press of Baltimore, Maryland, and the Smithsonian Institution Press in Washington, D.C.

Since its founding in 1873, the Naval Institute has encouraged research on naval history through forums, its press, the *Proceedings*, and its new journal, *Naval History*. Two current series demonstrate a long-term commitment to excellence on the part of the Naval Institute Press. *Classics of Sea Power*, edited by John B. Hattendorf and Wayne P. Hughes, contains works by Julian Corbett, Philip Howard Colomb, and Alfred Thayer Mahan. *Classics of Naval Literature*, edited by Jack Sweetman, embraces books by Herman Melville, James Fenimore Cooper, Frederick Marryat, and C.S. Forester as well as memoirs by Admirals Charles Clark, George Dewey, and Robley D. Evans.[83]

In the last two decades, the Naval Institute Press published three important works of collective biography: *Dictionary of Admirals of the U.S. Navy*, by William

---

Berkeley, 1993).

[81] Scheina, *U.S. Coast Guard Cutters and Craft, 1946–1990* (Annapolis: NIP, 1990), and *U.S. Coast Guard Cutters and Craft of World War II* (Annapolis: NIP, 1982).

[82] Ebbert and Hall, *Crossed Currents: Navy Women from World War I to Tailhook*, (Washington: Brassey's, Div. of Maxwell Macmillan Co., 1993).

[83] Hattendorf and Hughes, eds., *Classics of Sea Power*, 9 volumes. (Annapolis: NIP, 1988–1994); and Sweetman, ed., *Classics of Naval Literature*, 30 vols. (Annapolis: NIP, 1984–1993).

B. Cogar; *American Secretaries of the Navy*, edited by Paolo E. Coletta; and *The Chiefs of Naval Operations*, edited by Robert W. Love, Jr.[84] With this track record, the Naval Institute Press will remain the leading commercial publisher of American naval history and related technical writing for the remainder of the twentieth century.

Within the Navy, the Naval Historical Center has a long history of publishing edited collections of documents, bibliographies, and scholarly monographs under its own imprint, or under those of the Department of the Navy and the U.S. Government Printing Office.[85] Currently, the center is producing three important series: the three-volume set of documents on the War of 1812, edited by William S. Dudley; the *Contributions to Naval History Series* and the series known as *Naval History Bibliographies*. Somewhat less active is the Naval War College Press, which was founded in 1975. This press has produced a series of historical monographs based upon the college's own collections. The Naval War College Historical Monograph Series now encompasses eleven volumes of edited manuscripts, bibliographies, memoirs, conference proceedings, and theses, with several volumes forthcoming.

★ ★ ★

Scholarly and quasi-scholarly journals publish a large number of articles on U.S. naval history each year. The premier outlet for popular writing is *Naval History*, published by the Naval Institute. This new bimonthly publication complements the more scholarly *American Neptune*; the long-established *Naval War College Review*, which covers all aspects of sea power and military affairs in general; and the U.S. Naval Institute *Proceedings*, which is especially strong in technical studies.[86] For Marine Corps topics, the leading journal is *The Marine Corps Gazette*, with an irregular schedule of publication.[87]

Another important periodical venue is the National Maritime Historical Society's *Sea History*. The professional military historians' voice is *The Journal of Military History* published by the Virginia Military Institute and the George C. Marshall Foundation. The vital museum-related publications include *The*

---

[84] Cogar, *Dictionary of Admirals of the U.S. Navy*, vol. 1, 1862–1900; vol. 2, 1901–1918 (Annapolis: NIP, 1989, 1991); Coletta, ed., *American Secretaries of the Navy*, vol. 1, 1775–1913; vol. 2, 1913–1972 (Annapolis: NIP, 1980); and Love, ed., *The Chiefs of Naval Operations*, vol. 1, 1775–1941; vol. 2, 1942–1991 (Annapolis: NIP, 1980).

[85] In addition to titles cited elsewhere, in 1993 the Naval Historical Center published two original studies: Edward J. Marolda, *By Sea, Air, and Land: An Illustrated History of the U.S. Navy and the War in Southeast Asia* (Washington: U.S. Govt. Print. Off., 1993); and Curtis A. Utz, *Cordon of Steel: The U.S. Navy and the Cuban Missile Crisis*, The U.S. Navy in the Modern World, no. 1 (Washington: U.S. Govt. Print. Off., 1993).

[86] For the transition between the *Proceedings* and *Naval History*, see Clayton R. Barrow, Jr., ed., *America Spreads Her Sails: U.S. Sea Power in the 19th Century* (Annapolis: NIP, 1973).

[87] *The Marine Corps Gazette* (Quantico, Va.: Marine Corps Assoc., 1916–present).

American Neptune of the Peabody Museum of Salem, and those published by the Mystic Seaport Museum, the South Street Sea Port, the Manitowac Maritime Museum, and the National Maritime Museum in San Francisco.

The journals just named and those discussed in earlier sections contain reviews of books related to naval history, and these reviews are an essential tool for keeping up with a subdiscipline that lacks a strong academic institutional base.

Sources of Funding

The principal steady source of financial support for research and writing is the Naval Historical Center. Each year the center awards the Samuel Eliot Morison Scholarship of $3,000 to a naval officer, as well as two research grants of $2,500 each for established scholars, one of $8,000 for a doctoral candidate writing a dissertation in naval history, and the Ernest M. Eller Prize of $1,000 for an outstanding scholarly article. Additionally, the center administers an internship program and occasionally awards larger, multi-year grants for official histories. To mark the bicentennial of the USS *Constitution*, the Naval Historical Center will make an award of $750 for an article and one of $2,500 for a book related to the bicentennial theme and based on original research. The works must be published or accepted for publication between 1994 and 1998.[88] The Marine Corps Historical Center, also located in the Washington Navy Yard, offers similar grants.

Major private foundations support naval history on an *ad hoc* basis. The John D. and Catherine T. MacArthur Foundation in Chicago has traditionally provided institutional grants for graduate and post-graduate research in security studies. In 1994, the Chicago-based Robert R. McCormick Tribune Foundation joined with the U.S. Naval Institute in sponsoring two scholarly observances of the fiftieth anniversary of the Normandy landings, one at the Cantigny Museum in Wheaton, Illinois, the other in Annapolis, Maryland. The Eisenhower Center of the University of New Orleans sponsored a more popularly oriented conference on the same topic in May 1994. This was one of the Eisenhower Center's series of annual conclaves on World War II topics from which naval historians are not excluded.

The Harry and Lynde Bradley Foundation of Milwaukee has supported work such as the series of Yale conferences where this chapter was spawned. The John M. Olin Foundation in New York has engaged in this type of activity and has funded pre- and post-doctoral fellowships in military history at the Yale International Security Program, which is directed by Paul Kennedy, and in security studies at Harvard's Olin Institute, directed by Samuel Huntington. The Smith Richardson Foundation of Westport, Connecticut also funds work in this field. The competition for all of these awards is intense, and generally the grants

---

[88] The best way to keep up with the multifaceted activities of the Naval Historical Center is by subscribing to its newsletter, *Pull Together*.

go to the same few institutions. Some, such as the Eller Fellowship in naval history at East Carolina University, are restricted to a particular college or university.

Summary: The State of U.S. Naval History

The teaching of naval history has fallen on tough times. At the Naval Academy, where it ought to reign supreme, naval history receives lukewarm support. In many other departments nationally, it is denied a secure niche in the curriculum. By contrast, American naval museums are stronger than ever before, although their financial underpinnings are not as solid as they might be, and thus their future vitality is not guaranteed. Research and publication are surprisingly healthy activities, although many scholars have to work alone and isolated in departments indifferent or hostile to their field. And, as has always been the case, Washington and Annapolis remain the primary geographic centers for research because of their libraries, archives, and manuscript collections.

★ ★ ★

Despite pockets of encouraging activity, a recent reviewer said, "as a sub-specialty of historical study, U.S. naval history is a toddler."[89] That most naval historians agree on this is distressing. Remedies must be sought, and one possibility is to write histories that address the Navy along lines other than policy and strategy. Sociological, financial, and even psychological approaches should be brought into play in examining naval history.

The primary challenge facing naval historians is to embrace new methodologies, or risk being considered completely irrelevant to the profession as a whole. They must target and address those broad questions insufficiently studied, such as the social history of sailors, the commercial-cultural history of Navy yards, civil-military relations, and the technical-bureaucratic history of weapons systems. Next, they must establish a methodological framework for investigating recent naval history, an area where most high-level government documents will remain highly classified for some time.

Finally, naval historians ought to ask, what is the purpose of American naval history? Is it to eulogize heroes and instill patriotic virtues of self-sacrifice, as it was for much of the nineteenth century? Is it to enshrine a particular strategic concept, as it was for the first half of the twentieth century? Or is it to question prevailing interpretive orthodoxies, as much of it has been since the 1960s?

With the end of the Cold War—if not with the dawning of a particularly bright "new world order"—it is imperative that the historians of America's great sea service ask questions relevant to the United States Navy of the future, a navy

---

[89] John B. Hattendorf, review of *History of U.S. Navy*, by Robert W. Love, Jr., *Naval Institute Proceedings* (August, 1993) pp. 99–100.

diminished in size from its magnitude of 1950–1990, but still the world's most powerful. Are there historical antecedents in the American experience or in the experience of other nations that will suggest strategic, operational, technological, logistical, and administrative guidelines for the future?

Some historians do not believe in seeking lessons from the past as lodestars for the future, but if U.S. naval historians adopt this purist stance, they will become even less germane to the intellectual and political mainstreams of the United States than they are now. The chance to reach out to the American people is a happy, if daunting, prospect.[90]

[90] The authors wish to thank several people for their advice and help on this project, including: Paul M. Kennedy and John B. Hattendorf for crucial assistance and advice at every stage; David A. Rosenberg for information and guidance; James C. Bradford, Charles C. Campbell, John P. Cummings, Harold D. Langley, Jane H. Price, Jack Sweetman, Richard Hume Werking, and Stephen D. Wrage for their thoughtful reading and comments; Richard A. von Doenhoff for material on the National Archives; Dean C. Allard and Edward Marolda for data on the Naval Historical Center; Harold Langley for information about the Smithsonian; James W. Cheevers, senior curator of the Naval Academy Museum, for the section on museums; Erica Thomas for a jump-start with the footnotes; and Ann Jensen for editing of the very highest order. This chapter, however, represents only the views of the authors.

The cutoff for information in this essay was 30 January 1994. Suggestions and comments for future editions may be addressed to the editor at the Naval War College Press.

Kenneth J. Hagan, a retired captain in the U.S. Naval Reserve, is author of *American Gunboat Diplomacy and the Old Navy, 1877–1889* and *This People's Navy: The Making of American Sea Power*, and editor of *In Peace and War: Interpretations of American History, 1775–1984*. Hagan served on the faculty of the history department of the U.S. Naval Academy, 1973–1993, and was the academy's archivist and museum director from 1990 through 1993.

Mark R. Shulman is author of *Navalism and the Emergence of American Sea Power, 1882–1893* (Annapolis: NIP) and numerous articles. He has edited or co-edited *An Admiral's Yarn: The Autobiography of Harris Laning* and *the Laws of War: Constraints on Warfare in the Western World*. Shulman has taught history at Yale University and is now at The National Strategy Information Center, Washington, D.C.

Beyond Toddlerhood
Thoughts on the Future of U.S. Naval History

David Alan Rosenberg

"As a sub-specialty of historical study, U.S. naval history is a toddler." So notes Dr. John B. Hattendorf, the Ernest J. King Professor of Maritime History at the U.S. Naval War College and editor of the present volume, in his recent review of Robert W. Love, Jr.'s *History of the U.S. Navy*. Professors Hagan and Shulman, in their overview of the current state of American naval history, have taken note of this comment and have provided some general suggestions about how historians of American naval affairs can advance their field as a sub-specialty of scholarly endeavor. This paper presents some additional thoughts to challenge colleagues old and young as they attack their chosen subject. The challenge takes the form of three questions historians might ask to move American naval history toward the complexity and intellectual sophistication envisioned by Messrs. Hattendorf, Hagan, and Shulman.

The first such question is "*What was the U.S. Navy, and who belonged to it?*" For far too long, we have regarded the naval establishment very narrowly, concentrating on the uniformed service, both officers and enlisted personnel, and on primarily the seagoing, operational components at that. This has reinforced naval history's strong traditional focus on the "tip of the spear," the ships and men that have deployed overseas and met the enemy in battle. As a result, if we continue the metaphor, we still have only a vague sense of the spear shaft, which had a different length and a different composition at various times in the nation's history. Yet that shaft is just as much a part of the naval establishment as the spearhead, and the shaft may well have determined the nature and effectiveness of the tip that was sent into harm's way.

We need to know more about the naval establishment, broadly defined. This includes civilian shipbuilders, gun, mine and torpedo makers, airplane builders, sail and rope makers, coal and oil suppliers, producers of navigational charts, books and instruments, victuallers, and white collar bureaucrats. There is also much additional work to be done on analyzing the evolution of the naval officer corps and the enlisted ranks, from a professional as well as a sociological perspective. For example, navy wives and families not only developed their own brand of naval culture, but in the twentieth century had a profound role in shaping personnel policies, particularly with respect to base housing, medical care, deployment schedules, and support services.

The political underpinnings of the American Navy deserve much more attention as well. While urban and social historians have begun to explore the role that military bases have played in shaping the growth of cities and communities, naval historians have not reciprocated by analyzing how local politics have influenced the development of the American Navy's shore infrastructure. Surprisingly, the role of national politics in shaping naval development has also received much less attention in articles and monographs than it clearly merits.

The second question historians should ask is "*What did navies do?*" This question might appear to be an obvious one, and one which historians have already undertaken to address, but the task is far from complete. Certain aspects have been ignored. While the gross outlines and in many cases the details of American naval operations have been traced and analyzed, the internal workings of shipboard life are little understood. For too long we have implicitly accepted Samuel Johnson's aphorism: "being in a ship is being in jail, with a chance of being drowned . . .," and have paid little attention to how sailors occupied their time while at sea. But life at sea was not simply a punitive exercise. The drills and discipline applied were not designed just to control human nature, but to meet the needs of the ship.

In a similar vein, significant progress has been made in recent years in studying the history of naval invention, but equally important is the as yet unwritten history of the application of such invention to operations and combat at sea. What sailors do, and are capable of doing, surely influences technical innovation, just as technology shapes what is expected of sailors as they sail, steam, and fight their ships. It is a question of education, training, drills, responsibilities, and schedules, just as much as it is a question of big guns, planes and missiles, armor plate, boilers, nuclear reactors, radios, radar, and electronic warfare. All of these facets come to define naval tactics, tactical doctrine, and command and control. The extent to which all of these considerations came to shape American naval strategy has never been analyzed. They may in the end prove to have been as important as the writings of naval theorists, even Alfred Thayer Mahan himself.

The third area needing further attention is defined by the question: "*Why should other historians care?*" Naval history will not come into its own as an academic discipline until naval historians are more successful at spelling out the connections between their subject and the concerns of the broader historical profession. Opportunities for such research abound. The development of navies and naval technology is not only an important element in national strategy and diplomacy, but in the history of the industrial nation state. The very existence of a navy is dependent on the choice of a state to invest in developing and maintaining the industrial capacity to build and sustain it. The centrality of navies in the history of European states has long been acknowledged, particularly with reference to Renaissance Venice, imperial Spain, and modern Britain. In the United States, however, the relevance of the Navy to the era of nation-building has rarely been considered. In particular, the rise of the American Navy after the Civil War rested not just on national policy, but on the availability of industrial manpower, the advancement of steam technology, and major breakthroughs in understanding and applying the laws of thermodynamics.

During the twentieth century, the American Navy began to operate in three dimensions: on, over, and beneath the oceans, ultimately fostering and employing such technologies as nuclear power, nuclear weapons, guided and ballistic missiles, and a full spectrum of computer systems. The role played by the Navy in the creation of new technology has been acknowledged, but the part the naval establishment played in sustaining new industries and shaping them to meet its needs has not been assessed. Further, the role the Navy played in these matters in contrast to the Army and the Air Force offers a fruitful avenue for further research. As America moves to adapt to a post Cold War era and the end of nearly fifty years of constant mobilization for war, such analyses would be of great service.

But what of "traditional" naval history: of sea fights, and diplomatic accomplishments, and the evolution of policy and strategy? Certainly in the latter case, asking and answering as best we can the questions just outlined should enrich such studies. For too long the history of policy and strategy has been treated as the self-fulfilling motion from words to deeds, without careful attention to the means—economic and financial, scientific, technological and industrial—which would translate one into the other. Knowing who made up navies, what they do and why they matter cannot help but enhance our understanding of the long-standing concerns of naval historians, from preparation in peacetime to achievements and failures in times of war.